Directory of Unpublished
Experimental Mental Measures

VOLUME 6

BERT A. GOLDMAN

DAVID F. MITCHELL

...

Series Editor: Bert A. Goldman

American Psychological Association, Washington, DC

■ ■ ■

Fourth printing July 1998

Published by
American Psychological Association
750 First Street, NE
Washington, DC 20002

Copies may be ordered from
APA Order Department
P.O. Box 2710
Hyattsville, MD 20784

Typeset in Futura Bold and Bodoni Book by Innodata, Hanover, MD

Cover and Text Designer: Minker Design, Bethesda, MD
Printer: TechniGraphix, Reston, VA
Technical/Production Editor: Susan Bedford

ISBN: 1-55798-289-9

Printed in the United States of America

Contents

...

Preface

Purpose: This *Directory of Unpublished Experimental Mental Measures*, Volume 6, marks the sixth in a series of publications designed to fill a need for reference tools in behavioral and social science research. The authors believe there is an ongoing need for a directory such as this to enable researchers to determine what types of noncommercial experimental test instruments are currently in use. This reference provides researchers with ready access to information about recently developed or recently used experimental measurement scales. The instruments are not evaluated, but the information given about each test should make it possible for researchers to make a preliminary judgment of its usefulness. It does not provide all necessary information for researchers contemplating the use of a particular instrument. It does describe basic test properties and in most cases identifies additional sources from which technical information concerning an instrument can be obtained.

Development: Thirty-seven relevant professional journals available to the authors were examined. The following list includes those journals which, in the judgment of the authors, contained instruments of value to researchers in education, psychology, and sociology. Foreign journals were not surveyed for use in this directory. Measures identified in dissertations were excluded as a matter of expediency and because the microfilm abstracts generally contain minimal information.

American Journal of Sociology
Brain and Language
Career Development Quarterly
Child Development
Child Study Journal
Educational and Psychological Measurement
Educational Research Quarterly
Gifted Child Quarterly
Journal of Applied Psychology
Journal of College Student Development
Journal of College Student Personnel
Journal of Consulting and Clinical Psychology
Journal of Counseling Psychology
Journal of Creative Behavior
Journal of Educational Psychology
Journal of Educational Research
Journal of Experimental Child Psychology
Journal of Experimental Education
Journal of General Psychology
Journal of Marriage and the Family
Journal of Occupational Psychology
Journal of Personality Assessment
Journal of Psychopathology and Behavioral Assessment
Journal of Research and Development in Education

Journal of Research in Personality
Journal of School Psychology
Journal of Social Psychology
Journal of Vocational Behavior
Measurement and Evaluation in Counseling and Development
Perceptual and Motor Skills
Personnel Psychology
Psychological Reports
Research in Higher Education
Social Psychology Quarterly
Sociology of Education
Vocational Guidance Quarterly

Volume 6 lists tests described in the 1986–1990 issues of the previously cited journals. An attempt was made to omit commercially published standardized tests, task-type activities such as memory word lists used in serial learning research, and achievement tests developed for a single, isolated course of study. The reader should not assume that the instruments described herein form a representative sample of the universe of unpublished experimental mental measures.

Organization: Following is a brief description of each of the 24 categories under which the authors grouped the measures of Volume 6.

Achievement: Measure learning and/or comprehension in specific areas. Also includes tests of memory and tests of spatial ability.

Adjustment–Educational: Measure academic satisfaction. Also includes tests of school anxiety.

Adjustment–Psychological: Evaluate conditions and levels of adjustment along the psychological dimension including, for example, tests of mood, fear of death, anxiety, depression, etc.

Adjustment–Social: Evaluate aspects of interactions with others. Also includes tests of alienation, conformity, need for social approval, social desirability, instruments for assessing interpersonal attraction and sensitivity.

Adjustment–Vocational: Identify burnout, vocational maturity, job-related stress, job frustration, job satisfaction, etc.

Aptitude: Predict success in given attributes.

Attitude: Measure reaction to a variety of experiences and objects.

Behavior: Measure general and specific types of activities such as classroom behavior, drug-use behavior, abusive and violent behavior.

Communication: Evaluate information exchange. Also includes tests of self-disclosure and counselor/client interaction.

Concept Meaning: Test one's understanding of words and other concepts. Also includes tests of conceptual structure and style, and information processing.

Creativity: Measure ability to reorganize data or information into unique configurations. Also includes tests of divergent thinking.

Development: Measure emerging characteristics, primarily for preschool ages. Also includes tests of identity, cognitive, and moral development.

Family: Measure intrafamily relations. Also includes tests of marital satisfaction, nurturance, parental interest, and warmth.

Institutional Information: Evaluate institutions and their functioning, community and involvement satisfaction, and organizational climate.

Motivation: Measure goal strength. Also includes measures of curiosity and need to achieve.

Perception: Determine how one sees the self and other objects. Also includes tests dealing with empathy, imagery, locus of control, self-concept, self-esteem, and time.

Personality: Measure general personal attributes. Also includes biographical information, defense mechanisms, and temperament.

Preference: Identify choices. Also includes tests of preference for objects, taste preference, and sex-role preference.

Problem–Solving and Reasoning: Measure general ability to reason through a number of alternative solutions, to generate such solutions to problems, etc.

Status: Identify a hierarchy of acceptability.

Trait Measurement: Identify and evaluate unitary traits. Also includes tests of anger, anxiety, authoritarianism, blame, cheating, and narcissism.

Values: Measure worth one ascribes to an object or activity. Includes tests of moral, philosophical, political, and religious values.

Vocational Evaluation: Evaluate a person for a specific position.

Vocational Interest: Measure interest in specific occupations and vocations as well as interest in general categories of activity.

The choice of the category under which each test was grouped was determined by the purpose of the test and/or its apparent content. The authors attempted to include basic facts for each test. Three facts are always listed: test name, purpose, and source. In addition, at least four of the following facts (starred in the list below) had to be present in the source in order for the test to be listed in the *Directory*: number of items, time required, format, reliability, validity, or related research. Readers should note that if no information was given for any one of the starred facts, the heading was not included in the entry. For example, if no information about validity was given in the source, validity was not listed in the test entry.

Test Name

The name of the test listed in the directory was usually given by the author of the paper in which it was found. When a name was not given in the source, one was created for it by the authors of the *Directory*.

Purpose

The general purpose of each scale was usually stated in the source or was suggested by its name. When available, additional detail about the test's purpose is given.

Description

Number of Items: The number of items in a scale as stated in the source.

Time Required: Few scales are administered under a time constraint. When they are, the time requirements are specified here.

Format: The description of the format of the scales varied widely in the sources. The authors of the *Directory* have presented the essential characteristics of the format such as general type (Likert, true–false, checklist, and semantic differential). Less common formats are briefly described in additional detail as needed.

Statistics

Reliability: When available, reliabilities and the *N*s on which they were based are reported. Commonly reported reliabilities are Alpha, split-half, item-total, and KR-20.

Validity: When available, validity data were reported. The authors of the *Directory* have also included correlations with other tests and group difference information that help define the characteristic being measured by the test.

Source

Author

Title

Journal (includes date of publication, volume, and page number)

Related Research: The purpose of this section is to provide additional information about the test. In some cases the original source of the test is given. If an existing test was revised for use with a special population, the original version may be cited. In other cases, a publication that offered additional technical information is listed.

Readers should note that the numbers within the Indexes refer to test numbers, not page numbers.

As a convenience to readers, the authors have incorporated the subject indexes from the five previous volumes, and in doing so have converted all page numbers in Volume 1 to test numbers. Thus, numbers 1 through 339 refer to tests in Volume 1, numbers 340 through 1034 refer to tests in Volume 2, numbers 1035 through 1595 refer to tests in Volume 3, numbers 1596 through 2369 refer to tests in Volume 4, numbers 2370 through 3665 refer to tests in Volume 5, and numbers 3666 through 5363 refer to tests in Volume 6.

The authors thank Rebecca Turner and Detra Thompson for typing the manuscript. Special appreciation is expressed to Jean and Richard Allen for doing the complex and time-consuming final sorting and processing of the entries included in this volume. Their efforts made it possible to finish the manuscript on schedule. Further, the authors wish to thank the American Psychological Association for continuing the publication of the directories.

Bert Arthur Goldman

David F. Mitchell

CHAPTER 1

Achievement

3666

Test Name: ALZHEIMER'S DISEASE SURVEY

Purpose: To measure knowledge and beliefs about Alzheimer's disease.

Number of Items: 23

Format: Likert, checklist, and true–false formats used.

Reliability: Cronbach's alpha was .86. Test–retest (1 week) reliability was .81.

Validity: Knowledge correlated significantly with educational level, $F(3, 141) = 3.12$, $p = .03$.

Author: Rice, J. A., et al.

Article: Elderly persons' perceptions and knowledge of Alzheimer's disease.

Journal: *Psychological Reports*, April 1986, *58*(2), 419–424.

• • •

3667

Test Name: AUDITORY SELECTIVE ATTENTION TEST

Purpose: To measure selective attention.

Number of Items: 24

Format: Each item or task involves dichotic messages presented simultaneously for the subject to repeat.

Reliability: Test–retest (2 weeks) reliabilities ranged from .39 to .81. Coefficient alphas ranged from .61 to .88.

Validity: Correlations with other variables ranged from .04 to .57.

Author: Doverspike, D., et al.

Article: The Auditory Selective Attention Test: A review of field and laboratory studies.

Journal: *Educational and Psychological Measurement*, Winter 1986, *46*(4), 1095–1103.

Related Research: Gopher, D. (1982). A selective attention test as a predictor of success in flight training. *Human Factors, 24*, 173–183.

• • •

3668

Test Name: BASEBALL KNOWLEDGE TEST

Purpose: To assess baseball knowledge.

Number of Items: 39

Format: Multiple choice.

Reliability: Alpha was .81.

Author: Recht, D. R., and Leslie, L.

Article: Effect of prior knowledge on good and poor readers' memory test.

Journal: *Journal of Educational Psychology*, March 1988, *80*(1), 16–20.

Related Research: Spilich, G. (1979). Text processing of domain related information for individuals with high and low domain knowledge. *Journal of Verbal Learning and Verbal Behavior, 18*, 275–290.

• • •

3669

Test Name: COGNITION AND READING COMPREHENSION SCALES

Purpose: To measure knowledge of cognition, effects of instruction on cognition, and regulation of cognition.

Number of Items: Varies as needed by interview.

Format: Interview format.

Reliability: Interrater reliabilities were above .80.

Author: Meloth, M. S.

Article: Changes in poor readers' knowledge of cognition and the association of knowledge cognition with regulation of cognition and reading comprehension.

Journal: *Journal of Educational Psychology*, December 1990, *82*(4), 792–798.

Related Research: Duffy, G. G., et al. (1987). The effects of explaining the reasoning associated with using reading strategies. *Reading Quarterly, 22*, 347–368.

• • •

3670

Test Name: CONSULTATION JUDGMENT INVENTORY

Purpose: To assess the ability to make appropriate clinical judgments about what actions to take in consultations.

Number of Items: 33

Format: Each item is a dialogue followed by five possible actions.

Reliability: Kuder-Richardson formula was .87. Discrimination indexes ranged from −.09 to .91.

Author: Randolph, D. L., and D'llio, V. R.

Article: Measuring consultation judgment-making ability: Further development of the Consultation Judgment Inventory.

Journal: *Psychological Reports*, February 1989, *64*(1), 98.

Related Research: Randolph, D. L., et al. (1984). Teaching consultant interview-skills: Measuring student progress. *Teaching of Psychology, 11*, 242–243.

■ ■ ■

3671

Test Name: CUBES

Purpose: To measure spatial ability.

Number of Items: 20 (Lower Battery), 32 (Middle Battery), 32 (Upper Battery).

Time Required: 3 minutes.

Format: Subjects respond "same" if they determine that pictures of pairs of cubes with different designs on each surface are the same as a result of mentally rotating the cubes.

Reliability: Split-half (Spearman-Brown corrected) reliabilities ranged from .41 to .75.

Validity: Correlation with DAT-Space Relations was .64.

Author: Johnson, E. S., and Meade, A. C.

Article: Developmental patterns of spatial ability: An early sex difference.

Journal: *Child Development*, June 1987, *58*(3), 725–740.

Related Research: Thurstone, L. (1938). Primary mental abilities. *Psychometric Monograph*, No. 1. Chicago: University of Chicago Press.

■ ■ ■

3672

Test Name: EVERYDAY SKILLS COMPETENCE SCALE

Purpose: To measure whether children know how to perform everyday skills such as using a washing machine.

Number of Items: 20

Format: 4-point rating scales.

Reliability: Alpha was .83.

Author: Amato, P. R., and Ochiltree, G.

Article: Family resources and the development of child competence.

Journal: *Journal of Marriage and the Family*, February 1986, *48*(1), 47–56.

Related Research: Amato, P. R., & Ochiltree, G. (1984). *Children becoming independent: An investigation of children's knowledge and performance of practical life skills*. Unpublished manuscript, Institute of Family Studies, Melbourne, Australia.

■ ■ ■

3673

Test Name: FLAGS

Purpose: To measure spatial ability.

Number of Items: 12 (Kindergarten), 24 (Lower Battery), 48 (Middle Battery), 48 (Upper Battery).

Time Required: 2 minutes.

Format: Pairs of American flags are judged same or different.

Reliability: Split-half (Spearman-Brown corrected) reliabilities ranged from .65 to .91.

Validity: Correlation with DAT-Space Relations was .40.

Author: Johnson, E. S., and Meade, A. C.

Article: Developmental patterns of spatial ability: An early sex difference.

Journal: *Child Development*, June 1987, *58*(3), 725–740.

Related Research: Thurstone, L. (1938). Primary mental abilities. *Psychometric Monograph*, No. 1. Chicago: University of Chicago Press.

3674

Test Name: HANDS

Purpose: To measure spatial ability.

Number of Items: 12 (Kindergarten), 16 (Lower Battery), 49 (Middle Battery), 49 (Upper Battery).

Time Required: 2 minutes.

Format: Pictures of hands are presented for a right–left discrimination.

Reliability: Split-half (Spearman-Brown corrected) reliabilities ranged from .47 to .93.

Validity: Correlation with DAT-Space Relations was .30.

Author: Johnson, E. S., and Meade, A. C.

Article: Developmental patterns of spatial ability: An early sex difference.

Journal: *Child Development*, June 1987, *58*(3), 725–740.

Related Research: Thurstone, L. (1938). Primary mental abilities. *Psychometric Monograph*, No. 1. Chicago: University of Chicago Press.

■ ■ ■

3675

Test Name: INDIVIDUAL DIFFERENCES QUESTIONNAIRE

Purpose: To assess verbal and imaginal habits, preferences, and abilities of high school students.

Number of Items: 34

Format: Includes five factors: good verbal expression and fluency, habitual use of imagery, concern with correct use of words, self-reported reading difficulties, and vividness of daydreams and dreams. All items are presented.

Reliability: Coefficient alphas ranged from .28 to .74.

Author: Kardash, C. A., et al.

Article: Structural analysis of Paivio's Individual Differences Questionnaire.

Journal: *Journal of Experimental Education*, Fall 1986, *55*(1), 33–38.

Related Research: Paivio, A., & Harshman, R. (1983). Factor analysis of a questionnaire on imagery and verbal habits and skills. *Canadian Journal of Psychology, 37,* 461–483.

■ ■ ■

3676

Test Name: INFANT BEHAVIOR QUESTIONNAIRE

Purpose: To assess knowledge of infant behavior.

Number of Items: 56

Format: Respondents circled number of months that they believed infants first are able to do a behavior.

Reliability: Alphas ranged from .59 to .78.

Author: Gullo, D. F., and Paludi, M.

Article: Older adolescents' differential expectations of infants development.

Journal: *Psychological Reports*, December 1986, *59*(3), 1090–1096.

Related Research: Granger, C. (1982). Young adolescents' knowledge of infant abilities. *Dissertation Abstracts International, 42,* DA8211152.

■ ■ ■

3677

Test Name: INSTRUMENTAL COMPETENCE SCALE FOR YOUNG CHILDREN

Purpose: To measure the instrumental competence of young children.

Number of Items: 40

Format: Responses to each item are made on a 7-point Likert scale from 1 (*strongly disagree*) to 7 (*strongly agree*). An example is presented.

Validity: Correlations with other variables ranged from .38 to .74.

Author: Arbuckle, B. S., and MacKinnon, C. E.

Article: A conceptual model of the determinants of children's academic achievement.

Journal: *Child Study Journal*, 1988, *18*(2), 121–147.

Related Research: Lange, G., & MacKinnon, C. (1987). *Instrumental Competence Scale for Children.* Unpublished instrument, University of North Carolina—Greensboro, Department of Child Development and Family Relations.

■ ■ ■

3678

Test Name: JOB CAREER KEY

Purpose: To provide a test of information about a wide variety of occupations.

Number of Items: 157

Format: A multiple-choice format is used.

Reliability: Kuder-Richardson formulas ranged from .43 to .91. Test–retest (4 month) reliability (*N* = 19) was .62.

Author: Yanico, B. J., and Hardin, S. I.

Article: College students' self-estimated and actual knowledge of gender traditional and nontraditional occupations: A replication and extension.

Journal: *Journal of Vocational Behavior*, June 1986, *28*(3), 229–240.

Related Research: Blank, J. R. (1978). Job-career key: A test of occupational information. *Vocational Guidance Quarterly, 27,* 6–17.

■ ■ ■

3679

Test Name: KNOWLEDGE OF BEHAVIORAL PRINCIPLES AS APPLIED TO CHILDREN

Purpose: To measure teachers' knowledge of behavioral principles that may be applied to children.

Number of Items: 22

Format: Two 22-item forms.

Reliability: Kuder-Richardson formula was .94. Split-half reliabilities ranged from .71 to .88.

Author: Anderson, T. K., et al.

Article: Training teachers in behavioral consultation and therapy: An analysis of verbal behaviors.

Journal: *Journal of School Psychology*, Fall 1986, *24* (3), 229–241.

Related Research: O'Dell, S. L., et al. (1979). An instrument to measure knowledge of behavioral principles as applied to children. *Journal of Behavior Therapy and Experimental Psychiatry, 10,* 29–34.

■ ■ ■

3680

Test Name: MENTAL ROTATIONS

Purpose: To measure spatial ability.

Number of Items: 20 (Lower Battery), 42 (Middle Battery), 42 (Upper Battery).

Time Required: 4 minutes.

Format: Pairs of three-dimensional block figures are presented for a same–different response.

Reliability: Split-half (Spearman-Brown corrected) reliabilities ranged from .28 to .66.

Validity: Correlation with DAT-Space Relations was .52.

Author: Johnson, E. S., and Meade, A. C.

Article: Developmental patterns of spatial ability: An early sex difference.

Journal: *Child Development*, June 1987, *58*(3), 725–740.

Related Research: Lansman, M., et al. (1982). Ability factors and cognitive processes. *Intelligence, 6,* 347–386.

■ ■ ■

3681

Test Name: MINIMUM PROFICIENCY SKILLS TEST

Purpose: To measure minimum competency in consumer life skills.

Number of Items: 63

Format: Includes three domains: language arts, computation, and problem solving. Multiple-choice format.

Validity: Correlations with the Iowa Test of Basic Skills ranged from .55 to .77.

Author: Reynolds, A. J., and Bezruczko, N.

Article: Assessing the construct validity of a life skills competency test.

Journal: *Educational and Psychological Measurement,* Spring 1989, *49*(1), 183–193.

Related Research: Bezruczko, N., & Reynolds, A. J. (1987). *Minimum proficiency skills test: 1987 item pilot report.* Unpublished manuscript, Board of Education, Department of Research and Evaluation, Chicago.

■ ■ ■

3682

Test Name: PERSONAL SAFETY QUESTIONNAIRE

Purpose: To assess children's knowledge about sexual abuse.

Number of Items: 13

Time Required: 15 minutes.

Format: Yes–no format. Sample items presented.

Reliability: Kuder-Richardson formula was .78. Test–retest (1 week) was .64.

Author: Wurtele, S. K., et al.

Article: Teaching personal safety skills for potential prevention of

sexual abuse: A comparison of treatments.

Journal: *Journal of Consulting and Clinical Psychology,* October 1986, *54,* (5), 688–692.

■ ■ ■

3683

Test Name: POLICE PROCEDURES TEST

Purpose: To provide a job knowledge achievement examination.

Number of Items: 16

Format: Multiple-choice items.

Reliability: Split-half corrected reliabilities ranged from .37 to .64.

Validity: Correlations with Job Performance Rating Scales ranged from .10 to .32.

Author: Friedland, D. L., and Michael, W. B.

Article: The reliability of a promotional job knowledge examination scored by number of items right and by four confidence weighting procedures and its corresponding concurrent validity estimates relative to performance criterion ratings.

Journal: *Educational and Psychological Measurement,* Spring 1987, *47*(1), 179–188.

■ ■ ■

3684

Test Name: RAPE TRAUMA KNOWLEDGE TEST

Purpose: To measure knowledge of physical, emotional, and behavioral symptoms of sexual assault.

Number of Items: 20

Format: 5-point true–false format.

Reliability: Alpha was .79.

Validity: Correlations with other variables ranged from −.41 to .55.

Author: Hamilton, M., and Yee, J.

Article: Rape knowledge and propensity to rape.

Journal: *Journal of Research in Personality,* March 1990, *24*(1), 111–122.

■ ■ ■

3685

Test Name: RATING SCALE OF CHILD'S ACTUAL COMPETENCE

Purpose: To enable teachers to rate children.

Number of Items: 28

Format: Includes cognitive and social subscales.

Validity: Correlations with other variables ranged from −.90 to .81.

Author: McCombs, A., et al.

Article: Early adolescent functioning following divorce: The relationship to parenting and non-parenting ex-spousal interactions.

Journal: *Child Study Journal,* 1987, *17*(4), 301–310.

Related Research: Harter, S. (1982). The Perceived Competence Scale for Children. *Child Development, 53,* 87–97.

■ ■ ■

3686

Test Name: SELF-MONITORING SCALE

Purpose: To measure an individual's self-monitoring skills.

Number of Items: 25

Format: Includes three factors. All items are presented.

Reliability: Coefficient alpha was .75. Kuder-Richardson formula was .72. Reliability for the three factors ranged from .40 to .49.

Author: Ahmed, S. M. S., et al.

Article: Psychometric properties of Snyder's self-monitoring of expressive behavior scale.

Journal: *Perceptual and Motor Skills,* October, 1986, *63*(2), 495–500

Related Research: Snyder, M. (1974). Self-monitoring of expressive behavior. *Journal of Personality and Social Psychology, 30,* 526–537.

■ ■ ■

3687

Test Name: SEX KNOWLEDGE AND ATTITUDE TEST

Purpose: To measure sex knowledge and attitudes.

Number of Items: 106

Format: 35 Likert-type items and 71 true–false items.

Reliability: Internal consistency for knowledge items was .87. Likert items' alphas ranged from .68 to .86.

Author: Adame, D. D.

Article: Instruction and course content in sex knowledge and attitudes and internal locus of control.

Journal: *Psychological Reports,* February 1986, *58*(1), 91–94.

Related Research: Miller, W. R., & Lief, H. I. (1979). The sex knowledge and attitude test. *Journal of Sex and Marital Therapy, 5,* 282–287.

■ ■ ■

3688

Test Name: TEACHER RATING SCALE OF CHILDREN'S ACTUAL COMPETENCE

Purpose: To enable teachers to rate children's cognitive, social, and physical competence.

Format: Includes three subscales: cognitive, social, and physical. Teachers rate children on a scale from 1 (*least competent*) to 4 (*most competent*).

Reliability: Kuder-Richardson formulas ranged from .93 to .96.

Validity: Correlations with other variables ranged from −.36 to .50.

Author: Fuchs, D., et al.

Article: Psychosocial characteristics of handicapped children who perform suboptimally during assessment.

Journal: *Measurement and Evaluation in Counseling and Development,* January 1986, *18*(4), 176–184.

Related Research: Harter, S. (1982). The Perceived Competence Scale for Children. *Child Development, 53,* 87–97.

■ ■ ■

3689

Test Name: TEACHER'S RATING SCALE OF CHILD'S COMPETENCE

Purpose: To assess a child's competence.

Number of Items: 28

Format: Includes four subscales.

Reliability: Internal consistency reliabilities ranged from .93 to 96.

Author: Forehand, R., et al.

Article: Interparental conflict and paternal visitation following divorce:

The interactive effect on adolescent competence.

Journal: *Child Study Journal,* 1990, *20*(3), 193–202.

Related Research: Harter, S. (1982). The Perceived Competence Scale for Children. *Child Development, 53,* 87–96.

■ ■ ■

3690

Test Name: TEST OF PHONEMIC ANALYSIS AND BLENDING

Purpose: To measure phonemic analysis and blending.

Number of Items: 24

Format: Twelve items measured phonemic analysis and 12 items measured phonemic blending. All items were presented.

Reliability: Cronbach's alpha was .95.

Author: Bus, A. G.

Article: Preparatory reading instruction in kindergarten: Some comparative research into methods of auditory and auditory-visual training of phonemic analysis and blending.

Journal: *Perceptual and Motor Skills,* February, 1986, *62*(1), 11–24

Related Research: Lewkowicz, N. K. (1980). Phonemic awareness training: What to teach and how to teach it. *Journal of Educational Psychology, 72,* 686–700.

CHAPTER 2
Adjustment–Educational

3691

Test Name: ACADEMIC STRESS SCALE

Purpose: To measure stress in college students.

Number of Items: 35

Format: 1000-point stress rating scale (500 = stress of an exam).

Reliability: Cronbach's alpha was .92. Split-half reliability was .86.

Validity: Significant differences between ethnic groups, religious groups, and students with high and low grades.

Author: Kohn, J. P., and Frazer, G. H.

Article: An Academic Stress Scale: Identification and rated importance of academic stressors.

Journal: *Psychological Reports*, August 1986, *59*(1)I, 415–426.

■ ■ ■

3692

Test Name: ACHIEVEMENT ANXIETY TEST

Purpose: To measure general test anxiety.

Format: Consists of two scales: facilitating and debilitating.

Reliability: Test–retest (8 weeks) reliabilities were .75 and .76. Test–retest (10 weeks) reliabilities were .83 and .87.

Validity: Correlation with the Test Anxiety Questionnaire was .64.

Author: Kostka, M. P., and Wilson, C. D.

Article: Reducing mathematics anxiety in nontraditional-age female students.

Journal: *Journal of College Student Personnel*, November 1986, *27*(6), 530–534.

Related Research: Alpert, R., & Haber, R. N. (1960). Anxiety in academic and achievement situations. *Journal of Abnormal and Social Psychology*, *61*, 207–215.

■ ■ ■

3693

Test Name: ACHIEVEMENT ANXIETY TEXT

Purpose: To measure test anxiety.

Number of Items: 28

Format: Provides debilitative, facilitative, and debilitative–facilitative scores.

Reliability: Reliability was reported in the .80s.

Author: Smith, R. J., et al.

Article: Test-anxiety and academic competence: A comparison of alternative models.

Journal: *Journal of Counseling Psychology*, July 1990, *37*(3), 313–321.

Related Research: Alpert, R., & Haber, R. N. (1960). Anxiety in academic and achievement situations. *Journal of Abnormal and Social Psychology*, *61*, 207–215.

■ ■ ■

3694

Test Name: ACHIEVEMENT ANXIETY TEST

Purpose: To measure test anxiety.

Number of Items: 19

Format: Five-point Likert format.

Reliability: Alpha was .82.

Validity: Correlations with other variables ranged from −.48 to .43.

Author: Watson, J. M.

Article: Achievement Anxiety Test: Dimensionality and utility.

Journal: *Journal of Educational Psychology*, December 1988, *80*(4), 585–591.

Related Research: Alpert, R., & Haber, R. N. (1960). Anxiety in academic achievement situations. *Journal of Abnormal and Social Psychology*, *61*, 207–215.

■ ■ ■

3695

Test Name: ADJUSTMENT TO COLLEGE LIFE MEASURE

Purpose: To measure students' perceived adjustment to college life.

Number of Items: 52

Format: Includes four subscales: academic adjustment, social adjustment, personal adjustment, and institutional adjustment. Items are rated on a 9-point Likert scale ranging from 1 (*applies very closely to me*) to 9 (*does not apply at all to me*).

Reliability: Alpha coefficients ranged from .75 to .95.

Validity: Correlations with other variables ranged from −.25 to .69.

Author: Robbins, S. B., and Schwitzer, A. M.

Article: Validity of the Superiority and Goal Instability Scales as predictors of women's adjustment to college life.

Journal: *Measurement and Evaluation in Counseling and Development*, October 1988, *21*(3), 117–123.

Related Research: Baker, R. W., & Siryk, B. (1984). Measuring adjustment to college. *Journal of Counseling Psychology, 31,* 179–189.

■ ■ ■

3696

Test Name: ADJUSTMENT TO COLLEGE SCALE

Purpose: To measure adjustment to college.

Number of Items: 67

Format: Responses to each item are made on a 9-point scale. Includes four subscales: academic, social, personal/emotional, and attachment.

Reliability: Coefficient alphas ($Ns = 216$ and 163) ranged from .79 to .92.

Author: Baker, R. W., and Siryk, B.

Article: Exploratory intervention with a scale measuring adjustments to college.

Journal: *Journal of Counseling Psychology*, January 1986, *33*(1), 31–38.

Related Research: Baker, R. W., et al. (1985). Expectation and reality in freshman adjustment to college. *Journal of Counseling Psychology, 32,* 94–103.

■ ■ ■

3697

Test Name: CHILDREN'S ACADEMIC COPING INVENTORY

Purpose: To measure children's cognitive, affective, and behavioral responses to perceived academic failure.

Number of Items: 19

Format: Includes 4 styles of coping: positive, projection, denial, and anxiety amplification.

Reliability: Alpha reliabilities ranged from .70 to .85.

Author: Connell, J. P., and Ilardi, B. C.

Article: Self-system concomitants of discrepancies between children's and teachers' evaluations of academic competence.

Journal: *Child Development*, October 1987, *58*(5), 1297–1307.

Related Research: Tero, P., & Connell, J. P. (1984, April). *Children's academic coping inventory: A new self-report measure.* Paper presented at American Educational Research Association, Montreal, Quebec, Canada.

■ ■ ■

3698

Test Name: CLASS ATTENDANCE SURVEY

Purpose: To assess reasons for missing class.

Number of Items: 51

Format: Six-point importance scale for each item (reasons for missing class).

Validity: Correlation between different schools was .77.

Author: Lummis, G., and McCutcheon, L. E.

Article: Self-reported reasons for students' absenteeism at a predominantly Black urban university.

Journal: *Psychological Reports*, December 1988, *63*(3), 939–942.

Related Research: McCutcheon, L. E., & Beder, B. A. (1987). The causes of student absenteeism in community college classes. *Community/Junior College Quarterly, 11,* 283–293.

■ ■ ■

3699

Test Name: CLASSROOM AND SOCIAL INVOLVEMENT SCALES

Purpose: To describe various indicators of level of classroom and social involvement.

Number of Items: 10

Format: Includes two scales: classroom experience and social involvement. Sample items are presented.

Reliability: Alpha coefficients were .61 and .75.

Author: Terenzini, P. T., and Wright, T. M.

Article: Influences on students' academic growth during 4 years of college.

Journal: *Research in Higher Education*, 1987, *26*(2), 161–179.

Related Research: Terenzini, P. T., et al. (1982). An assessment of the academic and social influences on freshman year educational outcomes. *Review of Higher Education, 5,* 86–109.

■ ■ ■

3700

Test Name: COLLEGE ADAPTATION SCALE PARTICIPANT

Purpose: To assess self-rated adaptation.

Number of Items: 60

Format: Each item is a challenge that college students typically face. Response to each item is made on a 5-point scale ranging from 1 (*completely satisfied*) to 5 (*completely dissatisfied*). There is also a form to permit observer-rated adaptation.

Validity: Correlations with other variables ranged from .13 to –.67.

Author: Jones, L. K.

Article: Adapting to the first semester of college: A test of Heath's model of maturing.

Journal: *Journal of College Student Personnel*, May 1987, *28*(3), 205–211.

Related Research: Heath, D. H. (1976). Adolescent and adult predictors of vocational adaptation. *Journal of Vocational Behavior, 9,* 1–19.

Weissberg, M., et al. (1982). An assessment of the personal, career, and academic needs of undergraduate students. *Journal of College Student Personnel, 61,* 115–122.

■ ■ ■

3701

Test Name: COLLEGE ADJUSTMENT INVENTORY

Purpose: To measure adjustment to college.

Number of Items: 67

Format: Measures four aspects of adjustment to college: academic, social, personal, and goal commitment. Responses are made on a 9-point Likert scale.

Reliability: Cronbach's alpha coefficients ranged from .73 to .94.

Validity: Correlations with other variables ranged from −.64 to .23.

Author: Lopez, F. G., et al.

Article: Depression, psychological separation, and college adjustment: An investigation of sex differences.

Journal: *Journal of Counseling Psychology,* January 1986, *33*(1), 52–56.

Related Research: Baker, R. W., & Siryk, B. (1984). Measuring adjustment to college. *Journal of Counseling Psychology, 31,* 179–180.

■ ■ ■

3702

Test Name: COLLEGE DROPOUT SELF-REPORT SCREENING INVENTORY

Purpose: To identify students at risk of dropping out of college.

Number of Items: 14

Format: Includes items addressing social support and those addressing dropout intention. Thirteen items are

responded to on a 5-point Likert-type scale and remaining item is multiple choice. All items are presented.

Validity: Correlation of each item with persistence ranged from −.20 to .34 (*N* = 143).

Author: Mallinckrodt, B.

Article: Student retention, social support, and dropout intention: Comparison of Black and White students.

Journal: *Journal of College Student Development,* January 1988, *29*(1), 60–64.

Related Research: Sedlacek, W. E., & Brooks, G. C., Jr. (1976). *Racism in American education: A model for change.* Chicago: Nelson-Hall.

■ ■ ■

3703

Test Name: COLLEGE MALADJUSTMENT SCALE

Purpose: To discriminate between adjusted and maladjusted college students.

Number of Items: 43

Format: True–false items drawn from the MMPI.

Reliability: Test–retest reliability was .88. Alpha was .85.

Author: Wilson, R. J., et al.

Article: Commuter and resident students' personal and family adjustments.

Journal: *Journal of College Student Personnel,* May 1987, *28*(3), 229–233.

Related Research: Kleinmuntz, B. (1960). Identification of maladjusted college students. *Journal of Counseling Psychology, 7,* 209–211.

■ ■ ■

3704

Test Name: COLLEGE STUDENT SATISFACTION QUESTIONNAIRE—REVISED

Purpose: To measure college student satisfaction.

Number of Items: 32

Format: Responses to each item are made on a 5-point Likert scale indicating strength of agreement with each statement. Subscales include: quality of education, working conditions, compensation, social life, and recognition.

Reliability: Internal consistencies ranged from .69 to .91.

Author: Pennington, D. C., et al.

Article: Changes in college satisfaction across an academic term.

Journal: *Journal of College Student Development,* November 1989, *30*(6), 528–535.

Related Research: Betz, E. L., et al. (1971). A dimensional analysis of college student satisfaction. *Measurement and Evaluation in Guidance, 4,* 99–106.

■ ■ ■

3705

Test Name: COMPUTER ANXIETY SCALE

Purpose: To measure the perception held by students of their anxiety in different situations related to computers.

Number of Items: 20

Format: Each item is rated on a 5-point scale ranging from *not at all* to *very much.* All items are presented.

Reliability: Test–retest (10 weeks) reliability was .77. Coefficient alpha was .97.

Author: Marcoulides, G. A.

Article: Measuring computer anxiety: The Computer Anxiety Scale.

Journal: *Educational and Psychological Measurement,* Autumn 1989, *49*(3), 733–739.

Related Research: Endler, N., & Hunt, J. (1966). Sources of behavioral variance as measured by the S-R

Inventory of Anxiousness. *Psychological Bulletin, 65,* 336–339.

■ ■ ■

3706

Test Name: DEBILITATING ANXIETY SCALE

Purpose: To measure test anxiety.

Number of Items: 10

Format: Five-point scales.

Reliability: Test–retest reliability ranged from .87 (10 weeks) to .76 (8 months).

Author: Hunsley, J.

Article: Cognitive processes in mathematics anxiety and test anxiety: The role of appraisals, internal dialogue, and attributions.

Journal: *Journal of Educational Psychology,* December 1987, *79*(4), 388–392.

Related Research: Alpert, R., & Haber, R. N. (1960). Anxiety in academic achievement situations. *Journal of Abnormal and Social Psychology, 61,* 207–215.

■ ■ ■

3707

Test Name: EVALUATION ANXIETY SCALE

Purpose: To measure writing apprehension.

Number of Items: 66

Format: Responses to each item are made on a 5-point scale from *strongly agree* to *strongly disagree.* Sample items are presented.

Reliability: Test–retest reliability coefficient was .92.

Validity: Correlations with other variables ranged from −.53 to .12.

Author: Kean, D. K., et al.

Article: Writing persuasive documents: The role of students' verbal aptitude and evaluation anxiety.

Journal: *Journal of Experimental Education,* Winter 1987, *55*(2), 95–102.

Related Research: Daly, J. A., & Miller, M. D. (1975). The empirical development of an instrument to measure writing apprehension. *Research in the Teaching of English, 9,* 242–249.

■ ■ ■

3708

Test Name: FRESHMEN EXPERIENCE SURVEY

Purpose: To measure interaction among peers, with faculty, and with the institution and educational goal commitments that resulted from student integration into the social and academic systems of the university.

Number of Items: 34

Format: Includes 5 factors: informal relations with faculty, peer group relations, faculty concern for teaching and student development, academic intellectual development, and institutional and goal commitments. All items are presented.

Reliability: Alpha coefficients ranged from −.82 to .88.

Author: Allen, D. F., and Nelson, J. M.

Article: Tinto's model of college withdrawal applied to women in two institutions.

Journal: *Journal of Research and Development in Education,* Spring 1989, *22*(3), 1–11.

Related Research: Pascaarella, E., & Terenzini, P. (1980). Predicting persistence and voluntary dropout decisions from a theoretical model. *Journal of Higher Education, 61,* 60–75.
Bean, J. (1981). *Student attrition, intentions and confidence: Interaction effects in a path model.* Paper presented at the annual meeting of the American Educational Research Association, Los Angeles.

3709

Test Name: FRESHMAN TRANSITION QUESTIONNAIRE

Purpose: To assess students' success in adjusting to college.

Number of Items: 67

Format: Includes four subscales: academic adjustment, social adjustment, personal-emotional adjustment, and goal commitment–institutional attachment.

Reliability: Coefficient alphas ranged from .78 to .95.

Author: Martin, N. K., and Dixon, P. N.

Article: The effects of freshman orientation and locus of control on adjustment to college.

Journal: *Journal of College Student Development,* July 1989, *30*(4), 362–367.

Related Research: Baker, R. W., & Siryk, B. (1984). Measuring adjustment to college. *Journal of Counseling Psychology, 31,* 179–189.

■ ■ ■

3710

Test Name: HASSLES SCALE

Purpose: To identify the personal severity of daily hassles as an index of student stress.

Number of Items: 117

Format: Respondents indicate on a 3-point scale the severity of each relevant daily hassle. Provides two scores: frequency and intensity.

Reliability: Average test–retest reliabilities were .79 (frequency) and .48 (intensity).

Author: Elliott, T. R., and Gramling, S. E.

Article: Personal assertiveness and the effects of social support among college students.

Journal: *Journal of Counseling Psychology,* October 1990, *37*(4), 427–436.

Related Research: Kanner, A., et al. (1981). Comparison of two modes of stress measurement: Daily hassles and uplifts versus major life events. *Journal of Behavioral Medicine, 4,* 1–39.

■ ■ ■

3711

Test Name: INVENTORY OF TEACHER SOCIAL AND BEHAVIORAL STANDARDS

Purpose: To measure teachers' tolerance for appropriate and inappropriate classroom behavior.

Number of Items: 107

Format: Three-category acceptability scales.

Reliability: Alphas ranged from .93 to .96. Test–retest ranged from .82 to .87.

Author: McIntyre, L. L.

Article: Teaching standards and gender: Factors in special education referral?

Journal: *Journal of Educational Research,* January/February 1990, *83*(3), 166–172.

Related Research: Walker, H., & Rankin, R. (1983). Assessing the behavioral expectations and demands of less restrictive settings. *School Psychology Review, 12,* 274–284.

■ ■ ■

3712

Test Name: MANDLER-SARASON TEST ANXIETY SCALE

Purpose: To assess test anxiety.

Number of Items: 37

Format: Items are answered true/false. An example is presented.

Reliability: Coefficient alpha was .82.

Author: Crocker, L., and Schmitt, A.

Article: Improving multiple-choice test performance for examinees with different levels of test anxiety.

Journal: *Journal of Experimental Education,* Summer 1987, *55*(4), 201–205.

Related Research: Sarason, I. G. (1978). The test anxiety scale: Concept and research. In C. D. Spielberger & I. G. Sarason (Eds.), *Stress and anxiety* (Vol. 5). New York: Hemisphere/Wiley.

■ ■ ■

3713

Test Name: MASTERY AND PERFORMANCE SCALES

Purpose: To assess students' perceived mastery and performance in the classroom.

Number of Items: 34

Format: Five-point Likert format. Sample items presented.

Reliability: Alphas ranged from .77 to .88.

Validity: Correlations with other variables ranged from –.29 to .63.

Author: Ames, C., and Archer, J.

Article: Achievement goals in the classroom: Students' learning strategies and motivation process.

Journal: *Journal of Educational Psychology,* September 1988, *80*(3), 260–267.

■ ■ ■

3714

Test Name: MATH ANXIETY MEASURE

Purpose: To measure math anxiety.

Number of Items: 19

Format: Seven-point Likert format.

Reliability: Alphas ranged from .71 to .80.

Author: Meece, J. L., et al.

Article: Predictors of math anxiety and its influence on young adolescents' course enrollment intentions and performance in mathematics.

Journal: *Journal of Educational Psychology,* March 1990, *82*(1), 60–70.

Related Research: Wigfield, A., & Meece, J. L. (1988). Math anxiety in elementary and secondary students. *Journal of Educational Psychology, 80,* 210–216.

■ ■ ■

3715

Test Name: MATH ANXIETY QUESTIONNNAIRE

Purpose: To measure math anxiety.

Number of Items: 11

Format: Seven-point Likert format. All items presented.

Validity: Factor structure of two scales was consistent across comparison groups. Correlations ranged from –.60 to .62.

Author: Wigfield, A., and Meece, J. L.

Article: Math anxiety in elmentary and secondary school students.

Journal: *Journal of Educational Psychology,* June 1988, *80*(2), 210–216.

Related Research: Meece, J. (1981). *Individual differences in the affective reactions of middle and high school students to mathematics: A social cognitive perspective.* Unpublished doctoral dissertation, University of Michigan.

■ ■ ■

3716

Test Name: MATHEMATICS ANXIETY SCALE

Purpose: To measure mathematics anxiety of college students.

Number of Items: 10

Format: Items are scored on a 5-point Likert scale.

Reliability: Split-half reliability was .92.

Author: Lapan, R. T., et al.

Article: Self-efficacy as a mediator of investigative and realistic general occupational themes on the Strong-Campbell Interest Inventory.

Journal: *Journal of Counseling Psychology*, April 1989, *36*(2), 176–182.

Related Research: Betz, N. E. (1978). Prevalence, distribution, and correlates of math anxiety in college students. *Journal of Counseling Psychology*, *25*, 441–448. Fennema, E., & Sherman, J. A. (1976). Fennema-Sherman Mathematics Attitude Scales: Instruments designed to measure attitudes toward the learning of mathematics by females and males. *JSAS: Catalog of Selected Documents in Psychology*, *6*, 31. (Ms. No. 1225).

■ ■ ■

3717

Test Name: MATHEMATICS ANXIETY SCALE

Purpose: To assess children's mathematics anxiety.

Number of Items: 8

Format: For each item, children indicate on a 3-point scale the degree to which they identify themselves with a hypothetical child in a mathematics classroom. An example is presented.

Reliability: Kuder-Richardson reliability coefficient was .82.

Author: Mevarech, Z. R.

Article: Computer-assisted instructional methods: A factorial study within mathematics disadvantaged classrooms.

Journal: *Journal of Experimental Education*, Fall 1985, *54*(1), 22–27.

Related Research: Mevarech, Z. R., & Rich, Y. (1985). Effects of computer-assisted mathematics instruction on disadvantaged pupils' cognitive and affective development. *Journal of Educational Research*, *79*, 5–11.

3718

Test Name: MATHEMATICS ANXIETY RATING SCALE

Purpose: To measure mathematics anxiety.

Number of Items: 98

Format: Five-point format.

Reliability: Alpha was .97. Test–retest (7 weeks) reliability was .85.

Author: Hunsley, J.

Article: Cognitive processes in mathematics anxiety and test anxiety: The role of appraisals, internal dialogue, and attributions.

Journal: *Journal of Educational Psychology*, December 1987, *79*(4), 388–392.

Related Research: Richardson, F. C., & Suinn, R. M. (1972). The Mathematics Anxiety Rating Scale: Psychometric data. *Journal of Counseling Psychology*, *19*, 551–554.

■ ■ ■

3719

Test Name: MATHEMATICS ANXIETY SCALE FOR CHILDREN

Purpose: To measure mathematics anxiety of children in upper elementary grades and middle schools.

Number of Items: 22

Format: Children rate activities on a 4-point scale ranging from 1 (*not nervous*) to 4 (*very very nervous*).

Reliability: Coefficient alphas ranged from .90 to .92.

Validity: Correlations with other variables ranged from .71 to –.50.

Author: Chiu, L-H., and Henry, L. L.

Article: Development and validation of the Mathematics Anxiety Scale for Children.

Journal: *Measurement and Evaluation in Counseling and Development*, October 1990, *23*(3), 121–127.

3720

Test Name: MATHEMATICS EFFICACY SCALES

Purpose: To assess mathematics efficacy in terms of comparisons to others, evaluations by others, and math anxiety.

Number of Items: 15

Format: Five-point self-descriptive scales. All items presented.

Reliability: Alphas ranged from .69 to .84.

Validity: Degree of fit to hypothesized psychometric model was 80%.

Author: Matsui, T., et al.

Article: Mechanisms underlying math self-efficacy learning of college students.

Journal: *Journal of Vocational Behavior*, October 1990, *37*(2), 225–238.

■ ■ ■

3721

Test Name: MATHEMATICS MOTIVATION AND ATTITUDES SCALES

Purpose: To measure effort, acceptability of failure as part of learning, and negative and positive thoughts about failure in learning mathematics.

Number of Items: 24

Format: Likert format. Sample items are presented.

Reliability: Alphas ranged from .59 to .83 across scales.

Validity: Correlations between scales and other measures ranged from .18 to .59.

Author: Kloosterman, P.

Article: Self-confidence and motivation in mathematics.

Journal: *Journal of Educational Psychology*, September 1988, *80*(3), 345–351.

3722

Test Name: MATH SELF-CONCEPT AND LEARNING SCALES

Purpose: To measure math self-concept, expectations for success, value of math, and math problem solving strategies.

Number of Items: 30

Reliability: Alphas ranged from .55 to .90 across subscales.

Validity: Correlations with math performance ranged from −.06 to .71.

Author: Pokay, P., and Blumenfeld, P. C.

Article: Predicting achievement early and late in the semester: The role of motivation and use of learning strategies.

Journal: *Journal of Educational Psychology*, March 1990, *82*(1), 41–50.

Related Research: Pintrich, P. (1986). Anxiety, motivated strategies, and student learning. Paper presented at the International Congress of Applied Psychology, Jerusalem, Israel.

■ ■ ■

3723

Test Name: MEIER BURNOUT ASSESSMENT

Purpose: To measure college student burnout.

Number of Items: 27

Format: Employs a true–false format.

Reliability: Cronbach's alpha was .83.

Validity: Correlations with other variables ranged from −.13 to .62 (*N* = 360).

Author: McCarthy, M. E., et al.

Article: Pscyhological sense of community and student burnout.

Journal: *Journal of College Student Development*, May 1990, *31*(3), 211–216.

Related Research: Meier, S. T., & Schmeck, R. R. (1985). The burned-out college student: A descriptive profile. *Journal of College Student Personnel*, 25, 63–69.

■ ■ ■

3724

Test Name: NON-COGNITIVE QUESTIONNAIRE

Purpose: To assess factors related to minority student academic success.

Number of Items: 23

Format: Includes 2 categorical items on educational aspirations, 18 Likert-type items on expectations regarding college and self-assessment, and 3 open-ended items requesting information on present goals, past accomplishments, and other activities.

Reliability: Test–retest (2 weeks) reliability ranged form .70 to .94.

Author: Tracey, T. J., and Sedlacek, W. E.

Article: A comparison of white and black student academic success using noncognitive variables: A LISREL analysis.

Journal: *Research in Higher Education*, 1987, *27*(4), 333–348.

Related Research: Tracey, T. J., & Sedlacek, W. E. (1984). Noncognitive variables in predicting academic success by race. *Measurement and Evaluation in Guidance*, *16*, 171–178.

■ ■ ■

3725

Test Name: NON-COGNITIVE QUESTIONNAIRE—REVISED

Purpose: To assess eight noncognitive dimensions important in minority student academic success.

Number of Items: 38

Format: Includes eight noncognitive dimensions: academic positive self-concept, realistic self-appraisal, support of academic plans, leadership, long range goals, ability to establish community ties, understanding of racism, and academic familiarity. All items are presented.

Reliability: Alpha coefficients ranged from .37 to .84.

Author: Tracey, T. J., and Sedlacek, W. E.

Article: Factor structure of the Non-Cognitive Questionnaire—Revised across samples of Black and White college students.

Journal: *Educational and Psychological Measurement*, Autumn 1989, *49*(3), 637–648.

Related Research: Tracey, T. J., & Sedlacek, W. E. (1984). Noncognitive variables in predicting academic success by race. *Measurement and Evaluation in Guidance*, *16*, 171–178.

■ ■ ■

3726

Test Name: READING AND WRITING SELF-EFFICACY INSTRUMENTS

Purpose: To measure confidence in being able to read and understand an author's meaning.

Number of Items: 27 (reading) and 24 (writing).

Format: Items rated on 100-point rating scales. All items presented.

Reliability: Alphas ranged from .92 to .95.

Validity: Correlations between reading and writing scales ranged from .10 to .85.

Author: Shell, D. F., et al.

Article: Self-efficacy and outcome expectancy mechanisms in reading and writing achievement.

Journal: *Journal of Educational Psychology*, March 1989, *81*(1), 91–100.

3727

Test Name: SATISFACTION WITH SCHOOL SCALE

Purpose: To assess college students' satisfaction with school

Number of Items: 5

Format: Responses are made on a scale ranging from 1 to 7 where 7 indicates a high degree of the characteristic being measured. All items are presented.

Validity: Correlations with other variables ranged from –.66 to .38.

Author: Staats, S., and Partlo, C.

Article: Predicting intent to get a college degree.

Journal: *Journal of College Student Development*, May 1990, *31*(3), 245–249.

Related Research: Staats, S. (1983). Perceived sources of stress and happiness in married and single college students. *Psychological Reports, 52,* 179–184.

■ ■ ■

3728

Test Name: SCHOOL ADJUSTMENT INDEX

Purpose: To measure school adjustment including disruptiveness, destructiveness, fighting, showing of consideration, task performance, toleration of frustration.

Number of Items: 44

Format: Four-point frequency scale (1 = *rarely or never*).

Reliability: Split-half reliability was .98.

Validity: Positively related to changes in moral reasoning (beta was .455, p < .0001).

Author: Arbuthnat, J., and Gordon, D. A.

Article: Behavioral and cognitive effects of a moral reasoning

development intervention for high-risk behavior-disordered adolescents.

Journal: *Journal of Consulting and Clinical Psychology*, April 1986, *54*(2), 208–216.

■ ■ ■

3729

Test Name: SCHOOL ADJUSTMENT SCALE

Purpose: To measure school adjustments.

Number of Items: 6

Format: Items ask about success in and liking for school.

Reliability: Alpha was .85.

Validity: Correlations with other variables ranged from .33 to –.45.

Author: Oetting, E. R., and Beauvais, F.

Article: Peer cluster theory, socialization characteristics, and adolescent drug use: A path analysis.

Journal: *Journal of Counseling Psychology,* April 1987, *34*(2), 205–213.

■ ■ ■

3730

Test Name: SCHOOL ATTACHMENT MEASURE

Purpose: To provide a measure of school attachment.

Number of Items: 5

Format: Items are in question format. All items are presented.

Reliability: Coefficient alpha was .68.

Author: Ensminger, M. E.

Article: Sexual activity and problem behaviors among Black, urban adolescents.

Journal: *Child Development*, December 1990, *61*(6), 2032–2046.

Related Research: Hirschi, T. (1969). *Causes of delinquency*. Berkeley: University of California.

3731

Test Name: SCHOOL FAILURE TOLERANCE SCALE

Purpose: To measure school failure tolerance.

Number of Items: 36

Format: Includes three subscales: failure feelings, failure action, and preferred difficulty. An agree–disagree Likert scale is used. Sample items are presented.

Reliability: Alpha coefficients ranged from .80 to .90.

Validity: Correlations with other variables ranged from –.45 to –.66.

Author: Clifford, M. M., et al.

Article: Academic risk-taking: Developmental and cross-cultural observations.

Journal: *Journal of Experimental Education*, Summer 1989, *57*(4), 321–388.

Related Research: Clifford, M. M. (1988). Failure tolerance and academic risk-taking in ten- to twelve-year-old students. *British Journal of Educational Psychology, 58,* 15–27.

■ ■ ■

3732

Test Name: SCIENCE ACTIVITY QUESTIONNAIRE

Purpose: To measure task mastery, ego/social involvement and work-avoidance, active engagement and superficial engagement in science.

Format: Four-point (*very true*) to (*not at all true*) scales.

Reliability: Alphas ranged from .77 to .94.

Validity: Correlations between subscales and with other variables ranged from –.40 to .70.

Author: Meece, J. L., et al.

Article: Students' goal orientations and cognitive engagement in classroom activities.

Journal: *Journal of Educational Psychology,* September 1988, *80*(4), 514–523.

Related Research: Nolen, S. (1986). *The Role of Personal Goals in Students' Selection of Learning Strategies.* Unpublished doctoral dissertation, Purdue University, West Lafayette, Indiana.

■ ■ ■

3733

Test Name: SELF-EFFICACY FOR TECHNICAL/SCIENTIFIC FIELDS SCALE

Purpose: To measure subjects' confidence in completing educational requirements for science and engineering fields.

Number of Items: 15

Format: Ten-point rating scales.

Reliability: Test–retest reliability was .89. Alpha was .89.

Author: Lent, R. W., et al.

Article: Relation of self-efficacy to inventoried vocational interests.

Journal: *Journal of Vocational Behavior,* June 1989, *34*(3), 289–298.

Related Research: Lent, R. W., et al. (1984). Relation of self-efficacy expectations to academic achievement and persistence. *Journal of Counseling Psychology, 31,* 356–362.

■ ■ ■

3734

Test Name: SOCIAL INTEGRATION SCALE

Purpose: To assess student involvement with peers and faculty.

Number of Items: 6

Format: Responses are either *yes* or *no.* An example is presented.

Reliability: Coefficient alpha was .58.

Validity: Correlation with completion of a bachelor's degree ranged from .18 to .26.

Author: Pascarella, E. T.

Article: Racial differences in factors associated with bachelor's degree completion: A 9-year follow-up.

Journal: *Research in Higher Education,* 1985, *23*(4), 351–373.

■ ■ ■

3735

Test Name: STUDENT ADAPTATION TO COLLEGE QUESTIONNAIRE

Purpose: To measure four aspects of student adaptation to college.

Number of Items: 67

Format: Includes four subscales: academic adjustment, social adjustment, personal–emotional adjustment, and institutional attachment. Responses are made on a 9-point scale indicating how closely the items apply to the respondent.

Reliability: Alpha coefficients ranged from .81 to .91.

Validity: Correlations with other variables ranged from −.40 to .37 (male) and from −.34 to .42 (female).

Author: Lopez, F. G., et al.

Article: Family structure, psychological separation, and college adjustment: A canonical analysis and cross-validation.

Journal: *Journal of Counseling Psychology,* October 1988, *35*(4), 402–409.

Related Research: Baker, R. W., et al. (1985). Expectation and reality in freshman adjustment to college. *Journal of Counseling Psychology, 32,* 94–103.

■ ■ ■

3736

Test Name: STUDENT'S PERCEPTION OF ABILITY SCALE

Purpose: To assess how children feel about reading, spelling, language arts, arithmetic and penmanship.

Number of Items: 70

Format: Yes–no format.

Reliability: Internal consistency was .92. Test–retest (6 weeks) reliability was .83.

Validity: Correlations with Piers-Harris total score ranged from −.03 to .08 (not statistically significant).

Author: Lyon, M. A., and MacDonald, N. T.

Article: Academic self-concept as a predictor of achievement for a sample of elementary school students.

Journal: *Psychological Reports,* June 1990, *66*(3) II, 1135–1142.

Related Research: Boerma, F. J., & Chapman, J. W. (1978). Comparison of student's perception of ability scale with the Piers-Harris Childrens Self-Concept Scale. *Perceptual and Motor Skills, 47,* 827–832.

■ ■ ■

3737

Test Name: STUDENT WORRY SURVEY

Purpose: To assess student worries including: school, relationships, health and appearance, career, acceptance, money and time.

Number of Items: 35

Format: Four point frequency and intensity scales for each item.

Reliability: Alpha was .93. Test–retest (8 weeks) reliability was .75.

Validity: All worries correlated positively with laterality (left-handedness). Seven of eight correlations were significant at $p <$ .05.

Author: Dillon, K. M.

Article: Lateral preference and students' worries: A correlation.

Journal: *Psychological Reports,* October 1989, *65*(2), 496–498.

Related Research: McDaniel, P. S., & Eison, J. (1987). Assessing student worries. In V. P. Makosky et al. (Eds.),

Activities handbook for the teaching of psychology (Vol. 2, pp. 241–245). Washington, DC: American Psychological Association.

■ ■ ■

3738

Test Name: STUDY HABITS AND INTEREST INVENTORY

Purpose: To predict academic success in college from students' study habits and attitudes.

Number of Items: 31

Format: Item formats include multiple-choice and yes–no types. All items presented.

Reliability: Alpha was .77.

Validity: Correlated .66 with grade point average.

Author: Nixon, C. T., and Frost, A. G.

Article: The Study Habits and Attitude Inventory and its implications for student success.

Journal: *Psychological Reports*, June 1990, *66*(3) II, 1075–1085.

■ ■ ■

3739

Test Name: SUINN TEST ANXIETY BEHAVIOR SCALE

Purpose: To measure general test anxiety.

Number of Items: 50

Format: Likert scale.

Reliability: Test–retest reliability coefficients were .74 and .78.

Validity: Correlations with the Text Anxiety Scale were .50 and .60.

Author: Kostka, M. P., and Wilson, C. K.

Article: Reducing mathematics anxiety in nontraditional-age female students.

Journal: *Journal of College Student Personnel*, November 1986, *27*(6), 530–534.

Related Research: Suinn, R. M. (1969). The STABS, a measure of test anxiety for behavior therapy: Normative data. *Behavior Research and Therapy*, *7*, 335–339.

■ ■ ■

3740

Test Name: TEACHER–CHILD RATING SCALE

Purpose: To measure children's classroom adjustment.

Number of Items: 35

Format: Teachers rate children on a 5-point severity scale.

Reliability: Median alpha was .91. Twenty-week stability coefficients ranged from .61 to .88.

Author: Alpert-Gillis, L. J., et al.

Article: The children of divorce intervention program: Development, implementation and evaluation of a program for young urban children.

Journal: *Journal of Consulting and Clinical Psychology*, October 1989, *57*(5), 583–589.

Related Research: Hightower, A. D., et al. (1986). The Teacher Child Rating Scale: A brief objective measure of elementary children.s school problem behaviors and competencies. *School Psychology Review*, *15*, 393–409.

■ ■ ■

3741

Test Name: TEACHER-CLASSROOM ADJUSTMENT RATING SCALE

Purpose: To assess the difficulties of children in school by teacher ratings.

Number of Items: 18

Format: Five-point problem seriousness scales.

Reliability: Alphas ranged from .88 to .94 across subscales. Test–retest reliabilities ranged from .76 to .88 across subscales.

Author: Gralnick, W. S., and Ryan, R. M.

Article: Parent styles associated with children's self-regulation and competence in school.

Journal: *Journal of Educational Psychology*, June 1989, *81*(2), 143–154.

Related Research: Hightower, A. D., et al. (1986). The teacher-child rating scale: A brief objective measure of elementary children's school problem behaviors and competencies. *School Psychology Review*, *16*, 239–255.

■ ■ ■

3742

Test Name: TEXT ANXIETY INVENTORY

Purpose: To measure test anxiety as a situation-specific personality trait.

Number of Items: 20

Format: Frequency scales. Sample items presented.

Reliability: Test–retest reliability ranged from .62 to .81. Alpha was .95.

Validity: Correlations with other trait variables ranged from .54 to .83.

Author: Schaer, B., and Isom, S.

Article: Effectiveness of progressive relaxation on test anxiety and visual perceptions.

Journal: *Psychological Reports*, October 1988, *63*(2), 511–518.

Related Research: Liebert, R. M., & Morris, L. W. (1967). Cognitive and emotional components of test anxiety: A distinction and some initial data. *Psychological Reports*, *20*, 975–978.

■ ■ ■

3743

Test Name: TEST ANXIETY SCALE

Purpose: To measure test anxiety.

Number of Items: 37

Format: True–false.

Reliability: Test–retest reliability was .80.

Author: Blankstein, K. R., and Toney, B. B.

Article: Influence of social-desirability responding on the Sarason Test Anxiety Scale: Implications for selection of subjects.

Journal: *Psychological Reports*, August 1987, *61*(1), 65–69.

Related Research: Sarason, I. G. (1978). The Test Anxiety Scale: Concept and research. In C. D. Spielberger & I. G. Sarason (Eds.), *Stress and anxiety* (Vol. 5, pp. 193–216). Washington, DC: Hemisphere.

■ ■ ■

3744

Test Name: TEST ANXIETY SCALE FOR ADOLESCENTS

Purpose: To measure test anxiety.

Number of Items: 31

Format: True–false format. Sample items are presented.

Reliability: Alpha coefficients ranged from .62 to .87.

Validity: Correlations with the Metropolitan Achievement Test ranged from −.20 to −.42.

Author: Crocker, L., et al.

Article: Test anxiety and standardized achievement test performance in the middle school years.

Journal: *Measurement and Evaluation in Counseling and Development*, January 1988, *20*(4), 149–157.

Related Research: Schmitt, A. P., & Crocker, L. (1982). Test anxiety and its components for middle school students. *Journal of Early Adolescence, 2*, 267–275.

■ ■ ■

3745

Test Name: TEST ANXIETY SCALE FOR CHILDREN

Purpose: To identify test anxiety in children.

Number of Items: 30

Format: The test provides yes/no questions concerning children's attitude and experiences in test or testlike situations colored by anxiety.

Reliability: Test–retest reliabilities (2 month interval) ranged from .44 to .82.

Validity: Correlations with other variables ranged from −.48 to .27.

Author: Wapner, J. G., and Connor, K.

Article: The role of defensiveness in cognitive impulsivity.

Journal: *Child Development*, December 1986, *57*(6), 1370–1374.

Related Research: Sarason, S., et al. (1958). A test anxiety scale for children. *Child Development, 29*, 105–113.

■ ■ ■

3746

Test Name: TEST COMFORT INDEX

Purpose: To measure test anxiety.

Number of Items: 7

Format: Items deal specifically with the test situation. Yes/no responses are made to each item. A sample item is presented.

Reliability: Coefficient alphas were .67 and .78.

Validity: Correlations with other variables ranged from −.34 to .33.

Author: Finchan, F. D., et al.

Article: Learned helplessness, test anxiety, and academic achievement: A longitudinal analysis.

Journal: *Child Development*, February 1989, *60*(1), 138–145.

Related Research: Harnisch, D. L., et al. (1980, April). *Development of a shorter, more reliable and valid measure of test motivation.* Paper

presented at the Annual Meeting of the National Council on Measurement in Education, Boston.
Feld, S. C., & Lewis, J. (1969). The assessment of achievement anxieties in children. In C. P. Smith (Ed.), *Achievement related motives in children* (pp. 79–93). New York: Sage.

■ ■ ■

3747

Test Name: UNIVERSITY ALIENATION SCALE

Purpose: To measure components of alienation in college students, with reference to the university setting.

Number of Items: 25

Format: Likert-type items are used to measure the following components of alienation: powerlessness, meaninglessness, and social estrangement.

Reliability: Split-half reliabilities ranged from .72 to .92.

Validity: Correlations with other variables ranged rom −.46 to .31.

Author: Steward, R. J., et al.

Article: Alienation and interactional styles in a predominantly White environment: A study of successful Black students.

Journal: *Journal of College Student Development*, November 1990, *31*(6), 509–515.

■ ■ ■

3748

Test Name: UNIVERSITY EXPERIENCE QUESTIONNAIRE

Purpose: To assess three components of membership in the unversity community.

Number of Items: 32

Format: The three components assessed are: satisfaction with the university environment, academic involvement, and knowledge of the university environment.

Reliability: Alpha coefficients were .85 and .89. Test–retest reliability was .88.

Author: Russel, J. H., and Shinkle, R. R.

Article: Evaluation of peer-adviser effectiveness.

Journal: *Journal of College Student Development*, September 1990, *31*(5), 388–394.

Related Research: Russel, J. H., & Shinkle, R. (1988). *The University Experience Questionnaire: An instrument to measure membership in the university community.* Paper presented at the International Conference on the First Year Experience, Toronto, Ontario, Canada.

■ ■ ■

3749

Test Name: WORRY AND EMOTIONALITY SCALE

Purpose: To measure situational test anxiety immediately prior to a classroom examination.

Number of Items: 10

Format: Includes two 5-item subscales of emotionality and worry. Responses are made on a 5-point agreement scale.

Reliability: Internal consistency correlations ranged from .81 to .88.

Validity: Correlations with fear of failure ranged from .32 to .39 ($N = 215$). Correlations with college grade point average ranged from −.11 to −.24 ($N = 215$).

Author: Herman, W. E.

Article: Fear of failure as a distinctive personality trait measure of test anxiety.

Journal: *Journal of Research and Development in Education*, Spring 1990, *23*(3), 180–185.

Related Research: Morris, L. W., et al. (1981). Cognitive and emotionality components of anxiety: Literature review and a revised worry-emotionality scale. *Journal of Educational Psychology, 73*, 541–555.

3750

Test Name: WRITING APPREHENSION TEST

Purpose: To measure the affective dimension of writing.

Number of Items: 26

Format: Six items are intended for in-classroom use. The remaining 20 items are responded to on a 5-point scale ranging from *strongly agree* to *strongly disagree*. Examples are presented.

Reliability: Split-half reliability was .94. Test–retest reliability (1 week) was .92.

Author: Megel, M. E.

Article: Nursing scholars, writing dimensions, and productivity.

Journal: *Research in Higher Education*, 1987, *27*(3), 226–243.

Related Research: Daley, J. A., & Miller, M. D. (1975). The empirical development of an instrument to measure writing apprehension. *Research in the Teaching of English, 9*(Fall), 242–249.

CHAPTER 3
Adjustment–Psychological

3751

Test Name: ACTIVITIES OF DAILY LIVING SCALE

Purpose: To measure daily living activities of chronic pain patients.

Number of Items: 10

Format: Items are rated on a 0–10-point scale indicating the person's ability to participate in each activity. All items are presented.

Reliability: Test–retest reliability was .89. Internal consistency was .75.

Validity: Correlation with global ratings was .63 and with significant others was .77.

Author: Luiton, S. J.

Article: Activities of daily living scale for patients with chronic pain.

Journal: *Perceptual and Motor Skills*, December 1990, *71*(3) part 1, 722.

■ ■ ■

3752

Test Name: ADJUSTMENT SCALE

Purpose: To assess adjustment and social behavior of prepsychotic and ex-hospital patients.

Number of Items: 127

Format: Present–absent format for hospitalized subjects. Four-point rating scale for others.

Reliability: Internal consistency ranged from .41 to .87. Test–retest reliability ranged from .50 to .75.

Author: Parker, G., and Johnston, P.

Article: Reliability of parental reports using the Katz Adjustment Scales:

Before and after hospital admission for schizophrenia.

Journal: *Psychological Reports*, August 1989, *65*(1), 251–258.

Related Research: Katz, M. M., & Lyerly, S. B. (1963). Methods for measuring adjustment and social behavior in the community: Rationale, description, discriminative validity, and scale development. *Psychological Reports*, 13, 503–535.

■ ■ ■

3753

Test Name: ADOLESCENT PERCEIVED EVENTS SCALE

Purpose: To measure daily major stressful events during adolescence.

Number of Items: 159, 200, or 210 pairs of items depending on the age of respondent.

Format: Subjects 12–14 years of age respond on a 9-point desirability scale; older subjects respond, in addition, to a 9-point impact scale and a 9-point frequency scale.

Reliability: Test–retest reliability ranged from .74 to .89.

Validity: Subject's and subject's roommates appraisals agreed 87 to 91 percent of the time.

Author: Compas, B. E., et al.

Article: Assessment of major and daily stressful events during adolescence: The Adolescent Perceived Events Scale.

Journal: *Journal of Consulting and Clinical Psychology*, June 1987, *55*(3), 534–541.

3754

Test Name: ADOLESCENT PERCEIVED EVENTS SCALE

Purpose: To measure adolescents' major and daily stressful events.

Number of Items: 164

Format: Yes–no format for each item. If yes, respondents indicate desirability of the event on a 9-point scale.

Reliability: Test–retest (2 weeks) reliability was .86.

Validity: Correlations with other variables ranged from .02 to .70.

Author: Compas, B. E., et al.

Article: Risk factors for emotional/behavioral problems in young adolescents: A prospective analysis of adolescent and parental stress symptoms.

Journal: *Journal of Consulting and Clinical Psychology*, December 1989, *56*(6), 732–740.

Related Research: Compas, B. E., et al. (1987). Adjustment of major and daily stressful events during adolescence: The Adolescent Perceived Events Scale. *Journal of Consulting and Clinical Psychology*, 55, 534–541.

■ ■ ■

3755

Test Name: AFFECT BALANCE SCALE

Purpose: To measure positive affect.

Number of Items: 5

Format: Yes–no format.

Reliability: Alpha was .62.

Validity: Correlations with other variables ranged from .00 to .25.

Author: O'Bryant, S. L.

Article: Sibling support and older widows' well-being.

Journal: *Journal of Marriage and the Family*, February 1988, *50*(1), 173–183.

Related Research: Bradburn, N. M. (1969). *The structure of psychological well-being*. Chicago: Adline.

■ ■ ■

3756

Test Name: AFFECT-BALANCE SCALE

Purpose: To measure happiness.

Number of Items: 10

Format: Divided between positive- and negative-affect scales. *Yes* or *no* responses are made to each item.

Reliability: Test–retest (1 week or less) reliability ranged from .80 to .97.

Validity: Correlation with the Rosow Morale Scale was .61.

Author: Shoskes, J. E., and Glenwick, D. S.

Article: The relationship of the Depression Adjective Check List to positive affect and activity level in older adults.

Journal: *Journal of Personality Assessment*, Winter 1987, *51*(4), 565–571.

Related Research: Bradburn, N. M. (1969). *The structure of psychological well-being*. Chicago: Aldine.

■ ■ ■

3757

Test Name: AFFECT INTENSITY MEASURE

Purpose: To measure the intensity of emotional experiences.

Number of Items: 40

Format: Never–always frequency scales.

Reliability: Test–retest (from 1 to 3 months) reliability ranged from .80 to .81.

Author: Calloni, J. C., and Ross, M. J.

Article: Affect intensity and self- versus-other referent information processing.

Journal: *Psychological Reports*, April 1990, *66*(2), 495–498.

Related Research: Larsen, R., et al. (1986). Affect intensity and reactions to daily life events. *Journal of Personality and Social Psychology*, *51*, 803–814.

■ ■ ■

3758

Test Name: AGORAPHOBIC COGNITIONS QUESTIONNAIRE

Purpose: To provide a self-report by agoraphobic patients of typical thoughts concerning negative consequences of experiencing anxiety.

Number of Items: 14

Format: Respondents indicate on a 5-point scale the frequency of occurrence of each cognition. The scale runs from *thought never occurs* to *thought always occurs*.

Reliability: Spearman-Brown coefficients ranged from .66 to .88.

Author: Craske, M. G., et al.

Article: Mobility, cognitions, and panic.

Journal: *Journal of Psychopathology and Behavioral Assessment*, September 1986, *8*(3), 199–210.

Related Research: Chambless, D., et al. (1984). Assessment of fear in agoraphobics: The Body Sensations Questionnaire and the Agoraphobic Cognitions Questionnaire. *Journal of Consulting and Clinical Psychology*, *52*, 1090–1097.

3759

Test Name: ANGER INVENTORY

Purpose: To determine the degree to which situations would anger students.

Number of Items: 90

Format: Likert scale.

Validity: Correlations with other variables ranged from −.03 to .41.

Author: Hogg, J. A., and Deffenbacher, J. L.

Article: Irrational beliefs, depression, and anger among college students.

Journal: *Journal of College Student Personnel*, July 1986, *27*(4), 349–353.

Related Research: Novaco, R. W. (1975). *Anger control: The development and evaluation of an experimental treatment*. Lexington, MA: Lexington Books.

■ ■ ■

3760

Test Name: ANXIETY SCALE

Purpose: To assess the degree to which an individual feels tense, jittery, anxious, and so on.

Number of Items: 20

Reliability: Coefficient alpha was .85.

Validity: Correlations with other variables ranged from −.37 to .13.

Author: Latack, J. C., et al.

Article: Carpenter apprentices: Comparison of career transition for men and women.

Journal: *Journal of Applied Psychology*, August 1987, *72*(3), 393–400.

Related Research: Caplan, D., et al. (1975). Job demands and worker health. (NIOSH Publication No. 75-160). Washington, DC: US Department of Health, Education, and Welfare.

3761

Test Name: ANXIETY SCALE

Purpose: To measure prolonged anxiety.

Number of Items: 5

Format: Five-point scales. All items described.

Reliability: Internal consistency was .67. Alphas ranged from .68 to .74.

Validity: Correlations with other variables ranged from −.52 to .53.

Author: Shamir, B.

Article: Self-esteem and the psychological impact of unemployment.

Journal: *Social Psychology Quarterly*, March 1986, *49*(1), 61–72.

Related Research: Warr, P. B. (1978). A study of psychological well-being. *British Journal of Psychology*, *69*, 111–121.

■ ■ ■

3762

Test Name: ANXIETY SCALE

Purpose: To measure the emotional arousal associated with a task.

Number of Items: 10

Format: Responses are made on a Likert scale ranging from 1 (*strongly disagree*) to 4 (*strongly agree*). Examples are presented.

Reliability: Alpha coefficients ranged from .76 to .86.

Validity: Correlations with other variables ranged from −.48 to .47.

Author: Stumpf, S. A., and Brief, A. P.

Article: Self-efficacy expectations and coping with career-related events.

Journal: *Journal of Vocational Behavior*, August 1987, *31*(1), 91–108.

Related Research: Caplan, R. D., et al. (1975, April). *Job demands and worker health*. Washington, DC: U. S., Department of Health, Education, and Welfare.

■ ■ ■

3763

Test Name: AUTOMATIC THOUGHTS QUESTIONNAIRE

Purpose: To assess the frequency of occurrence of particular thoughts.

Number of Items: 30

Format: Each item is rated on a 5-point scale indicating frequency of rumination from 1 (*not at all*) to 5 (*all the time*).

Validity: Correlations with other variables ranged from .58 to .85.

Author: Hill, C. V., et al.

Article: An empirical investigation of the specificity and sensitivity of the Automatic Thoughts Questionnaire and Dysfunctional Attitudes Scale.

Journal: *Journal of Psychopathology and Behavioral Assessment*, December 1989, *11*(4), 291–311.

Related Research: Hollon, S. D., & Kendall, P. (1980). Cognitive self statements in depression: Development of an automatic thoughts questionnaire. *Cognitive Therapy and Research*, *4*, 383–395.

■ ■ ■

3764

Test Name: BECK ANXIETY INVENTORY

Purpose: To measure severity of anxiety in psychiatric populations.

Number of Items: 21

Format: Four-point severity rating scales. All items presented.

Reliability: Alpha was .92. Test–retest (1 week) reliability was .75.

Validity: Correlations with other measures ranged from .15 to .52.

Author: Beck, A. T., et al.

Article: An inventory for measuring clinical anxiety: Psychometric properties.

Journal: *Journal of Consulting and Clinical Psychology*, December 1988, *56*(6), 893–897.

■ ■ ■

3765

Test Name: BECK DEPRESSION INVENTORY—SHORT FORM

Purpose: To assess global marital satisfaction.

Number of Items: 13

Format: Scores range from 0 (*no depression*) to 39 (*severely depressed*).

Reliability: Test–retest reliability was .83.

Validity: Correlations with marital satisfaction ranged from −.16 to −.33.

Author: Beach, S. R. H., et al.

Article: The relationship of marital satisfaction and social support to depressive symptomatology.

Journal: *Journal of Psychopathology and Behavioral Assessment*, December 1986, *8*(4), 305–316

Related Research: Reynolds, W. M., & Gould, J. W. (1981). A psychometric investigation of the standard and short form Beck Depression Inventory. *Journal of Consulting and Clinical Psychology*, *49*, 306–307.

■ ■ ■

3766

Test Name: BECK DEPRESSION INVENTORY (PERSIAN VERSION)

Purpose: To measure depression.

Number of Items: 13

Format: Likert format.

Reliability: Item-total correlations ranged from .14 to .72 and alphas from .83 to .85. Test–retest reliability was .61.

Validity: Correlations with other scales ranged from .36 (misanthropy) to .60 (neuroticism).

Author: Hojat, M., et al.

Article: Psychometric properties of a Persian version of the Short Form of the Beck Depression Inventory for Iranian college students.

Journal: *Psychological Reports*, August 1986, *59*(1), 331–338.

■ ■ ■

3767

Test Name: BECK DEPRESSION INVENTORY—MODIFIED

Purpose: To measure depression.

Number of Items: 20

Format: Scores range from 0 to 60. Higher scores represent greater depression.

Reliability: Alpha reliability was .87.

Author: Hains, A. A., and Szyjakowski, M.

Article: A cognitive stress-reduction intervention program for adolescents.

Journal: *Journal of Counseling Psychology*, January 1990, *37*(1), 79–84.

Related Research: Reynolds, W. M., & Coats, K. I. (1986). A comparison of cognitive-behavioral therapy and relaxation training for the treatment of depression in adolescents. *Journal of Consulting and Clinical Psychology*, *54*, 653–660.

■ ■ ■

3768

Test Name: BECK DEPRESSION INVENTORY (DUTCH VERSION)

Purpose: To measure intensity of depression.

Number of Items: 21

Format: Cronbach's alpha was .82.

Reliability: Correlated .69 with Zung Depression Scale.

Author: Bosscher, R. J., et al.

Article: Reliability and validity of the Beck Depression Inventory in a Dutch college population.

Journal: *Psychological Reports*, June 1986, *58*(3), 696–698.

Related Research: Beck, A. T., et al. (1961). An inventory for measuring depression. *Archives of General Psychiatry*, *4*, 561–571.

■ ■ ■

3769

Test Name: BECK DEPRESSION INVENTORY

Purpose: To measure the intensity of depression.

Number of Items: 21

Format: The severity of each depressive symptom is rated on a 0 to 3 scale. All symptoms are presented.

Reliability: Split-half reliabilities reported in the .90s. Coefficient alpha was .87.

Validity: Correlations with clinical ratings of depression were above .50. Correlations with the Hamilton Psychiatric Rating Scale for Depression ranged from .54 to .86.

Author: Steer, R. A., et al.

Article: Relationships between the Beck Depression Inventory and the Hamilton Psychiatric Rating Scale for Depression in depressed outpatients.

Journal: *Journal of Psychopathology and Behavioral Assessment*, September 1987, *9*(3), 327–339.

Related Research: Beck, A. T., et al. (1979). *Cognitive therapy of depression*. New York: Guilford Press. Jarjoura, D., & O'Hara, M. W. (1987). A structural model for postpartum responses to the somatic and cognitive items on the Beck Depression Inventory. *Journal of Psychopathology and Behavioral Assessment*, *9*, 389–402.

3770

Test Name: BECK HOPELESSNESS SCALE

Purpose: To measure hopelessness.

Number of Items: 20

Format: Items are optimistic and pessimistic true–false statements.

Reliability: Kuder-Richardson reliability was .93.

Validity: Correlation with other variables ranged from −.42 to .70.

Author: Cole, D. A., and Milstead, M.

Article: Behavioral correlates of depression: Antecedents or consequences?

Journal: *Journal of Counseling Psychology*, October 1989, *36*(4), 408–416.

Related Research: Beck, A. T., et al. (1974). The measurement of pessimism: The Hoplessness Scale. *Journal of Consulting and Clinical Psychology*, *42*, 861–865.

■ ■ ■

3771

Test Name: BELL GLOBAL PSYCHOPATHOLOGY SCALE

Purpose: To measure psychological symptoms of stress.

Number of Items: 33

Format: Includes eight subscales. Responses are made on either a 5-point scale ranging from 1 (*never*) to 5 (*all the time*) or on a 2-point scale of 1 (*no*) or 2 (*yes*).

Reliability: Coefficient alpha and test–retest reliabilities were greater than .80.

Validity: Correlation with the Health Opinion Survey was .74. Correlations with other variables ranged from −.47 to .46.

Author: Mallinckrodt, B.

Article: Social support and the effectiveness of group therapy.

Journal: *Journal of Counseling Psychology*, April 1989, *36*(2), 170–175.

Related Research: Schwab, J. J., et al. (1979). *Social order and mental health: The Florida Health Study.* New York: Brunner/Mazel.

■ ■ ■

3772

Test Name: BELL OBJECT RELATIONS INVENTORY

Purpose: To assess object relations and reality testing.

Number of Items: 90

Format: Responses are either *true* or *false*. Includes seven subscales.

Reliability: For object relations subscales, alpha coefficients ranged from .78 to .90 and Spearman-Brown split-half reliabilities also ranged from .78 to .90.

Author: Heesacker, R. S., and Neimeyer, G. J.

Article: Assessing object relations and social cognitive correlates of eating disorder.

Journal: *Journal of Counseling Psychology*, October 1990, *37*(4), 419–426.

Related Research: Bell, M., et al. (1986). A scale of the assessment of object relations: Reliability, validity, and factorial invariance. *Journal of Clinical Psychology*, *42*, 733–741.

■ ■ ■

3773

Test Name: BIOGRAPHICAL AND EXPERIENCE QUESTIONNAIRE— REVISED

Purpose: To assess the physical compared with the psychological aspects of burnout.

Number of Items: 22

Format: Includes two subsets: physical symptoms and psychological symptoms. Frequency of experiencing each symptom is rated on a 6-point scale.

Validity: Correlations with other variables ranged from –.03 to .57 (*N* = 360).

Author: McCarthy, M. E., et al.

Article: Psychological sense of community and student burnout.

Journal: *Journal of College Student Development*, May 1990, *31*(3), 211–216.

Related Research: Moos, R., & Van Dort, B. (1977). Physical and emotional symptoms and campus health center utilization. *Social Psychiatry*, *2*, 107–115.

■ ■ ■

3774

Test Name: BLOMBERG-ERICKSON-LOWERY COMPUTER ATTITUDES TASK

Purpose: To measure computer anxiety.

Number of Items: 36

Format: Includes five subscales: computers as useful, liking computers, attitudes toward success with computers, computers as a male domain, and computer anxiety. Responses are made on 5-point Likert scales.

Reliability: Interitem reliability coefficients of the five subscales ranged from .71 to .81.

Validity: Correlations with other variables ranged from .75 to .89.

Author: Dukes, R. L., et al.

Article: Convergent validity of four computer anxiety scales.

Journal: *Educational and Psychological Measurement*, Spring 1989, *49*(1), 195–203.

Related Research: Erickson, T. E. (1987). Sex differences in student attitudes towards computers (Doctoral dissertation. Berkeley: University of California). Also presented at the Annual Meetings of the AERA, Portland, Oregon, November.

3775

Test Name: BOREDOM PRONENESS SCALE

Purpose: To measure one's proneness to boredom.

Number of Items: 28

Format: Responses may be *true* or *false* or placed on a 7-point Likert scale. Includes five factors: external stimulation, internal stimulation, affective responses, perception of time, and constraint. All items are presented.

Reliability: Alpha coefficients ranged from .59 to .83. Test–retest (1 week) reliability was .83 (*N* = 62).

Author: Vodanovich, S. J., and Kass, S. J.

Article: A factor analytic study of the Boredom Proneness Scale.

Journal: *Journal of Personality Assessment*, Fall 1990, *55*(1 and 2), 115–123.

Related Research: Farmer, R., & Sundberg, N. D. (1986). Boredom proneness: The development and correlates of a new scale. *Journal of Personality Assessment*, *50*, 4–17.

■ ■ ■

3776

Test Name: BORDERLINE SYNDROME INDEX

Purpose: To discriminate borderlines, schizotypals, and mixed patient groups from normals.

Number of Items: 52

Format: Yes–no format. Examples are presented.

Reliability: Kuder-Richardon formula was .92.

Author: Serban, G., et al.

Article: Borderline and schizotypal personality disorders: Mutually exclusive or overlapping?

Journal: *Journal of Personality Assessment*, Spring 1987, *51*(1), 15–22.

Related Research: Conte, H. R., et al. (1980). A self-report borderline scale: Discriminative validity and preliminary norms. *Journal of Nervous and Mental Disease, 172,* 254–265.

■ ■ ■

3777

Test Name: BRIEF SYMPTOM INVENTORY

Purpose: To assess severity of psychological symptoms by self-report.

Number of Items: 53

Format: Five-point rating scales.

Reliability: Alpha was .95.

Author: Rapp, S. R., et al.

Article: Psychological dysfunction and physical health among elderly medical inpatients.

Journal: *Journal of Consulting and Clinical Psychology,* December 1988, *56*(6), 851–855.

Related Research: Derogatis, L. R., & Melisaratos, N. (1983). The Brief Symptom Inventory: An introductory report. *Psychological Medicine, 13,* 595–605.

■ ■ ■

3778

Test Name: CANCER INVENTORY OF PROBLEM SITUATIONS

Purpose: To assess problems confronted by cancer patients.

Number of Items: 144

Format: Five-point rating scale (5 = *not at all a problem*).

Reliability: Alpha's averaged .84. Test–retest reliability coefficients were .80 or above.

Author: Telch, C. F., and Telch, M. J.

Article: Group coping skills instruction and supportive group therapy for cancer patients: A comparison of strategies.

Journal: *Journal of Consulting and Clinical Psychology,* December 1986, *54*(6), 802–808.

Related Research: Schag, C. C., et al. (1983). Cancer inventory of problem situations: An instrument for assessing cancer patients' rehabilitation needs. *Journal of Psychosocial Oncology, 1,* 11–24.

■ ■ ■

3779

Test Name: CENTER FOR EPIDEMIOLOGIC STUDIES DEPRESSION SCALE

Purpose: To measure depressive symptomatology in the general population.

Number of Items: 20

Format: Responses indicating how often the respondents felt were made on a 4-point scale ranging from *rarely or none of the time* to *most or all of the time.* An example is given.

Reliability: Internal consistency reliability estimate was .85. Test–retest reliability coefficients ranged from .32 (12 months) to .67 (4 weeks).

Author: Brief, A. P., et al.

Article: Should negative affectivity remain an unmeasured variable in the study of job stress?

Journal: *Journal of Applied Psychology,* May 1988, *73*(2), 193–198.

Related Research: Radloff, L. S. (1977). The CES-D Scale: A self-report depression scale for research in the general population. *Applied Psychological Measurement, 1,* 385–401.

■ ■ ■

3780

Test Name: CENTER FOR EPIDEMIOLOGICAL STUDIES DEPRESSION SCALE

Purpose: To measure depression.

Number of Items: 12

Format: Eight-point frequency scales.

Reliability: Alphas ranged from .84 to .79.

Author: Ulbrich, P. M.

Article: The determinants of depression in two-income marriages.

Journal: *Journal of Marriage and the Family,* February 1988, *50*(1), 121–131.

Related Research: Radloff, L. S. (1977). The CES-D scale: A self-report depression scale for the general population. *Applied Psychological Measurement, 1,* 385–401.

■ ■ ■

3781

Test Name: CHECKLIST OF PHYSICAL LIMITATIONS

Purpose: To measure disability by self-report.

Number of Items: 6

Format: Guttman format. Sample items presented.

Reliability: Internal consistency ranged from .81 to .83.

Author: Revenson, T. A., and Felton, B. J.

Article: Disability and coping as predictors of psychological adjustment to rheumatoid arthritis.

Journal: *Journal of Consulting and Clinical Psychology,* June 1989, *57*(3), 344–348.

Related Research: Rosow, I., & Breslau, N. (1966). A Guttman Health Scale for the aged. *Journal of Gerontology, 21,* 556–559. Meenan, R. F., et al. (1984). The Arthritis Impact Measurement Scales: Further investigation of a health status measure. *Arthritis and Rheumatism, 25,* 1048–1053.

3782

Test Name: CHILDREN'S
ABILITY–EFFORT SCALE

Purpose: To identify helpless
children.

Number of Items: 10

Format: The scale specifically
contrasts effort and ability
attributions for failure.

Reliability: Coefficient alphas were
.63 and .67.

Validity: Correlations with other
variables ranged from −.25 to .49.

Author: Fincham, F. D., et al.

Article: Learned helplessness, test
anxiety, and academic achievement:
A longitudinal analysis.

Journal: *Child Development*,
February 1989, *60*(1), 138–145.

Related Research: Finchman, F. D.,
& Cain, K. M. (1984). *The Children's
Ability-Effort Scale: A measure of
attributions in children*. Unpublished
manuscript.

■ ■ ■

3783

Test Name: CHILDREN'S
DEPRESSION INVENTORY

Purpose: To assess cognitive-
behavioral and neuro-vegetative signs
of depression.

Number of Items: 27

Format: Each item consists of three
statements from which the child
selects the one that best describes the
child over the past 2 weeks.

Reliability: Internal consistency,
split-half, and test–retest reliabilities
ranged from .94 to .38.

Author: Finch, A. J. Jr., et al.

Article: Brief Rorschach records with
children and adolescents.

Journal: *Journal of Personality
Assessment*, Winter 1990, *55*(3 and 4),
640–646.

Related Research: Kovacs, M.
(1985). Rating scales to assess
depression in school-aged children.
Acta Paedopsychiatry, *46*, 305–315.

■ ■ ■

3784

Test Name: CHILDREN'S
NEGATIVE COGNITIVE ERROR
QUESTIONNAIRE

Purpose: To measure four types of
negative cognitive errors derived from
Beck's cognitive theory of adult
depression.

Number of Items: 24

Format: Children respond to short
descriptions of events on a 5-point
rating scale (1 = *not at all like I would
think*). Sample items presented.

Reliability: Test–retest reliability
ranged from .44 to .59. Alphas ranged
from .60 to .89.

Author: Leitenberg, H., et al.

Article: Negative cognitive errors in
children: Questionnaire development,
normative data, and comparisons
between children with and without
self-reported symptoms of depression,
low self-esteem and evaluation
anxiety.

Journal: *Journal of Consulting and
Clinical Psychology*, August 1986,
54(4), 528–536.

Related Research: Lefebvre, M. F.
(1981). Cognitive distortion and
cognitive errors in depressed
psychiatric and low back pain
patients. *Journal of Consulting and
Clinical Psychology*, *49*, 517–525.

■ ■ ■

3785

Test Name: CLINICAL ANXIETY
SCALE

Purpose: To measure the amount of
anxiety a person currently
experiences.

Number of Items: 25

Format: Responses to each item are
made on a 5-point scale from 1
(rarely or none of the time) to 5 *(most
or all of the time)*. All items are
presented.

Reliability: Coefficient alpha was .94.

Validity: Discriminant validity
coefficient was .77 (*N* = 47). Phi
coefficient was .81.

Author: Westhuis, D., and Thyer, B. A.

Article: Development and validation
of the Clinical Anxiety Scale: A rapid
assessment instrument for empirical
practice.

Journal: *Educational and
Psychological Measurement*, Spring
1989, *49*(1), 153–163.

Related Research: American
Psychiatric Association. (1980).
*Diagnostic and statistical measure of
mental disorders* (3rd ed.).
Washington, DC: Author.

■ ■ ■

3786

Test Name: COGNITIVE ERROR
QUESTIONNAIRE (RHEUMATOID
ARTHRITIS VERSION)

Purpose: To measure cognitive
distortion.

Number of Items: 24

Format: Vignettes followed by four
types of illogical or distorted
inferences.

Reliability: Cronbach's alphas ranged
from .81 to .86 across subscales. Total
alpha was .90.

Author: Smith, T. W., et al.

Article: Cognitive distortion in
rheumatoid arthritis: Relation to
depression and disability.

Journal: *Journal of Consulting and
Clinical Psychology*, June 1988,
56(3), 412–416.

Related Research: Lefebvre, M. F.
(1981). Cognitive distortion and
cognitive errors in depressed
psychiatric and low back pain
patients. *Journal of Consulting and
Clinical Psychology*, *49*, 517–525.

3787

Test Name: COGNITIVE–SOMATIC ANXIETY QUESTIONNAIRE

Purpose: To measure cognitive–somatic anxiety.

Number of Items: 14

Format: Includes two subscales: cognitive and somatic.

Reliability: Cronbach's alphas ranged from .76 to .85.

Author: Freedland, K. E., and Carney, R. M.

Article: Factor analysis of the Cognitive–Somatic Anxiety Questionnaire.

Journal: *Journal of Psychopathology and Behavioral Assessment*, December 1988, *10*(4), 367–375.

Related Research: Schwartz, G. E., et al. (1978). Patterning of cognitive and somatic processes in the self-regulation of anxiety: Effects of meditation versus exercise. *Psychosomatic Medicine, 40,* 321–328.

■ ■ ■

3788

Test Name: COGNITIVE TRIAD INVENTORY

Purpose: To measure Beck's cognitive triad.

Number of Items: 23

Format: Seven-point Likert format. Sample items presented.

Reliability: Alphas ranged from .81 to .95.

Validity: Correlated .77 with the Beck Depression Inventory. Other validity data presented.

Author: Beckham, E. E., et al.

Article: Development of an instrument to measure Beck's Cognitive Triad: The Cognitive Triad Inventory.

Journal: *Journal of Consulting and Clinical Psychology*, August 1986, *54*(4), 566–567.

3789

Test Name: COLLEGE STUDENTS' LIFE EVENTS SCHEDULE

Purpose: To measure stressful life events.

Number of Items: 112

Format: Combination checklist and 4-point rating scale format.

Reliability: Alpha was .87.

Author: Porterfield, A. L.

Article: Does sense of humor moderate the impact of stress on psychological and physical well-being?

Journal: *Journal of Research in Personality*, September 1987, *21*(3), 306–317.

Related Research: Sandler, I. N., & Lakey, B. (1982). Locus of control as a stress moderator: The role of control perceptions and social support. *American Journal of Community Psychology, 10,* 65–80.

■ ■ ■

3790

Test Name: COMPETITIVE STATE ANXIETY INVENTORY—2

Purpose: To measure competitive state anxiety.

Number of Items: 27

Format: Includes three subscales: cognitive anxiety, somatic anxiety, and self-confidence.

Reliability: Internal reliability coefficients ranged from .79 to .90.

Author: Swain, A., et al.

Article: Interrelationships among multidimensional competitive state anxiety components as a function of the proximity of competition.

Journal: *Perceptual and Motor Skills*, December 1990, *71*(3) part 2, 1111–1114.

Related Research: Martens, R., et al. (1990). The Competitive State Anxiety Inventory-2 (C5AI-2). In R.

Martens, R. S. Vealy, & D. Burton (Eds.), *Competitive anxiety in sport* (pp. 2–12). Champaign, IL: Hurman Kinetics.

■ ■ ■

3791

Test Name: COMMUNITY COMPETENCE SCALE—REVISED

Purpose: To measure everyday living ability.

Number of Items: 78

Format: Includes 10 subscales: compensate for incapacities, manage money, communication, care of medical needs, personal hygiene, maintain household, utilize transportation, and acquire money.

Reliability: Test–retest (1 week) reliabilities ranged from .57 to .93.

Author: Searight, H. R., et al.

Article: Correlations of two competence assessment methods in a geriatric population.

Journal: *Journal of Perceptual Motor Skills*, June 1989, *68*(3) Part 1, 863–872.

Related Research: Anderten, P. S. (1981). The elderly, incompetency, and guardianship. Unpublished master's thesis, St. Louis University.

■ ■ ■

3792

Test Name: COMPUTER ANXIETY INDEX

Purpose: To measure computer anxiety.

Number of Items: 26

Format: Likert-type items employing a 6-point scale from *strongly agree* to *strongly disagree*.

Reliability: Alpha coefficients ranged from .94 to .96. Test–retest reliability was .90.

Validity: Correlation with the State Trait Anxiety Inventory was .32. Correlation with structured observations was .36. Correlations with other variables ranged from .75 to .89.

Author: Dukes, R. L., et al.

Article: Convergent validity of four computer anxiety scales.

Journal: *Educational and Psychological Measurement*, Spring 1989, *49*(1), 195–203.

Related Research: Rohner, D. J. (1981). Development and Validation of an index of computer anxiety among prospective teachers. Unpublished master's thesis. Ames: Iowa State University.

■ ■ ■

3793

Test Name: COMPUTER ANXIETY RATING SCALE

Purpose: To assess computer anxiety.

Number of Items: 19

Format: Employs a 5-point Likert-type response format.

Reliability: Alpha coefficients were .87 and .90.

Validity: Correlations with other variables ranged from .06 to .79.

Author: Zakrajsek, T. D., et al.

Article: Convergent validity of scales measuring computer-related attitudes.

Journal: *Educational and Psychological Measurement*, Summer 1990, *50*(2), 343–349.

Related Research: Heinssen, R. K., et al. (1987). Assessing computer anxiety: Development and validation of the Computer Anxiety Rating Scale. *Computers in Human Behavior, 3*, 49–59.

■ ■ ■

3794

Test Name: COMPUTER ANXIETY SCALE

Purpose: To measure computer anxiety.

Number of Items: 20

Format: Likert format. All items presented.

Reliability: Alpha was .94.

Validity: Correlated −.48 with total experience with computers (*p* < .001). No anxiety differences between males and females or between undergraduate and graduate students.

Author: Cohen, B. A., and Waugh, G. W.

Article: Assessing computer anxiety.

Journal: *Psychological Reports*, December 1989, *65*(3) I, 735–738.

■ ■ ■

3795

Test Name: COMPUTER ANXIETY SCALE

Purpose: To measure computer anxiety.

Number of Items: 30

Format: Contains Likert-type items employing 6-point ordered response scales ranging from *strongly agree* to *strongly disagree*. Includes three subscales: fear and anxiety about computers, enjoyment in working with computers, and confidence in the ability to use and to learn about computers.

Reliability: Reliability coefficients ranged from .86 to .95.

Validity: Correlations with other variables ranged from .76 to .89.

Author: Dukes, R. L., et al.

Article: Convergent validity of four computer anxiety scales.

Journal: *Educational and Psychological Measurement*, Spring 1989, *49*(1), 195–203.

Related Research: Loyd, B. H., & Gressard, C. (1984). Reliability and factoral validity of computer attitude scales. *Educational and Psychological Measurement, 44*, 501–505.

3796

Test Name: COMPUTER TECHNOLOGY HASSLES SCALE

Purpose: To assess severity of computer-related "hassles."

Number of Items: 69

Format: Four-point severity of hassle scale.

Reliability: Test–retest ranged from .58 to .78.

Author: Hudburg, R. A.

Article: Psychology of computer use: XVII. The Computer Technology Hassles Scale: Revision, reliability and some correlates.

Journal: *Psychological Reports*, December 1989, *65*(3), II, 1387–1394.

Related Research: Rosen, L., et al. (1987). Computerphobia. *Behavioral Research Methods, Instruments and Computers, 19*, 167–179.

■ ■ ■

3797

Test Name: COMPUTER TECHNOLOGY HASSLES SCALE

Purpose: To measure the irritating, frustrating, and distressing demands encountered in computer use.

Number of Items: 65

Format: Four-point severity scale.

Validity: Correlation with perceived stress was .20 (*p* < .05) and with hours of computer use was .21 (*p* < .05).

Author: Hudburg, R. A.

Article: Psychology of computer use: VII. Measuring technostress: Computer-related stress.

Journal: *Psychological Reports*, June 1989, *64*(3) I, 767–772.

Related Research: Kanner, A., et al. (1981). Comparison of two modes of stress measurement: Daily hassles and uplifts versus major life events. *Journal of Behavioral Medicine, 4*, 1–39.

3798

Test Name: COPING HUMOR SCALE

Purpose: To measure use of humor in times of stress.

Number of Items: 7

Format: Four-point Likert format.

Reliability: Alpha was .42.

Author: Porterfield, A. L.

Article: Does sense of humor moderate the impact of stress on psychological and physical well-being?

Journal: *Journal of Research in Personality*, September 1987, *21*(3), 306–317.

Related Research: Martin, R. A., & Lefcourt, H. M. (1983). Sense of humor as a moderator of the relation between stressors and moods. *Journal of Personality and Social Psychology*, *45*, 1313–1324.

■ ■ ■

3799

Test Name: COPING ORIENTATION FOR PROBLEM EXPERIENCES SCALE

Purpose: To assess behavior when faced with difficulties on when feeling tense.

Number of Items: 54

Format: Five-point frequency scale.

Reliability: Cronbach's alphas ranged from .36 to .76.

Author: Kurdek, L. A., and Sinclair, R. J.

Article: Adjustment of young adolescents in two-parent nuclear, stepfather and mother-custody families.

Journal: *Journal of Consulting and Clinical Psychology*, February 1988, *56*(1), 91–96.

Related Research: McCubbin, H. I., & Thompson, A. I. (Eds.). (1987). *Family assessment inventories*. Madison: University of Wisconsin Press.

3800

Test Name: COPING SCALE

Purpose: To assess coping.

Number of Items: 33

Format: Three-point frequency scales. Sample items presented.

Reliability: Alphas ranged from .87 to .97. Test–retest (1 month) reliability was .82.

Author: Jung, J., and Khalsa, H. K.

Article: The relationship of daily hassles, social support, and coping to depression in Black and White students.

Journal: *Journal of General Psychology*, October 1989, *116*(4), 407–417.

Related Research: Folkman, S., & Lazarus, R. S. (1980). An analysis of coping in a middle-aged community sample. *Journal of Health and Social Behavior*, *21*, 219–239.

■ ■ ■

3801

Test Name: COPING STRATEGIES INVENTORY

Purpose: To assess the coping strategies used in responding to the major life events that must change or disrupt an individual's usual activities.

Number of Items: 76

Format: Includes five factors: problem centered, cognitive restructuring, avoidance, social centered, and self-denigration.

Reliability: Alpha coefficients ranged from .71 to .94. Test–retest (two weeks) correlation coefficients ranged from .67 to .83.

Author: Larson, L. M., et al.

Article: Significant predictors of problem-solving appraisal.

Journal: *Journal of Counseling Psychology*, October 1990, *37*(4), 482–490.

Related Research: Tobin, D. L., et al. (1989). The hierarchial factor structure of the Coping Strategies Inventory. *Cognitive Therapy and Research*, *13*, 343–361.

■ ■ ■

3802

Test Name: COPING STRATEGIES QUESTIONNAIRE FOR SCD

Purpose: To measure how subjects with sickle cell disease cope with pain.

Number of Items: 80

Format: Seven-point Likert format adapted to a frequency-of-use scale.

Reliability: Alphas ranged from .72 to .88 across subscales.

Author: Gil, K. M., et al.

Article: Sickle cell disease pain: Relation of coping strategies to adjustment.

Journal: *Journal of Consulting and Clinical Psychology*, December 1989, *56*(6), 725–731.

Related Research: Rosenstiel, A. K., & Kaefe, F. J. (1983). The use of coping strategies in low back pain patients: Relationship to patient characteristics and current adjustment. *Pain*, *17*, 33–40.

■ ■ ■

3803

Test Name: COPING STYLES QUESTIONNAIRE

Purpose: To measure coping in seven dimensions: problem-focused, blaming-self, avoidance/advice seeking, wishful thinking, minimizing threat, seeking support, and emotional coping.

Number of Items: 275

Format: Cherklin format.

Reliability: Alphas ranged from .45 to .81.

Author: Rotheram-Borus, M. J., et al.

Article: Cognitive style and pleasant activities among female adolescent suicide attempters.

Journal: *Journal of Consulting and Clinical Psychology*, October 1990, *58*(5), 554–591.

Related Research: Lazarus, R. S. (1981). The stress and coping paradigm. In C. Eisdoifer, et al. (Eds.), *Models for clinical psychology* (pp. 177–214). Jamaica, NY: Spectrum Publications.

■ ■ ■

3804

Test Name: COUNSELING OUTCOME MEASURE

Purpose: To measure how much clients change overall and in their behavior, self-esteem, and self-understanding relative to when they first enter counseling.

Number of Items: 4

Format: Responses are made to each item on a 7-point Likert scale ranging from 1 (*much worse*) to 7 (*much improved*).

Reliability: Coefficient alpha was .89 (*N* = 39). Test–retest reliabilities ranged from .63 to .81.

Author: Tracey, T. J.

Article: Stage differences in the dependencies of topic intiation and topic following behavior.

Journal: *Journal of Counseling Psychology*, April 1987, *34*(2), 123–131.

Related Research: Gelso, C. J., & Johnson, D. H. (Eds.). (1983). *Explorations in time-limited counseling and psychotherapy*. New York: Teacher's College.

■ ■ ■

3805

Test Name: DEATH ANXIETY SCALE

Purpose: To measure preoccupation with issues surrounding death.

Number of Items: 15

Format: True–false format.

Reliability: Test–retest reliability was .83. Kuder-Richardson formula was .76.

Author: Schumaker, J. F., et al.

Article: Death anxiety in Malaysian and Australian university students.

Journal: *The Journal of Social Psychology*, February 1988, *128*(1), 41–47.

Related Research: Templer, D. I. (1970). The construction and validation of a death anxiety scale. *Journal of General Psychology, 82*, 165–177.

■ ■ ■

3806

Test Name: DEATH CONCERN SCALE

Purpose: To measure conscious contemplation of death and its negative evaluation.

Number of Items: 30

Format: Eleven frequency items and 19 agreement items.

Reliability: Alpha was .82.

Validity: Coefficients of congruence for matching factors were .92 and .96, and for non-matching factors, less than .20.

Author: Hammer, S. C., and Brookings J. B.

Article: Factor structure of the Death Concern Scale: A replication.

Journal: *Psychological Reports*, February 1987, *60*(1), 199–202.

Related Research: Klug, L., & Boss, M. (1976). Factorial structure of the Death Concern Scale. *Psychological Reports, 38*, 107–112.

■ ■ ■

3807

Test Name: DEPRESSION MEASURE

Purpose: To measure depression.

Number of Items: 6

Format: Four-point self-descriptive response scales.

Reliability: Alpha was .88.

VALIDITY: Correlation with MMPI Depression Scale was .70.

Author: Beehr, T. A., et al.

Article: Social support and occupational stress: Talking to supervisors.

Journal: *Journal of Vocational Behavior*, February 1990, *36*(1), 61–81.

RELATED RESEARCH: Caplan, R. D., et al. (1978). *Job demands and worker health: Main effects and occupational differences*. Ann Arbor, MI: Institute for Social Research.

■ ■ ■

3808

Test Name: DEPRESSION-PRONENESS RATING SCALE

Purpose: To measure a person's tendency to become depressed.

Number of Items: 10

Format: Frequency rating responses for items. All items listed.

Validity: Three factors extracted that account for 66% of total variance and are nearly identical to factors found for clinically depressed persons.

Author: Hong, S. M.

Article: Factor structure of the Depression-Proneness Rating Scale.

Journal: *Psychological Reports*, December 1987, *61*(3), 863–866.

Related Research: Zemore, R. (1983). Development of a self-report measure of depression proneness. *Psychological Reports, 52*, 223–230.

■ ■ ■

3809

Test Name: DEPRESSION SYMPTOM INVENTORY

Purpose: To measure affective, motivational, and somatic aspects of depression (in Dutch).

Number of Items: 22

Format: Five-point severity scales.

Reliability: Alpha was .92.

Validity: Correlated .81 with Beck's Depression Inventory.

Author: Bouman, T. K., et al.

Article: Mood Connotations of a Locus of Control Questionnaire.

Journal: *Psychological Reports*, December 1986, *59*(3), 1055–1059.

Related Research: Bouman, T. K. (1986). *The measurement of depression with questionnaires.* Unpublished doctoral dissertation. University of Groningen, The Netherlands.

■ ■ ■

3810

Test Name: DEROGATIS STRESS PROFILE

Purpose: To assess stress levels in environmental, personality, and emotional domains.

Number of Items: 77

Format: Includes 11 subscales.

Reliability: Alpha reliabilities ranged from .79 to .99. Test–retest coefficients ranged from .79 to .93.

Validity: Correlations with other measures ranged from .56 to .58.

Author: Bertock, M. R., et al.

Article: Reducing teacher stress.

Journal: *Journal of Experimental Education*, Winter 1989, *57*(2), 117–128.

Related Research: Derogatis, L. R. (1987). The Derogatis Stress Profile (DSP): Quantification of psychological stress. *Advances in Psychosomatic Medicine, 17*, 30–54.

3811

Test Name: DIRECT COPING SCALE

Purpose: To assess the use of instrumental, problem focused coping methods and avoidance of cognitive distortion and fantasy.

Number of Items: 17

Format: Examples are presented.

Reliability: Coefficient alpha was .69.

Validity: Correlations with other variables ranged from −.20 to .13 (*N* = 157).

Author: Parkes, K. R.

Article: Coping, negative affectivity, and the work environment: Additive and interactive predictors of mental health.

Journal: *Journal of Applied Psychology*, August 1990, *75*(4), 399–409.

Related Research: Parkes, K. R. (1984). Locus of control, cognitive appraisal, and coping in stressful episodes. *Journal of Personality and Social Psychology, 46*, 655–668.

■ ■ ■

3812

Test Name: DISPOSITIONAL STRESS SCALES

Purpose: To measure sources of stress.

Number of Items: 32

Format: Includes five factors: overload, lack of self-confidence, time urgency, need to keep busy, and anxiety. Subjects responded on a 4-point scale from 1 (*almost never true*) to 4 (*almost always true*). All items are presented.

Reliability: Coefficient alphas ranged from .73 to .88. Test–retest (1 week) reliability for each factor ranged from .68 to .97 (*N* = 25).

Validity: Correlations with other variables ranged from −.26 to .55.

Author: Albertson, L. M., and Kagan, D. M.

Article: Occupational stress among teachers.

Journal: *Journal of Research and Development in Education*, Fall 1987, *21*(1), 69–75.

Related Research: Girdano, D., & Everly, G. (1977). *Controlling stress and tension.* Englewood Cliffs, NJ: Prentice-Hall.

■ ■ ■

3813

Test Name: DYSFUNCTIONAL ATTITUDES SCALE—FORM A

Purpose: To measure the presence of beliefs or assumptions postulated to predispose individuals to depression.

Number of Items: 40

Format: Employs a modified 7-point Likert response format. A sample item is given.

Reliability: Test–retest reliability ranged from .73 to .81. Internal consistency ranged from .88 to .92.

Validity: Correlations with other variables ranged from .43 to .52.

Author: Vredenburg, K., et al.

Article: Depression in college students: Personality and experiential factors.

Journal: *Journal of Counseling Psychology*, October 1988, *35*(4), 419–425.

Related Research: Dobson, K. S., & Breiter, H. J. (1983). Cognitive assessment of depression: Reliability and validity of three measures. *Journal of Abnormal Psychology, 92*, 107–109.

■ ■ ■

3814

Test Name: ECONOMIC STRAIN SCALE

Purpose: To measure economic distress as a measure of general life stress.

Number of Items: 9

Format: Five-point Likert format.

Reliability: Alphas ranged from .87 to .92.

Validity: Correlated −.43 with per capita family income and .22 with husband work stability.

Author: Simons, R. L., et al.

Article: Husband and wife differences in determinants of parenting: A social learning and exchange model of parental behavior.

Journal: *Journal of Marriage and the Family*, May 1990, *52*(2), 375–392.

Related Research: Pearlin, L. I., et al. (1981). The stress process. *Journal of Health and Social Behavior, 22,* 337–356.

■ ■ ■

3815

Test Name: EVERYDAY VISION QUESTIONNAIRE

Purpose: To provide a self-report measure of visual functioning in daily living.

Number of Items: 20

Format: Responses are made on a scale ranging from 1 (*cannot see*) to 10 (*see very well*).

Reliability: Test–retest (1 to 2 weeks) reliability averaged .67.

Author: Cogan, R., and Staples, J.

Article: Self-reported visual function and academic success: Cattell revisited.

Journal: *Perceptual and Motor Skills,* April 1990, *70*(2), 673–674.

Related Research: Staples, J., & Cogan, R. (1989). Development of the everyday vision questionnaire. Paper presented at the meeting of the Southwestern Psychological Association, Houston, Texas.

3816

Test Name: EXPECTED BALANCE SCALE

Purpose: To measure expected positive feelings.

Number of Items: 18

Format: Includes separate scales measuring optimism and pessimism. Employs a 5-point response mode.

Reliability: Test–retest (9 weeks) reliability was .66.

Validity: Correlations with other variables ranged from −.83 to .73.

Author: Staats, S.

Article: Hope: A comparison of two self-report measures for adults.

Journal: *Journal of Personality Assessment,* Summer 1989, *53*(2), 366–375.

Related Research: Staats, S. (1987). Hope: Expected positive affect in an adult sample. *Journal of Geriatric Psychology, 148,* 357–364.

■ ■ ■

3817

Test Name: FEAR OF BODILY SENSATIONS QUESTIONNAIRE

Purpose: To measure how fearful people are of 14 body sensations.

Number of Items: 14

Format: Responses are made on a 5-point scale ranging from 0 (*not at all fearful*) to 4 (*extremely fearful*).

Reliability: Cronbach's alpha was .90 (*N* = 141).

Author: deRuiter, C., and Garssen, B.

Article: Social anxiety and fear of bodily sensations in panic disorder and agoraphobia: A matched comparison.

Journal: *Journal of Psychopathology and Behavioral Assessment,* June 1989, *11*(2), 175–184.

Related Research: Van den Hout, M. A., et al. (1987). Specificity of

interoceptive fear to panic disorders. *Journal of Psychopathology and Behavioral Assessment, 9,* 99–106.

■ ■ ■

3818

Test Name: FEAR OF COMMITMENT SCALE

Purpose: To assess fear of commitment.

Number of Items: 40

Format: Responses are made on a 6-point scale ranging from 1 (*strongly disagree*) to 6 (*strongly agree*). Examples are presented.

Reliability: Coefficient alpha was .91. Test–retest (2 weeks) reliability was .89.

Validity: Correlation with other variables ranged from −.49 to .68.

Author: Serling D. A., and Betz, N. E.

Article: Development and evaluation of a measure of fear of commitment.

Journal: *Journal of Counseling Psychology,* January 1990, *37*(1), 91–97.

■ ■ ■

3819

Test Name: FEAR OF CRIME SCALE

Purpose: To measure fear of crime.

Number of Items: 7

Format: *Not fearful* and *fearful* response categories. All items presented.

Reliability: Alpha was .90.

Author: Parker, K. D.

Article: Black–White differences in perceptions of fear of crime.

Journal: *The Journal of Social Psychology,* August 1988, *128*(4), 487–494.

Related Research: Lee, G. R. (1982). Residential location and fear of crime among the elderly. *Rural Sociology, 47,* 655–669.

3820

Test Name: FEAR OF DEATH SCALE

Purpose: To measure fear of death and dying.

Number of Items: 36

Format: Likert format. Sample items presented.

Reliability: Alpha ranged from .69 to .75.

Author: Lev, E. I.

Article: Effects of course in hospice nursing: Attitudes and behaviors of baccalaureate school of nursing undergraduates and graduates.

Journal: *Psychological Reports*, October 1986, *59*(2)II, 847–858.

Related Research: Lester, D. (1967). Experimental and correlational studies of the fear of death. *Psychological Bulletin*, *67*(1), 27–36.

■ ■ ■

3821

Test Name: FEAR OF FAILURE SCALE

Purpose: To measure fear of failure.

Number of Items: 45

Format: Includes 25 survey items embedded in a 45-item scale containing positive and avoidance statements.

Reliability: Kuder-Richardson 21 internal consistency was .74.

Validity: Correlations with emotionality and worry ranged from .32 to .39 (*N* = 215). Correlation with college grade point average was −.36 (*N* = 215).

Author: Herman, W. E.

Article: Fear of failure as a distinctive personality trait measure of test anxiety.

Journal: *Journal of Research and Development in Education*, Spring, 1990, *23*(3), 180–185.

Related Research: Herman, W. E. (1987). *Test anxiety: Emotionality, worry, and fear of failure*. Unpublished doctoral dissertation, University of Michigan.

■ ■ ■

3822

Test Name: FEAR OF NEGATIVE EVALUATION

Purpose: To measure anxiety.

Number of Items: 35

Format: Likert format.

Reliability: Test–retest (4 weeks) reliability was .79.

Validity: Correlated with social approval (.81) and the Situational Questionnaire (.75).

Author: Lemelin, M., et al.

Article: Consistency between self-report and actual proficiency in giving and taking criticism.

Journal: *Psychological Reports*, August 1986, *59*(1)I, 387–390.

Related Research: Watson, D., & Friend, R. (1969). Measurement of social-evaluation anxiety. *Journal of Consulting and Clinical Psychology*, *33*, 448–457.

■ ■ ■

3823

Test Name: FEAR QUESTIONNAIRE SUBSCALES

Purpose: To measure phobic concerns.

Number of Items: 15

Format: Includes the following subscales: blood injury, social phobia, and agoraphobia.

Reliability: Internal consistency coefficients ranged from .44 to .73.

Author: Trull, T. J., and Hillerbrand, E.

Article: Psychometric properties and factor of structure of the Fear Questionnaire Phobia subscale items in two normative samples.

Journal: *Journal of Psychopathology and Behavioral Assessment*, December 1990, *12*(4), 285–297.

Related Research: Marks, I. M., & Matthews, A. M. (1978). Brief self-rating for phobic patients. *Behavior Research and Therapy*, *17*, 263–267.

■ ■ ■

3824

Test Name: FINANCIAL CONCERNS SCALE

Purpose: To indicate frequency of worrying about being able to provide food, clothing, medical care, entertainment, and vacations at the quality to which they are accustomed.

Number of Items: 5

Format: Responses are made on a 5-point scale ranging from 1 (*seldom*) to 5 (*almost constantly*).

Reliability: Coefficient alpha was .83.

Validity: Correlations with other variables ranged from −.35 to .60.

Author: Mallinckrodt, B., and Fretz, B. R.

Article: Social support and the impact of job loss on older professionals.

Journal: *Journal of Counseling Psychology*, July 1988, *35*(3), 281–286.

Related Research: Pearlin, L. I., & Radabaugh, C. W. (1976). Economic strains and the coping functions of alcohol. *American Journal of Sociology*, *82*, 652–663.

■ ■ ■

3825

Test Name: FOUR SYSTEMS ANXIETY QUESTIONNAIRE

Purpose: To assess anxiety.

Number of Items: 60

Format: Includes four components: somatic, cognitive, behavioral, and feeling.

Reliability: Alpha coefficients ranged from .59 to .92.

Validity: Correlations with other variables ranged from .32 to .85.

Author: Koksal, F., and Power, K. G.

Article: Four Systems Anxiety Questionnaire (FSAQ): A self-report measure of somatic, cognitive, behavioral, and feeling components.

Journal: *Journal of Personality Assessment*, Summer 1990, *54*(3 and 4), 534–545.

■ ■ ■

3826

Test Name: GENERAL HEALTH QUESTIONNAIRE

Purpose: To measure level of general health.

Number of Items: 30

Format: Four-point severity scales. Sample items presented.

Reliability: Split-half reliability was .92.

Validity: People who have scored about 5 have been clinically identified as nonpsychotic and generally suited for outpatient treatment.

Author: Enos, D. M., and Handal, P. J.

Article: Relation of sex and age of White adolescents at the time of parental divorce to the youths' perception of family climate and psychological adjustment.

Journal: *Psychological Reports*, December 1987, *61*(3), 699–705.

Related Research: Goldberg, D. P. (1972). *The detection of psychiatric illness by questionnaire*. London: Oxford University Press.

■ ■ ■

3827

Test Name: GENERALIZED ANXIETY QUESTIONNAIRE

Purpose: To measure generalized anxiety.

Number of Items: 29

Format: Subjects rate the severity of symptoms for the previous month on a 7-point Likert scale ranging from *not at all* to *severe*.

Reliability: Alpha was .92.

Validity: Correlations with other variables ranged from .47 to .64.

Author: Gross, P. R., and Eifert, G. H.

Article: Delineating generalized anxiety: A preliminary investigation.

Journal: *Journal of Psychopathology and Behavioral Assessment*, December 1990, *12*(4), 345–358.

■ ■ ■

3828

Test Name: GENERALIZED CONTENTMENT SCALE

Purpose: To measure nonpsychotic depression.

Number of Items: 25

Format: Responses are made on a 5-point scale from 1 (*rarely or none of the time*) to 5 (*most or all of the time*).

Reliability: Test–retest reliability coefficients were .94 and .70.

Author: Payne, P. A., and Friedman, G. H.

Article: Group applications of hypnosis for college students.

Journal: *Journal of Student Personnel*, March 1986, *27*(2), 154–160.

Related Research: Hudson, W. W., & Proctor, E. K. (1977). Assessment of depressive affect in clinical practice. *Journal of Consulting and Clinical Psychology, 45*, 1206–1207.

■ ■ ■

3829

Test Name: GENERALIZED EXPECTANCY FOR NEGATIVE MOOD REGULATION

Purpose: To measure generalized expectancies for negative mood regulation.

Number of Items: 30

Format: Includes five types of items: general, cognitive, behavioral-alone, behavioral-social, and behavioral unspecified. Responses are made on a 5-point Likert scale ranging from 1 (*strong disagreement*) to 5 (*strong agreement*). All items are presented.

Reliability: Alpha coefficients ranged from .86 to .92. Test–retest (3–4 weeks) reliability was .74 (78 women) and .76 (31 men). Test–retest (6–8 weeks) reliability was .78 (138 women) and .67 (63 men).

Validity: Correlations with other variables ranged from −.58 to .23.

Author: Catanzro, S. J., and Mearns, J.

Article: Measuring generalized expectancies for negative mood regulation: Initial scale development and implications.

Journal: *Journal of Personality Assessment*, Summer 1990, *54*(3 and 4), 546–563.

■ ■ ■

3830

Test Name: GENERAL MENTAL HEALTH QUESTIONNAIRE

Purpose: To measure the tendency toward psychiatric disturbance.

Number of Items: 20

Format: Sample items presented.

Reliability: Alphas ranged from. .82 to .85.

Validity: Correlation with clinical assessment was .80.

Author: Mathieu, J. E., and Hamel, K.

Article: A causal model of the antecedents of organizational commitment among professionals and nonprofessionals.

Journal: *Journal of Vocational Behavior*, June 1989, *34*(3), 299–317.

Related Research: Goldberg, D. P. (1972). *The dectection of psychiatric illness by questionnaire.* Oxford, England: Oxford University Press.

■ ■ ■

3831

Test Name: GENERAL PHYSICAL HEALTH SYMPTOMS INVENTORY

Purpose: To assess general physical health symptoms.

Number of Items: 77

Format: Response to each health problem is made on a 3-point scale from 0 (*did not experience this problem*) to 2 (*experienced this problem quite a bit*).

Reliability: Alpha coefficient was .89.

Author: Jorgensen, R. S., and Richards, C. S.

Article: Negative affect and the reporting of physical symptoms among college students.

Journal: *Journal of Counseling Psychology,* October 1989, *36*(4), 501–504.

Related Research: Boaz, T. L. (1982). *Sensation-seeking, locus of control, and self-control as moderator variables in the relationship between life stress and physical and mental disorders.* Unpublished master's thesis. University of Kansas, Lawrence.

■ ■ ■

3832

Test Name: GERIATRIC DEPRESSION SCALE

Purpose: To assess depression in older adults by self-report.

Number of Items: 30

Format: True–false format.

Reliability: Alpha was .92.

Author: Rapp, S. R., et al.

Article: Psychological dysfunction and physical health among elderly medical inpatients.

Journal: *Journal of Consulting and Clinical Psychology,* December 1988, *56*(6), 851–855.

Related Research: Yescavage, J. A., et al. (1983). Development and validation of a geriatric depression screening scale: A preliminary report. *Journal of Psychiatric Research, 17,* 39–49.

■ ■ ■

3833

Test Name: GLOBAL ASSESSMENT SCALE

Purpose: To measure overall mental health.

Number of Items: 1

Format: Ten-interval 100-point rating scale. Each interval is defined such that judges can rate cases from 1 to 100.

Reliability: Interim reliability ranged from .83 to .92.

Validity: Correlations with other variables ranged from −.06 to −.76. Correlations with Health Sickness Rating Scale ranged from .85 to .92.

Author: Sohlberg, S.

Article: There's more in a number than you think: New validity data for the Global Assessment Scale.

Journal: *Psychological Reports,* April 1989, *64*(2), 455–461.

Related Research: Eudicatt, J., et al. (1976). The Global Assessment Scale. *Archives of General Psychiatry, 33,* 766–771.

■ ■ ■

3834

Test Name: GLOBAL HOPELESSNESS SCALE

Purpose: To assess respondent's level of pessimism about the future.

Number of Items: 5

Reliability: Cronbach's alpha was .84.

Validity: Correlations with other variables ranged from −.39 to .74.

Author: Cole, D. A., and Milstead, M.

Article: Behavioral correlates of depression: Antecedents or consequences?

Journal: *Journal of Counseling Psychology,* October 1989, *36*(4), 408–416.

Related Research: Cole, D. A. (1988). Hopelessness, social desirability, depression, and parasuicide in two college student samples. *Journal of Consulting and Clinical Psychology, 56,* 131–136.

■ ■ ■

3835

Test Name: GOAL INSTABILITY SCALE—MODIFIED

Purpose: To indicate the level of people's confusion about their present situations and about their future purposes and goals.

Number of Items: 10

Format: Responses are made on a 6-point Likert scale.

Reliability: Test–retest (2 weeks) reliability was .76. Coefficient alpha was .80.

Validity: Correlations with other variables ranged from .35 to .53.

Author: Smith, L. C., and Robbins, S. B.

Article: Validity of the Goal Instability Scale (Modified) as a predictor of adjustment in retirement-age adults.

Journal: *Journal of Counseling Psychology,* July 1988, *35*(3), 325–329.

Related Research: Robbins, S., & Patton, M. (1985). Self-psychology and career development: Development of the Superiority and Goal Instability scales. *Journal of Counseling Psychology, 32,* 221–231.

■ ■ ■

3836

Test Name: HAIR-LOSS CONCERN SCALE

Purpose: To measure concern about hair-loss.

Number of Items: 3

Format: All items presented. Response format not specified.

Reliability: Alpha was .87 for balding men and .80 for nonbalding men.

Author: Franzoi, S. L., et al.

Article: Individual differences in men's perceptions of and reactions to thinning hair.

Journal: *The Journal of Social Psychology*, April 1990, *130*(2), 209–218.

Related Research: Roll, S., & Verinis, J. S. (1971). Stereotypes of scalp and facial hair as measured by the semantic differential. *Psychological Reports, 28*, 975–980.

■ ■ ■

3837

Test Name: HAMILTON PSYCHIATRIC RATING SCALE FOR DEPRESSION

Purpose: To measure the severity of depression in patients already diagnosed as depressed.

Number of Items: 24

Format: Items are rated for severity on either a 3- or a 5-point scale. All symptoms are presented.

Reliability: Interrater reliabilities are within the .90s. Coefficient alpha was .80.

Validity: Correlations with the Beck Depression Inventory ranged from .54 to .86.

Author: Steer, R. A., et al.

Article: Relationships between the Beck Depression Inventory and the Hamilton Psychiatric Rating Scale for Depression in depressed outpatients.

Journal: *Journal of Psychopathology and Behavioral Assessment,* September 1987, *9*(3), 327–339.

Related Research: Hamilton, M. (1960). A rating scale for depression. *Journal of Neurology and Neurosurgical Psychiatry, 23*, 56–62.

■ ■ ■

3838

Test Name: HAMILTON RATING SCALE FOR DEPRESSION

Purpose: To measure clinical depression.

Number of Items: 17

Format: Each item is rated on either a 0–2 or a 0–4 scale for the presence of the symptom within the last week.

Reliability: Interrater reliability ranged from .80 to .90.

Author: Deluty, B. M., et al.

Article: Concordance between clinicians' and patients' ratings of anxiety and depression as mediated by private self-consciousness.

Journal: *Journal of Personality Assessment*, Summer 1986, *50*(1), 93–106.

Related Research: Hamilton, M. (1960). A rating scale for depression. *Journal of Neurology, Neurosurgery, and Psychiatry, 23*, 56–62.

■ ■ ■

3839

Test Name: HAPPINESS AND OPTIMISM OF GENERAL OUTLOOK QUESTIONNAIRE

Purpose: To measure happiness and optimisim of general outlook.

Number of Items: 21

Reliability: Alpha was .80.

Validity: Correlations with other variables ranged from −.13 to .29.

Author: Walker, I., and Gibbins, K.

Article: Expecting the unexpected: An explanation of category width.

Journal: *Journal of Perceptual and Motor Skills*, June 1989, *68*(3) Part 1, 715–724.

Related Research: Gibbins, K. (1968). Response sets and semantic differential. *British Journal of Social and Clinical Psychology, 7*, 253–263.

■ ■ ■

3840

Test Name: HEALTH INTERFERENCE SCALE

Purpose: To measure to what extent doctor-diagnosed health problems prevent carrying out daily activities.

Number of Items: 13

Format: Three-point disability scales.

Reliability: Alpha was .71.

Author: Coleman, L. M.

Article: Social roles in the lives of middle-aged and older black women.

Journal: *Journal of Marriage and the Family*, November 1987, *48*(4), 761–771.

Related Research: Chatters, L. M. (1983). *A causal analysis of subjective well-being among elderly blacks.* Unpublished doctoral dissertation, University of Michigan, Ann Arbor.

■ ■ ■

3841

Test Name: HEALTH WORRY SCALE

Purpose: To measure concern for one's health.

Number of Items: 1

Format: Vertical visual analog scale (10 intervals).

Reliability: Test–retest (1 week) reliability was .91.

Validity: Worry scores were significantly higher before receiving test results than after receiving test results. Correlated .68 with A-state of the State–Trait Anxiety Inventory.

Author: Byers, P. H., et al.

Article: Self-disclosure, anxiety, and health worry in unscheduled outpatients.

Journal: *Psychological Reports*, April 1988, *62*(2), 379–386.

■ ■ ■

3842

Test Name: HETEROSEXUAL BEHAVIOR HIERARCHY— FEMALE FORM

Purpose: To measure sexual anxiety.

Number of Items: 21

Format: Eight-point anxiety response categories ranging from *no anxiety* to *very much anxiety*.

Reliability: Test–retest reliability was .68. Kuder-Richardson formula was .90.

Author: Anderson, B. D., et al.

Article: Controlled prospective longitudinal study of women with Cancer: I. Sexual functioning outcomes.

Journal: *Journal of Consulting and Clinical Psychology*, December 1989, *56*(6), 683–691.

Related Research: Bentler, P. (1968). Heterosexual behavior assessment: 2. Females. *Behavior Research and Therapy, 6,* 27–30.

■ ■ ■

3843

Test Name: HOMOPHOBIA SCALE

Purpose: To measure homophobia.

Number of Items: 10

Format: Fifty-point scales.

Reliability: Alpha was .81. Test–retest (3 weeks) reliability was .90.

Author: Tintinger, J., and Simkins, L.

Article: Mandatory AIDS testing: Factors influencing public opinion.

Journal: *Psychological Reports*, December 1989, *65*(3) I, 835–843.

Related Research: Simkins, L., & Kushner, A. (1986). Attitudes toward AIDS, Herpes II, and toxic shock syndrome: Two years later. *Psychological Reports, 59,* 883–891.

■ ■ ■

3844

Test Name: HOPE INDEX

Purpose: To measure the cognitive component of hope.

Number of Items: 16

Format: Half the items are self-referenced and the remainder refer either to others or to global world circumstances. Exampes are presented.

Reliability: Test–retest (9 weeks) reliability was .74. Alpha coefficients ranged from .72 to .85.

Validity: Correlations with other variables ranged from −.39 to .72.

Author: Staats, S.

Article: Hope: A comparison of two self-report measures for adults.

Journal: *Journal of Personality Assessment*, Summer 1989, *53*(2), 366–375.

Related Research: Scheier, M., & Carver, C. (1985). Optimism, coping, and health: Assessment and implications of generalized outcome expectancies. *Health Psychology, 4,* 219–247.

■ ■ ■

3845

Test Name: HOPELESSNESS SCALE

Purpose: To assess negative expectancies or hopeless ideation about the future and the self.

Number of Items: 17

Format: Dichotomous responses.

Reliability: Internal consistency ranged from .75 to .97.

Author: Kashani, J. H., et al.

Article: Levels of hopelessness in children and adolescents: A developmental perspective.

Journal: *Journal of Consulting and Clinical Psychology*, August 1989, *57*(4), 496–499.

Related Research: Kazdin, A. E., et al. (1986). The Hopelessness Scale for Children: Psychometric characteristics and concurrent validity. *Journal of Consulting and Clinical Psychology, 54,* 241–245.

■ ■ ■

3846

Test Name: HOPELESSNESS SCALE

Purpose: To measure degree to which an individual's cognitive schemata are dominated by negative expectations of the future.

Number of Items: 20

Format: True–false.

Reliability: Kuder-Richardson formula was .93.

Author: Schotte, D. E., and Clum, G. A.

Article: Problem-solving skills in suicidal psychiatric patients.

Journal: *Journal of Consulting and Clinical Psychology*, February 1987, *55*(1), 49–54.

Related Research: Beck, A., et al. (1974). The measurement of pessimism: The Hopelessness Scale. *Journal of Consulting and Clinical Psychology, 42,* 861–865.

■ ■ ■

3847

Test Name: HOPELESSNESS SCALE FOR CHILDREN

Purpose: To measure negative expectations toward the future.

Number of Items: 17

Format: True–false. All items presented.

Reliability: Alpha was .97. Spearman-Brown split half reliability was .96.

Validity: Correlated with depression (.58), self-esteem (−.61), and social skills (−.39).

Author: Kazdin, A. E., et al.

Article: The Hopelessness Scale for Children: Psychometric characteristics and concurrent validity.

Journal: *Journal of Consulting and Clinical Psychology*, April 1986, *54*(2), 241–245.

■ ■ ■

3848

Test Name: HOPKINS SYMPTOM CHECKLIST

Purpose: To assess mental health.

Number of Items: 20

Format: Includes two subscales: state anxiety and depression.

Reliability: Alpha coefficients were .87 and .84.

Validity: Correlations with other variables ranged from −.75 to .71.

Author: Caplan, R. D., et al.

Article: Job seeking, reemployment, and mental health: A randomized field experiment in coping with job loss.

Journal: *Journal of Applied Psychology*, October 1989, *74*(5), 759–769.

Related Research: Derogatis, L. R., et al. (1974). The Hopkins Symptom Checklist (HSCL). In P. Pichot (Ed.), *Psychological measurements in psychopharmacology: Modern problems in pharmacopsychiatry* (Vol. 7, pp. 79–110). Basel: Karger.

■ ■ ■

3849

Test Name: HOSPITAL QUESTIONNAIRE

Purpose: To provide a rapid approximation of a clinical

psychiatric diagnostic interview (assesses six groups of symptoms and traits).

Number of Items: 48

Reliability: Ranged from .43 to .82 across subscales.

Validity: High school students scored higher on depression and phobic reactions than college students. Females scored higher than males on depression and anxiety.

Author: Makaremi, A.

Article: Mental health of Iranian high school and college students.

Journal: *Psychological Reports*, February 1989, *64*(1), 19–22.

Related Research: Crown, S., & Crisp, A. H. (1966). A short clinical diagnostic self-rating scale for psychoneurotic patients: The Middlesex Hospital Questionnaire (MHQ). *British Journal of Psychiatry*, *112*, 917–923.

■ ■ ■

3850

Test Name: HOSTILITY SCALES

Purpose: To measure overt and covert hostility.

Number of Items: 21

Format: Likert format. Sample items presented.

Reliability: Cronbach's alphas ranged from .67 to .77.

Validity: Correlations with other variables ranged from −.53 to .74.

Author: Schill, T., et al.

Article: Development of Covert and Overt Hostility Scales from the Buss-Durkee Inventory.

Journal: *Psychological Reports*, October 1990, *67*(2), 671–674.

Related Research: Buss, A. H., & Durkee, A. (1957). An inventory for assessing different kinds of hostility. *Journal of Consulting Psychology*, *21*, 343–349.

3851

Test Name: ILLNESS AND SICK-ROLE SCALES

Purpose: To measure illness management, expression, labeling, dependence, role strain, impairment, and sick-role support.

Number of Items: 37

Format: Likert format. All items presented.

Reliability: Alphas ranged from .47 to .74 across subscales.

Author: Nuttbrock, L.

Article: The management of illness among physically impaired older people: An interactionist interpretation.

Journal: *Social Psychology Quarterly*, June 1986, *49*(2), 180–191.

Related Research: Shanas, E. (1960). *The health of older people: A survey*. New York: The Free Press.

■ ■ ■

3852

Test Name: IMPACT OF EVENT SCALE

Purpose: To assess emotional sequelae of extreme stress.

Number of Items: 15

Format: Four-point frequency scale, 1 (*not at all*) to 4 (*often*), for each of 15 emotional reactions. All items presented.

Reliability: Alpha was .93.

Validity: All items but two distinguished between a combat stress reaction group, a combat control group, and a noncombat control group ($p < .01$).

Author: Schwartzwald, J., et al.

Article: Validation of the Impact of Event Scale for psychological sequelae of combat.

Journal: *Journal of Consulting and Clinical Psychology*, April 1987, *55*(2), 251–256.

Related Research: Horowitz, M., et al. (1979). Impact of Event Scale: A measure of subjective stress. *Psychosomatic Medicine, 41*, 209–218.

• • •

3853

Test Name: IOWA SELF-ASSESSMENT INVENTORY

Purpose: To assess functional characteristics of the elderly across six dimensions.

Number of Items: 120

Format: Includes six scales: social resources, economic resources, mental health, physical health, activities of daily living, and cognitive status. Responses are made on a 4-point scale: *true, more often true than not, more often false than not,* and *false.*

Reliability: Alpha coefficients ranged from .78 to .87.

Validity: Correlations with demographic variables ranged from –.32 to .36.

Author: Morris, W. W., et al.

Article: Issues related to the validation of the Iowa Self-Assessment Inventory.

Journal: *Educational and Psychological Measurement,* Winter 1989, *49*(4), 853–861.

Related Research: Morris, W. W., & Buckwalter, K. C. (1988). Functional assessment of the elderly: The Iowa Self-Assessment Inventory. In C. F. Waltz & O. L. Strickland (Eds.), *Measurement of nursing outcomes: Vol. 1. Measuring client outcomes.* New York: Springer.

• • •

3854

Test Name: INDEX OF ADULT ADJUSTMENT

Purpose: To identify markers of effective functioning likely to be observed over time in the lives of adult women.

Number of Items: 20

Format: Includes four subscales: career, social, physical health, and psychological health.

Validity: Correlations with other variables ranged from –.23 to .43.

Author: Picano, J. J.

Article: Development and validation of a life history index of adult adjustment for women.

Journal: *Journal of Personality Assessment,* Summer 1989, *53*(2), 308–318.

Related Research: Vaillant, G. E. (1975). Natural history of male psychological health III: Empirical dimensions of mental health. *Archives of General Psychiatry, 32*, 420–425.

• • •

3855

Test Name: INDEX OF HOMOPHOBIA

Purpose: To measure dread of and discomfort about homosexuals.

Number of Items: 26

Format: Five-point Likert format. Sample items presented.

Reliability: Internal consistency was .90.

Author: Young, M., et al.

Article: Attitudes of nursing students toward patients with AIDS.

Journal: *Psychological Reports,* October 1990, *67*(2), 491–497.

Related Research: Hudson, W., & Ricketts, W. A. (1980). A strategy for the measurement of homophobia. *Journal of Homosexuality, 5,* 357–372.

• • •

3856

Test Name: INTELLECTUAL ACHIEVEMENT RESPONSIBILITY SCALE

Purpose: To identify helpless children.

Number of Items: 34

Format: Each item depicts either a success or failure achievement situation followed by two alternative explanations for the event.

Reliability: Coefficient alphas were .54 and .66.

Validity: Correlations with other variables ranged from –.17 to .49.

Author: Fincham, F. D., et al.

Article: Learned helplessness, test anxiety, and academic achievement: A longitudinal analysis.

Journal: *Child Development,* February 1989, *60*(1), 138–145.

Related Research: Crandall, V. C., et al. (1965). Children's beliefs in their own control of reinforcements in intellectual-academic situations. *Child Development, 36*, 91–109.

• • •

3857

Test Name: INVENTORY OF COMMON PROBLEMS

Purpose: To measure the presenting problems of college students.

Number of Items: 24

Format: Includes six problem subgroups: depression, anxiety, interpersonal problems, academic problems, physical health problems, and substance-use problems. Each item is rated on a 5-point scale.

Reliability: Alpha was .85.

Validity: Correlations with other variables ranged from .01 to .43.

Author: Hoffman, J. A., and Weiss, B.

Article: Family dynamics and presenting problems in college students.

Journal: *Journal of Counseling Psychology,* April 1987, *34*(2), 157–163.

Related Research: Hoffman, J. A., & Weiss, B. (1986). A new system for conceptualizing problems of college students: Types of crises and the Inventory of Common Problems. *Journal of American College Health*, *34*, 259–266.

■ ■ ■

3858

Test Name: INVENTORY OF PHYSICAL SYMPTOMS

Purpose: To assess psychosomatic symptoms.

Number of Items: 33

Format: Five-point rating scale format.

Reliability: Alpha was .88.

Validity: Correlated .22 and .29 with use of student health facilities.

Author: Hershberger, P. J.

Article: Self-complexity and health promotion: Promising but premature.

Journal: *Psychological Reports*, June 1990, *66*(3) II, 1207–1216.

Related Research: Cohen, S., & Hoberman, H. M. (1983). Positive events and social supports as buffers of life change stress. *Journal of Applied Psychology*, *13*, 99–125.

■ ■ ■

3859

Test Name: INVENTORY TO DIAGNOSE DEPRESSION

Purpose: To measure subject symptoms consistent with diagnostic criteria for major depressive, endogenous, and melancholia classifications.

Number of Items: 22

Format: Responses are made on a 5-point Likert scale.

Reliability: Test–retest (2 days) reliability was .98. Internal consistency was .92.

Validity: Correlations with other variables ranged from −.15 to −.36.

Author: Elliott, T. R., and Gramling, S. E.

Article: Personal assertiveness and the effects of social support among college students.

Journal: *Journal of Counseling Psychology*, October 1990, *37*(4), 427–436.

Related Research: Zimmerman, M., & Coryel, W. (1987). The inventory to diagnose depression (IDD): A self-report scale to diagnose major depressive disorder. *Journal of Consulting and Clinical Psychology*, *55*, 55–59.

■ ■ ■

3860

Test Name: JALOWEIC COPING SCALE

Purpose: To identify coping strategies.

Number of Items: 40

Format: Includes three subscales: problem, emotional, and palliative behaviors.

Reliability: Alpha coefficients ranged from .70 to .85.

Author: Keller, C.

Article: Psychological and physical variables as predictors of coping strategies.

Journal: *Perceptual and Motor Skills*, August 1988, *67*(1), 95–100.

Related Research: Jaloweic, A., et al. (1984). Psychosomatic assessment of the Jaloweic Scale. *Nursing Research*, *3*, 157–161.

■ ■ ■

3861

Test Name: JANIS-FIELD FEELINGS OF INADEQUACY SCALE

Purpose: To identify feelings of inadequacy.

Number of Items: 20

Format: Half the items are positively worded and half are negatively worded. Five graded answer categories are provided.

Reliability: Split-half reliabilities were .84 and .88.

Author: Stoltz, R. F., and Galassi, J. P.

Article: Internal attributions and types of depression in college students: The learned helplessness model revisited.

Journal: *Journal of Counseling Psychology*, July 1989, *36*(3), 316–321.

Related Research: Eagly, A. H. (1967). Involvement as a determinant of response to favorable and unfavorable information. *Journal of Personality and Social Psychology*, *7*(3, Whole No. 643).

■ ■ ■

3862

Test Name: JOB AFFECT SCALE

Purpose: To measure individual affect.

Number of Items: 20

Format: Half of the items measure positive affect, the other half measure negative affect. Responses are made on a 5-point scale ranging from 1 (*very slightly or not at all*) to 5 (*very much*).

Reliability: Internal consistency reliabilities were .80 and .81.

Validity: Correlations with other variables ranged from −.39 to .63.

Author: George, J. M.

Article: Personality, affect, and behavior in groups.

Journal: *Journal of Applied Psychology*, April 1990, *75*(2), 107–116.

Related Research: Brief, A. P., et al. (1988). Should negative affectivity remain an unmeasured variable in the study of job stress? *Journal of Applied Psychology*, *73*, 193–198.

■ ■ ■

3863

Test Name: LIFE EVENTS SCALE

Purpose: To measure the subjective impart of life changes such as marriage, death of a family member, or changes in work.

Number of Items: 47

Format: Subjects endorse items that happened to them and then rate the import of them on a 7-point bipolar scale.

AUTHOR: Klar, Y., et al.

Reliability: Test–retest (5 or 6 weeks) reliability ranged from .56 to .88.

Article: Characteristics of participants in a large group awareness training.

Journal: *Journal of Consulting and Clinical Psychology*, February 1990, *58*(1), 99–108.

Related Research: Sarason, I. G., et al. (1978). Assessing the import of life change: Developing the Life Experiences Survey. *Journal of Consulting and Clinical Psychology*, *46*, 932–946.

■ ■ ■

3864

Test Name: LIFE EVENTS SCALE

Purpose: To measure life events during the past 12 months and the degree to which they were upsetting.

Number of Items: 31

Format: Four-point frequency scale ranging from 4 (*happened and was very upsetting*) to 1 (*hasn't happened in the past year*).

Validity: Correlations with other variables ranged from –.09 to .74.

Author: Monroe, S. M., et al.

Article: Social support, life events, and depressive symptoms: A 1-year prospective study.

Journal: *Journal of Consulting and Clinical Psychology*, August 1986, *54*(4), 424–431.

Related Research: Dohrenwend, B. S., et al. (1978). Exemplification of a method for scaling life events: The

PERI life events scale. *Journal of Health and Social Behavior*, *19*, 205–229.

■ ■ ■

3865

Test Name: LIFE EXPERIENCES SURVEY

Purpose: To list events that occurred over a 1-year period prior to testing.

Number of Items: 57

Format: Likert format indicates negative or positive experiences.

Reliability: Test–retest reliability ranged from .56 to .88.

Author: Frank, R. G., et al.

Article: Differences in coping styles among persons with spinal cord injury: A cluster-analytic approach.

Journal: *Journal of Consulting and Clinical Psychology*, October 1987, *55*(5), 727–731.

Related Research: Sarason, I. G., et al. (1978). Assessing the impact of life changes: Development of the Life Experiences Survey *Journal of Consulting and Clinical Psychology*, *46*, 932–946.

■ ■ ■

3866

Test Name: LIFE EXPERIENCES SURVEY

Purpose: To assess negative life stress.

Number of Items: 47

Format: Responses are made on a 7-point scale ranging from –3 to 3.

Reliability: Test–retest reliability ranged from .56 to .88.

Validity: Correlations with variables ranged from –.15 to .55.

Author: Nezu, A. M., and Ronan, G. F.

Article: Social problems solving as a moderator of stress-related depressive symptoms: A prospective analysis.

Journal: *Journal of Counseling Psychology*, April 1988, *35*(2), 134–138.

Related Research: Sarason, I. G., et al. (1978). Assessing the impact of life changes: Development of the Life Experiences Survey. *Journal of Consulting and Clinical Psychology*, *46*, 932–946.

■ ■ ■

3867

Test Name: LIFE EXPERIENCES SURVEY

Purpose: To assess life stress.

Number of Items: 60

Format: Students indicate on a 7-point scale the impact of stressful life events.

Reliability: Test–retest (6 weeks) reliability ranged from .63 to .64.

Validity: Correlations with other variables ranged from –.25 to .37.

Author: Rich, A. R., and Bonner, R. L.

Article: Support for a pluralistic approach to the treatment of depression.

Journal: *Journal of College Student Development*, September 1989, *30*(5), 426–431.

Related Research: Sarason, I. G., et al. (1978). Assessing the impact of life changes: Development of the Life Experiences Survey. *Journal of Consulting and Clinical Psychology*, *45*, 932–942.

■ ■ ■

3868

Test Name: LIFE EXPERIENCES SURVEY—MODIFIED

Purpose: To assess athletes' likely life stressors.

Number of Items: 8

Format: Each stressor experienced during the week was rated on a 5-point scale from 1 (*no stress*) to 5 (*a great deal of stress*).

Validity: Correlations with other variables ranged from −.40 to .30.

Author: Williams, D. A., and Jenkins, J. O.

Article: Role of competitive anxiety in the performance of black college basketball players.

Journal: *Perceptual and Motor Skills*, October, 1986, *63*(2), 847–853.

Related Research: Sarason, I. G., et al. (1978). Assessing the impact of life changes: Development of the life experience survey. *Journal of Consulting and Clinical Psychology, 46,* 934–946.

■ ■ ■

3869

Test Name: LIFE REGARD INDEX (DUTCH)

Purpose: To measure meaning in life on two dimensions: Framework in life and fulfillment in life.

Number of Items: 28

Format: Three-point Likert format. Sample items presented.

Reliability: Test–retest reliability was .94. Cronbach's alphas ranged from .79 to .86.

Validity: Correlations with other variables ranged from −.37 to .33.

Author: Debats, D. L.

Article: The Life Regard Scale.

Journal: *Psychological Reports*, August 1990, *67*(1), 27–34.

Related Research: Battista, J., & Almond, G. (1978). The development of meaning in life. *Psychiatry, 36,* 409–427.

■ ■ ■

3870

Test Name: LIFE SATISFACTION SCALE

Purpose: To measure life satisfaction.

Number of Items: 8

Format: Seven-point bipolar items. All items presented.

Reliability: Internal reliabilities ranged from .92 to .93.

Author: Arnold, J.

Article: Career decidedness and psychological well-being: A two-cohort longitudinal study of undergraduate students and recent graduates.

Journal: *Journal of Occupational Psychology*, June 1989, *62*(2), 163–176.

Related Research: Quinn, R. P., & Staines, C. L. (1979). *The 1977 Quality of Employment Survey*. Ann Arbor: Institute for Social Research, University of Michigan.

■ ■ ■

3871

Test Name: LIFE SATISFACTION SCALE

Purpose: To measure life satisfaction.

Number of Items: 15

Format: Assesses satisfaction with such aspects as individual's living space, state of health, education, family and social life, present government, moral standards, freedom and democracy in the country, and the state of law and order.

Validity: Correlations with other variables ranged from −.44 to .58.

Author: Fullagar, C., & Barling, J.

Article: A longitudinal test of a model of the antecedents and consequences of union loyalty.

Journal: *Journal of Applied Psychology*, April 1989, *74*(2), 213–227.

Related Research: Warr, P., et al. (1980). Scales for the measurement of some work attitudes and aspects of psychological well-being. *Journal of Occupational Psychology, 52,* 129–148.

3872

Test Name: LIFE SATISFACTION SCALE

Purpose: To measure eight aspects of satisfaction with life.

Number of Items: 9

Format: Responses made on a 7-point scale: 1 (*delighted*), 2 (*pleased*), 3 (*mostly satisfied*), 4 (*mixed/about equally satisfied and dissatisfied*), 5 (*mostly dissatisfied*), 6 (*unhappy*), and 7 (*terrible*).

Reliability: Alpha was .97.

Validity: Correlations with other variables ranged from .54 to −.31.

Author: Lounsbury, J. W., and Hoopes, L. L.

Article: A vacation from work: Changes in work and nonwork outcomes.

Journal: *Journal of Applied Psychology*, August 1986, *71*(3), 392–401.

Related Research: Andrews, F. M., & Withey, S. B. (1976). *Social indicators of well-being*. New York: Plenum.

■ ■ ■

3873

Test Name: LIFE SATISFACTION SCALE

Purpose: To assess change in individually identified problem areas.

Number of Items: 11

Format: Includes one scale for each of the following areas: health; financial; recreational; social relations; attitudes toward self; dating, sex, and marriage; family morals—religion; academic; career; and educational environments. Responses were made on a scale from 1 (*completely unhappy*) to 10 (*completely happy*).

Reliability: Test–retest (5 weeks) reliability was .66 (*N* = 54).

Validity: Average correlation with depression was –.58 and with anxiety was –.35.

Author: Payne, P. A., and Friedman, G. H.

Article: Group applications of hypnosis for college students.

Journal: *Journal of College Student Personnel*, March 1986, *27*(2), 154–160.

Related Research: Payne, P. A. (1972). The *Life Satisfaction Scale*. Unpublished manuscript, University of Cincinatti, Psychological Service Center.

■ ■ ■

3874

Test Name: LITIGAPHOBIA SCALE

Purpose: To measure fear of litigation.

Number of Items: 47

Format: Likert formal.

Reliability: Kuder-Richardson formula was .90.

Author: Breslin, F. A., et al.

Article: Development of a litigaphobia scale: Measurement of excessive fear of litigation.

Journal: *Psychological Reports*, April 1986, *58*(2), 547–550.

Related Research: Brodsky, S. L. (1983). Litigaphobia: The professional's disease. Review of B. Schurtz, "League liability in psychotherapy." *Contemporary Psychology, 28*, 204–205.

■ ■ ■

3875

Test Name: LOUISVILLE FEAR SURVEY SCHEDULE

Purpose: To assess children's fears.

Number of Items: 104

Format: Children rate the degree of their fear on a 5-point scale.

Reliability: Internal consistency reliabilities ranged from .64 to .87.

Author: Dollinger, S. J., and Cramer, P.

Article: Children's defensive responses and emotional upset following a disaster: A projective assessment.

Journal: *Journal of Personality Assessment*, Spring 1990, *54*(1,2), 116–127.

Related Research: Miller, L. C., et al. (1972). Factor structure of childhood fears. *Journal of Consulting and Clinical Psychology, 39*, 264–268.

■ ■ ■

3876

Test Name: MANIFEST ANXIETY SCALE

Purpose: To measure generalized anxiety.

Number of Items: 50

Format: True–false questionnaire.

Reliability: Test–retest (over 5 months) reliability was .81; test–retest (over 3 weeks) reliability was .89.

Author: Redding, C. A., and Livneh, H.

Article: Manifest anxiety: A cluster analytic study.

Journal: *Perceptual and Motor Skills*, October, 1986, *63*(2), 471–474.

Related Research: Taylor, J. A. (1953). A personality scale of manifest anxiety. *Journal of Abnormal and Social Psychology, 48*, 285–290.

■ ■ ■

3877

Test Name: MASCULINE GENDER-ROLE STRESS QUESTIONNAIRE

Purpose: To measure masculine gender-role stress.

Number of Items: 66

Format: Respondents rate each item according to the impact each would have on them using a 7-point Likert scale ranging from 1 (*not at all stressful*) to 7 (*extremely stressful*).

Reliability: Coefficient alphas were in the low .90s.

Validity: Correlations with other variables ranged from –.18 to .54.

Author: Eisler, R. M., et al.

Article: Masculine gender-role stress: Predictor of anger, anxiety, and health-risk behaviors.

Journal: *Journal of Personality Assessment*, Spring 1988, *52*(1), 133–141.

■ ■ ■

3878

Test Name: MENTAL HEALTH INVENTORY

Purpose: To assess mental health in terms of feelings of distress or well-being.

Number of Items: 38

Format: Five- and 6-point Likert formats.

Reliability: Alphas ranged from .81 to .92.

Validity: Correlates in the low .80s with the Beck Depression Inventory.

Author: Windle, M.

Article: Predicting temperament–mental health relationships: A covariance structure latent variable analysis.

Journal: *Journal of Research in Personality*, March 1989, *23*(1), 118–144.

Related Research: Viet, C. T., & Ware, J. H., Jr. (1983). The structure of psychological distress and well-being in general populations. *Journal of Consulting and Clinical Psychology, 5*, 730–742.

3879

Test Name: MENTAL HEALTH SCALE

Purpose: To assess mental health.

Number of Items: 9

Format: Includes measures of anger and self-esteem.

Reliability: Alpha coefficents were .88 (anger) and .72 (self-esteem).

Validity: Correlation with other variables ranged from −.59 to .72.

Author: Caplan, R. D., et al.

Article: Job seeking, reemployment, and mental health: A randomized field experiment in coping with job loss.

Journal: *Journal of Applied Psychology*, October 1989, *74*(5), 759–769.

Related Research: Caplan, R. D., et al. (1984). Tranquilizer use and well-being: A longitudinal study of social and psychological effects. Ann Arbor, MI: Research Report Series.

■ ■ ■

3880

Test Name: MENSTRUAL DISTRESS QUESTIONNAIRE— DUTCH

Purpose: To measure menstrual distress as an aid in the diagnosis of premenstrual syndrome (PMS).

Number of Items: 46

Format: Items are symptoms. Respondents indicate on visual analogue scales how much a symptom is descriptive of them. The questionnaire is given four times during the menstrual cycle.

Reliability: Alphas ranged from .69 to .91.

Validity: Four factors previously identified were replicated, but two others were not.

Author: Van der Ploeg, H. M.

Article: The factor structure of the Menstrual Distress Questionnaire— Dutch.

Journal: *Psychological Reports*, June 1990, *66*(3)1, 707–714.

Related Research: Moos, R. H. (1968). The development of a menstrual distress questionnaire. *Psychosomatic Medicine*, *30*, 853–867.

■ ■ ■

3881

Test Name: MISSISSIPPI SCALE FOR COMBAT-RELATED POST-TRAUMATIC STRESS DISORDER

Purpose: To assess severity of post-traumatic stress disorder.

Number of Items: 35

Format: Five-point rating scales.

Reliability: Alpha was .94. Average item-total correlation was .58. Test–retest reliability was .97.

Validity: Correlated .25 ($p < .0001$) with Combat Exposure Scale. Diagnostic accuracy ranged from 80% to 93%.

Author: Keane, T. M., et al.

Article: Mississippi Scale for Combat-Related Post-Traumatic Stress Disorder: Three studies in reliability and validity.

Journal: *Journal of Consulting and Clinical Psychology*, February 1988, *56*(1), 85–90.

■ ■ ■

3882

Test Name: MOBILITY INVENTORY FOR AGORAPHOBIA

Purpose: To identify types of situations typically avoided by agoraphobic patients.

Number of Items: 27

Format: Subjects rate the degree of avoidance for each situation using a 5-point scale from *never avoid* to *always avoid*. The number of panics during the previous 7 days is recorded.

Reliability: Spearman-Brown split-half reliability coefficients ranged from .87 to .94.

Author: Craske, M. G., et al.

Article: Mobility, cognitions, and panic.

Journal: *Journal of Psychopathology and Behavior Assessment*, September 1986, *8*(3), 199–210.

Related Research: Chambless, D., et al. (1985). The Mobility Inventory for Agoraphobia. *Behavior Research and Therapy*, *23*, 35–44.

■ ■ ■

3883

Test Name: MOBILITY INVENTORY FOR AGORAPHOBIA

Purpose: To measure self-reported severity of agoraphobic avoidance behavior.

Number of Items: 26

Format: Each item is a situation rated on a 5-point Likert scale according to how much the situation is avoided both if the person is alone and if the person is accompanied. Includes two factors: public, crowded, or social situations and enclosed or riding situations.

Validity: Correlations with other variables ranged from −.04 to .76.

Author: Kwon, S. M., et al.

Article: Factor structure of the Mobility Inventory for Agoraphobia: A validation study with Australian samples of agoraphobic patients.

Journal: *Journal of Psychopathology and Behavioral Assessment*, December 1990, *12*(4), 365–374.

Related Research: Chambless, D. L., et al. (1985). The mobility inventory for agoraphobia. *Behavior Research and Therapy*, *23*, 35–44.

■ ■ ■

3884

Test Name: MODIFIED FEAR SURVEY

Purpose: To assess fears experienced by victims of rape, animal fears, classical fears, social-interpersonal fears, tissue damage fears, and self-esteem fears.

Number of Items: 120

Reliability: Internal consistency was .98. Test–retest reliability was .73.

Validity: Fear scores decrease in response to two treatment programs to reduce fears.

Author: Alexander, P. C., et al.

Article: A comparison of group treatments of women sexually abused as children.

Journal: *Journal of Consulting and Clinical Psychology*, August 1989, 57(4), 479–483.

Related Research: Veroneen, L. J., & Kilpatrick, D. G. (1980). Reported fears of rape victims: A preliminary investigation. *Behavior Modification*, 4, 383–396.

■ ■ ■

3885

Test Name: MODIFIERS AND PERCEIVED STRESS SCALE

Purpose: To measure life events associated with stress.

Number of Items: 41

Format: Each item is rated on five 9-point scales: months ago it happened, stress, degree it was anticipated, degree responsible for it, and degree of support received. All items presented.

Reliability: Test–retest reliability ranged from .69 to .88.

Validity: Correlations with anxiety, depression, self-esteem, life satisfaction, and blood pressure ranged from .03 to .35.

Author: Linn, M.

Article: Modifiers and perceived stress scale.

Journal: *Journal of Consulting and Clinical Psychology*, August 1986, 54(4), 507–513.

Related Research: Holmes, T. H., & Rahe, R. M. (1967). The social readjustment rating scale. *Journal of Psychosomatic Research*, 11, 213–218.

■ ■ ■

3886

Test Name: MOOD CHECK LIST

Purpose: To measure the factorial structure of mood.

Number of Items: 60

Format: Respondents address each item on a 5-point scale ranging from 1 (*very slightly or not at all*) to 5 (*very much*). Most of the adjectives are presented.

Reliability: Internal consistencies of a short form version were .89 and .90.

Author: Almagor, M., and Ben-Porath, Y. S.

Article: The two-factor model of self-reported mood: Across-cultural replication.

Journal: *Journal of Personality Assessment*, Spring 1989, 53(1), 10–21.

Related Research: Tellegen, A. (1980). *The structure of mood states*. Unpublished manuscript, University of Minnesota, MN.

■ ■ ■

3887

Test Name: MULTIPLE SCLEROSIS INCAPACITY SCALE

Purpose: To inventory neurological and rehabilitative dysfunctions.

Number of Items: 16

Format: Five-point functioning rating scales.

Reliability: Alpha was .93. Interrater reliability was .94.

Validity: Construct = .81.

Author: Crawford, J. D., and McIvor, G. P.

Article: Stress management for multiple sclerosis patients.

Journal: *Psychological Reports*, October 1987, 61(2), 423–429.

Related Research: Kurtzke, J. F. (1981). A proposal for a uniform minimal record of disability in multiple sclerosis. *Acta Neurologica Scandinavica*, 64(Suppl. 87), 110–129.

■ ■ ■

3888

Test Name: NEGATIVE AFFECTIVITY SCALE

Purpose: To assess the global disposition of negative affectivity.

Number of Items: 21

Format: Respondents answer each item on a 6-point Likert scale indicating the extent of agreement or disagreement.

Reliability: Alpha coefficients ranged from .84 to .86 (Ns varied from 107 to 381).

Validity: Correlations with other variables ranged from −.74 to .64.

Author: Levin, I., and Stokes, J. P.

Article: Dispositional approach to job satisfaction: Role of negative affectivity.

Journal: *Journal of Applied Psychology*, October 1989, 74(5), 752–758.

■ ■ ■

3889

Test Name: NEGATIVE MOOD REGULATION SCALE

Purpose: To measure generalized expectancies for alleviating negative moods.

Format: Responses to each item are made on a 5-point scale from *strongly disagree* to *strongly agree*.

Reliability: Alpha coefficients ranged from .86 to .92.

Validity: Correlations with other variables ranged from −.42 to .31.

Author: Kirsch, I., et al.

Article: Mood-regulation expectancies as determinants of dysphoria in college students.

Journal: *Journal of Counseling Psychology*, July 1990, *37*(3), 306–312.

Related Research: Catanzaro, S. J., & Mearns, J. (1987, August). *A scale measuring generalized expectancies for coping with negative moods.* Paper presented at the meeting of the American Psychological Association, New York.

■ ■ ■

3890

Test Name: NEGATIVE MOOD SCALE

Purpose: To assess negative mood.

Number of Items: 7

Format: Respondents indicate on a 4-point scale how often they feel bored, angry with themselves, lonely, angry with society, happy, helpless, and depressed.

Reliability: Coefficient alpha was .67.

Author: Winefield, A. H., and Tiggermann, M.

Article: Employment status and psychological well-being: A longitudinal study.

Journal: *Journal of Applied Psychology*, August 1990, *75*(4), 455–459.

Related Research: Tiggermann, M., & Winefield, A. H. (1984). The effects of unemployment on mood, self-esteem, locus of control and depressive affect of school leavers. *Journal of Occupational Psychology*, *57*, 33–42.

■ ■ ■

3891

Test Name: NEUROTIC TRAIT SCREENING SCALE

Purpose: To measure neuroticism.

Number of Items: 20

Format: A true–false test. One point is awarded for each item answered in the "neurotic" direction. All items are presented.

Validity: Correlations with other variables ranged from .30 to .57.

Author: Young, L. D., et al.

Article: Comparison of the Milwaukee Neurotic Tract Screening Scale with the Symptom Check List.

Journal: *Perceptual and Motor Skills*, June 1987, *64*(3, Part 1), 855–859.

Related Research: Berkman, L. F., & Breslow, L. (1983). *Health and ways of living.* New York: Oxford University Press.

■ ■ ■

3892

Test Name: NOISE SENSITIVITY SCALE

Purpose: To measure noise sensitivity by addressing affective reactions to noise in a variety of situations.

Number of Items: 21

Format: Responses are made on a 6-point scale ranging from 0 (*agree strongly*) to 5 (*disagree strongly*).

Reliability: Split-half reliability coefficient was .85. Cronbach's alpha was .84.

Author: Ekehammar, B., and Dornic, S.

Article: Weinstein's noise sensitivity scale: Reliability and construct validity.

Journal: *Perceptual and Motor Skills*, February 1990, *70*(1), 129–130.

Related Research: Weinstein, N. D. (1978). Individual differences in reaction to noise: A longitudinal study in a college dormitory. *Journal of Applied Psychology*, *63*, 458–466.

■ ■ ■

3893

Test Name: OBSESSIVE-COMPULSIVE SCALE

Purpose: To reflect cognitions and behaviors associated with obsessive-compulsive disorders.

Number of Items: 22

Format: True–false format.

Reliability: Test–retest reliability was .82.

Author: Lambirth, T. T., et al.

Article: Use of a behavior-based personality instrument in aviation selection.

Journal: *Educational and Psychological Measurement*, Winter 1986, *46*(4), 973–978.

Related Research: Gibb, G., et al. (1983). The measurement of obsessive-compulsive personality. *Educational and Psychological Measurement*, *43*, 1233–1238.

■ ■ ■

3894

Test Name: PARENTAL STRESS SCALE

Purpose: To measure emotional stress.

Number of Items: 9

Format: Four-point rating scale.

Reliability: Alpha was .89.

Author: Demo, D. H., et al.

Article: Family relations and the self-esteem of adolescents and their parents.

Journal: *Journal of Marriage and the Family*, November 1987, *48*(4), 705–715.

Related Research: Pearlin, L., & Schooler, C. (1978). The structure of coping. *Journal of Health and Social Behavior*, *19*, 2–21.
Noh, S., & Avison, W. R. (1988). Spouses of discharged psychiatric patients: Factors associated with their experiences of burden. *Journal of Marriage and the Family*, *50*, 377–389.
Vega, W. A., et al. (1988). Marital strain, coping, and depression among

Mexican-American women. *Journal of Marriage and the Family, 50,* 391–403.

• • •

3895

Test Name: PATIENT SICK-ROLE SCALE

Purpose: To measure helplessness in psychiatric patients.

Number of Items: 13

Format: Likert format.

Reliability: Cronbach's alpha was .69.

Validity: Correlated .50 with the medical perception of mental illness. Correlated .42 with nurses ratings of patients.

Author: Augoustinos, M.

Article: Psychiatric inpatients' attitudes toward mental disorder and the tendency to adopt a sick role.

Journal: *Psychological Reports*, April 1986, *58*(2), 495–498.

• • •

3896

Test Name: PEER NOMINATION INDEX OF DEPRESSION

Purpose: To measure depression in children.

Number of Items: 13

Format: Students nominate classmates who are "sad" or have other indicators of depression. Depression scores are the proportion of the classmates who nominate a given individual summed over the 13 items.

Reliability: Reliability ranged from .71 to .85.

Author: Cole, D. A., and Carpentieri, S.

Article: Social status and the comorbidity of child depression in conduct disorder.

Journal: *Journal of Consulting and Clinical Psychology*, December 1990, *58*(6), 748–757.

Related Research: Lefkowitz, M. M., & Tesiny, E. P. (1980). Assessment of childhood depression. *Journal of Consulting and Clinical Psychology, 48*, 433–450.

• • •

3897

Test Name: PEOPLE KNOWING QUESTIONNAIRE

Purpose: To measure fear of success.

Number of Items: 64

Format: Items are answered either *true* or *false*.

Validity: Correlations with other variables ranged from −.32 to .24.

Author: Larkin, L.

Article: Identity and fear of success.

Journal: *Journal of Counseling Psychology*, January 1987, *34*(1), 38–45.

Related Research: Cohen, N. E. (1975). Exploration in the fear of success. (Doctoral dissertation, Columbia University, 1975). *Dissertation Abstracts International, 36*, 1425B-1426B.

• • •

3898

Test Name: PERCEIVED STRESS SCALE

Purpose: To assess stress.

Number of Items: 14

Format: Five-point rating scale format.

Reliability: Alphas ranged from .84 to .86. Test–retest (2 days) reliability was .85.

Author: Hershberger, P. J.

Article: Self-complexity and health promotion: Promising but premature.

Journal: *Psychological Reports*, June 1990, *66*(3) II, 1207–1216.

Related Research: Cohen, S., et al. (1983). A global measure of perceived stress. *Journal of Health and Social Behavior, 24*, 385–396.

3899

Test Name: PERINATAL GRIEF SCALE—SHORT VERSION

Purpose: To measure bereavement of pregnancy loss.

Number of Items: 33

Format: Likert-type items with responses varying from 1 (*strongly agree*) to 5 (*strongly disagree*). Includes three subscales: active grief, difficulty coping, and despair. All items are presented.

Reliability: Cronbach's alphas ranged from .86 to .95. Test–retest (12 to 15 months) reliability ranged from .59 to .66.

Author: Potvin, L., et al.

Article: Measuring grief: A short version of the Perinatal Grief Scale.

Journal: *Journal of Psychopathology and Behavioral Assessment*, March 1989, *11*(1), 29–45.

Related Research: Toedter, L., et al. (1988). The Perinatal Grief Scale: Development and initial validation. *American Journal of Orthopsychiatry, 58*, 435–449.

• • •

3900

Test Name: PERSONALITY STRESS INVENTORY

Purpose: To measure the probability of contracting different diseases (cancer, coronary heart disease, and others).

Number of Items: 182

Format: The inventory is administered twice with change scores the desired reading. Yes–no format. All items presented.

Validity: Factor analytic and proband validity data suggest that the inventory is valid.

Author: Grossarth-Maticek, R., and Eysenck, H. J.

Article: Personality, Stress and Disease: Description and validation of a new inventory.

Journal: *Psychological Reports*, April 1990, *66*(2), 355–373.

Related Research: Baltrusch, H., et al. (1988). Cancer from the behavioral perspective: The type C pattern. *Activas Nervosa Superior*, *30*, 18–20.

■ ■ ■

3901

Test Name: PHILADELPHIA GERIATRIC CENTER MORALE SCALE—REVISED

Purpose: To assess psychological well-being.

Number of Items: 17

Format: *Agree* or *disagree* is recorded for each item. Includes three subscales: agitation, attitude toward own aging, and lonely dissatisfaction. Sample items are presented.

Reliability: Alpha for total scale was .75 and ranged from .53 to .61 for the subscales.

Validity: Correlations with the Social Desirability Scale ranged from –.14 to .34.

Author: Mancini, J. A., and McKeel, A. J.

Article: Social desirability and psychological well-being reports in late life: A further inquiry.

Journal: *Educational and Psychological Measurement*, Spring 1986, *46*(1), 89–94.

Related Research: Lauton, M. P. (1975). The Philadelphia Geriatric Center Morale Scale: A revision. *Journal of Gerontology*, *30*, 85–89.

■ ■ ■

3902

Test Name: PLEASANT EVENTS INVENTORY

Purpose: To measure involvement in satisfaction and anticipated satisfaction in pleasant events.

Number of Items: 276

Format: Subjects endorse items they have experienced and indicate their degree of satisfaction with it. Respondents report anticipated satisfaction on non-enclosed items.

Reliability: Alpha was .81. Test–retest (1 month) reliability was .78.

Author: Rotheram-Borus, M. J., et al.

Article: Cognitive style and pleasant activities among female adolescent suicide attempters.

Journal: *Journal of Consulting and Clinical Psychology*, October 1990, *58*(5), 554–561.

Related Research: MacPhillamy, D. J., & Lewinsohn, P. M. (1982). The Pleasant Events Schedule: Studies on reliability, validity, and scale intercorrelations. *Journal of Consulting and Clinical Psychology*, *50*, 363–380.

■ ■ ■

3903

Test Name: PLEASURE CAPACITY SCALE

Purpose: To assess individual differences in hedonic capacity.

Number of Items: 36

Format: Each item, a potentially gratifying situation, is rated on a 5-point scale ranging from 1 (*no pleasure at all*) to 5 (*extreme and lasting pleasure*).

Validity: Correlations with measures of masculinity and femininity were .18 and .46 respectively (*N* = 99).

Author: Zeldow, P. B., et al.

Article: Masculinity, femininity, and psychosocial adjustment in medical students: A 2-year follow-up.

Journal: *Journal of Personality Assessment*, Spring 1987, *51*(1), 3–14.

Related Research: Fawcett, J., et al. (1983). Assessing anhedonia in psychiatric patients: The pleasure scale. *Archives of General Psychiatry*, *40*, 79–88.

3904

Test Name: POSITIVE AND NEGATIVE AFFECT SCALE

Purpose: To index positive and negative affect.

Number of Items: 20

Format: Responses are made on a 5-point scale ranging from 1 (*very slightly*) to 5 (*extremely*). Includes two factors: positive affect and negative affect.

Reliability: Test–retest (3–5 months) averaged .80 for negative affectivity with comparable support for positive affect. Alpha coefficients were .91 (positive affect) and .84 (negative affect).

Validity: Correlations with other variables ranged from –.38 to .44.

Author: Organ, D. W., and Konovsky, M.

Article: Cognitive versus affective determinants of organizational citizenship behavior.

Journal: *Journal of Applied Psychology*, February 1989, *74*(1), 157–164.

Related Research: Watson, D., & Tellegen, A. (1985). Toward a consensual structure of mood. *Psychological Bulletin*, *98*, 219–235.

■ ■ ■

3905

Test Name: PROBLEM CHECKLIST

Purpose: To assess frequency of current problems.

Number of Items: 9

Format: Subjects report frequency of problems over past 2 weeks.

Reliability: Test–retest reliability was .62. Alpha was .73.

Author: Nezu, A. M., and Perri, M. G.

Article: Social problem-solving therapy for unipolar depression: An initial dismantling investigation.

Journal: *Journal of Consulting and Clinical Psychology*, June 1989, *57*(3), 408–413.

Related Research: Nezu, A. M. (1986). Effects of stress from current problems: Comparison of major life events. *Journal of Clinical Psychology*, *42*, 847–852.

■ ■ ■

3906

Test Name: PROBLEM SEVERITY RATING SCALE

Purpose: To rate clients' overall psychological health.

Number of Items: 4

Format: The four areas measured include: severity of problems, subjective distress, quality of interpersonal functioning, and academic performance.

Reliability: Coefficient alpha was .70.

Author: Kokotovic, A. M., and Tracey, T. J.

Article: Working alliance in the early phase of counseling.

Journal: *Journal of Counseling Psychology*, January 1990, *37*(1), 16–21.

Related Research: Strupp, H. H., & Hadley, S. W. (1979). Specific versus nonspecific factors in psychotherapy: A controlled study of outcome. *Archives of General Psychiatry*, *46*, 1125–1136.

■ ■ ■

3907

Test Name: PSYCHIATRIC DISORDER CONCEPTUALIZATION SCALE

Purpose: To distinguish medical from psychosocial concept of disorders.

Number of Items: 24

Format: Likert format.

Reliability: Cronbach's alpha = .51. Test–retest = .74.

Validity: Correlated .50 with sick-role scale.

Author: Augoustinos, M.

Article: Psychiatric inpatients' attitudes toward mental disorder and the tendency to adopt a sick role.

Journal: *Psychological Reports*, April 1986, *58*(2), 495–498.

■ ■ ■

3908

Test Name: PSYCHIATRIC EPIDEMIOLOGY RESEARCH INSTRUMENT (PERI)

Purpose: To measure psychological symptoms.

Number of Items: 25

Format: Three-point frequency-of-occurrence scales.

Reliability: Alpha was .89.

Author: Dooley, D., et al.

Article: Job and non-job stressors and their moderators.

Journal: *Journal of Occupational Psychology*, June 1987, *60*(2), 115–132.

Related Research: Dohrenwend, B. P., et al (1980). What brief psychiatric screening scales measure. In S. Sudiman (Ed.), Health Survey Research Methods: Third Biennial Conference (pp. 188–198). Washington, DC: National Center for Health Sciences Research.

■ ■ ■

3909

Test Name: PSYCHOLOGICAL SEPARATION INVENTORY

Purpose: To measure factors underlying psychological separation during late adolescence.

Number of Items: 138

Format: Includes four factors: functional independence, emotional independence, attitudinal independence, and conflictual independence.

Reliability: Alpha coefficients ranged from .84 to .92. Test–retest (2 to 3 weeks) reliabilities ranged from .74 to .96.

Validity: Correlations with other variables ranged from –.44 to .37 (males) and from –.47 to .42 (females).

Author: Lopez, F. G., et al.

Article: Family structure, psychological separation, and college adjustment: A canonical analysis and cross-validation.

Journal: *Journal of Counseling Psychology*, October 1988, *35*(4), 402–409.

Related Research: Hoffman, J. (1984). Psychological separation of late adolescents from their parents. *Journal of Counseling Psychology*, *31*, 170–178.

■ ■ ■

3910

Test Name: PSYCHOLOGICAL SEPARATION INVENTORY

Purpose: To measure individuation as freedom from excessive guilt, anxiety, mistrust, responsibility, inhibition, resentment, and anger.

Number of Items: 25 paired items.

Format: Five-point Likert format.

Reliability: Cronbach's alphas ranged from .84 to .92. Test–retest reliability was .83.

Author: Transeau, G., and Eliot, J.

Article: Individuation and adult children of alcoholics.

Journal: *Psychological Reports*, August 1990, *67*(1), 137–142.

Related Research: Hoffman, J. A. (1984). Psychological separation of late adolescents from their parents. *Journal of Counseling Psychology*, *31*, 170–178.

■ ■ ■

3911

Test Name: PSYCHOLOGICAL WELL-BEING SCALES

Purpose: To measure psychiatric symptoms, positive affect, meaning, and agitation.

Number of Items: 33

Format: All items presented.

Reliability: Alphas ranged from .62 to .79.

Validity: Intercorrelations ranged from −.45 to .48. Correlations with other variables ranged from −.38 to .34.

Author: Umberson, D.

Article: Relationships with children: Explaining parents' psychological well-being.

Journal: *Journal of Marriage and the Family*, November 1989, *51*(4), 999–1012.

Related Research: Hughes, M. D., & Gove, W. R. (1981). Living alone, social integration and mental health. *American Journal of Sociology*, 87, 48–74.

■ ■ ■

3912

Test Name: PSYCHOPATHOLOGY CHECKLIST

Purpose: To assess psychopathy in criminal populations.

Number of Items: 22

Format: Three-point scales (does not apply, unable to score, does apply) use interview and file data.

Reliability: Alphas ranged from .79 to .90 across samples of inmates. Interrater reliability ranged from .76 to .90.

Validity: Global, clinical assessments of psychopathy correlated .80 and .65 with two factors that were reliably extracted in all samples.

Author: Harpur, T. J., et al.

Article: Factor structure of the psychopathy checklist.

Journal: *Journal of Consulting and Clinical Psychology*, October 1988, *56*(5), 741–747.

Related Research: Hare, R. D. (1985). *The Psychopathy Checklist.* Unpublished manuscript, University of British Columbia, Vancouver, Canada.

■ ■ ■

3913

Test Name: PSYCHOPATHY CHECKLIST

Purpose: To asses psychopathy in criminal populations.

Number of Items: 20

Format: Includes a 40-point scale.

Reliability: Interrater reliabilities ranged from .88 to .92. Test–retest reliabilities ranged from .85 to .90.

Author: Gacono, C. B., et al.

Article: A Rorschach investigation of narcissism and hysteria in antisocial personality.

Journal: *Journal of Personality Assessment*, Fall 1990, *55*(1 and 2), 270–279.

Related Research: Hare, R. (1980). A research scale for the assessment of psychopathy in criminal populations. *Personality and Individual Differences*, *1*, 111–119.

■ ■ ■

3914

Test Name: QUALITY OF LIFE MEASURE

Purpose: To assess quality of life.

Number of Items: 8

Reliability: Coefficient alpha was .87.

Validity: Correlations with other variables ranged from −.75 to .72.

Author: Caplan, R. D., et al.

Article: Job seeking, reemployment, and mental health: A randomized field experiment in coping with job loss.

Journal: *Journal of Applied Psychology*, October 1989, *31*(5), 759–769.

Related Research: Andrews, F. M., & Withey, S. B. (1976). *Social indicators of well-being: American's perceptions of life quality*. New York: Plenum Press.

■ ■ ■

3915

Test Name: QUALITY OF LIFE SCALE

Purpose: To assess quality of life.

Number of Items: 10

Format: The first eight items involve a 7-point bipolar scale and the remaining two are single item measures. Examples are presented.

Reliability: Coefficient alpha was .93.

Validity: Correlations with other variables ranged from −.39 to .49.

Author: Greenhaus, J. H., et al.

Article: Work experiences, job performance, and feelings of personal and family well-being.

Journal: *Journal of Vocational Behavior*, October 1987, *31*(2), 200–215.

Related Research: Staines, G. L., et al. (1986). Wives' employment and husbands' attitudes toward work and life. *Journal of Applied Psychology*, *71*, 118–128.

■ ■ ■

3916

Test Name: READING AND WRITING OUTCOME EXPECTANCY SCALE

Purpose: To rate importance of reading and writing for achieving life goals.

Number of Items: 40

Format: Seven-point Likert format. All items presented.

Reliability: Alpha was .90.

Validity: Correlations with canonical variates ranged from .29 to .45.

Author: Shell, D. F., et al.

Article: Self-efficacy and outcome expectancy mechanisms in reading and writing achievement.

Journal: *Journal of Educational Psychology*, March 1989, *81*(1), 91–100.

■ ■ ■

3917

Test Name: REASONS FOR LIVING INVENTORY

Purpose: To assess reasons for living as a cognitive component in suicide.

Number of Items: 48

Format: Each item is rated on a 6-point scale ranging from 1 (*extremely unimportant*) to 6 (*extremely important*). Includes 6 subscales: survival and coping beliefs, responsibility to family, child concerns, fear of suicide, fear of social disapproval, and moral objections.

Reliability: Cronbach alphas ranged from .72 to .89.

Author: Range, L. M., and Antonelli, K. B.

Article: A factor analysis of six commonly used instruments associated with suicide using college students.

Journal: *Journal of Personality Assessment*, Winter 1990, *55*(3 & 4), 804–811.

Related Research: Linehan, M. M., & Nielsen, S. L. (1981). Assessment of suicide ideation and parasuicide: Hopelessness and social desirability. *Journal of Consulting and Clinical Psychology*, *49*, 773–775.

■ ■ ■

3918

Test Name: RELAXATION INVENTORY

Purpose: To assess the effects of relaxation training.

Number of Items: 45

Format: Includes three scales: physiological tension, physical assessment, and cognitive tension. Responses are made on a 5-point Likert scale.

Reliability: Kuder-Richardson reliability coefficients ranged from .81 to .95. Test–retest (1 hr) reliabilities ranged from .80 to .99 (*M* = 26).

Author: Christ, D. A., et al.

Article: The Relaxation Inventory: Self-report scales of relaxation training effects.

Journal: *Journal of Personality Assessment*, Winter 1989, *53*(4), 716–726.

Related Research: Lehrer, P. M., & Woolfolk, R. L. (1982). Self-report assessment of anxiety: Somatic, cognitive, and behavioral modalities. *Behavioral Assessment*, *4*, 167–177.

■ ■ ■

3919

Test Name: REPRESSION–SENSITIZATION SCALE

Purpose: To measure the degree to which people repress or ruminate on negative feelings.

Number of Items: 127

Format: True–false.

Reliability: Alpha was .94.

Author: Finman, R., and Berkowitz, L.

Article: Some factors influencing the effect of depressed mood on anger and overt hostility toward another.

Journal: *Journal of Research in Personality*, March 1989, *23*(1), 70–84.

Related Research: Byrne, D. (1961). The repression–sensitization scale: Rationale, reliability, and validity. *Journal of Personality*, *29*, 334–349.

■ ■ ■

3920

Test Name: REPRESSION–SENSITIZATION SCALE

Purpose: To operationalize three basic styles of coping with anxiety: repression, sensitization, and a realistic coping style.

Number of Items: 124

Format: Yes–no responses. Low scores indicate predominantly avoiding, denying, repressing and high scores indicate predominantly approaching, intellectualizing, and obsessing.

Validity: Correlations with other variables were .61 and .78.

Author: Furnham, A., and Osborne, A.

Article: Repression–sensitization, self-image disparity, and mental health.

Journal: *Educational and Psychological Measurement*, Spring 1986, *46*(1), 125–133.

Related Research: Byrne, D., et al. (1963). Relations of the revised Repression-Sensitization Scale to measures of self-description. *Psychological Reports*, *13*, 323–334.

■ ■ ■

3921

Test Name: REVISED CHILDREN'S MANIFEST ANXIETY SCALE

Purpose: To identify children's manifest anxiety.

Number of Items: 28

Format: The examiner reads each question to the child and scores it either *yes* or *no*. Examples are presented.

Reliability: Kuder-Richardson coefficient was .83.

Validity: Correlations with other variables ranged from −.36 to .19.

Author: Fuchs, D., et al.

Article: Psychosocial characteristics of handicapped children who perform suboptimally during assessment.

Journal: *Measurement and Evaluation in Counseling and*

Development, January 1986, *18*(4), 176–184.

Related Research: Reynolds, C. R., & Richmond, B. O. (1978). What I think and feel: A revised measure of children's manifest anxiety. *Journal of Abnormal Child Psychology*, *6*, 271–280.

■ ■ ■

3922

Test Name: RIMON'S BRIEF DEPRESSION SCALE

Purpose: To measure depression.

Number of Items: 7. All items presented.

Format: Four-point severity scales.

Reliability: Ranged from .77 to .87 over factors.

Validity: No differences by sex. No systematic differences by age. Correlated .78 with Beck's depression scale.

Author: Keltikangas-Järvinen, L, and Rimon, R.

Article: Rimon's Brief Depression Scale, a rapid method for screening depression.

Journal: *Psychological Reports*, February 1987, *60*(1), 111–119.

■ ■ ■

3923

Test Name: SATISFACTION WITH LIFE SCALE

Purpose: To measure satisfaction with marital, financial, and other life domains.

Number of Items: 15

Format: Seven-point scales ranged from *delighted* to *terrible*.

Reliability: Cronbach's alpha was .90.

Author: Klar, Y., et al.

Article: Characteristics of participants in a large group awareness training.

Journal: *Journal of Consulting and Clinical Psychology*, February 1990, *58*(1), 99–108.

Related Research: Andrews, F. M., & Crandall, R. (1976). The validity of measures of self-reported well-being. *Social Indicators Research*, *3*, 1–19.

■ ■ ■

3924

Test Name: SATISFACTION WITH LIFE SCALE

Purpose: To measure global life satisfaction.

Number of Items: 5

Format: Seven-point Likert format. Sample item presented.

Reliability: Alphas ranged from .82 to .90. Test–retest reliability was .82.

Author: Noe, R. A., et al.

Article: An investigation of the Correlates of Career Motivation.

Journal: *Journal of Vocational Behavior*, December 1990, *37*(3), 340–356.

Related Research: Diener, E., et al. (1985). The satisfaction with life scale. *Journal of Personality Assessment*, *49*, 71–75.

■ ■ ■

3925

Test Name: SCALE FOR SUICIDE IDEATION

Purpose: To assess suicidal intention.

Number of Items: 19

Format: Includes three factors: active suicidal desire, passive suicidal desire, and specific plans for suicide.

Reliability: Cronbach alpha was .89.

Author: Range, L. M., and Antonelli, K. B.

Article: A factor analysis of six commonly used instruments

associated with suicide using college students.

Journal: *Journal of Personality Assessment*, Winter 1990, *55*(3 & 4), 804–811.

Related Research: Beck, A. T., et al. (1979). Assessment of suicidal intention: The Scale for Suicide Ideation. *Journal of Consulting and Clinical Psychology*, *47*, 353–352.

■ ■ ■

3926

Test Name: SCALE OF COMPETENCY IN INDEPENDENT LIVING SKILLS

Purpose: To measure everyday living ability.

Number of Items: 16

Format: Each item is rated on a 5-point scale by a relative, friend, or professional who knows the patient well. Items include personal hygiene, laundry, property maintenance, obtaining money, money management, driving, public transportation, shopping, cooking, diet, medical needs, communication by phone, communication by mail, social communication, emergencies, and compensation for difficulties.

Reliability: Test–retest reliability coefficient was .66.

Validity: Correlations with other variables ranged from −.59 to .10.

Author: Searight, H. R., et al.

Article: Correlations of two competence assessment methods in a geriatric population.

Journal: *Journal of Perceptual Motor Skills*, June 1989, *68*(3) Part 1, 863–872.

Related Research: Dunn, E. J. (1985). *The relationship of the Halstead-Reitan Neuropsychological Battery to functional daily living skills in a geriatric population.* Unpublished doctoral dissertation, St. Louis University.

3927

Test Name: SELF-CONSCIOUSNESS SCALE (SPANISH)

Purpose: To measure private and public self-consciousness and anxiety.

Number of Items: 22

Reliability: Alphas ranged from .73 to .94 across subscales and three groups (Normals, asthmatics, and depressives).

Validity: Spanish version had about the same factor structure as the English version.

Author: Baños, R. M., et al.

Article: Self-Consciousness Scale: A study of Spanish housewives.

Journal: *Psychological Reports*, June 1990, *66*(3)1, 771–774.

Related Research: Scherer, M. F., & Carver, C. S. (1985). The Self-Consciousness Scale: A revised version for the general population. *Journal of Applied Social Psychology*, *15*, 687–699.

■ ■ ■

3928

Test Name: SELF EVALUATION OF LIFE FUNCTION SCALE

Purpose: To address psychological factors that contribute to life satisfaction.

Number of Items: 54

Format: Includes six dimensions: physical disability, symptoms of aging, self-esteem, social satisfaction, depression, and personal control.

Reliability: Test–retest (3 to 5 days) reliabilities ranged from .36 to .99 for individual items.

Author: Morris, W. W., et al.

Article: Issues related to the validation of the Iowa Self-Assessment Inventory.

Journal: *Educational and Psychological Measurement*, Winter 1989, *49*(4), 853–861.

Related Research: Linn, M. W., & Linn, B. S. (1984). Self-evaluation of Life Function (SELF) Scale: A short comprehensive report of health for elderly adults. *Journal of Gerontology*, *39*, 603–612.

■ ■ ■

3929

Test Name: SELF-RATING ANXIETY SCALE

Purpose: To provide a rating instrument for anxiety disorders.

Number of Items: 20

Reliability: Split-half reliability was .71. Test–retest reliability was .73.

Validity: Correlation with anxiety assessed by an interviewer was .74.

Author: Payne, P. A., and Friedman, G. H.

Article: Group applications of hypnosis for college students.

Journal: *Journal of College Student Personnel*, March 1986, *27*(2), 154–160.

Related Research: Zung, W. W. K. (1971). A rating instrument for anxiety disorders. *Psychosomatics*, *12*, 371–379.

■ ■ ■

3930

Test Name: SELF-RATING DEPRESSION SCALE

Purpose: To evaluate the severity of depression.

Number of Items: 20

Format: For each item the subject indicates whether it applies *None or a little of the time, Some of the time, Good part of the time,* or *Most or all of the time.* The higher the score the greater the depression.

Validity: Correlations with: global ratings of depression ranged from .43 to .65; Correlations with the Minnesota Multiphasic Personality Inventory Depression Scale ranged from .59 to .75.

Author: Riedel, H. P. R., et al.

Article: Efficacy of booster sessions after training in assertiveness.

Journal: *Perceptual and Motor Skills*, June 1986, *62*(3), 791–798.

Related Research: Zung, W. W. K. (1965). A self-rating depression scale. *Archives of General Psychiatry*, *12*, 63–70.

■ ■ ■

3931

Test Name: SENSE OF COHERENCE SCALE

Purpose: To measure sense of coherence in daily living.

Number of Items: 13

Format: Seven-point Likert format.

Reliability: Alpha was .74.

Author: Margalit, M., and Eysenck, S.

Article: Prediction of conherence in adolescence: Gender differences in social skills, personality and family climate.

Journal: *Journal of Research in Personality*, December 1990, *24*(4), 510–521.

Related Research: Autonovsky, A. (1987). Unraveling the mystery of health. San Francisco: Jossey Bass.

■ ■ ■

3932

Test Name: SEPARATION ANXIETY TEST

Purpose: To measure psychological separation.

Number of Items: 12

Format: A projective instrument in which the subject responds to 12 pictures of a child in different separation scenes. Examples are described.

Reliability: Split-half reliability for the Total SAT was .89.

Author: Rice, K. G., et al.

Article: Separation–individuation, family cohesion, and adjustment to college: Measurement validation and test of a theoretical model.

Journal: *Journal of Counseling Psychology*, April 1990, *37*(2), 195–202.

Related Research: Hansburg, H. G. (1980). *Adolescent separation anxiety* (Vol. 2). New York: Krieger.

■ ■ ■

3933

Test Name: SITUATIONAL HUMOR RESPONSE QUESTIONNAIRE

Number of Items: 18

Format: Five-point amusement rating scale.

Reliability: Alpha was .77.

Author: Porterfield, A. L.

Article: Does sense of humor moderate the impact of stress on psychological and physical well-being?

Journal: *Journal of Research in Personality*, September 1987, *21*(3), 306–317.

Related Research: Martin, R. A., & Lefcourt, H. M. (1983). Sense of humor as a moderator of the relation between stressors and moods. *Journal of Personality and Social Psychology*, *45*, 1313–1324.

■ ■ ■

3934

Test Name: SOMATIC COMPLAINTS SCALE

Purpose: To assess somaticism.

Format: Contains the following categories: fatigue & sickness, gastrointestinal, cardiovascular, respiratory, genitourinary, classical psychosomatic, conversion, psychosexual, and pain. Responses were made on a scale from 1 (*never/rarely*) to 4 (*very often*).

Reliability: Test–retest (3 months) reliability was .76. Coefficient alpha was .88.

Validity: Correlations with other variables ranged from −.20 to .39.

Author: Norton, N. C.

Article: Three scales of alexithymia: Do they measure the same thing?

Journal: *Journal of Personality Assessment*, Fall 1989, *53*(3), 621–637.

Related Research: Brodman, K., et al. (1951). The Cornell Medical Index-Health Questionnaire II as a diagnostic instrument. *Journal of the American Medical Association*, *145*, 152–157.

■ ■ ■

3935

Test Name: S-R INVENTORY OF GENERAL TRAIT ANXIOUSNESS

Purpose: To provide a multidimensional measure of anxiety.

Format: Responses are made on a 5-point Likert scale.

Reliability: Internal consistency reliabilities ranged from .62 to .86.

Validity: Correlations with other variables ranged from −.28 to .49.

Author: Fuqua, D. R., et al.

Article: The relationship of career and anxiety: A multivariate examination.

Journal: *The Journal of Vocational Behavior*, April 1987, *30*(2), 175–186.

Related Research: Endler, N. S., & Okada, M. (1975). A multidimensional measure of trait anxiety: The S-R Inventory of General Trait Anxiousness. *Journal of Counseling and Clinical Psychology*, *43*, 319–329.

■ ■ ■

3936

Test Name: STRESS ADJECTIVE CHECKLIST

Purpose: To measure stress and arousal.

Number of Items: 20

Format: Responses to each item are made on a 4-point scale from 1 (*definitively yes*) to 4 (*definitely not*).

Reliability: Coefficient alphas ranged from .66 to .82.

Author: Fischer, D. G., and Donatelli, M. J.

Article: A measure of stress and arousal: Factor structure of the stress adjective cheklist.

Journal: *Educational and Psychological Measurement*, Summer 1987, *47*(2), 425–435.

Related Research: Mackay, C., et al. (1978). An inventory for the measurement of self-reported stress and arousal. *British Journal of Social and Clinical Psychology*, *17*, 283–284.

■ ■ ■

3937

Test Name: STRESS INVENTORY FOR CHILDREN OF CLERGY

Purpose: To measure the impact of ministerial careers on the children of clergy.

Number of Items: 42

Format: Five-point Likert format. All items presented.

Reliability: Cronbach's alpha was .91 (total) and ranged from .67 to .88 across subscales.

Validity: Correlations with the A-FILE Total Decent Life Changes Scales ranged from .32 to .53 ($p < .05$).

Author: Ostrander, D. L., et al.

Article: The Stressors of Clergy Children Inventory: Reliability and validity.

Journal: *Psychological Reports*, December 1990, *67*(3) I, 787–794.

■ ■ ■

3938

Test Name: STRESS-SYMPTOM RATING FORM

Purpose: To identify self-observable indicators of stress.

Number of Items: 25

Format: Subjects rate the frequency of each stress symptom for the previous year on a 6-point scale from 0 (*not at all*) to 5 (*more than once per day*).

Reliability: Coefficient alpha was .93.

Author: Heilbrun, Jr., A. B., and Friedberg, E. B.

Article: Type A personality, self-control, and vulnerability to stress.

Journal: *Journal of Personality Assessment*, Fall 1988, 52(3), 420–433.

Related Research: Heilbrun, Jr., A. B., & Pepe, V. (1985). Awareness of cognitive defences and stress management. *British Journal of Medical Psychology*, 58, 9–17.

■ ■ ■

3939

Test Name: STRESS SYMPTOMS SCALE

Purpose: To assess stress symptoms such as indigestion, sleeplessness, and loss of appetite.

Number of Items: 30

Format: Four-point frequency scales.

Reliability: Internal reliabilities ranged from .87 to .90.

Author: Feather, N. T., and O'Brien, G. E.

Article: A longitudinal study of the effects of employment and unemployment on school leaving.

Journal: *Journal of Occupational Psychology*, June 1986, 59(2), 121–144.

Related Research: O'Brien, G. E. (1981). Locus of control, previous occupation and satisfaction with retirement. *Australian Journal of Psychology*, 36, 57–74.

3940

Test Name: STRESS SYMPTOMS SCALE

Purpose: To measure self-observable symptoms of stress.

Number of Items: 25

Format: Rating scale format.

Reliability: Alpha was .93.

Validity: Anorexic, depressed females score higher than females without these conditions. Type A males score higher than other males.

Author: Heilbrun, A. B., Sr., and Renert, D.

Article: Type A behavior, cognitive defense, and stress.

Journal: *Psychological Reports*, April 1986, 58(2), 447–456.

■ ■ ■

3941

Test Name: STUDENT BEHAVIOR CHECKLIST

Purpose: To explore teacher reports as a means of identifying helpless children.

Number of Items: 24

Format: Includes 12 helpless and 12 mastery-oriented items. All items are presented.

Reliability: Coefficient alphas were .95 and .96.

Validity: Correlations with other variables ranged from –.56 to .49.

Author: Fincham, F. D., et al.

Article: Learned helplessness, test anxiety, and academic achievement: A longitudinal analysis.

Journal: *Child Development*, February 1989, 60(1), 138–145.

■ ■ ■

3942

Test Name: SUICIDE IDEATION SCALE

Purpose: To measure suicide ideation.

Number of Items: 18

Reliability: Alpha was .94.

Validity: Correlations with other suicide ideation measures ranged from .34 to .76.

Author: Miller, I. W., et al.

Article: To Modified Scale for Suicidal Ideation: Reliability and validity.

Journal: *Journal of Consulting and Clinical Psychology*, October 1986, 54(5), 724–725.

Related Research: Beck, A., et al. (1979). Assessment of suicidal intention: The Scale for Suicide Ideation. *Journal of Consulting and Clinical Psychology*, 47, 343–352.

■ ■ ■

3943

Test Name: SUPPRESSION SCALE

Purpose: To assess such strategies as withdrawal, restraint, compromise, and ignoring the problem.

Number of Items: 12

Format: Examples are presented.

Reliability: Coefficient alpha was .58.

Validity: Correlations with other variables ranged from –.17 to .18 (N = 157).

Author: Parkes, K. R.

Article: Coping, negative affectivity, and the work environment: Additive and interactive predictors of mental health.

Journal: *Journal of Applied Psychology*, August 1990, 75(4), 399–409.

Related Research: Parkes, K. R. (1984). Locus of control, cognitive appraisal, and coping in stressful episodes. *Journal of Personality and Social Psychology*, 46, 655–668.

■ ■ ■

3944

Test Name: SYMPTOM CHECKLIST–90

Purpose: To provide a self-report instrument to measure clinical states in psychiatric patients.

Number of Items: 90

Format: Each symptom is responded to on a 5-point scale ranging from *not at all* to *extremely*. Examples are presented.

Reliability: Coefficient alphas ranged from .79 to .89.

Author: Mazmanian, D., et al.

Article: Psychopathology and response styles to the SCL-90 responses of acutely distressed persons.

Journal: *Journal of Psychopathology and Behavioral Assessment*, June 1987, *9*(2), 135–148.

Related Research: Derogatis, L. R., et al. (1973). SCL-90: An outpatient psychiatric rating scale—preliminary report. *Psychopharmacology Bulletin*, *9*, 13–28.

■ ■ ■

3945

Test Name: SYMPTOM CHECKLIST–10

Purpose: To measure global psychological distress.

Number of Items: 10

Format: Examples are presented.

Reliability: Internal consistency was .88 and .84 (French-Canadian version). Temporal stability (4 months) was .59.

Validity: Correlation with the Psychiatric Symptom Inventory was .81. Correlation with other variables ranged from −.04 to −.52.

Author: Sabourin, S., et al.

Article: Social desirability, psychological distress, and consumer satisfaction with mental health treatment.

Journal: *Journal of Counseling Psychology.* July 1989, *36*(3), 352–356.

Related Research: Nguyen, T. D., et al. (1983). Assessment of patient satisfaction: Development and refinement of a service evaluation questionaire. *Evaluation and Program Planning*, 6, 299–314.

■ ■ ■

3946

Test Name: SYMPTOMS OF STRESS INVENTORY

Purpose: To identify the physiological, behavioral, and cognitive components of stress responses.

Number of Items: 94

Format: Includes 10 subscales.

Reliability: Internal consistency was .97. Test–retest reliability was .83.

Validity: Correlation with the SCL-90 was .82.

Author: Horvath, A. O., and Goheen, M. D.

Article: Factors mediating the success of defiance- and compliance-based interventions.

Journal: *Journal of Counseling Psychology*, October 1990, *37*(4), 363–371.

Related Research: Leckie, M. S., & Thompson, E. (1979). *Symptoms of stress inventory*. Seattle, WA: University of Washington Department of Psychosocial Nursing.

■ ■ ■

3947

Test Name: SYMPTOM SURVEY

Purpose: To measure psychological and psychophysiological complaints.

Number of Items: 22

Format: Presence–absence format.

Validity: Discriminates outpatients and expatients from nonpatients and those who are incapacitated.

Author: Enos, D. M., and Handal, P. J.

Article: Relation of sex and age of white adolescents at the time of parental divorce to the youths' perception of family climate and psychological adjustment.

Journal: *Psychological Reports*, December 1987, *61*(3), 699–705.

Related Research: Langer, T. S. (1962). A 22–item screening score of psychiatric symptoms indicating impairment. *Journal of Health and Human Behavior*, 3, 269–276.

■ ■ ■

3948

Test Name: SYMPTOM SURVEY

Purpose: To measure psychological distress.

Number of Items: 21

Format: Symptom checklist format. Yes–no responses.

Reliability: Internal consistency was .80.

Author: Handal, P. J., et al.

Article: Preliminary investigation of the relationship between religion and psychological distress in Black women.

Journal: *Psychological Reports*, December 1989, *65*(3) I, 971–975.

Related Research: Langner, T. S. (1962). A twenty-one item screening scale score of psychiatric symptoms indicating impairment. *Journal of Health and Human Behavior*, 3, 269–276.

■ ■ ■

3949

Test Name: TEACHERS' RATING OF DEPRESSION SCALE

Purpose: To enable teachers to rate the depression of their students.

Number of Items: 4

Format: Items deal with mood, attitude, motivation, and physical functioning. All items are presented.

Reliability: Test–retest (6 weeks) reliability was .75.

Validity: Correlations with: Children's Depression Inventory was .35; reading measures ranged from −.53 to .01.

Author: Henderson, Jr., J. G.

Article: Effects of depression upon reading: A case for distinguishing effortful from automatic processes.

Journal: *Perceptual and Motor Skills*, February 1987, *64*(1), 191–200.

Related Research: Lefkowitz, M. M., & Tesiny, E. P. (1980). Assessment of childhood depression. *Journal of Consulting and Clinical Psychology, 48*, 43–50.

■ ■ ■

3950

Test Name: TEDIUM BURNOUT SCALE

Purpose: To measure emotional, mental, and physical exhaustion.

Number of Items: 21

Format: Seven-point frequency scale.

Reliability: Cronbach's alpha was .91.

Author: Kahill, S.

Article: Relationship of burnout among professional psychologists to professional expectations and social support.

Journal: *Psychological Reports*, December 1986, *59*(3), 1043–1053.

Related Research: Pines, A., & Aronson, E. (1981). *Burnout: From tedium to personal growth*. New York: Free Press.

■ ■ ■

3951

Test Name: THREAT INDEX

Purpose: To assess threat.

Number of Items: 40

Format: Items are bipolar core constructs.

Reliability: Test–retest (4 to 9 weeks) reliability ranged from .87 to .90. Split-half internal consistency was .96.

Author: Froehle, T. C.

Article: Personal construct threat as a mediator of performance in counseling techniques.

Journal: *Journal of College Student Development*, November 1989, *30*(6), 536–540.

Related Research: Krieger, S. R., et al. (1979). Validity and reliability of provided constructs in assessing death threat: A self-administered form. *Omega, 10*, 87–95.

■ ■ ■

3952

Test Name: UNEMPLOYMENT COPING TACTICS SCALE

Purpose: To assess how individuals face difficulties resulting from unemployment.

Number of Items: 14

Format: 5-point frequency scales.

Reliability: Alpha was .60.

Author: Payne, R., and Hartley, J.

Article: A test of a model for explaining the affective experience of unemployed men.

Journal: *Journal of Occupational Psychology*, March 1987, *60*(1), 31–47.

Related Research: Folkman, S., & Lazarus, R. S. (1980). An analysis of coping in a middle-aged community sample. *Journal of Health and Social Behavior, 21*, 219–239.

■ ■ ■

3953

Test Name: VANDERBILT PSYCHOTHERAPY PROCESS SCALE

Purpose: To rate patient/therapist relationship, productiveness of sessions and patient activities and characteristics.

Number of Items: 80

Format: Observers rate sessions on a 5-point scale from 1 (*not at all*) to 5 (*a great deal*).

Reliability: Interrater reliabilities ranged from .63 to .83.

Author: Rounsaville, B. J., et al.

Article: The relation between specific and general dimensions of the psychotherapy process in interpersonal psychotherapy of depression.

Journal: *Journal of Consulting and Clinical Psychology*, June 1987, *55*(3), 379–384.

Related Research: Strupp, H. H., et al. (1984). *Vanderbilt Psychotherapy Process Scale*. Unpublished manuscript, Vanderbilt University.

■ ■ ■

3954

Test Name: VISUAL-ANALOGUE MOOD SCALES

Purpose: To measure depression, anxiety, and distress.

Number of Items: 3 100-mm visual line scales.

Format: Subjects indicated on each line their felt depression, anxiety, and distress.

Reliability: Test–retest ranged from .50 to .83.

Validity: Correlations between visual scores and several well-known conventional scales ranged from −.04 to .66. Of 18 correlations, 13 were statistically significant.

Author: Cella, D. F., and Perry, S. W.

Article: Reliability and concurrent validity of three visual-analogue mood scales.

Journal: *Psychological Reports*, October 1986, *59*(2)II, 827–833.

Related Research: Luria, R. E. (1975). The validity and reliability of the visual analogue mood scale. *Journal of Psychiatric Research, 12*, 51–57.

■ ■ ■

3955

Test Name: WAYS OF COPING CHECKLIST (REVISED)

Purpose: To measure coping.

Number of Items: 68

Format: Four-point rating scales (never used to used regularly). Sample items presented.

Reliability: Internal consistency ranged from .76 to .83.

Author: Vataliano, P. P., et al.

Article: Coping in chest pain patients with and without psychiatric disorders.

Journal: *Journal of Consulting and Clinical Psychology*, June 1989, *57*(3), 338–343.

Related Research: Vitaliano, P. P., et al. (1985). The Ways of Coping Checklist: Revision and psychometric properties. *Multivariate Behavioral Research*, *20*, 3–26.

■ ■ ■

3956

Test Name: WAYS OF COPING INSTRUMENT

Purpose: To measure coping.

Number of Items: 53

Format: Yes–no format. All items presented.

Reliability: Cronbach's alpha varied from .55 to .80 across subscales.

Author: Wright, T. A.

Article: The Ways of Coping Instrument: Reliability and temporal stability for a sample of employees.

Journal: *Psychological Reports*, August 1990, *67*(1), 155–162.

Related Research: Ways of coping checklist. (1980). Stress and Coping Project, Psychology Department, University of California, Berkeley, CA.

■ ■ ■

3957

Test Name: WAYS OF COPING QUESTIONNAIRE

Purpose: To measure coping using a contextual process approach.

Number of Items: 33

Format: Likert format.

Validity: Coefficients of congruence ranged from .95 to .98.

Author: Schere, R. F., et al.

Article: Dimensionality of coping: Factor stability using the Ways of Coping Questionnaire.

Journal: *Psychological Reports*, June 1988, *62*(3), 763–770.

Related Research: Folkman, S., & Lazarus, R. S. (1985). If it changes it must be process: Study of emotion and coping during three stages of a college examination. *Journal of Personality and Social Psychology*, *48*, 150–170.

■ ■ ■

3958

Test Name: WAYS OF COPING— REVISED

Purpose: To identify methods used to deal with stressful situations.

Number of Items: 66

Format: Includes eight scales: problem-focused coping, wishful thinking, detachment, seeking social support, focusing on the positive, self-blame, tension-reduction, and keep to self. Responses are made on a 4-point Likert scale from 0 (*does not apply and/or not used*) to 3 (*used a great deal*).

Reliability: Cronbach's alpha coefficients ranged from .59 to .88.

Validity: Correlations with the Ottens-Tucker Academic Anxiety Coping Scale ranged from −.27 to .60.

Author: Ottens, A. J., et al.

Article: The construction of an academic anxiety coping scale.

Journal: *Journal of College Student Development*, May 1989, *30*(3), 249–256.

Related Research: Folkman, S., & Lazarus, R. S. (1985). If it changes it must be process: Study of emotion and coping during three stages of a college examination. *Journal of Personality and Social Psychology*, *48*, 150–170.

■ ■ ■

3959

Test Name: WORK-RELATED FEAR OF AIDS SCALE

Purpose: To measure fear as an affective response to AIDS.

Number of Items: 5

Format: Likert format. All items presented.

Reliability: Test–retest reliability was .88. Kuder-Richardson formula was .92.

Validity: Correlated positively (.40) with likelihood of rejecting job applicants with AIDS and positively related to likelihood of firing someone with AIDS (.45).

Author: O'Brien, F. P.

Article: Work-related fear of AIDS and social-desirability response bias.

Journal: *Psychological Reports*, October 1989, *65*(2), 371–378.

■ ■ ■

3960

Test Name: WORRY SCALE

Purpose: To measure fears and worries among youth.

Number of Items: 20

Format: Four-point rating scale (not at all worried to very worried).

Reliability: Split-half reliability was .83.

Validity: Three factors were extracted: public issue worries, psychological worries, and personal/injury worries.

Author: Doctor, R. M., et al.

Article: Adolescents' attitudes about nuclear war.

Journal: *Psychological Reports*, April 1987, *60*(2), 599–614.

3961

Test Name: YOUTH SUICIDE SCALE

Purpose: To assess reactions to youth suicide and other types of childhood death.

Number of Items: 11

Format: Includes a brief, fictitious newspaper article about an 18-year-old male's suicide, four demographic questions, and eight 7-point Likert items.

Reliability: Test–retest reliability ranged from .30 to .61.

Author: Range, L. M. , et al.

Article: Factor Structure of Calhoun's Youth Suicide Scale

Journal: *Journal of Personality Assessment*, Summer, 1987, *51*(2), 262–266

Related Research: Calhoun, L. G., et al. (1980). Reactions to the parents of the child suicide: A study of social impressions. *Journal of Consulting and Clinical Psychology, 48*, 535–536.

■ ■ ■

3962

Test Name: ZUNG SELF-RATING DEPRESSION SCALE

Purpose: To measure depression.

Number of Items: 20

Format: True–false.

Reliability: Cronbach's alpha ranged from .72 to .77 across four groups of elderly males and females.

Validity: Factor structure differs across four groups of elderly males and females.

Author: Kirelä, S., and Pahkala, K.

Article: Sex and age differences of factor pattern and reliability of the Zung Self-Rating Depression Scale in a Finnish elderly population.

Journal: *Psychological Reports*, October 1986, *59*(2)I, 587–597.

Related Research: Zung, W. W. K. (1965). A self-rating depression scale. *Archives of General Psychiatry, 12*, 63–70.

CHAPTER 4
Adjustment–Social

3963

Test Name: ACCEPTANCE OF INDIVIDUAL DIFFERENCES MEASURE

Purpose: To assess the estimate of physical distance a person will allow for other people of similar age and sex who have characteristics usually rated negatively.

Number of Items: 12

Format: Subjects indicate on a "closeness wheel" how close they would like each of 12 children, representing a variety of disabilities, to come during free play.

Reliability: Test–retest reliability was .83 (seventh graders).

Validity: Correlations with other variables ranged from –.33 to .35.

Author: Chalmers, J. B., and Townsend, M. A. R.

Article: The effects of training in social perspective taking on socially maladjusted girls.

Journal: *Child Development*, February 1990, *61*(1), 178–190.

Related Research: Duke, M. P., & Nowicki, S. (1972). A new measure and social-learning model for interpersonal distance. *Journal of Experimental Research in Personality*, 6, 119–132.

• • •

3964

Test Name: ACCEPTANCE OF INTERPERSONAL VIOLENCE SCALE

Purpose: To indicate one's level of interpersonal violence acceptance.

Number of Items: 6

Format: Subjects indicate on a 7-point scale their level of agreement with each item. An example is presented.

Reliability: Cronbach's alpha was .59.

Author: Muehlenhard, C. L., and Linton, M. A.

Article: Date rape and sexual aggression in dating situations: Incidence and risk factors.

Journal: *Journal of Counseling Psychology*, April 1987, *34*(2), 186–196.

Related Research: Burt, M. R. (1980). Cultural myths and supports for rape. *Journal of Personality and Social Psychology*, *38*, 217–230.

• • •

3965

Test Name: ACCEPTANCE RATING SCALE

Purpose: To assess social acceptance among children.

Format: Children rate pictures of classmates on a 3-point scale from 1 (*don't like to play with*) to 3 (*like to play with*).

Reliability: Test–retest reliability produced a median correlation of .82.

Validity: Correlation with other variables ranged from .29 to .38.

Author: Bullock, J. R.

Article: Parental knowledge and role satisfaction and children's sociometric status.

Journal: *Child Study Journal*, 1989, *18*(4), 265–275.

Related Research: Singleton, L. C., & Asher, S. R. (1977). Peer preferences and social interactions among third grade children in an integrated school district. *Journal of Educational Psychology*, *69*, 330–336.

• • •

3966

Test Name: ACCULTURATION RATING SCALE FOR MEXICAN-AMERICANS

Purpose: To measure within-group differences among Mexican-American community college students.

Number of Items: 20

Format: Includes five dimensions: language, familiarity and usage, ethnic interaction, ethnic pride and identity, cultural heritage, and generational proximity. Employs a 5-point scale from 1 (*low*) to 5 (*high*).

Reliability: Coefficient alpha was .88. Test–retest reliability was .80.

Validity: Correlations with other variables were .81 and .76.

Author: Ponce, F. Q., and Atkinson, D. R.

Article: Mexican-American acculturation, counselor ethnicity, counseling style, and perceived counselor credibility.

Journal: *Journal of Counseling Psychology*, April 1989, *36*(2), 203–208.

Related Research: Cuellar, I., et al. (1980). An acculturation scale for

Mexican-American normal and clinical populations. *Hispanic Journal of Behavioral Sciences*, 2, 199–217.

■ ■ ■

3967

Test Name: ACCULTURATION RATING SCALE FOR PUERTO RICANS

Purpose: To measure level of acculturation for Puerto Ricans at 5 levels.

Number of Items: 5

Format: Questions are scored on a 5-point scale ranging from 1 (*Puerto Rican*) to 5 (*Anglo/English*).

Reliability: Split-half corrected reliability was .93 (*N* = 100).

Author: Pomales, J., and Williams, V.

Article: Effects of level of acculturation and counseling style on Hispanic students' perceptions of counselor.

Journal: *Journal of Counseling Psychology*, January 1989, *36*(1), 79–83.

Related Research: Cuellar, I., et al. (1980). An acculturation scale for Mexican-American normal and clinical populations. *Hispanic Journal of Behavioral Sciences*, 2, 199–217.

■ ■ ■

3968

Test Name: ADOLESCENT INTERPERSONAL COMPETENCE QUESTIONNAIRE

Purpose: To assess interpersonal competence.

Number of Items: 40

Format: Assesses five domains of competence: self-disclosure; providing emotional support to friends; management of conflicts; negative assertions; and initiation of friendships. Responses are made on a 5-point rating scale. Examples are presented.

Reliability: Alpha coefficients were .93 and .92.

Validity: Correlations with other variables ranged from −.30 to .68.

Author: Buhrmester, D.

Article: Intimacy of friendship, interpersonal competence, and adjustment during preadolescence and adolescence.

Journal: *Child Development*, August 1990, *61*(4), 1101–1111.

Related Research: Buhrmester, D., et al. (1988). Five domains of interpersonal competence in peer relations. *Journal of Personality and Social Psychology*, 55, 991–1008.

■ ■ ■

3969

Test Name: ALIENATION SCALE

Purpose: To measure alienation.

Format: Includes three subscales: powerlessness, normlessness, and social isolation. Employed a 5-point Likert format.

Reliability: Split-half reliability ranged from .73 to .84.

Validity: Correlations with other variables ranged from −.22 to−.52.

Author: Zimmerman, M. A.

Article: The relationship between political efficacy and citizen participation: Construct validation studies.

Journal: *Journal of Personal Assessment*, Fall 1989, *53*(3), 554–566.

Related Research: Dean, D. G. (1961). Alienation: Its meaning and measurement. *American Sociological Review*, 26, 753–758.

■ ■ ■

3970

Test Name: ANALOGUE MEASURE OF SOCIAL SKILLS

Purpose: To measure social skills when sociograms are impractical.

Number of Items: 17 situations.

Format: Children are presented 5 × 7 cards showing facial expressions with matching narratives. Ratings made on a 5-point desirability scale.

Reliability: Interrater agreement ranged from 79% to 87%.

Validity: Correlations with sociometric measures ranged from .48 to .66.

Author: Rinn, R. C., et al.

Article: Validation of an analogue measure of social skills in children.

Journal: *Psychological Reports*, August 1986, *59*(1), 95–99.

■ ■ ■

3971

Test Name: ATTRACTION QUESTIONNAIRE

Purpose: To assess interpersonal interest in people presented on videotape.

Number of Items: 13

Format: Six-point Likert format.

Reliability: Internal consistency was .93.

Author: Herr, P. N., et al.

Article: Interpersonal reactions to a depressed, schizotypal, or normal individual: An attributional perspective.

Journal: *Journal of Research in Personality*, December 1990, *24*(4), 454–467.

Related Research: Winer, D. L., et al. (1981). Depression and social attraction. *Motivation and Emotion*, 5, 153–166.

■ ■ ■

3972

Test Name: BALANCED INVENTORY OF DESIRABLE RESPONDING

Purpose: To assess two factors defining social desirability.

Number of Items: 40

Format: Includes two factors: self-deception and impression management.

Reliability: Alpha coefficients ranged from .70 to .80 (self-deception) and from .72 to .75 (impression management). Temporal stability (4 weeks) was .81 for self-deception.

Validity: Correlations with other variables ranged from −.52 to .20.

Author: Sabourin, S., et al.

Article: Social desirability, psychological distress, and consumer satisfaction with mental health treatment.

Journal: *Journal of Counseling Psychology*, July 1989, *36*(3), 352–356.

Related Research: Paulhus, D. L. (1984). Two-component models of socially desirable responding. *Journal of Personality and Social Psychology, 46*, 598–609.

■ ■ ■

3973

Test Name: BARRETT-LENNARD RELATIONSHIP INVENTORY

Purpose: To provide an indication of the status of the therapeutic relationship.

Number of Items: 85

Format: Includes five core concepts of client-centered theory: level of regard, empathetic understanding, congruence, unconditionality, and willingness to be known. Each statement is rated on 6-point scale ranging from −3 (*I strongly feel that it is not true*) to +3 (*I strongly feel that it is true*).

Reliability: Split-half reliability coefficients ranged from .82 to .93. Test–retest (4 weeks) reliability ranged from .78 to .90.

Author: Hayes, T. J., and Tinsley, H. E. A.

Article: Identification of the latent dimensions of instruments that measure perceptions of and expectations about counseling.

Journal: *Journal of Counseling Psychology*, October 1989, *36*(4), 492–500.

Related Research: Barrett-Lennard, G. T. (1962). Dimensions of therapists' response as causal factors in therapeutic change. *Psychological Monographs, 76*(43, Whole No. 562).

■ ■ ■

3974

Test Name: BARRETT-LENNARD RELATIONSHIP INVENTORY (SHORT)

Purpose: To measure the experience of the facilitative conditions in the supervisory relationship.

Number of Items: 40

Format: Six-point *true of me* scales.

Reliability: Cronbach's alphas ranged from .72 to .92.

Author: Schacht, A. J., et al.

Article: A short form of the Barrett-Lennard Relationship Inventory for Supervisory Relationships.

Journal: *Psychological Reports*, December 1988, *63*(3), 699–706.

Related Research: Barrett-Lennard, G. T. (1962). Dimensions of therapist response as causal factors in therapeutic change. *Psychological Monographs, 76*(43, Whole No. 562).

■ ■ ■

3975

Test Name: BEHAVIORAL ACCULTURATION SCALE—ADAPTED

Purpose: To identify acculturation level.

Number of Items: 24

Format: Items describe language, hobbies, and customs on a 5-point scale ranging from completely Puerto Rican to completely American.

Reliability: Coefficient alpha was .97. Test–retest reliability was .96.

Validity: Folensbee, R. W., et al.

Author: Impact of two types of counselor intervention on Black American, Puerto Rican, and Anglo-American analogue clients.

Article: *Journal of Counseling Psychology*, October 1986, *33*(4), 446–453.

Journal: Szapocznik, J., et al. (1978). Theory and measurement of acculturation. *Interamerican Journal of Psychology, 12*, 113–130.

■ ■ ■

3976

Test Name: BLACK ETHNOCENTRISM SCALE

Purpose: To measure ethnocentrism among Black adults.

Number of Items: 40

Format: Likert scale with two subscales: pro-Black scale and anti-White scale.

Reliability: Split-half reliability coefficients ranged from .87 to .91 (*N* = 99); Test–retest reliability coefficients ranged from .80 to .87.

Validity: Correlations with other measures ranged from −.22 to .60.

Author: Branch, C. W., and Newcombe, N.

Article: Racial attitude development among young Black children as a function of parental attitudes: A longitudinal and cross-sectional study.

Journal: *Child Development*, June 1986, *57*(3), 712–721.

Related Research: Chang, E., & Ritter, E. (1976). Ethnocentricism in Black college students. *Journal of Social Psychology, 100*, 89–98.

■ ■ ■

3977

Test Name: BLACK SEPARATISM SCALE

Purpose: To measure commitment to Black culture and Black separatism.

Number of Items: 6

Format: Four-point Likert format.

Reliability: Alpha was .61.

Author: Demo, D. H., and Hughes, M.

Article: Socialization and racial identity among Black Americans.

Journal: *Social Psychology Quarterly*, December 1990, *53*(4), 364–374.

Related Research: Allen, R. L., et al. (1989). A schema-based approach to modeling an African-American social belief system. *American Political Science Review*, *83*, 421–441.

■ ■ ■

3978

Test Name: BLOOD DONOR SCALES

Purpose: To measure the norms, donor role, and social relationships involved in donating blood.

Number of Items: 17

Format: Nine-item Likert format or 4-point rating scales. All items presented.

Reliability: Alphas ranged from .81 to .82.

Validity: Correlations between scales ranged from .13 to .50.

Author: Charng, H., et al.

Article: Role identity and reasoned action in the prediction of repeated behavior.

Journal: *Social Psychology Quarterly*, December 1988, *51*(4), 303–317.

■ ■ ■

3979

Test Name: CHILDHOOD SOCIAL NETWORK QUESTIONNAIRE

Purpose: To measure satisfaction with peer social support.

Number of Items: 11

Reliability: Kuder-Richardson formula was .92.

Validity: Factor analysis yielded one factor accounting for 68% of total variance.

Author: Friedrich, W. N., et al.

Article: Sex differences in depression in early adolescents.

Journal: *Psychological Reports*, April 1988, *62*(2), 475–481.

Related Research: Chan, D. A., & Perry, M. A. (1981). Child abuse: Discriminating factors toward positive outcome. Paper presented at the Biennial meeting of the Society for Research in Child Development, Boston, MA.

■ ■ ■

3980

Test Name: CHILDREN'S SELF-EFFICACY FOR PEER INTERACTION

Purpose: To measure children's perceptions of their competence at specific social skills.

Format: The child responds to each item on a 4-point scale (*HARD, hard, easy, EASY*), indicating how easy or difficult it would be to perform the specific task. An example is presented.

Reliability: Cronbach's alpha was .85.

Validity: Correlations with other variables ranged from −.21 to .38.

Author: Buzzelli, C. A.

Article: Parents' perceptions of reponsibility for promoting children's social competence.

Journal: *Child Study Journal*, 1989, *19*(4), 273–284.

Related Research: Wheeler, V. A., & Ladd, G. W. (1982). Assessment of children's self-efficacy for social interactions with peers. *Developmental Psychology*, *18*, 795–805.

3981

Test Name: CHILDREN'S SOCIAL SUPPORT SCALE

Purpose: To measure social support as reported by children.

Number of Items: 25

Format: Likert 5-point agreement format. Sample item presented.

Reliability: Cronbach's alpha was .71.

Author: Kudek, L. A., and Berg, B.

Article: Children's Beliefs about Parental Divorce Scale: Psychometric characteristics and concurrent validity.

Journal: *Journal of Consulting and Clinical Psychology*, October 1987, *55*(5), 712–718.

Related Research: Gottlieb, B. H. (1983). Social support as a focus for integrative research in psychology. *American Psychologist*, *38*, 278–287.

■ ■ ■

3982

Test Name: CHRONICITY OF LONELINESS SCALE

Purpose: To measure the length of time one has felt lonely.

Number of Items: 1

Reliability: Test–retest reliability was .73.

Validity: Correlation with UCLA Loneliness Scale was .49.

Author: Hojat, M., et al.

Article: Perception of childhood dissatisfaction with parents and selected personality traits in adulthood.

Journal: *Journal of General Psychology*, July 1990, *117*(3), 241–253.

Related Research: Hojat, M. (1983). Comparison of transitory and chronic loners on selected personality variables. *British Journal of Psychology*, *74*, 199–202.

3983

Test Name: COMMUNITY COMMITMENT SCALE

Purpose: To measure the identification and involvement of persons in their community.

Number of Items: 5

Format: Seven-point Likert format. Sample items presented.

Reliability: Alpha was .82.

Validity: Correlations with other variables ranged from −.19 to .40.

Author: Steffy, B. D., and Jones, J. W.

Article: The impact of family and career planning variables on the organizational, career, and community commitment of professional women.

Journal: *Journal of Vocational Behavior*, April 1988, *32*(2), 196–212.

■ ■ ■

3984

Test Name: COMPANION ANIMAL BONDING SCALE

Purpose: To measure extent of child–animal activity.

Number of Items: 8

Format: Five-point frequency scales (*always* to *never*). All items presented.

Reliability: Cronbach alphas ranged from .77 to .82.

Validity: Correlated with Pet Attitude Scale (.39) and Contemporary Bonding Scale (.40).

Author: Poresky, R. H., et al.

Article: The Companion Animal Bonding Scale: Internal reliability and construct validity.

Journal: *Psychological Reports*, June 1987, *60*(3)I, 743–746.

■ ■ ■

3985

Test Name: CONCERN FOR APPROPRIATENESS SCALE

Purpose: To measure tendencies to conform to group conformity pressures.

Number of Items: 20

Format: Responses are made on a 5-point Likert format ranging from 1 (*strongly agree*) to 5 (*strongly disagree*)

Reliability: Alpha coefficients ranged from .82 to .89. Test–retest (3 weeks) reliability was .84.

Author: Johnson, M. A.

Article: Concern for Appropriateness Scale and behavior conformity

Journal: *Journal of Personality Assessment*, Fall 1989, *53*(3), 567–574.

Related Research: Lennox, R. D., & Wolfe, R. N. (1984). Revision of the Self-Monitoring Scale. *Journal of Personality and Social Psychology*, 6, 1349–1364.

■ ■ ■

3986

Test Name: CONCERN WITH REGARD OF OTHERS SCALE

Purpose: To measure concern with regard of others.

Number of Items: 4

Format: Subjects indicate importance of being liked and respected by peers and faculty.

Validity: Correlations with measures of masculinity and femininity were −.14 and −.15 respectively (*N* = 99).

Author: Zeldow, P. B., et al.

Article: Masculinity, femininity, and psychosocial adjustment in medical students: A 2-year follow-up.

Journal: *Journal of Personality Assessment*, Spring 1987, *51*(1), 3–14.

Related Research: Zeldow, P. B., et al. (1985). Masculinity, femininity, Type A behavior, and psychosocial adjustment in medical students. *Journal of Personality and Social Psychology*, *48*, 481–492.

3987

Test Name: CONTRACEPTIVE SITUATIONS QUESTIONNAIRE

Purpose: To measure apprehension in cross-sex interaction involving contraception.

Number of Items: 18

Format: Five-point rating scales.

Reliability: Alpha was .83.

Author: Bruch, M. A., and Hynes, M. J.

Article: Heterosocial anxiety and contraceptive behavior.

Journal: *Journal of Research in Personality*, September 1987, *21*(3), 343–360.

Related Research: Byrne, D. (1983). Sex without contraception. In D. Byrne & A. W. Fisher (Eds.), *Adolescents, sex and contraception* (pp. 3–31). Hillsdale, NJ: Erlbaum, pp. 3–31.

■ ■ ■

3988

Test Name: COORDINATING STYLE SCALE

Purpose: To rate client interpersonal behavior from videotapes of the clinical intake interviews.

Number of Items: 6

Format: Utilized 4-point Likert-type items.

Reliability: Coefficient alpha was .88. Interrater reliability was .90.

Author: Westerman, M. A., et al.

Article: Client cooperative interview behavior and outcome in paradoxical and behavioral brief treatment approaches

Journal: *Journal of Counseling Psychology* January 1987, *34*(1), 99–102.

Related Research: Westerman, M. A., et al. (1986). The coordinating style construct: An approach to conceptualizing patient interpersonal behavior. *Psychotherapy, 23,* 540–547.

▪ ▪ ▪

3989

Test Name: COURTLY LOVE SCALE

Purpose: To measure acceptance of medieval rules of love.

Number of Items: 42

Format: Likert format. All items presented.

Reliability: Cronbach's alphas ranged from .33 to .46.

Validity: Correlations with Rubin's romantic love and liking scales ranged from .07 to .18.

Author: Rechtien, J. G., and Fiedler, E.

Article: Contributions to psychohistory: XIII. Courtly love today: Romance and socialization in interpersonal scripts.

Journal: *Psychological Reports,* December 1988, *63*(3), 683–695.

Related Research: Rubin, Z. (1970). Measurement of romantic love. *Journal of Personality and Social Psychology, 16,* 265–273.

▪ ▪ ▪

3990

Test Name: CO-WORKER COMMITMENT SCALE

Purpose: To assess loyalty to co-workers.

Number of Items: 6

Format: Five-point Likert format. All items presented.

Reliability: Alpha was .74.

Validity: Correlations with other variables ranged from −.03 to .47.

Author: McGinnis, S. K., and Morrow, P. C.

Article: Job attitudes among full- and part-time employees.

Journal: *Journal of Vocational Behavior,* February 1990, *36*(1), 82–96.

▪ ▪ ▪

3991

Test Name: CULTURAL MISTRUST INVENTORY

Purpose: To measure the degree to which Blacks mistrust Whites.

Number of Items: 48

Format: Responses are made on a 7-point scale ranging from 1 (*strongly agree*) to 7 (*strongly disagree*). Sample items are presented.

Reliability: Test–retest (2 weeks) reliability was .82.

Author: Watkins, Jr., C. E., et al.

Article: Cultural mistrust and its effects on expectational variables in Black client–White counselor relationships.

Journal: *Journal of Counseling Psychology,* October 1989, *36*(4), 447–450.

Related Research: Terrell, F., & Terrell, S. L. (1981). An inventory to measure cultural mistrust among blacks. *Western Journal of Black Studies, 5,* 180–184.

▪ ▪ ▪

3992

Test Name: DATING AND ASSERTION QUESTIONNAIRE

Purpose: To provide a self-report of assertion and dating competence.

Number of Items: 18

Format: Responses are made on a Likert scale ranging from 1 to 5. Includes two scales: dating and competence.

Reliability: Alpha coefficients were .92 (dating) and .85 (assertion).

Author: Kenny, M. E.

Article: College seniors' perceptions of parental attachments: The value and stability of family ties.

Journal: *Journal of College Student Development,* January 1990, *31*(1), 39–46.

Related Research: Levenson, R. W., & Gottman, J. M. (1978). Toward the assessment of social competence. *Journal of Consulting and Clinical Psychology, 46,* 453–468.

▪ ▪ ▪

3993

Test Name: DATING ANXIETY SURVEY

Purpose: To assess dating anxiety in males and females.

Number of Items: 23

Format: Responses are made on a 7-point Likert scale, 1 (*being least anxious*) to 7 (*being extreme anxiety*). Includes three subscales: passive, active, and dating.

Reliability: Coefficient alphas ranged from .87 to .93 (males) and from .90 to .92 (females).

Validity: Correlations with other variables ranged from −.38 to .65.

Author: Calvert, J. D., et al.

Article: Psychometric evaluation of the Dating Anxiety Survey: A self-report questionnaire for the assessment of dating anxiety in males and females.

Journal: *Journal of Psychopathology and Behavioral Assessment,* September 1987, *9*(3), 341–350.

▪ ▪ ▪

3994

Test Name: DEFINING ISSUES TEST

Purpose: To measure empathy and socialization.

Number of Items: 72

Format: Subjects rank and rate moral dilemmas.

Reliability: Test–retest reliability was .80. Cronbach's alpha ranged from .70 to .80.

Validity: Correlations with CPI scores ranged from −.60 to .69.

Author: Curtis, J., et al.

Article: Personality correlates of moral reasoning and attitudes toward authority.

Journal: *Psychological Reports*, December 1988, *63*(3), 947–954.

Related Research: Rent, J. R., et al. (1974). Judging the important issues in moral dilemmas—an objective measure of development. *Developmental Psychology*, *10*, 491–501.

■ ■ ■

3995

Test Name: DESPERATE LOVE SCALE

Purpose: To measure where people place themselves on a continuum from having no experience of desperate love to strong experience.

Number of Items: 12

Format: An example is presented.

Reliability: Test–retest correlation was .92. Coefficient alpha was .93.

Validity: Correlations with other variables ranged from −.39 to .34.

Author: Sperling, M. B.

Article: Ego identity and desperate love.

Journal: *Journal of Personality Assessment*, Winter 1987, *51*(4), 600–605.

Related Research: Sperling, M. B. (1985). Discriminant measures for desperate love. *Journal of Personality Assessment*, *49*, 324–328.

■ ■ ■

3996

Test Name: DIFFERENTIAL LONELINESS SCALE (FINNISH VERSION)

Purpose: To measure quantity and quality of social interaction.

Number of Items: 60

Format: Yes–no format.

Reliability: Cronbach's alpha was .92. Test–retest reliability ranged from .85 to .97.

Validity: Correlation with UCLA Loneliness was .70.

Author: Kalliopuska, M., and Laitinen, M.

Article: Testing loneliness on the Differential Loneliness Scale.

Journal: *Psychological Reports*, February 1987, *60*(1), 15–18.

Related Research: Schmidt, N., & Sermat, W. (1983). Measuring loneliness in different relationships. *Journal of Personality and Social Psychology*, *43*, 524–531.

■ ■ ■

3997

Test Name: DATING AND ASSERTION QUESTIONNAIRE

Purpose: To provide a self-report of assertion and dating competence.

Number of Items: 18

Format: Responses are made on a Likert scale ranging from 1 to 5. Includes two scales: dating and competence.

Reliability: Alpha coefficients were .92 (dating) and .85 (assertion).

Author: Kenny, M. E.

Article: College seniors' perceptions of parental attachments: The value and stability of family ties.

Journal: *Journal of College Student Development*, January 1990, *31*(1), 39–46.

Related Research: Levenson, R. W., & Gottman, J. M. (1978). Toward the assessment of social competence. *Journal of Consulting and Clinical Psychology*, *46*, 453–468.

■ ■ ■

3998

Test Name: DYADIC RELATIONSHIP SCALES

Purpose: To measure love, conflict, maintenance, ambivalence, and sexual components of intimate relationships.

Number of Items: 27

Format: Seven-point frequency scales. Items are described.

Reliability: Alphas ranged from .72 to .94.

Author: Felmlee, D., et al.

Article: The dissolution of intimate relationships: A hazzard model.

Journal: *Social Psychology Quarterly*, March 1990, *53*(1), 13–30.

Related Research: Braiker, H. B., & Kelley, H. H. (1979). Conflict in the development of close relationships. In P. L. Burgess & T. L. Huston (Eds.), *Social exchange in developing relationships* (pp. 135–169). New York: Academic Press.

■ ■ ■

3999

Test Name: EDWARDS'S SOCIAL DESIRABILITY SCALE

Purpose: To assess the subject's tendency to answer in a socially desirable fashion.

Number of Items: 39

Format: True–false items.

Validity: Correlations with other variables ranged from −.53 to .39.

Author: Cole, D. A., and Milstead, M.

Article: Bchavioral correlates of depression: Antecedents or consequences?

Journal: *Journal of Counseling Psychology*, October 1989, *36*(4), 408–416.

Related Research: Edwards, A. L. (1957). *The social desirability variable in personality assessment and research.* New York: Dryden.

■ ■ ■

4000

Test Name: EMOTIONAL AUTONOMY SCALE

Purpose: To measure affective and cognitive aspects of emotional autonomy.

Number of Items: 20

Format: Responses to each item are made on a 4-point Likert format. Includes four subscales: deidealization, individuation, nondependency, and parents as people.

Reliability: Cronbach's alpha for the total scale was .75.

Validity: Correlations with other variables ranged from −.41 to .20.

Author: Ryan, R. M., and Lynch, J. H.

Article: Emotional autonomy versus detachment: Revisiting the vicissitudes of adolescence and young adulthood.

Journal: *Child Development*, April 1989, *60*(2), 340–356.

Related Research: Steinberg, L., & Silverberg, S. (1986). The vicissitudes of autonomy in adolescence. *Child Development*, 57, 841 851.

■ ■ ■

4001

Test Name: EMOTIONAL AUTONOMY SCALE

Purpose: To assess the dimensions of acceptance versus rejection and the encouragement of independence versus overprotection.

Number of Items: 56

Format: Items are rated on a 5-point Likert scale.

Reliability: Alphas ranged from .82 to .91.

Author: Ryan, R. M., and Lynch, J. H.

Article: Emotional autonomy versus detachment: Revisiting the vicissitudes of adolescence and young adulthood.

Journal: *Child Development*, April 1989, *60*(2), 340–356.

Related Research: Ricks, M. H. (1985). The social transmission of parental behavior: Attachment across generations. In I. Bretherton & E. Waters (Eds.), Growing points of attachment theory and research (pp. 211–229). *Monographs of the Society for Research in Child Development*, *50*(1, Serial No. 209).

■ ■ ■

4002

Test Name: EMOTIONAL CLOSENESS SCALE

Purpose: To measure emotional closeness.

Number of Items: 10

Format: Seven-point scales. Sample item presented.

Reliability: Alpha was .96.

Author: Lee, T. R., et al.

Article: Sibling relationships in adulthood: Contact patterns and motivations.

Journal: *Journal of Marriage and the Family*, May 1990, *52*(2), 431 440.

Related Research: Walker, A. J. (1979). *The social networks of young marrieds: Distinguishing among relationship types*. Unpublished doctoral dissertation, Pennsylvania State University.

■ ■ ■

4003

Test Name: FREQUENCY OF DISAGREEMENTS CONFLICT RESOLUTION SCALES

Purpose: To measure disagreement among adults and how they resolve conflicts.

Number of Items: 21 disagreement items. Unknown number of resolutions.

Format: Six-point agreement scales.

Reliability: Alpha was .88.

Author: Ganong, L. H., and Coleman, M.

Article: Do mutual children cement bonds in stepfamilies?

Journal: *Journal of Marriage and the Family*, August 1988, *50*(3), 687–698.

Related Research: Pasley, K., & Ihinger-Tallman, M. (1984). *Remarried family life*. Unpublished instrument, Washington State University, Pullman.

■ ■ ■

4004

Test Name: FRIENDSHIP INTIMACY QUESTIONNAIRE

Purpose: To measure intimacy of friendship.

Format: Responses are made on a 5-point Likert scale ranging from 1 (*never or hardly ever*) to 5 (*very often or extremely much*).

Reliability: Alpha coefficients were both .93 for preadolescents and adolescents.

Validity: Correlations with other variables ranged from −.32 to .68.

Author: Buhrmester, D.

Article: Intimacy of friendship, interpersonal competence, and adjustment during preadolescence and adolescence.

Journal: *Child Development*, August 1990, *61*(4), 1101–1111.

Related Research: Furman, W., & Buhrmester, D. (1985). Children's perception of the personal relationship in their social network. *Developmental Psychology*, *21*, 1016–1024.

■ ■ ■

4005

Test Name: GENERAL OPINION SURVEY

Purpose: To measure interpersonal trust.

Number of Items: 40

Format: Includes 15 filler items to obscure the purpose of the test.

Reliability: Coefficient alpha was .72. Test–retest (1 week) reliability was .76 ($N = 39$).

Validity: Correlation with social desirability was –.34. Correlation with a trust item was –.06.

Author: Kumar, V. K., et al.

Article: The effects of disguising scale purpose on reliability and validity.

Journal: *Measurement and Evaluation in Counseling and Development*, January 1986, *18*(4), 163–167.

Related Research: Rotter, J. B. (1967). A new scale for the measurement of interpersonal trust. *Journal of Personality*, *35*, 651–665.

■ ■ ■

4006

Test Name: GLOBAL SEXUAL INTEREST SCALE

Purpose: To measure a person's perception of a couple's relationship as portrayed in taped scenarios.

Number of Items: 10

Format: Likert format. Sample items presented.

Reliability: Reliability was .81.

Author: Shotland, R. L., and Craig, J. M.

Article: Can men and women differentiate between friendly and sexually interested behavior?

Journal: *Social Psychology Quarterly*, March 1988, *51*(1), 66–73.

Related Research: Abbey, A., & Melby, C. (1986). The effects of nonverbal cues on gender differences in perceptions of sexual intent. *Sex Roles*, *15*, 283–298.

■ ■ ■

4007

Test Name: GROUP COHESION

Purpose: To measure group solidarity.

Number of Items: 18

Format: Likert format. All items presented.

Reliability: Split half reliability was .90.

Author: Summers, I., et al.

Article: Work-group cohesion.

Journal: *Psychological Reports*, October 1988, *63*(2), 627–636.

Related Research: Wheeless, L. R., et al. (1982). A research note on the relations among social and task perceptions in small groups. *Small Group Behavior*, *13*, 373–384.

■ ■ ■

4008

Test Name: GROUP COHESIVENESS SCALE

Purpose: To measure group cohesiveness.

Number of Items: 4

Format: Responses are made on a 4-point scale ranging from 5 (*great, couldn't be better*) to 1 (*not very good at all*).

Reliability: Coefficient alpha was .85.

Validity: Correlations with other variables ranged from –.25 to .50.

Author: George, J. M., and Bettenhausen, K.

Article: Understanding prosocial behavior, sales performance, and turnover: A group-level analysis in a service context.

Journal: *Journal of Applied Psychology*, December 1990, *75*(6), 698–709.

Related Research: O'Reilly, C. A. III, & Caldwell, D. F. (1985). The impact of normative social influence and cohesiveness on task perceptions and attitudes: A social information processing approach. *Journal of Occupational Psychology*, *58*, 193–206.

4009

Test Name: GROUP IDENTIFICATION SCALE

Purpose: To measure the value and emotional significance attached to group membership.

Number of Items: 10

Format: Five-point frequency scales. All items presented.

Reliability: Alpha was .71.

Author: Brown, R., et al.

Article: Explaining intergroup differentiation in an industrial organization.

Journal: *Journal of Occupational Psychology*, December 1986, *59*(4), 273–286.

Related Research: Driedger, L. (1976). Ethnic self-identity: A comparison of ingroup evaluations. *Sociometry*, *39*, 131–141.

■ ■ ■

4010

Test Name: GROUP IMPORTANCE INVENTORY

Purpose: To measure the importance of the group to its members.

Number of Items: 13

Format: Nine-point rating scales. Sample items presented.

Reliability: Split-half reliability was .85.

Validity: Correlations with group satisfaction ranged from .68 to .77.

Author: Meir, E. I., et al.

Article: Group importance as a mediator between personality–environment congruence and satisfaction.

Journal: *Journal of Vocational Behavior*, February 1986, *28*(1), 60–69.

■ ■ ■

4011

Test Name: INCURABLE DISEASE SOCIAL DISTANCE SCALE

Purpose: To measure social distance from dying patients, psychiatric patients, alcoholics, and AIDS patients.

Number of Items: 63

Format: Seven social distance ratings (all presented).

Reliability: Alpha ranged from .79 to .88.

Author: Lev, E. I.

Article: Effects of course in hospice nursing: Attitudes and behaviors of baccalaureate school of nursing undergraduates and graduates.

Journal: *Psychological Reports*, October 1986, *59*(2)II, 847–858.

Related Research: Bogardus, E. S. (1925). Measuring social distance. *Journal of Applied Sociology, 9,* 299–308.

■ ■ ■

4012

Test Name: INDIVIDUALISM–COLLECTIVISM SCALE

Purpose: To measure solidarity and concern for others.

Number of Items: 63

Format: Five-point Likert format. All items presented.

Reliability: Alphas ranged from the .40s to the .60s.

Validity: Correlations with other variables ranged from −.33 to .44.

Author: Hui, C. H.

Article: Measurement of individualism–collectivism.

Journal: *Journal of Research in Personality*, March 1988, *22*(1), 17–36.

■ ■ ■

4013

Test Name: INTERACTIONAL PROBLEM-SOLVING INVENTORY

Purpose: To measure to what extent couples are able to solve their interactional problems.

Number of Items: 17

Format: Five-point scales. All items presented in English.

Reliability: Cronbach's alphas were .86 (husbands) and .88 (wives).

Author: Lange, A., et al.

Article: Status inconsistency, traditionality and marital distress in the Netherlands.

Journal: *Psychological Reports*, December 1990, *67*(3) II, 1243–1253.

Related Research: Lange, A. (1983). *Interactionale probleem oplossing vragen lijst.* Deventer, The Netherlands: Van Loghum Staterus.

■ ■ ■

4014

Test Name: INTERPERSONAL ADJECTIVE SCALES—REVISED

Purpose: To measure interpersonal dispositions.

Number of Items: 64

Format: Items all rated as an 8-point scale ranging from 1 (*characteristic*) to 8 (*uncharacteristic*).

Validity: Correlations with the Inventory of Interpersonal Problems ranged from −.57 to .58.

Author: Alden, L. E., et al.

Article: Construction of circumplex scales for the Inventory of Interpersonal problems.

Journal: *Journal of Personality Assessment*, Winter 1990, *55*(3 and 4), 521–536.

Related Research: Wiggins, J. S., et al. (1988). Psychometric and geometric characteristics of the revised Interpersonal Adjective Scales (IAS-R). *Multivariate Behavioral Research, 23,* 517–530.

■ ■ ■

4015

Test Name: INTERPERSONAL CONFLICT SCALE

Purpose: To measure interpersonal conflict.

Number of Items: 4

Format: Responses to each item are made on a 5-point scale from *less than once per month* to *several times per day*.

Reliability: Coefficient alphas were .81 and .71 (*N*s = 154 and 152, respectively).

Validity: Correlations with other variables ranged from −.35 to .50 (*N*s = 148–156).

Author: Spector, P. E., et al.

Article: Relation of job stressors to affective, health, and performance outcomes: A comparison of multiple data sources.

Journal: *Journal of Applied Psychology*, February 1988, *73*(1), 11–19.

Related Research: Spector, P. E. (1987). Interactive effects of perceived control and job stressors on affective reactions and health outcomes for clerical workers. *Work and Stress, 1,* 155–162.

■ ■ ■

4016

Test Name: INTERPERSONAL JEALOUSY SCALE (REVISED)

Purpose: To measure jealousy among homosexual men.

Number of Items: 28

Format: Sample items presented.

Reliability: Spearman-Brown reliability coefficient was .95.

Validity: Correlations with other jealousy measures ranged from .24 to .65.

Author: Hawkins, R. O., Jr.

Article: Comparative study of three measures of sexual jealousy.

Journal: *Psychological Reports*, October 1987, *61*(2), 539–544.

Related Research: Mathes, E. W., et al. (1982). A convergent validity study of six jealousy scales. *Psychological Reports, 50,* 1143–1147.

• • •

4017

Test Name: INTERPERSONAL ORIENTATION SCALE

Purpose: To assess preferences for social interaction.

Number of Items: 29

Format: Responses are made on a 5-point Likert scale.

Reliability: Internal consistency was .71 and .70. Test–retest reliability was .76.

Validity: Correlations with other variables ranged from –.31 to .30.

Author: Vancouver, J. B., and Ilgen, D. R.

Article: Effects of interpersonal orientation and the sex-type of the tasks on choosing to work alone or in groups.

Journal: *Journal of Applied Psychology,* December 1989, 74(6), 927–934.

Related Research: Swap, W. C., & Rubin, J. Z. (1983). Measurement of interpersonal orientation. *Journal of Personality and Social Psychology, 44,* 208–219.

• • •

4018

Test Name: INTERPERSONAL RELATIONSHIPS SCALE

Purpose: To rate clients' level of hostility, quality of interpersonal relationships, and quality of relationship to family members.

Number of Items: 13

Format: Items are rated on a 7-point scale ranging from 1 (*never*) to 7 (*always*).

Reliability: Alpha coefficients ranged from .82 to .87.

Author: Kokotovic, A. M., and Tracey, T. J.

Article: Working alliance in the early phase of counseling.

Journal: *Journal of Counseling Psychology,* January 1990, 37(1), 16–21.

Related Research: Strupp, H. H., & Hadley, S. W. (1979). Specific versus nonspecific factors in psychotherapy: A controlled study outcome. *Archives of General Psychiatry, 46,* 1125–1136.

• • •

4019

Test Name: INTERPERSONAL TRUST SCALE

Purpose: To assess individual differences in interpersonal trust.

Number of Items: 23

Format: Responses were made on a 5-point scale ranging from 1 (*strongly disagree*) to 5 (*strongly agree*). Examples are presented.

Validity: Correlation with the Hypercompetitive Attitude Scale was .29 ($N = 45$).

Author: Ryckman, R. M., et al.

Article: Construction of a hypercompetitive attitude scale.

Journal: *Journal of Personality Assessment,* Winter 1990, 55(3 and 4), 630–639.

Related Research: Rotter, J. B. (1967). A new scale for the measurement of interpersonal trust. *Journal of Personality, 35,* 651–665.

• • •

4020

Test Name: INVENTORY OF ADOLESCENT ATTACHMENTS

Purpose: To provide indices of well-being within an adolescent population.

Format: Includes two dimensions: felt security and emotional utilization. Items are rated on 5-point Likert scales.

Reliability: Test–retest (2 weeks) reliability ranged from .70 to .89.

Validity: Correlations with emotional autonomy ranged from –.76 to .27.

Author: Ryan, R. M., and Lynch, J. H.

Article: Emotional autonomy versus detachment: Revisiting the vicissitudes of adolescence and young adulthood.

Journal: *Child Development,* April 1989, 60(2), 340–356.

Related Research: Greenberg, M. T., et al. (1983). The nature and importance of attachment relationships to parents and peers during adolescence. *Journal of Youth and Adolescence, 12,* 373–386.

• • •

4021

Test Name: INVENTORY OF INTERPERSONAL PROBLEMS

Purpose: To reflect a wide range of interpersonal problems.

Number of Items: 64

Format: Items are grouped into eight scales: domineering, vindictive, cold, socially avoidant, nonassertive, exploitable, overly nuturant, and intrusive. Items are rated on a 5-point scale ranging from 0 (*not at all*) to 4 (*extremely*). Sample items are presented.

Reliability: Alpha coefficients ranged from .72 to .85 ($N = 974$).

Validity: Correlations with the Revised Interpersonal Adjective Scales ranged from –.57 to .58.

Author: Alden, L. E., et al.

Article: Construction of circumplex scales for the Inventory of Interpersonal Problems.

Journal: *Journal of Personality Assessment,* Winter 1990, 55(3 and 4), 521–536.

Related Research: Horowitz, L. M., et al. (1988). Inventory of interpersonal problems: Psychometric properties and clinical applications. *Journal of Consulting and Clinical Psychology, 56*, 885–892.

■ ■ ■

4022

Test Name: INVENTORY OF INTERPERSONAL PROBLEMS

Purpose: To measure distress arising from interpersonal sources.

Number of Items: 127

Format: Five-point rating scales. A sample item is presented.

Reliability: Alphas ranged from .82 to .94 across subscales. Test–retest (10 weeks) reliability ranged from .80 to .90.

Validity: Correlations with other variables ranged from –.16 to .64. Residual gain correlation was .80 (indicating sensitivity to clinical improvement).

Author: Horowitz, L. M., et al.

Article: Inventory of interpersonal problems: Psychometric properties and clinical applications.

Journal: *Journal of Consulting and Clinical Psychology,* December 1988, *56*(6), 885–892.

■ ■ ■

4023

Test Name: INVENTORY OF SOCIALLY SUPPORTIVE BEHAVIORS

Purpose: To measure enacted and received support.

Number of Items: 12

Format: Four-point response categories. Sample items described.

Reliability: Alpha was .81.

Author: Norris, F. H., et al.

Article: Use of mental health services among victims of crime: Frequency, correlates, and subsequent recovery.

Journal: *Journal of Consulting and Clinical Psychology,* October 1990, *58*(5), 538–547.

Related Research: Barrera, M., et al. (1981). Preliminary development of a scale of social support: Studies on college students. *American Journal of Community Psychology, 9,* 435–447.

■ ■ ■

4024

Test Name: KIRTON ADAPTION–INNOVATION INVENTORY

Purpose: To determine from the subject how difficult it was to present themselves to others.

Number of Items: 32

Format: Eleven items are reversed. A 5-point response format from *very easy* to *very hard* was used.

Reliability: Reliability coefficients ranged from .84 to .69.

Validity: Correlations with other variables ranged from –.10 to .72.

Author: Goldsmith, R. E.

Article: Convergent validity of four innovativeness scales.

Journal: *Educational and Psychological Measurement,* Spring 1986, *46*(1), 81–87.

Related Research: Kirton, M. J. (1976). Adaptors and innovators: A description and measure. *Journal of Applied Psychology, 61,* 622–629.

■ ■ ■

4025

Test Name: LEAST PREFERRED CO-WORKER SCALE

Purpose: To measure people whose main concern is to develop and maintain good interpersonal relations.

Number of Items: 16

Format: Eight-point semantic differential.

Reliability: Alpha was .89.

Author: Bryman, A., et al.

Article: Leader orientation and organizational transience: An investigation using Fiedler's LPC scale.

Journal: *Journal of Occupational Psychology,* March 1987, *60*(1), 13–19.

Related Research: Fiedler, F. E. (1967). *A Theory of Leadership Effectiveness.* New York: McGraw-Hill.

■ ■ ■

4026

Test Name: LIFE ACTIVITIES INVENTORY

Purpose: To assess social adjustment.

Number of Items: 17

Format: Most items assess intensity of impairment and duration of impairment.

Reliability: Coefficient alpha was .78.

Author: Klein, D. N., et al.

Article: Social adjustment in the offspring of parents with bipolar affective disorder.

Journal: *Journal of Psychopathology and Behavioral Assessment,* December 1986, *8*(4), 355–366.

Related Research: Weissman, M. M., et al. (1981). The assessment of social adjustment: An update. *Archives of General Psychiatry, 38,* 1250–1258.

■ ■ ■

4027

Test Name: LIFE PRIORITIES, Q-SORT

Purpose: To measure the dimensions of interdependence–independence.

Number of Items: 84

Format: The cards are sorted into a normal distribution containing 9 categories from 1 (*lowest*) to 9 (*highest*).

Reliability: Test–retest (4–5 weeks) reliabilities ranged from .45 to .95.

Author: Hyman, R. B., and Woog, P.

Article: The relationship of age and marital status to women's needs for interdependence–independence.

Journal: *Measurement and Evaluation in Counseling and Development*, April 1987, *20*(1), 27–35.

Related Research: Baruch, G., et al. (1983). *Lifeprints: New patterns of love and work for today's women.* New York: New American Library.

■ ■ ■

4028

Test Name: LIKING FOR SUBORDINATE SCALE

Purpose: To measure superviser liking for the subordinate.

Number of Items: 4

Format: Responses are made on a 5-point Likert scale ranging from 1 (*I don't like this subordinate at all*) to 5 (*I like this subordinate very much*) for Item 1, and for the other items from 1 (*strongly disagree*) to 5 (*strongly agree*). All items are presented.

Reliability: Coefficient alphas were .94 and .86.

Validity: Correlations with other variables ranged from .45 to .74.

Author: Wayne, S. J., and Ferris, G. R.

Article: Influence tactics, affect, and exchange quality in supervisor–subordinate interactions: A laboratory experiment and field study.

Journal: *Journal of Applied Psychology,* October 1990, *75*(5), 487–499.

■ ■ ■

4029

Test Name: LOGIC OF CONFIDENCE QUESTIONNAIRE

Purpose: To measure logic of confidence.

Number of Items: 29

Format: Includes three dimensions: The myth of professionalism, avoidance, and overlooking. Sample items are presented.

Reliability: Estimates of internal consistency ranged from .79 to .91.

Author: Okeafor, K. R., and Teddlie, C.

Article: Organizational factors related to administrators' confidence in teachers.

Journal: *Journal of Research and Development in Education,* Fall 1989, *23*(1), 28–36.

Related Research: Okeafor, K., et al. (1987). Toward an operational definition of the logic of confidence. *Journal of Experimental Education, 56*, 47–54.

■ ■ ■

4030

Test Name: LONELINESS QUESTIONNAIRE—REVISED

Purpose: To measure loneliness.

Number of Items: 14

Reliability: Cronbach's alpha ranged from .90 to .93.

Validity: Correlations with other variables ranged from −.49 to .33.

Author: Lempers, J. D., et al.

Article: Economic hardship, parenting, and distress in adolescence.

Journal: *Child Development,* February 1989, *60*(1), 25–39.

Related Research: Asher, S. R., et al. (1984). Loneliness in children. *Child Development, 55*, 1456–1464.

■ ■ ■

4031

Test Name: LONELINESS RATING SCALE

Purpose: To measure student loneliness.

Number of Items: 24

Format: A 5-point Likert scale. All items are presented.

Reliability: Spearman-Brown reliability coefficients ranged from .84 to .93, *N* = 20.

Validity: Correlation with teacher ratings was r=.81.

Author: Luftig, R. L.

Article: Children's loneliness, perceived ease in making friends and estimated social adequacy: Development and social metacognition.

Journal: *Child Study Journal,* 1987, *17*(1), 35–53.

Related Research: Asher, S. R., et al. (1984). Loneliness in children. *Child Development, 55*, 1456–1464.

■ ■ ■

4032

Test Name: LOVE/HATE CHECKLIST

Purpose: To assess love/hate based on the perceived actions of people toward one another.

Number of Items: 90

Format: Checklist format. All items presented.

Reliability: Test–retest (3 weeks) reliability ranged from .84 to .97.

Validity: Correlations with the Personal Attribute Inventory ranged from .07 to .61.

Author: Parrish, T. S.

Article: The Love/Hate Checklist: A preliminary report.

Journal: *Psychological Reports,* August 1988, *63*(1), 67–70.

Related Research: Parrish, T. S., et al. (1976). The personal attribute inventory. *Perceptual and Motor Skills, 42*, 715–720.

Parrish, T. S. (1988). The Love/Hate Checklist: A further report. *Psychological Reports, 63,* 294.

∎ ∎ ∎

4033

Test Name: LOVE RELATIONSHIP SCALE

Purpose: To measure the underlying constructs of the concept of love.

Number of Items: 55

Format: All items presented.

Validity: Eight factors were extracted, one of which, Consummate Obsession, is similar to the g factor.

Author: Borrello, G. M., and Thompson, B.

Article: A replication bootstrap analysis of the structure underlying perceptions of stereotypic love.

Journal: *Journal of General Psychology,* July 1989, *116*(3), 317–327.

Related Research: Borrello, G. M., & Thompson, B. (1987, November). *Construct validity of a measure of love relationships and perceptions.* Paper presented at the annual meeting of the Mid-South Educational Research Association, Mobile, AL.

∎ ∎ ∎

4034

Test Name: MALE SOCIAL-SEXUAL EFFECTIVENESS SCALE

Purpose: To measure perceived effectiveness in dating and sexual-relating.

Number of Items: 14

Format: Likert format. All items presented.

Reliability: Cronbach's alpha was .85.

Author: Quackenbush, R. L.

Article: Assessing men's social-sexual effectiveness: A self-report instrument.

Journal: *Psychological Reports,* June 1989, *64*(3), I, 969–970.

Related Research: Abbey, A. (1982). Sex differences in attributions for friendly behavior: Do males misperceive females' friendliness? *Journal of Personality and Social Psychology, 42,* 830–838.

∎ ∎ ∎

4035

Test Name: MANAGER MENTORING SCALE

Purpose: To measure attraction to the manager as mentor.

Number of Items: 6

Format: Five-point Likert format.

Reliability: Internal consistency was .92.

Author: Carroll, S. J., et al.

Article: Reactions to the new minorities by employees of the future.

Journal: *Psychological Reports,* June 1987, *60*(3)I, 911–920.

Related Research: Hunt, D. M., & Michael, C. (1983). Mentorship: A career training and development tool. *Academy of Management Review, 8,* 475–485.

∎ ∎ ∎

4036

Test Name: MARLOWE-CROWNE SOCIAL DESIRABILITY SCALE

Purpose: To measure the degree to which subjects attempt to present themselves in a socially desirable manner.

Number of Items: 33

Format: Forced-choice (true–false) format. Sample items are presented.

Reliability: Kuder-Richardson reliability was .88. Test–retest correlation was .89.

Validity: Correlations with other variables ranged from –.13 to .41.

Author: Rice, K. G., et al.

Article: Separation–individuation, family cohesion, and adjustment to college: Measurement validation and test of a theoretical model.

Journal: *Journal of Counseling Psychology,* April 1990, *37*(2), 195–202.

Related Research: Crowne, D. P., & Marlowe, D. (1960). A new scale of social desirability independent of psychopathology.

∎ ∎ ∎

4037

Test Name: MARLOWE CROWNE SOCIAL DESIRABILITY SCALE—SHORT FORM

Purpose: To assess the social desirability response bias.

Number of Items: 13

Format: A high score indicates a strong tendency to give socially desirable answers to test questions.

Reliability: Coefficient alpha was .76.

Validity: Correlations with other variables ranged from –.16 to .20.

Author: Zorich, S., and Reynolds, W. M.

Article: Convergent and discriminant validation of a measure of social self-concept.

Journal: *Journal of Personality Assessment,* Fall 1988, *52*(3), 441–453.

Related Research: Reynolds, W. M. (1982). Development of reliable and valid short forms of the Marlowe-Crowne Social Desirability Scale. *Journal of Clinical Psychology, 38,* 119–125.

∎ ∎ ∎

4038

Test Name: MASLOWIAN ASSESSMENT SURVEY

Purpose: To measure safety, belongingness, affiliation, and esteem.

Number of Items: 195

Format: Five-point Likert format.

Reliability: Alphas ranged from .76 to .93 across subscales.

Validity: Correlations with other variables ranged from −.47 to .65.

Author: Williams, D. E., and Page, M. M.

Article: A multi-dimensional measure of Maslow's hierarchy of needs.

Journal: *Journal of Research in Personality*, June 1989, *23*(2), 192–213.

■ ■ ■

4039

Test Name: MULTIDIMENSIONAL SCALE OF PERCEIVED SOCIAL SUPPORT

Purpose: To provide a self-report measure of subjectively assessed social support.

Number of Items: 12

Format: Responses are made on a 7-point rating scale ranging from 1 (*very strongly disagree*) to 7 (*very strongly agree*). Includes three subscales: family, friends, and significant other. All items are presented.

Reliability: Coefficient alpha was .88 for total scale and ranged from .85 to .91 for the subscales. Test–retest (2 to 3 months) was .85 for total scale and ranged from .72 to .85 for the subscales.

Validity: Correlations with measures of depression and anxiety ranged from −.13 to −.25.

Author: Zimet, G. D., et al.

Article: The Multidimensional Scale of Perceived Social Support.

Journal: *Journal of Personality Assessment*, Spring 1988, *52*(1), 30–41.

■ ■ ■

4040

Test Name: NONCONFORMITY SCALE

Purpose: To assess an individual's tendency to break existing societal norms, laws, and regulations.

Number of Items: 30

Format: Subjects indicate the number of times they engaged in each nonconforming behavior never to very often.

Reliability: Coefficient alpha was .83. Test–retest (2 weeks) reliability was .94.

Author: Worthington, D. L., and Schlottmann, R. S.

Article: The predictive validity of subtle and obvious empirically derived psychological test items under faking conditions.

Journal: *Journal of Personality Assessment*, Summer 1986, *50*(2), 171–181.

Related Research: Gynther, M. D., et al. (1979). Do face-valid items have more predictive validity than subtle items? The case of the MMPI Pd scale. *Journal of Consulting and Clinical Psychology*, *47*, 295–300.

■ ■ ■

4041

Test Name: NORBECK SOCIAL SUPPORT QUESTIONNAIRE

Purpose: To measure multiple dimensions of perceived social support.

Format: Includes three composite variables: total functional, total network, and total loss.

Reliability: Test–retest reliability coefficients ranged from .90 to .96. Coefficient alphas ranged from .92 to .94.

Validity: Correlations with the Personal Resource Questionnaire Part II ranged from .35 to .44.

Author: Byers, P. H., and Mullis, M. R.

Article: Reliability and validity of the Norbeck Social Support Questionnairie in psychiatric inpatients.

Journal: *Educational and Psychological Measurement*, Summer 1987, *47*(2), 445–448.

Related Research: Norbeck, J. S., et al. (1983). Further development of the Norbeck Social Support Questionnaire: Normative data and validity testing. *Nursing Research*, *32*, 4–9.

■ ■ ■

4042

Test Name: OBJECTIVE AND SUBJECTIVE BURDEN SCALES

Purpose: To measure the consequences of living with a depressed person.

Number of Items: 33

Format: Five-point scale from 1 (*does not apply*) to 5 (*a great deal*). All items presented.

Reliability: Alphas ranged from .48 to .95 among four subscales.

Author: Coyne, J. C., et al.

Article: Living with a depressed person.

Journal: *Journal of Consulting and Clinical Psychology*, June 1987, *55*(3), 347–352.

Related Research: Montgomery, R. J., et al. (1985). Caregiving and the experience of subjective and objective burden. *Family Relations*, *34*, 19–36.

■ ■ ■

4043

Test Name: OTHER DYADIC PERSPECTIVE-TAKING SCALE

Purpose: To assess the extent to which one's partner is perceived to be a perspective-taker.

Number of Items: 20

Format: Includes two factors: strategies and cognizance. An example is presented.

Reliability: Alpha coefficients ranged from .87 to .93.

Author: Long, E. C. J.

Article: Measuring dyadic perspective-taking: Two scales for assessing perspective-taking in marriage and similar dyads.

Journal: *Education and Psychological Measurement*, Spring 1990, *50*(1), 91–103.

Related Research: Long, E. C. J. (1987). Perspective-taking as a determinant of marital adjustment and propensity to divorce (Doctoral dissertation, Oregan State University). *Dissertation Abstracts International*, *48*, 8A.

■ ■ ■

4044

Test Name: PEER RELATIONSHIP SATISFACTION SCALE

Purpose: To measure peer relationship satisfaction.

Number of Items: 11

Format: Responses to each item are made on a 5-point scale from *always true* to *not true at all*. All items are presented.

Reliability: Alpha coefficients were .80 (EMR sample) and .87 (non-EMR sample).

Author: Taylor, A. R., et al.

Article: The social adaptation of mainstreamed mildly retarded children.

Journal: *Child Development*, October 1987, *58*(5), 1321–1334.

Related Research: Asher, S. R., & Wheeler, V. A. (1985). Children's loneliness: A comparison of rejected and neglected status. *Journal of Consulting and Clinical Psychology*, *53*, 500–505.

■ ■ ■

4045

Test Name: PEER SOCIAL SUPPORT SCALE

Purpose: To measure students' perceptions of the extent to which

they were engaged in a supportive social network with their friends.

Number of Items: 12

Format: Assesses behavioral and evaluative components of friendship.

Reliability: Cronbach's alpha was .68.

Validity: Correlations with other variables ranged from −.52 to .46.

Author: Hirsch, B. J., and Rapkin, B. D.

Article: The transition to junior high school: A longitudinal study of self-esteem, psychological symptomatology, school life, and social support.

Journal: *Child Development*, October 1987, *58*(5), 1235–1243.

Related Research: Hirsch, B. J. (1981). Social networks and the coping process: Creating personal communities. In B. Gottlieb (Ed.), *Social networks and social support* (pp. 149–170). Beverly Hills, CA: Sage.

■ ■ ■

4046

Test Name: PEER SUPPORT SCALE FOR TEACHERS

Purpose: To measure how much teachers help fellow teachers contribute to the instructional program of a school.

Number of Items: 15

Format: Five-point Likert format. Sample items presented.

Reliability: Alpha was .79.

Validity: Correlations with other variables ranged from −.44 to .62.

Author: Brissie, J. S., et al.

Article: Individual, situational contributions to burnout.

Journal: *Journal of Educational Research*, November/December 1988, *82*(2), 106–112.

4047

Test Name: PERCEIVED SOCIAL SUPPORT: FRIENDS SCALE

Purpose: To measure perceived friend support.

Number of Items: 20

Format: Responses to each item are either *yes, no,* or *don't know.*

Reliability: Coefficient alpha ranged from .84 to .92.

Validity: Correlations with Perceived Social Support—Family Scale ranged from .18 to .42.

Author: Lyons, J. S., et al.

Article: Perceived social support from family and friends: Measurement across disparate samples.

Journal: *Journal of Personality Assessment*, Spring 1988, *52*(1), 42–47.

Related Research: Procidano, M., & Heller, K. (1983). Measures of perceived social support from friends and from family: Three validation studies. *American Journal of Community Psychology*, *11*, 1–24.

■ ■ ■

4048

Test Name: PERSONAL INTERACTION QUESTIONNAIRE

Purpose: To measure support for quitting smoking by a spouse or live-in partner.

Number of Items: 20

Format: Subjects responded to each item on a 5-point frequency scale. All items are presented.

Reliability: Cronbach's alphas ranged from .82 to .89.

Author: Cohen, S., and Lichtenstein, E.

Article: Partner behaviors that support quitting smoking.

Journal: *Journal of Consulting and Clinical Psychology*, June 1990, *58*(3), 304–309.

Related Research: Mermelstein, R., et al. (1983). Partner support and relapse in smoking cessation programs. *Journal of Consulting and Clinical Psychology, 51,* 456–466.

■ ■ ■

4049

Test Name: PERSONAL RELATIONSHIP MAINTENANCE DIFFICULTY SCALE

Purpose: To measure difficulty in maintaining personal relationships.

Number of Items: 5

Reliability: Alpha was .65.

Validity: Correlation with Maintenance Difficulty—Personal Scale was .54.

Author: Wright, P. H., and Conneran, P. J.

Article: Measuring strain in personal relationships: A refinement.

Journal: *Psychological Reports,* June 1989, *64*(3), II, 1321–1322.

Related Research: Wright, P. H. (1985). The Acquaintance Description Form. In S. Duck & D. Perlman (Eds.), *Understanding personal relationships: An interdisciplinary approach* (pp. 39–62). London: Sage.

■ ■ ■

4050

Test Name: PERSONAL RESOURCE QUESTIONNAIRE— PART II

Purpose: To measure five relational dimensions of social support.

Number of Items: 25

Format: Items are Likert scaled.

Validity: Correlations with the Norbeck Social Support Questionnaire ranged from .35 to .44.

Author: Byers, P. H., and Mullis, M. R.

Article: Reliability and validity of the Norbeck Social Support

Questionnaire in psychiatric inpatients.

Journal: *Educational and Psychological Measurement,* Summer 1987, *47*(2), 445–448.

Related Research: Brandt, P. A., & Weinert, C. (1981). The PRQ–A social support measure. *Nursing Research, 30,* 277–280.

■ ■ ■

4051

Test Name: PET ATTACHMENT AND ANTHROPOMORPHISM SCALES

Purpose: To measure emotional attachment to pets.

Number of Items: 18

Format: All items presented. Format not specified for all items.

Reliability: Alphas were .85 (attachment) and .69 (anthropomorphism).

Author: Albert, A., and Bulcroft, K.

Article: Pets, families, and the life course.

Journal: *Journal of Marriage and the Family,* May 1988, *50*(2), 543–552.

Related Research: Rubin, Z. (1973). *Liking and loving.* New York: Holt Rinehart and Winston.

■ ■ ■

4052

Test Name: PICTORIAL SCALE OF PERCEIVED COMPETENCE AND SOCIAL ACCEPTANCE FOR YOUNG CHILDREN

Purpose: To measure perceived competencies of pre-school and kindergarten children.

Number of Items: 24

Format: Children choose which of two verbal descriptions of pictures best describes themselves.

Reliability: Coefficients ranged from .62 to .83 across subscales.

Author: Gullo, D. F., and Ambrose, R. P.

Article: Perceived Competence and Social Acceptence in Kindergarten: Its relationship to Academic Performance.

Journal: *Journal of Educational Research,* September-October 1987, *81*(1), 28–32.

Related Research: Harter, S., & Pike, R. (1984). The pictorial scale of perceived competence and social acceptance for young children. *Child Development, 55,* 1969–1982.

■ ■ ■

4053

Test Name: POPULARITY/BEHAVIORAL ATTRIBUTE

Purpose: To provide a sociometric peer nominating form.

Number of Items: 7

Format: Respondent nominated three classmates who possess each attribute.

Reliability: Test–retest reliability coefficients ranged from .68 to .76.

Author: Luftig, R. L.

Article: Children's loneliness, perceived ease in making friends and estimated social adequacy: Development and social metacognition.

Journal: *Child Study Journal,* 1987, *17*(1), 35–53.

Related Research: Sherman, L. W. (1984). Social distance of elementary school children in age-heterogeneous and homogeneous classroom settings. *Perceptual and Motor Skills, 58,* 395–409.

■ ■ ■

4054

Test Name: POWERLESSNESS SCALE

Purpose: To measure expectancies of control over societal events.

Number of Items: 7

Format: Forced-choice formats.

Validity: Correlations with other variables ranged from −.21 to .39.

Author: Jackson, L. A., and Jeffers, D. L.

Article: The Attitudes About Reality Scale: A new measure of personal epistemology.

Journal: *Journal of Personal Assessment*, Summer 1989, *53*(2), 353–365.

Related Research: Neal, A., & Seeman, M. (1964). Organizations and powerlessness: A text of the mediational hypothesis. *American Sociological Review*, *29*, 216–225.

■ ■ ■

4055

Test Name: PRIVACY REGULATION RATING SCALE

Purpose: To assess the amount of desired privacy achieved for six kinds of privacy.

Number of Items: 6

Format: Subjects rate each kind of privacy on a 9-point scale ranging from −4 (*extremely less than desired*) through 0 (*same as desired*) to +4 (*extremely more than desired*). Types of privacy include: reserve, isolation, intimacy with family, solitude, intimacy with friends, and anonymity.

Validity: Correlations with the California Psychological Inventory ranged from −.53 to .36 (men) and −.36 to .35 (women).

Author: Pedersen, D. M.

Article: Correlates of privacy regulation.

Journal: *Perceptual and Motor Skills*, April 1988, *66*(2), 595–601.

Related Research: Pedersen, D. M. (1978). Dimensions of privacy. *Perceptual and Motor Skills*, *48*, 1291–1297.

■ ■ ■

4056

Test Name: PSYCHOLOGICAL SEPARATION INVENTORY

Purpose: To assess separation–individuation.

Number of Items: 138

Format: Responses are made on a 5-point Likert format ranging from *not at all true of me* to *very true of me*. Half the items refer to psychological separation from mother, the other half from father. Includes four subscales.

Reliability: Alpha coefficients ranged from .84 to .92. Test–retest stability ranged from .69 to .96.

Validity: Correlations with the College Adjustment Inventory ranged from −.14 to .31 (for freshmen) and from −.17 to .39 (for upperclassmen).

Author: Lapsley, D. K., et al.

Article: Psychological separation and adjustment to college.

Journal: *Journal of Counseling Psychology*, July 1989, *36*(3), 286–294.

Related Research: Hoffman, J. A. (1984). Psychological separation of late adolescents from their parents. *Journal of Counseling Psychology*, *31*, 170–178.

■ ■ ■

4057

Test Name: QUALITATIVE SOCIAL SUPPORT INDEX

Purpose: To measure the qualitative aspects of one's social resources.

Number of Items: 6

Format: Subjects indicate how frequently each of six specific behaviors occurred in a relationship deemed important to them. A 5-point scale from 1 (*never*) to 5 (*often*) was employed.

Reliability: Coefficient alpha was .74.

Validity: Correlation with other variables ranged from −.46 to .47.

Author: Brown, S. D., et al.

Article: Perceived social support among college students: Three studies of the psychometric characteristics and counseling uses of the social support inventory.

Journal: *Journal of Counseling Psychology*, July, 1987, *34*(3), 337–354

Related Research: Moos, R. H., et al. (1983). *Health and daily living form manual*. Unpublished manuscript, Stanford University, Social Ecology Laboratory.

■ ■ ■

4058

Test Name: RELATIONSHIP ASSESSMENT SCALE

Purpose: To measure satisfaction in close relationships.

Number of Items: 7

Format: Five-point satisfaction scales. All items presented.

Reliability: Item-total correlations ranged from .57 to .76.

Validity: Correlations with other variables ranged from −.53 to .80.

Author: Hendrick, S. S.

Article: A generic measure of relationship satisfaction.

Journal: *Journal of Marriage and the Family*, February 1988, *50*(1), 93–94.

Related Research: Hendrick, S. S. (1981). Self-disclosure and marital satisfaction. *Journal of Personality and Social Psychology*, *40*, 1150–1159.

■ ■ ■

4059

Test Name: RELATIONSHIP STRESS SCALE

Purpose: To measure stress in primary relationships.

Number of Items: 9

Format: All items presented.

Reliability: Alpha was .82. Test–retest (1 month) reliability was .85.

Validity: A single factor accounted for 43% of total variance.

Author: Jenner, J. R.

Article: The experience of work stress as a function of stress in a primary relationship.

Journal: *Psychological Reports*, June 1988, *62*(3), 711–717.

• • •

4060

Test Name: RESPONSIBILITY SCALE

Purpose: To measure social responsibility.

Number of Items: 56

Format: True–false format.

Reliability: Alpha was .80.

Author: Mellor, S., et al.

Article: Comparative trait analysis of long-term recovering alcoholics.

Journal: *Psychological Reports*, April 1986, *58*(2), 411–418.

Related Research: Gough, H. G., et al. (1952). A personality scale for social responsibility. *Journal of Abnormal and Social Psychology*, 47, 73–80.

• • •

4061

Test Name: REVISED CLASS PLAY

Purpose: To measure peer nominations in elementary school children.

Number of Items: 30

Format: Children nominate classmates for 15 positive and 15 negative roles in an imaginary class play.

Reliability: Test–retest reliability ranged from .77 to .87. Internal consistency ranged from .81 to .95.

Author: Schneider, B. H., et al.

Article: Social relations of gifted children as a function of age and school program.

Journal: *Journal of Educational Psychology*, March 1989, *81*(1), 48–56.

Related Research: Masten, A. S., et al. (1985). A revised class play method of peer assessment. *Developmental Psychology, 21,* 523–533.

• • •

4062

Test Name: REVISED SELF-MONITORING SCALE

Purpose: To identify high and low self-monitors.

Number of Items: 13

Format: Includes two factors: ability to modify self-presentation and sensitivity to the expressive behavior of others. Responses are made on a 6-point scale from 0 (*certainly, always false*) to 5 (*certainly, always true*).

Reliability: Alpha coefficients ranged from .66 to .83.

Author: Shuptrine, F. K., et al.

Article: An analysis of the dimensionality and reliability of the Lennox and Wolfe Revised Self-Monitoring Scale.

Journal: *Journal of Personality Assessment*, Summer 1990, *54*(3 and 4), 515–522.

Related Research: Lennox, R. D., & Wolfe, R. N. (1984). Revision of the Self-Monitoring Scale. *Journal of Personality and Social Psychology, 46,* 1349–1364.

• • •

4063

Test Name: ROOMMATE RAPPORT SCALE

Purpose: To measure roommate rapport.

Number of Items: 28

Format: Likert format. Sample items are presented.

Reliability: Internal consistency estimates ranged from .95 to .97.

Author: Carey, J. C., et al.

Article: Development of a short form of the Roommate Rapport Scale.

Journal: *Measurement and Evaluation in Counseling and Development*, January 1988, *20*(4), 175–180.

Related Research: Carey, J. C., et al. (1986). Development of an instrument to measure rapport between college roommates. *Journal of College Student Personnel, 27,* 269–273.

• • •

4064

Test Name: ROOMMATE RAPPORT SCALE—SHORT FORM

Purpose: To measure roommate rapport.

Number of Items: 10

Reliability: Guttman split-half reliability was .97. Cronbach's alpha was .97.

Validity: Correlations with other variables ranged from −.25 to .88.

Author: Saidla, D. D.

Article: Roommates' cognitive development, interpersonal understanding, and relationship rapport.

Journal: *Journal of College Student Development*, July 1990, *31*(4), 300–306.

Related Research: Carey, J., et al. (1988). Development of a short form of the Roommate Rapport Scale. *Measurement and Evaluation in Counseling and Development, 20,* 175–180.

• • •

4065

Test Name: SELF ACCEPTANCE AND ACCEPTANCE OF OTHERS SCALE

Purpose: To measure acceptance of self and generalized other.

Number of Items: 32

Format: Subjects rate themselves on each item on a 5-point *true of myself* scale.

Reliability: Alpha was .84. Item-total correlations ranged from .27 to .68.

Author: Rigby, K.

Article: Acceptance of authority, self, and others.

Journal: *Journal of Social Psychology,* August 1986, *126*(4), 493–501.

Related Research: Berger, E. M. (1952). The relation between expressed acceptance of need and experienced acceptance of others. *Journal of Abnormal Social Psychology, 47,* 778–782.

■ ■ ■

4066

Test Name: SELF-DESCRIPTION INVENTORY—REVISED

Purpose: To measure need for social approval.

Number of Items: 128

Format: True–false format.

Validity: Correlation with Marlowe-Crown Social Desirability Scale was .82.

Author: Adams, C. J., and Krasnoff, A. G.

Article: Social desirability effects in male prisoners.

Journal: *Journal of Research in Personality,* December 1989, *23*(4), 421–434.

Related Research: Jacobson, L. I., et al. (1983). A revised multidimensional social desirability inventory. *Bulletin of the Psychonomic Society, 21,* 391–392.

■ ■ ■

4067

Test Name: SELF DYADIC PERSPECTIVE-TAKING SCALE

Purpose: To assess a self-report dyadic perspective-taking measure.

Number of Items: 13

Format: Includes two factors: strategies and cognizance. An example is presented.

Reliability: Alpha coefficients ranged from .80 to .85.

Author: Long, E. C. J.

Article: Measuring dyadic perspective-taking: Two scales for assessing perspective-taking in marriage and simialr dyads.

Journal: *Educational and Psychological Measurement,* Spring 1990, *50*(1), 91–103.

Related Research: Long, E. C. J. (1987). Perspective-taking as a determinant of marital adjustment and propensity to divorce (Doctoral dissertation, Oregan State University). *Dissertation Abstracts International, 48,* 8A.

■ ■ ■

4068

Test Name: SELF-MONITORING SCALE

Purpose: To measure the degree to which individuals guide their behavior.

Number of Items: 25

Format: Items are true–false. Five components are included: concern for the social appropriateness of one's self-presentation, attention to social comparison information, ability to control or modify self-presentation, use of this ability in particular situations, and cross-situational variability of social behavior.

Reliability: Average internal consistency estimate was .58.

Author: Shuptrine, F. K., et al.

Article: An analysis of the dimensionality and reliability of the Lennox and Wolfe Revised Self-Monitoring Scale.

Journal: *Journal of Personality Assessment,* Summer 1990, *54*(3 and 4), 515–522.

Related Research: Snyder, M. (1974). Self-monitoring of expressive behavior. *Journal of Personality and Social Psychology, 30,* 526–537.

■ ■ ■

4069

Test Name: SELF-REPORT TRUST SCALE

Purpose: To measure interpersonal trust.

Number of Items: 8

Reliability: Alpha's ranged from .73 to .74 across two factors.

Validity: Bently hit for a two factor situation was .94.

Author: Lagace, R. R., and Rhoads, G. K.

Article: Evaluation of the MacDonald, Kessel, and Fuller Self-Report Trust Scale.

Journal: *Psychological Reports,* December 1988, *63*(3), 961–962.

Related Research: MacDonald, A. P., et al. (1972). Self-disclosure and two kinds of trust. *Psychological Reports, 30,* 143–148.

■ ■ ■

4070

Test Name: SEPARATION-INDIVIDUATION INVENTORY

Purpose: To measure disturbances in separation-individuation processes within adult populations.

Number of Items: 39

Format: Items are rated on a 10-point scale regarding how characteristic it is of the subject.

Reliability: Coefficient alpha was .92.

Validity: Correlations with other variables ranged from −.36 to .52 ($N = 104$).

Author: Ryan, R. M., and Lynch, J. H.

Article: Emotional autonomy versus detachment: Revisiting the vicissitudes of adolescence and young adulthood.

Journal: *Child Development*, April 1989, *60*(2), 340–356.

Related Research: Christenson, R. M., & Wilson, W. P. (1985). Assessing pathology in the separation-individuation process by an inventory. *Journal of Nervous and Mental Disease*, *173*, 561–565.

■ ■ ■

4071

Test Name: SOCIAL ADJUSTMENT AND EMPLOYMENT SCALES

Purpose: To measure adjustment to child and home activities, contact with friends, contact with relatives and recreation and hobbies.

Number of Items: 23

Format: Subjects give frequency estimates for the preceding month for each activity items.

Reliability: Internal consistency ranged from .48 to .68 across subscales.

Author: Andersen, B. L.

Article: Controlled prospective longitudinal study of women with cancer: II. Psychological outcomes.

Journal: *Journal of Consulting and Clinical Psychology*, December 1989, *56*(6), 692–697.

Related Research: Katz, M. M., & Lyerly, S. B. (1963). Methods for measuring adjustment and social behavior in the community: 1. Rationale, description, discriminative validity, and scale development. *Psychological Reports*, *13*, 503–535.

■ ■ ■

4072

Test Name: SOCIAL ANXIETY INDEX FOR ANXIETY

Purpose: To determine how anxious different social situations make respondents feel.

Number of Items: 105

Format: Items are rated on a 1–5 scale.

Reliability: Alpha was .98. Test–retest reliability was .80.

Validity: Correlations with other variables ranged from –.45 to .38.

Author: Cole, D. A., and Milstead, M.

Article: Behavioral correlates of depression: Antecedents or consequences?

Journal: *Journal of Counseling Psychology*, October 1989, *36*(4), 408–416.

Related Research: Curran, J. P., et al. (1980). Social skill and social anxiety. *Behavior Modification*, *4*, 493–512.

■ ■ ■

4073

Test Name: SOCIAL ANXIETY QUESTIONNAIRE

Purpose: To assess social anxiety and social skills.

Number of Items: 35

Format: Responses are made on a 5-point scale for discomfort and for frequency of social responses. Includes five subscales concerning: giving criticisms, expressing opinions, giving compliments, initiating conversations, and making positive self-assertions.

Reliability: Cronbach's alphas ranged between .91 and .96. Test–retest (6 weeks) reliabilities were .85 and .88.

Validity: Correlation with the Social Anxiety Schedule was .76.

Author: deRuiter, C., and Garssen, B.

Article: Social anxiety and fear of bodily sensations in panic disorder and agoraphobia: A matched comparison.

Journal: *Journal of Psychopathology and Behavioral Assessment*, June 1989, *11*(2), 175–184.

Related Research: van Dam-Baggen, R. (1987). *Social anxiety and nonassertiveness in psychiatric patients: Research in clinical practice.*

Lisse, The Netherlands: Swets & Zeitlinger.

■ ■ ■

4074

Test Name: SOCIAL ANXIETY INDEX FOR SKILL

Purpose: To assess social skill.

Format: Items are rated on a 1–5 scale.

Reliability: Alpha reliability coefficient was .98. Test–retest reliability was .71.

Validity: Correlations with other variables ranged from –.49 to .40.

Author: Cole, D. A., and Milstead, M.

Article: Behavioral correlates of depression: Antecedents or consequences?

Journal: *Journal of Counseling Psychology*, October 1989, *36*(4), 408–416.

Related Research: Curran, J. P., et al. (1980). Social skill and social anxiety. *Behavior Modification*, *4*, 493–512.

■ ■ ■

4075

Test Name: SOCIAL ANXIETY SCALE FOR CHILDREN

Purpose: To measure social anxiety as a situation-specific form of trait anxiety, reflecting individual differences in anxiety proneness in social situations.

Number of Items: 46

Format: Includes an additional 10–item social desirability scale.

Reliability: Internal consistency for social desirability, Kuder-Richardson was .72. Internal consistency for social anxiety, Kuder-Richardson was .91 (*N* = 2,149).

Author: Groot, M., and Prins, P.

Article: Children's social behavior: Reliability and concurrent validity of two self-report measures.

Journal: *Journal of Psychopathology and Behavioral Assessment*, September 1989, *11*(3), 195–207.

Related Research: Cohen, Kettenis, P. T., & Dekking, Y. M. (1980). *Cognitive aspects of social anxiety in children*. Lisse, The Netherlands: Swets & Zeitlinger.

■ ■ ■

4076

Test Name: SOCIAL AVOIDANCE AND DISTRESS SCALE

Purpose: To measure the level of anxiety experienced in social situations.

Number of Items: 28

Format: Employs a 5-point scale ranging from 1 (*never*) to 5 (*always*).

Reliability: Kuder-Richardson formula was .94.

Validity: Correlations with other variables ranged from −.53 to .56.

Author: Cole, D. A., and Milstead, M.

Article: Behavioral correlates of depression: Antecedents or consequences?

Journal: *Journal of Counseling Psychology*, October 1989, *36*(4), 408–416.

Related Research: Watson, D., & Friend, R. (1969). Measurement of social-evaluative anxiety. *Journal of Consulting and Clinical Psychology*, *33*, 448–457.

■ ■ ■

4077

Test Name: SOCIAL BEHAVIOR ASSESSMENT—REVISED—TEACHER RATING SCALE

Purpose: To provide a teacher rating of social competence.

Number of Items: 70

Format: Includes three factors: self-control/social convention, academic responsibility, and social participation. Paraphrased versions of each item are presented.

Reliability: Coefficient alphas were .93 and .96.

Author: Byrne, B. M., and Schneider, B. H.

Article: Student–teacher concordance on dimensions of student social competence: A multitrait-multimethod analysis.

Journal: *Journal of Psychopathology and Behavioral Assessment*, September 1986, *8*(3), 263–279.

Related Research: Byrne, B. M., & Schneider, B. H. (1985). Factorial validity of Stephen's Social Behavior Assessment. *Journal of Consulting and Clinical Psychology*, *53*, 259–260.

■ ■ ■

4078

Test Name: SOCIAL BEHAVIOR RATING SCALE

Purpose: To assess positive and negative behavior toward peers.

Number of Items: 16

Format: Includes two scales: positive social behavior and negative social behavior scales.

Reliability: Cronbach's alpha was .95.

Author: French, D. C.

Article: Heterogeneity of peer-rejected boys: Aggressive and nonaggressive subtypes.

Journal: *Child Development*, August 1988, *59*(4), 976–985.

Related Research: Walker, H. M., et al. (1978). *RECESS: Reprogramming environmental contingencies for effective social skills*. Eugene, OR: CORBEH.

■ ■ ■

4079

Test Name: SOCIAL DESIRABILITY SCALE—BRIEF VERSION

Purpose: To measure social desirability.

Number of Items: 6

Format: Includes two subscales: assert good; deny bad. All items are presented. Statements are answered either *true* or *false*.

Reliability: Alpha for total score was .55 and for each subscale alpha was .44.

Validity: Correlations with the Philadelphia Geriatric Center Morale Scale revised ranged from −.14 to .34.

Author: Mancini, J. A., and McKell, A. J.

Article: Social desirability and psychological well-being reports in late life: A further inquiry.

Journal: *Educational and Psychological Measurement*, Spring 1986, *46*(1), 89–94.

■ ■ ■

4080

Test Name: SOCIAL DISTANCE SCALES TOWARD MALE AND FEMALE HOMOSEXUALS

Purpose: To measure social distance with respect to homosexuals based on Bogardus' concept of social distance.

Number of Items: 5

Format: Guttman format. All items presented.

Reliability: For the male scale reproducibility was .95. Minimum marginal reproducibility was .68: Scalability was .83. For the female scale the values were .95, .67, and .84.

Validity: Correlations with other variables ranged from −.42 to .56.

Author: Gentry, C. S.

Article: Social distance regarding male and female homosexuals.

Journal: *Journal of Social Psychology*, April 1987, *127*(2), 199–208.

■ ■ ■

4081

Test Name: SOCIAL INTERACTION SELF-STATEMENT TEST

Purpose: To provide a measure of self-statements.

Number of Items: 30

Format: Half the items are positive and the others are negative.

Reliability: Internal consistency reliability coefficients ranged from .71 to .86.

Validity: Correlations with other variables ranged from −.58 to .68.

Author: Myszka, M. T., et al.

Article: Comparison of cognitive assessment methods with heterosocially anxious college women.

Journal: *Journal of Counseling Psychology*, October 1986, *33*(4), 401–407.

Related Research: Glass, C. R., & Arnkoff, D. B. (1982). Thinking cognitively: Selected issues in cognitive assessment and therapy. In P. C. Kendall (Ed.), *Advances in cognitive-behavior research and therapy*, *1*, 35–70. New York: Academic Press.

■ ■ ■

4082

Test Name: SOCIAL INTERACTION SCALE

Purpose: To measure social-evaluative anxiety.

Number of Items: 58

Format: Includes two subscales: Fear of negative evaluation and social avoidance distress.

Validity: Correlations with the Mobility Inventory for Agoraphobia ranged from −.04 to .59.

Author: Kwon, S. M., et al.

Article: Factor structure of the Mobility Inventory for Agoraphobia: A validational study with Australian samples of agoraphobic patients.

Journal: *Journal of Psychopathology and Behavioral Assessment*, December 1990, *12*(4), 365–374.

Related Research: Watson, D., & Friend, R. (1969). Measurement of social-evaluative anxiety. *Journal of Consulting and Clinical Psychology*, *33*, 448–457.

■ ■ ■

4083

Test Name: SOCIAL ISOLATION SCALE

Purpose: To assess frequency of contact with others.

Number of Items: 5

Format: Responses to each item are made on a scale from 1 (*never*) to 6 (*almost always*).

Reliability: Item-total correlations ranged from .53 to .64.

Validity: Correlations with Beck Depression Inventory—Short Form ranged from −.33 to −.35.

Author: Beach, S. R. H., et al.

Article: The relationship of marital satisfaction and social support to depressive symptomatology.

Journal: *Journal of Psychopathology and Behavioral Assessment*, December 1986, *8*(4), 305–316.

■ ■ ■

4084

Test Name: SOCIAL PROVISIONS SCALE

Purpose: To measure perceived social support.

Number of Items: 24

Format: Responses are made on a 4-point Likert scale ranging from 1 (*strongly disagree*) to 4 (*strongly agree*). Includes six social support domains: attachment, social integration, reassurance of worth, reliable alliance, guidance, and opportunity for nurturance. Examples are presented.

Reliability: Alpha coefficients ranged from .61 to .95. Test–retest reliabilities ranged from .37 to .66.

Validity: Correlations with other variables ranged from −.09 to .56.

Author: Mallinckrodt, B., and Fretz, B. R.

Article: Social support and the impact of job loss on older professionals.

Journal: *Journal of Counseling Psychology*, July 1988, *35*(3), 281–286.

Related Research: Cutrona, C. E., & Russell, D. W. (1988). The provisions of social relationships and adaptation to stress. In W. H. Jones & D. Perlman (Eds.), *Advances in personal relationships* (Vol. 1, pp. 37–67). Greenwich, CT: JAI Press.

■ ■ ■

4085

Test Name: SOCIAL PROVISIONS SCALE—MODIFIED

Purpose: To measure social support during pregnancy.

Number of Items: 6

Format: Includes six components of social support: attachment, social integration, opportunity for nurturance, reassurance of worth, reliable alliance, and guidance. Responses to each item are made on a 7-point scale from *not at all true* to *completely true*. All items are presented.

Reliability: Cronbach's alpha was .65.

Validity: Correlations with other variables ranged from .30 to .60.

Author: Cutrona, C. E., and Troutman, B. R.

Article: Social support, infant temperament, and parenting self-efficacy: A mediational model of postpartum depression.

Journal: *Child Development*, December 1986, *57*(6), 1507–1518.

Related Research: Russell, D., & Cutrona, C. E. (1984, August). *The provisions of social relationships and adaptation to stress.* Paper presented at the annual meeting of the American Psychological Association, Anaheim, CA.

4086

Test Name: SOCIAL SKILLS CHECKLIST

Purpose: To measure social skills behavior.

Number of Items: 40

Format: Five-point frequency scale.

Reliability: Alpha was .87.

Author: Margalit, M., and Eysenck, S.

Article: Prediction of conherence in adolescence: Gender differences in social skills, personality and family climate.

Journal: *Journal of Research in Personality*, December 1990, *24*(4), 510–521.

Related Research: Goldstein, A. P., et al. (1980). *Skillstreaming the adolescents*. Champaign, IL: Research Press.

■ ■ ■

4087

Test Name: SOCIAL SKILLS RATING SCALE FOR TEACHERS

Purpose: To measure the social skills of elementary school students.

Number of Items: 27

Format: Three-point rating scale.

Reliability: Alphas ranged from .75 to .92.

Author: Vaughn, S., et al.

Article: Peer acceptance, self-perceptions and social skills of learning disabled students prior to identification.

Journal: *Journal of Educational Psychology*, March 1990, *82*(1), 101–106.

Related Research: Gresham, F. M., & Elliot, S. (1966). Social skills rating scale for teachers. Baton Rouge: Lousiana State University.

■ ■ ■

4088

Test Name: SOCIAL SKILLS SURVEY—PEER

Purpose: To measure, by self-report, perceived level of social skills in situations involving peers.

Number of Items: 15

Format: Five-point Likert format.

Reliability: Cronbach's alpha was .93. Test–retest reliability was .79.

Author: Marlowe, H. A., Jr.

Article: Social intelligence: Evidence for multidimensionality and construct independence.

Journal: *Journal of Educational Psychology*, February 1986, *78*(1), 52–58.

Related Research: Marlowe, H. A., Jr., & Weinberg, R. B. (1983). *The Social Skills Survey: Construction and validation of the survey*. Unpublished manuscript. University of South Florida. Florida Mental Health Institute, Tampa FL.

■ ■ ■

4089

Test Name: SOCIAL SUPPORT INVENTORY

Purpose: To provide a measure of perceived social support based on a person–environment fit model of satisfaction.

Number of Items: 39

Format: Responses to each item are made on two scales: a need strength scale and a perceived supply scale. Both scales range from 1 (*none*) to 7 (*very much*).

Reliability: Cronbach's alpha ranged from .78 to .93.

Validity: Correlations with other variables ranged from .20 to .57.

Author: Brown, S. D., et al.

Article: Perceived social support among college students: Factor structure of the Social Support Inventory.

Journal: *Journal of Counseling Psychology*, October 1988, *35*(4), 472–478.

Related Research: Brown, S. D., et al. (1987). Perceived social support among college students: Three studies of the psychometric characteristics and counseling uses of the Social Support Inventory (Monograph). *Journal of Counseling Psychology*, *34*, 337–354.

■ ■ ■

4090

Test Name: SOCIAL SUPPORT SCALE

Purpose: To measure perceived social support by self-report.

Number of Items: 25

Format: Format not specified. All items presented.

Reliability: Alphas ranged from .73 to .91 across subscales.

Author: Dunn, S. E., et al.

Article: Social support and adjustment in gifted adolescents.

Journal: *Journal of Educational Psychology*, December 1987, *79*(4), 467–473.

Related Research: Fleming, R., et al. (1982). Mediating influences of social support on stress at Three Mile Island. *Journal of Human Stress*, *8*, 14–22.

■ ■ ■

4091

Test Name: SOCIAL SUPPORT SCALE

Purpose: To measure the perception or experience of social support.

Number of Items: Varies.

Format: Vignette format. Examples presented.

Reliability: Alpha was .78.

Author: Stemp, P. S., et al.

Article: Psychological distress in the postpartum period: The significance of social support.

Journal: *Journal of Marriage and the Family*, May 1986, *48*(2), 271–277.

Related Research: Kaplan, A. (1977). *Social support: The construct and its measurement*. Unpublished B. A. thesis, Department of Psychology, Brown University, Providence, RI.

∎ ∎ ∎

4092

Test Name: SOCIAL SUPPORT SCALE

Purpose: To measure the extent to which individuals reported feeling that their needs for support were satisfied.

Number of Items: 13

Format: Includes three areas of perceived support: the mother's family, the baby's father during pregnancy, and either the baby's father or a male who was "like a father" to the mother's baby at 8 months. Each item was rated on a 3-point scale from 1 (*not at all*) through 2 (*a little*) to 3 (*very much*). Examples are presented.

Reliability: Alphas ranged from .70 to .91.

Validity: Correlations with other variables ranged from −.08 to .50.

Author: Unger, D. G., and Wandersman, L. P.

Article: The relation of a family and partner support to the adjustment of adolescent mothers.

Journal: *Child Development*, August 1988, *59*(4), 1056–1060.

Related Research: Belle, D. (1982). Social ties and social support. In D. Belle (Ed.), *Lives in stress* (pp. 133–144). Beverly Hills, CA: Sage.

∎ ∎ ∎

4093

Test Name: SOCIAL SUPPORT SCALE FOR FRIENDS

Purpose: To measure social support.

Number of Items: 20

Format: Responses to each item are either *yes*, *no*, or *don't know*.

Reliability: Cronbach's alpha was .88.

Validity: Correlations with other variables ranged from −.37 to .33.

Author: Cole, D. A., and Milstead, M.

Article: Behavioral correlates of depression: Antecedents or consequences?

Journal: *Journal of Counseling Psychology*, October 1989, *36*(4), 408–416.

Related Research: Procidano, M., & Heller, K. (1983). Measures of perceived social support for friends and family: Three validation studies. *American Journal of Community Psychology*, *11*, 1–24.

∎ ∎ ∎

4094

Test Name: SOCIALLY DESIRABLE RESPONSE SET–5

Purpose: To measure socially desirable response set.

Number of Items: 5

Format: Responses are made on a 5-point scale from 1 (*definitely true*) to 5 (*definitely false*). All items are presented.

Reliability: Alpha reliabilities were .66 and .68 (*N*s were 614 and 3,053, respectively). Test–retest (1 month) reliability was .75 (*N* = 75).

Author: Hays, R. D., et al.

Article: A five-item measure of socially desirable response set.

Journal: *Educational and Psychological Measurement*, Autumn 1989, *49*(3), 629–636.

Related Research: Reynolds, W. M. (1982). Development of reliable and valid short forms of the Marlowe-Crowne Social Desirability Scale. *Journal of Clinical Psychology*, *38*, 119–125.

∎ ∎ ∎

4095

Test Name: SOCIOEMOTIONAL ADJUSTMENT QUESTIONNAIRE

Purpose: To measure several spheres of self-perception of socioemotional adjustment.

Number of Items: 40

Format: Responses are made on a 5-point Likert scale ranging from 1 (*never or not at all*) to 5 (*very often or very much*). Includes three dimensions: sociability, hostility, and anxiety/depression. Examples are presented.

Reliability: Cronbach's alpha coefficients ranged from .72 to .87.

Validity: Correlations with other variables ranged from −.32 to .63.

Author: Buhrmester, D.

Article: Intimacy of friendship, interpersonal competence, and adjustment during preadolescence and adolescence.

Journal: *Child Development*, August 1990, *61*(4), 1101–1111.

Related Research: Buhrmester, D. (1989). *Manual for the Socioemotional Adjustment Questionnaire*. Unpublished manuscript. Program in Psychology, University of Texas at Dallas: Richardson, Texas.

∎ ∎ ∎

4096

Test Name: SPHERES OF CONTROL SCALE

Purpose: To assess the multidimensional nature of the control dimension.

Number of Items: 30

Format: Includes three scales: personal efficacy, interpersonal control, and sociopolitical control.

Reliability: Alpha coefficients ranged from .45 to .57.

Validity: Correlations with university grades ranged from −.07 to −.22.

Author: Watkins, D., and Alfon, M.

Article: The Spheres of Control Scale: An attempt at cross-cultural validation.

Journal: *Educational and Psychological Measurement*, Summer 1988, *48*(2), 453–457.

Related Research: Paulhus, D. (1983). Sphere-specific measures of perceived control. *Journal of Personality and Social Psychology*, *44*, 1253–1265.

■ ■ ■

4097

Test Name: STRANGER ROLE SCALE

Purpose: To measure the cognitive approaches people make in dealing with strangers.

Number of Items: 7

Format: Five-point Likert format. All items described.

Reliability: Alpha was .72.

Author: Reitzes, D.

Article: Urban identification and downtown activities: A social psychological approach.

Journal: *Social Psychology Quarterly*, June 1986, *49*(2), 167–179.

Related Research: Lofland, L. A. (1973). *A world of strangers*. New York: Basic Books.

■ ■ ■

4098

Test Name: STRUCTURAL ANALYSIS OF SOCIAL BEHAVIOR QUESTIONNAIRES

Purpose: To assess interpersonal and intrapsychic dispositions from the clients' perspectives.

Number of Items: 108

Format: The instrument has three surfaces: other, self, and intrapsychic. Within each surface there is an affiliation axis and an independence axis. Examples are presented.

Reliability: Alpha coefficients ranged from .49 to .98.

Author: Quintana, S. M., and Meara, N. M.

Article: Internalization of therapeutic relationships in short-term psychotherapy.

Journal: *Journal of Counseling Psychology*, April 1990, *37*(2), 123–130.

Related Research: Benjamin, L. S. (1979). Structural analysis of differentiation failure. *Psychiatry, 42*, 1–23.

■ ■ ■

4099

Test Name: SUBJECTIVE SOCIAL SUPPORT SCALE

Purpose: To measure social support in the military.

Number of Items: 34

Format: Yes–no format.

Reliability: Cronbach's alpha was .92.

Author: Solomon, Z., et al.

Article: Objective versus subjective measurement of stress and social support: Combat-related reactions.

Journal: *Journal of Consulting and Clinical Psychology*, June 1987, *55*(3), 577–583.

Related Research: Moos, R. H. (1973). *Military Company Environment Inventory*. Stanford, CA: Stanford University.

■ ■ ■

4100

Test Name: SUINN-LEW ASIAN SELF-IDENTITY ACCULTURATION SCALE

Purpose: To measure Asian Americans' level of acculturation.

Number of Items: 21

Format: Includes items about: language, identity, friendship, choice, behaviors, generation and geography, and attitudes.

Reliability: Internal consistency reliability was .88.

Author: Leong, F. T. L., and Tata, S. P.

Article: Sex and acculturation differences in occupational values among Chinese-American children.

Journal: *Journal of Counseling Psychology*, April 1990, *37*(2), 208–212.

Related Research: Suinn, R. M., et al. (1987). The Suinn-Lew Asian Self-Identity Acculturation scale: An initial report. *Educational and Psychological Measurement, 47*, 401–407.
Gim, R. H., et al. (1990). Asian-American acculturation, severity of concerns, and willingness to see a counselor. *Journal of Counseling Psychology, 37*(3), 281–285.

■ ■ ■

4101

Test Name: SURVEY OF HETEROSEXUAL INTERACTIONS

Purpose: To assess the subject's ability to initiate heterosocial interactions.

Number of Items: 20

Format: Responses are made on a 7-point scale ranging from *unable to respond* to *able to carry out interaction*. The scale is appropriate for men only.

Reliability: Split-half reliability coefficient was .85. Test–retest (4 months) reliability coefficient was .85.

Validity: Correlations with other variables ranged from −.69 to .84.

Author: Zane, N. W. S.

Article: Change mechanisms in placebo procedures: Effects of suggestion social demand, and contingent success on improvement in treatment.

Journal: *Journal of Counseling Psychology*, April 1989, *36*(2), 234–243.

Related Research: Twentyman, C. T., & McFall, R. M. (1975). Training of social skills in shy males. *Journal of Consulting and Clinical Psychology, 43*, 384–395.

4102

Test Name: SURVEY OF HETEROSOCIAL INTERACTIONS—FEMALE

Purpose: To measure female heterosocial functioning.

Number of Items: 20

Format: Responses are made on a 7-point Likert scale from 1 (*unable to initiate a conversation*) to 7 (*able to initiate a conversation in every case*).

Validity: Correlations with other variables ranged from −.02 to .37.

Author: Jones, G. N., et al.

Article: Criterion-related validity of self-report measures of female heterosocial functioning.

Journal: *Journal of Psychopathology and Behavioral Assessment*, March 1988, *10*(1), 1–7.

Related Research: Williams, C. L., & Ciminero, A. R. (1978). Development and validation of a heterosocial skills inventory: The survey of heterosocial interactions for females. *Journal of Consulting and Clinical Psychology, 46*, 1547–1548.

■ ■ ■

4103

Test Name: TEXAS SOCIAL BEHAVIOR INVENTORY

Purpose: To measure social confidence and self-esteem.

Number of Items: 16

Format: Employs a 5-point rating scale.

Reliability: Internal consistency was .91. Test–retest reliability coefficient was .93 for women.

Validity: Correlations with other variables ranged from .19 to .74.

Author: Hollinger, C. L., and Fleming, E. S.

Article: Gifted and talented young women: Antecedents and correlates of life satisfaction.

Journal: *Gifted Child Quarterly*, Spring 1988, *32*(2), 254–259.

Related Research: Helmreich, R. L., et al. (1974). The Texas Social Behavior Inventory (TSBI): An objective measure of self-esteem for social competence. *JSAS Catalog of Selected Documents in Psychology, 4*, 79.

■ ■ ■

4104

Test Name: TRAUMATIC STRESS RESPONSE

Purpose: To measure distress arising from stress associated with membership in a group at high risk for AIDS.

Number of Items: 17

Format: Items adapted from Impart of Events Scale.

Reliability: Alpha was .87.

Author: Mactin, J. L.

Article: Psychological consequences of AIDS-related bereavement among gay men.

Journal: *Journal of Consulting and Clinical Psychology*, December 1988, *56*(6), 856–862.

Related Research: Horowitz, M. J., et al. (1979). Import of event scale. A study of subjective stress. *Psychosomatic Medicine, 41*, 209–218.

■ ■ ■

4105

Test Name: TRIANGULAR LOVE SCALE

Purpose: To measure intimacy, passion, and decision/commitment.

Number of Items: 45

Format: Nine-point Likert format.

Reliability: Cronbach's alphas were over .90. Test–retest (2 weeks) ranged from .75 to .81.

Validity: Correlations with self-disclosure ranged from .00 to .62.

Author: Chojnacki, J. T., and Walsh, W. B.

Article: Reliability and concurrent validity of the Sternberg Triangular Love Scale.

Journal: *Psychological Reports*, August 1990, *67*(1), 219–224.

Related Research: Sternberg, R. J. (1986). A triangular theory of love. *Psychological Review, 93*, 119–135.

■ ■ ■

4106

Test Name: UCLA LONELINESS SCALE—REVISED

Purpose: To measure loneliness.

Number of Items: 4

Format: Likert-type response options. Examples are presented.

Reliability: Cronbach's alpha was .63.

Validity: Correlations with other variables ranged from −.39 to .56.

Author: Hays, R. D., and DiMatteo, M. R.

Article: A short-form measure of loneliness.

Journal: *Journal of Personality Assessment*, Spring 1987, *51*(1), 69–81.

Related Research: Andersson, L. (1985). Intervention against loneliness in a group of elderly women: An impact evaluation. *Social Science and Medicine, 20*, 355–364. Franzoi, S. L., & Davis, M. H. (1985). Adolescent self-disclosure and loneliness: Private self-consciousness and parental influences. *Journal of Personality and Social Psychology, 48*, 768–780.

■ ■ ■

4107

Test Name: UCLA LONELINESS SCALE—REVISION

Purpose: To measure loneliness.

Number of Items: 8

Format: Likert-type response options. All items are presented.

Reliability: Cronbach's alpha was .84.

Validity: Correlations with other variables ranged from −.41 to .64.

Author: Hays, R. D., and DiMatteo, M. R.

Article: A short-form measure of loneliness.

Journal: *Journal of Personality Assessment*, Spring 1987, *51*(1), 69–81.

Related Research: Russell, D., et al. (1980). The revised UCLA Loneliness Scale: Concurrent and discriminant validity evidence. *Journal of Personality and Social Psychology*, *39*, 472–480.

■ ■ ■

4108

Test Name: UCLA LONELINESS SCALE

Purpose: To measure loneliness.

Number of Items: 20

Format: Likert-type response options. Several items are presented.

Reliability: Cronbach's alpha was .90.

Validity: Correlations with other variables ranged from −.46 to .65.

Author: Hays, R. D., and DiMatteo, M. R.

Article: A short-form measure of loneliness.

Journal: *Journal of Personality Assessment*, Spring 1987, *51*(1), 69–81.

Related Research: Russell, D., et al. (1978). Developing a measure of loneliness. *Journal of Personality Assessment*, *42*, 290–294.

■ ■ ■

4109

Test Name: UNEMPLOYMENT SUPPORT SCALE

Purpose: To measure how much support an unemployed person perceives to come from individuals and organizations.

Number of Items: 13

Format: Four-point helpfulness scales. Sample items presented.

Reliability: Alpha was .63.

Validity: Correlations with other variables ranged from −.12 to .25.

Author: Payne, R., and Hartley, J.

Article: A test of a model for explaining the affective experience of unemployed men.

Journal: *Journal of Occupational Psychology*, March 1987, *60*(1), 31–47.

■ ■ ■

4110

Test Name: UNION SOCIALIZATION SCALE

Purpose: To assess early socialization experiences.

Number of Items: 11

Format: Responses are made on a 3-point scale, where 2 (*yes*), 1 (*no*), 0 (*can't remember*).

Validity: Correlations with other variables ranged from −.43 to .56.

Author: Fullagar, C., and Barling, J.

Article: A longitudinal test of a model of the antecedents and consequences of union loyalty.

Journal: *Journal of Applied Psychology*, April 1989, *74*(2), 213–227.

Related Research: Gordon, M. E., et al. (1980). Commitment to the union: Development of a measure and an examination of its correlates. *Journal of Applied Psychology*, *65*, 479–499.

■ ■ ■

4111

Test Name: UNIVERSITY ALIENATION SCALE

Purpose: To provide information about students' feelings of alienation.

Number of Items: 24

Format: Likert-type scale ranging from 1 (*strongly disagree*) to 4

(*strongly agree*). Includes items measuring powerlessness, meaninglessness, and social estrangement.

Reliability: Split-half reliability was .92.

Author: Schram, J. L., and Lauver, P. J.

Article: Alienation in international students.

Journal: *Journal of College Student Development*, March 1988, *29*(2), 146–150.

Related Research: Burbach, H. J. (1972). The development of contextual measure of alienation. *Pacific Sociological Review*, *15*, 225–234.

■ ■ ■

4112

Test Name: WASHINGTON PSYCHOSOCIAL SEIZURE INVENTORY

Purpose: To measure psychosocial adjustment of epileptic patients.

Number of Items: 132

Reliability: Interrater reliability ranged from .80 to .94. Test–retest reliability ranged from .66 to .87.

Validity: Concurrent validity ranged from .56 to .75.

Author: Tellier, A., et al.

Article: Long-term effects of severe penetrating head injury on psychosocial adjustment.

Journal: *Journal of Consulting and Clinical Psychology*, October 1990, *58*(5), 531–537.

Related Research: Dodrill, C. B., et al. (1980). An objective method for the assessment of psychological and social problems among epileptics. *Epilepsia*, *21*, 123–135.

■ ■ ■

4113

Test Name: WAY OF LIFE SCALE

Purpose: To assess an individual's need for exaggerated forms of interpersonal control.

Number of Items: 21

Format: True–false. All items presented.

Reliability: Alpha was .63. Test–retest (3 weeks) reliability was .77.

Validity: Correlations with other variables ranged from −.09 to .53.

Author: Wright, L., et al.

Article: Exaggerated social control and its relationship to the type A behavior pattern.

Journal: *Journal of Research in Personality*, June 1990, *24*(2), 258–269.

■ ■ ■

4114

Test Name: WAYS I HELP OTHERS TO COPE

Purpose: To measure how we perceive ourselves to be helpful to others.

Number of Items: 69

Format: Employs a 9-point Likert scale from 1 (*very unhelpful*) to 9 (*very helpful*).

Reliability: Alpha coefficients ranged from .51 to .89 (*N* = 116). Test–retest reliability coefficients ranged from .46 to .72 (*N* = 45).

Author: Kottke, J. L., et al.

Article: Development of two scales of coping strategies: An initial investigation.

Journal: *Educational and Psychological Measurement*, Autumn 1988, *48*(3), 737–742.

Related Research: Lazarus, R., & Folkman, S. (1984). *Stress, appraisal, and coping*. New York: Springer.

■ ■ ■

4115

Test Name: WAYS OTHERS HELP ME COPE

Purpose: To measure the way we perceive others to be helpful to us in coping.

Number of Items: 67

Format: Employs a 9-point Likert scale ranging from 1 (*very unhelpful*) to 9 (*very helpful*).

Reliability: Alpha coefficients ranged from .55 to .83 (*N* = 116). Test–retest reliabilities ranged from .57 to .78 (*N* = 45).

Author: Kettke, J. L., et al.

Article: Development of two scales of coping strategies: An initial investigation.

Journal: *Educational and Psychological Measurement*, Autumn 1988, *48*(3), 737–742.

Related Research: Lazarus, R., & Folkman, S. (1984). *Stress, appraisal, and coping*. New York: Springer.

■ ■ ■

4116

Test Name: "WHAT IF" SITUATIONS TEST–III

Purpose: To measure ability of children to identify appropriate and inappropriate requests of adults.

Number of Items: 6

Format: Children respond to short vignettes. All items presented.

Reliability: Alpha was .84 (prevention score), test–retest

reliability was .66, and interrater reliability was .98.

Author: Wurtele, S. K., et al.

Article: Comparison of programs for teaching personal safety skills to preschoolers.

Journal: *Journal of Consulting and Clinical Psychology*, August 1989, *57*(4), 505–511.

Related Research: Wurtele, S. K., et al. (1988, August). *Development of an instrument to evaluate sexual abuse prevention programs*. Paper presented at the convention of the American Psychological Association, Atlanta, GA.

■ ■ ■

4117

Test Name: WORK SUPPORT SCALE

Purpose: To assess perceived social support.

Number of Items: 3

Format: Responses are made on a 6-point Likert scale ranging from 0 (*not at all supportive*) to 5 (*very supportive*).

Reliability: Coefficient alpha was .55.

Validity: Correlations with other variables ranged from −.30 to .13 (*N* = 157).

Author: Parkes, K. R.

Article: Coping, negative affectivity, and the work environment: Additive and interactive predictors of mental health.

Journal: *Journal of Applied Psychology*, August 1990, *75*(4), 399–409.

CHAPTER 5
Adjustment–Vocational

4118

Test Name: ABSENCE CONSEQUENCES SCALE

Purpose: To assess the consequences of being absent from work.

Number of Items: 4

Format: Responses are made on a 3-point Likert scale ranging from 1 (*never*) to 3 (*often*).

Reliability: Coefficient alpha was .50.

Validity: Correlations with other variables ranged from −.21 to .54.

Author: Baba, V. V.

Article: Methodological issues in modeling absence: A comparison of least squares and Tobit analyses.

Journal: *Journal of Applied Psychology*, August 1990, *75*(4), 428–432.

• • •

4119

Test Name: CAREER IMPATIENCE SCALE

Purpose: To measure acceptance of being patient with career progress.

Number of Items: 3

Format: Seven-point Likert format.

Reliability: Alpha was .71.

Author: Posner, B. Z., and Powell, G. N.

Article: A longitudinal investigation of work preferences among college graduates

Journal: *Psychological Reports*, June 1990, *66*(3), 1125–1134.

Related Research: Veiga, J. F. (1981). Plateaued versus nonplateaued managers: Career patterns, attitudes, and path potential. *Academy of Management Journal*, *24*, 566–578.

• • •

4120

Test Name: CAREER STRATEGY SCALE

Purpose: To measure strategies people believe will further their careers.

Number of Items: 18

Format: Seven-point Likert format.

Reliability: Alphas ranged from .61 to .73.

Author: Rynes, S. L., et al.

Article: Aspirations to manage: A comparison of engineering students and working engineers.

Journal: *Journal of Vocational Behavior*, April 1988, *32*(2), 239–253.

Related Research: Gould, S. U., & Penley, L. (1984). Career strategies and salary progression: A study of their relationships in a municipal bureaucracy. *Organizational Behavior and Human Performance*, *34*, 244–265.

• • •

4121

Test Name: CHARACTERISTICS OF LIFELONG LEARNERS IN THE PROFESSIONS.

Purpose: To measure characteristics of lifelong learners in the human service professions.

Number of Items: 36

Format: Responses are made on a 7-point Likert scale from 1 (*strongly disagree*) to 7 (*strongly agree*). Includes 7 factors: professional growth through learning, self-motivated achievement, educability, readiness for change, causation for learning participation, familial educational background, and future orientation.

Reliability: Cronbach's alpha was .91.

Author: Livneh, C., and Livneh, H.

Article: Factors differentiating high and low participants in lifelong learning.

Journal: *Educational and Psychological Measurement*, Autumn 1988, *48*(3), 637–646.

Related Research: Livneh, C. L. (1986). *Characteristics of lifelong learners in the human service professions.* Unpublished doctoral dissertation, Boston University, 1986.

• • •

4122

Test Name: COMPANY SATISFACTION SCALE

Purpose: To assess company satisfaction.

Number of Items: 14

Format: Responses are made on a 5-point scale ranging from 1 (*very dissatisfied*) to 5 (*highly satisfied*).

Reliability: Coefficient alpha was .90.

Validity: Correlations with other variables ranged from −.15 to .79.

Author: Mellor, S.

Article: The relationship between membership decline and union commitment: A field study of local unions in crisis.

Journal: *Journal of Applied Psychology,* June 1990, 75(3), 258–267.

Related Research: Stagner, R., & Eflal, B. (1982). Internal union dynamics during a strike: A quasi-experimental study. *Journal of Applied Psychology*, 67, 37–44.

■ ■ ■

4123

Test Name: COMPETENCE INDEX

Purpose: To measure sense of competence that results from experience at work.

Number of Items: 23

Reliability: Alpha ranged from .60 to .67 across subscales.

Validity: Factor structure does not yield a confidence dimension, but does reveal motivation, ability, and influence dimensions.

Author: Srinivasan, P. T., and Anantharaman, R. N.

Article: Multidimensionality of the Wagner and Vhorse Competence Index.

Journal: *Psychological Reports,* October 1989, 65(2), 621–622.

Related Research: Wagner, F. R., & Vhorse, J. J. (1975). A measure of individual sense of competence. *Psychological Reports*, 36, 451–459. Snyder, R. A. (1989). The factor structure of the Wagner and Vhorse Competence Index: Another view. *Psychological Reports*, 65, 673–674.

■ ■ ■

4124

Test Name: CONCERN ABOUT TEACHING SCALE

Purpose: To measure concerns about teaching among student-teachers.

Number of Items: 18

Format: Five-point Likert type format.

Reliability: Test–retest (1 week) reliability was .78.

Author: Evans, E. O., and Tribble, M.

Article: Perceived teaching problems, self-efficacy, and commitment to teaching among preservice teachers.

Journal: *Journal of Educational Research,* November-December 1986, 80(2), 81–85.

Related Research: Veenman, S. (1984). Perceived problems of beginning teachers. *Review of Educational Research*, 54(2), 143–178.

■ ■ ■

4125

Test Name: COPING WITH JOB LOSS SCALES

Purpose: To assess coping with involuntary job loss.

Number of Items: 20

Format: Five-point Likert format. All items presented.

Reliability: Alphas ranged from .61 to .82.

Validity: Subscale intercorrelations ranged from −.19 to .42. Correlations with other variables ranged from −.08 to .11.

Author: Kinicki, A. J., and Latack, J. C.

Article: Explication of the construct of coping with involuntary job loss.

Journal: *Journal of Vocational Behavior,* June 1990, 36(3), 339–360.

■ ■ ■

4126

Test Name: EMPLOYEE STOCK OWNERSHIP PLANS SATISFACTION MEASURE

Purpose: To measure employees' satisfaction with employees' stock ownership plans.

Number of Items: 8

Format: Responses are made on a 7-point scale ranging from 1 (*strongly disagree*) to 7 (*strongly agree*). A sample item is presented.

Reliability: .91.

Validity: Correlations with other variables ranged from −.20 to .28.

Author: Klein, K. J., and Hall, R. J.

Article: Correlates of employee satisfaction with stock ownership: Who likes an ESOP most?

Journal: *Journal of Applied Psychology,* November 1988, 73(4), 630–638.

■ ■ ■

4127

Test Name: ENERGY DEPLETION INDEX

Purpose: To measure occupational burnout.

Number of Items: 4

Format: Five-point frequency rating scale. All items presented.

Reliability: Alphas ranged from .79 to .87 across samples.

Author: Garden, A. M.

Article: Burnout: The effect of psychological type on research findings.

Journal: *Journal of Occupational Psychology,* September 1989, 62(3), 223–234.

Related Research: Garden, A. M. (1985). Burnout: The effect of personality. Unpublished doctoral dissertation. Massachusetts Institute of Technology 0373736.

■ ■ ■

4128

Test Name: FEAR OF CAREER STAGNATION SCALE

Purpose: To measure acceptance of career plateauing.

Number of Items: 4

Format: Seven-point Likert format.

Reliability: Alpha was .68.

Author: Posner, B. Z., and Powell, G. N.

Article: A longitudinal investigation of work preferences among college graduates.

Journal: *Psychological Reports*, June 1990, *66*(3), 1125–1134.

Related Research: Veiga, J. F. (1981). Plateaued versus non plateaued managers: Career patterns, attitudes, and path potential. *Academy of Management Journal, 24*, 566–578.

■ ■ ■

4129

Test Name: FRUSTRATION, EMOTIONAL REACTION AND HOSTILITY SCALES

Purpose: To measure environmental frustration at work.

Number of Items: 14

Format: Five-point Likert format.

Reliability: Alphas ranged from .74 to .85.

Author: West, M., and Rushton, R.

Article: Mismatches in the work-role transitions.

Journal: *Journal of Occupational Psychology*, December 1989, *62*(4), 271–286.

Related Research: Keenan, A., & Newton, T. J. (1984). Frustration in organizations: Relationships to role stress, climate and psychological strain. *Journal of Occupational Psychology, 57*, 57–65.

■ ■ ■

4130

Test Name: FRUSTRATION SCALE

Purpose: To measure secretarial frustration on the job.

Number of Items: 3

Format: Responses to each item were made on a 6-point scale from strongly disagree to strongly agree.

Reliability: Coefficient alpha was .83 (*N* = 155).

Validity: Correlations with other variables ranged from –.27 to .56 (*Ns* = 148–156).

Author: Spector, P. E., et al.

Article: Relation of job stressors to affective, health, and performance outcomes: A comparison of multiple data sources.

Journal: *Journal of Applied Psychology*, February 1988, *73*(1), 11–19.

Related Research: Peters, L. H., & O'Connor, E. J. (1910). Situational constraints and work outcomes: The influence of a frequently overlooked construct. *Academy of Management Review, 5*, 391–397.

■ ■ ■

4131

Test Name: GLOBAL JOB SATISFACTION QUESTIONNAIRE

Purpose: To measure global job satisfaction.

Number of Items: 15

Reliability: Alpha was .65. Test–retest (6 months) reliability was .63.

Validity: Correlations with other variables ranged from 53 to –.20.

Author: Barling, J., and Rosenbaum, A.

Article: Work stressors and wife abuse.

Journal: *Journal of Applied Psychology*, May 1986, *71*(2), 346–348.

Related Research: Warr, P. B., et al. (1979). Scales for the measurement of some work attitudes and aspects of psychological well-being. *Journal of Occupational Psychology, 52*, 129–148.

4132

Test Name: GOAL INSTABILITY SCALE

Purpose: To measure a lack of goal directedness and inhibition in work.

Number of Items: 10

Format: Utilizes 6-point Likert scales.

Reliability: Test–retest (2 weeks) reliability was .76. Coefficient alpha was .80.

Validity: Correlation with self-esteem was .64.

Author: Robbins, S. B., and Tucker, K. R., Jr.

Article: Relation of goal instability to self-directed and interactional career counseling workshops.

Journal: *Journal of Counseling Psychology*, October 1986, *33*(4), 418–424.

Related Research: Robbins, S., & Patton, M. (1985). Self-psychology and career development: Construction of the Superiority and Goal Instability Scales. *Journal of Counseling Psychology, 32*, 221–231.

■ ■ ■

4133

Test Name: GROWTH NEED STRENGTH MEASURE

Purpose: To provide a measure of employee need for growth on the job.

Number of Items: 12

Format: Forced-choice format.

Reliability: Test–retest (6 months) reliability was .65.

Author: Graen, G. B., et al.

Article: A field experimental test of the moderating effects of growth need strength on productivity.

Journal: *Journal of Applied Psychology*, August 1986, *71*(3), 484–491.

Related Research: Aldag, R. J., & Brief, A. P. (1979). Examination of a measure of higher-order need strength. *Human Relations, 8,* 705–718.

■ ■ ■

4134

Test Name: HEALTH PROFESSIONS STRESS INVENTORY

Purpose: To assess levels and sources of stress experienced by health professionals.

Number of Items: 30

Format: Likert format. All items presented.

Reliability: Alphas ranged from .88 to .89.

Validity: Correlations with Lyon's tension index ranged from .75 to .78.

Author: Wolfgang, A. P.

Article: The Health Professions Stress Inventory.

Journal: *Psychological Reports,* February 1988, *62*(1), 220–222.

Related Research: Lyons, T. F. (1971). Role, clarity, need for clarity, satisfaction, tension, and withdrawal. *Organizational Behavior and Human Performance, 6,* 99–110.

■ ■ ■

4135

Test Name: HOPPOCK JOB SATISFACTION BLANK

Purpose: To measure resident assistants' job satisfaction.

Number of Items: 4

Format: Items measure the degree to which resident assistants like their jobs, feel satisfied with their job, and like their job in comparison with other RAs, and how often they would consider changing jobs.

Reliability: Coefficient alpha was .87.

Validity: Correlations with other variables ranged from −.33 to .01.

Author: Deluga, R. J., and Winters, J. J., Jr.

Article: The impact of role ambiguity and conflict on resident assistants.

Journal: *Journal of College Student Development,* May 1990, *31*(3), 230–236.

Related Research: Hoppock, R. (1960). The Job Satisfaction Blank. In J. O. Crites (Ed.), *Vocational psychology* (p. 480). New York: McGraw-Hill.

■ ■ ■

4136

Test Name: INDEX OF JOB DESIRABILITY

Purpose: To measure how "good" a person's job is compared with an "average" job.

Number of Items: 14

Format: 13 nonmonetary job characteristics are followed by various appropriate response categories.

Validity: Correlations with other related variables ranged from .53 to .72.

Author: Jencks, C., et al.

Article: What is a good job? A new measure of labor-market services.

Journal: *American Journal of Sociology,* May 1988, *93*(6), 1322–1357.

Related Research: Duncan, O. D. (1961). A socio-economic index for all occupations. In A. J. Reiss (Ed.), *Occupations and professions* (pp. 109–161). New York: Free Press.

■ ■ ■

4137

Test Name: INDEX OF ORGANIZATIONAL REACTIONS

Purpose: To measure satisfaction.

Number of Items: 42

Format: Includes eight subscales assessing satisfaction with:

supervision, company identification, kind of work, amount of work, coworkers, physical work conditions, financial rewards, and career future. Responses are made on 5-point rating scales.

Reliability: Coefficient alpha was .89.

Validity: Correlations with other variables ranged from −.07 to .54.

Author: Meyer, J. P., et al.

Article: Organizational commitment and job performance: It's the nature of the commitment that counts.

Journal: *Journal of Applied Psychology,* February 1989, *74*(1), 152–156.

Related Research: Smith, F. J. (1976). Index of Organizational Reactions (OR). *JSAS Catalog of Selected Documents in Psychology,* *6*(54, No. 1265).

■ ■ ■

4138

Test Name: INDEX OF ORGANIZATIONAL REACTIONS

Purpose: To assess overall satisfaction with a new job.

Number of Items: 20

Format: Includes eight job facets: amount of work, career opportunities, coworkers, organization, physical conditions, pay, supervisor, and type of work.

Reliability: Coefficient alpha was .72.

Author: Taylor, M. S.

Article: Effects of college internships or individual participants.

Journal: *Journal of Applied Psychology,* August 1988, *73*(3), 393–401.

Related Research: Dunham, R. B., & Smith, F. J. (1979). *Organizational surveys.* Glenview, IL: Scott, Foresman.

4139

Test Name: INDSALES MEASURE

Purpose: To measure a salesperson's job satisfaction.

Number of Items: 61

Format: Likert format.

Reliability: Alphas ranged from .84 to .92 across seven subscales.

Author: Goldsmith, R. E., et al.

Article: Similarity of sales representatives' and supervisors' problem-solving styles and the satisfaction–performance relationship.

Journal: *Psychological Reports*, June 1989, *64*(3, Part I), 827–832.

Related Research: Childers, T. L., et al. (1980). Towards a more parsimonious measurement of job satisfaction for the industrial salesforce. In R. P. Bagozzi et al. (Eds.), *Marketing in the 80's: Changes and challenges* (pp. 344–349). Chicago, IL: American Marketing Association.

■ ■ ■

4140

Test Name: INTENT TO STAY IN JOB SCALE

Purpose: To assess a person's perceived opportunities for job mobility.

Number of Items: 3

Format: Seven-point Likert format.

Reliability: Alpha was .91.

Author: McGinnis, S. K., and Morrow, P. C.

Article: Job attitudes among full- and part-time employees.

Journal: *Journal of Vocational Behavior*, February 1990, *36*(1), 82–96.

Related Research: Landau, J., & Hammer, T. H. (1986). Clerical employees' perceptions of intra-organizational career opportunities. *Academy of Management Journal*, 2, 385–404.

4141

Test Name: INTENTION TO TURNOVER SCALE

Purpose: To assess the participant's intention to quit his or her job.

Number of Items: 34

Reliability: Coefficient alphas were .83 and .92.

Validity: Correlations with other variables ranged from −.47 to .24.

Author: Hatcher, L., and Crook, J. C.

Article: First-job surprises for college graduates: An exploratory investigation.

Journal: *Journal of College Student Development*, September 1988, *29*(5), 441–448.

Related Research: Seashore, S. E., et al. (1983). Assessing organizational change: A guide to methods, measures and practices. New York: Wiley.

■ ■ ■

4142

Test Name: INTERNAL REWARDS SCALE

Purpose: To measure feelings of professional fulfillment in work and the extent of recognition in work.

Number of Items: 7

Format: Five-point Likert format. Sample item presented.

Reliability: Alpha was .77.

Validity: Correlations with other variables ranged from −.49 to .56.

Author: Brissie, J. S., et al.

Article: Individual, situational contributions to burnout.

Journal: *Journal of Educational Research*, November/December 1988, *82*(2), 106–112.

■ ■ ■

4143

Test Name: JOB AFFECT SCALE

Purpose: To measure mood at work.

Number of Items: 20

Format: Half the items measure negative affect or mood at work and the other half measure positive affect or mood at work. Responses are made on a 5-point scale ranging from 1 (*very slightly or not at all*) to 5 (*very much*).

Reliability: Reliabilities for positive affect were .80 and .88; for negative affect they were .81 and .84.

Validity: Correlations with other variables ranged from −.38 to .34.

Author: George, J. M.

Article: Mood and absence.

Journal: *Journal of Applied Psychology*, April 1989, *74*(2), 317–324.

Related Research: Brief, A. P., et al. (1988). Should negative affectivity remain an unmeasured variable in the study of job stress? *Journal of Applied Psychology*, 73, 193–198.

■ ■ ■

4144

Test Name: JOB COGNITIONS SCALE—ADAPTED

Purpose: To measure cognitive appraisal of job outcomes.

Number of Items: 12

Format: Half of the items are concerned with pay and half with the job itself. Responses are made on a 5-point scale ranging from 1 (*very bad*) to 5 (*very good*). All items are presented.

Reliability: Alpha coefficients were .87 (job) and .92 (pay).

Validity: Correlations with other variables ranged from −.33 to .57.

Author: Organ, D. W., and Konovsky, M.

Article: Cognitive versus affective determinants of organizational citizenship behavior.

Journal: *Journal of Applied Psychology*, February 1989, *74*(1), 157–164.

Related Research: Scholl, R. W., et al. (1987). Referent selection to determining equity perceptions: Differential effects on behavioral and attitudinal outcomes. *Personnel Psychology, 40*, 113–124.

■ ■ ■

4145

Test Name: JOB DEPENDENCY SCALES

Purpose: To determine if individuals are dependent on the approval of others, and others are dependent on them, to do their jobs.

Format: Seven-point Likert format. Sample items presented.

Reliability: Alphas ranged from .60 to .89.

Validity: Perceived power was negatively related to dependence on others and positively related to others' dependence.

Author: Mainiero, L. A.

Article: An empirical investigation of the relationship between perceived position power and task and career sources of dependency in organizations.

Journal: *Psychological Reports*, August 1986, *59*(1), 431–438.

■ ■ ■

4146

Test Name: JOB-DESCRIPTIVE INDEX FOR ACCOUNTANTS

Purpose: To measure job satisfaction of accountants.

Number of Items: 30

Format: Likert format. All items presented.

Reliability: Alphas ranged from .84 to .90.

Author: Gregson, T.

Article: Measuring job satisfaction with a multiple-choice format of the Job Descriptive Index.

Journal: *Psychological Reports*, June 1990, *66*(3)1, 787–793.

Related Research: Smith, P. C., et al. (1969). *The measurement of satisfaction in work and retirement.* Chicago, IL: Rand McNally.

■ ■ ■

4147

Test Name: JOB DIAGNOSTIC SURVEY—SHORT VERSION

Purpose: To measure overall and facet job satisfaction.

Format: A 5-point scale was employed which ranged from 1 (*extremely dissatisfied*) to 5 (*extremely satisfied*). Includes: overall, security, supervisory, social, growth, coworkers, and management.

Reliability: Alpha coefficients ranged from .55 to .84.

Validity: Correlations with organizational commitment ranged from .16 to .62. Correlations with other variables ranged from −.20 to .25.

Author: Meglino, B. M., et al.

Article: A work values approach to corporate culture: A field test of the value congruence process and its relationship to individual outcomes.

Journal: *Journal of Applied Psychology*, June 1989, *74*(3), 424–432.

Related Research: Hackman, J. R., & Oldham, G. R. (1975). Development of the Job Diagnostic Survey. *Journal of Applied Psychology, 16*, 159–170.

■ ■ ■

4148

Test Name: JOB INVOLVEMENT SCALE

Purpose: To measure job involvement.

Number of Items: 6

Format: Responses are made on a 5-point scale ranging from 1 (*strongly disagree*) to 5 (*strongly agree*).

Reliability: Coefficient alpha was .77.

Validity: Correlations with other variables ranged from −.18 to .61.

Author: Mathieu, J. E., and Kohler, S. S.

Article: A cross-level examination of group absence influences on individual absence.

Journal: *Journal of Applied Psychology*, April 1990, *75*(2), 217–220.

Related Research: Lodahl, T., & Kejner, M. (1965). The definition and measurement of job involvement. *Journal of Applied Psychology, 49*, 24–33.

■ ■ ■

4149

Test Name: JOB PERFORMANCE CONSTRAINTS SCALE

Purpose: To assess the frequency of constraints that hinder job performance.

Number of Items: 11

Format: Responses to each item are made on a 5-point scale from less than once per month to several times per day.

Reliability: Coefficient alphas were .84 and .88 (*N* = 156).

Validity: Correlations with other variables ranged from −.47 to .57 (*N*s = 148–156).

Author: Spector, P. E., et al.

Article: Relation of job stressors to affective, health, and performance outcomes: A comparison of multiple data sources.

Journal: *Journal of Applied Psychology*, February 1988, *73*(1), 11–19.

Related Research: O'Connor, E. J., et al. (1982). Situational constraints and employee affective reactions: A partial field replication. *Group and Organizational Studies, 7,* 418–428.

■ ■ ■

4150

Test Name: JOB SATISFACTION BLANK

Purpose: To measure job satisfaction.

Number of Items: 4

Format: Seven-point format.

Reliability: Alphas ranged from .76 to .89.

Author: Rounds, J. B.

Article: The comparative and combined utility of work value and interest data in career counseling with adults.

Journal: *Journal of Vocational Behavior,* August 1990, *37*(1), 32–45.

Related Research: McNichols, C. W., et al. (1978). A validation of Hoppock's job satisfaction measure. *Academy of Management Journal, 21,* 737–742.

■ ■ ■

4151

Test Name: JOB SATISFACTION MEASURE

Purpose: To assess job satisfaction.

Number of Items: 15

Format: Employed a 3-point rating scale: *unhappy, not sure, happy.*

Reliability: Alpha was .81. Test–retest reliability was .69.

Validity: Correlations with other variables ranged from –.24 to .66.

Author: Barling, J., et al.

Article: Psychological functioning following an acute disaster.

Journal: *Journal of Applied Psychology,* November 1987, *72*(4), 683–690.

Related Research: Warr, P. B., et al. (1979). Scales for the measurement of

work attitudes and aspects of psychological well-being. *Journal of Occupational Psychology, 52,* 129–148.

■ ■ ■

4152

Test Name: JOB SATISFACTION MEASURE

Purpose: To provide an index of job satisfaction.

Number of Items: 38

Format: Includes: global questions about the respondent's job, comfort, challenge, financial rewards, promotion, resources, and relations with co-workers. Examples are presented.

Reliability: Coefficient alpha was .85.

Validity: Correlations with other variables ranged from .51 to –.20.

Author: Staines, G. L., et al.

Article: Wives' employment and husbands' attitudes towards work and life.

Journal: *Journal of Applied Psychology,* February 1986, *71*(1), 118–128.

Related Research: Quinn, R. P., & Staines, G. L. (1979). *The 1977 Quality of Employment Survey.* Ann Arbor, MI: Institute for Social Research.

■ ■ ■

4153

Test Name: JOB SATISFACTION QUESTIONNAIRE

Purpose: To measure job satisfaction.

Number of Items: 4

Format: Responses are made on a 7-point Likert format. The four aspects that the questions address are presented.

Reliability: Alpha coefficients ranged from .76 to .89.

Author: Chusmir, L. H., and Koberg, C. S.

Article: Creativity differences among managers.

Journal: *Journal of Vocational Behavior,* October 1986, *29*(2), 240–253.

Related Research: McNichols, C. W., et al (1978). A valuation of Hoppock's job satisfaction measure. *Academy of Management Journal, 21,* 737–742.

■ ■ ■

4154

Test Name: JOB SATISFACTION SCALE

Purpose: To evaluate general job satisfaction.

Number of Items: 8

Format: Responses to each statement are made by indicating whether the statement is very true, somewhat true, not too true, or not at all true.

Reliability: Reliability over 1 year was .67 for workers who changed neither employer nor occupation. For those who changed both occupation and employer the reliability was .25.

Validity: Correlations with other variables ranged from –.11 to .37.

Author: Gerhart, B.

Article: Voluntary turnover and alternative job opportunities.

Journal: *Journal of Applied Psychology,* October 1990, *75*(5), 467–476.

■ ■ ■

4155

Test Name: JOB SATISFACTION SCALE

Purpose: To measure job satisfaction.

Number of Items: 5

Format: Likert format.

Reliability: Alphas ranged from .83 to .87.

Validity: Correlations with other job related constructs ranged from –.46

(rate insufficiency) to .21 (rate responsibility).

Author: Lagace, R. R.

Article: Role-stress differences between salesmen and saleswomen: Effect on job satisfaction and performance.

Journal: *Psychological Reports*, June 1988, *62*(3), 815–825.

Related Research: Childers, T. L., et al. (1980). Towards a more parsimonious measurement of job satisfaction for the industrial sales force. In R. P. Bagozzi et al. (Eds.), *1980 Educators Conference Proceedings* (pp. 344–349). Chicago, IL: American Marketing Association.

■ ■ ■

4156

Test Name: JOB SATISFACTION SCALE

Purpose: To measure job satisfaction.

Number of Items: 4

Reliability: Coefficient alpha was .75.

Validity: Correlations with other variables ranged from −.37 to .54.

Author: Latack, J. C., et al.

Article: Carpenter apprentices: Comparison of career transitions for men and women.

Journal: *Journal of Applied Psychology*, August 1987, *72*(3), 393–400.

Related Research: McNichols, C. W., et al. (1978). A validation of Hoppock's job satisfaction measure. *Academy of Management Journal, 21,* 737–741.

■ ■ ■

4157

Test Name: JOB SATISFACTION SCALE

Purpose: To measure seven aspects of job satisfaction.

Number of Items: 7

Format: Includes items assessing satisfaction with co-workers, the work itself, pay and fringe benefits, the physical surroundings of the job, job supervision, promotion opportunities, and the job as a whole. Responses are made on a 7-point scale: 1 (delighted), 2 (pleased), 3 (mostly satisfied), 4 (mixed/about equally satisfied and dissatisfied), 5 (mostly dissatisfied), 6 (unhappy), and 7 (terrible).

Reliability: Alphas were .94 and .95.

Validity: Correlations with other variables ranged from .55 to −.53.

Author: Lounsbury, J. W., and Hoopes, L. L.

Article: A vacation from work: Changes in work and nonwork outcomes.

Journal: *Journal of Applied Psychology*, August 1986, *71*(3), 392–401.

Related Research: Andrews, F. M., & Withey, S. B. (1976). *Social indicators of well-being.* New York: Plenum. Quinn, R. P., & Staines, G. L. (1979). *The 1977 Quality of Employment Survey*, Ann Arbor, MI: Survey Research Center, Institute for Social Research.

■ ■ ■

4158

Test Name: JOB SATISFACTION SCALE

Purpose: To assess one's satisfaction with the present job.

Number of Items: 3

Format: Items dealt with: overall satisfaction, willingness to recommend the job to another person, and an indication that if given the opportunity they would choose the same job again. Responses are made on a 5-point scale ranging from 1 (*strongly disagree*) to 5 (*strongly agree*).

Reliability: Reliability coefficient was .87.

Validity: Correlations with other variables ranged from −.28 to .61.

Author: Pazy, A., and Zin, R.

Article: A contingency approach to consistency: A challenge to prevalent views.

Journal: *The Journal of Vocational Behavior*, February 1987, *30*(1), 84–101.

■ ■ ■

4159

Test Name: JOB SATISFACTION SCALE

Purpose: To measure job satisfaction.

Number of Items: 6

Format: Each item was answered on a 5-point scale ranging from 1 (*definitely not take job*) to 5 (*definitely take job*). All items are presented.

Reliability: Coefficient alpha was .90.

Validity: Correlations with other variables ranged from .07 to −.49.

Author: Pond, S. B., III, and Geyer, P. D.

Article: Employee age as a moderator of the relation between perceived work alternatives and job satisfaction.

Journal: *Journal of Applied Psychology*, November 1987, *72*(4), 552–557.

Related Research: Quinn, R. P., & Shepard, L. (1974). *The 1973–1974 quality of employment survey: Descriptive statistics*. Ann Arbor, MI: Institute for Social Research, Survey Research Center.

■ ■ ■

4160

Test Name: JOB SATISFACTION SCALE

Purpose: To measure job satisfaction.

Number of Items: 3

FORMAT: Seven-point semantic differential format. Sample item presented.

Reliability: Alpha was .68.

Author: Vecchio, R. P., et al.

Article: The predictive utility of the vertical dyad linkage approach.

Journal: *The Journal of Social Psychology*, October 1986, *126*(5), 617–625.

Related Research: Hoppock, R. (1935). *Job satisfaction*. New York: Harper.

■ ■ ■

4161

Test Name: JOB STRESS QUESTIONNAIRE

Purpose: To provide a perceptual measure of job related stress.

Number of Items: 13

Format: Includes four dimensions: work overload, role ambiguity, under-utilization of skills, and role conflict. Responses are made on a 7-point Likert format from 1 (*never*) to 7 (*always*). Examples are presented.

Reliability: Coefficient alphas ranged from −.32 to .89 (Ns = 157–603).

Author: Hamel, K., and Bracken, D.

Article: Factor structure of the Job Stress Questionnaire (JSQ) in the occupational groups.

Journal: *Educational and Psychological Measurement*, Autumn 1986, *46*(3), 777–786.

Related Research: Caplan, R., et al. (1975). *Demands and worker health: Main effects and organizational differences*. Washington, DC: U. S. Government Printing Office.

■ ■ ■

4162

Test Name: JOB TENSION SCALE

Purpose: To measure job tension.

Number of Items: 7

Format: Responses are made on a 5-point scale ranging from 1 (*strongly disagree*) to 5 (*strongly agree*).

Validity: Correlations with other variables ranged from −.42 to .44.

Author: Netemayer, R. G., et al.

Article: Analysis of role conflict and role ambiguity in a structural equations framework.

Journal: *Journal of Applied Psychology*, April 1990, 75(2), 148–157.

Related Research: House, R. J., & Rizzo, J. R. (1972). Role conflict and ambiguity as critical variables in a model of organizational behavior. *Organizational Behavior and Human Performance*, 7, 467–505.

■ ■ ■

4163

Test Name: MINNESOTA IMPORTANCE QUESTIONNAIRE

Purpose: To measure employee needs.

Number of Items: 21

Format: Includes 21 job facets: 13 focus on intrinsic job facets (e.g., achievement, moral values) and 8 focus on extrinsic job facets (e.g., pay, policies).

Reliability: Internal consistency coefficient was .74.

Author: Vandenberg, R. J., and Scarpello, V.

Article: The matching model: An examination of the processes underlying realistic job previews.

Journal: *Journal of Applied Psychology*, February 1990, 75(1), 60–67.

Related Research: Gay, E. G., et al. (1971). Manual for the Minnesota Importance Questionnaire. *Minnesota Studies in Vocational Rehabilitation*, Bulletin No. 28.

■ ■ ■

4164

Test Name: MINNESOTA JOB DESCRIPTION QUESTIONNAIRE

Purpose: To assess the perceptions of how rewarding the current job was among 21 job facets.

Number of Items: 21

Format: Includes 21 job facets: 13 focus on intrinsic job facets (e.g., achievement, moral values) and 8 focus on extrinsic job facets (e.g., pay, policies).

Reliability: Internal consistency was .74.

Author: Vandenberg, R. J., and Scarpello, V.

Article: The matching model: An examination of the processes underlying realistic job previews.

Journal: *Journal of Applied Psychology*, February 1990, 75(1), 60–67.

Related Research: Borgen, F. H., et al. (1968). The measure of occupational reinforcer patterns. *Minnesota Studies in Vocational Rehabilitation*, Bulletin No. 49.

■ ■ ■

4165

Test Name: MINNESOTA SATISFACTION QUESTIONNAIRE

Purpose: To measure job satisfaction.

Number of Items: 100

Format: Likert format.

Reliability: Alpha ranged from .82 to .96.

Author: Levinson, E. M.

Article: Job satisfaction among school psychologists: A replication study.

Journal: *Psychological Reports*, October 1989, *65*(2), 579–584.

Related Research: Weiss, D. J., et al. (1967). *Manual for the Minnesota Satisfaction Questionnaire*. Minneapolis, MN: University of Minnesota.

■ ■ ■

4166

Test Name: MINNESOTA SATISFACTION QUESTIONNAIRE

Purpose: To measure job satisfaction.

Number of Items: 20

Format: Five-point Likert format. Sample item presented.

Reliability: Alpha was .90.

Author: Ornstein, S., and Isabella, L.

Article: Age vs. stage models of career attitudes of women: A partial replication and extension.

Journal: *Journal of Vocational Behavior*, February 1990, *36*(1), 1–19.

Related Research: Weiss, D. J., et al. (1967). *Manual for the Minnesota Satisfaction Questionnaire.* Minneapolis: University of Minnesota, Industrial Relations Center.

■ ■ ■

4167

Test Name: MULTIDIMENSIONAL JOB SATISFACTION SCALE

Purpose: To measure job satisfaction.

Number of Items: 36

Format: Seven-point Likert format. All items prsented.

Reliability: Alphas ranged from .66 to .92 across subscales.

Validity: Correlations with other variables ranged from .14 to .74.

Author: Shouksmith, G., et al.

Article: Construction of a multidimensional scale of job satisfaction.

Journal: *Psychological Reports*, October 1990, *67*(2), 355–364.

■ ■ ■

4168

Test Name: NONWORK INFLUENCES OF JOB ATTRITION

Purpose: To measure reasons why women leave jobs.

Number of Items: 6

Format: Five-point Likert format.

Reliability: Alpha was .69.

Author: Rosin, H. M., and Korabik, K.

Article: Marital and family correlates of women managers' attrition from organizations.

Journal: *Journal of Vocational Behavior*, August 1990, *37*(1),104–120.

Related Research: Lee, T. W., & Mowday, R. T. (1987). Voluntarily leaving an organization: An empirical investigation of Steer's and Mowday's model of turnover. *Academy of Management Journal, 30,* 721–743.

■ ■ ■

4169

Test Name: NURSE STRESS INVENTORY

Purpose: To assess eight occupation stress factors for nurses: professional distress, patient care and motivation, time and workload management, personal time disruptions, emotional manifestations, fatigue, and physiological manifestations.

Number of Items: 66

Format: Likert format.

Reliability: Alphas ranged from .68 to .91 across subscales. Total alpha was .95.

Author: Fimian, M. J., et al.

Article: Stress in nursing and intentions of leaving the profession.

Journal: *Psychological Reports*, April 1988, *62*(2), 499–506.

Related Research: Finian, M. J. (1984). The development of an instrument to measure occupational stress in teachers: The Teacher Stress Inventory. *Journal of Occupational Psychology, 57,* 277–292.

■ ■ ■

4170

Test Name: NURSING ROLE CONFLICT SCALE

Purpose: To measure role conflict specific to nurses.

Number of Items: 4

Format: Five-point Likert format. All items presented.

Reliability: Alpha was .83.

VALIDITY: Correlation with general role conflict was .64.

Author: Beehr, T. A., et al.

Article: Social support and occupational stress: Talking to supervisors.

Journal: *Journal of Vocational Behavior*, February 1990, *36*(1), 61–81.

■ ■ ■

4171

Test Name: NURSING SATISFACTION SCALE

Purpose: To assess one's satisfaction with working in the nursing field.

Number of Items: 28

Reliability: Coefficient alpha was .94.

Validity: Correlations with other variables ranged from −.19 to .66.

Author: Kinicki, A. J., et al.

Article: Interviewer predictions of applicant qualifications and interviewer validity: Aggregate and individual analyses.

Journal: *Journal of Applied Psychology*, October 1990, *75*(5), 477–486.

Related Research: Griffeth, R. W., & Hom, P. W. (1983, August). *Test of Mobley's (1977) model to explain nursing turnover.* Paper presented at the 44th Annual Meeting of the Academy of Management, Dallas, TX.

■ ■ ■

4172

Test Name: OCCUPATIONAL QUESTIONNAIRE

Purpose: To measure degree of confidence people think they would have if they were to work in one of a number of occupations.

Number of Items: 20

Format: Rated on 11-point confidence scales. Examples presented.

Reliability: Test–retest reliability ranged from .74 to .89.

Validity: Correlation with General Self-Efficacy Scale was .42.

Author: Clement, S.

Article: The self-efficacy of expectations and occupational preferences of females and males.

Journal: *Journal of Occupational Psychology*, September 1987, *60*(3), 257–265.

■ ■ ■

4173

Test Name: OVERALL JOB SATISFACTION SCALE

Purpose: To assess job satisfaction.

Number of Items: 16

Format: Responses are made on a 7-point scale.

Reliability: Coefficient alpha was .88.

Validity: Correlations with other variables ranged from −.19 to .20.

Author: Bluen, S. D., et al.

Article: Predicting sales performance, job satisfaction, and depression by using the achievement strivings and impatience-irritability dimensions of type A behavior.

Journal: *Journal of Aplied Psychology*, April 1990, *75*(2), 212–216.

Related Research: Warr, P. B., et al. (1979). Scales for the measurement of work attitudes and aspects of psychological well-being. *Journal of Occupational Psychology, 52,* 129–148.

■ ■ ■

4174

Test Name: OVERALL JOB SATISFACTION SCALE

Purpose: To measure job satisfaction.

Number of Items: 15

Format: Includes 7 items measuring intrinsic satisfaction and 8 items measuring extrinsic satisfaction.

Validity: Correlations with other variables ranged from −.64 to .60.

Author: Fullagar, C., and Barling, J.

Article: A longitudinal test of a model of the antecedents and consequences of union loyalty.

Journal: *Journal of Applied Psychology*, April 1989, *74*(2), 213–227.

Related Research: Warr, P., et al. (1980). Scales for the measurement of some work attitudes and aspects of psychological well-being. *Journal of Occupational Psychology, 52,* 129–148.

■ ■ ■

4175

Test Name: OVERALL JOB-SATISFACTION SCALE

Purpose: To measure general level of satisfaction.

Number of Items: 3

Format: Responses to each item were made on a 6-point scale from *strongly disagree* to *strongly agree*.

Reliability: Coefficient alphas were .90 and .88 (*N*s= 155 and 156, respectively).

Validity: Correlations with other variables ranged from −.51 to .51 (*N*s = 148–156).

Author: Spector, P. E., et al.

Article: Relation of job stressors to affective, health, and performance outcomes: A comparison of multiple data sources.

Journal: *Journal of Applied Psychology*, February 1988, *73*(1), 11–19.

Related Research: Cammann, C., et al. (1979). *The Michigan*

Organizational Assessment Questionnaire. Unpublished manuscript, University of Michigan, Ann Arbor.

■ ■ ■

4176

Test Name: PARTICIPATION IN DECISION-MAKING INDEX

Purpose: To examine how much teacher participation the principal allows in the school's decision-making process.

Number of Items: 8

Format: Responses are made on a 7-point Likert scale ranging from 1 (*not at all true of my job*) to 7 (*extremely true of my job*). Examples are presented.

Reliability: Coefficient alpha was .95.

Validity: Correlations with other variables ranged from −.50 to .80.

Author: Schwab, R. E., et al.

Article: Educator burnout: Sources and consequences.

Journal: *Educational Research Quarterly*, 1985–1986, *10*(3), 14–30.

Related Research: House, R. J., & Mitchell, T. R. (1974). Path-goal theory of leadership. *Journal of Contemporary Business, 3,* 81–97. Vroom, V. H. (1959). Some personality determinants of the effect of participation. *Journal of Abnormal and Social Psychology, 59,* 322–327.

■ ■ ■

4177

Test Name: PAY SATISFACTION QUESTIONNAIRE

Purpose: To measure four aspects of compensation.

Number of Items: 18

Format: Includes four aspects of compensation: pay level, pay raises, pay structure-administration, and benefits. All items presented.

Reliability: Alpha coefficients ranged from .77 to .97.

Author: Scarpello, V., et al.

Article: Compensation satisfaction: Its measurement and dimensionality.

Journal: *Journal of Applied Psychology*, May 1988, *73*(2), 163–171.

Related Research: Heneman, H. G., & Schwab, D. P. (1985). Pay satisfaction: Its multidimensional nature and measurement. *International Journal of Psychology*, *20*, 129–141.

■ ■ ■

4178

Test Name: PAY SATISFACTION SCALE

Purpose: To measure pay satisfaction.

Number of Items: 4

Format: Responses are made on a 5-point agree–disagree Likert format. All items presented.

Reliability: Coefficient alpha was .88.

Validity: Correlations with other variables ranged from .06 to .50.

Author: Rice, R. W., et al.

Article: Multiple discrepancies and pay satisfaction.

Journal: *Journal of Applied Psychology*, August 1990, *75*(4), 386–393.

Related Research: Hackman, J. R., & Oldham, G. R. (1975). Development of the Job Diagnostic Survey. *Journal of Applied Psychology*, *60*, 159–170. Smith, P. C., et al (1969). *The measurement of satisfaction in work and retirement*. Chicago: Rand McNally.

■ ■ ■

4179

Test Name: PERCEIVED WORK ALTERNATIVES SCALE

Purpose: To assess employee beliefs about the availability of better work alternatives.

Number of Items: 8

Format: Responses are made on a 4-point scale ranging from 1 (*very unlikely*) to 4 (*very likely*). All items are presented.

Reliability: Coefficient alpha was .84.

Validity: Correlations with other variables ranged from .11 to −.49.

Author: Pond, S. B., III, and Geyer, P. D.

Article: Employee age as a moderator of the relation between perceived work alternatives and job satisfaction.

Journal: *Journal of Applied Psychology*, November 1987, *72*(4), 552–557.

■ ■ ■

4180

Test Name: PERCEIVED WORK LOAD SCALE

Purpose: To measure how busy and pressured workers perceive their jobs to be.

Number of Items: 4

Format: Seven-point rating scale.

Reliability: Alpha was .78.

Author: Kirmeyer, S. L., and Dougherty, T. W.

Article: Work load, tension, and coping: Moderating effects of supervisor support.

Journal: *Personnel Psychology*, Spring 1988, *41*(1), 125–139.

Related Research: Caplan, R. D., et al. (1975). Job demands and worker health (NIOSH Publication No. 75–100). Washington, DC: U. S. Department of Health, Education and Welfare.

■ ■ ■

4181

Test Name: PERSONAL STRAIN QUESTIONNAIRE

Purpose: To measure vocational, physical, interpersonal and psychological strain.

Number of Items: 40

Format: Likert format

Reliability: Alphas ranged from .71 to .89 across subscales.

Validity: Correlations with other variables ranged from .06 to .67.

Author: Osipow, S. H., and Davis, A. S.

Article: The relationship of coping resources to occupational stress and strain.

Journal: *Journal of Vocational Behavior*, February 1988, *32*(1), 1–15.

■ ■ ■

4182

Test Name: POLICE STRESS SURVEY

Purpose: To measure stress in police work.

Number of Items: 60

Format: Items were rated on 0–100-point response scales.

Reliability: Alpha was .97 (total); .95 and .94 for two subscales.

Validity: Correlations with job satisfaction measures ranged from −.42 to .67.

Author: Martelli, T., et al.

Article: The Police Stress Survey: Reliability and relation to job satisfaction and organizational commitment.

Journal: *Psychological Reports*, February 1989, *64*(1), 267–273.

Related Research: Spielberger, C. D., et al. (1981). *The Police Stress Survey: Sources of stress in law enforcement* (Monograph Series Three, No. 3). Tampa, FL: College of Social and Behavioral Science, University of South Florida.

■ ■ ■

4183

Test Name: PROFESSIONAL ROLE ORIENTATION SCALE FOR PHARMACISTS

Purpose: To measure the extent to which pharmacists believe that they should influence the distribution of drugs.

Number of Items: 10

Format: Five-point Likert format. All items presented.

Reliability: Alpha was .68.

Validity: Correlations with other variables ranged from −.04 to .05.

Author: Humphrys, P., and O'Brien, G. E.

Article: The relationship between skill utilization, professional orientation, and job satisfaction for pharmacists.

Journal: *Journal of Occupational Psychology*, December 1986, *59*(4), 315–326.

■ ■ ■

4184

Test Name: PROPENSITY TO LEAVE SCALE

Purpose: To assess a person's intention to leave the company after a specified period of time.

Number of Items: 4

Format: Responses are made on a 7-point scale ranging from 1 (*chance of quitting "terrible"*) to 7 (*chance of quitting "excellent"*).

Validity: Correlation with other variables ranged from −.59 to .48.

Author: Netemayer, R. G., et al.

Article: Analysis of role conflict and role ambiguity in a structural equations framework.

Journal: *Journal of Applied Psychology*, April 1990, *75*(2), 148–157.

Related Research: Bluedorn, A. C. (1982). A unified model of turnover from organizations. *Human Relations, 35*, 135–153.

■ ■ ■

4185

Test Name: PURDUE TEACHER OPIONNAIRE

Purpose: To measure reactions of teachers to their jobs.

Number of Items: 100

Format: Four-point agreement scales.

Reliability: Test–retest reliability ranged from .62 to .88.

Author: Schaer, B., and Trentham, L.

Article: Self-concept and job satisfaction: Correlations between two instruments.

Journal: *Psychological Reports*, June 1986, *58*(3), 951–956.

Related Research: Bentley, R. R., & Rempel, A. M. (1970). *Manual for the Purdue Teacher Opionnaire*. West Lafayette, IN: Purdue Research Foundation.

■ ■ ■

4186

Test Name: QUALITY OF TEACHER WORK LIFE SURVEY

Purpose: To measure satisfaction and stress.

Number of Items: 36

Format: Likert scales are used to rate each item.

Reliability: Alpha coefficients ranged from .46 to .91. Test–retest (1 year) reliability ranged from .52 to .74 ($N = 93$).

Validity: Correlations with other variables ranged from −.44 to .30.

Author: Pelsma, D. M., et al.

Article: The Quality of Teacher Work Life Survey: A measure of teacher stress and job satisfaction.

Journal: *Measurement and Evaluation in Counseling and Development*, January 1989, *21*(4), 165–176.

Related Research: Coates, T. J., & Thoreson, C. E. (1976). Teacher anxiety: A review with recommendations. *Review of Educational Research, 46*, 159–184. Kyraicou, C., & Sutcliffe, J. (1978).

Teacher stress: Prevalence, sources, and symptoms. *British Journal of Educational Psychology, 48*, 159–172.

■ ■ ■

4187

Test Name: QUALITY OF WORK LIFE MEASURE

Purpose: To assess quality of work life.

Number of Items: 9

Reliability: Coefficient was .77.

Validity: Correlations with other variables ranged from −.38 to .46.

Author: Caplan, R. D., et al.

Article: Job seeking, reemployment, and mental health: A randomized field experiment in coping with job loss.

Journal: *Journal of Applied Psychology*, October 1989, *74*(5), 759–769.

Related Research: Andrews, F. M., & Withey, S. B. (1976). Social indicators of well being: American's perceptions of life quality. New York; Plenum Press.

■ ■ ■

4188

Test Name: QUANTITATIVE WORK OVERLOAD SCALE

Purpose: To assess respondents' perceptions of having too much work to do.

Number of Items: 3

Format: Responses are made on a 5-point scale ranging from 1 (*strongly disagree*) to 5 (*strongly agree*). An example is presented.

Reliability: Coefficient alpha was .71

Validity: Correlations with other variables ranged from −.33 to .43.

Author: Frone, M. R., and McFarlin, D. B.

Article: Chronic occupational stressors, self-focused attention, and well being: Testing a cybernetic model of stress.

Journal: *Journal of Applied Psychology*, December 1989, *74*(6), 876–883.

Related Research: Seashore, S. E., et al. (1982). Observing and measuring organizational change: A guide to field practice. New York: Wiley.

■ ■ ■

4189

Test Name: ROLE PROBLEMS SCALE

Purpose: To measure strain in working relationships.

Number of Items: 5

Format: Four-point rating scales.

Reliability: Alphas ranged from .74 to .86.

Author: Yammarino, F. Y., and Dubinsky, A. J.

Article: Employee responses: Gender- or job-related differences?

Journal: *Journal of Vocational Behavior*, June 1988, *32*(3), 366–383.

Related Research: Dansereau, F. (1975). A vertical dyad linkage approach to leadership within formal organizations: A longitudinal investigation of the role-making process. *Organizational Behavior and Human Performance, 13*, 46–78.

■ ■ ■

4190

Test Name: SALARY EQUITY/SATISFACTION SCALE

Purpose: To measure perceived equity/satisfaction with salary after the disclosure.

Number of Items: 3

Format: Responses are made on three 10-point scales: 1 (*very unfavorably*) to 10 (*very favorably*); 1 (*strongly disagree*) to 10 (*agree*); and 1 (*very dissatisfied*) to 10 (*very satisfied*). All items are presented.

Reliability: Coefficient alpha was .86.

Validity: Correlations with other variables ranged from −.33 to .30.

Author: Manning, M. R., and Avolio, B. J.

Article: The impact of blatant pay disclosure in a university environment.

Journal: *Research in Higher Education*, 1985, *23*(2), 135–149.

■ ■ ■

4191

Test Name: SATISFACTION WITH MATERIAL REWARDS SCALE

Purpose: To measure satisfaction with pay and security.

Number of Items: 4

Format: Includes two subscales: satisfaction with pay and satisfaction with security. Examples are presented.

Reliability: Coefficient alpha was .85.

Validity: Correlations with other variables ranged from −.23 to .35.

Author: Puffer, S. M.

Article: Prosocial behavior, noncompliant behavior, and work performance among commission sales people.

Journal: *Journal of Applied Psychology*, November 1987, *72*(4), 615–621.

Related Research: Hackman, J. R., & Oldham, G. R. (1975). Development of the Job Diagnostic Survey. *Journal of Applied Psychology, 60*, 159–170.

■ ■ ■

4192

Test Name: SATISFACTION WITH PERFORMANCE APPRAISAL SCALE

Purpose: To measure employee satisfaction with performance appraisals.

Number of Items: 12

Format: Five-point scales with varying anchors. Sample items presented.

Reliability: Alphas ranged from .71 to .83.

Author: Waldman, D. A., et al.

Article: Leadership and outcomes of performance and appraisal processes.

Journal: *Journal of Occupational Psychology*, September 1987, *60*(3), 177–186.

Related Research: Einstein, W. O., & Waldman, D. A. (1984). In search of a satisfying appraisal system: The effects of individual personality characteristics and supervisory ratings. Presented at the meeting of the Academy of Management, Boston.

■ ■ ■

4193

Test Name: SEX-ROLE CONFLICT SCALE

Purpose: To measure sex-role conflict in the workplace.

Number of Items: 17

Format: Five-point Likert format.

Reliability: Alpha was .90.

Author: Koberg, C. S., and Chusmir, L. H.

Article: Relationships between sex-role conflict and work related variables: Gender and hierarchical differences.

Journal: *The Journal of Social Psychology*, December 1989, *129*(6), 779–791.

Related Research: Chusmir, L. H., et al. (1986). Development and validation of the sex-role conflict scale. *Journal of Applied Behavioral Science, 22*, 397–407.

■ ■ ■

4194

Test Name: SOMATIC COMPLAINTS SCALE

Purpose: To determine frequency of somatic complaints.

Number of Items: 17

Format: Subjects indicate the frequency of each complaint. An overall score is obtained by averaging the frequencies.

Reliability: Coefficient alpha was .87.

Validity: Correlations with other variables ranged from .19 to −.17.

Author: Ganster, D. C., et al.

Article: Role of social support in the experience of stress at work.

Journal: *Journal of Applied Psychology*, February 1986, *71*(1), 102–110.

■ ■ ■

4195

Test Name: SOMATIC COMPLAINTS SCALE

Purpose: To measure frequency of stressful events.

Number of Items: 10

Format: Asks how often a person experiences stressful events such as dizziness, trembling hands, loss of appetite, and sleeplessness.

Reliability: Coefficient alpha was .75.

Validity: Correlation with other variables ranged from −.12 to .46.

Author: Motowidlo, S. J., et al.

Article: Occupational stress: Its causes and consequences for job performance.

Journal: *Journal of Applied Psychology*, November 1986, *71*(4), 618–629.

Related Research: Caplan, R. D., et al. (1975). *Job demands and worker health.* Washington, DC: U. S. Department of Health, Education and Welfare.

■ ■ ■

4196

Test Name: STAGES OF CONCERN QUESTIONNAIRE

Purpose: To measure the stages of concern that teachers indicate when involved in the implementation of an innovation.

Number of Items: 35

Format: Responses are made on a Likert scale ranging from 0 to 7. An example is presented.

Reliability: Test–retest reliabilities ranged from .65 to .96. Internal consistency ranged from .80 to .93.

Author: Cicchelli, T., and Baecher, R.

Article: Microcomputers in the classroom: Focusing on teacher concerns.

Journal: *Educational Research Quarterly*, 1989, *13*(1), 37–46.

Related Research: James, R. K., & Hall, G. E. (1981). A study of the concerns of science teachers regarding an implementation of ISCS. *Journal of Research in Science Teaching*, *18*(6), 479–487.

■ ■ ■

4197

Test Name: STRESS AT WORK SCALE

Purpose: To measure chronic organizational stress.

Number of Items: 18

Format: All items presented, but response categories not reported.

Reliability: Cronbach's alpha was .91. Test–retest (1 month and 1 week, respectively) reliability ranged from .91 to .92.

Validity: Correlations with other variables ranged from −.13 to .52.

Author: Jenner, J. R.

Article: A measure of chronic organizational stress.

Journal: *Psychological Reports*, April 1986, *58*(2), 543–546.

Related Research: Adams, J. D. (1980). Understanding and managing

stress: A workbook in changing lifestyles (pp. 245–261). La Jolla, CA: University Association.

■ ■ ■

4198

Test Name: STRESS DIAGNOSTIC SURVEY

Purpose: To determine a resident assistant's stress resulting from the lack of clarity and confusion (ambiguity) as well as the incompatibility (conflict) of his or her role expectations.

Number of Items: 10

Format: Responses were made on a 7-point Likert scale ranging from 1 (*never*) to 7 (*always*). Half the items measure role ambiguity and half measure role conflict. Sample items are presented.

Reliability: Alpha coefficients were .86 (ambiguity) and .66 (conflict).

Validity: Correlations with other variables ranged from −.19 to .26 (ambiguity) and from −.21 to .27 (conflict).

Author: Deluga, R. J., and Winters, J. J., Jr.

Article: The impact of role ambiguity and conflict on resident assistants.

Journal: *Journal of College Student Development*, May 1990, *31*(3), 230–236.

Related Research: Ivancevich, J. M., & Matteson, M. T. (1980). *Stress and Work.* Glenview, IL: Scott, Foresman.

■ ■ ■

4199

Test Name: STRESS INTENSITY SCALE

Purpose: To measure the stress experienced by dental hygienists while on the job.

Number of Items: 31

Format: Five-point rating scales. Sample items presented.

Reliability: Alpha was .92.

Validity: Correlated .15 with the Brief Symptom Inventory.

Author: Lang, R. J., et al.

Article: Stress-related symptoms among dental hygienists.

Journal: *Psychological Reports*, June 1990, *66*(3)1, 715–722.

■ ■ ■

4200

Test Name: SUBJECTIVE STRESS SCALE

Purpose: To measure subjective stress.

Number of Items: 6

Format: Responses are made on a 5-point scale. Examples are presented.

Reliability: Coefficient alpha was .86.

Validity: Correlation with other variables ranged from −.11 to .46.

Author: Motowidlo, S. J., et al.

Article: Occupational stress: Its causes and consequences for job performance.

Journal: *Journal of Applied Psychology*, November 1986, *71*(4), 618–629.

■ ■ ■

4201

Test Name: TACTICS OF INFLUENCE SCALE

Purpose: To assess how employees influence superiors, co-workers and subordinates.

Number of Items: 58

Format: Five-point frequency of use scale for each of the 58 tactics.

Reliability: Alphas ranged from .54 to .59.

Author: Erez, M., et al.

Article: The two sides of the tactics of influence: Agent vs. target.

Journal: *Journal of Occupational Psychology*, March 1986, *59*(1), 25–39.

Related Research: Kipnis, D., et al. (1980). Intraorganizational influence tactics: Exploration in getting one's way. *Journal of Applied Psychology*, *65*, 440–452.

■ ■ ■

4202

Test Name: TASK SATISFACTION SCALE

Purpose: To measure task satisfaction.

Number of Items: 10

Format: Bipolar adjectives are employed. All bipolar adjectives are presented. Subjects respond on 7-point scales.

Reliability: Coefficient alpha was .97.

Author: Gardner, D. G.

Article: Activation theory and task design: An empirical test of several new predictions.

Journal: *Journal of Applied Psychology*, August 1986, *71*(3), 411–418.

Related Research: Stone, E. F. (1977). *Some personality correlates of perceptions of and reactions to task characteristics* (Paper No. 54). Institute for Research in the Behavioral, Economic, and Management Sciences, Purdue University.

■ ■ ■

4203

Test Name: TEACHER BURNOUT SCALE

Purpose: To measure whether school or teaching-induced stress is sufficient to make a teacher want to defect.

Number of Items: 7

Format: Five-point Likert format. Sample item presented.

Reliability: Alpha was .76.

Validity: Correlations with other variables ranged from −.49 to .50.

Author: Brissie, J. S., et al.

Article: Individual, situational contributions to burnout.

Journal: *Journal of Educational Research,* November/December 1988, *82*(2), 106–112.

■ ■ ■

4204

Test Name: TEACHER BURNOUT SCALE

Purpose: To measure public school teacher burnout.

Number of Items: 21

Format: Includes four factors: career satisfaction, perceived administrative support, coping with job-related stress, and attitudes toward students.

Reliability: Alpha coefficients ranged from .72 to .89. Test–retest reliability coefficients ranged from .56 to .82.

Validity: Correlations with teachers' reports ranged from .36 to .62. Correlations with the Maslach Burnout Inventory ranged from .39 to .72.

Author: Seidman, S. A., and Zager, J.

Article: The Teacher Burnout Scale.

Journal: *Educational Research Quarterly*, 1986–1987, *11*(1), 26–33.

■ ■ ■

4205

Test Name: TEACHER CONCERNS QUESTIONNAIRE

Purpose: To identify teachers' concerns about teaching.

Number of Items: 15

Format: Contains three subscales: self, task, and impact. Responses are made on a 5-point scale ranging from 1 (*not concerned*) to 5 (*extremely concerned*).

Reliability: Test–retest reliability coefficients were in the .70s. Alpha coefficients ranged from .67 to .83.

Author: Pigge, F. L., and Marso, R. N.

Article: A longitudinal assessment of affective impact of preservice training on prospective teachers.

Journal: *Journal of Experimental Education*, Summer 1990, *58*(4), 283–289.

Related Research: George, A. A. (1978). *Measuring self, task, and impact concerns: A manual for use of the teacher concerns questionnaire.* The Research and Development Center for Teacher Education, University of Texas at Austin.

■ ■ ■

4206

Test Name: TEACHER OCCUPATIONAL STRESS FACTOR QUESTIONNAIRE

Purpose: To describe potentially stressful perceptions or feelings specific to teaching.

Number of Items: 30

Format: Utilized a 5-point Likert scale.

Reliability: Coefficient alphas ranged from .80 to .91.

Validity: Correlations with other variables ranged from .00 to .55.

Author: Albertson, L. M., and Kagan, D. M.

Article: Occupational stress among teachers.

Journal: *Journal of Research and Development in Education*, Fall 1987, *21*(1), 69–75.

Related Research: Moracco, J., et al. (1982). The factorial validity of the Teacher Occupational Stress Factor Questionnaire. *Educational and Psychological Measurement, 42,* 275–283.

■ ■ ■

4207

Test Name: TEACHER STRESS INVENTORY

Purpose: To measure teacher stress.

Number of Items: 46

Format: Includes nine factors: role ambiguity, role overload, role conflict, nonparticipation, job satisfaction, management style, life satisfaction, task stress, and supervisory support. All items are presented.

Reliability: Alpha coefficients ranged from .68 to .86.

Author: Schutz, R. W., and Long, B. C.

Article: Confirmatory factory analysis, validation and revision of a teacher stress inventory.

Journal: *Educational and Psychological Measurement*, Summer 1988, *48*(2), 497–511.

Related Research: Pettegrew, L. S., & Wolf, G. E. (1982). Validating measures of teacher stress. *American Educational Research Journal, 19,* 373–396.

■ ■ ■

4208

Test Name: TEACHER STRESS INVENTORY

Purpose: To measure occupational stress in teachers of exceptional students.

Number of Items: 49 stressor/manifestation items plus 4 questions about general satisfaction and stress level.

Format: Includes six factors: personal/professional stressors, professional distress, discipline and motivation, emotional manifestations, biobehavioral manifestations, and physiological-fatigue manifestation. Responses are made on a 5-point Likert scale ranging from 1 (*no strength*) to 5 (*major strength*).

Reliability: Test–retest and split-half reliability estimates ranged from .89 to .95 for teachers.

Author: Vance, B., et al.

Article: Responses of laboratory school teachers to the teacher stress inventory.

Journal: *Journal of Perceptual and Motor Skills*, June 1989, *68*(3) Part 1, 939–944.

Related Research: Fimian, M. J. (1985). The development of an instrument to measure occupational stress in teachers of exceptional students. *Techniques: Journal for Remedial Education and Counseling, 1,* 270–285.

■ ■ ■

4209

Test Name: TEACHER STRESS INVENTORY—REVISED

Purpose: To measure teacher stress.

Number of Items: 36

Format: Includes seven factors: role ambiguity, role stress, organizational management, job satisfaction, life satisfaction, task stress, and supervisory support. All items are presented.

Reliability: Alpha coefficients ranged from .74 to .87.

Author: Schutz, R. W., and Long, B. C.

Article: Confirmatory factor analysis, validation, and revision of a teacher stress inventory.

Journal: *Educational and Psychological Measurement*, Summer 1988, *48*(2), 497–511.

Related Research: Pettegrew, L. S., & Wolf, G. E. (1982). Validating measures of teacher stress. *American Educational Research Journal, 19,* 373–396.

■ ■ ■

4210

Test Name: TEACHER STRESS MEASURE

Purpose: To assess stress levels on 14 variables.

Number of Items: 70

Format: Includes 14 variables.

Reliability: Alpha reliability coefficients ranged from .57 to .91.

Validity: Correlations with other variables ranged from .57 to .72.

Author: Bertoch, M. R.

Article: Reducing teacher stress.

Journal: *Journal of Experimental Education*, Winter 1989, *57*(2), 117–128.

Related Research: Pettegrew, L. S., & Wolf, G. E. (1982). Validing measures of teacher stress. *American Educational Research Journal*, *19* (3), 373–396.

■ ■ ■

4211

Test Name: TEACHING ANXIETY SCALE

Purpose: To measure teaching anxiety.

Number of Items: 29

Format: Responses are made on a 5-point scale ranging from 1 (*never*) to 5 (*always*).

Reliability: Test–retest coefficient of stability was .95. Alpha coefficients ranged from .87 to .94.

Validity: Correlations with other variables ranged from .24 to .62.

Author: Pigge, F. L., and Marso, R. N.

Article: A longitudinal assessment of affective impact of preservice training on prospective teachers.

Journal: *Journal of Experimental Education*, Summer 1990, *58*(4), 283–289.

Related Research: Parsons, J. J. (1973). *Assessment of anxiety about teaching using the Teacher Anxiety Scale: Manual and research report.* The Research and Development Center for Teacher Education, University of Texas at Austin.

■ ■ ■

4212

Test Name: TURNOVER INTENTIONS SCALE

Purpose: To measure intention to turnover.

Number of Items: 3

Format: Responses are made on a 7-point scale.

Reliability: Internal consistency was .87.

Validity: Correlations with other variables ranged from −.42 to .25.

Author: George, J. M.

Article: Mood and absence.

Journal: *Journal of Applied Psychology*, April 1989, *74*(2), 327–324.

Related Research: Cammann, C., et al. (1979). *The Michigan Organizational Assessment Questionnaire.* Unpublished manuscript, University of Michigan, Ann Arbor.

■ ■ ■

4213

Test Name: UNION SATISFACTION SCALE

Purpose: To assess the extent to which apprentices are satisfied with what the union provides.

Number of Items: 20

Reliability: Coefficient alpha was .91.

Validity: Correlations with other variables ranged from −.36 to .60.

Author: Latack, J. C., et al.

Article: Carpenter apprentices: Comparison of career transitions for men and women.

Journal: *Journal of Applied Psychology*, August 1987, *72*(3), 393–400.

Related Research: Hochner, A., et al. (1979). Thinking about democracy and participation in unions. In B. Dennis (Ed.), *Proceedings of the 32nd Annual Meeting of the Industrial Relations Research Association.* Atlanta, GA: Industrial Relations Research Association.

4214

Test Name: UNION SATISFACTION SCALE

Purpose: To assess union satisfaction.

Number of Items: 14

Format: Responses are made on a 5-point scale ranging from 1 (*very dissatisfied*) to 5 (*highly satisfied*).

Reliability: Coefficient alpha was .93.

Validity: Correlations with other variables ranged from −.16 to .79.

Author: Mellor, S.

Article: The relationship between membership decline and union commitment: A field study of local unions in crisis.

Journal: *Journal of Applied Psychology*, June 1990, *75*(3), 258–267.

Related Research: Stagner, R., & Eflal, B. (1982). Internal union dynamics during a strike: A quasi-experimental study. *Journal of Applied Psychology*, *67*, 37–44.

■ ■ ■

4215

Test Name: WITHDRAWAL COGNITIONS

Purpose: To measure the intention to quit one's job.

Number of Items: 3

Format: Seven-point likelihood scales.

Reliability: Alpha was .73.

Author: Blau, G. J.

Article: Locus of control as a potential moderator of the turnover process.

Journal: *Journal of Occupational Psychology*, March 1987, *60*(1), 21–29.

Related Research: Michaels, C., & Spector, P. (1982). Causes of employee turnover: A test of the Mobley, Griffeth, Hand and Meglino model. *Journal of Applied Psychology, 67,* 53–59.

■ ■ ■

4216

Test Name: WORKER OPINION SURVEY (WOS)

Purpose: To measure job satisfaction.

Number of Items: 48

Format: Four-point response categories. All items presented.

Validity: Confirmatory factor analysis revealed six correlated factors.

Author: Bell, R. C., and Weaver, J. R.

Article: The dimensionality and scaling of job satisfaction: An internal validation of the Worker Opinion Survey.

Journal: *Journal of Occupational Psychology,* June 1987, *60*(2), 147–155.

Related Research: Cross, D. (1973). The Worker Opinion Survey: A measure of shop-floor satisfaction. *Occupational Psychology, 47,* 193–208.

■ ■ ■

4217

Test Name: WORK EXPERIENCE SCALES

Purpose: To measure dimensions of work experience: confirmed expectations, job challenge, job satisfaction, commitment norm, organizational dependability, participation, peer cohesion, personal importance, role clarity, and self-expression.

Number of Items: 22

Format: Seven-point scales. Sample items presented.

Reliability: Alphas ranged from .53 to .91.

Author: Meyer, J. P., and Allen, N. J.

Article: Links between work experiences and organizational commitment during the first year of employment: A longitudinal analysis.

Journal: *Journal of Occupational Psychology,* September 1988, *60*(3), 195–209.

Related Research: Buchanan, B. (1974). Building organizational commitment: The socialization of managers in work organizations. *Administrative Science Quarterly, 19,* 533–546.

■ ■ ■

4218

Test Name: WORKLOAD SCALE

Purpose: To assess workload.

Format: Responses to each item were made on a 5-point scale from *less than once per month* to *several times per day.*

Reliability: Coefficient alpha was .85 ($N = 150$).

Validity: Correlations with other variables ranged from –.26 to .56 ($Ns = 148$–156).

Author: Spector, P. E., et al.

Article: Relation of job stressors to affective, health, and performance outcomes: A comparison of multiple data source.

Journal: *Journal of Applied Psychology,* February 1988, *73*(1), 11–19.

Related Research: Arsenault, A., & Dolan, S. (1983). The role of personality, occupation, and organization in understanding the relationships between job stress, performance and absenteeism. *Journal of Occupational Psychology, 56,* 227–240.
Caplan, R. D. (1971). *Organizational stress and individual strain: A social-psychological study of risk factors in coronary heart disease among administrators, engineers, and scientists.* (University Microfilms No. 72–14822). Ann Arbor: University of

Michigan, Institute for Social Research.
Payne, R., & Fletcher, B. C. (1983). Job demands, supports, and constraints as predictors of psychological strain among schoolteachers. *Journal of Vocational Behavior, 22,* 136–147.

■ ■ ■

4219

Test Name: WORK RELATED EMOTIONAL DISTRESS SCALE

Purpose: To assess the strength of negative emotional reaction to daily work experiences.

Number of Items: 6

Format: Responses are made on a 5-point scale ranging from 1 (*not at all*) to 5 (*extremely*).

Reliability: Coefficient alpha was .84.

Validity: Correlations with other variables ranged from –.51 to .53.

Author: Frone, M. R., and McFarlin, D. B.

Article: Chronic occupational stressors, self-focused attention, and well being: Testing a cybernetic model of stress.

Journal: *Journal of Applied Psychology,* December 1989, *74*(6), 876–883.

Related Research: Kandel, D. B., et al. (1985). The stressfulness of daily social roles for women: Marital, occupational, and household roles. *Journal of Health and Social Behavior, 26,* 64–78.

■ ■ ■

4220

Test Name: WORK-ROLE CENTRALITY SCALE

Purpose: To measure interest in work, importance of success at work, degree of concern about work, and identification with work.

Number of Items: 8

Format: 3-point response scales.

Reliability: Alpha was .58.

Author: Mannheim, B., and Angel, O.

Article: Pay systems and work-role centrality of industrial workers.

Journal: *Personnel Psychology*, Summer 1986, *39*(2), 359–378.

Related Research: Mannheim, B. (1975). A comparative study of work centrality, job rewards, and satisfaction. *Sociology of Work and Occupations, 2,* 79–101.

■ ■ ■

4221

Test Name: WORK SATISFACTION SCALE

Purpose: To measure work satisfaction.

Number of Items: 12

Format: Responses are made on a 5-point scale.

Reliability: Coefficient alpha was .77.

Validity: Correlations with other variables ranged from .15 to .64.

Author: Near, J. P., and Sorcinelli, M. D.

Article: Work and life away from work: Predictors of faculty satisfaction.

Journal: *Research in Higher Education*, 1986, *25*(4), 377–394.

Related Research: Quinn, R. P., & Shepard, L. J. (1974). The 1972–73 *Quality of Employment Study*. Ann Arbor: Institute for Social Research, University of Michigan.

4222

Test Name: WORK STRESS INVENTORY

Purpose: To assess stress.

Number of Items: 40

Format: Items are rated on a 5-point scale. Includes items pertaining to organizational stress and job risk.

Reliability: Test–retest reliabilities ranged from .83 to .91.

Validity: Correlations with other variables ranged from −.57 to .85.

Author: Barone, D. F., et al.

Article: The Work Stress Inventory: Organizational stress and job risk.

Journal: *Educational and Psychological Measurement*, Spring 1988, *48*(1), 141–154.

CHAPTER 6
Aptitude

4223

Test Name: CANADIAN READINESS TEST

Purpose: To predict reading and mathematics achievement for first-grade children.

Number of Items: 117

Time Required: 30–45 minutes.

Format: Various visual task formats used on seven subscales.

Reliability: Kuder-Richardson coefficients ranged from .75 to .95 across subscales.

Author: Ollilia, L. O., et al.

Article: Predicting first-grade students writing achievement using the Canadian Readiness Test and selected measures of cognitive development.

Journal: *Journal of Educational Research*, September–October 1986, *80*(1), 47–52.

Related Research: Canadian Readiness Test. (1975). Victoria, B. C.: University of Victoria.

■■■

4224

Test Name: COMPUTER APTITUDE SCALE-REVISED

Purpose: To assess the likelihood of success in computer science courses.

Number of Items: 18

Format: Includes four subscales: sequence, logic, simulation, and word problems.

Reliability: Coefficient alphas ranged from .67 to .76.

Author: Dambrot, F. H., et al.

Article: Psychology of computer use: II. Sex differences in prediction of course grades in a computer language course.

Journal: *Perceptual and Motor Skills*, April 1988, *66*(2), 627–636.

Related Research: Dambrot, F. H., et al. (1985). Correlates of sex differences in attitudes toward and involvement with computers. *Journal of Vocational Behavior*, *27*, 71–86.

■■■

4225

Test Name: COMPUTER APTITUDE SCALE

Purpose: To assess the likelihood of success in computer science courses.

Number of Items: 25

Reliability: Kuder-Richardson reliability was .76.

Validity: Predictive validity was .56.

Author: Danbrot, F. H., et al.

Article: Psychology of computer use: II. Sex differences in prediction of course grades in a computer language course.

Journal: *Perceptual and Motor Skills*, April 1988, *66*(2), 627–636.

Related Research: Konvalina, J., et al. (1983). Math proficiency: Key to success for computer science students. *Communications of the ACM*, *26*, 377–382.

■■■

4226

Test Name: FIGURAL INTERSECTIONS TEST

Purpose: To measure mental capacity.

Number of Items: 36

Format: Subjects are required to locate the one area of intersection of a number of geometric shapes.

Validity: Correlations with other variables ranged from .30 to .76 ($N = 162$).

Author: Johnson, J., and Pascual-Leone, J.

Article: Developmental levels of processing in metaphor interpretation.

Journal: *Journal of Experimental Child Psychology*, August 1989, *48*(1), 1–31.

Related Research: Pascual-Leone, J., & Ijaz, H. (1988). Mental capacity testing as a form of intellectual–developmental assessment. In R. Samuda, et al. (Eds.), *Assessment and placement of minority students*. Toronto: C. J. Hogrefe.

■■■

4227

Test Name: INDIVIDUAL READING READINESS INVENTORY

Purpose: To predict the extent to which children would profit from formal reading instruction in kindergarten.

Format: Includes six subtests: visual skills, auditory skills, visual-motor coordination, oral language, concept development, and readiness for books.

Reliability: Coefficient alphas ranged from .09 to .91 ($N = 113$).

Validity: Correlation with the Metropolitan Achievement Test was .49.

Author: Gold, S.

Article: Predicting reading achievement using an individual reading readiness inventory.

Journal: *Child Study Journal*, 1987, *17*(2), 97–103.

Related Research: Mangrum, C. T., & Forgan, H. W. (1979). *Developing competencies in teaching reading.* Columbus, OH: Charles E. Merrill.

4228

Test Name: NONCOGNITIVE QUESTIONNAIRE

Purpose: To measure seven noncognitive variables for prediction academic success.

Number of Items: 23

Format: Includes 2 nominal items, 18 Likert-type items, and 3 open-ended questions. The instrument measures seven noncognitive variables.

Reliability: Test–retest reliability coefficients ranged from .70 to .94. Interjudge agreement on open-ended items ranged from .83 to 1.00.

Author: O'Callaghan, K. W., and Bryant, C.

Article: Noncognitive variables: A key to Black American academic success at a military academy?

Journal: *Journal of College Student Development*, March 1990, *31*(2), 121–126.

Related Research: Tracey, T. J., & Sedlacek, W. E. (1984). Noncognitive variables in predicting academic success by race. *Measurement and Evaluation in Guidance, 16*, 171–176.

CHAPTER 7
Attitude

4229

Test Name: ABORTION ATTITUDE SCALE

Purpose: To measure abortion attitude.

Number of Items: 6

Format: Yes–no. All items presented.

Reliability: Alpha was .90.

Validity: Breslau, N.

Author: Abortion of defective fetuses: Attitudes of mothers of congenitally impaired children.

Article: *Journal of Marriage and the Family*, November 1987, *48*(4), 839–845.

Journal: Granberg, D., & Granberg, B. (1980). Abortion attitude, 1965–1980: Trends and determinants. *Family Planning Perspectives, 12,* 250–261.

. . .

4230

Test Name: ABSENCE ATTITUDE SCALE

Purpose: To measure attitude toward absence from work.

Number of Items: 5

Format: Responses are made on a 3-point Likert scale ranging from 1 (*not important*) to 3 (*very important*). Sample items are presented.

Reliability: Coefficient alpha was .76.

Validity: Correlations with other variables ranged from –.33 to .45 (*N* = 193).

Author: Baba, V. V.

Article: Methodological issues in modeling absence: A comparison of least squares and Tobit analyses.

Journal: *Journal of Applied Psychology*, August 1990, *75*(4), 428–432.

. . .

4231

Test Name: ACADEMIC ADJUSTMENT SCALE

Purpose: To measure attitudes toward academic goals and requirements, academic self-sufficiency, and application to studies.

Number of Items: 18

Format: Nine-point rating scales.

Reliability: Alphas ranged from .82 to .88.

Author: Lopez, F. G.

Article: Current family dynamics, trait anxiety, and academic adjustment: Test of a family-based model of vocational identity.

Journal: *Journal of Vocational Behavior*, August 1989, *35*(1), 76–87.

Related Research: Baker, R. W., & Siryk, B. (1984). Measuring adjustment to college. *Journal of Counseling Psychology, 31,* 179–189.

. . .

4232

Test Name: ADULT SURVEY OF READING ATTITUDES—REVISED

Purpose: To assess the reading attitudes of adults.

Number of Items: 40

Format: Includes five factors: reading activity and enjoyment, social reinforcement, reading modes, reading anxiety and difficulty, and reading assistance.

Reliability: Cronbach's alpha was .93. Split-half corrected correlation was .93. Test–retest (6 weeks) reliability was .87.

Validity: Correlations with other variables ranged from .24 to .43.

Author: Smith, M. C.

Article: The development and use of an instrument for assessing adults' attitudes toward reading.

Journal: *Journal of Research and Development in Education*, Spring 1990, *23*(3), 156–161.

Related Research: Wallbrown, F. H., et al. (1981). Sex differences in reading attitudes. *Reading Improvement, 18,* 226–234.

. . .

4233

Test Name: AIDS AND HOMOSEXUALITY ATTITUDE SCALE

Purpose: To measure attitudes about homosexuality and about AIDS.

Number of Items: 18

Format: Five-point Likert format. Sample items presented.

Reliability: Alpha was .86. Split-half correlation was .83.

Author: Austin, D., et al.

Article: Some determinants of fear about AIDS among Australian college students.

Journal: *Psychological Reports*, June 1987, *63*(4, Part II), 1239–1244.

Related Research: Royce, D., et al. (1987). Undergraduate and graduate students' attitudes towards AIDS. *Psychological Reports*, *60*, 1185–1186.
Larsen, K. S., et al. (1980). Attitudes of heterosexuals toward homosexuality: A Likert-type scale and construct validity. *Journal of Sex Research*, *16*, 245–257.

■ ■ ■

4234

Test Name: ATTITUDE FUNCTIONS INVENTORY

Purpose: To measure attitude functions by matching a target attitude with experimental/schematic, social-expressive, defensive, and value-expressive endings.

Number of Items: 10

Format: All items presented and explained for a sample target.

Reliability: Alphas ranged from .41 to .87.

Validity: Correlations with other variables ranged from .25 to .40.

Author: Herek, G. M.

Article: Can functions be measured? A new perspective on the functional approach to attitudes.

Journal: *Social Psychology Quarterly*, December 1987, *50*(4), 285–303.

■ ■ ■

4235

Test Name: ATTITUDES ABOUT REALITY SCALE

Purpose: To measure implicit causal assumptions about the relationship between persons and their physical and social reality.

Number of Items: 40

Format: Includes three factors: societal determinism, individual determinism, and variable determinism. Degree of agreement or disagreement is made on a 7-point Likert scale for each item. Several items are presented.

Reliability: Alpha coefficients ranged from .50 to .69.

Validity: Correlations with the other variables ranged from −.22 to .19.

Author: Jackson, L. A., and Jeffers, D. L.

Article: The attitudes about reality scale: A new measure of personal epistemology.

Journal: *The Journal of Personality Assessment*, Summer 1989, *53*(2), 353–365.

Related Research: Unger, R. K., et al. (1986). Personal epistemology and personal experience. *Journal of Social Issues*, *42*, 67–79.

■ ■ ■

4236

Test Name: ATTITUDES TOWARD AIDS VICTIMS SCALE

Purpose: To measure attitudes towards AIDS victims.

Number of Items: 20

Format: All items presented. Response format not specified.

Reliability: Alpha was .91. Split-half correlation was .87.

Validity: Correlations with authoritarianism and dogmatism were small but statistically significant (.17 and .20, respectively).

Author: Larson, K. S., et al.

Article: Authoritarianism and attitudes toward AIDS victims.

Journal: *The Journal of Social Psychology*, February 1990, *130*(1), 77–80.

Related Research: Larson, K. S., et al. (1988). *Acquired Immune Deficiency Syndrome (AIDS):* International attitudinal comparisons. Corvallis: Oregan State University, Department of Psychology.

4237

Test Name: ATTITUDE TOWARD COMPUTER USAGE SCALE (REVISED)

Purpose: To measure attitudes toward computers and computerized machinery.

Number of Items: 20

Format: Employs a 7-point Likert scale.

Reliability: Coefficient alpha was .84.

Validity: Correlations with other variables ranged from .06 to .79.

Author: Zakrajsek, T. D., et al.

Article: Convergent validity of scales measuring computer related attitudes.

Journal: *Educational and Psychological Measurement*, Summer 1990, *50*(2), 343–349.

Related Research: Popovich, P. M., et al. (1985). The development of the Attitude Toward Computer Usage Scale. *Educational and Psychological Measurement,45*, 261–269.

■ ■ ■

4238

Test Name: ATTITUDES TOWARD CONTROVERSY SCALE

Purpose: To measure liking of controversy in group settings.

Number of Items: 5

Format: Five-point Likert format.

Reliability: Alpha was .94.

Author: Smith, K. A., et al.

Article: The effects of controversy and concurrence seeking on effective decision making.

Journal: *The Journal of Social Psychology*, April 1986, *126*(2), 237–248.

Related Research: Johnson, D. W., et al. (1978). The effects of cooperative and individualized instruction on student attitudes and achievement. *Journal of Social Psychology, 104*, 207–216.

4239

Test Name: ATTITUDES TOWARD FEMINISM SCALE

Purpose: To measure college women's subjective reactions to feminist ideology and the women's movement.

Number of Items: 32

Format: Includes 22 masking items, 9 Thurstone attitudinal scale items, and 1 item to assess participants' subjective identification with feminism. Responses were made on a 5-point scale from 1 (*strongly disagree*) to 5 (*strongly agree*).

Reliability: Test–retest (2 weeks) reliability was .81.

Validity: Correlations with other variables ranged from .38 to .68.

Author: Enns, C. Z., and Hackett, G.

Article: Comparison of feminist and nonfeminist women's reactions to variants of nonsexist and feminist counseling.

Journal: *Journal of Counseling Psychology*, January 1990, *37*(1), 33–40.

Related Research: Fassinger, R. E. (1985). *Development of the Attitudes Toward Feminism Scale*. Unpublished manuscript, Ohio State University, Columbus.

■ ■ ■

4240

Test Name: ATTITUDES TOWARD FINANCIAL ACCOUNTING

Purpose: To measure attitudes toward financial accounting.

Number of Items: 36

Format: Contains three subscales. Responses are made on a 5-point Likert scale ranging from *strongly agree* to *strongly disagree*.

Reliability: Coefficient alpha was .92.

Validity: Correlations with performance ranges from .15 to .41.

Author: Geiger, M. A.

Article: Discriminating levels of development through attitudes: An empirical analysis.

Journal: *Educational and Psychological Measurement*, Autumn 1988, *48*(3), 763–771.

■ ■ ■

4241

Test Name: ATTITUDES TOWARD HOMOSEXUALITY SCALE

Purpose: To assess attitudes toward homosexuality.

Number of Items: 28

Format: Likert-type format.

Reliability: Internal consistency reliability was .93.

Author: Fennell, R.

Article: The impact of a credit course on AIDS at the collegiate level.

Journal: *Journal of College Student Development*, September 1990, *31*(5), 467–469.

Related Research: MacDonald, A. P., Jr., et al. (1973). Attitudes towards homosexuality: Preservation of sex morality or the double standard. *Journal of Consulting and Clincial Psychology*, *40*, 155–166.

■ ■ ■

4242

Test Name: ATTITUDES TOWARD LESBIANS AND GAY MEN SCALE—REVISED

Purpose: To assess attitudes toward lesbians and gay men.

Number of Items: 10

Format: Responses are answered on a 9-point Likert format. All items are presented.

Validity: Correlations with other variables ranged from −.44 to .45.

Author: D'Angelli, A. R., and Rose, M. L.

Article: Homophobia in a university community: Attitudes and experiences of heterosexual freshmen.

Journal: *Journal of College Student Development*, November 1990, *31*(6), 484–491.

Related Research: Herek, G. M. (1988). Heterosexuals' attitudes toward lesbians and gay men: Correlates and gender differences. *Journal of Sex Research*, *25*, 451–477.

■ ■ ■

4243

Test Name: ATTITUDES TOWARD MALE NURSES SURVEY

Purpose: To measure attitudes toward male nurses.

Number of Items: 21

Format: True–false format.

Reliability: Kuder-Richardson formula was .86.

Author: LaRoche, E. J., and Livneh, H.

Article: The factorial structure of American attitudes toward male nurses.

Journal: *The Journal of Social Psychology*, October 1986, *126*(5), 679–680.

Related Research: LaRoche, E., & Livneh, H. (1983). Regressional analysis of attitudes toward male nurses. *Journal of Psychology*, *113*, 67–71.

■ ■ ■

4244

Test Name: ATTITUDES TOWARD MARRIAGE SCALE

Purpose: To measure attitudes toward marriage.

Number of Items: 14

Format: Five-point Likert format.

Reliability: Alpha was .92.

Author: Kinnaird, K. L., and Garrard, M.

Article: Premarital sexual behavior and attitudes toward marriage and divorce among young women as a function of their mother's marital status.

Journal: *Journal of Marriage and the Family*, November 1986, *48*(4), 757–765.

Related Research: Wallin, P. (1954). Marital happiness of parents and their children's attitude toward marriage. *American Sociological Review*, *19*, 20–23.

■ ■ ■

4245

Test Name: ATTITUDES TOWARD MEN SCALE

Purpose: To measure attitudes toward men's roles in contemporary society.

Number of Items: 34

Format: Responses to each item are made on a 4-point scale ranging from 1 (*strongly agree*) to 4 (*strongly disagree*).

Reliability: Test–retest (2 weeks) reliabilities were .94 (men) and .90 (women). Alpha coefficients ranged from .84 to .90.

Validity: Correlations with other variables ranged from .57 to .84.

Author: Good, G. E., et al.

Article: Male role and gender role conflict: Relations to help-seeking in men.

Journal: *Journal of Counseling Psychology*, July 1989, *36*(3), 295–300.

Related Research: Downs, A. C., & Engleson, S. A. (1982). The Attitudes Toward Men Scale: An analysis of the role and status of men and masculinity. *JASA: Catalog of Selected Documents in Psychology*, *12*, 45 (Ms. No. 2503).

■ ■ ■

4246

Test Name: ATTITUDES TOWARD RAPE QUESTIONNAIRE

Purpose: To reflect societal attitudes toward rape.

Number of Items: 25

Format: Responses to each item are made on a 6-point Likert scale ranging from 1 (*strongly agree*) to 6 (*strongly disagree*). Examples are presented.

Reliability: Mean estimated reliability was .62.

Validity: Correlation with Rape Empathy Scale was .64.

Author: Borden, L. A., et al.

Article: Effects of a university rape prevention program on attitudes and empathy toward rape.

Journal: *Journal of College Student Development*, March 1988, *29*(2), 132–136.

Related Research: Thornton, B., et al. (1982). The relationships of observer characteristics to beliefs in the causal responsibility of victims of sexual assault. *Human Relations*, *35*, 321–330.

■ ■ ■

4247

Test Name: ATTITUDES TOWARD SEEKING PROFESSIONAL PSYCHOLOGICAL HELP REVISED

Purpose: To measure attitudes toward seeking psychological help.

Number of Items: 29

Format: Responses to each statement were made on a 4-point scale ranging from 0 (*agree*) to 3 (*disagree*).

Reliability: Test–retest (2 weeks) reliability was .89. Test–retest (8 weeks) reliability was .84. Internal consistency was .83 and .84.

Author: Good, G. E., et al.

Article: Male role and gender role conflict: Relations to help-seeking in men.

Journal: *Journal of Counseling Psychology*, July 1989, *36*(3), 295–300.

Related Research: Fischer, E. H., & Turner, J. L. (1970). Orientation to seeking professional psychological help: Development and research utility of an attitude scale. *Journal of Consulting and Clinical Psychology*, *35*, 79–90.

■ ■ ■

4248

Test Name: ATTITUDES TOWARD SEX ROLE SCALE

Purpose: To measure responses to statements about appropriate sex role behavior.

Number of Items: 35

Format: Includes five subscales: woman as partner, woman as ingenue, woman as homemaker, woman as competitor, and woman as knower. Responses are made on a 7-point scale ranging from 1 (*disagree very strongly*) to 7 (*agree very strongly*).

Reliability: Internal consistency coefficients ranged from .85 to .93. Test–retest (2 weeks) stability coefficient was .86 (*N* = 42).

Author: Glidden, C. E., and Tracey, T. J.

Article: Women's perceptions of personal versus sociocultural counseling interventions.

Journal: *Journal of Counseling Psychology*, January 1989, *36*(1), 54–62.

Related Research: Hawley, P. (1977). *Attitudes toward sex roles*. Unpublished manuscript, San Diego State University, San Diego, CA.

■ ■ ■

4249

Test Name: ATTITUDES TOWARD STATISTICS

Purpose: To measure attitudes toward statistics.

Number of Items: 29

Format: Five-point Likert scoring is used.

Reliability: Alpha reliability was .91.

Validity: Correlations with other variables ranged from −.11 to .88.

Author: Roberts, D. M., and Reese, C. M.

Article: A comparison of two scales measuring attitudes toward statistics.

Journal: *Educational and Psychological Measurement*, Autumn 1987, *47*(3), 759–764.

Related Research: Wise, S. L. (1985). The development and validation of a scale measuring attitudes toward statistics. *Educational and Psychological Measurement*, *45*, 401–405.

■ ■ ■

4250

Test Name: ATTITUDES TOWARDS THE GRIEVANCE SYSTEM

Purpose: To measure the fairness of a grievance system.

Number of Items: 15

Format: Five-point Likert format. Sample items presented.

Reliability: Alphas ranged from .66 to .74.

Author: Gordon, M. E., and Bowlby, R. A.

Article: Propositions about grievance settlements: Finally, consultation with grievants.

Journal: *Personnel Psychology*, Spring 1987, *41*(1), 107–123.

Related Research: Folger, R., & Greenberg, J. (1985). Procedural justice: An interpretive analysis of personnel systems. In K. M. Rowland & G. R. Ferris (Eds.), *Research in personnel and human resources management* (Vol. 3, pp. 141–183). Greenwich, CT: JAI Press.

■ ■ ■

4251

Test Name: ATTITUDES TOWARDS WOMEN SCALE—SHORT FORM

Purpose: To determine attitudes toward rights and roles appropriate for women in vocational, educational, intellectual, and social areas.

Number of Items: 25

Format: Responses are made on a 4-point scale from *agree strongly* to *disagree strongly*.

Reliability: Coefficient alpha reliabilities were .82 or higher.

Author: Greeley, A. T., and Tinsley, H. E. A.

Article: Autonomy and intimacy development in college students: Sex differences and predictors.

Journal: *Journal of College Student Development*, November 1988, *29*(6), 512–520.

Related Research: Spence, J. T., et al. (1973). A short version of the Attitudes Toward Women Scale. Bulletin of the *Psychonomic Society*, *2*, 219–220.

■ ■ ■

4252

Test Name: ATTITUDES TOWARD WOMEN SCALE

Purpose: To measure attitudes toward the rights and roles of women in contemporary society.

Number of Items: 55

Format: Includes six content areas: vocational, educational and intellectual roles; freedom and independence; dating, courtship, and etiquette; drinking, swearing, and dirty jokes; sexual behavior; and marital relationships and obligations. Responses are made on a 4-point scale ranging from *agree strongly* to *disagree strongly*.

Reliability: Internal reliability ranged from .92 to .93. Test–retest reliability ranged from .89 to .95.

Author: McEwen, M. K.

Article: Biographical correlates of student leaders' attitudes toward women.

Journal: *Journal of College Student Development*, November 1990, *31*(6), 500–508.

Related Research: Spence, J. T., & Helmreich, R. L. (1972). The attitudes toward women scale: An objective instrument to measure attitudes toward the rights and roles of women in contemporary society. *JSAS Catalog of Selected Documents in Psychology*, *2*, 66.

■ ■ ■

4253

Test Name: ATTITUDES TOWARD WOMEN CARPENTERS SCALE

Purpose: To measure attitudes toward women's nontraditional role as carpenters.

Number of Items: 21

Format: Adopted from Women as Managers Scale to apply to job of carpenter.

Reliability: Coefficient alpha was .92.

Author: Latack, J. C., et al.

Article: Carpenter apprentices: Comparison of career transitions for men and women.

Journal: *Journal of Applied Psychology*, August 1987, *72*(3), 393–400.

Related Research: Peters, L. H., et al. (1974). Women as Managers Scale (WAMS): A measure of attitudes toward women in management positions. *JSAS Catalog of Selected Documents in Psychology*, *4*, 24 (Ms. No. 585).

■ ■ ■

4254

Test Name: ATTITUDES TOWARD WOMEN SCALES

Purpose: To measure contemporary attitudes toward women.

Number of Items: 15-, 25-, and 55-item versions.

Format: Positive items are scored from 0 (*most traditional, conservative* *attitude*) to 3 (*most liberal, profeminist attitude*). For negative items, scoring is reversed. The higher the score, the more liberal the attitudes.

Reliability: Cronbach's alphas ranged from .85 to .92; Spearman-Brown split-half reliability ranged form .83 to .93.

Author: Daugherty, C. G., and Dambrot, F. H.

Article: Reliability of the Attitudes Toward Women Scale.

Journal: *Educational and Psychological Measurement*, Summer 1986, *46*(2), 449–453.

Related Research: Spence, J. T., & Helmreich, R. L. (1978). *Masculinity and femininity: Their psychological dimensions, correlates, and antecedents.* Austin, TX: University of Texas Press.

■ ■ ■

4255

Test Name: ATTITUDES TOWARD WOMEN SCALE

Purpose: To enable parents to rate their sex-role attitudes.

Number of Items: 15

Format: Responses are made on a 4-point scale. A sample is presented.

Reliability: Alpha coefficients were .87 (fathers) and .85 (mothers).

Author: McHale, S. M., et al.

Article: Children's housework and psychosocial functioning: The mediating effects of parents' sex-role behaviors and attitudes.

Journal: *Child Development*, October 1990, *61*(5), 1413–1426.

Related Research: Spence, J., & Helmreich, R. (1972). The attitudes toward women scale: An objective instrument to measure attitudes toward the rights and roles of women in contemporary society. *JSAS Catalog of Selected Documents in Psychology*, 2, 66 (Mss. No. 153).

4256

Test Name: ATTITUDES TOWARD WOMEN SCALE

Purpose: To measure traditionality of respondents' attitudes toward women and sex roles.

Number of Items: 55

Format: Level of agreement with each item is recorded on a 4-point scale. An example is presented.

Reliability: Test–retest (2 weeks) reliability coefficient was .94. Cronbach's alpha was .91.

Author: Muehlenhard, C. L., and Linton, M. A.

Article: Date rape and sexual aggression in dating situations: Incidence and risk factors.

Journal: *Journal of Counseling Psychology*, April 1987, *34*(2), 186–196.

Related Research: Muehlenhard, C. L., & Scardino, T. J. (1985). What will he think? Men's impressions of women who initiate dates and achieve academically. *Journal of Counseling Psychology*, 32, 560–569.

■ ■ ■

4257

Test Name: ATTITUDES TOWARD WOMEN SCALE—SHORT FORM

Purpose: To measure attitudes about the societal rights and roles of women.

Number of Items: 25

Format: Responses are made on a 4-point scale ranging from *agree strongly* to *disagree strongly*.

Reliability: Alpha coefficients were .82 and .89.

Author: Foss, C. J., and Slaney, R. B.

Article: Increasing nontraditional career choices in women: Relation of attitudes toward women and responses to a career intervention.

Journal: *Journal of Vocational Behavior*, June 1986, *28*(3), 191–202.

Related Research: Spence, J. T., et al. (1973). A short version of the Attitudes Toward Women Scale. *Bulletin of the Psychonomic Society*, 2, 219–220.

■ ■ ■

4258

Test Name: ATTITUDES TOWARD WOMEN SCALE—SHORT FORM

Purpose: To measure attitudes about societal rights and roles of women.

Number of Items: 25

Format: Four-point agreement scales.

Reliability: Alphas ranged from .82 to .89.

Validity: Correlation with long form was .97.

Author: Foss, C. J., and Slaney, R. B.

Article: Increasing nontraditional career choices in women: Relation of attitudes toward women and responses to career intervention.

Journal: *Journal of Vocational Behavior*, June 1986, *28*(3), 191–202.

Related Research: Spence, J. T., et al. (1973). A short version of the attitudes toward women scale. *Bulletin of the Psychonomic Society*, 2, 219–220.

■ ■ ■

4259

Test Name: ATTITUDES TOWARD CHRISTIANITY SCALE

Purpose: To measure attitudes toward Christianity.

Number of Items: 24

Format: Likert format.

Reliability: Alpha was .86.

Author: Francis, L. J., and McCarron, M. M.

Article: Measurement of attitudes toward Christianity among Nigerian secondary students.

Journal: *The Journal of Social Psychology*, August 1989, *129*(4), 569–571.

Related Research: Francis, L. J. (1978). Attitude and longitude: A study in measurement. *Character Potential, 8,* 119–130.

■ ■ ■

4260

Test Name: ATTITUDES TOWARD WOMEN SCALE FOR ADOLESCENTS

Purpose: To measure sex role attitudes, or the extent to which the adolescent approves of the gender-based division of roles.

Number of Items: 12

Format: Responses are made on a 4-point scale ranging from *agree strongly* to *disagree strongly.* An example is presented.

Validity: Correlation with other variables ranged from −.08 to .20.

Author: Galambos, N. L., et al.

Article: Masculinity, femininity, and sex role attitudes in early adolescence: Exploring gender intensification.

Journal: *Child Development,* December 1990, *61*(6), 1905–1914.

Related Research: Galambos, N. L., et al. (1985). The Attitudes Toward Women Scale for adolescents (AWSA): A study of reliability and validity. *Sex Roles, 13,* 343–356.

■ ■ ■

4261

Test Name: ATTITUDE TOWARD ACADEMIC ACCELERATION OF THE GIFTED SCALE

Purpose: To rate the extent of agreement with presumed effects of acceleration.

Number of Items: 22

Format: Likert format. Scale includes four dimensions: academic adjustment, social development, emotional adjustment both in school and later in life, and inhibition in the development of leadership. All items are presented.

Reliability: Cronbach's alpha was .94.

Author: Southern, W. T., et al.

Article: Practitioner objections to the academic acceleration of gifted children.

Journal: *Gifted Child Quarterly,* Winter 1989, *33*(1), 29–35.

Related Research: Uphoff, J. K., & Gilmore, J. (1987). Pupil age and school entrance—How many are ready for success? *Dimensions, 8*(7), 3–5.

■ ■ ■

4262

Test Name: ATTITUDE TOWARD FULL-SERVICE RESTAURANTS SCALE

Purpose: To measure attitudes towards full-service restaurants.

Number of Items: 22

Format: From 4 to 10 minutes.

Reliability: Thrustone format.

Validity: Odd–even reliability was .80. Parallel forms reliability was .88.

Article: Bleumenfeld, W. S., et al.

Journal: Development of parallel forms of a generalized scale of attitudes toward full-service restaurants.

Related Research: *Psychological Reports,* April 1986, *58*(2), 605–606.

■ ■ ■

4263

Test Name: ATTITUDE TOWARD HUMAN RESOURCE MANAGEMENT INNOVATION

Purpose: To measure attitudes toward innovation in HRM.

Number of Items: 10

Format: Five-point Likert format.

Reliability: Reliabilities ranged from .72 to .88 across subscales.

Author: Kossek, E. E.

Article: The acceptance of human resource innovation by multiple constituencies.

Journal: *Personnel Psychology,* Summer 1989, *42*(2), 263–281.

Related Research: Kossek, E. E. (1987). Human resources management innovation. *Human Resource Management, 26,* 71–92.

■ ■ ■

4264

Test Name: ATTITUDE TOWARD LOVE SCALE

Purpose: To measure attitude toward love along the romantic–compassionate love continuum.

Number of Items: 29

Format: All items reflect a romantic attitude toward love. Examples are presented.

Reliability: Test–retest correlation was .78.

Validity: Correlations with other variables ranged from −.31 to .34.

Author: Sperling, M. B.

Article: Ego identity and desperate love.

Journal: *Journal of Personality Assessment,* Winter 1987, *51*(4), 600–605.

Related Research: Knox, D. H., & Sporakowski, M. J. (1968). Attitude of college students toward love. *Journal of Marriage and the Family, 30*(4), 638–642.

■ ■ ■

4265

Test Name: ATTITUDE TOWARD MANAGING WORK AND CHILD CARE

Purpose: To measure attitudes about managing child care and work.

Number of Items: 8

Format: Five-point Likert format. Sample items presented.

Reliability: Alpha was .82.

Author: Kossek, E. E.

Article: Diversity in child care assistance needs: Employee problems, preferences and work-related outcomes.

Journal: *Personnel Psychology*, Winter 1990, *43*(4), 769–791.

Related Research: Kopelman, R. E., et al. (1983). A model of work, family and interrole conflict: A construct validity study. *Organizational Behavior and Human Performance*, *32*, 198–215.

■ ■ ■

4266

Test Name: ATTITUDE TOWARD SCHOOL SCALE

Purpose: To measure affective and cognitive dimensions of school attitude.

Number of Items: 35

Format: Five-point Likert format. Sample items presented.

Reliability: Thetas were .75 or greater.

Author: Margoribanks, K.

Article: Ability and attitude correlates of academic achievement: Family-Group Differences.

Journal: *Journal of Educational Psychology*, June 1987, *79*(2), 171–178.

Related Research: Bagozzi, R. P., & Burnkrant, R. E. (1985). Attitude organization and the attitude-behavior relation: A reply to Dillon and Kumar. *Journal of Personality and Social Psychology*, *49*, 47–57.

■ ■ ■

4267

Test Name: ATTITUDE TOWARD SCIENCE SCALE

Purpose: To measure attitudes of the gifted toward science.

Number of Items: 31

Format: Includes four factors: instrumental value of science, active participation in science, difficulty and complexities of science, and general attitude toward school. All items are presented.

Reliability: Alpha reliabilities ranged from .55 to .99.

Author: Vitale, P. A., and Johnson, B. K.

Article: A factor analysis study of the attitudes of gifted secondary students toward science.

Journal: *Educational and Psychological Measurement*, Winter 1988, *48*(4), 1011–1018.

Related Research: Vargas-Gomez, R. G., & Yager, R. E. (1987). Attitudes of students in exemplary programs toward their science teachers. *Journal of Research in Science Teaching*, *24*(1), 87–91.

■ ■ ■

4268

Test Name: ATTITUDE TOWARD STATISTICS SCALE

Purpose: To measure attitude toward statistics.

Number of Items: 29

Format: Employs a 5-point response scale. Includes two subscales: Attitude Toward the Field and Attitude Toward Course.

Reliability: Internal consistency reliabilities ranged from .83 to .91.

Validity: Correlations with the Statistics Attitude Survey were .73 and .83.

Author: Waters, L. K., et al.

Article: Factor analyses of two measures of attitudes toward statistics.

Journal: *Educational and Psychological Measurement*, Winter 1988, *48*(4), 1037–1041.

Related Research: Wise, S. L. (1985). The development and validation of a scale measuring attitudes toward statistics. *Educational and Psychological Measurement*, *45*, 401–405.

■ ■ ■

4269

Test Name: ATTITUDE TOWARD TEACHING AS A CAREER SCALE

Purpose: To measure attitude toward teaching as a career.

Number of Items: 11

Format: Responses are made on a 6-point scale ranging from 1 (*strongly disagree*) to 6 (*strongly agree*).

Reliability: Test–retest reliability was .79.

Author: Pigge, F. L., and Marso, R. N.

Article: A longitudinal assessment of affective impact of preservice training on prospective teachers.

Journal: *Journal of Experimental Education*, Summer 1990, *58*(4), 283–289.

Related Research: Merwin, J. C., & DiVesta, F. J. (1959). The study of need theory and career choice. *Journal of Counseling Pschology*, *6*, 302–308.

■ ■ ■

4270

Test Name: ATTITUDE TOWARD WOMEN SCALE

Purpose: To measure abstract attitudes about the rights and roles of women vis-à-vis men.

Number of Items: 25

Format: Scored such that higher scores indicate less traditional, more egalitarian attitudes.

Validity: Correlations with the Sex Role Behavior Scale—Short Form ranged from −.37 to .31.

Author: Orlofsky, J. L., and O'Heron, C. A.

Article: Development of a short-form sex role behavior scale.

Journal: *Journal of Personality Assessment*, Summer 1989, *51*(2), 267–277

Related Research: Spence, J. T., et al. (1973). A short version of the Attitudes Toward Women Scale (AWS). *Bulletin of the Psychonomic Society, 2*, 219–220.

■ ■ ■

4271

Test Name: BARNETT LIKING OF CHILDREN SCALE

Purpose: To assess the extent to which individuals have a favorable attitude toward children.

Number of Items: 14

Format: Extent of agreement with each item is recorded on a 7-point scale ranging from 1 (*strongly disagree*) to 7 (*strongly agree*). All items are presented.

Reliability: Cronbach's alpha was .93.

Validity: Correlations with other variables ranged from −.57 to .58.

Author: Barnett, M. A., and Sinisi, C.

Article: The initial validation of a liking of children scale.

Journal: *Journal of Personality Assessment*, Fall 1990, *55*(1 and 2), 161–167.

■ ■ ■

4272

Test Name: BEHAVIORAL INDEX OF TROUBLED EMPLOYEES

Purpose: To measure supervisors' attitudes toward impaired and problem workers.

Number of Items: 23

Format: Seven-point Likert format.

Reliability: Alphas ranged from .68 to .89.

Author: Bayer, G. A., and Gerstein, L. H.

Article: EAP referrals and troubled employees: An analogue study of supervisors' decisions.

Journal: *Journal of Vocational Behavior*, June 1990, *36*(3), 304–319.

Related Research: Bayer, G., & Gerstein, L. (1988). Supervisory attitudes toward impaired workers: A factor analytic study of the behavioral index of troubled employees (BITE). *Journal of Applied Social Psychology, 18*, 23–37.

■ ■ ■

4273

Test Name: BODY DISTORTION QUESTIONNAIRE

Purpose: To identify abnormal attitudes concerning body appearance and functioning.

Number of Items: 82

Format: Response to each item was either *yes, no,* or *undecided.*

Reliability: Kuder-Richardson formula was .95.

Validity: Correlations with other variables ranged from −.66 to .43.

Author: Gleghorn, A. A., et al.

Article: The psychometric properties of several measures of body image.

Journal: *Journal of Psychopathology and Behavioral Assessment*, June 1987, *9*(2), 203–218.

Related Research: Fisher, S. (1970). *Body experience in fantasy and behavior.* New York: Appleton-Century-Crofts.

■ ■ ■

4274

Test Name: CHEATING ATTITUDE QUESTIONNAIRE

Purpose: To measure perceptions and beliefs about academic cheating.

Number of Items: 120

Format: Likert format. Sample items are presented.

Reliability: Alphas ranged from .71 to .90 across subscales.

Author: Evans, E. D., and Craig, D.

Article: Teacher and student perceptions of academic cheating in middle and senior high schools.

Journal: *Journal of Educational Research*, September/October 1990, *84*(1), 44–52.

Related Research: Bushway, A., & Nash, W. R. (1977). School cheating behavior. *Review of Educational Research, 47*, 623–632.

■ ■ ■

4275

Test Name: CHILDREN'S ATTITUDES TOWARD HANDICAPPED SCALE

Purpose: To identify children's attitudes toward handicapped peers.

Number of Items: 20

Format: Children circle descriptions that best represent what they think children with disabilities are really like. Examples are presented.

Reliability: Coefficient alpha was .70.

Author: Archie, V. W., and Sherrill, C.

Article: Attitudes toward handicapped peers of mainstreamed and nonmainstreamed children in physical education.

Journal: *Journal of Perceptual and Motor Skills*, August 1989, *69*(1), 319–322.

Related Research: Rapier, J., et al. (1972). Changes in childrens' attitudes toward the physically handicapped. *Exceptional Children, 39*, 219–233.

■ ■ ■

4276

Test Name: CHILDREN'S SCALE OF SOCIAL ATTITUDES

Purpose: To measure conservative attitudes among children.

Number of Items: 17

Format: Yes–no format. All items presented.

Reliability: Alpha ranged from .52 to .83 across subscales.

Validity: "Oriental" Israeli students scored higher than "Western" students.

Author: Katz, V. J.

Article: Conservatism of Israeli junior high school students: Interethnic differences.

Journal: *Psychological Reports*, October 1989, *65*(2), 635–641.

Related Research: Insel, P. M., & Wilson, G. D. (1971). Measuring social attitudes in children. *British Journal of Social and Clinical Psychology*, *10*, 84–86.

■■■

4277

Test Name: COCKPIT MANAGEMENT ATTITUDES QUESTIONNAIRE—REVISED

Purpose: To provide an index of the cockpit-management attitudes of crew members.

Number of Items: 19

Format: Responses are made on a 5-point Likert scale ranging from 1 (*strongly disagree*) to 5 (*strongly agree*). Includes three factors: Communication and coordination, command responsibility, and recognition of stressor effects.

Reliability: Alpha coefficients ranged from .47 to .67.

Author: Gregorich, S. E., et al.

Article: The structure of cockpit management attitudes.

Journal: *Journal of Applied Psychology*, December 1990, *75*(6), 682–690.

Related Research: Helmreich, R. L. (1984). Cockpit management

attitudes. *Human Factors, 26,* 583–589.

■■■

4278

Test Name: COLLINS ATTITUDES TOWARD COMPUTERS SURVEY—SHORT FORM

Purpose: To measure attitudes toward computers.

Number of Items: 24

Format: Items are rated on a 5-point Likert scale ranging from 1 (*strongly disagree*) to 5 (*strongly agree*).

Reliability: Alpha internal consistency reliability was .85.

Author: Temple, L., and Lips, H. M.

Article: Reliability and generalizability of the Collins Attitudes toward Computers Survey.

Journal: *Educational Research Quarterly*, 1989, *13*(4), 6–9.

Related Research: Collins, B. (1984). *The development of an instrument to measure attitudes of secondary school males and females toward computers*. Unpublished doctoral dissertation, University of Victoria, Victoria, B. C., Canada.

■■■

4279

Test Name: COMMUNITY SATISFACTION SCALE

Purpose: To measure attitudes toward community life.

Number of Items: 54

Format: Five-step truthfulness scales.

Reliability: Item-total correlations all exceeded .30.

Author: Hughey, J. B., and Bardo, J. W.

Article: Social psychological dimensions of community satisfaction and quality of life: Some obtained relations.

Journal: *Psychological Reports*, August 1987, *61*(1), 239–246.

Related Research: Hughey, J. B., & Bardo, J. W. (1984). The structure of community satisfaction in a southeastern American city. *Journal of Social Psychology*, *123*, 91–99.

■■■

4280

Test Name: COMPUTER ANXIETY SCALE

Purpose: To measure computer attitude.

Number of Items: 23

Format: Includes three factors: computer liking, computer confidence, and computer achievement. All items are presented.

Reliability: Alpha coefficients ranged from .90 to .96.

Author: Bandalos, D., and Benson, J.

Article: Testing the factor structure invariance of a computer attitude scale over two grouping conditions.

Journal: *Educational and Psychological Measurement*, Spring 1990, *50*(1), 49–60.

Related Research: Loyd, B. H., & Gressard, C. P. (1984). Reliability and factorial validity of computer attitude scales. *Education and Psychological Measurement*, *44*, 501–505.

■■■

4281

Test Name: COMPUTER ATTITUDE SCALE

Purpose: To measure attitude toward computers.

Number of Items: 34

Format: Includes two factors: the computer as a controlling device and the computer as a challenging instrument. Responses were made on a 5-point Likert scale ranging from 1 (*agree strongly*) to 5 (*disagree strongly*).

Reliability: Alpha coefficients were .77 and .82.

Validity: Correlations with other variables ranged from −.03 to .18.

Author: Koslowsky, M., et al.

Article: Validating an attitude toward computer scale.

Journal: *Educational and Psychological Measurement,* Summer 1988, *48*(2), 517–521.

■ ■ ■

4282

Test Name: COMPUTER ATTITUDE SCALE

Purpose: To provide a range of attitudes towards computers.

Number of Items: 40

Format: Includes four subscales: computer anxiety, computer liking, computer confidence, and computer usefulness.

Reliability: Stability coefficients ranged from .37 to .73.

Validity: Correlations with other variables ranged from .11 to .54.

Author: Roszkowski, M. J., et al.

Article: Validity and temporal stability issues regarding two measures of computer aptitudes and attitudes.

Journal: *Educational and Psychological Measurement,* Winter 1988, *48*(4), 1029–1035.

Related Research: Loyd, B. H., & Loyd, D. E. (1985). The reliability and validity of an instrument for the assessment of computer attitudes. *Educational and Psychological Measurement, 45,* 903–908.

■ ■ ■

4283

Test Name: COMPUTER ATTITUDE SCALE

Purpose: To measure computer attitude.

Number of Items: 14

Format: Employs a 5-point Likert-type format. Includes two subscales:

cognitive computer attitude and affective computer attitude.

Reliability: Coefficient alphas ranged from .56 to .93.

Validity: Correlations with other variables ranged from −.06 to .80.

Author: Zakrjsek, T. D., et al.

Article: Convergent validity of scales measuring computer-related attitudes.

Journal: *Educational and Psychological Measurement,* Summer 1990, *50*(2), 343–349.

Related Research: Bannon, S. H., et al. (1985). Cognitive and affective computer attitude scales: A validity study. *Educational and Psychological Measurement, 45,* 679–681.

■ ■ ■

4284

Test Name: COMPUTER ATTITUDE SCALE (CATT)

Purpose: To measure computer attitude.

Number of Items: 20

Format: Employs a Likert scale.

Reliability: Coefficient alpha was .86.

Validity: Correlations with other variables ranged from .19 to .78.

Author: Zakrajsek, T. D., et al.

Article: Convergent validity of scales measuring computer-related attitudes.

Journal: *Educational and Psychological Measurement,* Summer 1990, *50*(2), 343–349.

Related Research: Dambrot, F. H., et al (1985). Correlates of sex differences in attitudes toward and involvement with computers. *Journal of Vocational Behavior, 27,* 71–86.

■ ■ ■

4285

Test Name: COMPUTER ATTITUDE SCALE (NCAS)

Purpose: To measure computer attitude.

Number of Items: 20

Format: Employs a 5-point Likert scale.

Reliability: Alpha coefficients were .81 and .82.

Validity: Correlation with other variables ranged from .07 to .78.

Author: Zakrajsek, T. D., et al.

Article: Convergent validity of scales measuring computer-related attitudes.

Journal: *Educational and Psychological Measurement,* Summer 1990, *50*(2), 343–349.

Related Research: Nickell, G. S., & Pinto, J. N. (1986). The Computer Attitude Scale. *Computers in Human Behavior, 2,* 301–306.

■ ■ ■

4286

Test Name: COOPERATIVE/COMPETITIVE STRATEGY SCALE

Purpose: To measure attitudes toward cooperative and competitive strategies for success and attitudes toward success outcomes.

Number of Items: 24

Format: Five-point frequency scale (*always* to *never*). All items presented.

Reliability: Test–retest (6 weeks) reliabilities ranged from .75 to .81.

Validity: Three factors were extracted. Correlations with fear of success ranged from −.23 to .44 over the three subscales.

Author: Simmons, C. H., et al.

Article: The Cooperative/Competitive Strategy Scale: A measure of motivation to use cooperative or competitive strategies for success.

Journal: *The Journal of Social Psychology,* April 1988, *128*(2), 199–205.

4287

Test Name: CYBERNETICS ATTITUDE SCALE

Purpose: To measure an individual's response to computerization in each of 10 sectors of society.

Number of Items: 32

Format: Includes five factors; computers as servants of humans, the difference between computers and humans, reflecting affective reactions toward the use of computers in traditional professional roles, the speed and accuracy of computers, and the use of the memory function of computers to benefit society. Responses are made on a 7-point Likert-type response format.

Reliability: Alpha coefficients ranged from .39 to .75.

Validity: Correlations with other variables ranged from −.06 to .53.

Author: Zakrajsek, T. D., et al.

Article: Convergent validity of scales measuring computer-related attitudes.

Journal: *Educational and Psychological Measurement*, Summer 1990, *50*(2), 343–349.

Related Research: Wagman, M. (1983). A factor analytic study of the psychological implications of the computer for the individual and society. *Behavior Research Methods and Instrumentation*, *15*, 413–419.

■ ■ ■

4288

Test Name: DISABILITY EVALUATION SCALE

Purpose: To evaluate disabilities.

Number of Items: 20

Format: Semantic differential.

Reliability: Alpha was .78.

Author: Zernitsky-Shurka, E.

Article: Ingroup and outgroup evaluations by disabled individuals.

Journal: *The Journal of Social Psychology*, August 1988, *128*(4), 465–472.

Related Research: Shurka, E., & Katz, S. (1976). Evaluation of persons with a disability: The influence of disability context and personal responsibility for the disability. *Rehabilitation Psychology*, *23*, 61–75.

■ ■ ■

4289

Test Name: DYSFUNCTIONAL ATTITUDE SCALE

Purpose: To assess attitudes and beliefs that reflect an individual's predisposition to depression.

Number of Items: 40

Format: Responses are made on a 7-point scale ranging from 1 (*totally agree*) to 7 (*totally disagree*). An example is presented.

Reliability: Internal consistency estimates were .90 (men) and .88 (women).

Validity: Correlation with the Beck Depression Inventory was .86.

Author: Strohmer, D. C., et al.

Article: Personal hypothesis testing: The role of consistency and self-schema.

Journal: *Journal of Counseling Psychology*, January 1988, *35*(1), 56–65.

Related Research: Weissman, A. N., & Beck, A. T. (1978, September). *Development and validation of the Dysfunctional Attitudes Scale: A preliminary investigation.* Paper presented at the American Educational Research Association Annual Convention, Toronto, Ontario, Canada.

■ ■ ■

4290

Test Name: EATING ATTITUDES TEST

Purpose: To measure the degree to which respondents possess a variety of behaviors and attitudes associated with disordered eating.

Number of Items: 40

Format: Items are rated on a 6-point Likert scale ranging from *always* to *never*.

Reliability: Alpha coefficients ranged from .79 to .94.

Validity: Correlations with other variables ranged from −.10 to .78.

Author: Heesacker, R., and Neimeyer, G. J.

Article: Assessing object relations and social cognitive correlates of eating disorders.

Journal: *Journal of Counseling Psychology*, October 1990, *37*(4), 419–426.

Related Research: Garner, D. M., & Garfinkel, P. E. (1979). The Eating Attitudes Test: An index of the symptoms of anorexia nervosa. *Psychological Medicine*, *9*, 273–279.

■ ■ ■

4291

Test Name: ETHNIC STEREOTYPE CHECKLIST

Purpose: To measure positive and negative stereotypical traits associated with ethnic groups.

Number of Items: 84

Format: Checklist format. All items presented.

Reliability: Alpha was .96.

Author: Lobel, S. A.

Article: Effects of personal versus impersonal rater instructions on relative favorability of 13 ethnic group stereotypes.

Journal: *The Journal of Social Psychology*, February 1988, *128*(1), 29–39.

Related Research: Katz, D., & Braly, K. W. (1933). Racial stereotypes of 100 college students. *Journal of Abnormal and Social Psychology*, *28*, 280–290.

4292

Test Name: FACULTY ATTITUDES ABOUT UNIONS SCALE

Purpose: To assess attitudes about issues and problems of collective bargaining in education.

Number of Items: 22

Format: Thurstone equal-appearing intervals format. All items and item ratings presented. Scoring suggestions also presented.

Validity: Discriminated between union members and those not in a union. Not correlated with sex, academic rank, and tenure status. Attitudes differed significantly by academic unit.

Author: Rodriguez, C., and Reardon, J.

Article: Attitudes of faculty toward unionization.

Journal: *Psychological Reports*, December 1989, *65*(3, Part I), 995–1000.

Related Research: Allen, R. E., & Keaveny, T. J. (1981). Correlates of university faculty interest in unionization: A replication and extension. *Journal of Applied Psychology, 66*, 582–588.

■ ■ ■

4293

Test Name: FEAR OF AIDS SCALE

Purpose: To measure attitudes toward the fear of AIDS.

Number of Items: 14

Format: Responses to each item are made by indicating whether represented strongly agree, agree, undecided, disagree, or strongly disagree. All items are presented.

Reliability: Cronbach alpha reliability was .80.

Validity: Correlations with the Homophobia Scale were .55 and .52 (males), .58 (females).

Author: Bouton, R. A., et al.

Article: Scales for measuring fear of AIDS and homophobia.

Journal: *Journal of Personality Assessment*, Winter 1987, *51*(4), 606–614.

Related Research: Allen, M. J., & Yen, W. M. (1979). *Introduction to measurement theory.* Monterey, CA: Brooks/Cole.

■ ■ ■

4294

Test Name: FEMINIST IDENTITY SCALE

Purpose: To assess a woman's attitude toward herself as a feminist.

Number of Items: 99

Format: Likert format.

Reliability: Alpha exceeded .85 on all subscales. Test–retest ranged from .83 to .93.

Author: Rickard, K. M.

Article: The effect of feminist identity level on gender prejudice toward artists' illustrations.

Journal: *Journal of Research in Personality*, June 1990, *24*(2), 145–162.

Related Research: Rickard, K. M. (1987). *Feminist identity development: Scale development and initial validity studies.* Paper presented at the Association for Women in Psychology, Denver, CO.

■ ■ ■

4295

Test Name: GENERAL ATTITUDE TOWARDS INSTITUTIONAL AUTHORITY SCALE

Purpose: To measure attitudinal acceptance of authority.

Number of Items: 20

Format: Five-point Likert format.

Reliability: Alpha was .88.

Validity: Correlated .72 with the Attitude Behavior Inventory.

Author: Rigby, K.

Article: Acceptance of authority, self, and others.

Journal: *The Journal of Social Psychology,* August 1986, *126*(4), 493–501.

Related Research: Rigby, K. (1982). A concise scale for the assessment of attitudes toward institutional authority. *Australian Journal of Psychology, 34*, 195–204.

■ ■ ■

4296

Test Name: HARDY DIVORCE SCALE

Purpose: To measure attitudes toward divorce.

Number of Items: 12

Format: Likert format.

Reliability: Test–retest reliability was .83. Cronbach's alpha was .82. Split-half reliability was .69.

Validity: Correlations with other variables were as follows: not religious (.45), liberal (.35), progressive (.24), and individualistic (.22).

Author: Ganong, L. H., and Coleman, M.

Article: Psychometric properties of the Hardy Divorce Scale.

Journal: *Psychological Reports,* April 1987, *60*(2), 531–536.

Related Research: Hardy, K. R. (1957). Determinants of conformity and attitude change. *Journal of Abnormal and Social Psychology, 54*, 289–294.

■ ■ ■

4297

Test Name: HOMOPHOBIA SCALE

Purpose: To measure attitude toward homosexuality.

Number of Items: 7

Format: Responses to each item are made by indicating whether respondents strongly agree, agree, are undecided, disagree, or strongly disagree. All items are presented.

Reliability: Cronbach's alpha reliability was .89.

Validity: Correlation with Fear of AIDS scale was .55 and .52 (males), .58 (females).

Author: Bouton, R. A., et al.

Article: Scales for measuring fear of AIDS and homophobia.

Journal: *Journal of Personality Assessment*, Winter 1987, *51*(4), 606–614

Related Research: Allen, M. J., & Yen, W. M. (1979). *Introduction to measurement theory*. Monterey, CA: Brooks/Cole.

■ ■ ■

4298

Test Name: HOSPICE ATTITUDE SCALE

Purpose: To measure predisposition to use hospice care of the terminally ill.

Number of Items: 5

Format: Six-point agreement scale. All items presented.

Reliability: Alphas ranged from .48 to .66 on two subscales.

Validity: Two factors extracted by factor analysis. No items correlated with scores on the Templer Death Anxiety Scale.

Author: Neubauer, B. J., & Lai, JY.

Article: Death anxiety and attitudes towards hospice care.

Journal: *Psychological Reports*, August 1988, *63*(1), 195–198.

■ ■ ■

4299

Test Name: HYPERMASCULINITY INVENTORY

Purpose: To measure sex attitudes as calloused, violent, and dangerous.

Number of Items: 30

Format: Forced choice.

Reliability: Alphas ranged from .71 to .89.

Validity: Correlations with Aggressive Sexual Behavior Scale ranged from .05 to .53.

Author: Mosher, D. L., and Anderson, R. D.

Article: Macho personality, sexual aggression, and reactions to guided imagery of rape.

Journal: *Journal of Research in Personality*, March 1986, *20*(1), 77–94.

Related Research: Mosher, D. L., & Sirkin, M. (1984). Measuring a macho personality constellation. *Journal of Research in Personality*, *18*, 150–163.

■ ■ ■

4300

Test Name: JOB ATTITUDES INSTRUMENT

Purpose: To assess job involvement, psychological success, and job challenge.

Number of Items: 14

Format: Responses are made on 6-point Likert scales.

Reliability: Alpha coefficients ranged from .79 to .80.

Author: Stout, S. K., et al.

Article: Career transitions of superiors and subordinates.

Journal: *The Journal of Vocational Behavior*, April 1987, *30*(2), 124–137.

Related Research: Lodahl, T. M., & Kejner, M. M. (1965). The definition and measurement of job involvement. *Journal of Applied Psychology*, *49*, 24–33.
Hall, D., et al. (1978). Effects of top-down departmental and job change upon perceived employee behavior and attitudes: A national field experiment. *Journal of Applied Psychology*, *63*, 62–72.
Hall, D., & Lawler, E. (1970). Job characteristics and pressures and

organizational integration of professionals. *Administrative Science Quarterly*, *15*, 271–281.

■ ■ ■

4301

Test Name: LEISURE ETHIC SCALE

Purpose: To measure attitudes towards leisure.

Number of Items: 10

Format: Seven-point Likert format.

Reliability: Alpha was .76. Test–retest reliability ranged from .59 to .87.

Validity: Correlation with Leisure Ethic Scale (Burdge) was .54 and with Affinity for Leisure (Neulinger) was .50.

Author: Tang, T. L.

Article: Effects of Type A personality and leisure ethic on Chinese college students' leisure activities and academic performance.

Journal: *The Journal of Social Psychology*, April 1988, *128*(2), 153–164.

Related Research: Crandall, R., & Slivken, K. (1980). Leisure attitudes and their measurement in S. E. Iso-Ahola (Ed.), *Social psychological perspectives on leisure and recreation* (pp. 261–284). Springfield, IL: Charles C Thomas.
Burdge, R. J. (1961). *The development of a Leisure Orientation Scale*. Unpublished master's thesis, Ohio State University.
Neulinger, J. (1971). *The psychology of leisure research: Approaches to the study of leisure*. Springfield, IL: Charles C Thomas.

■ ■ ■

4302

Test Name: MASTURBATION ATTITUDE SCALE

Purpose: To measure attitudes towards masturbation.

Number of Items: 30

Format: Five-point Likert format. Sample items presented.

Reliability: Split-half reliability was .75.

Author: Houck, E. L., and Abramson, P. R.

Article: Masturbatory guilt and the psychological consequences of sexually transmitted diseases among women.

Journal: *Journal of Research in Personality*, September 1986, *20*(3), 267–275.

Related Research: Abramson, P. R., & Monher, D. L. (1975). Development of a measure of negative attitudes toward masturbation. *Journal of Consulting and Clinical Psychology*, *43*, 485–490.

■ ■ ■

4303

Test Name: MATHEMATICS LEARNING IN THE CLASSROOM QUESTIONNAIRE

Purpose: To measure intentions and attitudes about help-seeking.

Number of Items: 17

Format: Five-point rating scales.

Reliability: Alphas ranged from .65 to .74.

Author: Newman, R. S.

Article: Children's help-seeking in the classroom: The role of motivational factors and attitudes.

Journal: *Journal of Educational Psychology*, March 1990, *82*(1), 71–80.

Related Research: Newman, R. S., & Goldin, L. (1990). Children's reluctance to seek help with schoolwork. *Journal of Educational Psychology*, *82*, 92–100.

■ ■ ■

4304

Test Name: MERIT PAY ATTITUDE SCALE

Purpose: To measure a global attitude toward merit pay.

Number of Items: 16

Format: Responses are made on a 4-point Likert scale ranging from 1 (*agree*) to 4 (*disagree*). All items are presented.

Reliability: Alpha coefficients ranged from .87 to .93.

Author: Weber, L.

Article: An instrument for assessing attitudes about merit pay.

Journal: *Educational Research Quarterly*, 1988, *12*(2), 2–7.

Related Research: Carter, E. L. (1983). *Merit pay programs for teachers: Perceptions of school board members in Virginia*. Unpublished doctoral dissertation, Virginia Polytechnic Institute and State University, VA.

■ ■ ■

4305

Test Name: MICROCOMPUTER ATTITUDE SCALE

Purpose: To assess attitudes about microcomputers.

Number of Items: 16

Format: *True about you* to *false about you* scales.

Reliability: Alpha was .82.

Author: Perkins, D., et al.

Article: Individual and dyad-assisted instruction.

Journal: *Psychological Reports*, April 1988, *62*(2), 407–413.

Related Research: Anderson, R. G., et al. (1979). *Minnesota computer literacy and awareness assessment*. St. Paul, MN: Minnesota Educational Computing Corp.

■ ■ ■

4306

Test Name: MODERNITY ATTITUDE SCALE

Purpose: To measure the modernity of attitudes towards religion, marriage, status of women, and education.

Number of Items: 80

Format: Five-point Likert format.

Reliability: Split-half reliability was .76. Test–retest (15 days) reliability ranged from .43 to .66 across subscales and was .86 for the total scale.

Validity: Correlated .44 with the Smith and Inkeles modernity score.

Author: Sudhir, M. A., and Lalrinkimi.

Article: Modernity in the context of education and socio-cultural factors: A study of social attitudes in Mizoram.

Journal: *The Journal of Social Psychology*, June 1986, *126*(3), 375–380.

Related Research: Anand, C. L., & Sudhir Kumar, M. A. (1982). Developing a modernity attitude scale. *Indian Educational Review, 17,* 28–41.
Smith, H., & Inkeles, A. (1966). The OM Scale: A comparative socio-psychological measure of individual modernity. *Sociometry, 29,* 353–377.

■ ■ ■

4307

Test Name: NUCLEAR ATTITUDES QUESTIONNAIRE.

Purpose: To measure nuclear concern, nuclear support, fear for the future, and nuclear denial.

Number of Items: 15

Format: Five-point Likert format. All items presented.

Reliability: Test–retest (8 weeks) reliability ranged from .77 to .90 across the scales.

Validity: Correlations between SCL-90–R subscales and nuclear attitude subscales ranged from −.18 to .40.

Author: Newcomb, M. D.

Article: Assessment of nuclear anxiety among American students: Stability over time, secular trends, and emotional correlates.

Journal: *The Journal of Social Psychology*, October 1989, *129*(5), 591–608.

Related Research: Newcomb, M. D. (1986). Nuclear attitudes and reactions: Associations with depression, drug use, and quality of life. *Journal of Personality and Social Psychology, 50*, 906–920.

• • •

4308

Test Name: OBERLEDER ATTITUDE SCALE

Purpose: To measure attitude toward elderly people.

Number of Items: 25

Format: Responses are made on a 4-point scale ranging from 4 (*strongly agree*) to 1 (*strongly disagree*).

Reliability: Reliabilities ranged from .88 to .75.

Author: Dillard, B. G., and Feather, B. L.

Article: Attitudes of in-home care aides toward elderly persons: Refinement of the Oberleder Scale.

Journal: *Journal of Perceptual and Motor Skills*, December 1989, *69*(3, Part 2), 1103–1106.

Related Research: Oberleder, M. (1962). An attitude to determine adjustment in institutions for the aged. *Journal of Chronic Disease, 15*, 915–923.

• • •

4309

Test Name: PACE SCALE OF ATTITUDES TOWARD MARRIED WOMEN'S EMPLOYMENT

Purpose: To identify attitudes toward married women's employment.

Number of Items: 20

Format: Total scores can range from 20 (very negative attitudes) to 100 (very positive attitudes).

Reliability: Internal consistency produced a Hoyt value was .75.

Author: Pearson, H. M., and Kahn, S. E.

Article: Women clerical workers: Sex-role socialization, work attitudes, and values.

Journal: *The Career Development Quarterly*, March 1989, *37*(3), 249–256.

Related Research: Pace, L. W. (1970). *A study of attitudes of married women towards married women's employment*. Columbia, MO: University Press.

• • •

4310

Test Name: PERSONAL COMPUTER USE ATTITUDE SCALE

Purpose: To measure attitudes toward using personal computers.

Number of Items: 26

Format: Five-point Likert format. Sample item presented.

Reliability: Alpha was .92.

Validity: Correlations with other variables ranged from −.23 to .42.

Author: Stone, R. A.

Article: Leadership style and managers' attitudes toward using personal computers: A field study.

Journal: *Psychological Reports*, December 1990, *67*(3, Part I), 915–922.

• • •

4311

Test Name: POWER APPREHENSION SCALE

Purpose: To provide an objective self-report measure of negative attitudes toward power.

Number of Items: 15

Format: Includes two scales: fear of own power and fear of others' power.

Reliability: Coefficient alpha was .78. Test–retest (8 weeks) reliability ranged from .73 to .84 (*N* = 83).

Validity: Correlations with other variables ranged from −.47 to .41.

Author: Offermann, L. R.

Article: The development and validation of the Power Apprehension Scale.

Journal: *Educational and Psychological Measurement*, Summer 1986, *46*(2), 437–441.

Related Research: Offermann, L. R., & Schrier, P. E. (1985). Social influence strategies: The impact of sex, role, and attitudes toward power. *Personality and Social Psychology Bulletin, 11*, 286–300.

• • •

4312

Test Name: PREMARITAL SEXUAL PERMISSIVENESS SCALE

Purpose: To measure premarital sexual permissiveness.

Number of Items: 15

Format: Six-point agreement scales. Items are described.

Validity: Scores differ in successive relationship stages.

Author: Sprecher, S., et al.

Article: A revision of the Reiss premarital sexual permissiveness scale.

Journal: *Journal of Marriage and the Family*, August 1988, *50*(3), 821–828.

Related Research: Reiss, I. L. (1964). The scaling of premarital sexual permissiveness. *Journal of Marriage and the Family, 26*, 188–198.

• • •

4313

Test Name: PRESCHOOL READING ATTITUDES SCALE

Purpose: To assess attitudes toward reading.

Number of Items: 12

Format: Children respond to each item on a 1–3 scale. Items were grouped into four categories: school reading activities, nonschool reading activities, library reading activities, and general reading activities.

Reliability: Test–retest (2 weeks) reliability coefficients ranged from .92 to .98. Internal consistency reliability coefficients ranged from .84 to .86.

Author: Saracho, O. N.

Article: The development of the Preschool Reading Attitude Scale.

Journal: *Child Study Journal*, 1986, *16*(2), 113–124.

Related Research: Teale, W. H., & Lewis, R. (1981). The nature of measurement of secondary students' attitudes toward reading. *Reading Horizons*, *21*, 94–102.

■ ■ ■

4314

Test Name: PUPIL CONTROL IDEOLOGY FORM

Purpose: To measure the extent to which the pupil control ideology of educators was custodial or humanistic.

Number of Items: 20

Format: Responses are made on a 5-point Likert scale ranging from *strongly agree* to *strongly disagree*. Examples are presented.

Reliability: Corrected split-half reliabilities were .91 and .95.

Validity: Correlations with other variables ranged from −.26 to .17.

Author: Lunenburg, F. C., and Schmidt, L. J.

Article: Pupil control ideology, pupil control behavior, and the quality of school life.

Journal: *Journal of Research and Development in Education*, Summer 1989, *22*(4), 36–44.

Related Research: Willower, D. J., et al. (1973). *The school and pupil control ideology* (Penn State Studies Monograph No. 24). University Park, Pennsylvania State University.

■ ■ ■

4315

Test Name: RACIAL IDENTITY ATTITUDE SCALE

Purpose: To assess racial identity attitudes.

Number of Items: 30

Format: Responses are made on a 5-point Likert scale ranging from 1 (*strongly disagree*) to 5 (*strongly agree*). Includes four groups of attitudes: pre-encounter, encounter, immersion–emersion, and internalization.

Reliability: Internal consistency reliability ranged from .66 to .72.

Author: Austin, N. L., et al.

Article: The role of racial identity on Black students' attitudes toward counseling and counseling centers.

Journal: *Journal of College Student Development*, May 1990, *31*(3), 237–244.

Related Research: Hell, W. A., et al. (1972). Stages in the development of Black awareness: An empirical investigation. In R. L. Jones (Ed.), *Black psychology* (pp. 156–165). New York: Harper & Row.

■ ■ ■

4316

Test Name: RACIAL IDENTITY ATTITUDE SCALE

Purpose: To measure Black attitudes toward racial identity.

Number of Items: 48

Format: Items deal with four stages: pre-encounter, encounter, immersion, and internalization.

Reliability: Internal consistency ranged from .67 to .72.

Author: Williams, T. M., and Leonard, M. M.

Article: Graduating Black undergraduates: The step beyond retention.

Journal: *Journal of College Student Development*, January 1988, *29*(1), 69–75.

Related Research: Parham, T. A., & Helms, J. E. (1981). The influence of Black students' racial identity attitudes on preference for counselor's race. *Journal of Counseling Psychology*, *28*, 250–257.

■ ■ ■

4317

Test Name: RATIONAL BELIEFS INVENTORY

Purpose: To assess the first four stages of Cross's Negro-to-Black conversion model.

Number of Items: 30

Format: Responses to each item are made on a 5-point Likert scale ranging from 1 (*strongly disagree*) to 5 (*strongly agree*).

Reliability: Internal consistency reliabilities ranged from .66 to .72.

Author: Carter, R. T., and Helms, J. E.

Article: The relationship of Black value-orientations to racial identity attitudes.

Journal: *Measurement and Evaluation in Counseling and Development*, January 1987, *19*(4), 185–195.

Related Research: Parham, T. A., & Helms, J. E. (1981). The influence of Black students' racial identity attitudes on preference for counselor race. *Journal of Counseling Psychology*, *28*, 250–257.

■ ■ ■

4318

Test Name: REASONING ABOUT ABORTION QUESTIONNAIRE

Purpose: To measure how persons view abortion.

Number of Items: 20

Format: Responses are made on a 5-point Likert scale ranging from *strongly agree* to *strongly disagree*. All items are presented.

Reliability: Coefficient alpha was .94. Test–retest (8 days) reliability was .98.

Author: Parsons, N. K., et al.

Article: Validation of a scale to measure reasoning about abortion.

Journal: *Journal of Counseling Psychology*, January 1990, *37*(1), 107–112.

Related Research: Smetana, J. (1982). *Concepts of self and morality: Women's reasoning about abortion.* New York: Praeger.

■ ■ ■

4319

Test Name: RESTRAINT SCALE

Purpose: To measure attitudes toward eating, frequency of dieting, and weight fluctuations.

Number of Items: 10

Format: Includes two subscales: concern for dieting and weight fluctuations. Sample items are presented.

Validity: Correlation with the Dutch Eating Behavior Questionnaire— Restrained subscale was .72.

Author: Jansen, A., et al.

Article: Nonregulation of food intake in restrained, emotional, and external eaters.

Journal: *Journal of Psychopathology and Behavioral Assessment*, December 1988, *10*(4), 345–354.

Related Research: Herman, C. P., et al. (1978). Distractability in dieters and nondieters: An alternative view of "externality." *Journal of Personality and Social Psychology*, *36*, 536–548.

4320

Test Name: RIAS

Purpose: To measure the attitude components of a four-stage theory known as the "Negro-to-Black Conversion Experience."

Number of Items: 30

Format: Responses are made on a 5-point Likert scale ranging from 1 (*strongly disagree*) to 5 (*strongly agree*).

Reliability: Alpha coefficients ranged from .35 to .79.

Author: Ponterotto, J. G., et al.

Article: Afro-American preferences for counselor characteristics: A replication and extension.

Journal: *Journal of Counseling Psychology*, April 1988, *35*(2), 175–182.

Related Research: Parham, T. A., & Helms, J. E. (1981). The influence of Black students' racial identity attitudes on preferences for counselor's race. *Journal of Counseling Psychology*, *28*, 250–257.

■ ■ ■

4321

Test Name: SCIENCE ATTITUDE SCALES

Purpose: To measure understanding, usefulness, and teacher interest in science.

Number of Items: 81

Format: Likert format.

Reliability: Alphas ranged from .72 to .82 across subscales.

Validity: Correlations between subscales and with other variables ranged from −.24 to .45.

Author: Walberg, H. J., et al.

Article: A test of a model of educational productivity among senior high school students.

Journal: *Journal of Educational Research*, January/February 1986, *79*(3), 133–139.

Related Research: Hueftle, S., et al. (1983). *Images of Science: A summary of Results from the 1981–82 National Assessment in Science.* Minneapolis: Minnesota Research and Evaluation Center, University of Minnesota.

■ ■ ■

4322

Test Name: SEX-ROLE EGALITARIANISM SCALE (SHORT FORM)

Purpose: To measure sex-role attitudes.

Number of Items: 25

Format: Five-point Likert format.

Reliability: Ranged from .91 to .94.

Author: Royse, D., and Clawson, D.

Article: Sex-role egalitarianism, feminisim, and sexual identity.

Journal: *Psychological Reports*, August 1988, *63*(1), 160–162.

Related Research: King, L. A., & King, D. W. (1986). Validity of the Sex-Role Egalitarianism Scale: Discriminating egalitarianism from feminism. *Sex Roles*, *15*, 207–214.

■ ■ ■

4323

Test Name: SEXUAL ATTITUDE SCALE

Purpose: To measure attitudes toward sexual expression on a continuum from liberal to conservative.

Number of Items: 25

Format: Statements are rated on a 5-point scale from 1 (*strongly disagree*) to 5 (*strongly agree*). Sample items are presented.

Reliability: Coefficient alpha was .92.

Author: Holland, A. L., et al.

Article: Effects of sexual attitude and sex similarity on perceptions of the counselor.

Journal: *Journal of Counseling Psychology*, July 1987, *34*(3), 322–325.

Related Research: Hudson, W., et al. (1983). A short-form scale to measure liberal vs. conservative orientations toward human sexual expression. *Journal of Sex Research, 19*, 258–272.

■ ■ ■

4324

Test Name: SOCIAL-RELIGIOUS-POLITICAL SCALE

Purpose: To measure social, religious, and political attitudes of adult respondents.

Number of Items: 60

Format: Includes two factors: religious attitudes and sociopolitical attitudes.

Reliability: Cronbach's alpha reliability coefficients ranged from .92 to .94.

Author: Katz, Y. J.

Article: A validation of the Social-Religious-Political Scale.

Journal: *Educational and Psychological Measurement*, Winter 1988, *48*(4), 1025–1028.

Related Research: Katz, Y. J. (1984). *The influence of some attitudes on intelligence.* Unpublished doctoral dissertation, University of the Witwatersrand.

■ ■ ■

4325

Test Name: SOCIAL SCALE

Purpose: To measure non-Black students' attitudes toward Blacks.

Number of Items: 8

Format: Responses to each item are made on a 7-point scale from 1 (*very uncomfortable*) to 7 (*very comfortable*). All items are presented.

Reliability: Alpha reliability coefficient was .90. Test–retest

($N = 30$) reliability coefficient was .94.

Validity: Correlations with Modern Racism Scale was .48 and with Social Scenarios Scale was .62 ($N = 286$).

Author: Byrnes, D. A., and Kiger, G.

Article: Contemporary measures of attitudes toward Blacks.

Journal: *Educational and Psychological Measurement*, Spring 1988, *48*(1), 107–118.

■ ■ ■

4326

Test Name: STATISTICS ATTITUDE SURVEY

Purpose: To measure attitude toward statistics.

Number of Items: 33

Format: Employs a 5-point response format.

Reliability: Coefficient alpha reliabilities were .92 and .93.

Validity: Correlations with the Attitude Toward Statistics scale ranged from .73 to .83.

Author: Waters, L. K., et al.

Article: Factor analyses of two measures of attitudes toward statistics.

Journal: *Educational and Psychological Measurement*, Winter 1988, *48*(4), 1037–1041.

Related Research: Roberts, D. M., & Reese, C. M. (1987). A comparison of two scales measuring attitudes towards statistics. *Educational and Psychological Measurement, 47*, 759–764.

■ ■ ■

4327

Test Name: STEREOTYPED ATTITUDE SCALE

Purpose: To measure stereotyped attitudes of Whites toward Blacks.

Number of Items: 20

Format: Five-point Likert format.

Reliability: Test–retest reliability was .71.

Author: Barnard, W. A., and Benn, M.

Article: Belief congruence and prejudice reduction in an interracial contact setting.

Journal: *The Journal of Social Psychology*, February 1988, *128*(1), 125–134.

Related Research: Otis, S. W. (1976). The relationship between locus of control and stereotyped attitudes of select Black and White college freshman (sic). (Doctoral dissertation, East Texas State University, 1976). *Dissertation Abstracts International, 77*, 500–A.

■ ■ ■

4328

Test Name: STUDENT SEXUAL ATTITUDE SCALE

Purpose: To measure aggressive attitudes toward women: rape myth acceptance, acceptance of interpersonal violence, adversarial sexual beliefs, sex-role stereotypes.

Number of Items: 113

Format: Seven-point Likert format.

Reliability: Reliability ranged from .59 to .88 across subscales.

Author: Peterson, D. L., and Pfost, K. S.

Article: Influence of rock videos on attitudes of violence against women.

Journal: *Psychological Reports*, February 1989, *64*(1), 319–322.

Related Research: Malamuth, N. M. (1983). Factors associated with rape as predictors of laboratory aggression against women. *Journal of Personality and Social Psychology, 45*, 432–442.

■ ■ ■

4329

Test Name: STUDENT SOCIAL ORIENTATIONS QUESTIONNAIRE

Purpose: To measure Israeli high school students' orientations toward social issues.

Number of Items: 43

Format: Includes five factors: occupational awareness, social image, study motivation, social integration, and good citizenship.

Reliability: Alpha reliability coefficients ranged from .64 to .86.

Author: Katz, Y. J., and Schmida, M.

Article: The validation of the Student Social Orientations Questionnaire.

Journal: *Educational and Psychological Measurement*, Spring 1988, *48*(1), 137–140.

Related Research: Schmida, M., & Katz, Y. J. (1987). The differential effect of three educational structures on the realization of academic and social variables. *Research in Education*, *37*, 1–11.

■ ■ ■

4330

Test Name: SUBSTANCE ABUSE ATTITUDE SURVEY

Purpose: To measure drug attitudes in medical education.

Number of Items: 50

Format: Likert format. All items presented.

Reliability: Test–retest reliability ranged from .65 to .86. Internal consistency ranged form .74 to .78.

Validity: Factor analysis yielded these factors.

Author: Jenkins, S. J., et al.

Article: Factor analysis of the Substance Abuse Attitude Survey with college undergraduates.

Journal: *Psychological Reports*, February 1990, *66*(1), 331–336.

Related Research: Chappel, N. J., et al. (1985). The Substance Abuse Attitude Survey: An instrument for measuring attitudes. *Journal of Studies on Alcohol*, *46*, 48–52.

4331

Test Name: TEACHER ATTITUDE SCALE

Purpose: To measure teachers' attitudes toward the teaching profession.

Number of Items: 19

Format: Measures three attributes: belief in using professional colleagues as a major reference, service to the public and a sense of calling to the field, and a belief in the right to self-regulation and autonomy. Responses to each item were made on a 4-point scale from 1 (*strongly agree*) to 4 (*strongly disagree*).

Reliability: Reliability coefficients ranged from .79 to .99.

Author: Ross, G. S., et al.

Article: Attitudes of Georgia public school teachers toward teaching as a profession.

Journal: *Perceptual and Motor Skills*, June 1988, *66*(3), 280–282.

Related Research: Uhlan, E. A. (1979). The development of an instrument to differentiate among public school teachers on the basis of attitudes toward professionalism. *Dissertation Abstracts International*, *40* (02A), 601. (University Microfilms No. DEL 79–17132)

■ ■ ■

4332

Test Name: TEACHER BEHAVIORS QUESTIONNAIRE

Purpose: To inventory attitudes regarding research-based teaching behaviors.

Number of Items: 37

Format: A form response Likert-type scale was employed. Sample items are presented.

Reliability: Alpha coefficient was .76.

Author: Marchant, G. J.

Article: An attitude inventory for research-based effective teaching behaviors.

Journal: *Educational and Psychological Measurement*, Spring 1990, *50*(1), 167–174.

Related Research: Marchant, G. J. (1988, October). Attitudes toward research-based effective teaching behaviors from teachers, principals, and college faculties and students. Paper presented at the annual meeting of Mid-Western Educational Research Association, Chicago. (ERIC Document Reproduction Service No. ED 303449).

■ ■ ■

4333

Test Name: TEST ATTITUDE SURVEY

Purpose: To measure the extent to which test-takers do their best.

Number of Items: 45

Format: Seven-point Likert format. All items presented.

Reliability: Alphas ranged from .56 to .85 across subscales.

Author: Arvey, R. D., et al.

Article: Motivational components of test taking.

Journal: *Personnel Psychology*, Winter 1990, *43*(4), 695–716.

Related Research: Campbell, J. P., & Pritchard, R. D. (1976). Motivation theory in industrial and organizational psychology. In M. D. Durnette (Ed.), *Handbook of industrial and organizational psychology* (pp. 63–130). Chicago: Rand-McNally.

■ ■ ■

4334

Test Name: THERAPIST PERSONAL REACTION QUESTIONNAIRE

Purpose: To measure counselor attitudes toward clients.

Number of Items: 15

Format: Includes 9 positive and 6 negative items answered on a 5-point scale. Responses are made on a 5-point scale ranging from 1 (*not characteristic*) to 5 (*highly characteristic*). All items are presented.

Reliability: Alpha coefficients ranged from .79 to .89.

Author: Tryon, G. S.

Article: The Therapist Personal Reaction Questionnaire: A cluster analysis.

Journal: *Measurement and Evaluation in Counseling and Development*, January, 1989, *21*(4), 149–156.

Related Research: Lewis, K. N., et al. (1981). Attractive versus unattractive clients: Mediating influences on counselors' perceptions. *Journal of Counseling Psychology, 28,* 309–314.

■ ■ ■

4335

Test Name: TRAINING UTILITY SCALE

Purpose: To measure managers' attitudes concerning training programs.

Number of Items: 5

Format: Seven-point Likert format.

Reliability: Internal consistency was .87.

Validity: Correlations with other variables ranged from −.04 to .22.

Author: Ford, J. K., and Noe, R. A.

Article: Self-assessed training needs: The effects of attitudes toward training, managerial level, and functions.

Journal: *Personnel Psychology,* Spring 1987, *40*(1), 39–53.

■ ■ ■

4336

Test Name: TRANSPERSONAL ORIENTATION TO LEARNING SCALE

Purpose: To measure a general orientation toward the transpersonal approach to education.

Number of Items: 40

Format: Includes four factors: fantasy techniques applied to schools, mysticism preferred to science as an epistemology, mystical/occult/paranormal techniques applied in schools, and transcendent consciousness. Responses are made on a 5-point Likert scale from *strongly agree* to *strongly disagree.*

Reliability: Cronbach's alpha reliabilities ranged from .82 to .96. Split-half reliability was .98.

Validity: Correlations with other variables ranged from .15 to .46.

Author: Shapiro, S. B., and Fitzgerald, L. F.

Article: The development of an objective scale to measure a transpersonal orientation to learning.

Journal: *Educational and Psychological Measurement,* Summer 1989, *49*(2), 375–384.

Related Research: Shapiro, S. B. (1987). The instructional values of humanistic educators: An expanded empirical analysis. *The Journal of Humanistic Education and Development, 25*(4), 155–170.

■ ■ ■

4337

Test Name: TREATMENT OF ANIMALS SCALE

Purpose: To measure attitudes toward use of animals in research.

Number of Items: 30

Format: Likert format. Sample items are presented.

Reliability: Alpha was .90.

Author: Bowd, A. D., and Boylan, C. P.

Article: High school biology and attitudes toward treatment of animals.

Journal: *Psychological Reports,* June 1986, *58*(3), 890.

Related Research: Bowd, A. D. (1984). Development and validation of a scale of attitudes toward the treatment of animals. *Educational and Psychological Measurement, 44,* 513–516.

■ ■ ■

4338

Test Name: UNIVERSITY COUNSELING AND TESTING CENTER ATTITUDES SURVEY

Purpose: To identify student attitudes toward university counseling and testing centers.

Number of Items: 29

Format: Includes five subscales: effectiveness of counseling, stigma of counseling, counseling readiness information about the counseling process, and information about the counseling center. Responses are made on a 5-point scale ranging from 1 (*strongly disagree*) to 5 (*strongly agree*).

Reliability: Alpha coefficients ranged from .64 to .78.

Author: Austin, N. L., et al.

Article: The role of racial identity in Black students' attitudes toward counseling and counseling centers.

Journal: *Journal of College Student Development,* May 1990, *31*(3), 237–244.

Related Research: Snyder, J. F., et al. (1972). Why some students do not use counseling facilities. *Journal of Counseling Psychology, 19,* 262–268.

■ ■ ■

4339

Test Name: WIN-AT-ANY-COST SPORTS COMPETITION SCALE

Purpose: To identify attitude toward athletic competition.

Number of Items: 22

Format: Responses are made on a 5-point scale ranging from 1 (*strongly*

disapprove) to 5 (*strongly approve*). Examples are presented.

Validity: Correlations with other variables ranged from −.10 to .24.

Author: Ryckman, R. M., et al.

Article: Construction of a hypercompetitive attitude scale.

Journal: *Journal of Personality Assessment*, Winter 1990, *55*(3 and 4), 630–369.

Related Research: Lakie, W. L. (1964). Expressed attitudes of various groups of athletes toward athletic competition. *Research Quarterly*, *35*, 497–503.

■ ■ ■

4340

Test Name: WOMEN AS MANAGERS SCALE

Purpose: To provide a measure of attitudes toward women in management positions.

Number of Items: 21

Format: Responses are made on a 7-point scale ranging from 1 (*strongly disagree*) to 7 (*strongly agree*).

Reliability: Split-half reliability was .83.

Author: Russell, J. E. A., and Rush, M. C.

Article: A comparative study of age-related variation in women's views of a career in management.

Journal: *Journal of Vocational Behavior*, June 1987, *30*(3), 280–294.

Related Research: Peters, L. H., et al. (1974). Women as Managers Scale

(WAMS): A measure of attitudes toward women in management positions. *JSAS Catalog of Selected Documents in Psychology*, No. 585.

■ ■ ■

4341

Test Name: WOMEN'S WORK ROLE ATTITUDE SCALE

Purpose: To measure attitudes regarding the participation of women in work.

Number of Items: 5

Format: Five-point Likert format.

Reliability: Alpha was .74.

Validity: Correlations with other variables ranged from −.42 to .34.

Author: Hardesty, C., and Bokemeier, J.

Article: Finding time and making do: Distribution of household labor in nonmetropolitan marriages.

Journal: *Journal of Marriage and the Family*, February 1989, *51*(1), 253–267.

■ ■ ■

4342

Test Name: WORK ROLE SALIENCE SCALE

Purpose: To assess general attitude toward work.

Number of Items: 27

Format: Responses to each statement are made on a scale from *strongly disagree* to *strongly agree*. Examples are presented.

Reliability: Cocfficient alpha was .81.

Author: Greeley, A. T., and Tinsley, H. E. A.

Article: Autonomy and intimacy development in college students: Sex differences and predictors.

Journal: *Journal of College Student Development*, November 1988, *29*(6), 512–520.

Related Research: Greenhaus, J. H. (1971). An investigation of the role of career salience in vocational behavior. *Journal of Vocational Behavior*, *1*, 209–216.

■ ■ ■

4343

Test Name: WRITING ATTITUDE SCALE FOR STUDENTS

Purpose: To measure preference, perception and process of writing.

Number of Items: 40

Format: Five-point Likert format.

Reliability: Alphas ranged from .60 to .72.

Author: Katstra, J., et al.

Article: The Effects of Peer Evaluation on Attitudes Toward Writing and Writing Fluency of Ninth Grade Students.

Journal: *Journal of Educational Research*, January-February 1987, *80*(3), 168–172.

Related Research: Emig, J., & King, B. (1979). *Emig-King Attitude Scale for Students*. New Brunswick, NJ: Rutgers University Douglass College. (ERIC Document Reproduction Service No. ED 236630)

CHAPTER 8
Behavior

4344

Test Name: ABUSIVE VIOLENCE SCALE

Purpose: To measure experience of abusive violence related to post-traumatic stress disorder.

Number of Items: 4

Format: Yes–no. All items presented.

Reliability: Cronbach's alpha was .81.

Validity: Correlations with other variables raged from .28 to .58.

Author: Hendrix, C., and Schuman, W.

Article: Reliability and validity of the Abusive Violence Scale.

Journal: *Psychological Reports*, June 1990, *66*(3, Part II), 1251–1258.

Related Research: Uhlan, E. A. (1979). The development of an instrument to differentiate among public school teachers on the basis of attitudes toward professionalism. *Dissertation Abstracts International*, *40* (02A), 601. (University Microfilms No. DEL 79–17132)

■ ■ ■

4345

Test Name: ACADEMIC SELF-REGULATION QUESTIONNAIRE

Purpose: To measure children's styles of regulating academic behavior on an external–internal continuum.

Number of Items: 26

Format: Four-point Likert format.

Reliability: Alphas ranged from .75 to .85 across subscales.

Author: Gralnick, W. S., and Ryan, R. M.

Article: Parent styles associated with children's self-regulation and competence in school.

Journal: *Journal of Educational Psychology*, June 1989, *81*(2), 143–154

Related Research: Connell, J. P., & Ryan, R. M. (1986). *Manual for the ASRQ: A theory and assessment of self-regulation within the academic domain*. Unpublished manuscript. University of Rochester, Rochester, N. Y.

■ ■ ■

4346

Test Name: ADELAIDE-CONNERS PARENT RATING SCALE

Purpose: To identify syndromes of child behavior disorder.

Number of Items: 96

Format: Includes 12 factorily defined scales plus a number of nonsyndromic items.

Reliability: Coefficient alphas ranged from .53 to .85 ($N = 1,454$). Test–retest (1 year) reliability ranged from .09 to .71.

Author: Glow, R. A., et al.

Article: Parent-perceived child behavior problems: Comparison of normative and clinical factors of the Adelaide-Conners Parent Rating Scale.

Journal: *Journal of Psychopathology and Behavioral Assessment*, September 1987, *9*(3), 255–280.

Related Research: Conners, C. K. (1973). Rating scales for use in drug studies with children. *Psychopharmacology Bulletins: Special Issue 1973, Pharmacotherapy with Children*, 24–84.

■ ■ ■

4347

Test Name: ADOLESCENT ACTIVITIES CHECKLIST

Purpose: To measure pleasant and unpleasant activities.

Number of Items: 100

Format: Respondents rate frequency and degree of pleasantness of each item.

Reliability: Alphas ranged from .92 to .95.

Validity: Unpleasant scores correlated with depression.

Author: Carey, M. P., et al.

Article: Relationship of activity to depression in adolescents: Development of the adolescent activities checklist.

Journal: *Journal of Consulting and Clinical Psychology*, June 1986, *54*(3), 320–322.

■ ■ ■

4348

Test Name: AGGRESSIVE SEXUAL BEHAVIOR INVENTORY

Purpose: To measure use of sexual aggression to gain sexual access.

Number of Items: 33

Format: Seven-point frequency scales. All items presented.

Reliability: Alpha was .94.

Validity: Correlations with Hypermasculinity Inventory ranged from .05 to .53.

Author: Mosher, D. L., and Anderson, R. D.

Article: Macho personality, sexual aggression, and reactions to guided imagery of rape.

Journal: *Journal of Research in Personality*, March 1986, *20*(1), 77–94.

■ ■ ■

4349

Test Name: AGITATION BEHAVIOR MAPPING INSTRUMENT

Purpose: To measure agitated behavior in the natural environment.

Time Required: Observations of one person last 3 consecutive minutes per hour.

Format: Nonobtrusive observation format using stratified random time-sampling.

Reliability: Interobserver agreement was .93.

Author: Marx, M. S., et al.

Article: Agitation and touch in the nursing home.

Journal: *Psychological Reports*, June 1989, *64*(3), II, 1019–1026.

Related Research: Cohen-Mansfield, J., et al. (1989, Fall). An observational study of agitation in agitated nursing home residents. *International Psychogeriatrics*, *1*(2), 153–155.

■ ■ ■

4350

Test Name: ALCOHOLISM TREATMENT SURVEY

Purpose: To measure treatment behaviors of alcoholics by self-report.

Number of Items: 6

Format: Likert format.

Reliability: Test–retest ranged from .83 to .90 (2 weeks).

Validity: Self-reported Alcoholics Anonymous (AA) attendance correlated .84 with participants' report of attendance of AA session and .81 with AA records of attendance.

Author: Williams, J. M., et al.

Article: Comparison of the importance of alcoholics anonymous and outpatient counseling to maintenance of sobriety among alcohol abusers.

Journal: *Psychological Reports*, June 1986, *58*(3), 803–806.

■ ■ ■

4351

Test Name: ATTENTION CHECKLIST

Purpose: To measure attention of adolescent educable mentally handicapped students in the classroom.

Number of Items: 12

Format: Checklist format. All items presented.

Reliability: Alpha was .96.

Validity: Correlated .84 with the Conners Rating Scale.

Author: Das, J. P., and Melnyk, L.

Article: Attention checklist: A rating scale for mildly mentally handicapped adolescents.

Journal: *Psychological Reports*, June 1989, *64*(3, Part II), 1267–1274.

Related Research: Conners, C. K. (1973). Rating scales for use in drug studies with children. *Psychopharmacology Bulletin* (Special Issue: Pharmacotherapy), *126*, 24–28.

■ ■ ■

4352

Test Name: AUTHORITY BEHAVIOR INVENTORY

Purpose: To assess acceptance of authority.

Number of Items: 24

Format: Responses to each item were made on a 5-point scale of *never, rarely, occasionally, frequently,* and *very frequently.* All items are presented.

Reliability: Coefficient alpha was .84.

Validity: Correlations with the General Attitude Towards Institutional Authority Scale were .71 and .77.

Author: Rigby, K.

Article: An authority behavior inventory.

Journal: *Journal of Personality Assessment*, Winter 1987, *51*(4), 615–625.

Related Research: Rigby, K. (1982). A concise scale for the assessment of attitudes towards institutional authority. *Australian Journal of Psychology*, *34*, 195–204.

■ ■ ■

4353

Test Name: AUTHORITY BEHAVIOR INVENTORY

Purpose: To measure the behavioral acceptance of authority.

Number of Items: 16

Format: Five-point *always* to *never* response categories.

Reliability: Alpha was .75.

Validity: Correlated .72 with the General Attitude Toward Institutional Authority Scale.

Author: Rigby, K.

Article: Acceptance of authority, self, and others.

Journal: *The Journal of Social Psychology*, August 1986, *126*(4), 493–501.

Related Research: Rigby, K. (1984). Acceptance of authority and directiveness as indicators of authoritarianism: A new framework. *Journal of Social Psychology, 122,* 171–180.

■ ■ ■

4354

Test Name: BEHAVIORAL CHECKLIST

Purpose: To measure submissive, assertive, and aggressive behavior in adolescents.

Number of Items: 32

Format: Checklist format.

Reliability: Interrater reliabilites typically exceeded .90.

Author: Lo Presto, C. T., and Deluty, R. H.

Article: Consistency of aggressive, assertive, and submissive behavior in male adolescents.

Journal: *The Journal of Social Psychology,* October 1988, *125*(5), 619–632.

Related Research: Deluty, R. H. (1984). Behavioral validation of the Children's Action Tendency Scale. *Journal of Behavioral Assessment, 6,* 115–130.

■ ■ ■

4355

Test Name: BEHAVIORAL DIMENSIONS RATING SCALE

Purpose: To provide an overview of behavioral patterns exhibited by school-age students.

Number of Items: 30

Format: Responses are made to pairs of items on a 7-point scale. Includes four subscales: aggressive and acting out, socially assertive, irresponsible and inattentive, and tense and fearful.

Reliability: Internal consistency reliabilities ranged from .73 to .95.

Author: Wilson, M. J., et al.

Article: Factorial invariance of the Behavioral Dimensions Rating Scale.

Journal: *Measurement and Evaluation in Counseling and Development*, April 1987, *20*(1), 11–17.

Related Research: Bullock, L. M., & Wilson, M. J. (1986). Behavioral Dimensions Rating Scale. *The Pointer, 30,* 21–24.

■ ■ ■

4356

Test Name: BEHAVIORAL RATING SCALE

Purpose: To measure relaxation behavior in patients with Huntington's Disease.

Number of Items: 8

Time Required: 15-second observation periods.

Format: Presence or absence of behavior rated by judges.

Reliability: Interrater agreement was .71 ($p < .01$).

Author: Fecteau, G. W., and Boyne, J.

Article: Behavioral Relaxation Training with Huntington's Disease patients: A pilot study.

Journal: *Psychological Reports*, August 1987, *61*(1), 151–157.

Related Research: Schilling, D. J., & Poppen, R. (1983). Behavioral relaxation training and assessment. *Journal of Behavior Therapy and Experimental Psychiatry, 14,* 99–107.

■ ■ ■

4357

Test Name: BEHAVIORAL ROLE-PLAY TEST

Purpose: To provide a measure of overt aggressive behavior.

Number of Items: 10

Format: Each item was a situation requiring the child to respond overtly in the situation. Examples of situations: teased by peers, mildly provoked or accused by an adult, expressing anger. The response was

scored for
5-point rat

Reliability:
ranged from

Validity: Cor
Interview for ..... .vior
ranged from .0. .o .36.

Author: Kazdin, A. E., and Esveldt-Dawson, K.

Article: The Interview for Antisocial Behavior: Psychometric characteristics and concurrent validity with child psychiatric inpatients.

Journal: *Journal of Psychopathology and Behavioral Assessment*, December 1986, *8*(4), 289–303.

■ ■ ■

4358

Test Name: BULIMIA TEST

Purpose: To identify bulimics.

Number of Items: 32

Format: Multiple-choice questionnaire.

Validity: Overall validity coefficient reported to be .82.

Author: Smith, J. E., and Morgan, C. D.

Article: The neglected bulimic: The nonpurger.

Journal: *Journal of Psychopathology and Behavioral Assessment*, June 1990, *12*(2), 103–118.

Related Research: Smith, M. C., & Thelen, M. H. (1984). Development and validation of a test for bulimia. *Journal of Consulting and Clinical Psychology, 52,* 863–872.

■ ■ ■

4359

Test Name: BULIT

Purpose: To assess clinical symptoms of bulimia.

Number of Items: 32

Format: Responses are made on a 5-point Likert scale.

...ty: Test–retest (2 months) ...bility was .87.

Validity: Correlations with group membership were .54 and .82.

Author: Thelen, M. H., et al.

Article: Bulimia and interpersonal relationships: A longitudinal study.

Journal: *Journal of Counseling Psychology*, January 1990, *37*(1), 85–90.

Related Research: Smith, M. C., & Thelen, M. H. (1984). Development and validation of a test for bulimia. *Journal of Consulting and Clinical Psychology*, 52, 863–872.

■ ■ ■

4360

Test Name: CHILD BEHAVIOR CHECKLIST

Purpose: To measure child characteristics: speech and language, feeding, bowel/bladder, motor skills, sleeping, and behavior problems.

Number of Items: 53

Format: Three-point checklist.

Reliability: Alpha was .90.

Author: Cohen, D. S., and Wilturner, L. S.

Article: Family relations and marital quality when a mentally handicapped child is present.

Journal: *Psychological Reports*, December 1987, *61*(3), 911–919.

Related Research: Friedrich, W. N. (1979). Predictors of the coping behavior of mothers of handicapped children. *Journal of Consulting and Clinical Psychology*, 47, 1140–1141.

■ ■ ■

4361

Test Name: CHILD BEHAVIOR RATING SCALE

Purpose: To describe normal and maladjusted behavior in children age range 6 to 14 years.

Number of Items: 146

Format: Includes eight prosocial scales: security; self-concept; impulse control; appropriate activity; physical concern and body awareness; moral development; general interpersonal skills; and relation to adults. Also includes eight problem scales: school problems; eating problems; sleep problems; inappropriate attention-seeking; avoidance; outer aggression, passive, and inner aggression; and pathology. Responses are made on a 4-point scale ranging from *almost always* to *almost never*.

Reliability: Test–retest reliabilities (10 days) ranged from .73 to .97.

Author: Duncan, P., and Kilpatrick, D.

Article: Use of extreme rating categories in ratings of child behavior.

Journal: *Child Study Journal*, 1989, *19*(1), 51–64.

Related Research: Duncan, P., & Kilpatrick, D. L. (1975). *The Child Behavior Rating Scale*. Unpublished. (Available from P. Duncan, Department of Psychology, University of Victoria, Victoria, BC, Canada).

■ ■ ■

4362

Test Name: CHILD BEHAVIORS INVENTORY OF PLAYFULNESS

Purpose: To measure playfulness.

Number of Items: 30

Format: Rating scale. Sample items presented.

Reliability: Cronbach's alpha ranged from .62 to .94.

Author: Tegano, D. W.

Article: Relationship of tolerance of ambiguity and playfulness to creativity.

Journal: *Psychological Reports*, June 1990, *66*(3)1, 1047–1056.

Related Research: Rogers, C. S., et al. (1987). Measuring playfulness:

Development of the Child Behaviors Inventory of Playfulness. Paper presented at the Southwest Conference on Human Development, New Orleans.

■ ■ ■

4363

Test Name: CHILDREN'S ACTION TENDENCY SCALE

Purpose: To measure aggressiveness, submissiveness and assertiveness in children in response to problematic social situations.

Number of Items: 10

Format: Paired comparison format.

Reliability: Split-half reliability ranged from .63 to .73. Test–retest reliability ranged from .44 to .70.

Validity: Correlations with other variables ranged from −.54 to .52.

Author: Broad, J., et al.

Article: Clinical application of the Children's Action Tendency Scale.

Journal: *Psychological Reports*, August 1986, *59*(1), 71–74.

Related Research: Deluty, R. H. (1979). Children's Action Tendency Scale: A self-report measure of aggressiveness, assertiveness, and submissiveness in children. *Journal of Consulting and Clinical Psychology*, 47, 1061–1071.

■ ■ ■

4364

Test Name: CHILDREN'S ACTION TENDENCY SCALE

Purpose: To assess how a child would respond in 13 situations involving provocation, frustration, or conflict.

Number of Items: 13

Format: Provides subscale scores for aggressiveness, assertiveness, and submissiveness.

Reliability: Test–retest reliabilities ranged from .44 to .77. Split-half reliabilities ranged from .63 to .77. Internal consistency ranged from .34 to .76.

Validity: Correlations with other variables ranged from −.40 to .54.

Author: Groot, M., and Prins, P.

Article: Children's social behavior: Reliability and concurrent validity of two self-report measures.

Journal: *Journal of Psychopathology and Behavioral Assessment,* September 1989, *11*(3), 195–207.

Related Research: Deluty, R. H. (1979). Children's Action Tendency Scale: A self-report measure of aggressiveness, assertiveness, and submissiveness in children. *Journal of Consulting and Clinical Psychology, 47,* 1061–1071.

■ ■ ■

4365

Test Name: CHILDREN'S ASSERTIVE BEHAVIOR SCALE

Purpose: To assess children's self-reported responses in both positive and negative interpersonal situations.

Number of Items: 27

Format: Responses are made on a scale ranging from −2 (*a very passive response*) to +2 (*a very aggressive response*).

Reliability: Internal consistency ranged from .57 to .80. Test–retest (4 weeks) reliability ranged from .66 to .86.

Validity: Correlations with other variables ranged from −.45 to .54.

Author: Groot, M., and Prins, P.

Article: Children's social behavior: Reliability and concurrent validity of two self-report measures.

Journal: *Journal of Psychopathology and Behavioral Assessment,* September 1989, *11*(3), 195–207.

Related Research: Michelson, L., & Wood, R. (1982). Development and psychometric properties of the

Children's Assertive Behavior Scale. *Journal of Behavioral Assessment, 4,* 3–13.

■ ■ ■

4366

Test Name: CHILDREN'S INTERVENTION RATING PROFILE

Purpose: To measure how children perceive interventions after they have misbehaved.

Number of Items: 7

Format: Likert format. All items presented.

Reliability: Alpha was .75.

Author: Turco, T. L., and Elliot, S. N.

Article: Assessment of student's acceptability ratings of teacher-initiated interventions for classroom misbehavior.

Journal: *Journal of School Psychology,* Fall 1986, *24*(3), 227–283.

Related Research: Witt, J. C., & Elliot, S. N. (1983). Assessment in behavioral consultation: The initial interview. *School Psychology Review, 12,* 42–49.

■ ■ ■

4367

Test Name: COMMUNITY COMPETENCE SCALE

Purpose: To assess competence in daily living.

Number of Items: 78

Format: Two or three category response scales.

Reliability: Various measures of reliability ranged from .57 to .98.

Author: Searight, H. R., et al.

Article: Relation of cognitive functioning to daily living skills in a geriatric population.

Journal: *Psychological Reports,* April 1989, *64*(2), 399–404.

Related Research: Loeb, P. A. (1983). *Validity of the Community Competence Scale with the elderly.* Unpublished dissertation, St. Louis University.

■ ■ ■

4368

Test Name: COMPULSIVE EATING AND DIETARY CONCERN WITH WEIGHT SCALES.

Purpose: To assess attitudes and eating behavior.

Number of Items: 55

Format: Includes three parts: stress, dieting and concern with weight, and compulsive eating.

Reliability: Coefficient alpha was .86.

Author: Koszewksi, W. M., et al.

Article: Effect of a nutrition education program on the eating attitudes and behavior of college women.

Journal: *Journal of College Student Development,* May 1990, *31*(3), 203–210.

Related Research: Kagan, D. M., & Squires, R. L. (1984). Compulsive eating, dieting, stress, and hostility among college students. *Journal of College Student Personnel, 25,* 213–210.

■ ■ ■

4369

Test Name: COMPULSIVE EATING SCALE

Purpose: To provide a behavioral measure of bulimia.

Number of Items: 16

Format: Includes three factors: negative affect in relation to food, concern about diet and body size, and eating as a means of obtaining pleasure or reducing tension. Responses are made on a 5-point Likert scale ranging from 1 (*never or rarely*) to 5 (*almost always*). An example is given.

Validity: Correlations with other variables ranged from −.29 to .52.

Author: Golden, B. R., et al.

Article: Parameters of bulimia: Examining the compulsive eating scale.

Journal: *Measurement and Evaluation in Counseling and Development*, July 1986, *19*(2), 84–92.

Related Research: Dunn, P., & Ondercin, P. (1985). Personality variables related to compulsive eating in college women. *Journal of Clinical Psychology*, *37*, 43–49.

■ ■ ■

4370

Test Name: CONSUMER EXCHANGE SCALE

Purpose: To measure the dimensions of exchange in consumer behavior including passion, intimacy, affection, friendship, affiliations, freedom/creativity, cooperation, satisfaction, compliance, and dependence.

Number of Items: 14

Format: Seven-point Likert format.

Reliability: Reliabilities ranged from .85 to .89 across two dimensions.

Validity: The exchange dimensions correlated significantly with "free time" shopping, "open-ended shopping desire," and comparison of alternatives. The obsessive-attraction dimension correlated only with comparison of alternatives.

Author: McConocha, D. M., and Lesser, J. A.

Article: Dimensions of consumer exchange.

Journal: *Journal of General Psychology*, April 1990, *117*(1), 125–142.

■ ■ ■

4371

Test Name: COOPERATIVE ATTITUDE IN SCHOOL SETTINGS SCALE

Purpose: To measure how cooperative attitudes appear in school settings.

Number of Items: 10

Format: Responses to each item are either *yes* or *no*. Sample items are presented.

Reliability: The internal consistency estimate of reliability, Kuder-Richardson formula, was .57.

Author: Engelhard, Jr., G., and Monsaas, J. A.

Article: Academic performance, gender, and the cooperative attitudes of third, fifth, and seventh grades.

Journal: *Journal of Research and Development in Education*, Fall 1988, *22*(1), 13–17.

Related Research: Muraki, E., & Engelhard, G. (1985, April). Affective outcome of schooling: Full-information item factor analysis of a student questionnaire. Paper presented at the annual meeting of the American Educational Research Association, Chicago. (ERIC Document Reproduction No. ED 257 872)

■ ■ ■

4372

Test Name: CREDIBILITY SCALE

Purpose: To assess credibility of personal injury claimants.

Number of Items: 100

Format: True–false.

Reliability: Split-half reliability was .95.

Validity: Discriminated between students who were instructed to be malingerous and those who were instructed to be credible.

Author: Lees-Haley, P. R.

Article: Provisional normative data for a credibility scale for assessing personal injury claimants.

Journal: *Psychological Reports*, June 1990, *66*(3, Part II), 1355–1360.

4373

Test Name: CREDIBILITY SCALE

Purpose: To measure trust, expertise and dynamism.

Number of Items: 6

Format: Likert format.

Reliability: Alpha was .90.

Validity: Correlations with leadership qualities ranged from .40 to .67.

Author: Posner, B. Z., and Kouzes, J. M.

Article: Relating leadership and credibility.

Journal: *Psychological Reports*, October 1988, *63*(2), 527–530.

Related Research: Berlo, D. K., et al. (1969). Dimensions for evaluating the acceptability of message sources. *Public Opinion Quarterly*, *33*, 563–576.

■ ■ ■

4374

Test Name: CRISIS CALL OUTCOME RATING SCALE

Purpose: To rate caller behavior on a hotline facility.

Number of Items: 36

Format: Seven-point agree–disagree format. All items presented.

Reliability: Item-total correlations ranged from .38 to .92. Alpha was .95.

Validity: Correlations with judges ratings of success were .94.

Author: Bonneson, M. G., and Hartsaugh, D. M.

Article: Development of the Crisis Call Outcome Rating Scale.

Journal: *Journal of Consulting and Clinical Psychology*, June 1987, *55*(3), 612–614.

■ ■ ■

4375

Test Name: COUNSELING OUTCOME MEASURE

Purpose: To measure the extent of client change relative to beginning counseling in the areas of behavior, self-esteem, self-understanding, and overall change.

Number of Items: 4

Format: Responses are made on a 7-point Likert-type format ranging from 1 (*much worse*) to 7 (*much improved*).

Reliability: Coefficient alpha was .89. Test–retest (3 weeks) reliability ranged from .63 to .81.

Author: Tracey, T. J., and Dundon, M.

Article: Role anticipations and preferences over the course of counseling.

Journal: *Journal of Counseling Psychology*, January 1988, *35*(1), 3–14.

Related Research: Gelso, C. J., & Johnson, D. H. (Eds.). (1983). *Explorations in time-limit counseling and psychotherapy*. New York: Teachers College.

∎ ∎ ∎

4376

Test Name: CURRENT SEXUAL ACTIVITIES SCALE

Purpose: To measure the range of sexual activity.

Number of Items: 24

Format: Yes–no format.

Reliability: Test–retest reliability was .72. Kuder-Richardson was .84.

Author: Andersen, B. L., et al.

Article: Controlled prospective longitudinal study of women with cancer: I. Sexual functioning outcomes.

Journal: *Journal of Consulting and Clinical Psychology*, December 1989, *56*(6), 683–691.

Related Research: Derogatis, L. R., & Melisaratos, N. (1979). The DSFI: A multidimensional measure of sexual functioning. *Journal of Sex and Marital Therapy*, 5, 244–281.

4377

Test Name: DANGEROUSNESS OF MENTAL PATIENTS SCALE

Purpose: To measure the perceived dangerousness of mental patients.

Number of Items: 8

Format: Four-point scales. All items presented.

Reliability: Alpha was .85.

Author: Link, B. G., et al.

Article: The social rejection of former mental patients: Understanding why labels matter.

Journal: *American Journal of Sociology*, May 1987, *92*(6), 1461–1500.

Related Research: Link, B., & Cullen, F. (1983). Reconsidering the social rejection of ex-mental patients: Levels of attitudinal response. *American Journal of Community Psychology*, *11*, 261–73.

∎ ∎ ∎

4378

Test Name: DATING BEHAVIOR INSTRUMENT

Purpose: To measure causes of approach/avoidance behaviors in dating.

Number of Items: 50

Format: Likert format. Sample items presented.

Reliability: Nunnally's reliability ranged from .80 to .93 across subscales.

Validity: Two factors, satisfaction with dating and frequency of dating, accounted for 71 % of the variance.

Author: Prisbell, M.

Article: Factors affecting college students' perceptions of satisfaction in and frequency of dating.

Journal: *Psychological Reports*, April 1987, *60*(2), 659–664.

4379

Test Name: DECISION INFLUENCE MEASURE

Purpose: To measure subordinate decision influence with the leader.

Number of Items: 8

Format: Likert-style format.

Reliability: Cronbach's alpha was .90.

Validity: Correlations with other variables ranged from .25 to .41.

Author: Scandura, T. A., et al.

Article: When managers decide not to decide autocratically: An investigation of leader–member exchange and decision influence.

Journal: *Journal of Applied Psychology*, November 1986, *71*(4), 579–584.

Related Research: Novak, M. A. (1984). *A study of leader resources as determinants of leader-member exchange*. Unpublished doctoral dissertation, University of Cincinnati.

∎ ∎ ∎

4380

Test Name: DEPENDENCE PRONENESS SCALE

Purpose: To assess conformity, evasion of responsibility, affection-affiliation, and lack of internal control.

Number of Items: 20

Format: Five-point agreement scales.

Reliability: Ranged between .67 and .94.

Author: Vats, A.

Article: Birth order, sex, and dependence proneness in Indian students.

Journal: *Psychological Reports*, February 1986, *58*(1), 284–286.

Related Research: Sinha, J. B. P. (1968). Some of the concomitant and background variables of dependence proneness in India. *Journal of General and Applied Psychology*, *1*, 44–49.

■ ■ ■

4381

Test Name: DIABETES HEALTH QUESTIONNAIRES

Purpose: To assess severity, susceptibility to complications, adherence to regimen, cost of regimen, and knowledge of management skills of diabetic patients.

Number of Items: 78

Format: Five-point rating scales.

Reliability: Cronbach's alpha ranged form .10 to .79 across seven subscales.

Validity: Severity and susceptibility predicted glycosylated hemoglobin levels for adolescents. Costs and benefits predicted glycosylated hemoglobin levels for adults.

Author: Brownlee-Duffeck, M., et al.

Article: The role of health beliefs in regimen adherence and metabolic control of adolescents and adults with diabetes mellitus.

Journal: *Journal of Consulting and Clinical Psychology*, April 1987, *55*(2), 139–144.

■ ■ ■

4382

Test Name: DOMINANCE-ACCOMMODATION SCALE

Purpose: To measure dominance in interactive settings.

Number of Items: 100

Format: Likert Format.

Reliability: Odd–even ranged from .50 to .91.

Validity: Correlations with other variables ranged from .30 to .54.

Author: Hoskins, C. N.

Article: Measuring perceived dominance–accommodation: Development of a scale.

Journal: *Psychological Reports*, April 1986, *58*(2), 627–642.

■ ■ ■

4383

Test Name: DRINKING PRACTICES QUESTIONNAIRE

Purpose: To measure extent and context of alcohol consumption.

Number of Items: 122

Format: Seven-point frequency scale (80 items). Rating scale (40 items).

Reliability: Theta was .97.

Author: Williams, J. G., and Kleinfelter, K. J.

Article: Perceived problem-solving skills and drinking patterns among college students.

Journal: *Psychological Reports*, December 1989, *65*(3, Part II), 1235–1244.

Related Research: McCrady, B., & Zitter, R. (1979). *The Drinking Patterns Questionnaire*. Center of Alcohol Studies. Smith Hall, Busch Campus, Rutgers University.

■ ■ ■

4384

Test Name: DRUG USE QUESTIONNAIRE

Purpose: To measure drug use.

Number of Items: 12

Reliability: Cronbach's alpha ranged from .66 to .87.

Validity: Correlations with other variables ranged from −.14 to .37.

Author: Lempers, J. D., et al.

Article: Economic hardship, parenting, and distress in adolescence.

Journal: *Child Development*, February 1989, *60*(1), 25–39.

Related Research: Elliott, D. S., et al. (1985). *Explaining delinquency and drug use*. Beverly Hills, CA: Sage.

4385

Test Name: DSM-III BULIMIA QUESTIONNAIRE

Purpose: To determine the degree to which participants conform to DSM-III specifications for bulimia.

Number of Items: 13

Format: Subjects indicate whether each item applies to their current behavior.

Validity: Correlations with other variables ranged from .22 to .52.

Author: Golden, B. R., et al.

Article: Parameters of bulimia: Examining the compulsive eating scale.

Journal: *Measurement and Evaluation in Counseling and Development*, July 1986, *19*(2), 84–92.

Related Research: Brant, K. W. (1983). *Symptoms of bulimia in college students and obese women: Sex differences in a proposed typology*. Unpublished master's thesis, Virginia Commonwealth University, Richmond.

■ ■ ■

4386

Test Name: EATING, DRINKING AND SMOKING SCALES

Purpose: To measure extent of eating, drinking, and smoking.

Number of Items: 16

Format: Varies by item. All items presented.

Reliability: Item-total correlations ranged form .37 to .87. Alphas ranged from .81 to .93.

Validity: Eating correlated .34 and .38 with an obesity index. Smoking and drinking responses corresponded to known national (Australian) data.

Author: Beckwith, J.

Article: Eating, drinking, and smoking and their relationship in adult women.

Journal: *Psychological Reports*, December 1986, *59*(3), 1075–1089.

■ ■ ■

4387

Test Name: EATING RELATED CHARACTERISTICS QUESTIONNAIRE

Purpose: To identify eating-related characteristics.

Number of Items: 179

Format: Includes two subsets: eating characteristics relating to obesity and anorecticlike characteristics in the general population. Responses are made on a 9-point Likert scale which ranged from +4 (*very strong agreement*) to 0 (*neither agreement nor disagreement*) to −4 (*very strong disagreement*). Sample items are presented.

Reliability: Kuder-Richardson reliability coefficients were .67 and .69.

Validity: Correlations with temperament scales ranged from −.57 to .30 (*N* = 260).

Author: Mehrabian, A., and Riccioni, M.

Article: Measures of eating-related characteristics for the general population: Relationships with temperament.

Journal: *Journal of Personality Assessment*, Winter 1986, *50*(4), 610–629.

Related Research: Mehrabian, A., et al. (1986). Individual difference correlates and measures of predisposition to obesity and to anorexia. *Imagination, Cognition, and Personality, 5*, 339–355.

■ ■ ■

4388

Test Name: EVALUATION OF SCHOOL FUNCTIONING INDEX

Purpose: To measure evaluations of student functioning in school by parents, teachers, and the students themselves.

Number of Items: 25

Format: True–false rating scales.

Reliability: Test–retest reliability ranged from .82 to .93.

Validity: Correlated .47 with Purdue Self-Concept Scale.

Author: Ensink, T., and Corroll, J. L.

Article: Comparisons of parents', teachers', and students' perceptions of self-concept in children from one- and two-parent families.

Journal: *Psychological Reports*, August 1989, *65*(1), 201–202.

Related Research: Smith, R. R. (1970). *Evaluation of School Functioning Index.* Unpublished manuscript, Spring Valley, NY.

■ ■ ■

4389

Test Name: EVERYDAY SPATIAL ACTIVITIES TEST

Purpose: To measure the contribution of differential spatial experiences to educational and vocational behaviors.

Number of Items: 20

Format: 5-point Likert format. All items presented.

Validity: Correlations between various reasoning and ability tests ranged from .11 to .68.

Author: Lunneborg, P. W., and Lunneborg, C. E.

Article: Everyday spatial activities test for studying differential spatial experience and vocational behavior.

Journal: *Journal of Vocational Behavior*, April 1986, *28*(2), 135–141.

Related Research: Lunnebogh, P. W. (1982). Sex differences in self-assessed, everyday spatial abilities. *Perceptual and Motor Skills, 55*, 200–202.

4390

Test Name: EYEBERG CHILD BEHAVIOR INVENTORY

Purpose: To inventory behavior problems in children aged 2–16 years of age.

Number of Items: 36

Format: Yes–no and 7-point intensity scales.

Reliability: Alpha was .98. Test–retest reliability was .86.

Author: Webster-Stratton, C.

Article: Mothers' and fathers' perceptions of child deviance: Roles of parent and child behaviors and parent adjustment.

Journal: *Journal of Consulting and Clinical Psychology*, December 1988, *56*(6), 909–915.

Related Research: Robinson, E. A., et al. (1980). The standardization of an inventory of child conduct problems behaviors. *Journal of Clinical Child Psychology, 9*, 22–28.

■ ■ ■

4391

Test Name: GENERAL CAUSALITY ORIENTATIONS SCALE

Purpose: To measure autonomy, control, and impersonal orientations in motivational processes.

Number of Items: 12

Format: Subjects choose one of three responses to each of 12 vignettes.

Reliability: Internal consistency ranged from .69 to .74. Test–retest reliability ranged from .71 to .78.

Author: Bluestein, D. L.

Article: The relationship between motivational processes and career exploration.

Journal: *Journal of Vocational Behavior*, June 1988, *32*(3), 345–357.

RELATED RESEARCH: Deci, E. L., & Ryan, R. M. (1985). The general causality orientations scale: Self-determination in personality. *Journal of Research in Personality*, 19, 109–134.

■ ■ ■

4392

Test Name: HEALTH SURVEY

Purpose: To provide inquiry about four areas of health.

Number of Items: 22

Format: Includes four areas: quality of sleep, problems of digestion and elimination, headaches, and respiratory problems.

Reliability: Coefficient alphas for men and women were .82 and .83, respectively.

Validity: Correlations with other measures ranged from −.31 to .08.

Author: Spence, J. T., et al.

Article: Impatience versus achievement strivings in the Type A pattern: Differential effects on students' health and academic achievement.

Journal: *Journal of Applied Psychology*, November 1987, 72(4), 522–528.

■ ■ ■

4393

Test Name: HUMOR OBSERVATION SYSTEM

Purpose: To measure behavior that initiates laughing or smiling.

Number of Items: 4

Format: Behavior observation. Examples presented.

Reliability: Alphas ranged from .81 to .91 across observers.

Author: Fabrizi, M. S., and Pollio, H. R.

Article: Are funny teenagers creative?

Journal: *Psychological Reports*, December 1987, 61(3), 751–761.

Related Research: Fabrizi, M. S., & Pollio, H. R. (1987). Laughing and smiling in the third, seventh and eleventh grades. *Merrill-Palmer Quarterly*, 33, 107–128.
Kubo, C. (1979). A multivariate approach to the study of humor in preschool children. Unpublished doctoral dissertation, University of Tennessee, Knoxville.

■ ■ ■

4394

Test Name: INAPPROPRIATE JOB-RELATED BEHAVIOR RATING SCALE

Purpose: To measure job-related behavior deemed inappropriate by supervisors.

Number of Items: 40. All items presented.

Format: Six-point intensity scales.

Reliability: Alpha was .91. Guttman split-half reliability was .82.

Validity: Correlation between male and female ratings was .93.

Author: Ward, E.

Article: Effects of supervisors: Age, sex, number of subordinates, and tenure on disciplinary intentions.

Journal: *Psychological Reports*, February 1987, 60(1), 287–294.

■ ■ ■

4395

Test Name: INCONSISTENCY SCALE (FOR THE CHILD ABUSE POTENTIAL INVENTORY)

Purpose: To detect inconsistent responders and distinguish them from random responders when using the Child Abuse Potential Inventory.

Number of Items: 20 (chosen from the 160 item ABUSE inventory).

Format: Similar and dissimilar item pairs.

Validity: A 5% misclassification was found when respondents were told to be consistent and inconsistent.

Author: Robertson, K. R., and Milner, J. S.

Article: An inconsistency scale for the Child Abuse Potential Inventory.

Journal: *Psychological Reports*, June 1987, 60(3)I, 699–703.

Related Research: Milner, J. S., & Robertson, K. R. (1985). Development of a random response scale for the Child Abuse Potential Inventory. *Journal of Clinical Psychology*, 41, 639–643.

■ ■ ■

4396

Test Name: INSTRUMENTAL AND EXPRESSIVE BEHAVIOR INVENTORY

Purpose: To measure instrumental and expressive behavior.

Number of Items: 40

Format: Five-point Likert format.

Reliability: Alphas ranged from .45 to .82 across subscales.

Validity: Correlations with other variables ranged from −.34 to .51.

Author: Holmbeck, G. N., and Bale, P.

Article: Relations between instrumental and expressive personality characteristics and behaviors: A test of Spence and Helmreich's theory.

Journal: *Journal of Research in Personality*, March 1988, 22(1), 37–59.

■ ■ ■

4397

Test Name: INTELLIGENT AND UNINTELLIGENT BEHAVIOR SCALE

Purpose: To assess what type of children's behavior is perceived to be intelligent or unintelligent.

Number of Items: 150

Format: Four-point rating scale from 1 (*never describes*) to 5 (*unrelated to intelligence*). All items presented.

Reliability: Interitem correlations within six scales ranged from .86 to .94.

Author: Murrone, J., and Gynther, M. D.

Article: Implicit theories or halo effect? Conceptions about children's intelligence.

Journal: *Psychological Reports*, December 1989, *65*(3, Part II), 1187–1193.

Related Research: Sternberg, R. J., et al. (1981). People's conception of intelligence. *Journal of Personality and Social Psychology*, *41*, 37–55.

■ ■ ■

4398

Test Name: INTENT TO ENGAGE IN ASSERTIVE INTERVIEW BEHAVIOR

Purpose: To assess the individual's subjective estimate of the likelihood that he or she would actually engage in certain interview behaviors.

Number of Items: 16

Format: Responses are made on a 5-point scale from 1 (*not at all likely*) to 5 (*very likely*).

Reliability: Internal consistency was .75.

Validity: Correlations with variables ranged from –.02 to .71.

Author: Phillips, S. D., and Bruch, M. A.

Article: Shyness and dysfunction in career development.

Journal: *Journal of Counseling Psychology*, April 1988, *35*(2), 159–165.

Related Research: Cianni-Surridge, M., & Horan, J. J. (1983). On the wisdom of assertive job-seeking behavior. *Journal of Counseling Psychology*, *30*, 209–214.

■ ■ ■

4399

Test Name: INTERVIEW FOR ANTISOCIAL BEHAVIOR

Purpose: To measure antisocial behaviors in children by means of a structured interview.

Number of Items: 30

Format: Parents rate the degree of severity of each item on a 5-point scale from 1 (*none at all*) to 5 (*very much*). All items are presented.

Reliability: Internal consistency provided a coefficient alpha of .91. Spearman-Brown coefficient was .87.

Validity: Correlations with other variables ranged from –.29 to .69.

Author: Kazdin, A. E., and Esveldt-Dawson, K.

Article: The interview for antisocial behavior: Psychometric characteristics and concurrent validity with child psychiatric inpatients.

Journal: *Journal of Psychopathology and Behavioral Assessment*, December 1986, *8*(4), 289–303.

■ ■ ■

4400

Test Name: INVENTORY OF LEARNING PROCESSES

Purpose: To identify behaviors in which students may engage while learning in the academic setting.

Number of Items: 32

Format: Includes two scales: Deep Processing and Elaborative Processing.

Reliability: Test–retest (2 weeks) reliabilities were .88 and .80 (*N* = 95).

Author: York, D. C., and Tinsley, H. E. A.

Article: The relationship between cognitive styles and Holland's personality types.

Journal: *Journal of College Student Personnel*, November 1986, *27*(6), 535–541.

Related Research: Schmeck, R. R., et al. (1977). Development of a self-report inventory for assessing individual differences in learning processes. *Applied Psychological Measurement*, *1*, 413–431.

■ ■ ■

4401

Test Name: INVENTORY OF SOCIALLY SUPPORTIVE BEHAVIORS

Purpose: To measure the frequency of supportive actions from others.

Number of Items: 40

Format: All items presented.

Reliability: Alphas ranged from .84 to .94. Test–retest reliability was .88.

Validity: Correlations with other variables ranged from .32 to .42.

Author: Hill, G. A.

Article: Social support and health: The role of affiliative need as a moderator.

Journal: *Journal of Research in Personality*, June 1987, *21*(2), 127–147.

Related Research: Barrera, M., Jr., et al. (1981). Preliminary development of a scale of social support: Studies on college students. *American Journal of Community Psychology*, *9*, 435–447.

■ ■ ■

4402

Test Name: JEALOUSY COPING SCALE

Purpose: To measure jealous behaviors.

Number of Items: 12

Format: Includes four factors: resolutional, redefinition/reassurance, revenge/retaliation, and manipulation.

Reliability: Cronbach's alpha was .74.

Validity: Correlation with the Ways of Coping Scale was .70.

Author: Mcintosh, E. G.

Article: Development of a scale to assess jealous behaviors.

Journal: *Perceptual and Motor Skills,* October 1988, *67*(2), 554.

■ ■ ■

4403

Test Name: JOB REACTIONS SURVEY

Purpose: To measure behavioral reactions to frustration.

Number of Items: 29

Format: Six-point frequency scales.

Reliability: Alpha was .89.

Validity: Correlations with other variables ranged from .16 to .45.

Author: Storms, P. L., and Spector, P. E.

Article: Relationships of organizational frustration with reported behavioral reactions: The moderating effect of locus of control.

Journal: *Journal of Occupational Psychology,* September 1987, *60*(3), 227–234.

Related Research: Spector, P. E. (1975). Relationships of organizational frustration with reported behavioral reactions of employees. *Journal of Applied Psychology, 60,* 635–637.

■ ■ ■

4404

Test Name: LEADER–MEMBER EXCHANGE SCALE

Purpose: To measure the vertical dyad linkage construct of negotiating latitude.

Number of Items: 7

Format: Multiple-choice format. Responses are made on scale ranging from 4 (*positive*) to 1 (*negative*) indicating which of four alternatives was most descriptive of the relationship with the respondent's supervisor.

Reliability: Internal consistency reliability was .86.

Validity: Correlations with the climate scales ranged from .09 to .60.

Author: Kozlowski, S. W. J., and Doherty, M. L.

Article: Integration of climate and leadership: Examination of a neglected issue.

Journal: *Journal of Applied Psychology,* August 1989, *74*(4), 546–553.

Related Research: Scandura, T. A., & Gaen, G. B. (1984). Moderating effects of initial leader-member exchange status on the effects of a leadership intervention. *Journal of Applied Psychology, 69,* 428–436.

■ ■ ■

4405

Test Name: LEADER MEMBER EXCHANGE SCALE

Purpose: To measure relationships between group leaders and group members.

Number of Items: 5

Format: Five-point effectiveness rating scales. Sample items presented.

Reliability: Alpha was .82.

Author: Vecchio, R. P., et al.

Article: The predictive utility of the vertical dyad linkage approach.

Journal: *The Journal of Social Psychology,* October 1986, *126*(5), 617–625.

Related Research: Graen, G., et al. (1982). Role of leadership in the employee withdrawal process. *Journal of Applied Psychology, 67,* 868–872.

■ ■ ■

4406

Test Name: LEADERSHIP ASSESSMENT SCALES

Purpose: To assess leadership behavior and characteristics.

Number of Items: 230

Format: Items are rated on a 7-point Likert scale from 1 (*never*) to 7 (*always*). Includes 13 subscales: coaching and mentoring others, sensitivity to others, integrity in dealing with others, participative behaviors, criticism of others, self-serving behavior, charismatic behavior, incisiveness, risk taking, hesitancy, directness, future orientation, and motivation.

Reliability: Alpha coefficients ranged from .70 to .95 ($N = 1,965$).

Author: Morgan, R. B.

Article: Reliability and validity of a factor analytically derived measure of leadership behavior and characteristics.

Journal: *Educational and Psychological Measurement,* Winter 1989, *49*(4), 911–919.

Related Research: Morgan, R. B. (1988). *Factor analysis and development of a leadership assessment and development instrument* (Research Report LDR-1). Plymouth, MI: Human Synergistics.

■ ■ ■

4407

Test Name: LEADERSHIP PRACTICES INVENTORY

Purpose: To measure the behaviors of leaders.

Number of Items: 30

Format: Includes five leadership practices: challenging the process, inspiring a shared vision, enabling others to act, modeling the way, and encouraging the heart. There are two forms: self and other. Responses were made on a 5-point Likert scale.

Reliability: Internal reliability coefficients ranged from .77 to .91 (*n* ranged from 708 to 2,876). Test–retest reliability coefficients ranged from .93 to .95, ($N = 57$).

Validity: Correlations with the Marlowe-Crowne Personal Reaction Inventory ranged from .04 to .29.

Author: Posner, B. Z., and Kouzes, J. M.

Article: Development and validation of the Leadership Practices Inventory.

Journal: *Educational and Psychological Measurement*, Summer 1988, *48*(2), 483–496.

■ ■ ■

4408

Test Name: LEADERSHIP SCALE FOR SPORTS

Purpose: To assess wrestlers' perceptions of their coaches' leadership styles concerning training and instruction, democratic behavior, autocratic behavior, social support, and positive feedback.

Number of Items: 40

Format: Responses are made on a 5-point Likert response format ranging from 1 (*never*) to 5 (*always*).

Reliability: Alpha coefficients ranged from .59 to .93.

Author: Dwyer, J. J. M., and Fischer, D. G.

Article: Wrestlers' perceptions of coaches' leadership as predictors of satisfaction with leadership.

Journal: *Perceptual and Motor Skills*, October 1990, *71*(2), 511–517.

Related Research: Chelladurai, P., & Saleh, S. D. (1978). Preferred leadership in sports. *Canadian Journal of Applied Sport Sciences, 3,* 85–92.

■ ■ ■

4409

Test Name: LEADERSHIP SUBSTITUTES SCALE

Purpose: To measure individual, task, and organizational characteristics that substitute for, neutralize, or supplement the influence of managers.

Number of Items: 44

Format: 5-point rating scales. All items presented.

Reliability: Cronbach's alpha ranged from .39 to .82 across subscales.

Validity: Congruency coefficients ranged from .97 to .24.

Author: Childers, T. I.

Article: On the psychometric properties of a scale to measure leadership substitutes.

Journal: *Psychological Reports*, December 1986, *59*(3), 1215–1226.

■ ■ ■

4410

Test Name: LENIENCY SCALE

Purpose: To measure leniency in leader behavior descriptions.

Number of Items: 23

Format: Items consist of extreme statements about other individuals to which *true* or *false* responses are given. Examples are presented.

Reliability: Test–retest and internal consistency reliability estimates are reported as in excess of .85.

Author: Bannister, B. D., et al.

Article: A new method for the statistical control of rating error in performance ratings.

Journal: *Educational and Psychological Measurement*, Autumn 1987, *47*(3), 583–597.

Related Research: Schriesheim, C., et al. (1979). The effect of leniency on leader behavior description. *Organizational Behavior and Human Performance, 23,* 1–29.

■ ■ ■

4411

Test Name: LETHAL BEHAVIORS SCALE

Purpose: To assess inclination to engage in lethal behaviors.

Number of Items: 22

Reliability: Alpha was .68.

Validity: Correlations with Zuckerman's Sensation-Seeking Scale ranged from −.28 to .60.

Author: Thorson, J. A., and Powell, F. C.

Article: Construct validity of the Lethal Behaviors Scale.

Journal: *Psychological Reports*, December 1989, *65*(3, Part I), 844–846.

Related Research: Thorson, J. A., & Powell, F. C. (1987). Factor structure of a Lethal Behaviors Scale. *Psychological Reports, 61,* 807–810.

■ ■ ■

4412

Test Name: MANAGEMENT BEHAVIOR QUESTIONNAIRE

Purpose: To measure direction of managerial effort.

Number of Items: 21

Format: Six-point rating scales.

Validity: Three subscales account for 51% of the variance.

Author: Blau, G.

Article: The relationship of management level to effort level, direction of effort, and managerial performance.

Journal: *Journal of Vocational Behavior*, October 1986, *29*(2), 226–239.

Related Research: Tornow, W., & Pinto, P. (1976). The development of a managerial job taxonomy: A system for describing, classifying, and evaluating executive positions. *Journal of Applied Psychology, 61,* 410–418.

■ ■ ■

4413

Test Name: MANAGEMENT BEHAVIOR SURVEY

Purpose: To measure supervisory behavior through descriptions furnished by immediate subordinates.

Number of Items: 115

Format: Includes 23 dimensions each represented by 5 statements describing the supervisor to which respondents indicate on a 5-point scale from 1 (*never*) to 5 (*almost always*) the frequency with which the supervisor displays the behaviors. Examples are presented.

Reliability: Interrater reliabilities ranged from .44 to .82 (*N*s = 247–457).

Author: Charters, Jr., W. W., and Pitner, N. J.

Article: The application of the Management Behavior Survey to the measurement of principal leadership behaviors.

Journal: *Educational and Psychological Measurement*, Winter 1986, *46*(4), 811–824.

Related Research: Yukl, G. (1981). *Leadership in organization.* Englewood Cliffs, NJ: Prentice Hall.

■ ■ ■

4414

Test Name: MATTHEWS YOUTH TEST FOR HEALTH

Purpose: To rate children's Type A behaviors by the children's classroom teachers.

Number of Items: 17

Format: Includes two subscales: competitive–achievement and impatience–aggression. Each item is rated on a 5-point scale from 1 (*extremely uncharacteristic of the child*) to 5 (*extremely characteristic of the child*). Sample items are presented.

Reliability: Test–retest (3 months) reliability was .79. Interrater reliability was .58.

Author: Visintainer, P. F., and Matthews, K. A.

Article: Stability of overt Type A behaviors in children: Results from a two- and five-year longitudinal study.

Journal: *Child Development*, December 1987, *58*(6), 1586–1591.

Related Research: Matthews, K. A., & Amgulo, J. (1980). Measurement of the Type A behavior pattern in children: Assessment of children's competitiveness, impatience-anger, and aggression. *Child Development, 51*, 466–475.

■ ■ ■

4415

Test Name: MCGILL PAIN QUESTIONNAIRE

Purpose: To measure pain by verbal report.

Number of Items: 20 sets of adjectives that describe subcategories of pain.

Format: Respondents choose best adjective in each of the 20 sets.

Validity: Discriminates between known patient subgroups better than chance and performs as well as or better than alternate forms. It is not clear whether subscale scores or total scores discriminate best.

Author: Hand, D. J., and Reading, A. E.

Article: Discriminant Function Analysis of the McGill Pain Questionnaire.

Journal: *Psychological Reports*, October 1986, *59*(2)II, 763–770.

Related Research: Melzack, R. (1975). The McGill Pain Questionnaire: Major properties and scoring method. *Pain, 23*, 101–112.

■ ■ ■

4416

Test Name: MORROW ASSESSMENT OF NAUSEA AND EMESIS

Purpose: To assess the frequency, severity, and duration of pre- and posttreatment nausea and vomiting associated with all previous chemotherapy administrations.

Number of Items: 17

Format: Frequency of symptoms are rated on a 5-point Likert scale ranging from *occurring at every treatment* to *never occurring*. Severity ratings of symptoms were made on a 6-point Likert scale ranging from *very mild* to *intolerable*.

Reliability: Test–retest (6 weeks) correlations ranged from −.01 to .78.

Author: Carnriek, Jr., C. L. M., et al.

Article: Test–retest and concurrent validity of the Morrow Assessment of Nausea and Emesis (MANE) for the assessment of cancer chemotherapy-related nausea and vomiting.

Journal: *Journal of Psychopathology and Behavior Assessment*, June 1988, *10*(2), 107–116.

Related Research: Morrow, G. R. (1984). The assessment of nausea and vomiting: Past problems, current issues, and suggestions for future research. *Cancer, 53*(10, Suppl.), 2267–2280.

■ ■ ■

4417

Test Name: MULTIFACTOR LEADERSHIP QUESTIONNAIRE

Purpose: To measure transactional and transformational leadership behavior.

Number of Items: 37

Format: Five-point frequency scales. Sample items presented.

Reliability: Alphas ranged from .70 to .94 across subscales.

Author: Waldman, D. A., et al.

Article: Leadership and outcomes of performance and appraisal processes.

Journal: *Journal of Occupational Psychology*, September 1987, *60*(3), 177–186.

Related Research: Bass, B. M. (1985). *Leadership and Performance Beyond Expectations.* New York: Free Press.

4418

Test Name: MYSTICISM SCALE (FORM D)

Purpose: To measure experiences associated with the mystical state.

Number of Items: 32

Format: Likert format.

Reliability: Item-total correlations ranged from .29 to .55.

Author: Smurthwaite, T. J., and McDonald, R. D.

Article: Examining ecological concern among persons reporting mystical experiences.

Journal: *Psychological Reports*, April 1987, *60*(2), 591–596.

Related Research: Hood, R. W., Jr. (1975). The construction and preliminary validation of a measure of reported mystical experience. *Journal for the Scientific Study of Religion*, *14*, 29–41.

■ ■ ■

4419

Test Name: NUCLEAR ACTIVISIM QUESTIONNAIRE

Purpose: To measure self-reported pro-nuclear and anti-nuclear past behaviors.

Number of Items: 14

Format: Half the items are pro-nuclear and half are anti-nuclear. Response to each item is made on a 4-point scale ranging from 0 (*never, no times*) to 3 (*three or more times*) indicating the number of times they had performed the activity in the past 4 years.

Reliability: Alpha coefficients were .78 and .83 (*N* = 166).

Validity: Correlations with the Nuclear Locus of Control Scales ranged from −.17 to .32 (*N* = 166).

Author: Rounds, J. B., and Erdahl, P.

Article: Nuclear Locus of Control Scales: Information on development, reliability, and validity.

Journal: *Educational and Psychological Measurement*, Summer 1988, *48*(2), 387–395.

Related Research: Werner, P., & Roy, P. (1985). Measuring activism regarding the nuclear arms race. *Journal of Personality Assessment*, *49*, 181–186.

■ ■ ■

4420

Test Name: OTTENS-TUCKER ACADEMIC ANXIETY COPING SCALE

Purpose: To ascertain whether students tend to employ functional or dysfunctional coping behaviors in response to critical evaluative situations.

Number of Items: 150

Format: Contains six functional coping behaviors categories: preexam preparation, task-directed self-instructions, overt tension reduction methods, active problem solving, positive attentional focus, and normalizing self-talk. There are also six dysfunctional coping behaviors categories: compulsive, misdirected attention, avoidance/resignation, worry, expressions of self-disgust, and impulsiveness. Responses are made on a 5-point continuum. Sample items are presented.

Reliability: Test–retest (6 weeks) reliability coefficient was .72 (*N* = 22). Alpha coefficients ranged from .89 to .91.

Validity: Correlations with other variables ranged from −.66 to .74.

Author: Ottens, A. J., et al.

Article: The construction of an academic anxiety coping scale.

Journal: *Journal of College Student Development*, May 1989, *30*(3), 249–256.

■ ■ ■

4421

Test Name: PEAK PERFORMANCE AND PEAK EXPERIENCE QUESTIONNAIRE

Purpose: To measure optimal functioning.

Number of Items: 42

Format: Five-point Likert format. All items presented.

Reliability: Total test reliability was .70. Item reliabilities ranged from .10 to .88. Test–retest reliability was .70.

Author: Privette, G., and Sherry, D.

Article: Reliability and readability of a questionnaire: Peak performance and peak experience.

Journal: *Psychological Reports*, April 1986, *58*(2), 491–494.

Related Research: Privette, G. (1983). Peak experience, peak performance and flow: A comparative analysis of positive human experiences. *Journal of Personality and Social Psychology*, *45*, 1361–1368.

■ ■ ■

4422

Test Name: PEER-DIRECTED BEHAVIOR OBSERVATION

Purpose: To measure how infants spend their time together in a typical daycare setting.

Number of Items: 18-category behavioral taxonomy.

Time Required: Seven-second intervals needed to measure "general" behavior; 2-second intervals needed for "molecular" behavior.

Reliability: Between observer reliability was 85%.

Author: Wescombe, N. R., et al.

Article: Peer-directed behaviors and interactions of infants in group care.

Journal: *Psychological Reports*, October 1986, *59*(2)I, 632–634.

Related Research: Wescombe, N. R. (1985). *Peer directed behaviors and interactions of 12–month-old and 14–month-old infants in a group care*

setting. Unpublished Master's thesis, University of California, Davis, CA.

■ ■ ■

4423

Test Name: PEER DRUG ASSOCIATIONS SCALE

Purpose: To measure peer drug associations.

Number of Items: 17

Format: Items focus on number of friends using drugs, whether friends asked them to try drugs, how strongly they would try to prevent friends from using drugs, and how strongly friends would try to prevent their use of drugs.

Reliability: Alpha was .91.

Validity: Correlations with other variables ranged from .74 to −.45.

Author: Oetting, E. R., and Beauvais, F.

Article: Peer cluster theory, socialization characteristics, and adolescent drug use: A path analysis.

Journal: *Journal of Counseling Psychology*, April 1987, *34*(2), 205–213.

■ ■ ■

4424

Test Name: POLITICAL ORIENTATION QUESTIONNAIRE

Purpose: To measure political behavior tendencies.

Number of Items: 50

Format: True–false.

Reliability: Kuder-Richardson formula was .78. Equal-length, unequal length, and Gutnam split-half reliabilities were .88.

Validity: Correlated .56 with the Mach IV scale.

Author: DuBrin, A. J.

Article: Career maturity, organizational rank, and political behavioral tendencies: A

correlational analysis of organizational politics and career experience.

Journal: *Psychological Reports*, October 1988, *63*(2), 531–537.

Related Research: DuBrin, A. J. (1978). Winning at office politics: 50 questions to help you play like a pro. *Success, 46*, 26–28.

■ ■ ■

4425

Test Name: POST-TRANSGRESSION REACTION SCALE

Purpose: To assess self-rated reactions after lying.

Number of Items: 17

Format: Semantic differential format.

Reliability: Alphas were greater than .90 on all subscales.

Author: Forsyth, D. R., and Nye, J. L.

Article: Personal moral philosophies and moral choice.

Journal: *Journal of Research in Personality*, December 1990, *24*(4), 398–414.

Related Research: Forsyth, D. R., & Berger, R. E. (1982). The effects of ethical ideology on moral behavior. *Journal of Social Psychology, 117*, 53–56.

■ ■ ■

4426

Test Name: PREDICTED BEHAVIOR OF AN ADOLESCENT QUESTIONNAIRE

Purpose: To measure behavior of adolescents and their families.

Number of Items: 12

Format: Seven-point bipolar scales.

Reliability: Alphas ranged from .83 to .86.

Author: Ganong, L., et al.

Article: Effects of behavior and family structure on perceptions.

Journal: *Journal of Educational Psychology*, December 1990, *82*(4), 820–825.

Related Research: Santrock, J., & Tracy, R. (1978). Effects of children's family structure status on the development of stereotypes by teachers. *Journal of Educational Psychology, 70*, 754–757.

■ ■ ■

4427

Test Name: PRESCHOOL BEHAVIOR QUESTIONNAIRE

Purpose: To measure (by teacher report) problem behavior of children 3–7 years of age.

Number of Items: 30

Format: Three-point rating scales.

Reliability: Test–retest reliability ranged from .60 to .99.

Author: Webster-Stratton, C.

Article: The relationship of marital support, conflict, and divorce to parent perceptions, behaviors, and childhood conduct problems.

Journal: *Journal of Marriage and the Family*, May 1989, *51*(2), 417–430.

Related Research: Behar, L. (1977). The preschool behavior questionnaire. *Journal of Abnormal Child Psychology, 5*, 265–275.

■ ■ ■

4428

Test Name: PRINCIPAL POWER TACTICS SURVEY

Purpose: To measure the subordinates' perception of their supervisor's use of power strategies.

Number of Items: 35

Format: Includes seven subscales: Assertiveness, sanctions, upward appeal, ingratiation, rationality, exchange, coalition, personal power, and position power. Responses to each item were made on a 5-point scale.

Reliability: Alpha coefficients ranged from .44 to .84.

Author: Landry, R. G., et al.

Article: The principal's power tactics survey: The measurement of administrative power strategies of elementary school principals.

Journal: *Educational and Psychological Measurement*, Spring 1989, *49*(1), 221–226.

Related Research: Kipnis, D., et al. (1980). Intraorganizational influence tactics: Explorations in getting one's way. *Journal of Applied Psychology*, *65*, 440–452.

• • •

4429

Test Name: PRINCIPAL SUPPORT SCALE

Purpose: To measure actions of the principal that facilitate instruction.

Number of Items: 24

Format: Five-point Likert format. Sample item presented.

Reliability: Alpha was .91.

Validity: Correlations with other variables ranged from –.49 to .62.

Author: Brissie, J. S., et al.

Article: Individual, situational contributions to burnout.

Journal: *Journal of Educational Research*, November/December 1988, *82*(2), 106–112.

• • •

4430

Test Name: PROBLEM SITUATION INVENTORY

Purpose: To assess drug abusers' skills in dealing with a range of high risk situations.

Number of Items: 51

Format: Scored by raters who assess 21 response categories and who also judge if a response is aggressive, passive, or poorly executed.

Reliability: Interrater reliability was 91%. Alphas ranged from .63 to .92.

Validity: Subscale scores correlate with each other. Correlations ranged from –.44 to .66. Correlations were higher at posttest than at pretest.

Author: Hawkins, J. D., et al.

Article: Measuring effects of a skills training intervention for drug abusers.

Journal: *Journal of Consulting and Clinical Psychology*, October 1986, *54*(5), 661–664.

• • •

4431

Test Name: PROCRASTINATION INVENTORY

Purpose: To measure procrastination in work-study, household chores, and interpersonal responsibilities.

Number of Items: 54

Format: Five-point self-rating scales. Sample items presented.

Reliability: Alpha was .91.

Validity: Correlations with other variables ranged from –.41 (self control) to .62 (effective study time).

Author: Stoham-Salomon, V., et al.

Article: You're changed if you do and changed if you don't: Mechanisms underlying paradoxical interventions.

Journal: *Journal of Consulting and Clinical Psychology*, October 1989, *57*(5), 590–598.

Related Research: Sroloff, B. (1963). *An empirical research of procrastination as a state/trait phenomenon.* Unpublished Master's Thesis, Tel-Aviv University, Israel.

• • •

4432

Test Name: PROCRASTINATION SCALE

Purpose: To measure procrastination behavior.

Number of Items: 20

Format: True–false format.

Reliability: Alphas ranged from .82 to .83.

Validity: Correlations with other variables ranged from –.49 to –.03.

Author: Lay, C. H.

Article: At last, my research article on procrastination.

Journal: *Journal of Research in Personality*, December 1986, *20*(3), 474–495.

• • •

4433

Test Name: PSYCHOLOGICAL REACTANCE SCALE

Purpose: To assess reaction to real or threatened loss of freedom.

Number of Items: 18

Format: Four-point Likert format.

Reliability: Split-half reliability was .77. Cronbach's alpha was .80.

Validity: Factor analysis does not replicate earlier studies of dimensionality.

Author: Hong, S. M., and Ostini, R.

Article: Further evaluation of Merz's Psychological Reactance Scale.

Journal: *Psychological Reports*, June 1989, *64*(3), 707–710.

Related Research: Tucker, R. K., & Byers, P. Y. (1987). Factorial validity of Merz's Psychological Reactance Scale. *Psychological Reports*, *61*, 811–815.

• • •

4434

Test Name: PUPIL CONTROL BEHAVIOR

Purpose: To measure an educator's pupil control behavior along a custodial–humanistic continuum.

Number of Items: 20

Format: Responses are made on a Likert scale ranging from *always* to *never*. Examples are presented.

Reliability: Cronbach's alpha was .92.

Validity: Correlations with other variables ranged from –.79 to .17.

Author: Lunenburg, F. C., and Schmidt, L. J.

Article: Pupil control ideology, pupil control behavior and the quality of school life.

Journal: *Journal of Research and Development in Education*, Summer 1989, *22*(4), 36–44.

Related Research: Helsel, A. R., & Willower, D. J. (1974). Toward definition and measurement of pupil control behavior. *Journal of Educational Administration, 12,* 114–123.

▪ ▪ ▪

4435

Test Name: PUPIL DISRUPTIVE BEHAVIOR SCALE

Purpose: To measure pupil disruptive behavior.

Number of Items: 29

Format: Responses were made on an 8-point Likert scale ranging from *no action* to *expulsion*. Includes three factors. All items are presented.

Reliability: Alpha coefficients ranged from .73 to .93.

Author: Lunenburg, F. C., and Schmidt, L. J.

Article: Pupil disruptive behavior: Development and factor structure of an operational measure.

Journal: *Educational and Psychological Measurement*, Winter 1987, *47*(4), 1081–1085.

Related Research: Willower, D. (1971). Social control in schools. In L. Deighton (Ed.), *Encyclopedia of education* (Vol. 8, pp. 245–253). New York: MacMillan.

4436

Test Name: RAPE RESPONSIBILITY QUESTIONNAIRE

Purpose: To assess a subject's response to a hypothetical rape case.

Number of Items: 12

Format: Eleven-point Likert format.

Validity: Correlations with other variables ranged from –.57 to.56.

Author: Quackenbush, R. L.

Article: A comparison of androgynous, masculine sex-typed and undifferentiated males on dimensions of attitudes toward rape.

Journal: *Journal of Research in Personality*, September 1989, *23*(3), 318–342.

Related Research: Deitz, S. R., & Byrnes, L. E. (1981). Attribution of responsibility for sexual assault: The influence of observer empathy and defendant occupation and attractiveness. *Journal of Psychology, 108,* 17–29.

▪ ▪ ▪

4437

Test Name: REACTIVITY TO EVENTS SCALE

Purpose: To assess reactivity to good and bad events.

Number of Items: 11

Format: Five-point scales.

Reliability: Alphas ranged from .73 to .84 across subscales.

Author: Lehman, A. K., and Rodin, J.

Article: Styles of self-nurturance and disordered eating.

Journal: *Journal of Consulting and Clinical Psychology*, February 1989, *57*(1), 117–122.

Related Research: Bryant, F., & Weaver, F. M. (1985, August). *Perceived control and subjective mental health: Testing a theoretical model.* Paper presented at the

meeting of the American Psychological Association, Los Angeles.

▪ ▪ ▪

4438

Test Name: REPORT OF CHILD BEHAVIOR

Purpose: To assess child behavior perceived and reported by parents.

Number of Items: 25

Format: Includes five scales: positive relationships, obedience, control problems, detachment, and independence. Examples are given.

Reliability: Internal consistency ranged from .69 to .95.

Author: Mullis, R. L., et al.

Article: Reports of child behavior by single mothers and married mothers.

Journal: *Child Study Journal*, 1987, *17*(3), 211–225.

Related Research: Schaefer, E. S., & Finkelstein, N. W. (1975, August). *Child behavior toward parent: An inventory and factor analysis.* Paper presented at the meeting of the American Psychological Association, Chicago.

▪ ▪ ▪

4439

Test Name: RIGOROUS EATING SCALE

Purpose: To measure hunger, deprivation, and restraint in eating style.

Number of Items: 13

Format: Six-point (*always* to *never*) scale. All items presented.

Reliability: Cronbach's alphas ranged from .82 to .88.

Author: Smead, V.

Article: A psychometric investigation of the Rigorous Eating Scale.

Journal: *Psychological Reports*, October 1990, *67*(2), 555–561.

Related Research: Smead, V. S., & Boyd, J. R. (1987). Correlates of eating related difficulties among college students: A preliminary investigation. *Addictive Behaviors, 12,* 185–188.

■ ■ ■

4440

Test Name: SELF-CARE INVENTORY

Purpose: To measure general health habits.

Number of Items: 29

Format: Includes the following health habits: self-care, rest and sleep, personal hygiene, substance use and abuse, and exercise and fitness practices.

Reliability: Cronbach's alpha coefficient was .76.

Author: Benedict, J. O., and Mondloch, G. J.

Article: Factors affecting burnout in paraprofessional residence hall staff members.

Journal: *Journal of College Student Development,* July 1989, *30*(4), 293–297.

Related Research: Pardine, P., et al. (1982, August). *The direct and indirect effects of stress on illness.* Paper presented at the meeting of the American Psychological Association, Washington, DC.

■ ■ ■

4441

Test Name: SELF-CONTROL SCHEDULE

Purpose: To assess the tendencies of individuals to apply self-management methods to the solution of common behavioral problems.

Format: Concerned with self-regulation, freedom from impulsivity, and independence from external environmental cues.

Reliability: Test–retest (over 4 weeks) reliability was .86. Internal

consistency reliabilities ranged from .78 to .84.

Validity: Correlations with the Religious Orientation Scale were .38 (intrinsic) and –.19 (extrinsic) with $N = 33$.

Author: Bergin, A. E., et al.

Article: Religiousness and mental health reconsidered: A study of an intrinsically religious sample.

Journal: *Journal of Counseling Psychology,* April 1987, *34*(2), 197–204.

Related Research: Richards, P. S. (1985). Construct validation of the Self-Control Schedule. *Journal of Research in Personality, 19,* 208–218. Rosenbaum, M. (1980). A schedule for assessing self-control behaviors: Preliminary findings. *Behavior Therapy, 11,* 109–121.

■ ■ ■

4442

Test Name: SELF-EXPRESSION INVENTORY

Purpose: To measure immature forms of grandiosity and the general instability or absence of orienting goals.

Number of Items: 20

Format: Includes two scales: superiority and goal instability. Responses are made on a 5-point Likert scale.

Reliability: Test–retest (2 weeks) reliability was .80 for superiority and .76 for goal instability. Alpha coefficients were .76 for superiority and .80 for goal instability.

Validity: Correlations with other variables ranged from .67 to .79.

Author: Mahalik, J. R., and Kivlighan, D. M., Jr.

Article: Self-help treatment for depression: Who succeeds?

Journal: *Journal of Counseling Psychology,* July 1988, *35*(3), 237–242.

Related Research: Robbins, S. R., & Patton, M. J. (1985). Self-psychology and career development: Construction of the superiority and goal instability scales. *Journal of Counseling Psychology, 32,* 221–231.

■ ■ ■

4443

Test Name: SELF-REPORTED EARLY DELINQUENCY INSTRUMENT

Purpose: To identify "norm-violating" and more serious illegal behavior.

Number of Items: 58

Format: Includes "norm-violating" behaviors and more serious illegal behaviors.

Reliability: Test–retest reliability (1 month) was .85. Kuder-Richardson Formula 20 internal consistency was .90.

Validity: Correlation with parental report of subjects' socialized aggressive behaviors was .43.

Author: Moffitt, T. E.

Article: Juvenile delinquency and attention deficit disorder: Boys' developmental trajectories from age 3 to age 5.

Journal: *Child Development,* June 1990, *61*(3), 893–910.

Related Research: Moffitt, T. E., & Silva, P. A. (1988). Self-reported delinquency: Results from an instrument for New Zealand. *Australian and New Zealand Journal of Criminology, 21,* 227–240.

■ ■ ■

4444

Test Name: SELF-REPORT MEASURE OF FOOD CONSUMPTION

Purpose: To provide a self-report measure of food consumption under specific emotional conditions.

Number of Items: 12

Format: Subjects respond to each item on a 9-point Likert scale ranging from +4 (*very strong agreement*) to −4 (*very strong disagreement*). Examples are presented.

Reliability: Kuder Richardson formula reliability coefficients were .88 and .92.

Author: Mehrabian, A., and Riccioni, M.

Article: Measures of eating-related characteristics for the general population: Relationships with temperament.

Journal: *Journal of Personality Assessment*, Winter 1986, *50*(4), 610–629.

Related Research: Mehrabian, A. (1980). *Basic dimensions for a general psychological theory*. Cambridge, MA: Oelgeschlager, Gunn & Hain.

■ ■ ■

4445

Test Name: SENSE OF AUTONOMY SCALE

Purpose: To measure teachers' sense of power and autonomy.

Number of Items: 24

Format: Four-point Likert format.

Reliability: Internal consistency was .91.

Author: Licatar, J. W., et al.

Article: Principal vision, teacher sense of autonomy, and environmental robustness.

Journal: *The Journal of Educational Research*, November-December 1990, *84*(2), 93–99.

Related Research: Charters, W. W. (1974) *Sense of teacher work autonomy: Measurement and findings*. Eugene, OR: Project MITT/Management Implications of Team Teaching, Center for Educational Policy and Management, University of Oregon.

4446

Test Name: SEX HISTORY QUESTIONNAIRE

Purpose: To obtain retrospective and current data regarding women's consensual and abusive sexual experiences and the effects of these experiences.

Number of Items: 478

Format: Structured interview format.

Reliability: Test–retest (2 years) reliability ranged from .65 to .98. Interrater reliability was averaged .90.

Author: Wyatt, G. E., and Newcomb, M.

Article: Internal and external mediators of women's sexual abuse in childhood.

Journal: *Journal of Consulting and Clinical Psychology*, December 1990, *58*(6), 758–767.

Related Research: Wyatt, G. E. (1985). The sexual abuse of Afro-American and White-American women in childhood. *Child Abuse and Neglect*, *9*, 507–519.

■ ■ ■

4447

Test Name: SEXUAL ABUSE SCALE

Purpose: To measure sexual abuse.

Number of Items: 4

Format: Times per week frequency scales. All items described.

Reliability: Total scale reliabilities ranged from .78 to .80.

Author: Burke, P. J., et al.

Article: Gender identity, self-esteem, and sexual abuse in dating relationships.

Journal: *Social Psychology Quarterly*, September 1988, *51*(3), 272–285.

Related Research: Sigalman, C. K., et al. (1984). Violence in college

students' dating relationships. *Journal of Applied Social Psychology*, *50*, 237–246.

■ ■ ■

4448

Test Name: SEXUAL AROUSABILITY INDEX

Purpose: To assess sexual arousal in women by self-report.

Number of Items: 28

Format: Five-point rating scales. All items presented.

Reliability: SR reliabilities ranged from .93 to .96. Kuder-Richardson formula reliabilities ranged from .92 to .93. Test–retest ranged from .68 to .90.

Validity: Five factors extracted. Factor congruence (repeatability in new samples) ranged from .76 to .96.

Author: Andersen, B. L., et al.

Article: A psychometric analysis of the Sexual Arousability Index.

Journal: *Journal of Consulting and Clinical Psychology*, February 1989, *57*(1), 123–130.

Related Research: Hoon, E. F., et al. (1976). An inventory for the measurement of female sexual arousability: The SAI. *Archives of Sexual Behavior*, *5*, 291–300.

■ ■ ■

4449

Test Name: SEXUAL EXPERIENCE SCALE

Purpose: To assess range of heterosexual experiences

Number of Items: 24

Format: Respondents endorse any behavior that occurred in the last month.

Reliability: Kuder-Richardson formula was .84. Test–retest reliability was .69.

Author: Andersen, B. L., et al.

Article: A psychometric analysis of the sexual arousability index.

Journal: *Journal of Consulting and Clinical Psychology*, February 1989, *57*(1), 123–130.

Related Research: Derogatis, L. R., & Melisaratus, N. (1979). The DSFI: A multidimensional measure of sexual functioning. *Journal of Sex and Marital Therapy, 5*, 244–281.

■ ■ ■

4450

Test Name: SHOPPING ORIENTATION SCALE

Purpose: To identify shoppers' styles that place particular emphasis on certain activities.

Number of Items: 42

Format: Responses are made on a 5-point Likert scale ranging from 1 (*strongly disagree*) to 5 (*strongly agree*).

Reliability: Alpha coefficients ranged from .61 to .87.

Author: Shim, S., and Kotsiopulos, A.

Article: Women's physical size, body-cathexis, and shopping for apparel.

Journal: *Perceptual and Motor Skills*, December 1990, *71*(3, Part 1), 1031–1042.

Related Research: Shim, S., & Drake, M. F. (1990). Consumer intention to shop through an electronic mall: The Fishbein behavioral intention model. *Journal of Direct Marketing, 4*(3), 22–33.

■ ■ ■

4451

Test Name: SOCIAL SCENARIOS SCALE

Purpose: To measure non-Black students' willingness to engage in discriminatory or anti-discriminatory behavior when confronted with racial conflict situations.

Number of Items: 12

Format: Respondents choose one of four possible responses to each racial conflict situation. All items are presented.

Reliability: Alpha reliability coefficient was .75. Test–retest reliability coefficient was .93 (*N* = 30).

Validity: Correlations with Modern Racism Scale was .42. Correlations with Social Scale was .62 (*N* = 286).

Author: Byrnes, D. A., and Kiger, G.

Article: Contemporary measures of attitudes toward Blacks.

Journal: *Educational and Psychological Measurement*, Spring 1988, *48*(1), 107–118.

■ ■ ■

4452

Test Name: SOMATIC RESPONSE SURVEY

Purpose: To assess patterns of normal physical responses during stressful situations.

Number of Items: 27

Format: Four-point frequency scale (*never* to *always*).

Reliability: Cronbach's alphas ranged from .49 to .89 across subscales.

Validity: Four factors accounted for 91% of the variance. The survey discriminated between males and females.

Author: McCroskery, J. H., and Reihman, J.

Article: Development of the Somatic Response Survey.

Journal: *Psychological Reports*, December 1990, *67*(3) II, 1097–1098

■ ■ ■

4453

Test Name: SPATIAL ACTIVITIES QUESTIONNAIRE

Purpose: To measure amount of participation in spatial activities.

Number of Items: 81

Format: Subjects rate their participation in spatial activities on a 6-point scale ranging from *never participated* to *participated more than once a week*. Includes three subscales.

Reliability: Internal consistency ranged from .79 to .92.

Author: Newcombe, N., et al.

Article: Associations of timing of puberty, spatial ability, and lateralization in adult women.

Journal: *Child Development*, February 1989, *60*(1), 246–254.

Related Research: Signorella, M. L., et al. (1986). A short version of a Spatial Activity Questionnaire. *Sex Roles, 14*, 475–479.

■ ■ ■

4454

Test Name: STABLE DISPOSITIONS CONCEPT MEASURE

Purpose: To measure the stable dispositions concept.

Number of Items: 16

Format: Two items measure each of eight different types of behaviors. Items are scored either 1 or 0 depending on whether the subjects predicted a new behavior congruent with the disposition implied in the first behavior. Sample items are presented.

Validity: Correlated .37 with age.

Author: Rholes, W. S., et al.

Article: Children's understanding of personal dispositions and its relationship to behavior.

Journal: *Journal of Experimental Child Psychology*, February 1988, *45*(1), 1–17.

Related Research: Rholes, W. S., & Ruble, D. N. (1984). Children's understanding of dispositional characteristics of others. *Child Development, 55*, 550–560.

4455

Test Name: STANTON SURVEY

Purpose: To screen job applicants to determine if they are theft-prone.

Number of Items: 70

Format: Fifty-two dichotomous items. Eighteen multiple-choice items.

Reliability: Reliability was .92.

Validity: Validity was .90.

Author: Harris, W. G.

Article: A components analysis of a preemployment integrity measure: A replicated study.

Journal: *Psychological Reports*, June 1987, *60*(3), 1051–1055.

Related Research: Klump, C. S., & Perman, S. (1980). *The Stanton Survey manual: Description and evaluation*. Chicago, IL: Stanton.

■ ■ ■

4456

Test Name: STRUCTURE RATING SCALE

Purpose: To rate the structure of assertion training.

Number of Items: 6

Format: Agreement with each item is rated on a 7-point scale ranging from 1 (*strongly agree*) to 7 (*strongly disagree*). Examples are presented.

Reliability: Interrater agreement was .85.

Author: Stoppard, J. M., and Henri, G. S.

Article: Conceptual level matching and effects of assertion training.

Journal: *Journal of Counseling Psychology*, January 1987, *34*(1), 55–61.

Related Research: Bachman, K. T. (1977). Conceptual level and degree of structure matching in counseling analogues. *Dissertation Abstracts International, 37,* 5821B–5822B. (University Microfilms No. 77–10, 486)

4457

Test Name: STUDENT DRINKING INFORMATION SCALE— ADAPTED

Purpose: To measure college students' attitudes, knowledge, and behavior related to alcohol use.

Number of Items: 120

Format: Includes eight sections: quantity–frequency, alcohol knowledge, negative consequences, responsible attitudes, peer pressure, family history, positive expectations, and health locus of control.

Reliability: For seven sections coefficient alphas ranged from .36 to .80. The eighth section, quantity-frequency, had a test–retest (2 months) reliability coefficient of .79 ($N = 90$).

Author: Sherry, P., and Stolberg, V.

Article: Factors affecting alcohol use by college students.

Journal: *Journal of College Student Personnel*, July 1987, *28*(4), 350–355.

Related Research: Gonzalez, G. M. (1982). Alcohol education can prevent alcohol problems: A summary of some unique research findings. *Journal of Alcohol and Drug Education, 27,* 2–12.

■ ■ ■

4458

Test Name: SUBORDINATE INFLUENCE TACTICS SCALE

Purpose: To measure subordinate influence tactics.

Number of Items: 24

Format: Responses are made on a 7-point scale ranging from 1 (*never*) to 7 (*always*). Includes three factors: job-focused, supervisor-focused, and self-focused tactics. All items presented.

Reliability: Coefficient alpha ranged from .71 to .87.

Validity: Correlation with other variables ranged from –.02 to .26.

Author: Wayne, S. J., and Ferris, G. R.

Article: Influence tactics, affect, and exchange quality in supervisor–subordinate interactions: A laboratory experiment and field study.

Journal: *Journal of Applied Psychology*, October 1990, *75*(5), 487–499.

■ ■ ■

4459

Test Name: SUBSTANCE USE SCALE

Purpose: To measure cigarette, alcohol, and marijuana use.

Number of Items: 28

Format: Subjects check substances used and their frequency of use.

Reliability: Test–retest reliability ranged from .75 to .87.

Author: Rhodes, J. E., and Jason, L. A.

Article: A social stress model of substance abuse.

Journal: *Journal of Consulting and Clinical Psychology*, August 1990, *58*(4), 395–401.

Related Research: Botvin, G. L., et al. (1984). A cognitive-behavioral approach to substance abuse prevention. *Addictive Behaviors, 9,* 137–147.

■ ■ ■

4460

Test Name: SUBSTITUTES FOR LEADERSHIP QUESTIONNAIRE

Purpose: To measure contextual factors (characteristics of staff, teaching, and the organization structure) known as leadership substitutes.

Number of Items: 41

Format: Includes 10 scales.

Reliability: Internal-consistency reliability estimates ranged from .60 to .85.

Author: Pitner, N. J.

Article: Leadership substitutes: Their factorial validity in educational organizations.

Journal: *Educational and Psychological Measurement*, Summer 1988, *48*(2), 307–315.

Related Research: Kerr, S. (1977). Substitutes for leadership: Some implications for organizational design. *Organization and Administrative Sciences*, *8*, 135–146.

■ ■ ■

4461

Test Name: SUPERVISORY STYLES INVENTORY

Purpose: To measure the degree to which a supervisor or trainee endorses behaviors representative of each of three factorially derived orthogonal dimensions of supervisory style.

Number of Items: 33

Format: Includes three dimensions: attractive, impersonally sensitive, and task-oriented. Eight of the items are filler items. Responses are made on a 7-point Likert scale ranging from 1 (*not very*) to 7 (*very*). There are two forms: one for supervisors and one for trainees.

Reliability: Alpha coefficients ranged from .70 to .93. Test–retest (2 weeks) reliability ranged form .78 to .94.

Validity: Correlations with other variables ranged from –.14 to .78.

Author: Efstation, J. F., et al.

Article: Measuring the working alliance in counselor supervision.

Journal: *Journal of Counseling Psychology*, July 1990, *37*(3), 322–329.

Related Research: Friedlander, M. L., & Ward, L. G. (1984). Development and validation of the

Supervisory Styles Inventory. *Journal of Counseling Psychology*, *31*, 541–557.

■ ■ ■

4462

Test Name: SURVEY OF EATING PATTERNS

Purpose: To provide a diagnosis for bulimia.

Number of Items: 14

Format: Provides two measures: a bivariate classification of bulimic or nonbulimic, and a continuous total scale score assessing the severity of bulimia.

Reliability: Cronbach's alpha was .82.

Validity: Correlation with the BULIT was .83.

Author: Berg, K. M.

Article: The prevalence of eating disorders in co-ed versus single-sex residence halls.

Journal: *Journal of College Student Development*, March 1988, *29*(2), 125–131.

Related Research: Shatford, L. A., & Evans, D. R. (1986). Bulimia as a manifestation of the stress process: A LISREL causal modeling analysis. *International Journal of Eating Disorders*, *5*, 451–474.

■ ■ ■

4463

Test Name: SYMPTOM QUESTIONNAIRE

Purpose: To measure symptoms of withdrawal from drug use.

Number of Items: 39

Format: Subject rated each symptom on a 5-point severity scale.

Reliability: Cronbach's alpha was .92.

Author: Hall, S. M., et al.

Article: Commitment to abstinence and acute stress in relapse to alcohol, opiates and nicotine.

Journal: *Journal of Consulting and Clinical Psychology*, April 1990, *58*(2), 175–181.

Related Research: Bachman, J. B. (1981). Withdrawal scale for cigarette smokers. Unpublished manuscript.
Hershon, H. (1977). Alcohol withdrawal symptoms and drinking behavior. *Journal of Studies on Alcohol*, *38*, 953–970.

■ ■ ■

4464

Test Name: TEACHER–CHILD RATING SCALE

Purpose: To enable teachers to rate the extent to which the child exhibits certain behaviors.

Number of Items: 43

Format: Includes two parts: Problem Behavior Scale and Competent Behavior Scale.

Reliability: Internal consistency reliabilities ranged from .85 to .95.

Author: Dubow, E. F., and Tisak, J.

Article: The relation between stressful life events and adjustment in elementary school children: The role of social support and social problem-solving skills.

Journal: *Child Development*, December 1989, *60*(6), 1412–1423.

Related Research: Hightower, A. D., et al. (1986). The teacher–child rating scale: A brief objective measure of elementary children's school problem behaviors and competencies. *School Psychology Review*, *15*, 393–409.

■ ■ ■

4465

Test Name: TEACHER PARTICIPATION SCALE

Purpose: To measure the involvement of teachers in decisions that affect instructional programs.

Number of Items: 6

Format: Five-point Likert format. Sample items presented.

Reliability: Alpha was .67.

Validity: Correlations with other variables ranged from −.47 to .65.

Author: Brissie, J. S., et al.

Article: Individual, situational contributions to burnout.

Journal: *Journal of Educational Research,* November/December 1988, *82*(2), 106–112.

■ ■ ■

4466

Test Name: TEACHER SELF-CONTROL RATING SCALE

Purpose: To measure self-control in children.

Number of Items: 15

Format: Five-point frequency scale for each of 15 behaviors. All items presented.

Reliability: Cronbach's alphas ranged from .84 to .90.

Author: Work, W. C., et al.

Article: Replication and extension of the Teacher Self-Control Rating Scale.

Journal: *Journal of Consulting and Clinical Psychology,* February 1987, *55*(1), 115–116.

Related Research: Humphrey, L. L. (1982). Children's and teacher's perspectives on children's self-control: The development of two rating scales. *Journal of Consulting and Clinical Psychology, 50,* 624–633.

■ ■ ■

4467

Test Name: TEACHER'S PERCEPTIONS QUESTIONNAIRE

Purpose: To measure positive and negative behavioral reactions to prevention training.

Number of Items: 13

Format: Teachers indicate frequency of behaviors on a 7-point scale. All items are presented.

Reliability: Alpha was .68.

Author: Wurtele, S. K., et al.

Article: Comparison of programs for teaching personal and safety skills to preschoolers.

Journal: *Journal of Consulting and Clinical Psychology,* August 1989, *57*(4), 505–511.

Related Research: Wurtele, S. K., & Miller-Perrin, C. C. (1987). An evaluation of side effects associated with participation in a sexual abuse prevention program. *Journal of School Health, 57,* 228–231.

■ ■ ■

4468

Test Name: TEACHER'S RATING SCALE

Purpose: To measure behavioral manifestations of anxiety in a school environment.

Number of Items: 17

Format: Includes a 5-point scale.

Validity: Correlations with other variables ranged from −.56 to .37 (22 boys) and from −.21 to .22 (28 girls).

Author: Kleinman, M. J, and Russ, S. W.

Article: Primary process thinking and anxiety in children.

Journal: *Journal of Personality Assessment,* Summer 1988, *52*(2), 254–262.

Related Research: Sarason, S. B., et al. (1960). *Anxiety in elementary school children.* New York: Wiley.

■ ■ ■

4469

Test Name: TEACHER TREATMENT INVENTORY REVISED

Purpose: To measure children's perceptions of the frequency of 30

teacher behaviors toward a hypothetical male or female high or low achieving student.

Number of Items: 30

Format: The children respond to each item by marking one of four responses: always, often, sometimes, or never. All items are presented.

Reliability: Internal consistency coefficients (Cronbach's alpha) ranged from .58 to .84 (*N*s ranged from 87 to 137). Test–retest reliability coefficients (2 weeks) ranged from .65 to .83.

Author: Weinstein, R. S., et al.

Article: Pygmalion and the student: Age and classroom differences in children's awareness of teacher expectations.

Journal: *Child Development,* August 1987, *58*(4), 1079–1093.

Related Research: Weinstein, R. S., et al. (1982). Student perceptions of differential teacher treatment in open and traditional classrooms. *Journal of Educational Psychology, 75,* 678–692.

■ ■ ■

4470

Test Name: TEENAGER'S SELF-TEST: DRUG USE

Purpose: To measure use of cigarettes, alcohol and marijuana, the characteristics of users and perceived benefits of use.

Number of Items: 31

Format: Five-point Likert format.

Reliability: Alphas ranged from .73 to .78.

Author: Botvin, G. J., et al.

Article: Preventing adolescent drug abuse through a multimodel cognitive–behavioral approach: Results of a 3-year study.

Journal: *Journal of Consulting and Clinical Psychology,* August 1990, *58*(4), 437–446.

Related Research: U. S. Public Health Service. (1974). *Teenager's self-test: Cigarette smoking* (DHEW Publication No. CDC 74–8723). Bethesda, MD: U. S. Department of Health, Education, and Welfare, National Clearing House for Smoking and Health.

■ ■ ■

4471

Test Name: TERMINATION BEHAVIOR CHECKLIST

Purpose: To identify client behaviors during termination phase of counseling.

Number of Items: 18

Format: Clients check behaviors that occurred during termination phase of counseling and identified any additional behaviors that occurred. All items are presented.

Reliability: Pearson coefficient was .88 for items checked on two occasions ($N = 20$).

Author: Marx, J. A., and Gelso, C. J.

Article: Termination of individual counseling in a university counseling center.

Journal: *Journal of Counseling Psychology*, January 1987, *34*(1), 3–9.

Related Research: Marx, J. A. (1983). An exploratory study of the termination of individual counseling in a university counseling center. *Dissertation Abstracts International*, *44*, 3938B. (University Microfilms No. 84–05.684)

■ ■ ■

4472

Test Name: TEXAS SOCIAL BEHAVIOR INVENTORY—SHORT FORM

Purpose: To measure social behavior.

Number of Items: 16

Format: Utilizes a true–false format.

Reliability: Corrected split-half reliability was .72.

Author: Pickering, G. S., and Galvin-Schaefers, K.

Article: An empirical study of reentry women.

Journal: *Journal of Counseling Psychology*, July 1988, *35*(3), 298–303.

Related Research: Helmreich, R., & Stapp, J. (1974). Short forms of the Texas Social Behavior Inventory, an objective measure of self-esteem. *Bulletin of the Psychonomic Society*, *4*, 473–475.

■ ■ ■

4473

Test Name: THERAPEUTIC REACTANCE SCALE

Purpose: To measure subjects' reactance potential.

Number of Items: 28

Format: Includes two subscales: verbal and behavioral reactance.

Reliability: Internal consistency reliabilities ranged from .75 to .84. Test–retest reliabilities were .76 (1 week, total scale) .59 (3 weeks, total scale) and .57 and .60 (3 weeks) for verbal and behavioral subscales, respectively.

Validity: Correlations with other variables ranged from –.12 to .11.

Author: Dowd, E. T., et al.

Article: Compliance-based and defiance-based intervention strategies and psychological reactance in the treatment of free and unfree behavior.

Journal: *Journal of Counseling Psychology*, October 1988, *35*(4), 370–376.

Related Research: Dowd, E. T., et al. (1984, August). *The therapeutic reactance scale: Development and reliability.* Paper presented at the meeting of the American Psychological Association, Toronto.

■ ■ ■

4474

Test Name: TIME MANAGEMENT BEHAVIOR SCALE

Purpose: To measure how time management behaviors are used.

Number of Items: 46

Format: Five-point rating scales. All items are presented.

Reliability: Interitem reliabilities ranged from .59 to .89.

Validity: Correlations with other variables ranged from –.55 to .32.

Author: Macan, T. H., et al.

Article: College students' time management: Correlations with academic performance and stress.

Journal: *Journal of Educational Psychology*, December 1990, *82*(4), 671–682.

■ ■ ■

4475

Test Name: TIME STRUCTURE QUESTIONNAIRE

Purpose: To measure use of time.

Number of Items: 5

Format: Seven-point agreement scales. All items presented.

Reliability: Alpha was .65.

Author: Rowley, K. M., & Feather, N. T.

Article: The impact of unemployment in relation to age and length of unemployment.

Journal: *Journal of Occupational Psychology*, December 1987, *60*(4), 323–332.

Related Research: Feather, N. T., & Bond, M. J. (1983). Time structure and purposeful activity among employed and unemployed university graduates. *Journal of Occupational Pscyhology*, *56*, 241–254.

4476

Test Name: UNETHICAL BEHAVIORS INVENTORY

Purpose: To identify frequency of involvement in unethical academic behaviors.

Number of Items: 18

Format: Responses are made on a 5-point scale ranging from *never* to *always*. All items are presented.

Reliability: Correlations with other variables ranged from –.20 to .20.

Author: Calabrese, R. L., and Cochran, J. T.

Article: The relationship of alienation to cheating among a sample of American adolescents.

Journal: *Journal of Research and Development in Education*, Winter 1990, *23*(2), 65–72.

Related Research: Stevens, G. (1984). Ethical inclinations of tomorrow's citizens: Actions speak louder. *Journal of Business Education*, *59*, 147–152.

■ ■ ■

4477

Test Name: VOLUNTARY SIMPLICITY SCALE

Purpose: To measure behavior of and motivation to enter a lifestyle of low consumption, self-sufficiency, and ecological responsibility.

Number of Items: 18

Format: Various multiple-choice frequency scales. All items presented.

Validity: Factor structure and correlations with a criterion variable were similar in three different cities.

Author: Shama, A.

Article: The voluntary simplicity consumer: A comparative study.

Journal: *Psychological Reports*, December 1988, *63*(3), 859–869.

Related Research: Leonard-Barton, D. (1981). Voluntary simplicity lifestyles and energy conservation. *Journal of Consumer Research*, *8*, 243–252(b).

CHAPTER 9
Communication

4478

Test Name: AFFECTIVE CONTENTS OF COMMUNICATION SCALE

Purpose: To measure contents of communication between nurses and supervisors.

Number of Items: 12

Format: Five-point frequency scales. All items presented.

Reliability: Alphas ranged from .75 to .92 across subscales.

Author: Beehr, T. A., et al.

Article: Social support and occupational stress: Talking to supervisors.

Journal: *Journal of Vocational Behavior*, February 1990, *36*(1), 61–81.

Related Research: Fenlason, K. J. (1989). *The effects of contents of supportive communications on work stress: A replication and extension.* Paper presented at the annual meeting of the Midwestern Psychological Association, Chicago.

■ ■ ■

4479

Test Name: COMMUNICATION QUALITY SCALE

Purpose: To assess the extent to which respondents perceived that their boss clearly communicated job expectations and provided useful information.

Number of Items: 6

Format: Responses are made on a 5-point scale ranging from 1 (*to a very little extent*) to 5 (*a very great extent*).

Reliability: Coefficient alpha was .86.

Validity: Correlations with other variables ranged from −.40 to .37.

Author: Frone, M. R., and McFarlin, D. B.

Article: Chronic occupational stressors, self-focused attention, and well being: Testing a cybernetic model of stress.

Journal: *Journal of Applied Psychology*, December 1989, *74*(6), 876–883.

Related Research: Frone, M. C., & Major, B. (1988). Communication quality and job satisfaction among managerial nurses: The moderating influence of job involvement. *Group and Organization Studies, 13,* 332–347.

■ ■ ■

4480

Test Name: DECISION CONFLICT AND COOPERATION QUESTIONNAIRE

Purpose: To assess decision conflict and cooperation.

Number of Items: 10

Format: Includes three factors: disagreement, openness, and control. All items are presented.

Reliability: Alpha coefficients ranged from .73 to .84.

Author: Dalton, D. R., and Cosier, R. A.

Article: Development and psychometric properties of the Decision Conflict and Cooperation Questionnaire (DCCQ).

Journal: *Educational and Psychological Measurement*, Autumn 1989, *49*(3), 697–700.

Related Research: Cosier, R. A., & Dalton, D. R. (1988). Presenting information under conditions of uncertainty and availability: Some recommendations. *Behavioral Science, 33,* 272–281.

■ ■ ■

4481

Test Name: INFORMATION EXCHANGE

Purpose: To measure in-group and out-group memberships.

Number of Items: 8

Format: Responses are made on a 7-point scale ranging from 1 (*very much so*) to 7 (*not at all*).

Reliability: Internal consistency reliability was .84.

Validity: Correlation with the Leader-Member Exchange scale was .73. Correlations with the Climate Scale ranged from −.04 to .44.

Author: Kozlowski, S. W. J., and Doherty, M. L.

Article: Integration of climate and leadership: Examination of a neglected issue.

Journal: *Journal of Applied Psychology*, August 1989, *74*(4), 546–553.

Related Research: Vecchio, R. P., & Gobdel, B. C. (1984). The vertical dyad linkage model of leadership: Problems and prospects. *Organizational Behavior and Human Performance, 34,* 5–20.

4482

Test Name: INTERNAL DIALOGUE MEASURE

Purpose: To measure covert internal dialogue related to counselor training.

Number of Items: 23

Format: Seven-point Likert format (*very dissimilar* to *very similar*). All items presented.

Reliability: Cronbach's alpha was .86 (task-facilitative items) and .93 (task-distractive items).

Validity: Pretest and posttest means not significantly different. Correlation between facilitative and distractive scores was .40. Correlated from .49 to .55 with anxiety and from .40 to .46 across several personality measures.

Author: Fuqua, D. A., et al.

Article: Preliminary study of internal dialogue in a training setting.

Journal: *Psychological Reports*, February 1986, *58*(1), 163–172.

■ ■ ■

4483

Test Name: INTERPERSONAL COMMUNICATION COMPETENCE SCALE

Purpose: To measure interpersonal communication competence.

Number of Items: 36

Format: Includes 5 dimensions of competence: affiliation/support, social relaxation, empathy, behavioral flexibility, and interaction management.

Reliability: Cronbach's alpha was .90.

Author: Jones, T. S., et al.

Article: Perceptions of style and competence in communication.

Journal: *Perceptual and Motor Skills*, December, 1986, *63*(3), 1224–1226

Related Research: Wiemann, J. (1977). Explication and test of a model of communicative competence.

Human Communication Research, 3, 195–213.

■ ■ ■

4484

Test Name: INTERPERSONAL NETWORK QUESTIONNAIRE

Purpose: To measure constructs of social networks including: social participation, confidant supports, size, and frequency of contact.

Number of Items: 31

Format: Formats include: list, Likert, and yes–no. Includes three parts: mutuality of relationships, network size, and frequency of contact.

Reliability: Alpha coefficients ranged from .56 to .77.

Validity: Correlation with the Inventory of Socially Supportive Behaviors was .31.

Author: Pearson, J. E.

Article: The Interpersonal Network Questionnaire: A tool for social network assessment.

Journal: *Measurement and Evaluation in Counseling and Development*, October 1987, *20*(3), 99–105.

■ ■ ■

4485

Test Name: OPENNESS TO EXPERIENCE INVENTORY

Purpose: To measure agreement with statements reflecting an openness to experience in six domains.

Number of Items: 48

Format: True–false format including six domains: fantasy, feelings, esthetics, actions, ideas, and values.

Validity: Correlation with the Levels of Emotional Awareness Scale was .33.

Author: Lane, R. D., et al.

Article: The Levels of Emotional Awareness Scale: A cognitive–developmental measure of emotion.

Journal: *Journal of Personality Assessment*, Fall 1990, *55*(1 and 2), 124–134.

Related Research: Coan, R. W. (1972). Measurable components of openness to experience. *Journal of Consulting and Clinical Psychology, 39,* 346.

■ ■ ■

4486

Test Name: PATIENT SELF-DISCLOSURE INSTRUMENT—IMPORTANT SCALE

Purpose: To measure the patient's rating of the importance of discussing each item with the clinician.

Number of Items: 21

Format: Includes three areas: personal problems and feelings, responses to health care, and lifestyle. Items are rated for both difficulty and importance of discussing the item with the clinician.

Reliability: Internal consistency ranged from .82 to .91. Test–retest reliability ranged from .81 to .88.

Validity: Correlations with Jourard's SD-25 inventory ranged from .26 to .57.

Author: Byers, P. H., et al.

Article: Validity of health self-disclosure importance ratings.

Journal: *Educational and Psychological Measurement*, Spring 1989, *49*(1), 171–175.

Related Research: Dawson, C., et al. (1984). A patient self-disclosure instrument. *Research in Nursing and Health, 7,* 135–147.

■ ■ ■

4487

Test Name: SD-25

Purpose: To measure the patient's rating of the importance of disclosing each item to the clinician.

Number of Items: 25-, 40-, and 60-item versions.

Format: Items address such topics as attitudes, opinions, money, hobbies, and work. Items are rated on a 7-point importance scale.

Reliability: Split-half reliabilities ranged from .75 to .99. Test–retest reliabilities ranged from .61 to .86.

Validity: Productive validity was .78. Concurrent validity was .63. Correlations with Dawson's Patient Self-Disclosure Instrument ranged from .26 to .57.

Author: Byers, P. H., et al.

Article: Validity of health self-disclosure importance ratings.

Journal: *Educational and Psychological Measurement*, Spring 1989, *49*(1), 171–175.

Related Research: Chelune, G. J. (1978). Nature and assessment of self-disclosing behavior. In P. McReynolds (Ed.), *Advances in psychological measurement* (Vol. 4). San Francisco: Jossey-Bass.

■ ■ ■

4488

Test Name: SELF-DISCLOSURE INVENTORY FOR ADOLESCENTS—REVISED

Purpose: To measure self-disclosure for adolescents.

Number of Items: 36

Format: Includes six categories: health and physical development, personal concerns, boy–girl relations, home and family, school concerns, and money and status concerns. Responses are made on a Likert scale ranging from 1 (*never talk about with*) to 4 (*often talk about with*).

Reliability: Alpha coefficients ranged from .63 to .88.

Author: Garcia, P. A., and Geisler, J. S.

Article: Sex and age/grade differences in adolescents' self-disclosure.

Journal: *Perceptual and Motor Skills*, October 1988, *67*(2), 427–432.

Related Research: West, L. W. (1971). A study of the validity of the Self-Disclosure Inventory for Adolescents. *Perceptual and Motor Skills*, *33*, 91–100.

■ ■ ■

4489

Test Name: SELF-DISCLOSURE SCALE

Purpose: To measure self-disclosure.

Number of Items: 25-, 40-, and 60-item versions are available.

Format: Self-report.

Reliability: Various measures of reliability ranged from .61 to .99.

Author: Byers, P. H., et al.

Article: Self-disclosure, anxiety, and health worry in unscheduled outpatients.

Journal: *Psychological Reports*, April 1988, *62*(2), 379–386.

Related Research: Jourard, S. M. (1971). *Self disclosure: An experimental analysis of the transparent self.* New York: Wiley Interscience.

■ ■ ■

4490

Test Name: SELF-DISCLOSURE SENTENCE COMPLETION BLANK

Purpose: To measure self-disclosive behavior.

Number of Items: 20

Format: Each item is a sentence stem stated by an interviewer and completed verbally with a candid, immediate response by the subject. Each response is later rated by three raters on a 5-level scoring system from *Very revealing* (Level 1) to *Very evasive* (Level 5).

Reliability: Interrater reliability was .93 and interater agreement was .75.

Author: Stevens, M. J., et al.

Article: Effect of eye gaze on self-disclosure.

Journal: *Perceptual and Motor Skills*, June 1986, *62*(3), 939–942.

Related Research: Greene, R. (1964). A sentence completion procedure for measuring self-disclosure. Unpublished Master's thesis, Ohio State University.

■ ■ ■

4491

Test Name: WORKING ALLIANCE INVENTORY

Purpose: To provide a self-report instrument for measuring the quality of alliance.

Number of Items: 36

Format: Responses to each item are made on a 7-point scale. There are two versions of the instrument: client and counselor. The instruments include 3 constituent components: tasks, bonds, and goals. All items of the client form are presented.

Reliability: Reliability estimates ranged from .85 to .88 (client's form) and from .68 to .87 (counselor's form).

Validity: Correlations with other variables ranged from .09 to .65 (client's form) and from .16 to .68 (counselor's form).

Author: Horvath, A. O., and Greenberg, L. S.

Article: Development and validation of the Working Alliance Inventory.

Journal: *Journal of Counseling Psychology*, April 1989, *36*(2), 223–233.

Related Research: Bordin, E. S. (1980, June). *Of human bonds that bind or free.* Presidential address delivered at the meeting of the Society for Psychotherapy Research, Pacific Grove, CA.

CHAPTER 10
Concept Meaning

4492

Test Name: BELIEF SYSTEMS TEST

Purpose: To measure conceptual level.

Format: Five-point Likert format. Sample items presented.

Reliability: Alpha ranged from .62 to .96 across 11 subscales.

Validity: Correlations with stress scales ranged from −.40 to .33.

Author: Kagan, D. M.

Article: Construct validity of belief systems subscales.

Journal: *The Journal of Social Psychology*, December 1986, *126*(5), 725–734.

Related Research: Gore, E. J. (1985). *Development of an Objective Measure of Belief Systems.* Unpublished doctoral dissertation. University of Colorado, Boulder.

■ ■ ■

4493

Test Name: CONCEPTUAL LEVEL SCALE

Purpose: To assess conceptual level.

Number of Items: 6

Format: Employs the paragraph completion method.

Reliability: Interrater reliability coefficient was .92.

Author: Stoppard, J. M., and Henri, G. S.

Article: Conceptual level matching and effects of assertion training.

Journal: *Journal of Counseling Psychology*, January 1987, *34*(1), 55–61.

Related Research: Hunt, D. E., et al. (1978). *Assessing conceptual level by the paragraph completion method.* Toronto, Ontario, Canada: Ontario Institute for Studies in Education.

CHAPTER 11
Creativity

4494

Test Name: CREATIVE
ACTIVITIES CHECK LIST

Purpose: To identify ratings of
children's creativity.

Number of Items: 55

Format: Frequency of involvement
for each activity is indicated on a
four-choice scale ranging from *never*
to *six or more times*. Includes four
domains: math-science, art, crafts,
and writing. Examples are
presented.

Reliability: Alpha coefficient ranged
from .64 to .91 across the domains.

Author: Runco, M. A., et al.

Article: Agreement between mothers
and sons on ratings of creative activity.

Journal: *Educational and
Psychological Measurement,* Autumn
1990, *50*(3), 673–680.

Related Research: Runco, M. A., &
Okuda, S. M. (1988). Problem
finding, divergent thinking, and the
creative process. *Journal of Youth
and Adolescence, 17,* 211–220.

...

4495

Test Name: CREATIVE PRODUCT
SEMANTIC SCALE

Purpose: To enable judgment of the
creativity of a product.

Number of Items: 70

Format: Items are bipolar adjectives
answered on 7-point scales. All items
are presented.

Reliability: Coefficient alphas ranged
from .69 to .91.

Author: Besemer, S. P., and O'Quin,
K.

Article: Analyzing creative products:
Refinement and test of a judging
instrument.

Journal: *Journal of Creative
Behavior,* 1986, *20*(2), 115–126.

Related Research: Besemer, S. P., &
Treffinger, D. J. (1981). Analysis of
creative products: Review and
synthesis. *Journal of Creative
Behavior, 15*(3), 158–178.

CHAPTER 12
Development

4496

Test Name: BELIEFS AND ACTIONS INVENTORY

Purpose: To assess Eriksonian stage development by examining placement in the eighth stages of Erikson's hierarchy.

Number of Items: 64

Format: Employs a forced-choice, true–false format.

Reliability: Cronbach's alpha ranged from .44 to .74.

Author: Kriegsman, K. H., and Hershenson, D. B.

Article: A comparison of able-bodied and disabled college students on Erikson's ego stages and Maslow's needs levels.

Journal: *Journal of College Student Personnel*, January 1987, *28*(1), 48–53.

Related Research: Hershenson, D. B. (1964). *Erikson's sense of identity, occupational fit, and enculturation in adolescence.* Unpublished doctoral dissertation, Boston University.

• • •

4497

Test Name: EGO IDENTITY SCALE

Purpose: To assess the extent to which the Erikson's first five stages have been resolved.

Number of Items: 60

Format: True–false items.

Reliability: Spearman-Brown corrected correlation coefficient was .85. Coefficient alpha was .85.

Author: Wilson, R. J., et al.

Article: Commuter and resident students' personal and family adjustment.

Journal: *Journal of College Student Personnel*, May 1987, *28*(3), 229–233.

Related Research: Rasmussen, J. E. (1964). Relationship of ego identity to psychosocial effectiveness. *Psychological Reports*, *15*, 815–825.

• • •

4498

Test Name: ERIKSON PSYCHOSOCIAL STAGE INVENTORY—REVISED

Purpose: To assess adolescent and young adult psychosocial maturity.

Number of Items: 54

Format: Responses are made on a 5-point Likert scale. Seven factors are included: initiative, industry, identity, friendship, dating, goal clarity, and self-confidence.

Reliability: Coefficient alphas ranged from .54 to .83.

Author: McPhail, M., et al.

Article: Erikson Psychosocial Stage Inventory: A factor analysis.

Journal: *Educational and Psychological Measurement*, Winter 1986, *46*(4), 979–983.

Related Research: Rosenthal, D. A., et al. (1981). From trust to intimacy: A new inventory for examining Erikson's stages of psychological development. *Journal of Youth and Adolescence*, *10*, 525–535.

4499

Test Name: FAMILY INTERACTION QUESTIONNAIRE

Purpose: To measure the developmental level of parents.

Number of Items: 2

Format: Subjects write 5-minute descriptions of their mothers and fathers, which are then scored by judges on a 9-point development scale.

Reliability: Correlation between raters was .92 (mother) and .94 (father).

Author: Raynes, E., and Auerbach, C.

Article: Level of object representation and psychic structure deficit in obese persons.

Journal: *Psychological Reports*, February 1989, *64*(1), 291–294.

Related Research: Blatt, S. J., et al. (1981). *The assessment of qualitative and structure dimensions of object relations.* New Haven, CT: Yale University Press.

• • •

4500

Test Name: GOAL INSTABILITY SCALE

Purpose: To measure consolidation of goals reflective of the idealized self.

Number of Items: 10

Format: Responses to each item are made on a 6-point Likert scale ranging from 1 (*strongly like me*) to 6 (*not at all like me*).

Reliability: Test–retest (2 weeks) reliability was .81.

Validity: Correlations with other variables ranged from .10 to .69.

Author: Robbins, S. B., and Schwitzer, A. M.

Article: Validity of the Superiority and Goal Instability Scales as predictors of women's adjustment to college life.

Journal: *Measurement and Evaluation in Counseling and Development*, October 1988, *21*, (3), 117–123.

Related Research: Robbins, S., & Patton, M. J. (1985). Self-psychology and career development: Construction of the superiority and goal instability scales. *Journal of Counseling Psychology*, *32*, 221–231.

■ ■ ■

4501

Test Name: IDENTITY ACHIEVEMENT SCALE

Purpose: To assess identity achievement.

Number of Items: 24

Format: Forced-choice items with scores ranging from 0 to 24.

Reliability: Test–retest (1 week) reliability was .76.

Author: Jones, L. K.

Article: Measuring a three-dimensional construct of career indecision among college students: A version of the Vocational Decision Scale—The Career Decision Profile.

Journal: *Journal of Counseling Psychology*, October 1989, *36*(4), 477–486.

Related Research: Simmons, D. D. (1973). *Research manual for the Identity Achievement Scale.* Unpublished manuscript, Oregon State University, Corvallis.

4502

Test Name: INFANT DEVELOPMENT QUESTIONNAIRE

Purpose: To determine mothers' understanding of when specific infant behaviors emerge.

Number of Items: 56

Format: Includes four domains: motor, language, cognitive, and social.

Reliability: Split-half reliability coefficients ranged from .59 to .78.

Author: Gullo, D. F.

Article: A comparative study of adolescent and older mothers' knowledge of infant abilities.

Journal: *Child Study Journal*, 1988, *18*(3), 223–231.

Related Research: Granger, C. (1982). Young adolescents' knowledge of infant abilities. *Dissertation Abstracts International*, *42*, DA8211152.

■ ■ ■

4503

Test Name: INVENTORY OF PSYCHOSOCIAL BALANCE

Purpose: To assess the eight Erisksonian psychosocial stages.

Number of Items: 120

Format: Responses are made on a 5-point Likert response format ranging from 1 (*strongly agree*) to 5 (*strongly disagree*).

Reliability: Alpha coefficients ranged from .48 to .74 (102 college students) and from .64 to .79 (73 elderly). Test–retest (1 month) reliability ranged from .78 to .90.

Validity: Correlations with other variables ranged form −.37 to .56.

Author: Domino, G., and Affanso, D. D.

Article: A personality measure of Erikson's life stages: The Inventory of Psychosocial Balance.

Journal: *Journal of Personality Assessment*, Summer 1990, *54*(3 and 4), 576–588.

■ ■ ■

4504

Test Name: IOWA PEGBOARD FINE-MOTOR TASK

Purpose: To measure fine-motor task development of preschool and school-age children.

Number of Items: 50

Time Required: 60 seconds.

Format: Subject places as many pegs as possible within 60 seconds in a 50-hole pegboard arranged in 5 rows of 10 holes each.

Reliability: Test–retest (4 to 8 weeks) reliability was .80 ($N = 73$).

Validity: Correlations with California Scale of Infant Development was .66 and with age was .63.

Author: Malby, J. N., et al.

Article: The Iowa Pegboard Fine-Motor Task: Normative performance and research applications.

Journal: *Perceptual and Motor Skills*, June 1987, *64*(3, Part 1), 995–1002.

Related Research: Pease, D. (1978, June 29). *Of pegs and beads: Development of fine-motor performance tests.* Paper presented at the meeting of the American Home Economics Association, New Orleans.

■ ■ ■

4505

Test Name: KENT INFANT DEVELOPMENT SCALE (MODIFIED)

Purpose: To measure developmental status of infants aged 2 to 13 months by asking the caregiver questions about an infant's abilities.

Number of Items: 252

Format: Yes–no format.

Validity: The test predicted Bayley scores and Stanford-Binet IQ.

Author: Marrow-Tlucak, et al.

Article: The Kent Infant Development Scale: Concurrent and predictive validity of a modified administration.

Journal: *Psychological Reports*, June 1987, *60*(3)I, 887–894.

Related Research: Katoff, L., et al. (1981). *The Kent Infant Development Scale*. Kent, OH: Kent Developmental Metrics.

• • •

4506

Test Name: MEASURE OF EPISTEMOLOGICAL REFLECTION

Purpose: To assess intellectual development.

Format: Addresses six domains of thinking related to learning: decision making; role of the learner, instructor, peers, and evaluation in the learning process; and the nature of knowledge. An example is presented.

Reliability: Interrater reliability was .80 (*N* = 752). Internal consistency was .74 (*N* = 752).

Validity: Correlation with interview scores was .93.

Author: Magolda, M. B. B.

Article: Comparing open-ended interviews and standardized measures of intellectual development.

Journal: *Journal of College Student Personnel*, September 1987, *28*(5), 443–448.

Related Research: Taylor, M. B. (1983). The development of the Measure of Epistemological Reflection. *Dissertation Abstracts International*, *44*, 1065A. (University Microfilms No. DA83–18, 441)

• • •

4507

Test Name: MEN'S ADULT LIFE EXPERIENCES INVENTORY

Purpose: To assess the frequency and intensity of 11 developmentally related domains of concerns of middle-aged men.

Number of Items: 97

Format: Yes–no for each item. If yes, a 4-point intensity scale follows.

Reliability: Total alpha was .97; across subscales alphas ranged from .79 to .86.

Validity: Age was a significant predictor (*F* = 4.05, *p* <.04). Factor analytic results also presented.

Author: DeLuccie, M. F., et al.

Article: The Men's Adult Life Experience Inventory: An instrument for assessing developmental concerns of middle age.

Journal: *Psychological Reports*, April 1989, *64*(2), 479–485.

• • •

4508

Test Name: MUTUALITY OF AUTONOMY SCALE

Purpose: To assess the structure of a person's object representations across a developmental continuum.

Format: Subject's responses are rated on a 7-point scale representing progressive levels of the development of mature object representations.

Reliability: Reliability between two raters was 98%.

Validity: Correlations with other variables ranged from .10 to .60.

Author: Hart, B., and Hilton, I.

Article: Dimensions of personality organization as predictors of teenage pregnancy risk.

Journal: *Journal of Personality Assessment*, Spring 1988, *52*(1), 116–132.

Related Research: Urist, J. (1977). Some structural considerations in the relationship between M and empathy. *Journal of Personality Assessment*, *41*, 573–578.

4509

Test Name: OCCUPATIONAL IDENTITY SCALE

Purpose: To measure the level of identity development specifically within the occupational domain.

Number of Items: 28

Format: Includes four factors: achievement, moratorium, foreclosure, and diffusion. Responses are made on a 5-point Likert scale ranging from 5 (*strongly agree*) to 1 (*strongly disagree*).

Reliability: Reliability coefficients ranged from .70 to .87.

Validity: Correlations with similar instruments ranged from .43 to .79.

Author: Neimeyer, G. J., and Metzler, A.

Article: The development of vocational schemas.

Journal: *The Journal of Vocational Behavior*, February 1987, *30*(1), 16–32.

Related Research: Melgosa, J. (1985). *Occupational identity assessment among middle and late adolescents*. Unpublished doctoral dissertation, Andrews University.

• • •

4510

Test Name: PERCEIVED SELF QUESTIONNAIRE

Purpose: To measure comprehensively the model of maturing.

Number of Items: 50

Format: Response to each of the bipolar items is made on an 8-point scale. Examples are presented.

Reliability: Test–retest correlation coefficients ranged from .47 to .78.

Validity: Correlations with other variables ranged from .26 to −.69.

Author: Jones, L. K.

Article: Adapting to the first semester of college: A test of Heath's model of maturing.

Journal: *Journal of College Student Personnel*, May 1987, *28*(3), 205–211.

Related Research: Heath, D. H. (1968). *Growing up in college: Liberal education and maturity*. San Francisco: Jossey-Bass.

■ ■ ■

4511

Test Name: PERSONAL MATURITY SCALE

Purpose: To measure the maturity of children.

Number of Items: 14

Format: Six-point scales. All items presented.

Reliability: Alpha was .87.

Validity: Standardized regression coefficients with verbal and math test scores ranged from .39 to 1.05.

Author: Entwistle, D., et al.

Article: A social psychological model of the schooling process over first grade.

Journal: *Social Psychology Quarterly*, September 1988, *51*(3), 173–189.

■ ■ ■

4512

Test Name: PHONEMIC AWARENESS TEST

Purpose: To measure phonemic awareness.

Number of Items: 42

Format: Administered orally. Sample items presented.

Reliability: Alphas were greater than .70 for all subscales.

Author: Juel, C., et al.

Article: Acquisition of literacy: A longitudinal study of children in first and second grade.

Journal: *Journal of Educational Psychology*, August 1986, *78*(4), 243–255.

Related Research: Roper/Schneider, H. D. W. (1984). *Spelling, Word Recognition, and Phonemic Awareness Among First Grade Children*. Unpublished doctoral dissertation, University of Texas.

■ ■ ■

4513

Test Name: PRINT AWARENESS TEST

Purpose: To assess how children comprehend the purposes of print media.

Number of Items: 15

Format: Children are presented with problems to solve in which one solution is using print media. Sample items are presented.

Reliability: Internal consistency was .85. Test–retest reliability was .91.

Validity: Correlations with reading comprehension ranged from .62 to .69. ($p < .05$).

Author: Huba, M. E., et al.

Article: Prereaders' understanding of the purposes of print and subsequent reading achievement.

Journal: *Journal of Educational Research*, March/April, 1989, *82*(4), 210–215.

Related Research: Huba, M. E., et al. (1987). *Print awareness: An aspect of language development*. Paper presented at the annual meeting of the Iowa Educational Research and Evaluation Association, Ames, IA.

■ ■ ■

4514

Test Name: PSYCHOLOGICAL STAGE INVENTORY (MODIFIED)

Purpose: To measure Erikson's eight stages of development.

Number of Items: 92

Time Required: 20 minutes.

Reliability: Alphas ranged from .75 to .97 across subscales.

Author: Darling-Fisher, C. S., and Leidy, N. K.

Article: Measuring Eriksonian development in the adult: The Modified Erikson Psychosocial Stage Inventory.

Journal: *Psychological Reports*, June 1988, *62*(3), 747–754.

Related Research: Rosenthal, D., et al. (1981). From trust to intimacy: A new inventory for examining Erikson's stages of psychosocial development. *Journal of Youth and Adolescence*, *10*, 525–537.

■ ■ ■

4515

Test Name: SCALE OF INTELLECTUAL DEVELOPMENT

Purpose: To measure cognitive development.

Number of Items: 101

Format: Includes four subscales: dualism, relativism, commitment, and empathy. Employs a 4-point Likert format.

Reliability: Cronbach's coefficient of internal consistency ranged from .70 to .81.

Validity: Correlations with Allen Paragraph Completion Instrument ranged from −.39 to .17.

Author: Stonewater, B. B., et al.

Article: Intellectual development using the Petty scheme: An exploratory comparison of two assessment instruments.

Journal: *Journal of College Student Personnel*, November 1986, *27*(6), 542–547.

Related Research: Erwin, T. D. (1983). The Scale of Intellectual Development: Measuring Penny's scheme. *Journal of College Student Personnel*, *24*, 6–12.

4516

Test Name: SENTENCE COMPLETION TEST

Purpose: To measure psychological maturity.

Number of Items: 36

Format: Items each consist of the completion of a sentence stem.

Validity: Correlation with the Levels of Emotional Awareness Scale was .40.

Author: Lane, R. D., et al.

Article: The Levels of Emotional Awareness Scale: A cognitive–developmental measure of emotion.

Journal: *Journal of Personality Assessment*, Fall 1990, *55*(1 and 2), 124–134.

Related Research: Loevinger, J., & Wessler, R. (1970). *Measuring ego development. Volume I: Construction and use of a sentence completion test.* San Francisco: Jossey-Bass.

■ ■ ■

4517

Test Name: SENTENCE COMPLETION TEST— SHORTENED FORM

Purpose: To assess ego development.

Number of Items: 18

Format: Respondents complete each sentence with their own thoughts.

Reliability: Interrater reliability ranged from .85 to .94.

Author: Locke, D. C., and Zimmerman, N. A.

Article: Effects of peer-counseling training on psychological maturity of Black students.

Journal: *Journal of College Student Personnel*, November 1987, *28*(6), 525–532.

Related Research: Loevinger, J., & Wessler, R. (1970). *Measuring ego development*. San Francisco: Jossey-Bass.

■ ■ ■

4518

Test Name: SOCIOMORAL REFLECTION OBJECTIVE MEASURE (SHORT FORM)

Purpose: To measure developmental status of justifications for moral decisions.

Time Required: 20 minutes.

Format: Multiple choice.

Reliability: Alphas ranged from .58 to .70. Test–retest reliability ranged from .46 to .75.

Validity: Concurrent validity ranged from .21 to .47. Construct validity ranged from .34 to .49.

Author: Basinger, K. S., and Gibbs, J. C.

Article: Validation of the Sociomoral Reflection Objective Inventory— Short Form.

Journal: *Psychological Reports*, August 1987, *61*(1), 139–146.

Related Research: Gibbs, J. C., et al. (1982). Construction and validation of a simplified, group administered equivalent to the Moral Judgment Interview. *Child Development*, 55, 527–536.

■ ■ ■

4519

Test Name: SUPERIORITY SCALE

Purpose: To measure one's level of development in grandiosity.

Number of Items: 10

Format: Items are rated on a 6-point Likert scale ranging from 1 (*strongly agree*) to 6 (*strongly disagree*). Sample items are presented.

Reliability: Test–retest reliability was .80. Cronbach's alpha was .76.

Author: Robinson, D. A. G., and Cooper, S. E.

Article: The relationship of Kohut's self-psychology to career choice certainty and satisfaction.

Journal: *Journal of College Student Development*, May 1988, *29*(3), 228–232.

Related Research: Robbins, S., & Patton, M. (1985). Self psychology and career development: Construction of the superiority and goal instability scales. *Journal of Counseling Psychology*, 33, 221–231.

■ ■ ■

4520

Test Name: WASHINGTON UNIVERSITY SENTENCE COMPLETION TEST

Purpose: To assess personality development.

Number of Items: 36

Format: Sentence completion items each scored on one of nine levels. Descriptions of the levels are presented.

Reliability: Reliability estimate between two raters was 90%.

Validity: Correlations with other variables ranged from .31 to .53.

Author: Hart, B., and Hilton, I.

Article: Dimensions of personality organization as predictors of teenage pregnancy risk.

Journal: *Journal of Personality Assessment*, Spring 1988, *52*(1), 116–132.

Related Research: Loevinger, J., & Redmore, C. (1978). *Measuring ego development* (Vol. 2). San Francisco: Jossey-Bass.

Family

4521

Test Name: ATTITUDES TOWARD WIFE ABUSE SCALE

Purpose: To measure attitudes toward wife abuse along a conservative to nontraditional continuum.

Number of Items: 8

Format: Seven-point Likert format. All items presented.

Reliability: Alpha was .63.

Author: Briere, J.

Article: Predicting self-reported likelihood of battering: Attitudes and childhood experiences.

Journal: *Journal of Research in Personality*, March 1987, *21*(1), 61–69.

Related Research: Briere, J., & Malamuth, N. M. (1983). Self-reported likelihood of sexual aggression: Attitudinal versus sexual explanations. *Journal of Research in Personality*, *17*, 315–323.

4522

Test Name: ATTITUDES TOWARD WORKING MOTHERS SCALE

Purpose: To assess attitudes toward the dual roles of mother and worker and the effects of these roles on the woman and her family.

Number of Items: 32

Format: Employs a Likert scale.

Reliability: Cronbach's alpha was .95.

Author: Etaugh, C., and Study, G. G.

Article: Demographic predictors of college students' attitudes toward working mothers.

Journal: *Journal of College Student Development*, September 1989, *30*(5), 465–466.

Related Research: Tetenbaum, T. J., et al. (1983). The construct validation of an Attitudes Toward Working Mothers Scale. *Psychology of Women Quarterly*, *8*, 69–78.

4523

Test Name: BELIEFS ABOUT THE CONSEQUENCES OF MATERNAL EMPLOYMENT FOR CHILDREN

Purpose: To assess beliefs about effects of maternal employment on children.

Number of Items: 24

Format: Six-point Likert format.

Reliability: Alphas ranged from .88 to .91.

Author: Greenberger, E., and O'Neil, R.

Article: Parents' concerns about their child's development: Implications for fathers' and mothers' well-being and attitudes toward work.

Journal: *Journal of Marriage and the Family*, August 1990, *52*(3), 621–635.

Related Research: Greenberger, G., et al. (1988). Beliefs about the consequences of maternal employment for children. *Psychology of Women Quarterly*, *12*, 35–39.

4524

Test Name: BLOCK CHILD-REARING PRACTICES REPORT Q-SORT

Purpose: To assess the quality of parent–child relationships.

Number of Items: 91

Format: Includes 21 subscales comprising two clusters: positive parenting and authoritarian control. Subjects sort the items into a nine-step distribution.

Reliability: Test–retest reliability was .71.

Author: Deal, J. E., et al.

Article: Parental agreement on child-rearing orientations: Relations to parental, marital, family, and child characteristics.

Journal: *Child Development*, October 1989, *60*(5), 1025–1034.

Related Research: Block, J., et al. (1981). Parental agreement–disagreement on child-rearing orientations and gender-related personality correlates in children. *Child Development*, *52*, 965–974.

4525

Test Name: CATEGORY SYSTEM FOR PARTNER'S INTERACTION

Purpose: To measure interpersonal communication in families.

Number of Items: 12

Format: Verbal categories (all presented) are rated by observers.

Reliability: Interobserver agreement was .80 (kappa) or higher.

Author: Hahlweg, K., et al.

Article: Expressed emotion and patient-relative interaction in families of recent onset schizophrenics.

Journal: *Journal of Consulting and Clinical Psychology*, February 1989, *57*(1), 11–18.

Related Research: Hahlweg, K., et al. (1984). Development and validity of a new system to analyze interpersonal communication. In K. Hahlweg & N. S. Jacobson (Eds.), *Marital interaction: Analysis and modification* (pp. 182–198). New York: Guilford Press.

∎ ∎ ∎

4526

Test Name: CHILD BEHAVIOR TOWARD THE PARENT INVENTORY

Purpose: To assess adolescent affection and positive sentiment by parental report.

Number of Items: 6

Format: Four-point rating scales.

Reliability: Alpha was .85.

Author: Demo, D. H., et al.

Article: Family relations and the self-esteem of adolescents and their parents.

Journal: *Journal of Marriage and the Family*, November 1987, *48*(4), 705–715.

Related Research: Schaefer, E. S., et al. (1979). *Parent report of child behavior to the Parent Inventory*. Chapel Hill, NC: Carolina Institute for Research on Early Education of the Handicapped.

∎ ∎ ∎

4527

Test Name: CHILD-CARE PROBLEM SCALE

Purpose: To measure extent of problems including: availability, cost,

quality, location, sick care, emergencies, and dependability.

Number of Items: 9

Format: Four-point rating scales.

Reliability: Alpha was .90.

Author: Kossek, E. E.

Article: Diversity in child care assistance needs: Employee problems, preferences, and work-related outcomes.

Journal: *Personnel Psychology*, Winter 1990, *43*(4), 769–791.

Related Research: Fernandez, J. P. (1986). *Child care and corporate productivity*. Lexington, MA: Lexington Books.

∎ ∎ ∎

4528

Test Name: CHILD RATING SCALE

Purpose: To assess parents' views of children's feelings.

Number of Items: 36

Format: Four-point true–false scales. Sample items presented.

Reliability: Alpha was .84. Test–retest (2 weeks) reliability was .72.

Author: Alpert-Gillis, L. J., et al.

Article: The children of divorce intervention program: Development, implementation, and evaluation of a program for young urban children.

Journal: *Journal of Consulting and Clinical Psychology*, October 1989, *57*(5), 583–589.

Related Research: Hightower, A. D., et al. (1987). The Child Rating Scale: The development and psychometric refinement of a socio-emotional self-rating scale for elementary school children. *School Psychology Review*, *16*, 239–255.

∎ ∎ ∎

4529

Test Name: CHILDREN'S BELIEFS ABOUT PARENTAL DIVORCE SCALE

Purpose: To measure five beliefs children express about divorce: peer ridicule and avoidance, paternal and maternal blame, fear of abandonment, hope of reunification, and self-blame.

Number of Items: 36

Format: Yes–no. All items presented.

Reliability: Cronbach's alpha ranged from .54 to .78. Test–retest correlations ranged from .41 to .72 (9 weeks).

Validity: Correlations with other variables ranged from −.49 to .54.

Author: Kurdek, L. A., and Berg, B.

Article: Children's Beliefs about Parental Divorce Scale: Psychometric characteristics and concurrent validity.

Journal: *Journal of Consulting and Clinical Psychology*, October 1987, *55*(5), 712–718.

∎ ∎ ∎

4530

Test Name: CHILDREN'S DIVORCE ADJUSTMENT SCALE

Purpose: To assess childrens' feelings about families.

Number of Items: 17

Format: Three-point scales (*usually yes* to *usually no*). Sample items presented.

Reliability: Test–retest reliability was .62.

Author: Alpert-Gillis, L. J., et al.

Article: The children of divorce intervention program: Development, implementation, and evaluation of a program for young urban children.

Journal: *Journal of Consulting and Clinical Psychology*, October 1989, *57*(5), 583–589.

Related Research: Sterling, S. (1986). *School-based intervention program for young children of divorce*. Unpublished doctoral dissertation, University of Rochester, Rochester, NY.

4531

Test Name: CHILDREN'S PERCEPTION QUESTIONNAIRE

Purpose: To measure interparent discord.

Number of Items: 12

Format: True–false.

Reliability: Cronbach's alpha was .86.

Author: Kurdek, L. A., and Sinclair, R. J.

Article: Adjustment of young adolescents in two-parent nuclear, stepfather, and mother-custody families.

Journal: *Journal of Consulting and Clinical Psychology*, February 1988, *56*(1), 91–96.

Related Research: Emery, R. E., & O'Leary, K. D. (1982). Children's perceptions of marital discord and behavior problems of boys and girls. *Journal of Abnormal Child Psychology, 10*, 11–24.

■ ■ ■

4532

Test Name: CONFLICT BEHAVIOR QUESTIONNAIRE

Purpose: To assess the parent–adolescent relationship.

Number of Items: 75

Format: Responses to each item are either *true* or *false*. Examples are presented.

Reliability: Alpha coefficients were above .88.

Author: Wierson, M., et al.

Article: Buffering young male adolescents against negative parental divorce influences: The role of good parent–adolescent relations.

Journal: *Child Study Journal*, 1989, *19*(2), 101–115.

Related Research: Prinz, R. J., et al. (1979). Multivariate assessment of conflict in distressed and non-

distressed mother-adolescent dyads. *Journal of Applied Behavior Analysis, 12*, 691–700.

■ ■ ■

4533

Test Name: CONJUGAL UNDERSTANDING MEASURE

Purpose: To assess to what degree spouses engage in stimulus discrimination between themselves or with others.

Number of Items: 13

Format: Five-point Likert format. Sample items presented.

Reliability: Alphas ranged from .67 to .87.

Author: de Turk, M. A., and Miller, G. R.

Article: The effects of husbands' and wives' social cognition on their marital adjustment, conjugal power and self-esteem.

Journal: *Journal of Marriage and the Family*, November 1986, *48*(4), 715–724.

Related Research: de Turk, M. A., & Miller, G. R. (1984, October). *Conceptualizing and measuring social cognition in marital communication: A validation study*. Paper presented at the National Council on Family Relations, San Francisco.

■ ■ ■

4534

Test Name: COOPERATIVENESS IN CONFLICT SCALE

Purpose: To measure verbal attacks by spouse, avoidance of confrontation, and compromise.

Number of Items: 15

Format: Five-point scales.

Reliability: Alphas ranged from .85 to .87.

Author: Godwin, D. D., and Scanzoni, J.

Article: Couple consensus during marital joint decision-making: A context, process, outcome model.

Journal: *Journal of Marriage and the Family*, November 1989, *51*(4), 943–956.

Related Research: Rands, M., et al. (1981). Patterns of conflict resolution and marital satisfaction. *Journal of Family Issues, 2*, 297–321.

■ ■ ■

4535

Test Name: COPING-HEALTH INVENTORY OF PARENTS

Purpose: To measure methods of coping with family problems.

Number of Items: 45

Format: Four-point helpfulness rating scale.

Validity: Internal consistency ranged from .71 to .79 across subscales.

Author: Powers, G. M., et al.

Article: Coping patterns of parents of chronically ill children.

Journal: *Psychological Reports*, October 1986, *59*(2)I, 519–522.

Related Research: McCubbin, H. I., et al. (1983). CHIP—*Coping-Health Inventory for Parents*. Madison, WI: Family Stress, Coping and Health Project, University of Wisconsin (available from the first author).

■ ■ ■

4536

Test Name: CORNELL PARENT BEHAVIOR DESCRIPTION

Purpose: To measure perceived parental support and control.

Number of Items: 4

Format: Five-point rating scales.

Reliability: Alphas ranged from .27 to .57.

Author: Clark, C. A., et al.

Article: The transmission of religious beliefs and practices from parents to firstborn adolescent sons.

Journal: *Journal of Marriage and the Family*, May 1988, *50*(2), 463–472.

Related Research: Rogers, R. R. (1966). *The Cornell parent behavior description—the proposed short form.* Unpublished report, Cornell University.
Whitbeck, L. B., & Gecas, V. (1988). Value attributions and value transmission between parents and children. *Journal of Marriage and the Family, 50*, 829–840.

■ ■ ■

4537

Test Name: CORNELL PARENT BEHAVIOR INVENTORY

Purpose: To describe mothers' and fathers' child rearing behavior.

Format: Includes three factors: support, discipline, and covert control.

Reliability: Cronbach's coefficient alphas ranged from .70 to .82.

Validity: Correlations with other variables ranged from −.42 to .22.

Author: Aquilino, W. S.

Article: Children's perceptions of marital interaction.

Journal: *Child Study Journal*, 1986, *16*(3), 159–172.

Related Research: Devereux, E., et al. (1969). Child rearing in England and the United States. *Journal of Marriage and the Family, 31*, 257–270.

■ ■ ■

4538

Test Name: CORNELL PARENTING ACTIVITIES LIST

Purpose: To measure the quality of workers' relationships to their children.

Number of Items: 10

Format: Five-point rating scales. Sample item presented.

Reliability: Alpha was .92.

Author: Small, S. E., and Riley, D.

Article: Toward a multidimensional assessment of work spillover into family life.

Journal: *Journal of Marriage and the Family*, February 1990, *52*(1), 51–61.

Related Research: Cochran, M., & Henderson, C. R. (1985). *Comparative ecology of human development project: Wave II instruments* (Appendix to the final report to the National Institute of Education). Ithaca, NY: Cornell University.

■ ■ ■

4539

Test Name: DECISION CONTROL INDEX

Purpose: To assess power in decision-making between parents and adolescents.

Number of Items: 15

Format: Five-point dominance scales.

Reliability: Alpha was .88.

Author: Demo, D. H., et al.

Article: Family relations and the self-esteem of adolescents and their parents.

Journal: *Journal of Marriage and the Family*, November 1987, *48*(4), 705–715.

Related Research: Elder, G. H., Jr. (1962). Structural variations in the child rearing relationship. *Sociometry, 34*, 466–482.

■ ■ ■

4540

Test Name: DISAGREEMENT OVER CHILDREN SCALE

Purpose: To measure parental disagreement over how to raise children.

Number of Items: 10

Format: Four-point rating scales.

Reliability: Alpha was .78.

Author: Ganong, L. H., and Coleman, M.

Article: Do mutual children cement bonds in stepfamilies?

Journal: *Journal of Marriage and the Family*, August 1988, *50*(3), 687–698.

Related Research: Ahrons, C. (1984). *Binuclear family questionnaire.* Unpublished instrument. University of Wisconsin, Madison.

■ ■ ■

4541

Test Name: DYADIC ADJUSTMENT SCALE

Purpose: To measure adjustment for dyadic relationships.

Number of Items: 32

Format: Includes four factors: dyadic consensus, dyadic satisfaction, dyadic cohesion, and affectional expression.

Reliability: Alpha coefficients were .91 and .96.

Validity: Correlations with the Marital Adjustment test were .86 and .88.

Author: Burnett, P.

Article: Assessing marital adjustment and satisfaction: A review.

Journal: *Measurement and Evaluation in Counseling and Development*, October 1987, *20*(3), 113–121.

Related Research: Spanier, G. B. (1976). Measuring dyadic adjustment: New scales for assessing the quality of marriage and similar dyads. *Journal of Marriage and the Family, 38*, 15–28.

■ ■ ■

4542

Test Name: DYADIC ADJUSTMENT SCALE—REVISED

Purpose: To assess the quality of marital and nonmarital heterosexual relationships.

Number of Items: 15

Format: Includes three factors: affectional expression, companionship, and marital tension.

Reliability: Coefficient alphas ranged from .74 to .78.

Validity: Correlations with other variables ranged from −.42 to .19.

Author: Aquilino, W. S.

Article: Children's perceptions of marital interaction.

Journal: *Child Study Journal*, 1986, *16*(3), 159–172.

Related Research: Spanier, G. (1976). Measuring dyadic adjustment: New scales for assessing the quality of marriage and similar dyads. *Journal of Marriage and the Family*, *38*, 15–28.

■ ■ ■

4543

Test Name: ECONOMIC HARDSHIP QUESTIONNAIRE

Purpose: To measure family economic hardship.

Number of Items: 12

Format: The first 10 items are answered on a 4-point scale from *never* to *very often*. The 11th item is answered on a 5-point scale from *increased very much* to *decreased very much*. The 12th item is answered on a 4-point scale from *no problems* to *extreme problems*. All items are presented.

Reliability: Cronbach's alphas ranged from .82 to .87.

Validity: Correlations with other variables ranged from −.25 to .33.

Author: Lempers, J. D., et al.

Article: Economic hardship, parenting, and distress in adolescence.

Journal: *Child Development*, February 1989, *60*(1), 25–39.

■ ■ ■

4544

Test Name: EMOTIONAL AUTONOMY SCALE

Purpose: To measure emotional autonomy.

Number of Items: 20

Format: Includes four subscales: Perceives parents as people, parental deidealization, nondependency on parents, and individuation. All items are presented.

Reliability: Cronbach's alpha was .75.

Validity: Correlations with feelings of self-reliance for 6th and 8th grade girls were −.23 and −.27, respectively.

Author: Steinberg, L., and Silverberg, S. B.

Article: Th vicissitudes of autonomy in early adolescence.

Journal: *Child Development*, August 1986, *57*(4), 841–851.

■ ■ ■

4545

Test Name: ENVIRONMENTAL ASSESSMENT INDEX

Purpose: To assess the educational/development quality of home environments of 3-year-old through 11-year-old children.

Number of Items: 44

Format: Responses to each item are either *yes* or *no*. All items are presented.

Reliability: Cronbach's alpha reliability was .74. Test–retest correlation coefficients were .73 (1 year) and .66 (2 years).

Validity: Correlations with IQ ranged from .12 to .66.

Author: Poresky, R. H.

Article: Environmental Assessment Index: Reliability, stability, and validity of the long and short forms.

Journal: *Educational and Psychological Measurement*, Winter 1987, *47*(4), 969–975.

Related Research: Technical Committee, North Central Regional Project Number 124 (Clark, S., et al.). (1981). *Life span analysis of mental and social development of rural children* (Technical Manual, Vol. 1, North Central Research Publication Number 285).

■ ■ ■

4546

Test Name: ENVIRONMENTAL ASSESSMENT INDEX—SHORT FORM

Purpose: To assess the educational/developmental quality of home environments of 3-year-old through 11-year-old children.

Number of Items: 24

Format: Items are answered *yes* or *no*. All items are presented.

Reliability: Cronbach's alpha was .82. Test–retest correlation coefficients were .80 (1 year) and .72 (2 years).

Validity: Correlations with IQ ranged from −.01 to .66.

Author: Poresky, R. H.

Article: Environmental Assessment Index: Reliability, stability, and validity of the long and short forms.

Journal: *Educational and Psychological Measurement*, Winter 1987, *47*(4), 969–975.

Related Research: NC-124. (1981). Technical Committee, North Central Regional Project Number 124 (Clark, S., et al.). *Life span analysis of mental and social development of rural children*. Technical Manual, Vol. 1. North Central Research Publication Number 2851.

■ ■ ■

4547

Test Name: FAMILISM SCALE

Purpose: To measure familism.

Number of Items: 5

Format: Four-point agreement scales. Sample item presented.

Reliability: Alphas ranged from .56 to .76.

Author: Rogler, L. H., and Procidano, M. E.

Article: Marital heterogamy and marital quality in Puerto Rican families.

Journal: *Journal of Marriage and the Family*, May 1989, *51*(2), 363–372.

Related Research: Kahl, J. A. (1965). Some measures of achievement motivation. *American Sociological Review, 70,* 669–681.

■ ■ ■

4548

Test Name: FAMILY ADAPTATION SCALE

Purpose: To measure satisfaction with family and family relations and communication.

Number of Items: 10

Format: Seven-point satisfaction rating scales. All items presented.

Reliability: Alpha was .87.

Validity: Correlations with Sense of Coherence Scale ranged from .85 to .89.

Author: Antonovsky, A., and Sourani, T.

Article: Family sense of coherence and family adaptation.

Journal: *Journal of Marriage and the Family*, February 1988, *50*(1), 79–92.

■ ■ ■

4549

Test Name: FAMILY ADAPTABILITY AND COHESION SCALES (FACES II)

Purpose: To assess family interaction as defined by the circumplex model.

Number of Items: 30

Format: Five-point Likert format.

Reliability: Cronbach's alphas ranged from .78 to .90. Test–retest reliability ranged from .80 to .84.

Validity: Factor analysis did not replicate the results in the FACES manual.

Author: Eigen, C. A., and Hartman, B. W.

Article: Replicating the Factor Structure of Family Adaptability and Cohesion Scales II.

Journal: *Psychological Reports*, June 1987, *60*(3)I, 775–782.

Related Research: Olson, D. H., et al. (1982). Manual for Faces II: Family Adaptability and Cohesion Scales. St. Paul: University of Minnesota, Family Social Science.

■ ■ ■

4550

Test Name: FAMILY ADAPTABILITY AND COHESION EVALUATION SCALES

Purpose: To measure family cohesion and family adaptability.

Number of Items: 20

Format: Employs a 5-point Likert-type format.

Reliability: Internal consistency coefficients were .62 and .77. Test–retest (4–5 weeks) reliability coefficients were .80 and .83.

Validity: Correlations with other variables ranged from −.54 to .75.

Author: Ryan, R. M., and Lynch, J. H.

Article: Emotional autonomy versus detachment: Revisiting the vicissitudes of adolescence and young adulthood.

Journal: *Child Development*, April 1989, *60*(2), 340–356.

Related Research: Olson, D. H., et al. (1983). *Families: What makes them work.* Beverly Hills, CA: Sage.

4551

Test Name: FAMILY AFFECT MEASURE

Purpose: To measure family behavior of depressed normal subjects in seven affect codes: happy, caring, irritated, dysphoric, sarcastic, whining, and neutral.

Number of Items: 7

Format: Observers record observational codes on hand-held computers.

Reliability: Observers who were trained for 6 months yielded Kappa coefficients that ranged from .64 to .65 across the seven affect codes.

Author: Hops, H., et al.

Article: Home observations of family interactions of depressed women.

Journal: *Journal of Consulting and Clinical Psychology*, June 1987, *55*(3), 341–346.

Related Research: Arthur, J. E., et al. (1982). *LIFE (Living in Familial Environment) coding system.* Unpublished manuscript, Oregon Research Institute, Eugene.

■ ■ ■

4552

Test Name: FAMILY ASSESSMENT DEVICE

Purpose: To provide information on six separate family functions.

Format: Includes six separate family functions and general functioning.

Reliability: Internal consistency ranged from .72 to .92. Test–retest reliability estimates ranged from .66 to .73.

Validity: Correlations with other variables ranged from −.63 to .78.

Author: Perosa, L. M., and Perosa, S. L.

Article: Convergent and discriminant validity for family self-report measures.

Journal: *Educational and Psychological Measurement,* Winter 1990, *50*(4), 855–868.

Related Research: Epstein, N., et al. (1983). The McMaster Family Assessment Device. *Journal of Marital and Family Therapy, 9*(2), 171–180.

■ ■ ■

4553

Test Name: FAMILY BEHAVIOR CHECKLIST

Purpose: To measure the health of family functioning.

Number of Items: 47

Format: Includes two dimensions: cohesion and adaptability. Students respond to each item on a 5-point scale indicating how often the statement applied to their family.

Reliability: Test–retest (1 week) reliability coefficients were .74 and .69.

Author: Lopez, F. G., et al.

Article: Construction of current family functioning among depressed and nondepressed college students.

Journal: *Journal of College Student Development,* May 1989, *30*(3), 221–228.

Related Research: Lemberg, R., & Levy, L. (1984). Family Behavior Checklist as a training device. *Journal of Strategic and Systemic Therapies, 3,* 25–29.

■ ■ ■

4554

Test Name: FAMILY ENVIRONMENT SCALE— HEBREW SHORT FORM

Purpose: To measure perceptions of family environment/climate.

Number of Items: 50

Format: Four-point Likert format.

Reliability: Alphas ranged from .62 to .89.

Author: Margalit, M., and Eysenck, S.

Article: Prediction of coherence in adolescence: Gender differences in social skills, personality, and family climate.

Journal: *Journal of Research in Personality,* December 1990, *24*(4), 510–521.

Related Research: Moos, R. H., & Moos, B. S. (1976). A typology of family social environments. *Family Process, 15,* 357–371.

■ ■ ■

4555

Test Name: FAMILY INTRUSION AT WORK SCALE

Purpose: To measure frequency of family intrusions at work.

Number of Items: 12

Format: Five-point frequency scales.

Reliability: Alpha was .74.

Validity: Correlations with other variables ranged from −.14 to .38.

Author: Loerch, K. J., et al.

Article: The relationships among family domain variables and work–family conflict for men and women.

Journal: *Journal of Vocational Behavior,* December 1989, *35*(3), 231–253.

■ ■ ■

4556

Test Name: FAMILY LIVING AND TRADITIONAL VALUES SCALES

Purpose: To measure cohesion in the family and traditional values.

Number of Items: 27

Format: Likert format. Sample items presented.

Reliability: Alphas were .83 on each of two subscales.

Author: Amato, P. R.

Article: Parental divorce and attitudes toward marriage and family life.

Journal: *Journal of Marriage and the Family,* May 1988, *50*(2), 453–461.

Related Research: Glezer, H. (1984). Antecedents and correlates of marriage and family attitudes in young Australian men and women. *Proceedings of the XXth International CFR Seminar on Social Change and Family Policies, Key Papers, Part 1.* Melbourne: Australian Institute of Family Studies.

■ ■ ■

4557

Test Name: FAMILY PERCEPTION GRID

Purpose: To assess a subject's construing of herself, significant others, men in general, and women in general.

Number of Items: 100

Format: Subjects rate 10 figures on 10 interpersonal constructs on 13-point Likert scales.

Reliability: Alphas ranged from .61 to .89 across constructs.

Author: Harter, S., et al.

Article: Long-term effects of incestuous child abuse in college women: Social adjustment, social cognition, and family characteristics.

Journal: *Journal of Consulting and Clinical Psychology,* February 1988, *56*(1), 5–8.

Related Research: Niemeyer, G. J., & Niemeyer, R. A. (1981). Personal construct perspectives on cognitive assessment. In T. Merluzzi et al. (Eds.), *Cognitive assessment* (pp. 188–232). New York: Guilford Press.

■ ■ ■

4558

Test Name: FAMILY PROVERBS SCALE

Purpose: To assess connectedness, responsibility, independence, and equality.

Number of Items: 15

Time Required: 90 minutes were required for interviews.

Format: Nine-point rating scale presented for each of 15 family proverbs (0 = *no value*, 8 = *enormous value*). All items presented.

Validity: Two factors were extracted that had eigen values greater than one and that accounted for 41% of the variance.

Author: Page, M. H., and Washington, N. D.

Article: Family proverbs and value transmission of single Black mothers.

Journal: *Journal of Social Psychology,* February 1987, *127*(1), 49–58.

■ ■ ■

4559

Test Name: FAMILY ROLE BEHAVIOR INVENTORY

Purpose: To measure the domains of family behavior identified by S. Wegscheider.

Number of Items: 46

Format: Five-point rating scales.

Reliability: Alphas ranged from .74 to .85 across subscales.

Validity: Content validity (Kappa) ranged from .81 to .91. Construct and cross validity were also reported.

Author: Verdiano, D. L., et al.

Article: Toward an empirical confirmation of the Wegscheider Role Theory.

Journal: *Psychological Reports*, June 1990, *66*(3)1, 723–730.

■ ■ ■

4560

Test Name: FAMILY SANCTIONS SCALE

Purpose: To identify family actions against drugs.

Number of Items: 7

Format: Focuses on alcohol, marijuana, inhalants, and others.

Reliability: Alpha was .86.

Validity: Correlations with other variables ranged from .35 to −.36.

Author: Oetting, E. R., and Beauvais, F.

Article: Peer cluster theory, socialization characteristics, and adolescent drug use: A path analysis.

Journal: *Journal of Counseling Psychology*, April 1987, *34*(2), 205–213.

■ ■ ■

4561

Test Name: FAMILY SENSE OF COHERENCE SCALE

Purpose: To measure sense of coherence as a global orientation.

Number of Items: 26

Format: Seven-point rating scale. All items presented.

Reliability: Alpha was .92.

Validity: Correlation with Family Adaptation Scale was .89 (for men) and .85 (for women).

Author: Antonovsky, A., and Sourani, T.

Article: Family sense coherence and family adaptation.

Journal: *Journal of Marriage and the Family*, February 1988, *50*(1), 79–92.

■ ■ ■

4562

Test Name: FAMILY STRENGTH SCALE

Purpose: To measure family strength.

Number of Items: 4

Format: Includes family intactness and whether the family cares.

Reliability: Coefficient alpha was .76.

Validity: Correlations with other variables ranged from −.24 to .35.

Author: Oetting, E. R., and Beauvais, F.

Article: Peer cluster theory, socialization characteristics, and adolescent drug use: A path analysis.

Journal: *Journal of Counseling Psychology*, April 1987, *34*(2), 205–213.

■ ■ ■

4563

Test Name: FAMILY STRUCTURE SURVEY

Purpose: To measure characteristic family interactions (structure) that have been previously associated with college student maladjustment.

Number of Items: 50

Format: Responses to each item are made on a 5-point rating scale indicating how descriptive the item was of current process in their family environments. Includes four subscales: parent–child role reversal, parent–child overinvolvement, marital conflict, and fear of separation.

Reliability: Alpha coefficients ranged from .51 to .90.

Validity: Correlations with other variables ranged from −.44 to .35 (males) and from −.47 to .32 (females).

Author: Lopez, F. G., et al.

Article: Family structure, psychological separation, and college adjustment: A canonical analysis and cross-validation.

Journal: *Journal of Counseling Psychology*, October 1988, *35*(4), 402–409.

Related Research: Lopez, F. G. (1986). Family structure and depression: Implications for the counseling of depressed college students. *Journal of Counseling and Development*, 64, 508–511.

■ ■ ■

4564

Test Name: FAMILY SYSTEM TEST

Purpose: To spatially represent family relationships.

Format: Consists of a 45 × 45-cm monochromatic square board divided into 81 squares, each 5 × 5 cm; male and female schematic wooden figures each 8 cm in height; and cylindrical blocks of three sizes: 1.5, 3, and 4.5 cm.

Reliability: Test–retest (1 week) reliability ranged from .57 to .86.

Validity: Correlations with other variables ranged from an average of .18 to .38.

Author: Feldman, S. S., and Gehring, T. M.

Article: Changing perceptions of family cohesion and power across adolescence.

Journal: *Child Development*, August 1988, *59*(4), 1034–1045.

Related Research: Gehring, T. M., & Wyler, I. L. (1986). Family-System Test (FAST): A three-dimensional approach to investigate family relationships. *Child Psychiatry and Human Development*, *16*, 235–248.

■ ■ ■

4565

Test Name: FILIAL PIETY SCALE

Purpose: To measure feelings about expected sibling support.

Number of Items: 6

Format: Five-point Likert format. Sample items presented.

Reliability: Alpha was .87.

Author: Lee, T. R., et al.

Article: Sibling relationships in adulthood: Contact patterns and motivations.

Journal: *Journal of Marriage and the Family*, May 1990, *52*(2), 431–440.

Related Research: Seelbach, W. C. (1978). Correlates of aged parents' filial responsibility expectations and realizations. *Family Coordinator*, *27*, 341–350.

4566

Test Name: HANDICAP-RELATED PROBLEMS FOR PARENTS INVENTORY

Purpose: To measure stress parents experience related to having a handicapped child.

Number of Items: 17

Format: Eight-point frequency scales.

Reliability: Alpha was .87. Test–retest reliability ranged from .58 to .62.

Author: Wallander, J. L., et al.

Article: Child functional independence and maternal psychosocial stress as risk factors threatening adaptation of mothers of physically or socially handicapped children.

Journal: *Journal of Consulting and Clinical Psychology*, December 1990, *58*(6), 818–824.

Related Research: Wallander, J. L., & Marullo, D. (1989). *The Handicapped Related Problems for Parents Inventory: An inventory to measure the stress for parents related to having a handicapped child.* Submitted for publication.

■ ■ ■

4567

Test Name: HOME OBSERVATION FOR MEASUREMENT OF THE ENVIRONMENT

Purpose: To measure child rearing environments.

Number of Items: 55

Format: Yes–no format.

Validity: The total HOME score differed significantly between intact and divorced families, $F(1, 18) = 5.96, p < .05$.

Author: Karr, S. K., and Easley, B.

Article: Exploration of effects of divorce on the Preschool Home Environment.

Journal: *Psychological Reports*, October 1986, *59*(2)I, 569–622.

Related Research: Coldwell, B. M., & Bradley, R. H. (1979). *Home Observation for Measurement of the Environment.* Little Rock, AR: University of Arkansas at Little Rock, Center for Child Development and Education.

■ ■ ■

4568

Test Name: HUSBAND SOCIAL SUPPORT SCALE

Purpose: To measure the perceived social support of husbands.

Number of Items: 3

Format: Five-point rating scale. All items presented.

Reliability: Alphas ranged from .78 to .88.

Author: Stemp, P. S., et al.

Article: Psychological distress in the postpartum period: The significance of social support.

Journal: *Journal of Marriage and the Family*, May 1986, *48*(2), 271–277.

Related Research: Paykel, E. S., et al. (1980). Life events and social support in puerperal depression. *British Journal of Psychiatry*, *136*, 339–346.

■ ■ ■

4569

Test Name: IMPORTANCE OF PARENTING SCALE

Purpose: To measure how much parents believe parenting behavior affects children.

Number of Items: 5

Format: Four-point Likert format.

Reliability: Alphas ranged from .50 to .59.

Author: Simons, R. L., et al.

Article: Husband and wife differences in determinants of parenting: A social learning and exchange model of parental behavior.

Journal: *Journal of Marriage and the Family*, May 1990, *52*(2), 375–392.

Related Research: Simons, R. L., et al. (1988). *Differences between husbands and wives in the impact of conceptions of parenting*. Unpublished manuscript, Department of Sociology, Iowa State University.

■ ■ ■

4570

Test Name: INFANT ATTRIBUTION SCALE

Purpose: To assess the mother's tendency to make internal/external, stable/unstable, and global/specific attributions for positive and negative outcomes for affiliative and infant care.

Number of Items: 12

Format: Reponses are made on a 7-point Likert scale. An example is presented.

Reliability: Alpha coefficients ranged from .38 to .69.

Author: Donovan, W. L., et al.

Article: Maternal self-efficacy: Illusory control and its effects on susceptibility to learned helplessness.

Journal: *Child Development*, October 1990, *61*(5), 1638–1647.

Related Research: Peterson, C., et al. (1982). The attributional style questionnaire. *Cognitive Therapy and Research, 6*, 287–299.

■ ■ ■

4571

Test Name: INTERGENERATIONAL FUSION SCALE

Purpose: To measure the degree to which a person operates in a fused or individuated manner with parents.

Number of Items: 7

Format: Each item is rated on a 5-point scale ranging from 5 (*strongly agree*) to 1 (*strongly disagree*). Examples are presented.

Reliability: Cronbach's alpha ranged from .76 to .87. Test–retest correlation was .55.

Validity: Correlation with the Sheely Symptom Index was –.29.

Author: Wilson, R. J., et al.

Article: Commuter and resident students' personal and family adjustment.

Journal: *Journal of College Student Personnel*, May 1987, *28*(3), 229–233.

Related Research: Bray, J., et al. (1984). Personal authority in the family system: Development of a questionnaire to measure personal authority in intergenerational family processes. *Journal of Marital and Family Therapy, 10*, 167–178.

■ ■ ■

4572

Test Name: INTERPARENTAL CONFLICT SCALE

Purpose: To measure parental conflict.

Number of Items: 37

Format: Subjects use a 7-point scale to indicate how frequently their parents have argued or conflicted over each issue during the past 5 years.

Reliability: Coefficient alpha was .98. Test–retest (1 week) reliability was .83.

Author: Hoffman, J. A., and Weiss, B.

Article: Family dynamics and presenting problems in college students.

Journal: *Journal of Counseling Psychology*, April 1987, *34*(2), 157–163.

Related Research: Schwarz, J. C., & Getter, H. (1980). Parental conflict and dominance in late adolescent

maladjustment: A triple interaction model. *Journal of Abnormal Psychology, 89*, 573–580.

■ ■ ■

4573

Test Name: INTERPARENTAL INFLUENCE SCALE

Purpose: To measure marital decision-making dominance.

Number of Items: 13

Format: For each item the subject indicates on a scale ranging from 1 (*always mother*) to 5 (*always father*) who makes the decision.

Reliability: Coefficient alpha was .68.

Author: Hoffman, J. A., and Weiss, B.

Article: Family dynamics and presenting problems in college students.

Journal: *Journal of Counseling Psychology*, April 1987, *34*(2), 157–163.

Related Research: Schwarz, J. C., & Getter, H. (1980). Parental conflict and dominance in late adolescent maladjustment: A triple interaction model. *Journal of Abnormal Psychology, 89*, 573–580.

■ ■ ■

4574

Test Name: INTERPARENT CONFLICT SCALE

Purpose: To measure interparent conflict.

Number of Items: 37

Format: Seven-point frequency ratings.

Reliability: Cronbach's alpha was .95.

Author: Kurdek, L. A., and Sinclair, R. J.

Article: Adjustment of young adolescents in two-parent nuclear, stepfather, and mother-custody families.

Journal: *Journal of Consulting and Clinical Psychology*, February 1988, *56*(1), 91–96.

Related Research: Schwarz, J. C., & Getter, H. (1980). Parental conflict and dominance in late adolescent maladjustment. *Journal of Abnormal Psychology*, *89*, 573–580.

■ ■ ■

4575

Test Name: KANSAS FAMILY LIFE SATISFACTION SCALE

Purpose: To measure satisfaction with marital relationships, parent–child relationships, sibling relationships, and general family relationships.

Number of Items: 4

Format: Five-point scales.

Reliability: Cronbach's alpha was .71.

Validity: Correlations were .47 with the Bray Scale and .06 with the PERI Life Events Scale.

Author: McCollum, E. E., et al.

Article: Reliability and validity of the Kansas Life Satisfaction Scale in a predominantly middle-aged sample.

Journal: *Psychological Reports*, February 1988, *62*(1), 95–98.

■ ■ ■

4576

Test Name: KANSAS MARITAL SATISFACTION SCALE

Purpose: To measure marital satisfaction.

Number of Items: 3

Format: Seven-point satisfaction scale. All items presented.

Reliability: Alpha was .93.

Validity: Correlations with other variables ranged from .53 to .91.

Author: Schumm, W. R., et al.

Article: Concurrent and discriminant validity of the Kansas Marital Satisfaction Scale.

Journal: *Journal of Marriage and the Family*, May 1986, *48*(2), 381–387.

Related Research: Lee, G. (1988). Marital satisfaction in later life: The effects of nonmarital roles. *Journal of Marriage and the Family*, *50*, 775–783.

■ ■ ■

4577

Test Name: KINSHIP RESPONSIBILITY INDEX

Purpose: To determine the number of constraints imposed on an individual by his or her relatives.

Number of Items: 6

Format: Includes four components: marriage, children, respondents' relatives, and respondent's spouse's relatives. All items are presented.

Reliability: Test–retest (8 months) reliabilities ranged from .81 to .94.

Validity: Correlations with other variables ranged form −.20 to .131.

Author: Blegen, M. A., et al.

Article: Measurement of kinship responsibility for organizational research.

Journal: *Journal of Applied Psychology*, August 1988, *73*(3), 402–409.

■ ■ ■

4578

Test Name: LIFEROLE SALIENCE SCALES

Purpose: To assess expectations about work, marriage, parenting, and homecare roles.

Number of Items: 40

Format: Likert format. All items presented.

Reliability: Alphas ranged from .49 to .94 across subscales.

Author: Amatea, E. S., et al.

Article: Assessing the work and family role expectations of career-oriented men and women: The Life Role Salience Scales.

Journal: *Journal of Marriage and the Family*, November 1986, *48*(4), 831–838.

Related Research: Clark, J. E. (1984). *A validational study of the life role expectations scales*. Unpublished doctoral dissertation, University of Florida.

■ ■ ■

4579

Test Name: MARITAL ADJUSTMENT SCALE

Purpose: To assess marital adjustment.

Number of Items: 15

Format: Taps such things as degree of happiness, agreement/disagreement between spouses, and mutuality in resolving disagreements.

Reliability: Coefficient alpha was .78.

Validity: Correlations with other variables ranged from −.19 to .49.

Author: Greenhaus, J. H., et al.

Article: Work experiences, job performance, and feelings of personal and family well-being.

Journal: *Journal of Vocational Behavior*, October 1987, *31*(2), 200–215.

Related Research: Locke, H. J., & Wallace, K. M. (1959). Short marital adjustment and prediction tests: Their reliability and validity. *Marriage and Family Living, 21*, 251–255.

■ ■ ■

4580

Test Name: MARITAL CONFLICT SCALE

Purpose: To measure frequency of thinking about marital problems, discussing divorce, seeking professional intervention, and leaving home after a fight.

Number of Items: 5

Format: Cronbach's alpha was .75. Test–retest (1 year) reliability was .71.

Reliability: Correlation with marital support was –.48. Correlations with depression were .38 and .36.

Validity: Monroe, S. M., et al.

Author: Social support, life events, and depressive symptoms: A 1-year prospective study.

Article: *Journal of Consulting and Clinical Psychology*, August 1986, *54*(4), 424–431.

Journal: Spanier, G. B. (1976). Measuring dyadic adjustment: New scales for assessing the quality of marriage and similar dyads. *Journal of Marriage and the Family, 38,* 15–28.

■ ■ ■

4581

Test Name: MARITAL COPING INVENTORY

Purpose: To measure how married couples cope with their perceived marital troubles.

Number of Items: 64

Format: Five-point frequency scales. All items presented.

Reliability: Alphas ranged from .77 to .88 across subscales.

Author: Bowman, M.

Article: Coping efforts and marital satisfaction: Measuring marital coping and its correlates.

Journal: *Journal of Marriage and the Family*, May 1990, *52*(2), 463–474.

Related Research: Menaghan, E. G. (1983). Individual coping efforts and family studies: Conceptual and methodological issues. *Marriage and Family Review, 6,* 113–135.

■ ■ ■

4582

Test Name: MARITAL INFLUENCE SCALE

Purpose: To measure frequency of use of influence strategies by marital partners.

Number of Items: 16

Format: Seven-point scales from 1(*not at all true*) to 7 (*absolutely true*).

Reliability: Reliabilities ranged from .71 to .89.

Author: Sexton, C. S., and Perlman, D. S.

Article: Couples' career orientation, gender role orientation, and perceived equity as determinants of marital power.

Journal: *Journal of Marriage and the Family*, November 1989, *51*(4), 933–941.

Related Research: Davis, S. F. (1975). Intimacy and perceived influence: A correlational study of rated use of resource types as bases of influence within heterosexual dyads of three levels of intimacy. (Doctoral dissertation, Northwestern University). *Dissertation Abstracts International, 36,* 5861B.

■ ■ ■

4583

Test Name: MARITAL RELATIONSHIP SCALE

Purpose: To measure the quality of the marital relationship.

Number of Items: 11

Format: All items presented. Yes–no format implied.

Reliability: Alphas were .79 (power subscale) and .81 (support subscale).

Author: Brodbar-Nemzer, J. Y.

Article: Marital relationships and self-esteem: How Jewish families are different.

Journal: *Journal of Marriage and the Family*, February 1986, *48*(1), 89–98.

Related Research: Chi, S. K., & Houseknecht, S. K. (1985). Protestant fundamentalism and marital success:

A comparative approach. *Sociology and Social Research, 69,* 351–375.

■ ■ ■

4584

Test Name: MARITAL SATISFACTION AND PROBLEM-SOLVING SCALES

Purpose: To measure satisfaction with marriage and spouse.

Number of Items: 12

Format: Nine-point satisfaction scales. All items presented.

Reliability: Alphas were .86 (satisfaction) and .79 (problem-solving).

Validity: Correlations with other variables ranged from –.19 to .59.

Author: Steffy, B. D., and Jones, J. W.

Article: The impact of family and career planning variables on the organizational, career, and community commitment of professional women.

Journal: *Journal of Vocational Behavior*, April 1988, *32*(2), 196–212.

Related Research: Rusbult, C. E. (1982). Unpublished questionnaire. University of Kentucky, Lexington, Kentucky.

■ ■ ■

4585

Test Name: MARITAL SATISFACTION SCALE

Purpose: To measure marital satisfaction.

Number of Items: 48

Format: Responses are made on a 5-point scale from *strongly agree* to *strongly disagree.*

Reliability: Coefficient alpha was .97 (70-item version). Test–retest reliability was .76 (70-item version).

Validity: Correlation with the Marital Adjustment Test was .79 (70-item version). Correlation with social desirability was .33 (70-item version).

Author: Burnett, P.

Article: Assessing marital adjustment and satisfaction: A review.

Journal: *Measurement and Evaluation in Counseling and Development*, October 1987, *20*(3), 113–121.

Related Research: Roach, A. J., et al. (1981). The Marital Satisfaction Scale: Development of a measure for intervention research. *Journal of Marriage and the Family, 43,* 537–546.

■ ■ ■

4586

Test Name: MARITAL TRANSGRESSION SCALE

Purpose: To measure frequency of provocative marital behaviors.

Number of Items: 18

Format: 5-point frequency scales.

Reliability: Alpha was .81.

Validity: Correlations with other variables ranged from –.41 to .20.

Author: Smolen, R. C., and Spiegel, D. A.

Article: Marital locus of control as a modifier of the relationship between the frequency of provocation by spouse and marital satisfaction.

Journal: *Journal of Research in Personality*, March 1987, *21*(2), 70–80.

■ ■ ■

4587

Test Name: MATERNAL BEHAVIOR SCALE

Purpose: To assess the sensitivity and warmth of the mother toward her infant.

Number of Items: 10

Format: Scales include: amount of looking at the infant, response to the

infant's cues, and the amount of expressed positive emotion.

Reliability: Coefficient alpha was .96.

Validity: Correlations with other variables ranged from .00 to .30.

Author: Unger, D. G., and Wandersman, L. P.

Article: The relation of family and partner support to the adjustment of adolescent mothers.

Journal: *Child Development*, August 1988, *59*(4), 1056–1060.

Related Research: Bakeman, R., & Brown, J. V. (1978). *Assessing early interaction: Methodologies and limitations.* Paper presented at the Southeastern Conference on Human Development, Atlanta.

■ ■ ■

4588

Test Name: MATERNAL SEPARATION ANXIETY SCALE

Purpose: To measure the concept of maternal separation anxiety.

Number of Items: 35

Format: Includes three factors: maternal separation anxiety, perception of separation effects on the child, and employment-related separation concerns. Responses to each item are made on a 5-point Likert scale from 1 (*strongly disagree*) to 5 (*strongly agree*). All items are presented.

Reliability: Cronbach's alphas ranged from .71 to .91.

Author: Hock, E., et al.

Article: Maternal separation anxiety: Mother–infant separation from the maternal perspective.

Journal: *Child Development*, August 1989, *60*(4), 793–802.

Related Research: Mosher, D. L. (1979). The meaning and measurement of guilt. In C. E. Izard (Ed.), *Emotions in personality and*

psychopathology (pp. 105–124). New York: Plenum Press.

■ ■ ■

4589

Test Name: MOTHER-FATHER-PEER SCALE: MATERNAL ACCEPTANCE SUBSCALE

Purpose: To assess the mother's developmental history.

Number of Items: 10

Format: Items refer to the mother's relationship with her mother during childhood.

Reliability: Cronbach's alpha was .91.

Validity: Correlation with other variables ranged from –.29 to .38.

Author: Crockenberg, S.

Article: Predictors and correlates of anger toward and punitive control of toddlers by adolescent mothers.

Journal: *Child Development*, August 1987, *58*(4), 964–975.

Related Research: Epstein, S. (1983). *The mother-father-peer scale.* Unpublished manuscript, University of Massachusetts, Amherst.

■ ■ ■

4590

Test Name: NURTURANCE RATING TASK

Purpose: To assess degree of self-nurturance, perceptions of parents as nurturant, and the degree to which food is used as a source of nurturance.

Number of Items: 42

Format: Five-point rating scales.

Reliability: Alphas ranged from .75 to .92 across subscales.

Author: Lehman, A. K., and Rodin, J.

Article: Styles of self-nurturance and disordered eating.

Journal: *Journal of Consulting and Clinical Psychology*, February 1989, *57*(1), 117–122.

Related Research: Katz, I., et al. (1963). Effect of one type of need complementarity on marriage partners' conformity to one another's judgments. *Journal of Abnormal Psychology, 67,* 8–14.

■ ■ ■

4591

Test Name: O'LEARY-PORTER SCALE

Purpose: To assess the frequency of overt parental conflict that occurs in the child's presence.

Number of Items: 10

Format: Parents rate each item on a 5-point Likert scale ranging from *very often* to *never.*

Reliability: Test–retest (2 weeks) reliability was .96.

Validity: Correlation with Marital Adjustment Test was .63. Correlations with other variables ranged from –.23 to .23.

Author: Forehand R., et al.

Article: Home predictors of young adolescents' school behavior and academic performance.

Journal: *Child Development,* December 1986, *57*(6), 1528–1533.

Related Research: Porter, B., & O'Leary, K. D. (1980). Marital discord and childhood behavior problems. *Journal of Abnormal Child Psychology, 80,* 287–295.

■ ■ ■

4592

Test Name: PARENTAL ACCEPTANCE SCALE

Purpose: To measure parental acceptance.

Format: Parents indicate on a 5-point scale their degree of acceptance toward the child.

Reliability: .86.

Validity: Correlations with variables of the Pictorial Scale of Perceived

Competence and Social Acceptance for Young Children ranged from –.05 to .37.

Author: Bullock, J. R., and Pennington, D.

Article: The relationship between parental perceptions of the family environment and children's perceived competence.

Journal: *Child Study Journal,* 1988, *18*(1), 17–31.

Related Research: Porter, B. M. (1954). Measurement of parental acceptance in children. *Journal of Home Economics, 46,* 117–184.

■ ■ ■

4593

Test Name: PARENTAL ACCEPTANCE-REJECTION QUESTIONNAIRE

Number of Items: 35

Format: Children rate on a 4-point scale the degree to which each item is like or not like the parent in question. An example is presented.

Reliability: Alpha coefficients were .90 (father–child) and .91 (mother–child).

Author: McHale, S. M., et al.

Article: Children's housework and psychosocial functioning: The mediating effects of parents' sex-role behaviors and attitudes.

Journal: *Child Development,* October 1990, *61*(5), 1413–1426.

Related Research: Rohner, R. (1980). *Handbook for the Study of Parental Acceptance and Rejection.* Unpublished manuscript, University of Connecticut.

■ ■ ■

4594

Test Name: PARENTAL ATTACHMENT QUESTIONNAIRE

Purpose: To identify college students' perceived parental attachment.

Number of Items: 55

Format: Includes three factors: quality of the parental relationship, parental role in providing emotional support, and parental role in fostering autonomy. Responses are made on a 5-point Likert scale ranging from 1 (*not at all*) to 5 (*very much*).

Reliability: Alpha coefficients ranged from .88 to .96.

Author: Kenny, M. E.

Article: College seniors' perceptions of parental attachments: The value and stability of family ties.

Journal: *Journal of College Student Development,* January 1990, *31*(1), 39–46.

Related Research: Kenny, M. E. (1987). The extent and function of parental attachment among first-year college students. *Journal of Youth and Adolescence, 16,* 17–27.

■ ■ ■

4595

Test Name: PARENTAL BONDING INSTRUMENT

Purpose: To measure warmth and control in parent–child interaction.

Number of Items: 25

Format: Four-point Likert format.

Reliability: Test–retest reliability ranged from .63 to .76. Split-half reliability ranged from .74 to .88.

Author: Truant, G. S., et al.

Article: Parental representations in two Canadian groups.

Journal: *Psychological Reports,* December 1987, *61*(3), 1003–1008.

Related Research: Parker, G., et al. (1979). A parental bonding instrument. *British Journal of Medical Psychology, 52,* 1–10.

■ ■ ■

4596

Test Name: PARENTAL HOME ASSESSMENT INDEX

Purpose: To obtain parents' assessments of the educational/developmental quality of their young children's home environments.

Number of Items: 23

Format: Each item is rated on a 5-point scale from 1 (*never*) to 5 (*always*). All items are presented.

Reliability: Alpha coefficients were .56 (mothers) and .65 (fathers).

Validity: Correlations with the Iowa Social Competency Scales ranged from −.41 to .36.

Author: Poresky, R. H.

Article: Parental Home Assessment Index: Internal and interparent reliability and construct validity.

Journal: *Educational and Psychological Measurement*, Winter 1989, *49*(4), 993–998.

Related Research: Poresky, R. H. (1987). Environmental assessment index: Reliability, stability, and validity of the long and short forms. *Educational and Psychological Measurement*, 47, 969–975.

■ ■ ■

4597

Test Name: PARENTAL NURTURANCE SCALE

Purpose: To appraise nurturance received from one's mother and father.

Number of Items: 5

Format: Five-point Likert format.

Reliability: Test–retest (2 weeks) was .92 (mother) and .94 (father). Alphas were .95 and .93, respectively.

Validity: Correlations with other variables ranged from −.20 to .49.

Author: Buri, J. R., et al.

Article: Familial correlates of self-esteem in young American adults.

Journal: *The Journal of Social Psychology*, December 1987, *127*(6), 583–588.

4598

Test Name: PARENTAL SATISFACTION WITH THEIR CHILD SCALE

Purpose: To measure parents' overall degree of satisfaction with their child.

Number of Items: 16

Format: Parents responded on a 4-point scale from 1 (*strongly dissatisfied*) to 4 (*strongly satisfied*). Examples are presented.

Reliability: Split-half reliability coefficient was .81.

Validity: Correlations with other variables ranged from −.30 to .29 (fathers) and −.36 to .39 (mothers).

Author: Bullock, J. R.

Article: Parental knowledge and role satisfaction and children's sociometric status.

Journal: *Child Study Journal*, 1988, *18*(4), 265–275.

■ ■ ■

4599

Test Name: PARENT BEHAVIOR FORM

Purpose: To assess childrearing behavior including: hostile control, rejection, achievement control, strict control, punitive control, lax control, warmth, active involvement, egalitarianism, cognitive independence, and others.

Number of Items: 135

Format: Three-point rating scales.

Reliability: Median alpha (15 subscales) ranged from .67 to .83 across rating groups.

Validity: Correlations with scores from the Child's Report of Parent Behavior Inventory ranged from −.86 to .81.

Author: Schwartz, J. C., and Mearns, J.

Article: Assessing parental childrearing behaviors: A comparison

of parent, child and aggregate ratings from two instruments.

Journal: *Journal of Research in Personality*, December 1989, *23*(4), 450–468.

Related Research: Schaefer, E. S. (1965). Children's reports of parental behavior: An inventory. *Child Development*, 36, 417–424.

■ ■ ■

4600

Test Name: PARENT BEHAVIOR SCALE

Purpose: To measure parental behavior as their child undergoes painful medical procedures.

Number of Items: 8

Format: Yes–no format.

Reliability: Interrater reliability ranged from .55 to .98.

Author: Jay, S. M., and Elliott, C. H.

Article: A stress inoculation program for parents whose children are undergoing painful medical procedures.

Journal: *Journal of Consulting and Clinical Psychology*, December 1990, *58*(6), 799–804.

Related Research: Jay, S. M., & Woody, P. D. (1985). *The Parent Behavior Scale*. Unpublished.

■ ■ ■

4601

Test Name: PARENT–CHILD RELATIONSHIP SCALES

Purpose: To measure intimacy, responsibility, and developmental problems in parent–child relationships.

Number of Items: 29

Format: Items rated on 5- and 9-point rating scales. All items presented.

Reliability: Alphas ranged from .64 to .73.

Validity: Correlations with other variables ranged from −.27 to .22.

Author: Risman, B. J., and Park, K.

Article: Just the two of us: Parent–child relationships in single-parent homes.

Journal: *Journal of Marriage and the Family*, November 1988, *51*(4), 1049–1062.

● ● ●

4602

Test Name: PARENT DAILY REPORTS

Purpose: To measure negative behaviors mothers report as a problem.

Number of Items: 19

Format: Checklist format.

Reliability: Test–retest reliability ranged from .60 to .82.

Author: Webster-Stratton, C.

Article: The relationship of marital support, conflict, and divorce to parent perceptions, behaviors, and childhood conduct problems.

Journal: *Journal of Marriage and the Family*, May 1989, *50*(2), 417–430.

Related Research: Chamberlain, P., & Reid, J. B. (1987). Parent observation and report of child symptoms. *Behavioral Assessment, 9*, 97–109.

● ● ●

4603

Test Name: PARENTING DAILY HASSLES

Purpose: To measure typical everyday events in parenting and parent–child interactions.

Number of Items: 20

Format: Includes two factors: parenting tasks and challenging behavior. Frequency responses are made on a 4-point scale ranging form *rarely* to *constantly*. Degree or intensity responses are made on a

5-point scale ranging from 1 (*no hassle*) to 5 (*big hassle*).

Reliability: Alpha coefficients ranged from .81 to .90.

Validity: Correlations with other variables ranged from −.49 to .47.

Author: Crnic, K. A., and Greenberg, M. T.

Article: Minor parenting stresses with young children.

Journal: *Child Development*, October 1990, *61*(5), 1628–1637.

● ● ●

4604

Test Name: PARENTING QUESTIONNAIRE

Purpose: To identify adolescents' perceptions of how their parents behaved toward them during the 6 months preceding testing.

Number of Items: 29

Format: Items are answered on a 4-point scale from *never* to *very often*. All items are presented.

Reliability: Cronbach's alpha ranged from .76 to .81.

Validity: Correlations with other variables ranged from −.47 to .32.

Author: Lampers, J. D., et al.

Article: Economic hardship, parenting, and distress in adolescence.

Journal: *Child Development*, February 1989, *60*(1), 25–39.

Related Research: Schaefer, E. S. (1965). Children's reports of parental behavior: An inventory. *Child Development, 36*, 413–426. Roberts, G. C., et al. (1984). Continuity and change in parents' child-rearing practices. *Child Development, 55*, 586–597.

● ● ●

4605

Test Name: PARENTING Q-SORT

Purpose: To provide an observational measure of parenting.

Number of Items: 38

Format: Includes three cluster scores of: love, control, and task orientation.

Reliability: Alpha coefficients ranged from .53 to .71.

Author: Deal, J. E.

Article: Parental agreement on child-rearing orientations: Relations to parental, marital, family, and child characteristics.

Journal: *Child Development*, October 1989, *60*(5), 1025–1034.

Related Research: Buss, D. (1981). Predicting parent-child interactions from children's activity level. *Developmental Psychology, 17*, 59–65.

● ● ●

4606

Test Name: PARENTING SENSE OF COMPETENCE SCALE

Purpose: To assess self-efficacy in the parenting role.

Number of Items: 8

Format: Each item is rated on 6-point scales from *strongly agree* to *strongly disagree*. Examples are presented.

Reliability: Cronbach's alpha was .72.

Validity: Correlation with the Coopersmith Self-Esteem Inventory was .48.

Author: Cutrona, C. E., and Troutman, B. R.

Article: Social support, infant temperament, and parenting self-efficacy: A mediational model of postpartum depression.

Journal: *Child Development*, December 1986, *57*(6), 1507–1518.

Related Research: Gibaud-Wallson, J. A. (1977). Self-esteem and situational stress: Factors related to sense of competence in new parents. (Doctoral dissertation, George Peabody College for Teachers, 1977). *Dissertation Abstracts International*, *39*, 379B. (University Microfilms No. DDK78–09936)

■ ■ ■

4607

Test Name: PARENT OPINION QUESTIONNAIRE

Purpose: To assess appropriateness of expecting various child behaviors.

Number of Items: 80

Format: Agree–disagree format. Sample items presented.

Reliability: Test–retest (6 weeks) reliability was .85.

Validity: Correctly classified 75% of abusive mothers and 93% of mothers whose spouse or boyfriend was the abuser.

Author: Azar, S. T., and Rohrbeck, C. A.

Article: Child abuse and unrealistic expectations: Further validation of the Parent Opinion Questionnaire.

Journal: *Journal of Consulting and Clinical Psychology*, December 1986, *54*(6), 867–868.

Related Research: Azar, S. T., et al. (1984). Unrealistic expectations and problem solving ability in maltreating and comparison mothers. *Journal of Consulting and Clinical Psychology*, *52*, 687–691.

■ ■ ■

4608

Test Name: PARENT QUESTIONNAIRE

Purpose: To identify parents' perceptions of their competence in promoting children's social skills; parents' perceptions of children's competence at several tasks; and parents' degree of responsibility for supporting their children's abilities at the tasks they assigned to themselves, their children's teachers, their

children's classmates, and their children.

Number of Items: 24

Format: Includes eight social tasks: making friends, getting along with peers, joining an activity, dealing with a child who is mean, being liked by classmates, liking oneself, seeing oneself as good, and feeling satisfied with one's accomplishments.

Reliability: Cronbach's alpha coefficients ranged from .73 to .83.

Validity: Correlations with other variables ranged from –.21 to .16.

Author: Buzzelli, C. A.

Article: Parents' perceptions of reponsibility for promoting children's social competence.

Journal: *Child Study Journal*, 1989, *19*(4), 273–284.

Related Research: Harter, S. (1982). The Perceived Competence Scale for Children. *Child Development*, *53*, 87–97.

■ ■ ■

4609

Test Name: PERCEIVED PARENTAL REARING PRACTICES SCALES

Purpose: To measure parental rearing practices as perceived by adults.

Number of Items: 80

Format: Four-point frequency scales. All items presented.

Reliability: Alphas ranged from .42 to .90 across scales, across sex, and across a Dutch and Hungarian sample.

Validity: Correlations with age and sex ranged from –.07 to .23.

Author: Arrendel, W. A., et al.

Article: Cross-national generalizability of dimensions of perceived parental rearing practices: Hungary and the Netherlands; a correction and repetition with healthy adolescents.

Journal: *Psychological Reports*, December 1989, *65*(3, Part II), 1079–1088.

■ ■ ■

4610

Test Name: PERCEIVED SOCIAL SUPPORT—FAMILY SCALE

Purpose: To measure perceived family support.

Number of Items: 20

Format: Responses to each item are either *yes, no,* or *don't know.*

Reliability: Coefficient alpha ranged from .89 to .92.

Validity: Correlations with Perceived Social Support—Friends Scale ranged from .18 to .42.

Author: Lyons, J. S., et al.

Article: Perceived social support from family and friends: Measurement across disparate samples.

Journal: *Journal of Personality Assessment*, Spring 1988, *52*(1), 42–47.

Related Research: Procidano, M., & Heller, K. (1983). Measures of perceived social support from friends and from family: Three validation studies. *American Journal of Community Psychology*, *11*, 1–24.

■ ■ ■

4611

Test Name: PERMEABILITY OF BOUNDARIES SCALE

Purpose: To identify the frequency during the preceding few years of parental behaviors that indicate intrusiveness in their child's life with respect to appearance, thoughts, space, property, and outside relationships.

Number of Items: 34

Format: Responses are made on a 5-point scale from 1 (*never*) to 5 (*often*). Sample items are presented.

Reliability: Alpha coefficients ranged from .76 to .77.

Author: Friedlander, M. L., and Siegal, S. M.

Article: Separation–individuation difficulties and cognitive–behavioral indicators of eating disorders among college women.

Journal: *Journal of Counseling Psychology*, January 1990, *37*(1), 74–78.

Related Research: Olver, R., et al. (1989). Self-other differentiation and the mother–child relationship: The effects of sex and birth order. *Journal of Genetic Psychology*, *150*, 311–321.

■ ■ ■

4612

Test Name: PROPENSITY TO DIVORCE SCALE

Purpose: To measure propensity to divorce.

Number of Items: 14

Format: Yes–no. All items presented.

Reliability: Total scale reliability was .91.

Author: Bitter, R. G.

Article: Late marriage and marital instability: The effects of heterogeneity in inflexibility.

Journal: *Journal of Marriage and the Family*, August 1986, *48*(3), 631–640.

Related Research: Booth, A., et al. (1981). *Female labor force participation and marital instability: Methodology report*. Unpublished manuscript.

■ ■ ■

4613

Test Name: PSYCHOLOGICAL SEPARATION INVENTORY

Purpose: To measure the student's psychological separation from parents.

Number of Items: 138

Format: Includes four scales: functional independence, emotional

independence, conflictual independence, and attitudinal independence.

Reliability: Cronbach's alpha coefficients ranged from .84 to .92.

Author: Lopez, F. G., et al.

Article: Constructions of current family functioning among depressed and nondepressed college students.

Journal: *Journal of College Student Development*, May 1989, *30*(3), 221–228.

Related Research: Hoffman, J. A. (1984). Psychological separation of late adolescents from their parents. *Journal of Counseling Psychology*, *31*, 170–178.

■ ■ ■

4614

Test Name: PURDUE HOME SIMULATION INVENTORY

Purpose: To measure physical and social parameters of the infant's home.

Number of Items: 41

Format: Includes physical and social environment items.

Reliability: Median interobserver agreement (physical environment) was .85. Median test–retest reliability (physical environment) was .69. Median interrater agreement (social environment) was .71. Median test–retest (12 months) reliability (social environment) was .49.

Author: Wachs, T. D., and Chan, A.

Article: Specificity of environmental action, as seen in environment correlates of infants' communication performance.

Journal: *Child Development*, December 1986, *57*(6), 1464–1474.

Related Research: Wachs, T. D., & Gandour, M. (1983). Temperament, environment and six months cognitive-intellectual development. *International Journal of Behavioral Development*, *6*, 135–152.

4615

Test Name: Q-SORT INVENTORY OF PARENTING BEHAVIORS

Purpose: To identify different parenting behaviors.

Number of Items: 72

Format: Statements are sorted into nine categories along a continuum from *most like me* to *least like me*.

Reliability: Test–retest (2 weeks) correlation coefficient was .72.

Author: Pease, D., et al.

Article: Reliability of the Q-Sort Inventory of Parenting Behaviors.

Journal: *Educational and Psychological Measurement*, Spring 1989, *49*(1), 11–17.

Related Research: Lawton, J., et al. (1983). A Q-sort assessment of parents' beliefs about parenting in six midwestern states. *Infant Mental Health Journal*, *4*, 344–351.

■ ■ ■

4616

Test Name: QUESTIONNAIRE ON RESOURCES AND STRESS-FRIEDRICH SHORT FORM

Purpose: To provide a measure of ecological stress in families with children who are handicapped.

Number of Items: 52

Format: Includes four factors. All items are presented.

Reliability: Alpha coefficients ranged from .77 to .85.

Author: Scott, R. L., et al.

Article: Structure of a short form of the Questionnaire on Resources and Stress: A bootstrap factor analysis.

Journal: *Educational and Psychological Measurement*, Summer 1989, *49*(2), 409–419.

Related Research: Friedrich, W. N., et al. (1983). A short form of the Questionnaire on Resources and Stress. *American Journal of Mental Deficiency*, *88*, 41–48.

4617

Test Name: SATISFACTION WITH PARENTING SCALE

Purpose: To assess mother's degree of pleasure with her child and satisfaction with parenting role.

Number of Items: 12

Reliability: Alpha was .68.

Validity: Correlations with the Satisfaction with Parenting Scale were −.33 (frequency scale) and −.49 (intensity scale).

Author: Crnic, K. A., and Greenberg, M. T.

Article: Minor parenting stresses with young children.

Journal: *Child Development*, October 1990, *61*(5), 1628–1637.

Related Research: Crnic, K. A., & Greenberg, M. T. (1987). Transactional relationships between perceived family style, risk status, and mother-child interactions in two-year-olds. *Journal of Pediatric Psychology, 12*, 343–362.

■ ■ ■

4618

Test Name: SHORT MARITAL ADJUSTMENT TEST

Purpose: To assess marital satisfaction.

Number of Items: 15

Reliability: Test–retest reliability was .54.

Validity: Correlations with other variables ranged from −.35 to .65.

Author: Barling, J., et al.

Article: Psychological functioning following an acute disaster.

Journal: *Journal of Applied Psychology*, November, 1987, *72*(4), 683–690

Related Research: Locke, H. J., & Wallace, K. M. (1959). Short marital adjustment and prediction tests: Their reliability and validity.

Marriage and Family Living, 21, 251–255.

■ ■ ■

4619

Test Name: SIBLING RELATIONSHIPS QUESTIONNAIRE

Purpose: To identify perceptions of sibling relationships.

Number of Items: 45

Format: Includes 15 scales of three items each. Responses are made on a 5-point Likert scale ranging from 1 (*hardly at all*) to 5 (*extremely much*).

Reliability: Alpha coefficients ranged from .53 to .79.

Author: Buhrmester, D., and Furman, W.

Article: Perceptions of sibling relationships during middle childhood and adolescence.

Journal: *Child Development*, October 1990, *61*(5), 1387–1398.

Related Research: Furman, W., et al. (1989). Children's, parents', and observers' perceptions of sibling relationships. In P. G. Zukow (Ed.), *Sibling Interaction Across Culture* (pp. 163–180). New York: Springer-Verlag.

■ ■ ■

4620

Test Name: SOCIAL SUPPORT APPRAISALS SCALE

Purpose: To measure the child's perceptions or appraisals of family, peer, and teacher support.

Number of Items: 31

Format: Response to each item is on a 5-point scale form 1 (*always*) to 5 (*never*). A sample item is presented.

Reliability: Cronbach's alpha was .88.

Validity: Correlations with other variables ranged from −.28 to .25.

Author: Dubow, E. F., and Tisak, J.

Article: The relation between stressful life events and adjustment in

elementary school children: The role of social support and social problem-solving skills.

Journal: *Child Development*, December 1989, *60*(6), 1412–1423.

Related Research: Dubow, E. F., & Ullman, D. G. (1989). Assessing social support in elementary school children: The survey of children's social support. *Journal of Clinical Child Psychology, 18*, 52–64.

■ ■ ■

4621

Test Name: SOCIAL SUPPORT FROM FAMILY INVENTORY

Purpose: To measure extent to which individuals perceive that support, information, and feedback needs are fulfilled by family.

Number of Items: 20

Format: *Yes, no, don't know* format.

Reliability: Alpha was .90.

Author: Gaston, L., et al.

Article: Relation of patient pretreatment characteristics to the therapeutic alliance in disease psychotherapies.

Journal: *Journal of Consulting and Clinical Psychology*, August 1988, *56*(4), 483–489.

Related Research: Procidano, M. E., & Heller, K. (1983). Measures of perceived social support from friends and family: Three validation studies. *American Journal of Community Psychology, 11*, 1–24.

■ ■ ■

4622

Test Name: SOCIAL SUPPORT SCALE

Purpose: To measure social support from family and friends.

Number of Items: 15

Format: Five-point rating scales. Sample items presented.

Reliability: Cronbach's alpha ranged from .78 to .85.

Author: Kahill, S.

Article: Relationship of burnout among professional psychologists to professional expectations and social support.

Journal: *Psychological Reports*, December 1986, *59*(3), 1043–1053.

Related Research: Turner, R. T., et al. (1983). Social support: Conceptualization, measurement, and implications for mental health. *Research in Community and Mental Health, 3*, 67–111.

■ ■ ■

4623

Test Name: SOCIAL SUPPORT SCALE

Purpose: To measure husband–wife social support.

Number of Items: 6

Reliability: Cronbach's alpha was .79. Test–retest (1 year) reliability was .67.

Validity: Correlation with marital conflict was −.48; correlations with depression were −.03 and −.19.

Author: Munroe, S. M., et al.

Article: Social support, life events, and depressive symptoms: A 1-year prospective study.

Journal: *Journal of Consulting and Clinical Psychology*, August 1986, *54*(4), 424–431.

Related Research: Pearlin, L. I., & Shooler, C. (1978). The structure of coping. *Journal of Health and Social Behavior, 19*, 2–21.

■ ■ ■

4624

Test Name: SOCIOEMOTIONAL SUPPORT INVENTORY

Purpose: To measure mothers' perception of support from her husband.

Number of Items: 16

Format: Eleven-point likeness scales. All items presented.

Reliability: Alpha was .86.

Author: Durrett, M. E., et al.

Article: Mother's involvement with infant and her perception of spousal support: Japan and America.

Journal: *Journal of Marriage and the Family*, February 1986, *48*(1), 187–194.

Related Research: Taylor, J. (1974). *Systometrics*. Unpublished manuscript, University of Pittsburgh.

■ ■ ■

4625

Test Name: SPOUSE SPECIFIC AGGRESSION SCALE

Purpose: To assess psychological aggression and passive aggressive behavior in marriage.

Number of Items: 12

Format: Six-point self-rating scales. Sample items presented.

Reliability: Alpha was .81.

Author: Murphy, C. M., and O'Leary, K. D.

Article: Psychological aggression predicts physical aggression early in marriage.

Journal: *Journal of Consulting and Clinical Psychology*, October 1989, *57*(5), 579–582.

Related Research: O'Leary, K. D., & Auley, A. D. (1986). Assertion and family violence: Correlates of spouse abuse. *Journal of Marital and Family Therapy, 12*, 281–289.

■ ■ ■

4626

Test Name: STRAUS CONFLICT TACTICS SCALE

Purpose: To assess interparent hostility.

Number of Items: 19

Format: Includes three subscales: reasoning, verbal aggression, and physical violence.

Reliability: Alpha coefficients ranged from .50 to .88.

Author: Cummings, J. S., et al.

Article: Children responses to angry adult behavior as a function of marital distress and history of interparent hostility.

Journal: *Child Development*, October 1989, *60*(5), 1035–1043.

Related Research: Straus, M. A. (1979). Measuring intrafamily conflict and violence: The Conflict Tactics (CT) Scales. *Journal of Marriage and the Family, 41*, 75–88.

■ ■ ■

4627

Test Name: STRUCTURAL FAMILY INTERACTION SCALE—REVISED

Purpose: To identify elements of family structure.

Format: Includes six scales. Examples are presented.

Reliability: Internal consiste

ncy coefficients ranged from .77 to .94.

Validity: Correlations with other variables ranged from −.65 to .64.

Author: Perosa, L. M., and Perosa, S. L.

Article: Covergent and discriminant validity for family self-report measures.

Journal: *Educational and Psychological Measurement*, Winter 1990, *50*(4), 855–868.

Related Research: Perosa, S., & Perosa, L. (1987, August). The relationship between family structure, identity status, and coping style. Paper presented at the meeting of the American Psychological Association, New York.

■ ■ ■

4628

Test Name: STRUCTURAL FAMILY SYSTEM RATINGS

Purpose: To rate family structure in six areas: structure, flexibility, resonance, developmental stage, identified parenthood, and conflict resolution.

Number of Items: 3

Time Required: 15 minutes.

Format: Three 5-minute tasks are given to parents and rated by scorers.

Reliability: Internal consistencies ranged from .52 to .97.

Author: Szapocznik, J., et al.

Article: Structural family versus psychodynamic child therapy for problematic Hispanic boys.

Journal: *Journal of Consulting and Clinical Psychology*, October 1989, *57*(5), 571–578.

Related Research: Szapocznik, J., et al. (1986). *Structural family systems rating: A manual* [Mimeo]. Miami: University of Miami School of

Medicine.

■ ■ ■

4629

Test Name: TEACHERS' BELIEFS ABOUT PARENTS

Purpose: To measure respondents' beliefs about parents of nonhandicapped students (Form A) or about parents of handicapped students (Form B).

Number of Items: 17

Format: Includes forms A and B. Sample items are presented.

Reliability: Cronbach's alpha was .95.

Validity: Correlations with other variables ranged from .29 to .56.

Author: Feldman, D., et al.

Article: Teachers' beliefs about administrators and parents of handicapped and nonhandicapped students.

Journal: *Journal of Experimental Education*, Fall 1989, *58*(1), 43–54.

Related Research: Feldman, D., & Gerstein, L. H. (1988). A factor analytic study of three teacher belief scales. *Measurement and Evaluation in Counseling and Development*, *21*, 72–80.

■ ■ ■

4630

Test Name: UNREVEALED DIFFERENCES QUESTIONNAIRE

Purpose: To assess patterns of family relations.

Number of Items: 9

Format: Each family member ranks responses to each item according to personal preferences. Then the family discusses the rankings while being tape recorded. Raters then assess the interactions.

Reliability: Interrater reliabilities

ranged from .63 to .99.

Author: Mann, B. J., et al.

Article: An investigation of systemic conceptualizations of parent–child coalitions and symptom change.

Journal: *Journal of Consulting and Clinical Psychology*, June 1990, *58*(3), 336–344.

Related Research: Borduin, C. M., et al. (1989). *Multisystemic treatment of juvenile offenders: A replication and extension*. Manuscript in preparation.

■ ■ ■

4631

Test Name: WORK-FAMILY CONFLICT SCALE

Purpose: To measure work–family conflict.

Number of Items: 8

Format: Responses are made on a 5-point scale ranging from *a strong negative impact* to a *strong positive impact*.

Reliability: Coefficient alpha was .91.

Validity: Correlations with other variables ranged from −.37 to .44.

Author: Greenhaus, J. H., et al.

Article: Work experiences, job performance, and feelings of personal and family well-being.

Journal: *Journal of Vocational Behavior*, October 1987, *31*(2), 200–215.

Related Research: Burke, R. J., et al. (1979). Type A behavior of administrators and wives' reports of marital satisfaction and well-being. *Journal of Applied Psychology*, *64*, 57–65.

■ ■ ■

4632

Test Name: WORK SPILLOVER SCALE

CHAPTER 14
Institutional Information

4633

Test Name: ACADEMIC AND SOCIAL INTEGRATION INVENTORY

Purpose: To measure five dimensions related to the college environment.

Number of Items: 34

Format: The dimensions include: intellectual development, peer group interactions, quality of student interaction with faculty, institutional and goal commitments, and faculty concern for student development.

Reliability: .71.

Author: Williams, T. M., & Leonard, M. M.

Article: Graduating Black undergraduates: The step beyond retention.

Journal: *Journal of College Student Development*, January 1988, *29*(1), 69–75.

Related Research: Pascarella, E. T., & Terenzini, P. T. (1980). Predicting freshman persistence and voluntary drop-out decisions from a theoretical model. *Journal of Higher Education*, *51*, 61–73.

● ● ●

4634

Test Name: CARPENTER APPRENTICE PROGRAM QUESTIONNAIRE

Purpose: To measure four factors of a carpenter apprentice program.

Number of Items: 44

Format: Includes four factors: program satisfaction, affirmative action support, co-worker acceptance, and job assignments.

Reliability: Coefficient alphas ranged from .78 to .86.

Validity: Correlations with other variables ranged from .60 to –.53.

Author: Latack, J. C., et al.

Article: Carpenter apprentices: Comparison of career transitions for men and women.

Journal: *Journal of Applied Psychology*, August 1987, *72*(3), 393–400.

● ● ●

4635

Test Name: CLIENT SATISFACTION QUESTIONNAIRE—SHORT

Purpose: To measure overall satisfaction with mental health services.

Number of Items: 3

Format: Employs a 4-point Likert-type format. All items are included.

Reliability: Alphas were .93 and .92.

Validity: Correlation with the therapists' estimates of client satisfaction was .42.

Author: Kokotovic, A. M., and Tracey, T. J.

Article: Premature termination at a university counseling center.

Journal: *Journal of Counseling Psychology*, January 1987, *34*(1), 80–82.

Related Research: Larsen, D. L., et al. (1979). Assessment of client/patient satisfaction: Development of a general scale.

Evaluation and Program Planning, *2*, 197–207.

● ● ●

4636

Test Name: CLIENT SATISFACTION QUESTIONNAIRE

Purpose: To assess consumer satisfaction with mental health care treatment.

Number of Items: 8

Format: Includes eight dimensions: physical surroundings; kind or type of service; treatment staff; quality of service; amount, length, or quantity of service; outcome of service, general satisfaction, and procedures. Each question has four response choices.

Reliability: Alpha coefficients ranged from .85 to .93.

Validity: Correlations with other variables ranged from –.04 to .20.

Author: Sabourin, S., et al.

Article: Social desirability, psychological distress, and consumer satisfaction with mental health treatment.

Journal: *Journal of Counseling Psychology*, July 1989, *36*(3), 352–356.

Related Research: Larsen, D. L., et al. (1979). Assessment of client/patient satisfaction: Development of a general scale. *Evaluation and Program Planning*, *6*, 211–236.

● ● ●

4637

Test Name: CLIENT SATISFACTION QUESTIONNAIRE

Purpose: To measure client satisfaction with mental health services.

Number of Items: 18

Format: Each item is answered on a 4-point scale. Sample items are presented.

Reliability: Alpha coefficients ranged from .82 to .93.

Author: Tryon, G. S.

Article: Session depth and smoothness in relation to the concept of engagement in counseling.

Journal: *Journal of Counseling Psychology*, July 1990, *37*(3), 248–253.

Related Research: Larsen, D. L., et al. (1979). Assessment of client/patient satisfaction: Development of a general scale. *Evaluation and Program Planning, 2*, 197–207.

■ ■ ■

4638

Test Name: COUNSELING ATTITUDE SCALE—REVISED

Purpose: To measure perceptions of helpfulness of a college counseling center.

Number of Items: 8

Format: Ratings were made on a 5-point scale ranging from 1 (*strongly disagree*) through 5 (*strongly agree*).

Reliability: Coefficient alpha was .91.

Author: Puchkoff, S. C., and Lewin, P. G.

Article: Student responsiveness to specialized college services: Contribution of personality variables and perceptions of services.

Journal: *Journal of Counseling Psychology*, July 1987, *34*(3), 330–332.

Related Research: Form, A. L. (1955). The construction of a scale on attitudes towards counseling. *Journal of Counseling Psychology, 2*, 96–102.

4639

Test Name: COUNSELING EVALUATION INVENTORY

Purpose: To evaluate counseling.

Number of Items: 19

Format: Includes three dimensions: counseling climate, counselor comfort, and client satisfaction. A 5-point Likert format is used.

Reliability: Test–retest reliability was .72.

Author: Fuqua, D. R., et al.

Article: Variability across sources of performance ratings: Further evidence.

Journal: *Journal of Counseling Psychology*, July 1986, *33*(3), 353–356.

Related Research: Linden, J. D., et al. (1965). Development and evaluation of an inventory for rating counseling. *Personnel and Guidance Journal, 44*, 267–276.

■ ■ ■

4640

Test Name: COUNSELING PERFORMANCE SCALE

Purpose: To measure six dimensions of counseling performance related to specific course objectives.

Number of Items: 6

Format: Each item measures one dimension of counseling performance related to a specific course objective.

Reliability: Interrater reliabilities were .74 and .76.

Author: Fuqua, D. R., et al.

Article: Variability across sources of performance ratings: Further evidence.

Journal: *Journal of Counseling Psychology*, July 1986, *33*(3), 353–356.

Related Research: Fuqua, D. R., et al. (1984). Variability across sources

of performance ratings. *Journal of Counseling Psychology, 31*, 249–252.

■ ■ ■

4641

Test Name: COUNSELOR EVALUATION INVENTORY

Purpose: To assess client satisfaction with counseling.

Number of Items: 21

Reliability: Test–retest reliability was .83.

Validity: Clients' satisfaction scores are reported as correlating significantly with their counselors' practicum grades.

Author: Stoppard, J. M., and Henri, G. S.

Article: Conceptual level matching and effects of assertion training.

Journal: *Journal of Counseling Psychology*, January 1987, *34*(1), 55–61.

Related Research: Linden, J. D., et al. (1965). Development and evaluation of an inventory for rating counseling. *Personnel and Guidance Journal, 44*, 267–276.

■ ■ ■

4642

Test Name: CULTURAL PARTICIPATION SCALE—SHORT FORM

Purpose: To identify the number of different kinds of material read by the students and the number of different kinds of educational and recreational equipment that are in the home.

Number of Items: 29

Reliability: Cronbach's alphas were .66 and .72.

Validity: Correlations with other variables ranged from −.10 to .38.

Author: King, S.

Article: Background and family variables in a causal model of career maturity: Comparing hearing and hearing-impaired adolescents.

Journal: *The Career Development Quarterly*, March 1990, *38*(3), 240–260.

Related Research: Lerman, A., & Guilfoyle, G. R. (1970). *The development of prevocational behavior in deaf adolescents*. New York: Teachers College.

■ ■ ■

4643

Test Name: DECISION LATITUDE SCALE

Purpose: To measure the extent to which respondents' work environment allowed control over job-related decision making.

Number of Items: 7

Format: Responses are made on a 5-point scale ranging from 1 (*none at all*) to 5 (*an extraordinary amount*). An example is presented.

Reliability: Coefficient alpha was .82.

Validity: Correlations with other variables ranged from –.51 to .38.

Author: Frone, M. R., and McFarlin, D. B.

Article: Chronic occupational stressors, self-focused attention, and well being: Testing a cybernetic model of stress.

Journal: *Journal of Applied Psychology*, December 1989, *74*(6), 876–883.

Related Research: Karasek, R., et al. (1981). Job decision latitude, job demands, and cardiovascular disease: A prospective study of Swedish men. *American Journal of Public Health*, *71*, 694–705.

■ ■ ■

4644

Test Name: DEPTH SCALE

Purpose: To measure the perceived value and power of individual counseling sessions.

Number of Items: 5

Format: Consists of pairs of adjectives presented on a semantic differential. An example is presented.

Reliability: Alpha coefficients were .91 (counselor ratings) and .87 (client ratings).

Validity: Correlations with other variables ranged from –.54 to .27.

Author: Kelly, K. R., et al.

Article: Relation of counselor intention and anxiety to Brief Counseling Outcome.

Journal: *Journal of Counseling Psychology*, April 1989, *36*(2), 158–162.

Related Research: Stiles, W. B., & Snow, J. S. (1984). Counseling session impact as viewed by novice counselors and their clients. *Journal of Counseling Psychology*, *31*, 3–12.

■ ■ ■

4645

Test Name: DEVELOPMENT OPPORTUNITIES SCALE

Purpose: To assess a worker's perceptions of opportunities for career development in his or her current position.

Number of Items: 4

Format: Seven-point Likert format. Sample item presented.

Reliability: Internal consistency was .81.

Validity: Correlations with other variables ranged from –.47 to .19.

Author: Noe, R. A., et al.

Article: An investigation of the factors influencing employees' willingness to accept mobility opportunities.

Journal: *Personnel Psychology*, Summer 1988, *41*(2), 559–580.

■ ■ ■

4646

Test Name: ENVIRONMENTAL ROBUSTNESS SCALE

Purpose: To measure school environments using dramaturgical metaphors.

Number of Items: 10

Format: Semantic differential format.

Reliability: Test–retest reliability ranged from .77 to .78.

Author: Licatar, J. W., et al.

Article: Principal vision, teacher sence of autonomy, and environmental robustness.

Journal: *The Journal of Educational Research*, November–December 1990, *84*(2), 93–99.

Related Research: Licatar, J. W., & Willower, D. J. (1978). Toward an operational definition of environmental robustness. *Journal of Educational Research*, *71*, 218–222.

■ ■ ■

4647

Test Name: ENVIRONMENTAL SATISFACTION INVENTORY

Purpose: To measure students' reactions to relationships with peers and faculty, services of the university, and opportunities for recreation and extracurricular activities.

Number of Items: 46

Format: Includes five factors: peer socialization, institutional perception, faculty contact, friendships, and community.

Reliability: Cronbach's alpha ranged from .72 to .74.

Author: Cuyjet, M. J., and Rode, D. L.

Article: Follow-up of orientation contacts: Effects on freshmen environmental satisfaction.

Journal: *Journal of College Student Personnel*, January 1987, *28*(1), 21–27.

Related Research: Astin, A. W. (1968). *The college environment*. Washington, DC: American Council on Education.

4648

Test Name: FOLLOW-UP QUESTIONNAIRE ON INDIVIDUAL COUNSELING

Purpose: To enable clients to evaluate their satisfaction with counseling and the amount of change that resulted.

Number of Items: 8

Format: Responses are made on a 5-point Likert format. Includes two parts: satisfaction and change.

Reliability: Alpha coefficients were .95 (satisfaction) and .86 (change). Test–retest (5 months) reliabilities ranged from .82 to .87 (satisfaction) and from .64 to .85 (change).

Author: Tracey, T. J., and Dundon, M.

Article: Role anticipations and preferences over the course of counseling.

Journal: *Journal of Counseling Psychology*, January 1988, *35*(1), 3–14.

Related Research: Tracey, T. J., & Ray, P. B. (1984). The stages of successful time-limited counseling: An interactional examination. *Journal of Counseling Psychology*, *31*, 13–27.

■ ■ ■

4649

Test Name: GENERAL COMMUNITY SATISFACTION SCALE

Purpose: To assess satisfaction with living in a suburb.

Number of Items: 24

Format: Five-point Likert format. All items presented.

Reliability: Alpha was .76.

Validity: Concurrent validity estimates were .78 and .85.

Author: Vreugdenhil, A., and Rigby, K.

Article: Assessing generalized community satisfaction.

Journal: *The Journal of Social Psychology*, August 1987, *127*(4), 367–374.

Related Research: Rigby, K., & Vreugdenhil, A. (1987). The relationship between generalized community satisfaction and residual social status. *The Journal of Social Psychology*, *127*, 381–390.

■ ■ ■

4650

Test Name: GROUP CLIMATE QUESTIONNAIRE

Purpose: To measure climate of psychotherapeutic groups, primarily affiliativeness.

Number of Items: 10

Reliability: Member–observer ratings correlated .86.

Validity: Member–observer mean differences were significant for all but one item.

Author: Hurley, J. R., and Brooks, L. A.

Article: Primacy of affiliativeness in ratings of group climate.

Journal: *Psychological Reports*, February 1988, *62*(1), 123–133.

Related Research: Mackenzie, K. R. (1981). Measurement of group climate. *International Journal of Group Psychotherapy*, *31*, 287–296.

■ ■ ■

4651

Test Name: GROUP EVALUATION FORM

Purpose: To enable participants to evaluate their group counseling experience.

Number of Items: 25

Format: A self-report measure employing 5-point Likert scales. Includes six dimensions.

Reliability: Coefficient alphas ranged from .81 to .90.

Author: Robbins, S. B., and Tucker, Jr., K. R.

Article: Relation of goal instability to self-directed and interactional career counseling workshops.

Journal: *Journal of Counseling Psychology*, October 1986, *33*(4), 418–424.

Related Research: Kivlighan, D., et al. (1981). Effects of matching treatment approaches and personality types in group vocational counseling. *Journal of Counseling Psychology*, *28*, 315–320.

■ ■ ■

4652

Test Name: INDUSTRIAL RELATIONS CLIMATE SCALE

Purpose: To measure the norms and attitudes reflecting union-management relations in an organization.

Number of Items: 26

Format: Five-point rating scale. All items presented.

Reliability: Alphas ranged from .65 to .91 across subscales.

Author: Dastmalchian, A., et al.

Article: Industrial relations climate: Testing a construct.

Journal: *Journal of Occupational Psychology*, March 1989, *62*(1), 21–32.

Related Research: Derber, M., et al. (1958). Environmental variables and union-management accommodation. *Industrial and Labor Relations Review*, *11*, 413–428.

■ ■ ■

4653

Test Name: INNOVATION STRATEGY SCALE

Purpose: To measure managers' perception of the extent to which their company was concerned with innovation.

Number of Items: 21

Format: Four-point importance scales.

Reliability: Alphas ranged from .65 to .73.

Author: Jackson, S. E., et al.

Article: Organizational characteristics as predictors of personnel practices.

Journal: *Personnel Psychology,* Winter 1989, *42*(4), 727–786.

Related Research: Dess, G. G., & Davis, P. S. (1984). Porter's (1980) generic strategies as determinants of strategic group membership and organizational performance. *Academy of Management Journal, 27,* 467–488.

■ ■ ■

4654

Test Name: JOB ATTRIBUTES QUESTIONNAIRE

Purpose: To measure characteristics of jobs including: work or company environment, job security, and fringe benefits.

Number of Items: 25

Format: Five-point likelihood scales. All items presented.

Reliability: Alphas ranged from .68 to .82 across subscales.

Validity: Correlations with other variables ranged from −.04 to .48.

Author: Harris, M. M., and Fink. L. S.

Article: A field study of applicant reactions to employment opportunities: Does the recruiting make a difference?

Journal: *Personnel Psychology,* Winter 1987, *40*(4), 765–784.

■ ■ ■

4655

Test Name: MANAGERIAL SUPPORT SCALE

Purpose: To measure the degree to which managers provided feedback, career encouragement, and challanges to employees.

Number of Items: 10

Format: Five-point Likert format. Sample item presented.

Reliability: Internal consistency was .91.

Validity: Correlations with other variables ranged from −.06 to .49.

Author: Noe, R. A., et al.

Article: An investigation of the correlates of career motivation.

Journal: *Journal of Vocational Behavior,* December 1990, *37*(3), 340–356.

■ ■ ■

4656

Test Name: MODERN LIFE SCALE

Purpose: To measure naturalistic, technological, and occupational features of modern life.

Number of Items: 29

Format: Three-point good–bad scales. Sample item presented.

Reliability: Cronbach's alpha was .78 (total). Alphas ranged from −.24 to −.33.

Validity: Correlations with anomy ranged from −.24 to −.33.

Author: Worsley, A., and Worsley, A. J.

Article: Naturalistic and technological values in the modern world.

Journal: *Psychological Reports,* June 1989, *63*(4, Part II), 1192–1194.

■ ■ ■

4657

Test Name: MULTIMETHOD JOB DESIGN QUESTIONNAIRE: SELF-REPORT

Purpose: To assess the quality of a job's design on the basis of each of four approaches.

Number of Items: 48

Format: Includes four scales: motivational, mechanistic, biological, and perceptual/motor. All items are presented. Responses to each item are made on a 5-point scale from 1 (*strongly agree*) to 5 (*strongly disagree*).

Reliability: Interrater reliability ranged from .78 to .95 (average correlations) and from .40 to .65 (mean absolute agreement).

Validity: Correlations with other variables ranged from −.77 to .81.

Author: Campion, M. A.

Article: Interdisciplinary approaches to job design: A constructive replication with extensions.

Journal: *Journal of Applied Psychology,* August 1988, *73*(3), 467–481.

Related Research: Campion, M. A. (1985). The Multimethod Job Design Questionnaire (MJDQ). *Psychological Documents, 15*(1, Ms. No. 2695).

■ ■ ■

4658

Test Name: MY CLASS INVENTORY

Purpose: To assess classroom learning environment.

Number of Items: 25

Format: Yes–no format.

Reliability: Alphas ranged from .58 to .81 across subscales.

Author: Richardson, A. G.

Article: Classroom learning environment and creativity: Some Caribbean findings.

Journal: *Psychological Reports,* June 1988, *62*(3), 939–942.

Related Research: Fraser, B. J., & O'Brien, P. (1985). Student and teacher perceptions of the environment of elementary school classrooms. *The Elementary School Journal, 85,* 568–580.

■ ■ ■

4659

Test Name: NOXIOUS PHYSICAL ENVIRONMENT SCALE

Purpose: To assess respondents' perceptions of whether their physical work environment exposed them to noxious elements.

Number of Items: 4

Format: Responses are made on a 5-point scale ranging from 1 (*strongly disagree*) to 5 (*strongly agree*)

Reliability: Coefficient alpha was .80.

Validity: Correlations with other variables ranged from −.30 to .53.

Author: Frone, M. R., and McFarlin, D. B.

Article: Chronic occupational stressors, self-focused attention, and well being: Testing a cybernetic model of stress.

Journal: *Journal of Applied Psychology*, December 1989, *74*(6), 876–883.

■ ■ ■

4660

Test Name: NURSES TRAINING EXPERIENCES SCALE

Purpose: To measure nurse training experiences.

Number of Items: 27

Format: Four-point experience scales from 1 (*little or none*) to 4 (*a great deal*).

Reliability: Alphas ranged from .78 to .81.

Validity: Correlations with other variables ranged from −.20 to .28.

Author: Arnold, J.

Article: Predictors of career commitment: A test of three theoretical models.

Journal: *Journal of Vocational Behavior*, December 1990, *37*(3), 285–302.

Related Research: Numerof, R. E., & Abrams, M. N. (1984). Sources of stress amongst nurses: An empirical investigation. *Journal of Human Stress, 10,* 84–100.

4661

Test Name: OCCUPATIONAL AGE QUESTIONNAIRE

Purpose: To measure perceived age of persons holding various jobs.

Number of Items: 59

Format: Subjects reported their best estimate of workers' ages in occupations.

Reliability: Test–retest (4 weeks) was .75. Within subject reliability was .80.

Validity: Perceived age correlated with actual age ($r = .75, p = .0001$).

Author: Gordon, R. A.

Article: Perceived and actual ages of workers.

Journal: *Journal of Vocational Behavior*, February 1986, *28*(1), 21–28.

Related Research: Meir, E. I. (1968). *Structural elaborations of Roe's classification of occupations.* Jerusalem, Israel: University of Jerusalem.

■ ■ ■

4662

Test Name: ORGANIZATIONAL CHARACTERISTICS INVENTORY

Purpose: To measure perceptions of organizational climate: management.

Number of Items: 24

Format: Likert format.

Reliability: Alphas ranged from .69 to .88 across subscales.

Author: Vardi, Y., et al.

Article: The value content of organizational mission as a factor in the commitment of members.

Journal: *Psychological Reports*, August 1989, *65*(1), 27–34.

Related Research: James, L. R., & Jones, A. P. (1974). Organizational climate: A review of theory and research. *Psychological Bulletin, 81,* 1096–1112.

4663

Test Name: ORGANIZATIONAL CLIMATE DESCRIPTION QUESTIONNAIRE

Purpose: To measure school climate.

Number of Items: 64

Format: Likert format.

Reliability: Split-half ranged from .26 to .84 (median .64).

Author: Porter, A. W., et al.

Article: School climate and administrative power strategies of elementary school principals.

Journal: *Psychological Reports*, December 1989, *65*(3), II, 1267–1271.

Related Research: Halpin, A. W., & Croft, D. B. (1963). *The organizational climate of schools.* Chicago, IL: University of Chicago Press.

■ ■ ■

4664

Test Name: ORGANIZATIONAL FAIRNESS SCALE

Purpose: To measure perceived equity in organizations.

Number of Items: 43

Format: Seven-point agreement scales. All items presented.

Reliability: Alphas ranged from .58 to .89 across subscales.

Validity: Congruency coefficients from a target analysis ranged from .60 to .96. Correlations with other organizational variables were .69 and .33.

Author: Lim, C. U., et al.

Article: A psychometric assessment of a scale to measure organizational fairness.

Journal: *Psychological Reports*, August 1988, *63*(1), 211–214.

Related Research: Dittrich, J. E., et al. (1985). Perceptions of equity, job satisfaction, and intention to quit among data processing personnel. *Information and Management*, 8, 67–75.

■ ■ ■

4665

Test Name: ORGANIZATIONAL HEALTH INVENTORY

Purpose: To measure the seven elements of school health.

Number of Items: 44

Format: Includes seven scales: institutional integrity, principal influence, consideration, initiating structure, resource support, morale, and academic emphasis. Responses are made on a 4-point Likert scale ranging from *rarely* to *very frequently*. Examples are presented.

Reliability: Alpha coefficients ranged from .87 to .95.

Author: Tarter, C. J., et al.

Article: School health and organizational commitment.

Journal: *Journal of Research and Development in Education*, Summer 1990, *23*(4), 236–242.

Related Research: Hoy, W. K., & Feldman, J. A. (1987). Organizational health: The concept and its measure. *Journal of Research and Development in Education*, *20*(4), 30–37.

■ ■ ■

4666

Test Name: ORGANIZATIONAL STRESS SCALE

Purpose: To assess sources of stress in schools.

Number of Items: 45

Format: Five-point response scales.

Reliability: Alpha was .95.

Author: Bhagat, R. S., and Allie, S. M.

Article: Organizational stress, personal life stress, and symptoms of life strains: An examination of the moderating role of sense competence.

Journal: *Journal of Vocational Behavior*, December 1989, *35*(3), 231–253.

Related Research: Kyriacou, C., and Sutcliff, J. (1978). Teacher stress: Prevalance, sources, and symptoms. *British Journal of Educational Psychology*, *48*, 159–167.

■ ■ ■

4667

Test Name: PERCEIVED CLIMATE QUESTIONNAIRE—REVISED

Purpose: To measure organizational climate.

Number of Items: 73

Format: Includes six factors: conflict and ambiguity; leadership facilitation and support; top-level work group cooperation, friendliness, and trust; leader goal-directed orientation; immediate work group cooperation, friendliness, and trust; and professional and organizational esprit. Responses are made on a 7-point scale.

Reliability: Alpha coefficients ranged from .61 to .84.

Author: Lysons, A.

Article: Taxonomies of higher educational institutions predicted from organizational climate.

Journal: *Research in Higher Education*, April 1990, *31*(2), 115–128.

Related Research: Jones, A. P., & James, L. R. (1979). Psychological climate: Dimensions and relationships of individual and aggregated work environment perceptions. *Organizational Behavior and Human Performance*, *23*, 201–250.

■ ■ ■

4668

Test Name: PERCEIVED QUALITY OF ACADEMIC LIFE SCALE

Purpose: To measure college students' perception of the quality of academic life.

Number of Items: 6

Format: Responses to each item are on a 7-point scale ranging from *delighted* to *terrible*. All items are presented.

Reliability: Alpha coefficients ranged from .74 to .86.

Validity: Correlations with intent to get a degree ranged from −.27 to −.34.

Author: Staats, S., and Partlo, C.

Article: Predicting intent to get a college degree.

Journal: *Journal of College Student Development*, May 1990, *31*(3), 245–249.

Related Research: Okun, M. A., et al. (1986). Measuring perceptions of the quality of academic life among college students. *Journal of College Student Personnel*, *27*, 447–482.

■ ■ ■

4669

Test Name: PERSONAL ATTRIBUTES INVENTORY

Purpose: To provide a global evaluation of counseling.

Number of Items: 100

Format: An adjective checklist consisting of 50 positive and 50 negative descriptors from which respondents select 30 that describe the counselor.

Reliability: Test–retest (2 days) reliability for 89 freshmen was .90. Test–retest (1 week) reliability for 32 juniors and seniors was .94 and for 17 graduate students was .95.

Validity: Correlations with other variables ranged from .46 to .66.

Author: Hayes, T. J., and Tinsley, H. E. A.

Article: Identification of the latent dimensions of instruments that measure perceptions of and expectations about counseling.

Journal: *Journal of Counseling Psychology*, October 1989, *36*(4), 492–500.

Related Research: Parish, T. S., et al. (1976). The Personal Attribute Inventory. *Perceptual and Motor Skills, 42,* 715–720.

■ ■ ■

4670

Test Name: POSSIBLE BARRIERS TO MANAGEMENT ENTRY SCALE

Purpose: To assess possible barriers to management entry.

Number of Items: 28

Format: Includes six factors: inadequate management traits, family/social concerns, organizational barriers, limited education/experience, femininity concerns, and future subordinate resistance. Responses are made on a 7-point scale ranging from 1 (*would not hinder at all*) to 7 (*would completely hinder*).

Reliability: Alpha coefficients ranged from .81 to .93.

Author: Russell, J. E. A., and Rush, M. C.

Article: A comparative study of age-related variation in women's views of a career in management.

Journal: *Journal of Vocational Behavior,* June 1987, *30*(3), 280–294.

Related Research: Fitzgerald, L. F., & Betz, N. E. (1983). Issues in the vocational psychology of women. In W. B. Walsh & S. H. Osipow (Eds.), *Handbook of Vocational Psychology. Vol. 1: Foundations* (pp. 83–159). Hillsdale, NJ: Erlbaum.

■ ■ ■

4671

Test Name: REACTION TO SKILL ASSESSMENT

Purpose: To assess participants' perceptions of the assessment center.

Number of Items: 15

Format: Responses are made on a 5-point scale ranging from 1 (*strongly agree*) to 5 (*strongly disagree*).

Reliability: Internal consistency was .91.

Validity: Correlations with other variables ranged from –.10 to .52.

Author: Noe, R. A., and Steffy, B. D.

Article: The influence of individual characteristics and assessment center evaluation or career exploration behavior and job involvement.

Journal: *The Journal of Vocational Behavior,* April 1987, *30*(2), 187–202.

■ ■ ■

4672

Test Name: SCHOOL ORGANIZATIONAL RIGIDITY SCALE

Purpose: To measure freedom that teachers have to take instructional action.

Number of Items: 6

Format: Five-point Likert format. Sample item presented.

Reliability: Alpha was .73.

Validity: Correlations with other variables ranged from –.65 to .50.

Author: Brissie, J. S., et al.

Article: Individual, situational contributions to burnout.

Journal: *Journal of Educational Research,* November/December 1988, *82*(2), 106–112.

■ ■ ■

4673

Test Name: SCHOOL RELATED CURIOSITY SCALE

Purpose: To assess positive reactions to new classroom environments, a need to know more about classroom topics, expressions of interest in classroom activities, and asking questions.

Number of Items: 4

Format: Yes–no format.

Reliability: Kuder-Richardson formula was .61.

Author: Engelhard, G., Jr.

Article: Grade level, gender, and school related curiosity in urban elementary schools.

Journal: *Journal of Educational Research,* September/October 1988, *82*(1), 22–26.

Related Research: Engelhard, G. (1985). The discovery of educational goals and outcomes: A view of the latent curriculum of schooling. (Doctoral dissertation, University of Chicago, 1985). *Dissertation Abstracts International, 46,* 2176-A.

■ ■ ■

4674

Test Name: SENSE OF COMMUNITY INDEX—SHORT FORM

Purpose: To measure sense of community for university communities.

Number of Items: 12

Format: Employs a true–false format. Includes four dimensions of psychological sense of community: membership, influence, fufillment of needs, and shared emotional connection.

Reliability: Cronbach's alpha was .71.

Validity: Correlations with other variables ranged from –.03 to .16 (*N* = 360).

Author: McCarthy, M. E., et al.

Article: Psychological sense of community and student burnout.

Journal: *Journal of College Student Development,* May 1990, *31*(3), 211–216.

Related Research: Chavis, D. M., et al. (1986). Sense of community through Brunswick's lens: A first look. *Journal of Community Psychology, 14,* 24–40.

■ ■ ■

4675

Test Name: SEX-BASED EQUAL OPPORTUNITY SCALE

Purpose: To measure equal opportunity climate on university campuses.

Number of Items: 49

Format: Five-point scales 1 (*not at all likely*) to 5 (*extremely likely*).

Reliability: Cronbach's alpha ranged from .83 to .95 across three subscales.

Author: Hooper, S. K., et al.

Article: Construction and validation of a Sex-Based Equal Opportunity Measure for the college campus.

Journal: *Psychological Reports*, June 1989, *64*(3, Part II), 1231–1238.

Related Research: Fisher, G. (1988). Equal opportunity climate: Development and initial validation of an assessment instrument and its relationship with organizational outcomes. Unpublished doctoral dissertation. The University of Mississippi, Oxford, MS.

■ ■ ■

4676

Test Name: SEXUAL EXPERIENCES QUESTIONNAIRE

Purpose: To measure the nature and extent of sexual harassment in the university setting.

Number of Items: 28

Format: Four-point frequency scales. Sample items presented.

Reliability: Alpha was .92. Test–retest was .86. Split-half ranged from .62 to .86.

Author: Fitzgerald, L. F., et al.

Article: The incidence and dimensions of sexual harassment in academia and the workplace.

Journal: *Journal of Vocational Behavior*, April 1988, *32*(2), 152–175.

Related Research: Till, F. (1980). *Sexual harassment: A report on the sexual harassment of students*. Washington, DC: National Advisory

Council on Women's Educational Programs.

■ ■ ■

4677

Test Name: STRUCTURAL CENTRALIZATION SCALE

Purpose: To measure functional dependence and centralization and formalization in organziations.

Number of Items: 4

Format: Four-point frequency scales. Sample item presented.

Reliability: Alpha was .74.

Author: Dornstein, M., and Matalon, Y.

Article: A comprehensive analysis of the predictors of organizational commitment: A study of voluntary army personnel in Israel.

Journal: *Journal of Vocational Behavior*, April 1989, *34*(2), 192–203.

Related Research: Aiken, M., & Hage, J. (1967). Relationship of centralization to other structural properties. *Administrative Science Quarterly*, *12*, 72–92.

■ ■ ■

4678

Test Name: SUBSTITUTES FOR LEADERSHIP SCALES.

Purpose: To measure factors in the workplace that may negate leadership efforts.

Number of Items: 55

FORMAT: Five-point Likert format. All items presented.

Reliability: Reliabilities ranged from .35 to .85.

Validity: Correlations with Social Desirability Scales ranged from −.10 to .17.

Author: Williams, M. L., et al.

Article: A preliminary analysis of the construct validity of Kerr and

Jermier's Substitutes for Leadership scales.

Journal: *Journal of Occupational Psychology*, December 1988, *61*(4), 307–333.

Related Research: Kerr, S., & Jermier, J. M. (1978). Substitutes for leadership: Their meaning and measurement. *Organizational Behavior and Human Performance*, *22*, 375–403.

■ ■ ■

4679

Test Name: SUPERVISION LEVEL SCALE

Purpose: To provide classification of predominant developmental level of supervisees and supervision environments.

Number of Items: 40

Format: Includes two scales: person scale and environment scale.

Reliability: Test–retest (2 weeks) reliability ranged from .71 to .89 for the person scale and ranged from .83 to .95 for the environment scale.

Author: Wiley, M. O., and Ray, P. B.

Article: Counseling supervision by developmental level.

Journal: *Journal of Counseling Psychology*, October 1986, *33*(4), 439–445.

Related Research: Stoltenberg, C. (1981). Approaching supervision from a developmental perspective: The Counselor Complexity Model. *Journal of Counseling Psychology*, *28*, 59–65.

■ ■ ■

4680

Test Name: SURVEY OF PERCEIVED ORGANIZATIONAL SUPPORT

Purpose: To measure the extent to which employees perceived that the organization valued their contribution and cared about their well-being.

Number of Items: 17

Format: Responses are made on a 7-point Likert-type scale ranging from 1 (*strongly disagree*) to 7 (*strongly agree*). Examples are presented.

Reliability: Cronbach's alpha was .97.

Author: Eisenberger, R., et al.

Article: Perceived organizational support and employee diligence, commitment, and motivation.

Journal: *Journal of Applied Psychology*, February 1990, 75(1), 51–59.

Related Research: Eisenberger, R., et al. (1987). Reciprocation ideology. *Journal of Personality and Social Psychology*, 53, 743–750.

■ ■ ■

4681

Test Name: SURVEY OF PERCEIVED ORGANIZATIONAL SUPPORT

Purpose: To measure employees' beliefs about an organization's support of them.

Number of Items: 36

Format: Responses are made on a 7-point Likert scale from 1 (*strongly disagree*) to 7 (*strongly agree*). Examples are presented.

Reliability: Alpha coefficients were .96 and .97.

Validity: Correlation with the Survey of Perceived Supervisory Support was .13.

Author: Kottke, J. L., and Sharafinski, C. E.

Article: Measuring perceived supervisory and organizational support.

Journal: *Educational and Psychological Measurement*, Winter 1988, 48(4), 1075–1079.

Related Research: Eisenberger, R., et al. Perceived organizational support. *Journal of Applied Psychology*, 71, 500–507.

4682

Test Name: SURVEY OF PERCEIVED SUPERVISORY SUPPORT.

Purpose: To assess employees' perceptions of supervisory support.

Number of Items: 16

Format: Employs a 7-point Likert scale ranging from 1 (*strongly disagree*) to 7 (*strongly agree*). All items are presented.

Reliability: Coefficient alpha was .98.

Validity: Correlation with the Survey of Perceived Organizational Support was .98.

Author: Kottke, J. L., and Sharafinski, C. E.

Article: Measuring perceived supervisory and organizational support.

Journal: *Educational and Psychological Measurement*, Winter 1988, 48(4), 1075–1079.

■ ■ ■

4683

Test Name: TEMPORAL DIMENSIONS QUESTIONNAIRE.

Purpose: To measure temporal dimensions of organization culture.

Number of Items: 49

Format: Includes 13 scales: schedules and deadlines, punctuality, future orientation, time boundaries between work and nonwork, quality versus speed, synchronization and coordination of work with others through time, awareness of time use, work pace, allocation of time, sequencing of tasks through time, intraorganizational time boundaries, autonomy of time use, and variety versus routine.

Reliability: Cronbach's alpha ranged from .52 to .80.

Author: Schriber, J. B., and Gutek, B. A.

Article: Some time dimensions of work: Measurement of an underlying aspect of organization culture.

Journal: *Journal of Applied Psychology*, November 1987, 72(4), 642–650.

Related Research: Schriber, J. B. (1985). *An exploratory study of the temporal dimensions of work organizations*. Unpublished doctoral dissertation, The Claremont Graduate School, Claremont, CA.

■ ■ ■

4684

Test Name: THERAPIST SATISFACTION SCALE

Purpose: To measure overall counselor satisfaction with the process of individual counseling sessions.

Number of Items: 7

Format: An example is presented.

Reliability: Alpha coefficients were .80 and .93. Test–retest reliability was .55.

Author: Kokotovic, A. M., and Tracey, T. J.

Article: Working alliance in the early phase of counseling.

Journal: *Journal of Counseling Psychology*, January 1990, 37(1), 16–21.

Related Research: Tracey, T. J. (1986). Interactional correlates of premature termination. *Journal of Counseling and Clinical Psychology*, 54, 45–51.

■ ■ ■

4685

Test Name: UNION ORGANIZATION QUESTIONNAIRE

Purpose: To measure two factors of union organization.

Number of Items: 27

Format: Includes two factors of: organizational acceptance and union commitment.

Reliability: Coefficient alphas were .70 and .67.

Validity: Correlations with other variables ranged from .53 to −.44.

Author: Latack, J. C., et al.

Article: Carpenter apprentices: Comparison of career transitions for men and women.

Journal: *Journal of Applied Psychology*, August 1987, *72*(3), 393–400.

■ ■ ■

4686

Test Name: UNIVERSITY CLIMATE SCALE

Purpose: To measure perceptions of the general university climate.

Number of Items: 99

Format: Includes 11 subscales. Responses are made on a 4-point Likert scale from 4 (*always true*) to 1 (*always false*). An example is presented.

Reliability: Alpha coefficients ranged from .47 to .86.

Author: Reynolds, A. J.

Article: Social environmental conceptions of male homosexual behavior: A university climate analysis.

Journal: *Journal of College Student Development*, January 1989, *30*(1), 62–69.

Related Research: Stern, G. G. (1970). *People in context: Measuring person-environment congruence in education and industry*. New York: Wiley.

■ ■ ■

4687

Test Name: VANDERBILT PSYCHOTHERAPY PROCESS SCALE

Purpose: To assess relationship qualities, patient participation, and therapist techniques in the psychotherapy process.

Number of Items: 44

Format: Judges rate 10-minute tape recorded therapy sessions on a 5-point Likert scale.

Reliability: Interrater correlations ranged from .78 to .91 across scales.

Validity: Correlations with other variables ranged from −.45 to .44.

Author: Windholz, M. J., et al.

Article: Vanderbilt Psychotherapy Process Scale: A replication with adult outpatients.

Journal: *Journal of Consulting and Clinical Psychology*, February 1988, *56*(1), 56–60.

Related Research: O'Malley, S. S., et al. (1983). The Vanderbilt Psychotherapy Process Scale: A report of scale development and a process-outcome study. *Journal of Consulting and Clinical Psychology*, *51*, 581–586.

■ ■ ■

4688

Test Name: WORK CLIMATE INSTRUMENT

Purpose: To assess an organization's internal work climate.

Number of Items: 55

Format: Includes 11 subscales: work structure, job understanding, personal accountability, responsibility, supervisor work employees, participation supportive supervision, teamwork, intergroup cooperation, management awareness and concern, and communications flow. Responses are made on a 5-point scale ranging from 1 (*strongly disagree*) to 5 (*strongly agree*).

Reliability: Internal consistency reliabilities ranged from .56 to .89.

Author: Kozlowski, S. W. J., and Doherty, M. L.

Article: Integration of climate and leadership: Examination of a neglected issue.

Journal: *Journal of Applied Psychology*, August 1989, *74*(4), 546–553.

Related Research: Joyce, W. F., & Slocum, J. W. (1984). Collective climate: Agreement as a basis for defining aggregate climates in organizations. *Academy of Management Journal*, *27*, 721–742.

■ ■ ■

4689

Test Name: WORK DEMAND SCALE

Purpose: To assess perceived demand, particularly time pressure, and quantitative overload.

Number of Items: 7

Format: Responses are made on a 4-point scale.

Reliability: Coefficient alpha was .86.

Validity: Correlations with other variables ranged from −.13 to .33 ($n = 157$).

Author: Parkes, K. R.

Article: Coping, negative affectivity, and the work environment: Additive and interactive predictors of mental health.

Journal: *Journal of Applied Psychology*, August 1990, *75*(4), 399–409.

Related Research: Karasek, R. A. (1979). Job demands, job decision latitude, and mental strain: Implications for job redesign. *Administrative Science Quarterly*, *24*, 285–308.

■ ■ ■

4690

Test Name: WORK ENVIRONMENT SCALES

Purpose: To measure a person's immediate work environment.

Format: Includes five scales: supervisory style, performance/reward systems, decision making, pressure to produce, and visibility.

Reliability: Alpha coefficients ranged from .54 to .92.

Author: Stout, S. K., et al.

Article: Career transitions of superiors and subordinates.

Journal: *The Journal of Vocational Behavior*, April 1987, *30*(2), 124–137.

Related Research: Newman, J. (1977). Development of a measure of perceived work environment. *Academy of Management Journal, 20,* 520–534.

Slocum, J. W. Jr., et al. (1985). Business strategy and the management of platcaued employees. *Academy of Management Journal, 28,* 133–154.

■ ■ ■

4691

Test Name: WORK EXPERIENCES QUESTIONNAIRE

Purpose: To measure four work experiences.

Number of Items: 19

Format: Includes four factors: autocracy, pressure, nonsupport, and reward inequity. Responses are made on a 7-point scale ranging from *very rarely* to *continually*. Examples are presented.

Reliability: Alpha coefficients ranged from .73 to .90.

Validity: Correlations with other variables ranged from –.39 to .51.

Author: Greenhaus, J. H., et al.

Article: Work experiences, job performance, and feelings of personal and family well-being.

Journal: *Journal of Vocational Behavior*, October 1987, *31*(2), 200–215.

Related Research: Schnake, M. E. (1983). An empirical assessment of the effects of affective response in the measurement of organizational climate. *Personnel Psychology, 36,* 791–807.

■ ■ ■

4692

Test Name: YOUTH LEVEL OF SERVICE INVENTORY

Purpose: To quantify narrative intake records of clients in youth services programs.

Number of Items: 87

Format: Yes–no.

Reliability: Interrater reliability was .87.

Validity: Discriminates youths in group homes from those in active treatment homes.

Author: Andrews, D. A., et al.

Article: Risk principle of case classification in the prevention of residential placements: An outcome evaluation of Parenting Program.

Journal: *Journal of Consulting and Clinical Psychology*, April 1986, *54*(2), 203–207.

Related Research: Andrews, D. A., et al. (1985). *The Fourth Level of Service Inventory: Risk/needs assessment in child welfare.* Unpublished manuscript, Carleton University, Department of Psychology, Ottawa, Ontario, Canada.

CHAPTER 15
Motivation

4693

Test Name: ACHIEVEMENT MOTIVATION QUESTIONNAIRE

Purpose: To assess orientation toward success.

Number of Items: 13

Format: Employs a five-point response scale. Included items measuring need for achievement, aspiration level, persistence, and preference for achievement-related activities.

Reliability: Coefficient alpha was .77.

Author: James, L. A., and James, L. R.

Article: Integrating work environment perceptions: Explorations into the measurement of meaning.

Journal: *Journal of Applied Psychology*, October 1989, *74*(5), 739–751.

Related Research: James, L. R., et al. (1979). Correlates of psychological influence: An illustration of the psychological climate approach to work environment perceptions. *Personnel Psychology, 32*, 563–588.

$\bullet\bullet\bullet$

4694

Test Name: ACHIEVEMENT MOTIVATION SCALE

Purpose: To measure achievement motivation as work ethic acquisitiveness, dominance, excellence, competitiveness, status aspiration, and mastery.

Number of Items: 49

Format: Yes–no format. All items presented.

Reliability: Alphas ranged from .55 to .81. Split-half reliability ranged from .52 to .81.

Validity: Correlations with other variables ranged from .04 to .89.

Author: Cassidy, T., and Lynn, R.

Article: A multifactorial approach to achievement motivation: The development of a comprehensive measure.

Journal: *Journal of Occupational Psychology*, December 1987, *62*(4), 301–312.

$\bullet\bullet\bullet$

4695

Test Name: ACHIEVEMENT MOTIVATION SCALES

Purpose: To assess various aspects of achievement motivation in college students.

Number of Items: 20

Format: Forced choice (subjects choose descriptions of high or low achievers).

Reliability: Ranged from .67 to .75 across subscales.

Author: Neumann, Y., et al.

Article: Achievement motivation factors and students' college outcomes.

Journal: *Psychological Reports*, April 1988, *62*(2), 555–560.

Related Research: Hermans, H. J. M. (1970). A questionnaire measure of achievement motivation. *Journal of Applied Psychology, 54*, 353–363.

4696

Test Name: ACHIEVEMENT MOTIVATION TEST

Purpose: To assess school-aged children's motivation to achieve.

Number of Items: 30

Format: Self-report questions. An example is presented.

Validity: Correlations with other variables ranged from −.51 to .55.

Author: Arbuckle, B. S., and MacKinnon, C. E.

Article: A conceptual model of the determinants of children's academic achievement.

Journal: *Child Study Journal*, 1988, *18*(2), 121–147.

Related Research: Russell, I. (1969). Motivation for school achievement: Measurement and validation. *Journal of Educational Research, 62*, 261–266.

$\bullet\bullet\bullet$

4697

Test Name: ACHIEVEMENT MOTIVE SCALE

Purpose: To assess achievement motives and failure motives.

Format: Four-point rating scale.

Reliability: Cronbach's alphas were .73 (success) and .86 (failure).

Validity: Correlations with other variables ranged from −.25 to .25.

Author: Halvari, H.

Article: The relations between competitive experiences in mid-childhood and achievement motives among male wrestlers.

Journal: *Psychological Reports*, December 1989, *65*(3, Part II), 979–988.

Related Research: Halvari, H. (1987). Effects of achievement motives on wrestling ability, oxygen intake, speed of movement, muscular strength, and technical performance. *Perceptual and Motor Skills*, *65*, 255–270.

■ ■ ■

4698

Test Name: ACTION CONTROL SCALE

Purpose: To assess action versus state orientation.

Number of Items: 60

Format: Includes three subscales: performance, failure, and decision-making.

Reliability: Coefficient alphas ranged from .70 to .82.

Validity: Correlations with the Scale of Intellectual Development ranged from –.47 to .42.

Author: Erwin, T. D., and Marcus-Mendoza, S. T.

Article: Motivation and students' participation in leadership and group activities.

Journal: *Journal of College Student Development*, July 1988, *29*(4), 356–361.

Related Research: Kuhl, J. (1982). Action vs. state-orientation as a mediation between motivation and action. In Wittacker, W. Volpert, & M. von Cranach (Eds.), *Cognitive and motivational aspects of action*. Amsterdam: North-Holland.

■ ■ ■

4699

Test Name: CHILDREN'S ACADEMIC MOTIVATION INVENTORY

Purpose: To measure academic achievement motivation.

Number of Items: 60

Format: Responses are made on a 6-point Likert-scale ranging from 1 (*strongly agree*) to 6 (*strongly disagree*).

Reliability: Coefficient alpha was .81.

Validity: Correlations with other variables ranged from .12 to .37.

Author: Hughes, K. R., et. al.

Article: The Children's Academic Motivation Inventory: A research note on psychometric properties.

Journal: *Measurement and Evaluation in Counseling and Development*, October 1989, *22*(3), 137–142.

Related Research: Hughes, K. R., & Redfield, D. L. (1985, November). *Achievement motivation in children*. Paper presented at the annual meeting of the Mid-South Educational Research Association, Biloxi, MS.

■ ■ ■

4700

Test Name: COMPETITIVENESS QUESTIONNAIRE

Purpose: To measure goal competitiveness and interpersonal competitiveness.

Number of Items: 15

Format: Includes two subscales: Goal competitiveness and interpersonal competitiveness. Responses are made on a 5-point Likert scale ranging from 1 (*strongly disagree*) to 5 (*strongly agree*). All items are presented.

Reliability: Coefficient alphas were .45 and .76.

Validity: Correlations with other instruments ranged from .62 to –.45.

Author: Griffin-Pierson, S.

Article: The Competitiveness Questionnaire: A measure of two components of competitiveness.

Journal: *Measurement and Evaluation in Counseling and Development*, October 1990, *23*(3), 108–115.

■ ■ ■

4701

Test Name: COUNSELING SITUATIONS INVENTORY

Purpose: To measure subjects' willingness to see the counselors.

Number of Items: 18

Format: Subjects respond to hypothetical counseling problems on a 5-point Likert type scale from *not willing* (1) to *willing* (5) to discuss each problem with a counselor.

Reliability: Cronbach's alpha was .91. Test–retest correlation was .79 (*n* = 18).

Author: Mallinckrodt, B., and Helms, J. E.

Article: Effect of disabled counselors' self-disclosures on client perceptions of the counselor.

Journal: *Journal of Counseling Psychology*, July 1986, *33*(3), 343–348.

Related Research: Mitchell, D. C., & Frederickson, W. A. (1975). Preferences for physically disabled counselors in hypothetical counseling situations. *Journal of Counseling Psychology*, *22*, 477–482.

■ ■ ■

4702

Test Name: DECISION MAKING INFORMATION NEEDS QUESTIONNAIRE

Purpose: To determine need for specific information.

Number of Items: 8

Format: Likert-type format ranging from 1 (*definitely yes*) to 4 (*definitely no*).

Reliability: Coefficient alpha reliability was .70.

Author: Bull, K. S., and Newman, D. L.

Article: The effect of audience role and decision context on school evaluation information needs.

Journal: *Journal of Research and Development in Education*, Fall 1986, *20*(1), 28–36.

Related Research: Newman, D. L., et al. (1983). School boards' and administrators' use of evaluation information: Influencing factors. *Evaluation Review*, 7, 110–125.

■ ■ ■

4703

Test Name: DEFERMENT OF GRATIFICATION SCALE

Purpose: To measure deferment of gratification.

Number of Items: 12

Format: Yes–no format.

Reliability: Alpha was .72. All items presented.

Author: Ray, J. J., and Najman, J. M.

Article: The generalizability of deferment of gratification.

Journal: *The Journal of Social Psychology*, February 1986, *126*(1), 117–119.

Related Research: Wormith, J. S., & Hasenpusch, B. (1979). Multidimensional measurement of delayed gratification preference with incarcerated offenders. *Journal of Clinical Psychology*, 35, 218–225.

■ ■ ■

4704

Test Name: EXPECTANCY MOTIVATION

Purpose: To measure expectancy motivation.

Number of Items: 23

Reliability: Alpha coefficients ranged from .71 to .83.

Validity: Includes three subscales: expectancy, valence, and instrumentality.

Author: Kottkamp, R. B., et al.

Article: Teachers expectancy motivation, open to closed climate, and pupil control ideology in high schools.

Journal: *Journal of Research and Development in Education*, Winter 1987, *20*(2), 9–18.

Related Research: Miskel, C., et al. (1980). A test of expectancy motivation theory in educational organizations. *Educational Administration Quarterly*, *16*(1), 70–92.

■ ■ ■

4705

Test Name: GOAL ASSESSMENT SCALE

Purpose: To assess importance of goals.

Number of Items: 17

Format: Five-point importance scales. All items presented.

Reliability: Test–retest (1 month) reliability was .82.

Author: Emmons, R. A., and Diener, E.

Article: A goal-affect analysis of everyday situational choices.

Journal: *Journal of Research in Personality*, September 1986, *20*(3), 309–326.

Related Research: Graham, J. A., et al. (1980). The goal structure of situations. *European Journal of Social Psychology*, *10*, 345–366.

■ ■ ■

4706

Test Name: GOAL COMMITMENT MEASURE

Purpose: To provide a unidimensional measure of goal commitment.

Number of Items: 7

Format: All items are presented.

Reliability: Coefficient alpha was .88.

Validity: Correlations with other variables ranged from −.18 to .36.

Author: Hollenbeck, J. R., et al.

Article: An empirical examination of the antecedents of commitment to difficult goals.

Journal: *Journal of Applied Psychology*, February 1989, *74*(1), 18–23.

■ ■ ■

4707

Test Name: GOAL DIMENSION QUESTIONNAIRE

Purpose: To measure value, expectancy, effort, persistence, and attributions for goal attainment.

Number of Items: 58

Format: Seven-point true–false and certainty scales. Sample items presented.

Reliability: Test–retest (3-days) ranged from .67 to .91.

Author: Zaleski, Z.

Article: Attributions and emotions related to future goal attainment.

Journal: *Journal of Educational Psychology*, September 1988, *80*(4), 563–568.

Related Research: Zaleski, Z. (1987). Behavioral effects of the self-set goals for different time ranges. *International Journal of Psychology*, *22*, 17–38.

■ ■ ■

4708

Test Name: GOAL DIRECTEDNESS SCALE

Purpose: To assess goal setting among adolescents.

Number of Items: 16

Format: True–false. Sample item presented.

Reliability: Cronbach's alpha was .78.

Author: Kurdek, L. A., and Sinclair, R. J.

Article: Adjustment of young adolescents in two-parent nuclear, stepfather, and mother-custody families.

Journal: *Journal of Consulting and Clinical Psychology*, February 1988, *56*(1), 91–96.

Related Research: Ford, M. E. (1982). Social cognition and social competence in adolescence. *Developmental Psychology, 18,* 323–340.

● ● ●

4709

Test Name: GOAL INSTABILITY SCALE

Purpose: To measure a lack of goal directedness and inhibition in work.

Number of Items: 10

Format: Responses are made on a 10-point Likert scale.

Reliability: Test–retest (2 weeks) reliability was .76 (*n* = 133). Alpha was .80.

Validity: Correlations with other variables ranged from −.58 to .12.

Author: Robbins, S. B.

Article: Predicting changes in career indecision from a self-psychology perspective.

Journal: *The Career Development Quarterly*, June 1987, *35*(4), 288–296.

Related Research: Robbins, S., & Patton, M. (1985). Self-psychology and career development: Construction of the Superiority and Goal Instability Scales. *Journal of Counseling Psychology, 32,* 220–231.

● ● ●

4710

Test Name: HARDINESS SCALE

Purpose: To measure presence of high commitment, high control, and desire for challenge.

Number of Items: 36

Format: Likert format (25 items). Forced choice (11 items). Sample items presented.

Reliability: Alpha was .86. Stability (5 years) was .61.

Author: Nagy, S., and Nix, C.

Article: Relations between preventive health behavior and hardiness.

Journal: *Psychological Reports,* August 1989, *65*(1), 339–345.

Related Research: Kobasa, S. C., et al. (1982). Personality and exercise as buffers in the stress-illness relationship. *Journal of Behavioral Medicine, 4,* 391–404.

● ● ●

4711

Test Name: HYPERCOMPETITIVE ATTITUDE SCALE

Purpose: To provide an individual difference measure of general hypercompetitive attitude.

Number of Items: 26

Format: Responses are made on a 5-point scale from 1 (*never true of me*) to 5 (*always true of me*). All items are presented.

Reliability: Coefficient alpha was .91. Test–retest was .81 (*n* = 101).

Validity: Correlations with other variables ranged from −.64 to .51.

Author: Ryckman, R. M., et al.

Article: Construction of a hypercompetitive attitude scale.

Journal: *Journal of Personality Assessment,* Winter 1990, *55*(3 and 4), 630–639.

● ● ●

4712

Test Name: INDEX OF PERSONAL REACTIONS

Purpose: To measure need for power and need for influence.

Number of Items: 48

Format: Five-point self-rating scales. All items presented.

Reliability: Alphas ranged from .75 to .88 across subscales. Test–retest reliabilities ranged from .60 to .87.

Validity: Correlations with other variables ranged from −.46 to .68.

Author: Bennett, J. B.

Article: Power and influence as distinct personality traits: Development and validation of a psychometric measure.

Journal: *Journal of Research in Personality*, September 1988, *22*(3), 361–394.

● ● ●

4713

Test Name: INNOVATIVENESS SCALE

Purpose: To measure willingness to change.

Number of Items: 20

Format: Employs a 7-point Likert-type format.

Reliability: Reliability coefficient was .89.

Validity: Correlations with other variables ranged from −.10 to .81 (*N* = .98).

Author: Goldsmith, R. E.

Article: Convergent validity of four innovativeness scales.

Journal: *Educational Psychological Measurement*, Spring 1986, *46*(1), 81–87.

Related Research: Hurt, H. T., et al. (1977). Scales for the measurement of innovativeness. *Human Communications Research, 4,* 58–65.

● ● ●

4714

Test Name: LIFE ACTIVITIES ACHIEVEMENT SCALE

Purpose: To measure achievement motivation.

Number of Items: 36

Format: Includes five factors: group involvement, home achievement, academic achievement, personal excellence, and anti-achievement. Responses are made on a scale from 0 (*never*) to 4 (*very frequently*). All items are presented.

Reliability: Alpha coefficients ranged from .63 to .81.

Author: Piedmont, R. L.

Article: The Life Activities Achievement Scale: An act-frequency approach to the measurement of motivation.

Journal: *Educational and Psychological Measurement*, Winter 1989, *49*(4), 863–874.

Related Research: Buss, D. M., & Craik, K. H. (1983). The act-frequency approach to personality. *Psychological Review, 90*, 105–126.

■ ■ ■

4715

Test Name: MANIFEST NEEDS QUESTIONNAIRE

Purpose: To assess needs for achievement, affiliation, autonomy, and dominance.

Number of Items: 20

Format: Responses to each item are made on a 7-point scale ranging from always to never.

Reliability: Alpha coefficients ranged from .17 to .73. Test–retest (2 weeks) correlations averaged .78.

Validity: Correlations with the Miner Sentence Completion Scale ranged from −.07 to .42.

Author: Eberhardt, B. J., and Yap, C. K.

Article: A psychometric evaluation of the multiple-choice version of the Miner Sentence Completion Scale.

Journal: *Educational and Psychological Measurement*, Spring 1988, *48*(1), 119–126.

Related Research: Steers, R. M., & Braunstein, D. N. (1976). A behaviorally based measure of manifest needs in work settings. *Journal of Vocational Behavior, 9*, 251–266.

■ ■ ■

4716

Test Name: MANIFEST NEEDS QUESTIONNAIRE

Purpose: To measure the manner in which people overtly seek to satisfy needs.

Number of Items: 10

Format: Seven-point Likert format.

Reliability: Alphas ranged from .66 to .83.

Author: Koberg, C. S., and Chusmir, L. H.

Article: Relationships between sex-role conflict and work related variables: Gender and hierarchical differences.

Journal: *The Journal of Social Psychology*, December 1989, *129*(6), 779–791.

Related Research: Steers, R. M., & Braunstein, D. N. (1976). A behaviorally-based measure of manifest needs in work settings. *Journal of Vocational Behavior, 9*, 251–266.

■ ■ ■

4717

Test Name: MANIFEST NEEDS QUESTIONNAIRE

Purpose: To measure need for achievement and need for autonomy.

Number of Items: 8

Format: Includes two subscales: need for achievement and need for autonomy. Examples are presented.

Reliability: Coefficient alphas were .60 (need for achievement) and .65 (need for autonomy).

Validity: Correlations with other variables ranged from −.17 to .25 for need for achievement and from −.29 to .17 for need for autonomy.

Author: Puffer, S. M.

Article: Prosocial behavior, noncompliant behavior, and work preference among commission sales people.

Journal: *Journal of Applied Psychology*, November 1987, *72*(4), 615–621.

Related Research: Steers, R. M., & Braunstein, D. N. (1976). A behaviorally based measure of manifest needs in work settings. *Journal of Vocational Behavior, 9*, 251–266.

■ ■ ■

4718

Test Name: MOTIVATION ASSESSMENT SCALE

Purpose: To assess staff perceptions of the motivators of specific maladaptive behavior.

Number of Items: 16

Format: All items presented (yes–no or frequency scales implied).

Reliability: Cronbach's alphas ranged from .69 to .81.

validity: Factor structures were similar to that found by Durrand and Crimmins.

Author: Bihm, E. M., et al.

Article: Factor structure of the Motivation Assessment Scale for persons with mental retardation.

Journal: *Psychological Reports*, December 1990, *67*(3, Part II), 1235–1238.

Related Research: Durrand, V. M., & Crimmins, D. B. (1988). Identifying the variables maintaining self-injuring behavior. *Journal of*

Autism and Developmental Disorders,
18, 99–117.

■ ■ ■

4719

Test Name: MOTIVATION FOR
MARRIAGE SCALE

Purpose: To assess desire to get
married.

Number of Items: 3

Format: Likert format.

Reliability: Alpha was .68.

Validity: Correlations with other
variables ranged from –.40 to .46.
Females scored significantly higher
than males ($p < .05$).

Author: Ingilis, A., and Greenglass,
E. R.

Article: Motivation for marriage
among men and women.

Journal: *Psychological Reports,*
December 1989, *65*(3, Part I),
1035–1042.

■ ■ ■

4720

Test Name: MOTIVATION TO
CHANGE SCALE—MODIFIED

Purpose: To assess motivation to
change.

Number of Items: 12

Format: Responses are made on a
7-point continuum. Four unscored
filler items are included.

Reliability: Alpha coefficients were
.67 and .75.

Author: Sharking, B. S., et al.

Article: Application of the foot-in-
the-door effect to counseling.

Journal: *Journal of Counseling*
Psychology, April 1989, *36*(2),
248–251.

Related Research: Claiborn, C. D.,
et al. (1983). Effects of intervention
discrepancy in counseling for
negative emotions. *Journal of*
Counseling Psychology, 30, 164–171.

4721

Test Name: MOTIVATION TO
TRAIN FOR NEW TECHNOLOGIES
SCALE

Purpose: To measure motivation to
technological training.

Number of Items: 14

Format: Five-point Likert format.
Sample items presented.

Reliability: Alpha was .74.

Author: Breakwell, G. M., et al.

Article: Parental influence and
teenagers' motivation to train for
technological jobs.

Journal: *Journal of Occupational*
Psychology, March 1988, *61*(1),
79–88.

Related Research: Breakwell, G. M.,
et al. (1986). Attitudes to new
technology in relation to social beliefs
and group memberships: A
preliminary investigation. *Current*
Psychological Research and Reviews,
5, 34–47.

■ ■ ■

4722

Test Name: MY EDUCATION
SCALE

Purpose: To measure motivation.

Number of Items: 50

Format: Multiple-choice with four
responses from *strongly agree* to
strongly disagree.

Reliability: Split-half reliability
coefficient was .85.

Author: White, W. F., and Cass, M.

Article: Factor structure of the My
Education Scale.

Journal: *Perceptual and Motor Skills,*
June 1988, *66*(3), 829–830.

Related Research: Uguroglu, M., &
Walberg, H. (1986). Predicting
achievement and motivation. *Journal*
of Research and Development in
Education, 19, 1–12.

4723

Test Name: MY EDUCATION

Purpose: To provide a motivation-
type questionnaire.

Number of Items: 55

Format: Includes nine factors: home
environment, motivation, media, peer
group, social environment, time on
task, quality of instruction, grade, and
sex. All items are presented.

Validity: Correlations with the
Degrees of Reading Power ranged
from .19 to .41.

Author: White, W. F., et al.

Article: Perception of home
environment and school abilities as
predictors of reading power and
school achievements.

Journal: *Perceptual and Motor Skills,*
June 1986, *62*(3), 819–822.

Related Research: Uguroglu, M. E.,
& Walberg, H. J. (1986). Predicting
achievement and motivation. *Journal*
of Research and Development in
Education, 19(3), 1–12.

■ ■ ■

4724

Test Name: NEED FOR
ACHIEVEMENT SCALE

Purpose: To measure achievement
motivation.

Number of Items: 10

Format: Yes–no. All items presented.

Reliability: Alphas ranged from .16
to .61 across subscales.

Author: Ward, E. A.

Article: An international comparison
and psychometric analysis of Need for
Achievement scores on the Ray
Scale.

Journal: *Psychological Reports,* June
1990, *66*(3)1, 755–758.

Related Research: Ray, J. J. (1986).
Measuring achievement motivation by
self-report. *Psychological Reports, 58,*
525–526.

4725

Test Name: NEED FOR COGNITION SCALE

Purpose: To assess the tendency for an individual to engage in and enjoy thinking.

Number of Items: 34

Format: A Likert-type rating scale is employed with nine response options for each item.

Validity: Correlation with: time perception was r −.53 ($N = 44$); anagram score was .24 ($N = 44$).

Author: Baugh, B. T., and Mason, S. E.

Article: Need for cognition related to time perception.

Journal: *Perceptual and Motor Skills*, April 1986, *62*(2), 540–542.

Related Research: Cacioppo, J. T., & Petty, R. E. (1982). The need for cognition. *Journal of Personality and Social Psychology, 42*, 116–131.

■ ■ ■

4726

Test Name: NEED FOR COGNITION SCALE

Purpose: To measure the tendency to engage in and enjoy thinking.

Number of Items: 30

Reliability: Interitem reliability was .89.

Validity: Correlation with Objectivism was .47.

Author: Leary, M. R., et al.

Article: Objectivism in information utilization: Theory and measurement.

Journal: *Journal of Personality Assessment*, Spring 1986, *50*(1), 32–43.

Related Research: Cacioppo, J. T., & Petty, R. E. (1982). The need for cognition. *Journal of Personality and Social Psychology, 42*, 116–131.

4727

Test Name: NEED FOR COGNITION SCALE (SHORT FORM)

Purpose: To measure need for cognition.

Number of Items: 16

Format: Likert (implied). All items presented.

Reliability: Alpha was .88.

Validity: Correlated with health care involvement (.20, $p < .05$). Factor structure similar to long version.

Author: Perri, M., III, and Wolfgang, A. P.

Article: A modified measure of need for cognition.

Journal: *Psychological Reports*, June 1988, *62*(3), 955–957.

Related Research: Cacioppo, J. T., & Petty, R. E. (1982). The need for cognition. *Journal of Personality and Social Psychology, 42*, 116–131.

■ ■ ■

4728

Test Name: NEED SATISFACTION IN NONWORK SETTINGS SCALE

Purpose: To measure satisfaction in nonwork settings.

Number of Items: 7

Format: Responses are made on a 5-point Likert scale ranging from 1 (*strongly agree*) to 5 (*strongly disagree*).

Reliability: Coefficient alpha was .77.

Validity: Correlations with other variables ranged from −.15 to .22.

Author: Baba, V. V.

Article: Methodological issues in modeling absence: A comparison of least squares and Tobit analyses.

Journal: *Journal of Applied Psychology*, August 1990, *75*(4), 428–432.

4729

Test Name: OPEN PROCESSING SCALE

Purpose: To measure the willingness to try new things.

Number of Items: 24

Format: Self-report measure with 12 content reversed items employing a 5-point Likert scale.

Reliability: Parallel form reliability was .72.

Validity: Correlations with other variables ranged from .06 to .81 ($N = 98$).

Author: Goldsmith, R. E.

Article: Convergent validity of four innovativeness scales.

Journal: *Educational and Psychological Measurement*, Spring 1986, *46*(1), 81–87.

Related Research: Leavitt, C., & Walton, J. R. (1975). Development of a scale for innovativeness. In M. J. Schlinger (Ed.), *Advances in consumer research*, Vol. 2 (pp. 545–554). Ann Arbor, MI: Association for Consumer Research.

■ ■ ■

4730

Test Name: PERSONAL INCENTIVES FOR EXERCISE QUESTIONNAIRE

Purpose: To assess an individual's personal goals in exercise.

Number of Items: 48

Format: Responses are made on a 5-point Likert scale. Includes nine factors: appearance, competition, mental benefits, affiliation, mastery, flexibility/agility, social recognition, health benefits, and weight management. Examples are presented.

Reliability: Alpha coefficients ranged from .74 to .94. Test–retest (2 weeks) correlations ($N = 106$) ranged from .58 to .86.

Author: Duda, J. L., and Tappe, M. K.

Article: The Personal Incentives for Exercise Questionnaire: Preliminary development.

Journal: *Journal of Perceptual and Motor Skills*, June 1989, *68*(3) Part 2, 1122.

Related Research: Duda, J. L. and Tappe, M. K. (1988). Predictors of personal investment in physical activity among middle aged and older adults. *Perceptual and Motor Skills*, *66*, 543–549.

■ ■ ■

4731

Test Name: PERSONAL INCENTIVES FOR EXERCISE QUESTIONNAIRE—VERSION 1

Purpose: To assess exercise incentives.

Number of Items: 49

Format: Five-point Likert-type items assess seven categories of personal incentives related to exercise: mastery, competition, social affiliation, recognition, health benefits, coping with stress, and physical fitness.

Reliability: Cronbach's alpha ranged from .68 to .91.

Author: Duda, J. L., and Tappe, M. K.

Article: Predictors of personal investment in physical activity among middle-aged and older adults.

Journal: *Perceptual and Motor Skills*, April 1988, *66*(2), 543–549.

Related Research: Duda, J. L., & Tappe, M. K. (1987). Personal investment in exercise: The development of the Personal Incentives for Exercise Questionnaire. Paper presented at the annual meeting of the Association for the Advancement of Applied Sport Psychology, Newport Beach, CA.

■ ■ ■

4732

Test Name: POWER MOTIVE QUESTIONNAIRE

Purpose: To measure power motive with an objective self-report.

Number of Items: 27

Format: True–false.

Reliability: Test–retest of .60 is possible if test instructions are favorable.

Validity: Correlations between power motivation and self-reported behavior ranged from .03 to .48.

Author: Moser, K., and Gerth, A.

Article: Construction and validation of a power motive questionnaire.

Journal: *Psychological Reports*, February 1986, *58*(1), 83–86.

Related Research: Winter, D. G., & Stewart, A. J. (1977). Power motive reliability as a function of retest instructions. *Journal of Consulting and Clinical Psychology*, *45*, 436–440.

■ ■ ■

4733

Test Name: PSYCHOLOGICAL REACTANCE SCALE

Purpose: To measure the motivation to reestablish threatened or lost personal freedom.

Number of Items: 14

Format: Five-point Likert format. All items presented.

Reliability: Test–retest (2 weeks) reliability was .89. Cronbach's alpha was .77. Theta was .78. Omega was .82.

Author: Hong, S. M., and Page, S.

Article: A Psychological Reactance Scale: Development, factor structure, and reliability.

Journal: *Psychological Reports*, June 1989, *63*(4, Part II), 1323–1326.

Related Research: Tucker, R. K., & Byers, P. Y. (1987). Factorial validities of Cherz's Psychological Reactance Scale. *Psychological Reports*, *61*, 811–815.

4734

Test Name: REASONS FOR QUITTING SCALE

Purpose: To measure motivation to stop smoking.

Number of Items: 20

Format: Varied formats depending on item.

Reliability: Cronbach's alpha ranged from .53 to .81.

Validity: Correlations with smokers characteristics ranged from –.16 to .58. Subjects above 75th percentile were two times as likely to quit smoking as subjects below the 25th percentile.

Author: Curry, S., et al.

Article: Instrinsic and extrinsic motivation for smoking cessation.

Journal: *Journal of Consulting and Clinical Psychology*, June 1990, *58*(3), 310–316.

Related Research: Cohen, S., et al. Debunking myths about self-quitting: Evidence from ten prospective studies of persons quitting smoking by themselves. *American Psychologist*, *44*, 1355–1365.

■ ■ ■

4735

Test Name: RISK SCALES

Purpose: To measure the "taste for risk" and the risk of getting caught.

Number of Items: 5

Format: Likert format. All items presented.

Reliability: Alphas were .67 (taste for risk) and .76 (risk of getting caught).

Author: Hagan, J., et al.

Article: Class in the household: A power-control theory of gender and delinquency.

Journal: *American Journal of Sociology*, January 1987, *92*(4), 788–816.

Related Research: Jensen, G. F., et al. (1978). Perceived risk of punishment and self-reported delinquency. *Social Forces*, *57*, 57–78.

■ ■ ■

4736

Test Name: SCHOOL MOTIVATION SCALE

Purpose: To assess teachers' perceptions of their students' motivation.

Number of Items: 14

Format: Includes four dimensions: external, introjected, identified, and intrinsic. Teachers respond to each item on a 4-point scale: *very true, sort of true, not very true, not at all true.*

Reliability: Alpha reliabilities ranged from .75 to .83.

Author: Connell, J. P., and Ilardi, B. C.

Article: Self-system concomitants of discrepancies between children's and teachers' evaluations of academic competence.

Journal: *Child Development*, October 1987, *58*(5), 1297–1307.

Related Research: Connell, J. P., & Ryan, R. (1987). A developmental theory of motivation in the classroom. *Teacher Education Quarterly*, *11*, 64–77.

■ ■ ■

4737

Test Name: SELF-MOTIVATION INVENTORY

Purpose: To measure what is and is not characteristic of an individual.

Number of Items: 40

Format: Five-point rating scales.

Reliability: Stability ranged from .86 to .92.

Author: Welsh, M. C., et al.

Article: Cognitive strategies and personality variables in adherence to exercise.

Journal: *Psychological Reports*, Deccember 1990, *67*(3, Part II), 1327–1335.

Related Research: Dishman, R. K., & Ickes, W. (1981). Self-motivation and adherence to therapeutic exercise. *Journal of Behavioral Medicine*, *4*, 421–438.

■ ■ ■

4738

Test Name: SELF-REGULATORY STYLE QUESTIONNAIRE

Purpose: To identify children's reasons for doing homework, classwork, wanting to do well in school, and answering questions in class.

Number of Items: 26

Format: Includes four dimensions of self-regulatory style: external regulation, introjected regulation, identified regulation, and level of intrinsic motivation. Examples are presented.

Reliability: Alpha reliabilities ranged from .75 to .88.

Author: Connell, J. P., and Ilardi, B. C.

Article: Self-system concomitants of discrepancies between children's and teachers' evaluations of academic competence.

Journal: *Child Development*, October 1987, *58*(5), 1297–1307.

Related Research: Connell, J. P., & Ryan, R. (1987). A developmental theory of motivation in the classroom. *Teacher Education Quarterly*, *11*, 64–77.

■ ■ ■

4739

Test Name: SENSATION-SEEKING SCALE (SHORT FORM)

Purpose: To measure an individual's need for an optimal level of stimulation.

Number of Items: 10. All items presented.

Format: Paired statements format.

Reliability: Test–retest reliability was .78. Cronbach's alpha was .43. Kuder-Richardson formula ranged from .13 to .24.

Validity: Correlated positively with alcohol use (.31), drug use (.27), and cigarette use (.17). Did not correlate well with Marlowe-Crown Social Desirability (.06). Rotter I-E (.08), or authoritarianism (-.05).

Author: Madsen, D. B., et al.

Article: A Short Sensation-Seeking Scale.

Journal: *Psychological Reports*, June 1987, *60*(3)II, 1179–1184.

Related Research: Zukerman, M. K., et al. (1964). Development of a sensation-seeking scale. *Journal of Consulting Psychology*, *28*, 477–482.

■ ■ ■

4740

Test Name: SEXUAL RESPONSE CYCLE

Purpose: To measure sexual desire.

Number of Items: 5

Format: Yes–no format. Sample items presented.

Reliability: Internal consistency was .75.

Author: Andersen, B. L., et al.

Article: Controlled prospective longitudinal study of women with cancer: I. Sexual functioning outcomes.

Journal: *Journal of Consulting and Clinical Psychology*, December 1989, *56*(6), 683–691.

Related Research: Kaplan, H. S. (1979). Disorders of sexual desire. New York: Brunner/Mazel.

■ ■ ■

4741

Test Name: SOCIAL ORIENTATION INVENTORY

Purpose: To measure social power motivation.

Number of Items: 28

Format: Self-report. Subject indicates like or dislike for power behavior.

Validity: A three factor solution was consistent with the theoretical basis of the construct.

Author: Freeman, B., and Lanning, W.

Article: A factorial validation study of the Social Orientation Inventory.

Journal: *Psychological Reports*, June 1989, *64*(3, Part II), 1119–1123.

Related Research: Good, L. R., & Good, K. C. (1972). An objective measure of the motive to attain social power. *Psychological Reports*, *30*, 247–251.

■ ■ ■

4742

Test Name: SUPERIORITY SCALE

Purpose: To measure consolidation of ambitions reflective of the grandiose self.

Number of Items: 10

Format: Responses are made on a 6-point scale ranging from 1 (*strongly like me*) to 6 (*not at all like me*). Examples are presented.

Reliability: Test–retest reliability was .76.

Validity: Correlations with other variables ranged from –.25 to .18.

Author: Robbins, S. B., and Schwitzer, A. M.

Article: Validity of the Superiority and Goal Instability Scales as predictors of women's adjustment to college life.

Journal: *Measurement and Evaluation in Counseling and Development*, October 1988, *21*(3), 117–123.

Related Research: Robbins, S., & Patton, M. J. (1985). Self-psychology and career development: Construction of the superiority and goal instability scales. *Journal of Counseling Psychology*, *32*, 221–231.

■ ■ ■

4743

Test Name: WORK PREFERENCES SCALE

Purpose: To measure work-related motives.

Number of Items: 17

Format: Five-point importance scales.

Reliability: Alphas ranged from .62 to .69.

Author: West, M. A., and Nicholson, N.

Article: The outcomes of job change.

Journal: *Journal of Vocational Behavior*, June 1989, *34*(3), 335–349.

Related Research: Bailyn, L. (1980). *Living with technology: Issues at mid-career*. Cambridge, Massachusetts: MIT Press.

■ ■ ■

4744

Test Name: WORK VALUES SCALE

Purpose: To assess the needs that women satisfy by working for pay.

Number of Items: 84

Format: Includes six factors: dominance–recognition, economic, independence, interesting activity, mastery-achievement, and social.

Reliability: Test–retest reliabilities ranged form .52 to .81. Another study revealed reliabilities that ranged from .46 to .64. Alpha coefficients ranged from .71 to .83 for men and from .62 to .92 for women.

Author: Vodanovich, S. J., and Kramer, T. J.

Article: An examination of the work values of parents and their children.

Journal: *The Career Development Quarterly*, June 1989, *37*(4), 365–374.

Related Research: Eyde, L. D. (1961). *Work values and background factors as predictions of women's desire to work* (Research Monograph No. 108). Columbus: Ohio State University, Bureau of Business Research.

CHAPTER 16
Perception

4745

Test Name: ABSORPTION SCALE

Purpose: To measure imaginative involvement in one's experiences.

Number of Items: 20

Format: Yes–no format.

Reliability: Internal consistency was .89.

Validity: Correlated .27 with hypnotic suggestibility.

Author: Jennings, P. S., et al.

Article: Personality correlates of reflectivity.

Journal: *Psychological Reports*, August 1986, *59*(1), 87–94.

Related Research: Tullegen, A., & Atkinson, G. (1974). Openness to absorbing and self-altering experiences ("absorption"), a trait related to hypnotic susceptibility. *Journal of Abnormal Psychology, 83*, 268–277.

■ ■ ■

4746

Test Name: ACADEMIC SELF-CONCEPT SCALE

Purpose: To elicit a student's own assessments and perceptions of teacher and parent assessments of academic performance and potential.

Number of Items: 6

Format: Five-point rating scales. Sample item presented.

Reliability: Alpha was .80.

Author: Smith, T. E.

Article: Parental separation and the academic self-concepts of

adolescents: An effort to solve the puzzle of separation effects.

Journal: *Journal of Marriage and the Family*, February 1990, *52*(1), 107–118.

Related Research: Griffore, R. J., & Bianchi, L. (1984). The effects of ordinal position on academic self-concept. *Psychological Reports, 55*, 263–268.

■ ■ ■

4747

Test Name: ACADEMIC SELF-DESCRIPTION QUESTIONNAIRES

Purpose: To assess academic self-concept across subject areas.

Number of Items: A total of 78 items for Grades 5–6. 96 items for Grades 7–10.

Format: Six-point rating scales. Sample items presented.

Reliability: Alphas ranged from .88 to .94.

Author: Marsh, H. W.

Article: The structure of academic self-concept: The Marsh/Shavelson model.

Journal: *Journal of Educational Psychology*, December 1990, *82*(4), 623–636.

Related Research: Marsh, H. W., & Shavelson, R. J. (1985). Self-concept: Its multifaceted, hierarchical structure. *Educational Psychologist, 20*, 107–125.

■ ■ ■

4748

Test Name: ACADEMIC SELF-EFFICACY SCALE

Purpose: To measure task saliency, confidence, and self-efficacy in academic roles.

Number of Items: 78

Format: Five- and 9-point rating scales. All items presented.

Reliability: Alphas ranged from .90 to .96.

Validity: Correlations between subscales and perceived frequency of performance ranged from .29 to .68.

Author: Gail, L., et al.

Article: An investigation of the self-efficacy of male and female academics.

Journal: *Journal of Vocational Behavior*, June 1988, *32*(3), 307–320.

Related Research: Ladino, R. A., & Owen, S. V. (1988). Self-efficacy in university faculty. *Journal of Vocational Behavior, 33*, 1–14.

■ ■ ■

4749

Test Name: ACADEMIC SELF-ESTEEM SCALE

Purpose: To measure the general feeling of doing well in school and satisfaction with achievement.

Number of Items: 7

Format: Four-point rating scales. Sample items presented.

Reliability: Alphas ranged from .80 to .81. Test–retest reliability was .78.

Author: Skaalvik, E. M., and Rankin, R. J.

Article: Math, verbal and general academic self-concept: The internal–external frame of reference model and gender differences in group structure.

Journal: *Journal of Educational Psychology*, September 1990, *82*(3), 546–554.

Related Research: Skaalvik, E. M. (1990). Gender differences in general academic self-esteem and success expectations on defined academic problems. *Journal of Educational Psychology, 82*, 593–598.

■ ■ ■

4750

Test Name: ACADEMIC SELF-IMAGE TEST

Purpose: To measure academic self-image.

Number of Items: 23

Format: Includes three factors. Each item is an activity scored from 1 (*I am very bad at ___*) to 5 (*I am very good at ___*). All items are presented.

Reliability: Test–retest (1 year) correlations ranged from .53 to .73. Homogeneity reliability was .88 (boys) and .85 (girls).

Author: Entwisle, D. R., et al.

Article: The emergent academic self-image of first graders: Its response to social structures.

Journal: *Child Development*, October 1987, *58*(5), 1190–1206.

Related Research: Dickstein, E. (1972). *The development of self-esteem: Theory and measurement.* Unpublished doctoral dissertation, Johns Hopkins University.

■ ■ ■

4751

Test Name: ADULT NOWICKI-STRICKLAND INTERNAL–EXTERNAL CONTROL SCALE—ABBREVIATED

Purpose: To assess mothers' beliefs about personal control.

Number of Items: 20

Format: Mothers responded *yes* or *no* to each item.

Reliability: Coefficients alphas ranged from .70 to .87.

Author: Stevens, J. H., Jr.

Article: Social support, locus of control, and parenting in three low-income groups of mothers: Black teenagers, Black adults, and White adults.

Journal: *Child Development*, June 1988, *59*(3), 635–642.

Related Research: Nowicki, S., & Duke, N. F. (1974). A locus of control scale for college as well as non-college adults. *Journal of Personality Assessment, 38*, 136–137.

■ ■ ■

4752

Test Name: ADULT NOWICKI-STRICKLAND INTERNAL–EXTERNAL LOCUS OF CONTROL

Purpose: To measure locus of control.

Number of Items: 40

Format: Responses are in a yes–no format. An example is presented.

Reliability: Split-half reliabilities ranged from .74 to .86 (*N* = 156). Test–retest (6 weeks) reliability was .83 (*N* = 48).

Author: Larson, L. M., et al.

Article: Significant predictors of problem-solving appraisal.

Journal: *Journal of Counseling Psychology*, October 1990, *37*(4), 482–490.

Related Research: Nowicki, S., & Duke, M. P. (1974). A locus of control scale for non-college as well as college adults. *Journal of Personality Assessment, 38*, 136–137.

■ ■ ■

4753

Test Name: ADVERSARIAL SEXUAL BELIEFS SCALE

Purpose: To measure adversarial sexual beliefs.

Number of Items: 9

Format: Subjects indicate level of agreement with each item by responding on a 7-point scale. A sample item is presented.

Reliability: Cronbach's alpha was .80.

Author: Muehlenhard, C. L., and Linton, M. A.

Article: Date rape and sexual aggression in dating situations: Incidence and risk factors.

Journal: *Journal of Counseling Psychology*, April 1987, *34*(2), 186–196.

Related Research: Burt, M. R. (1980). Cultural myths and supports for rape. *Journal of Personality and Social Psychology, 38*, 217–230.

■ ■ ■

4754

Test Name: AFRICAN SELF-CONCIOUSNESS SCALE

Purpose: To assess the Black personality construct African self-conciousness.

Number of Items: 42

Format: Measures four competency dimensions: awareness and recognition of one's African-American identity and heritage; general ideological and identity priorities placed on Black survival, liberation, and proactive affirmative development; specific activity priorities placed on self-knowledge and self-affirmation (i.e., Afrocentric values, customs, and institutions); and a posture of resolute resistance to anti-Black forces and threats to Black survival in general. Sample items are presented.

Reliability: Kuder-Richardson formula reliability coefficients ranged from .77 to .90.

Author: Cheatham, H. E., et al.

Article: The African self-conciousness construct and African-American students.

Journal: *Journal of College Student Development*, November 1990, *31*(6), 492–499.

Related Research: Baldwin, J. A., & Bell, Y. (1982). *The African Self-Conciousness Scale Manual.* Tallahassee, FL: A&M University.

∎ ∎ ∎

4755

Test Name: AFTER-COLLEGE QUESTIONNAIRE

Purpose: To measure self-acceptance/identity, social interaction, self-esteem, and locus of control.

Number of Items: 20

Format: Five-point Likert or other rating scales.

Reliability: Alphas ranged from .59 to .85.

Author: Richardson, T. M., and Benbow, C. P.

Article: Long-term effects of acceleration on the social-emotional adjustment of mathematically precocious youth.

Journal: *Journal of Educational Psychology*, September 1990, *82*(3), 464–470.

Related Research: Peng, S. S., et al. (1981). *High School and Beyond.* Washington, DC: National Center for Education Statistics.

∎ ∎ ∎

4756

Test Name: AIDS VICTIM EMPLOYMENT SCALE

Purpose: To measure managers' beliefs about employing AIDS victims.

Number of Items: 15

Format: Five-point Likert format. All items presented.

Reliability: Cronbach alphas ranged from .81 to .91.

Validity: Three factors explain 65% of the variance.

Author: Vest, M. J., et al.

Article: Perceived consequences of employing AIDS victims: Development and validation of a scale.

Journal: *Psychological Reports*, June 1990, *66*(3, Part II), 1367–1374.

∎ ∎ ∎

4757

Test Name: APPROPRIATENESS CHECKLIST—REVISED

Purpose: To assess perceptions of relevance

Number of Items: 14

Format: Responses to each item were made on a 5-point scale which ranged from 1 (*definitely inappropriate*) to 5 (*most appropriate*).

Reliability: Coefficient alpha was .90.

Author: Puchkoff, S. C., and Lewin, P. G.

Article: Student responsiveness to specialized college services: Contribution of personality variables and perceptions of services.

Journal: *Journal of Counseling Psychology*, July, 1987, *34*(3), 330–332

Related Research: Warman, R. E. (1960). Differential perceptions of a counseling role. *Journal of Counseling Psychology*, 7, 269–274.

∎ ∎ ∎

4758

Test Name: ARTICULATION OF THE BODY-CONCEPT SCALE

Purpose: To assess field-dependence/independence.

Format: The child is asked to draw a male and a female each on a separate sheet of paper. At least two judges independently rate the drawings on a 5-point scale. The drawings are rated according to form level, degree of sex identity differentiated, and the level of detail.

Reliability: Test–retest reliability ranged from .75 to .99. Interrater reliability estimates ranged from .88 to .99.

Validity: Correlations with the Goodenough-Harris Drawing Test ranged from .85 to .97. Correlations with the Preschool Embedded Figures Test ranged from .85 to .92. Correlations with the Children's Embedded Figures Test ranged from .11 to .21.

Author: Saracho, O. N.

Article: Validation of two cognitive measures to assess field-dependence/independence.

Journal: *Perceptual and Motor Skills*, August, 1986, *63*(1), 255–263

Related Research: Witkin, H. A., et al. (1974). Psychological differentiation: Studies of development. Potomac, MD: Erlbaum.

∎ ∎ ∎

4759

Test Name: ASPECTS OF IDENTITY QUESTIONNAIRE

Purpose: To measure the degree to which identities are based on personal and social attributes.

Number of Items: 21

Format: Subjects indicate how important personal and social attributes are in determining "who they are."

Reliability: Alphas ranged from .73 to .82.

Author: Barnes, B. D., et al.

Article: Reactions to social vs. self-evaluation: Moderating effects of personal and social identity orientations.

Journal: *Journal of Research in Personality*, December 1989, *23*(4), 513–524.

Related Research: Cheeks, J. M. (1982). *The Aspects of Identity Questionnaire: Revised scales assessing personal and social identity.*

Unpublished manuscript, Wellesley College, Wellesley, MA.

• • •

4760

Test Name: ATTRIBUTIONAL STYLE QUESTIONNIARE

Purpose: To measure external and internal attributional styles in college students.

Number of Items: 10

Format: Subjects choose one item in a pair and indicate its likelihood. Sample item presented.

Reliability: Semipartial correlation internal consistency was .82 forinternal and .77 for external.

Author: Koestner, R., et al.

Article: Attributional style, comparison focus of praise, and intrinsic motivation.

Journal: *Journal of Research in Personality*, March 1990, *24*(1), 87–100.

Related Research: Crandall, V. C., et al. (1965). Children's beliefs in their own control of reinforcements in intellectual academic achievement situations. *Child Development*, *36*, 91–109.

• • •

4761

Test Name: ATTRIBUTIONAL STYLE QUESTIONNAIRE

Purpose: To measure internality, stability, globality, and controllability.

Number of Items: 24

Format: Each item consists of a hypothetical situation describing a negative outcome for which the subject rates the cause on 7-point scales for degree of internality, stability, globality, and controlability.

Reliability: Internal consistency reliabilities ranged from .66 to .88.

Validity: Correlation with other variables ranged from −.65 to .64.

Author: Stoltz, R. F., and Galassi, J. P.

Article: Internal attributions and types of depression in college students: the learned helplessness model revisited.

Journal: *Journal of Counseling Psychology*, July 1989, *36*(3), 316–321.

Related Research: Peterson, C., & Seligman, M. E. P. (1984). Causal explanations as a risk factor for depression: Theory and evidence. *Psychological Review*, *91*, 347–374.

• • •

4762

Test Name: AUTONOMOUS LEARNING BEHAVIOR SCALE

Purpose: To measure attributional styles in mathematics.

Number of Items: 30

Format: Likert format.

Reliability: Alphas ranged from .71 to .80.

Author: Kloosterman, P.

Article: Self-confidence and motivation in mathematics.

Journal: *Journal of Educational Psychology*, September 1988, *80*(3), 345–351.

Related Research: Fennema, G., & Peterson, P. (1984). *Classroom processes, sex differences, and autonomous learning in mathematics: Final report to the National Science Foundation.* Available from author. University of Wisconsin, Madison.

• • •

4763

Test Name: AUTONOMY SCALE

Purpose: To assess autonomy.

Number of Items: 3

Format: Responses to each item were made on a 7-point scale from *very little* to *very much*.

Reliability: Coefficient alphas were .70 and .75 (*N* = 156).

Validity: Correlations with other variables ranged from −.36 to .51 (*N* = 148–156).

Author: Spector, P. E., et al.

Article: Relation of job stressors to affective, health, and performance outcomes: A comparison of multiple data courses.

Journal: *Journal of Applied Psychology*, February 1988, *73*(1), 11–19.

Related Research: Hackman, J. R., & Oldham, G. R. (1975). Development of the Job Diagnostic Survey. *Journal of Applied Psychology*, *60*, 159–170.

• • •

4764

Test Name: BALANCED INVENTORY OF DESIRABLE RESPONDING

Purpose: To measure the self-deception and impression management variables.

Number of Items: 40

Format: Includes equal numbers of self-deception and impression management items. Responses are made on a 7-point scale ranging from 1 (not true) to 7 (very true). Sample items are presented.

Reliability: Alpha coefficients were .72 (impression management) and .68 (self deception).

Author: Lautenschlager, G. J., and Flaherty, V. L.

Article: Computer administration of questions: More desirable or more social desirability?

Journal: *Journal of Applied Psychology*, June 1990, *75*(3), 310–314.

Related Research: Paulhus, D. L. (1986). Self-deception and impression management in test responses. In A. Angleitner & J. S. Wiggins (Eds.), Personality assessment via questionnaire (pp.143–165). Berlin: Springer-Verlag.

4765

Test Name: BARRETT-LENNARD RELATIONSHIP INVENTORY

Purpose: To measure visible racial/ethnic group supervisees' perceptions of their cross-cultural supervisory relationship.

Number of Items: 64

Format: Includes four dimensions: empathic understanding, level of regard, unconditionality of regard, and congruence. Responses are made on a 6-point scale ranging from 3 (*strongly feel that it is true*) to −3 (*strongly feel that it is not true*). Examples are presented.

Reliability: Split-half reliability coefficients ranged from .75 to .94.

Author: Cook, D. A., and Helms, J. E.

Article: Visible racial/ethnic group supervisees' satisfaction with cross-cultural supervision as predicted by relationship characteristics.

Journal: *Journal of Counseling Psychology*, July 1988, *35*(3), 268–274.

Related Research: Barrett-Lennard, G. T. (1962). Dimensions of therapist response as causal factors in therapeutic change. *Psychological Monographs Applied*, *76*(43, Whole No. 562).

■ ■ ■

4766

Test Name: BEHAVIORAL CORRELATES SCALE—REVISED

Purpose: To assess the counselor's perception of how the client behaved in-session on four role expectations.

Number of Items: 34

Format: Responses are made on a 7-point Likert scale ranging from 1 (*not at all evident*) to 7 (*highly evident*).

Reliability: Test–retest (1 week) reliability ranged from .62 to .75. Internal consistency alphas ranged from .77 to .85.

Author: Tracey, T. J., and Dundon, M.

Article: Role anticipations and preferences over the course of counseling.

Journal: *Journal of Counseling Psychology*, January 1988, *35*(1), 3–14.

Related Research: Rickers-Ovsiankina, M. A., et al. (1971). Patients' role expectancies in psychotherapy: A theoretical and measurement approach. *Psychotherapy: Theory, Research, and Practice, 8*, 124–126.

■ ■ ■

4767

Test Name: BELIEF IN PERSONAL CONTROL SCALE

Purpose: To provide a multidimensional measure of the belief in personal control construct.

Number of Items: 85

Format: Subjects respond to each item on a 5-point scale including the points: *always true, often true, sometimes true, rarely true*, and *never true*. Includes three factors: General External Control, Exaggerated Internal Control, and God-Mediated Control. All items are presented.

Reliability: Test–retest coefficients (1, 2, and 4–week intervals) ranged from .80 to .97.

Validity: Correlations with other variables ranged from −.55 to .45.

Author: Berrenberg, J. L.

Article: The Belief in Personal Control Scale: A measure of God-mediated and exaggerated control.

Journal: *Journal of Personality Assessment*, Summer, 1987, *51*(2). 194–206

■ ■ ■

4768

Test Name: BLOOD DONOR IDENTITY SCALE

Purpose: To measure the extent that blood donor is viewed as part of the self.

Number of Items: 5

Format: Nine-point Likert format. All items presented.

Reliability: Alpha was .81.

Author: Callero, P. L., et al.

Article: Helping behavior as role behavior: Disclosing social structure and history in the analysis of prosocial action.

Journal: *Social Psychology Quarterly*, September 1987, *50*(3), 247–256.

Related Research: Callero, P. L. (1985). Role identity salience. *Social Psychology Quarterly, 48*, 203–214.

■ ■ ■

4769

Test Name: BODILY FEELING SCALE

Purpose: To provide a measure of self-reported bodily feelings.

Number of Items: 35

Format: Each item is rated on a 9-point Likert scale. Includes seven factors.

Reliability: Coefficient alphas ranged from .54 to .94.

Validity: Correlations with other factors ranged from .14 to .59.

Author: Alpher, V. S., et al.

Article: Multifactor measurement of bodily feelings: Conceptual development, scale construction, and empirical validation.

Journal: *Journal of Psychopathology and Behavioral Assessment*, December 1987, *9*(4), 403–421.

■ ■ ■

4770

Test Name: BODY AWARENESS QUESTIONNAIRE

Purpose: To assess self-reported attentiveness to normal nonemotive body processes.

Number of Items: 18

Format: Items are rated on a 7-point scale ranging from 1 (*not at all true about me*) to 7 (*very true about me*). All items are presented.

Reliability: Alpha coefficients ranged from .77 to .83. Test–retest (2 weeks) reliability was .80.

Validity: Correlations with other variables ranged from −.15 to .66.

Author: Shields, S. A., et al.

Article: The Body Awareness Questionnaire: Reliability and validity.

Journal: *Journal of Personality Assessment*, Winter 1989, *53*(4), 802–815.

■ ■ ■

4771

Test Name: BODY-CATHEXIS SCALE

Purpose: To measure one's feelings about one's body.

Number of Items: 46

Format: Subjects rate on a 5-point Likert scale from 1 (*wishes for change*) to 5 (*considers self fortunate*).

Reliability: Reported reliability is .83. Split-half reliability is .81.

Author: Dworkin, S. H., and Kerr, B. A.

Article: Comparison of interventions for women experiencing body image problems.

Journal: *Journal of Counseling Psychology*, April 1987, *34*(2), 136–140.

Related Research: Secord, P. F., & Jourard, S. M. (1953). The appraisal of body cathexis and the self. *Journal of Consulting Psychology, 17,* 343–347.

4772

Test Name: BODY CATHEXIS SCALE—REVISED

Purpose: To measure body-image.

Number of Items: 40

Format: Responses to each item are made on a 5-point Likert scale that ranged from 1 (*strong negative*) to 5 (*strong positive*).

Reliability: Test–retest (2 weeks) reliability was .89.

Validity: Correlations with the Tennessee Self-Concept Scale ranged from −.05 to .62.

Author: Balogun, J. A.

Article: Reliability and construct validity of the Body Cathexis Scale.

Journal: *Perceptual and Motor Skills*, June 1986, *62,*(3), 927–935.

Related Research: Tucker, L. A. (1985). Dimensionality and factor satisfaction of the body image construct: A gender comparison. *Sex Roles, 12,* 931–937.

■ ■ ■

4773

Test Name: BODY CATHEXIS SCALE—MODIFIED

Purpose: To measure satisfaction with the body and its separate parts.

Number of Items: 24

Format: Body parts are rated on a 5-point Likert scale ranging from *very satisfied* to *very dissatisfied*.

Reliability: Cronbach's alpha was .80.

Author: Markee, N. L., et al.

Article: Body cathexis and clothed body cathexis: Is there a difference?

Journal: *Perceptual and Motor Skills*, June 1990, *70*(3, Part 2), 1239–1244.

Related Research: Davis, L. L. (1985). Perceived somatotype, body-cathexis, and attitude toward clothing among college females. *Perceptual and Motor Skills, 61,* 1199–1205.

4774

Test Name: BODY CATHEXIS SCALE—MODIFIED

Purpose: To evaluate satisfaction of individual body parts and processes.

Number of Items: 32

Format: Responses to each item are made on a 5-point Likert scale from 1 (*very satisfied*) to 5 (*very dissatisfied*).

Validity: Zero-order correlations of satisfaction ratings and corresponding body parts ($N = 41$) ranged from −.33 to .48.

Author: Ward, T. E., and McKeown, B. C.

Article: Association of body cathexis and morphological variables on college-aged females in an exercise setting.

Journal: *Perceptual and Motor Skills*, February 1987, *64*(1), 179–190.

Related Research: Secord, P. F., & Jourard, S. M. (1953). The appraisal of body cathexis and the self. *Journal of Clinical Psychology, 17,* 343–347.

■ ■ ■

4775

Test Name: BODY-CONSCIOUSNESS INVENTORY

Purpose: To measure body-consciousness.

Number of Items: 15

Format: Includes three scales: private body-consciousness, public body-consciousness, and body-competence.

Validity: Correlations with other variables ranged from .03 to .48.

Author: Kelson, T. R., et al.

Article: Body-image and body-beautification among female college students.

Journal: *Perceptual and Motor Skills*, August 1990, *71*(1), 281–289.

Related Research: Miller, L. C., et al. (1981). Consciousness of body:

Private and public. *Journal of Personality and Social Psychology, 41*, 397–406.

■ ■ ■

4776

Test Name: BODY CONSCIOUSNESS QUESTIONNAIRE

Purpose: To measure body competence and private and public body consciousness.

Number of Items: 14

Format: Includes measures of covert bodily processes, chronic awareness of observable body aspects, and body competence. Examples are presented.

Validity: Correlations with other measures ranged from −.46 to .63 (*N*s = 193 and 150).

Author: Franzoi, S. L., and Herzog, M. E.

Article: The body esteem scale: A convergent and discriminant validity study.

Journal: *Journal of Personality Assessment*, Spring 1986, *50*(1), 24–31.

Related Research: Miller, L. C., et al. (1981). Consciousness of body: Private and public. *Journal of Personality and Social Psychology, 41*, 397–406.

■ ■ ■

4777

Test Name: BODY ESTEEM SCALE—FEMALE SUBSCALES

Purpose: To measure dimensions of body esteem.

Number of Items: 35

Format: Includes three subscales: weight concern, sexual attractiveness, and physical condition.

Validity: Correlations with other variables ranged from −.81 to −.68.

Author: Thomas, C. D., and Freeman, R. J.

Article: The Body Esteem Scale: Construct validity of the female subscales.

Journal: *Journal of Personality Assessment*, Spring 1990, *54*(1/2), 204–212.

Related Research: Franzoi, S., & Shields, S. (1984). The Body Esteem Scale: Multidimensional structure and sex differences in a college population. *Journal of Personality Assessment, 48*, 173–178.

■ ■ ■

4778

Test Name: BODY PARTS SATISFACTION SCALE

Purpose: To determine body satisfaction.

Number of Items: 24

Format: Body parts are rated on a 6-point scale ranging from 1 (*extremely dissatisfied*) to 6 (*extremely satisfied*).

Reliability: Cronbach's alphas were .91 (men) and .89 (women).

Validity: Correlations with other variables ranged from −.61 to −.66.

Author: Keeton, W. P., et al.

Article: Body image or body images? Comparative, multidimensional assessment among college students.

Journal: *Journal of Personality Assessment*, Spring 1990, *54*(1/2), 213–230.

Related Research: Berscheid, E., et al. (1973, November). The happy American body: A survey report. *Psychology Today*, pp., 119–131.

■ ■ ■

4779

Test Name: BODY PARTS SATISFACTION QUESTIONNAIRE—REVISED

Purpose: To assess respondents' satisfaction with their body parts.

Number of Items: 26

Format: Response to each item is made on a 7-point Likert scale.

Reliability: Coefficient alpha was .92.

Validity: Correlations with other variables ranged from −.07 to −.66.

Author: Gleghorn, A. A., et al.

Article: The psychometric properties of several measures of body image.

Journal: *Journal of Psychopathology and Behavioral Assessment*, June 1987, *9*(2), 203–218.

Related Research: Berscheid, E., et al. (1973, November). The happy American body: A survey report. *Psychology Today, 7* (6), 119–131.

■ ■ ■

4780

Test Name: BODY-SELF RELATIONS QUESTIONNAIRE

Purpose: To assess physical appearance.

Number of Items: 140

Format: Five-point Likert format.

Reliability: Alphas ranged from .68 to .91 across subscales. Test–retest reliability ranged from .65 to .91.

Author: Sullivan, L. A., and Harnish, R. J.

Article: Body image: Differences between high and low self-monitoring males and females.

Journal: *Journal of Research in Personality*, September 1990, *24*(3), 291–302.

Related Research: Umstead, B. A., & Cash, T. F. (1984). *Reliability and validity of the Body-Self Relations Questionnaire: A new measure of body image.* Paper presented at the meeting of the Southeastern Psychological Association, New Orleans, LA.

■ ■ ■

4781

Test Name: BODY-SELF RELATIONS QUESTIONNAIRE

Purpose: To assess affective, cognitive, and behavioral

components of appearance-related body image.

Number of Items: 54

Format: Includes three subscales: Appearance attention/importance, appearance evaluation, and appearance action. Responses are made on a 5-point Likert-type response format.

Reliability: Cronbach's alpha ranged from .83 to .92.

Validity: Correlations with other variables ranged from −.42 to .16.

Author: Cash, T. F., and Green, G. K.

Article: Body weight and body image among college women: Perception, cognition, and affect.

Journal: *Journal of Personality Assessment*, Summer 1986, *50*(2), 290–301.

Related Research: Noles, S. W., et al. (1985). Body image, physical attractiveness, and depression. *Journal of Consulting and Clinical Psychology, 53*, 88–94.

■ ■ ■

4782

Test Name: BROWN LOCUS OF CONTROL SCALE

Purpose: To measure locus of control.

Number of Items: 25

Format: Includes three dimensions: internal, external, and external other.

Reliability: Test–retest (2 weeks) reliability coefficients ranged from .84 to .91. Alpha coefficients ranged from .66 to .87.

Validity: Correlations with other variables ranged from −.43 to .58.

Author: Brown, R.

Article: The construct and concurrent validity of the social dimension of the Brown Locus of Control Scale.

Journal: *Educational and Psychological Measurement*, Summer 1990, *50*(2), 377–382.

Related Research: Brown, R. (1983). Locus of control and sex role orientation of women graduate students. *College Students Journal, 17*(1), 10–12.

■ ■ ■

4783

Test Name: BULIMIA COGNITIVE DISTORTIONS SCALE

Purpose: To measure irrational beliefs and cognitive distortions associated with bulimia.

Number of Items: 25

Format: Responses are made on a 5-point scale from 1 (*strongly disagree*) to 5 (*strongly agree*).

Reliability: Coefficient alpha was .97.

Validity: Correlations with other variables ranged from .19 to .77.

Author: Schulman, R. G., et al.

Article: The development of a scale to measure cognitive distortions in bulimia.

Journal: *Journal of Personality Assessment*, Winter 1986, *50*(4), 630–639.

■ ■ ■

4784

Test Name: CANCER LOCUS OF CONTROL SCALE (ENGLISH VERSION)

Purpose: To predict illness-related behavior of cancer patients.

Number of Items: 17

Format: All items presented. Response categories implied but not presented.

Reliability: Alphas ranged from .77 to .80 across subscales.

Validity: Correlations with Mental Adjustment to Cancer Scale ranged from −.19 to .34.

Author: Watson, M., et al.

Article: Locus of control and adjustment to cancer.

Journal: *Psychological Reports*, February 1990, *66*(1), 39–48.

Related Research: Pryun, J. F. A., et al. (1988). De locus of control— Schaal voor kankerpatienten (The locus of control scale for cancer patients). *Tijdschift voor Sociale Mezndheidszorj, 66*, 404–408.

■ ■ ■

4785

Test Name: CANCER PERCEIVED SELF-EFFICACY SCALE

Purpose: To measure patients' beliefs concerning their ability to cope when behavior is made difficult by cancer.

Number of Items: 38

Format: Ten-point confidence scales.

Reliability: Cronbach's alphas ranged from .77 to .92. Test–retest reliability was .95.

Author: Telch, C. F., and Telch, M. J.

Article: Group coping skills instruction and supportive group therapy for cancer patients: A comparison of strategies.

Journal: *Journal of Consulting and Clinical Psychology*, December 1986, *54*(6), 802–808.

Related Research: Telch, C. F., & Telch, M. J. (1982). *Stanford Inventory of Cancer Patient Adjustment*. Unpublished scales, Stanford University.

■ ■ ■

4786

Test Name: CAREER DEVELOPMENT LOCUS OF CONTROL SCALE

Purpose: To measure locus of control as it relates to the career process among college students.

Number of Items: 18

Format: A true–false format is employed. All items are presented.

Reliability: Test–retest (3 weeks) reliability coefficient was .93. Kuder-

Richardson formula results ranged from .78 to .82.

Validity: Correlations with Rotter I-E scale was .52 for women. Correlation with Marlowe-Crowne scale was −.13 for men.

Author: Trice, A. D., et al.

Article: A career locus of control scale for undergraduate students.

Journal: *Journal of Perceptual and Motor Skills*, October 1989, *69*(2), 555–561.

■ ■ ■

4787

Test Name: CAUSAL DIMENSION SCALE

Purpose: To measure how individuals perceive causes.

Number of Items: 9

Format: Nine-point Likert format.

Reliability: Internal consistency ranged from .73 to .87 across subscales.

Validity: Does not correlate with Beck Depression Inventory.

Author: Endlich, E.

Article: Depression and attributions for problems and solutions in college students.

Journal: *Psychological Reports*, August 1989, *65*(1), 131–141.

Related Research: Russell, D. (1982). The Causal Dimension Scale: A measure of how individuals perceive causes. *Journal of Personality and Social Psychology*, *42*, 1137–1145.

■ ■ ■

4788

Test Name: CHANCE SCALE

Purpose: To measure locus of control.

Number of Items: 8

Format: Six-point Likert format.

Reliability: Alpha was .76.

Author: Blau, G. J.

Article: Locus of control as a potential moderator of the turnover precess.

Journal: *Journal of Occupational Psychology*, March 1987, *60*(1), 21–29.

Related Research: Levenson, H. (1973). Multidimensional locus of control in psychiatric patients. *Journal of Consulting and Clinical Psychology*, *41*, 397–404.

■ ■ ■

4789

Test Name: CHILDREN'S ATTRIBUTIONAL STYLE QUESTIONNAIRE

Purpose: To measure beliefs about causes of events as set out in learned helplessness theory.

Number of Items: 48

Format: Each item is a positive or negative event followed by two explanations of it. Subjects choose the one most characteristic of them.

Reliability: Internal consistency ranged from .50 to .73.

Author: Curry, J. F., and Craighead, W. E.

Article: Attributional style in clinically depressed and conduct disordered adolescents.

Journal: *Journal of Consulting and Clinical Psychology*, February 1990, *58*(1), 109–115.

Related Research: Seligman, M. E. P., et al. (1984). Attributional style and depressive symptoms among children. *Journal of Abnormal Psychology*, *93*, 235–238.

■ ■ ■

4790

Test Name: CHILDREN'S PERCEIVED CONTROL SCALE

Purpose: To measure perceptions of control.

Number of Items: 48

Format: Four-point scale (*very true* to *not at all true*).

Reliability: Alphas ranged from .56 to .66.

Validity: Correlations with other variables ranged from −.34 to .57.

Authors: Marsh, H. W., and Gouvernet, P. J.

Article: Multidimensional self-concept and perceptions of control: Constant validation of responses by children.

Journal: *Journal of Educational Psychology*, March 1989, *81*(1), 57–69.

Related Research: Connell, J. P. (1985). A new multidimensional measure of children's perceptions of control. *Child Development*, *56*, 1018–1041.

■ ■ ■

4791

Test Name: CHILDREN'S SELF DESCRIPTION QUESTIONNAIRE

Purpose: To measure self-concept including: physical appearance, peer relations, relations with parents, reading, math, and school subjects.

Number of Items: 62

Format: Five-point true–false format.

Reliability: Cronbach's alphas ranged from .87 to .92.

Author: Kudek, L. A., and Berg, B.

Article: Children's Beliefs about Parental Divorce Scale: Psychometric characteristics and concurrent validity.

Journal: *Journal of Consulting and Clinical Psychology*, October 1987, *55*(5), 712–718.

Related Research: Marsh, H. W., et al. (1983). Self-concept: The construct validity of interpretations based on the SDQ. *Journal of Personality and Social Psychology*, *45*, 173–187.

4792

Test Name: CHILDREN'S SELF-EFFICACY FOR PEER INTERACTION SCALE

Purpose: To measure children's perceptions of their ability to perform specific social skills (verbal persuasive behaviors) in peer situations.

Number of Items: 22

Format: Includes two subscales representing two-types of situational constraints: conflict and nonconflict. For each item children indicate on a 4-point scale from *Easy* to *Hard,* their ease or difficulty in performing a specific goal-directed behavior. Examples are presented.

Validity: Correlations with: peer ratings ranged from .18 to .30 (*N*s from 36 to 114); friendship nominations ranged from .20 to .39 (*N*s from 36 to 114).

Author: Ladd, G. W., and Frice, J. M.

Article: Promoting children's cognitive and social competence: The relation between parents' perceptions of task difficulty and children's perceived and actual competence.

Journal: *Child Development,* April 1986, *57*(2), 446–460.

Related Research: Wheeler, V. A., & Ladd, G. W. (1982). Assessment of children's self-efficacy for social interactions with peers. *Developmental Psychology, 18,* 795–805.

■ ■ ■

4793

Test Name: CHILD'S ATTRIBUTIONAL STYLES QUESTIONNAIRE

Purpose: To measure attributional styles.

Number of Items: 48

Format: Each item describes a situation and is followed by two attributions.

Reliability: Internal consistency ranged from .57 to .73. Test–retest (1 week) reliability was .74.

Validity: Correlated .42 with Beck Depression Inventory.

Author: Rotheram-Borus, M. J., et al.

Article: Cognitive style and pleasant activities among female adolescent suicide attempters.

Journal: *Journal of Consulting and Clinical Psychology,* October 1990, *58*(5), 554–561.

Related Research: Kaslow, N. J., et al. (1978). *The Kasten: A child's attributional styles questionnaire.* Unpublished manuscript, University of Pennsylvania, Philadelphia.

■ ■ ■

4794

Test Name: CHRONIC DISEASE IMPRESSION RATING SCALES

Purpose: To measure how people evaluate people with chronic disease.

Number of Items: 17

Format: Semantic differential (all items presented).

Reliability: Alphas ranged from .64 to .79 across five subscales.

Validity: Across types of chronic diseases, the correlations ranged from .25 to .55. The five subscales varied systematically across disease types.

Author: Katz, I., et al.

Article: Lay people's and health care professional's perceptions of cancer, AIDS, cardiac and diabetic patients.

Journal: *Psychological Reports,* April 1987, *60*(2), 615–629.

■ ■ ■

4795

Test Name: CIVIL-LIBERTIES CLIMATE SCALE

Purpose: To measure an individual's perception of tolerance (the civil-liberties "climate") in his or her place of work.

Number of Items: 19. Sample items presented.

Format: Likert format.

Reliability: Alpha was .80.

Validity: Correlation with preferred climate was .17 (not significant).

Author: Sheinfeld, D., and Zalkind, S. S.

Article: Does civil liberties climate in organizations correlate with job satisfaction and work alienation?

Journal: *Psychological Reports,* April 1987, *60*(2), 467–477.

Related Research: Zalkind, S. S., et al. (1975). Civil liberties attitudes and personality measures: Some exploratory research. *Journal of Social Issues, 31,* 77–83.

■ ■ ■

4796

Test Name: COGNITIVE PROCESS SURVEY

Purpose: To assess sex differences in dream recall as a function of degree of imaginal life, orientation toward imaginal life, degree of suppression of feelings and number of dreams recalled weekly.

Number of Items: 39

Format: Includes three subscales: degree of imaginal life, orientation toward imaginal life, and degree of suppression. Responses are made on a Likert scale. All items are presented.

Reliability: Reliability coefficents ranged from .72 to .78.

Author: Martinetti, R. F.

Article: Sex differences in dream recall and components of imaginal life.

Journal: *Journal of Perceptual and Motor Skills,* October 1989, *69*(2), 643–649.

Related Research: Martinetti, R. F. (1983). Dream recall, imaginal processes and short-term memory, a pilot study. *Perceptual and Motor Skills, 57,* 718.

4797

Test Name: COLLEGE INTERACTION SELF-EFFICACY QUESTIONNAIRE

Purpose: To provide a measure of self-efficacy expectations concerning interaction with same-sex students who do and do not have physical disabilities.

Number of Items: 40

Format: Responses are made on a 6-point scale from 1 (*very uncomfortable*) to 6 (*very comfortable*). All items are presented.

Validity: Correlations with other variables ranged from −.70 to .60.

Author: Fichten, C. S., et al.

Article: Validation of the College Interaction Self-Efficacy Questionnaire: Students with and without disabilities.

Journal: *Journal of College Student Personnel*, September 1987, *28*(5), 449–458.

Related Research: Bandura, A. (1977). Self-efficacy: Toward a unifying theory of behavioral change. *Psychological Review*, *84*, 191–215.

■ ■ ■

4798

Test Name: COMPANION ANIMAL SEMANTIC DIFFERENTIAL

Purpose: To assess the respondent's perceptions of a childhood companion animal.

Number of Items: 18

Format: Items are bipolar semantic differential word pairs. All items are presented.

Reliability: Cronbach's alpha coefficient was .90.

Validity: Correlations with other variables were .31 and .54.

Author: Poresky, R. H., et al.

Article: The Companion Animal Semantic Differential: Long and short form reliability and validity.

Journal: *Educational and Psychological Measurement*, Spring 1988, *48*(1), 255–260.

■ ■ ■

4799

Test Name: COMPANION ANIMAL SEMANTIC DIFFERENTIAL— SHORT FORM

Purpose: To assess the respondent's perception of a childhood companion animal.

Number of Items: 9

Format: Items are bipolar semantic differential word pairs. All items are presented.

Reliability: Cronbach's alpha coefficient was .88.

Validity: Correlations with other variables were .24 and .50.

Author: Poresky, R. H., et al.

Article: The Companion Animal Semantic Differential: Long and short form reliability and validity.

Journal: *Educational and Psychological Measurement*, Spring 1988, *48*(1), 255–260.

■ ■ ■

4800

Test Name: COMPUTER SELF-EFFICACY SCALE

Purpose: To measure perceptions of capability regarding specific computer-related knowledge and skills.

Number of Items: 32

Format: Includes three factors: beginning level computer skills, advanced level computer skills, and mainframe computer skills. Responses are made on a 5-point Likert scale. All items are presented.

Reliability: Alpha coefficients ranged from .92 to .97.

Author: Murphy, C. A., et al.

Article: Development and validation of the Computer Self-Efficacy Scale.

Journal: *Educational and Psychological Measurement*, Winter 1989, *49*(4), 893–899.

Related Research: Schunk, D. H. (1989). Self-efficacy and cognitive skill learning. In C. Ames & R. Ames (Eds.), *Research on motivation in education* (Vol. 3, pp. 13–14). San Diego: Academic Press.

■ ■ ■

4801

Test Name: CONFIDENCE SCALE

Purpose: To assess self-esteem.

Number of Items: 20

Format: Ten true-keyed and 10 false-keyed items that express expectations of success in work competition, feeling of self-assurance, and a sense of pride in abilities and accomplishment.

Reliability: Coefficient alphas were .86, .85, and .80 (*N*s were 189, 521, and 178, respectively).

Validity: Correlations with: Popularity Scale was .42 (*N* = 178); Rosenberg's Self-Esteem Scale was .65 (*N* = 178).

Author: Lorr, M., and Wunderlich, R. A.

Article: Two objective measures of self-esteem.

Journal: *Journal of Personality Assessment*, Spring 1986, *50*(1), 18–23.

■ ■ ■

4802

Test Name: CONTROLLABILITY SCALE—REVISED

Purpose: To measure the extent to which subjects attributed their procrastination to factors under their direct control.

Number of Items: 7

Format: Responses are made on a 7-point scale.

Reliability: Coefficient alpha was .66.

Author: Olson, D. H., and Claiborn, C. D.

Article: Interpretation and arousal in the counseling process.

Journal: *Journal of Counseling Psychology*, April 1990, *37*(2), 131–137.

Related Research: Strong, S. R., et al. (1979). Motivational and equipping functions of interpretation in counseling. *Journal of Counseling Psychology*, *26*, 98–107.

■ ■ ■

4803

Test Name: COUNSELOR RATING FORM

Purpose: To assess subjects' perceptions of the therapist's expertness, attractiveness, and trustworthiness.

Number of Items: 36

Format: Items are bipolar adjectives arranged on three dimensions.

Reliability: Split-half reliabilities ranged from .84 to .90.

Validity: Correlation with postcounseling outcome was .53.

Author: Carter, R. L., and Motta, R. W.

Article: Effects of intimacy of therapist's self-disclosure and formality on perceptions of credibility in an initial interview.

Journal: *Perceptual and Motor Skills*, February 1988, *66*(1), 167–173.

Related Research: LaCrosse, M. B., & Barak, A. (1976). Differential perception of counselor behavior. *Journal of Counseling Psychology*, *23*, 170–172.

■ ■ ■

4804

Test Name: CRITICISM CONCERNS SCALE

Purpose: To assess irrational beliefs concerning giving and taking criticism.

Number of Items: 21

Format: True–false format. Sample items presented.

Reliability: Test–retest (4 weeks) reliability was .72.

Validity: Correlated .23 (giving) and 31 (taking) with reported self-esteem.

Author: Lemelin, M., et al.

Article: Consistency between self-report and actual proficiency in giving and taking criticism.

Journal: *Psychological Reports*, August 1986, *59*(1)I, 387–390.

■ ■ ■

4805

Test Name: DAHLHAUSER FOOTBALL LOCUS OF CONTROL SCALE

Purpose: To measure locus of control within a subenvironment of college life.

Number of Items: 29

Format: Forced-choice opinionnaire including six filler items.

Reliability: Test–retest Pearson correlation was .84.

Validity: Correlation with the Rotter Locus of Control Scale was .46.

Author: Gross, W. C., et al.

Article: Situation-specific expertise and perceived control.

Journal: *Perceptual and Motor Skills*, April 1987, *64*(2), 659–662.

Related Research: Dahlhauser, M. M. (1977). *Visual disembedding and locus of control as variables in high school football injuries*. Unpublished Master's thesis, Tennessee State University, Nashville, Tennessee.

■ ■ ■

4806

Test Name: DEPRESSION LOCUS OF CONTROL SCALE

Purpose: To determine the degree of perceived self-control over feelings of depression in particular and over behavior in general.

Number of Items: 8

Format: Each item is a pair of statements from which respondents select the one with which they most strongly agree. An example is presented.

Reliability: Internal consistency estimates ranged from .75 to .78.

Validity: Correlations with other variables ranged from .35 to .43.

Author: Vredenburg, K., et al.

Article: Depression in college students: Personality and experiential factors.

Journal: *Journal of Counseling Psychology*, October 1988, *35*(4), 419–425.

Related Research: Vredenburg, K., & Krames, L. (1987). *Depression locus of control*. Unpublished manuscript.

■ ■ ■

4807

Test Name: DEPRESSION LOCUS OF CONTROL SCALE

Purpose: To measure internality and externality in adolescents.

Number of Items: 12

Format: Likert format.

Reliability: Test–retest reliability was .55. Cronbach's alphas ranged from .63 to .73 across subscales.

Validity: Correlations with Health Locus of Control Scale ranged from −.07 to .54 across three subscales identified by factor analysis.

Author: Whitman, L., et al.

Article: Development of a Depression Locus of Control Scale.

Journal: *Psychological Reports*, April 1987, *60*(2), 583–589.

■ ■ ■

4808

Test Name: DETENTION LOCUS OF CONTROL SCALE

Purpose: To measure perceived locus of control of persons in detention for political reasons.

Number of Items: 25

Format: Paired comparison. All items presented.

Reliability: Cronbach's alphas ranged from .67 to .81 across subscales.

Validity: Correlation with the Rotter I-E Scale was .26 (not significant). Correlation with political scale was .50 (significant).

Author: Perkel, A., and Govender, R.

Article: Development and testing of a scale to measure locus of control in South African political detainees.

Journal: *Psychological Reports*, October 1990, *67*(2), 387–395.

■ ■ ■

4809

Test Name: DIABETES LOCUS OF CONTROL SCALE

Purpose: To measure internality or externality about control of diabetes.

Number of Items: 25

Format: Likert format. All items presented.

Reliability: Test–retest ranged from .66 to .77. Alpha ranged from .72 to .77.

Validity: Correlations with other variables ranged from −.21 to .64.

Author: Ferraro, L. A., et al.

Article: Development of a diabetes locus of control scale.

Journal: *Psychological Reports*, December 1987, *61*(3), 763–770.

■ ■ ■

4810

Test Name: DIETING BELIEFS SCALE

Purpose: To measure weight locus of control.

Number of Items: 16

Format: Responses are made on a 6-point scale from 1 (*not at all descriptive of my beliefs*) to 6 (*very descriptive of my beliefs*). All items are presented.

Reliability: Cronbach's alpha was .68. Test–retest (6 weeks) reliability was .81 (*N* = 43).

Validity: Correlations with other variables ranged from .05 to .41.

Author: Stotland, S., and Zuroff, D. C.

Article: A new measure of weight locus of control: The Dieting Beliefs Scale.

Journal: *Journal of Personality Assessment*, Spring 1990, *54*(1/2), 191–203.

■ ■ ■

4811

Test Name: DIFFERENTIATION OF SELF SCALE

Purpose: To identify the subject's perceived self-other differentiation.

Number of Items: 11

Format: Each item is rated on a 4-point scale ranging from *never* to *always*. An example is presented.

Reliability: Internal consistency reliability was .91.

Author: Friedlander, M. L., and Siegel, S. M.

Article: Separation-individuation difficulties and cognitive-behavioral indicators of eating disorders among college women.

Journal: *Journal of Counseling Psychology*, January 1990, *37*(1), 74–78.

Related Research: Olver, R., et al. (1989). Self-other differentiation and the mother-child relationship: The effects of sex and birth order. *Journal of Genetic Psychology*, *150*, 311–321.

■ ■ ■

4812

Test Name: DIFFERENT SITUATIONS INVENTORY

Purpose: To measure locus of control orientation.

Number of Items: 20

Format: Items are situations for which one of two responses is chosen: one response reflects an internal control, the other reflects an external control.

Reliability: Test–retest reliability was .90. Internal consistency reliability estimates were .51 and .26.

Validity: Correlation with the Rotter Internal–External Scale was .66.

Author: King, S.

Article: Background and family variables in a causal model of career maturity: Comparing hearing and hearing-impaired adolescents.

Journal: *The Career Development Quarterly*, March 1990, *38*(3), 240–260.

Related Research: Gardner, D. C., & Warren, S. A. (1977). *Careers and disabilities: A career education approach*. Stamford, CT: Greylock.

■ ■ ■

4813

Test Name: DRINKING EXPECTANCY QUESTIONNAIRE

Purpose: To measure alcohol-related expectancies.

Number of Items: 80

Format: Includes nine factors: assertiveness, sexual enhancement, affective change, social enhancement, relaxation, aggression, dependence, cognitive impairment, and carelessness. Responses to each item are made on a 5-point scale ranging from 1 (*strongly disagree*) to 5 (*strongly agree*). Sample items are presented.

Reliability: Alpha coefficients ranged from .22 to .94.

Author: Young, R. M., and Knight, R. G.

Article: The Drinking Expectancy Questionnaire: A revised measure of alcohol-related beliefs.

Journal: *Journal of Psychopathology and Behavioral Assessment*, March 1989, *11*(1), 99–112.

Related Research: Brown, S. A., et al. (1987). The Alcohol Expectancy Questionnaire: An instrument for the assessment of adolescent and adult alcohol expectancies. *Journal of Studies on Alcohol, 48* (5), 483–491.

■ ■ ■

4814

Test Name: DYSFUNCTIONAL ATTITUDES SCALE

Purpose: To assess irrational beliefs and faulty assumptions about reality to determine emotional disturbance.

Number of Items: 50

Format: Responses to each item are made on a 7-point scale from totally agree to totally disagree.

Reliability: Cronbach's alpha was .93. Test–retest reliability was .71.

Author: Beach, S. R. H., et al.

Article: Cognitive and marital factors in depression.

Journal: *Journal of Psychopathology and Behavioral Assessment*, March 1988, *10*(1), 93–105.

Related Research: Weissman, A. N., & Beck, A. T. (1978). *Development and validation of the Dysfunctional Attitude Scale: A preliminary investigation*. Paper presented at the annual meeting of the American Education Research Association, Toronto, Ontario, Canada.

■ ■ ■

4815

Test Name: DYSFUNCTIONAL ATTITUDES SCALE—FORM A

Purpose: To measure beliefs held by depressed individuals.

Number of Items: 40

Format: Items are rated on a 7-point degree of belief scale ranging from 1 (*not at all*) to 7 (*totally*). An example is presented.

Validity: Correlations with other variables ranged from .54 to .58.

Author: Hill, C. V., et al.

Article: An empirical investigation of the specificity and sensitivity of the Automatic Thoughts Questionnaire and Dysfunctional Attitudes Scale.

Journal: *Journal of Psychopathology and Behavioral Assessment*, December 1989, *11*(4), 291–311.

Related Research: Weissman, A. N., & Beck, A. J. (1978). *Development and validation of the Dysfunctional Attitudes Scale: A preliminary investigation*. Paper presented at the Annual Meeting of the American Educational Research Association, Toronto, Ontario, Canada.

■ ■ ■

4816

Test Name: EDUCATION BELIEF SCALES

Purpose: To measure abstract and concrete beliefs about education.

Number of Items: 14

Format: Likert format. All items presented.

Reliability: Alphas ranged from .67 (concrete beliefs) to .71 (abstract beliefs).

Validity: Correlation with other variable ranged from −.34 to .36.

Author: Mickelson, R. A.

Article: The attitude-achievement paradox among Black adolescents.

Journal: *Sociology of Education*, January 1990, *63*(1), 44–61.

■ ■ ■

4817

Test Name: ESTIMATION QUESTIONNAIRE

Purpose: To measure estimates of widths.

Number of Items: 20

Format: Includes two parts: Part A requires estimates of the maximum

value, Part B requires estimates of the minimum value.

Reliability: Pearson correlation between halves across a 1-month interval was .74 (Spearman-Brown corrected). Coefficient alpha was .88.

Validity: Correlations with other variables ranged from .11 to .31.

Author: Walker, I., and Gibbins, K.

Article: Expecting the unexpected: An explanation of category width.

Journal: *Journal of Perceptual and Motor Skills*, June 1989, *68*(3) Part 1, 715–724.

Related Research: Pettigrew, T. F. (1958). The measurement and correlates of category width as a cognitive variable. *Journal of Personality, 26*, 532–544.

■ ■ ■

4818

Test Name: ETHNIC IDENTITY SCALE

Purpose: To measure subjective ethnic identity.

Number of Items: 5

Format: Open-ended questions. All items presented.

Reliability: Alpha was .78.

Validity: Correlations with other variables ranged from −.05 to .65.

Author: Stephan, C. W., and Stephan, W. G.

Article: After intermarriage: Ethnic identity among mixed-heritage Japanese-Americans and Hispanics.

Journal: *Journal of Marriage and the Family*, May 1989, *51*(2), 507–519.

■ ■ ■

4819

Test Name: EXPECTATIONS ABOUT COUNSELING—B

Purpose: To assess client expectations.

Number of Items: 52

Format: Includes four areas: counselor's attitudes and behaviors, clients' attitudes and behaviors, counselors' characteristics, and characteristics of the counseling process and outcome. responses are made on a 7-point scale.

Reliability: Internal consistancy reliabilities ranged from .69 to .82.

Author: Craig, S. S., and Hennessy.

Article: Personality differences and expectations about counseling.

Journal: *Journal of Counseling Psychology,* October 1989, *36*(4), 401–407.

Related Research: Washington, K., & Tinsley, H. E. A. (1982, August). Measurement of clients' expectancies about counseling. In H. E. A. (Chain), studies of the nature and impact of expectancies about counseling. Symposium conducted at the annual meeting of the American Psychological Association, Washington, DC.

■ ■ ■

4820

Test Name: EXPECTATIONS ABOUT COUNSELING QUESTIONNAIRE

Purpose: To assess some of the constructs that may affect social influence processes.

Number of Items: 135

Format: Includes 13 scales.

Reliability: Internal consistency reliabilities ranged between .69 and .82.

Author: Dorn, F. J.

Article: An examination of client motivation and career certainty.

Journal: *Journal of College Student Development,* May 1989, *30*(3), 237–241.

Related Research: Tinsley, H., et al. (1980). Factor analysis of the domain of client expectations about counseling. *Journal of Counseling Psychology, 27,* 561–570.

4821

Test Name: EXPECTATIONS ABOUT COUNSELING—BRIEF FORM

Purpose: To measure students' expectations about counseling.

Number of Items: 53

Format: Includes 17 scales: responsibility, motivation, openness, acceptance, confrontation, genuineness, directiveness, empathy, self-disclosure, nurturance, attractiveness, expertness, trustworthiness, tolerance, immediacy, concreteness, and outcome. Responses are made on a 7-point scale ranging from *not true* to *definitely true.*

Reliability: Internal consistency reliabilities (*N* = 446) ranged from .69 to .82. Test–retest (2 months) reliabilities ranged from .47 to .87.

Author: Hayes, T. J., and Tinsley, H. E. A.

Article: Identification of the latent dimensions of instruments that measure perceptions of and expectations about counseling.

Journal: *Journal of Counseling Psychology,* October 1989, *36*(4), 492–500.

Related Research: Tinsley, H. E. A. (1982). *Expectations about counseling.* Unpublished test manual, Southern Illinois University, Department of Psychology, Carbondale.

■ ■ ■

4822

Test Name: EXPECTATIONS ABOUT COUNSELING—BRIEF FORM

Purpose: To measure students' expectations about counseling.

Number of Items: 66

Format: Includes four general areas: client attitudes and behaviors, counselor attitudes and behaviors, counselor characteristics, and counselor process and outcome.

Reliability: Internal consistency reliabilities ranged from .69 to .82 (*N* = 446). Test–retest (2 months) reliabilities ranged from .74 to .87.

Author: Tinsley, H. E. A., and Westcot, A. M.

Article: Analysis of the cognitions stimulated by the items on the Expectations about Counseling— Brief Form: An analysis of construct validity.

Journal: *Journal of Counseling Psychology,* April 1990, *37*(2), 223–226.

Related Research: Tinsley, H. E. A. (1982). *Expectations about counseling.* Unpublished test manual, Southern Illinois University at Carbondale, Department of Psychology. Kunkel, M. A. (1990). Expectations about counseling in relation to acculturation in Mexican-American and Anglo-American student samples. *Journal of Counseling Psychology, 37*(3), 286–292.

■ ■ ■

4823

Test Name: EXPRESSED ACCEPTANCE OF SELF

Purpose: To assess levels of self-esteem or self-acceptance.

Number of Items: 36

Format: Each item is ranked between 1 and 5 ranging from *definitely true of myself* to *not at all true of myself.*

Validity: Correlation with Type A behavior was .16.

Author: Kirschner, C., et al.

Article: Personality and performance: An examination of type A and B constructs.

Journal: *Journal of Perceptual and Motor Skills,* June 1989, *68*(3) Part 2, 1107–1114.

Related Research: Berger, E. (1952). The relation between expressed acceptance of self and expressed acceptance of others. *Journal of Abnormal Psychology, 47,* 778–782.

4824

Test Name: FAMILY OF ORIGIN SCALE

Purpose: To measure perceptions of health in family of origin.

Number of Items: 40

Reliability: Test–retest reliability was .97 (2 weeks).

Validity: Correlated .23 (total), .27 (men), and .22 (women) with Texas Social Behavior Inventory.

Author: Bonnington, S. B.

Article: Self-esteem and perceived health of the family of origin: Are there sex differences?

Journal: *Psychological Reports*, June 1989, *64*(3) I, 811–814.

Related Research: Hovestadt, A. J., et al. (1985). A family of origin scale. *Journal of Marital and Family Therapy*, *11*, 287–297.

■ ■ ■

4825

Test Name: FATALISM SCALE

Purpose: To measure fatalism.

Number of Items: 6

Format: Four-point agreement scales. Sample item presented.

Reliability: Alphas ranged from .60 to .74.

Author: Rogler, L. H., and Procidano, M. E.

Article: Marital heterogamy and marital quality in Puerto Rican families.

Journal: *Journal of Marriage and the Family*, May 1989, *50*(2), 363–372.

Related Research: Kahl, J. A. (1965). Some measures of achievement motivation. *American Sociological Review*, *70*, 669–681.

■ ■ ■

4826

Test Name: FETAL HEALTH LOCUS OF CONTROL SCALE

Purpose: To measure perceived control over health of the fetus.

Number of Items: 18

Format: Nine point graphic agreement scales. All items presented.

Reliability: Cronbach's alpha ranged from .76 to .88. Test–retest (2-weeks) reliability ranged form .67 to .80.

Validity: Correlations with cigarette and caffeine consumption were related to the scale as were intentions to participate in childbirth classes.

Author: Labs, S. M., and Wurtele, S. K.

Article: Fetal Health Locus of Control Scale: Development and validation.

Journal: *Journal of Consulting and Clinical Psychology*, December 1986, *54*(6), 814–819.

■ ■ ■

4827

Test Name: FIGURE RATINGS TASK

Purpose: To assess body shape perception and dissatisfaction.

Number of Items: 9

Format: Each item is a silhouette drawing of a woman. The drawings range from 1 to 9 where 1 is the thinnest. Subjects indicate the body shapes best representing their current figure, their ideal figure, and the figure thought to be most attractive to men.

Validity: Correlations with other variables ranged from −.08 to −.66.

Author: Thomas, C. D., and Freeman, R. J.

Article: The Body Esteem Scale: Construct validity of the female subscales.

Journal: *Journal of Personality Assessment*, Spring 1990, *54*(1/2), 204–212.

Related Research: Stunkard, A., et al. (1983). Use of the Danish

Adoption Register for the study of obesity and thinness. In S. Kety et al. (Eds.), *The genetics of neurological and psychiatric disorders* (pp. 15–120). New York: Raven.

■ ■ ■

4828

Test Name: GENERALIZED EXPECTANCY FOR SUCCESS SCALE

Purpose: To measure adults' expectations of attaining distant goals in a variety of realms.

Number of Items: 30

Format: Includes two factors: optimism and pessimism. Most items are presented.

Reliability: Coefficient alpha was .79 (optimism) and .65 (pessimism).

Validity: Correlations with Piers-Harris Self-Concept Scale ranged from −.44 to .35.

Author: Fischer, M., and Leitenberg, H.

Article: Optimism and pessimism in elementary school aged children.

Journal: *Child Development*, February 1986, *57*(1), 241–248.

Related Research: Fibel, B., & Hale, W. D. (1978). The generalized expectancy for success scale: A new measure. *Journal of Consulting and Clinical Psychology*, *46*, 924–931.

■ ■ ■

4829

Test Name: GENERAL SELF-EFFICACY

Purpose: To measure a subject's judgment about his/her ability to do a job.

Number of Items: 11

Format: Five-point Likert format. Sample item presented.

Reliability: Alphas ranged from .77 to .83.

Author: Pond III, S. B., and Hay, M. S.

Article: The impact of task preview information as a function of recipient self-efficacy.

Journal: *Journal of Vocational Behavior*, August 1989, *35*(1), 17–29.

Related Research: Pond III, S. B., et al. (1987). *The measurement of general self-efficacy* (Technical Report No. 87–10). Raleigh: North Carolina State University, Department of Psychology.

■ ■ ■

4830

Test Name: GENERAL STATEMENTS QUESTIONNAIRE

Purpose: To assess subjects' beliefs about and reactions to both specific features of computers and potential uses and applications of computers.

Number of Items: 23

Format: Employs a 7-point Likert-type response format.

Reliability: Coefficient alpha was .62.

Validity: Correlation with other variables ranged from .09 to .90.

Author: Zakrajsek, T. D., et al.

Article: Convergent validity of scales measuring computer-related attitudes.

Journal: *Educational and Psychological Measurement*, Summer 1990, *50*(2), 343–349.

Related Research: Zoltan, E., & Chapanis, A. (1982). What do professional persons think about computers? *Behavioral and Information Technology, 1*, 55–68.

■ ■ ■

4831

Test Name: GENERAL STATEMENTS QUESTIONNAIRE

Purpose: To assess subjects' beliefs about and reactions to both specific features of computers and potential uses and applications of computers.

Number of Items: 12

Format: Employs a 7-point Likert-type response format.

Reliability: Coefficient alpha was .66.

Validity: Correlation with other variables ranged from .03 to .90.

Author: Zakrajsek, T. D., et al.

Article: Convergent validity scales measuring computer-related attitudes.

Journal: *Educational and Psychological Measurement*, Summer 1990, *50*(2), 343–349.

Related Research: Zoltan, E., & Chapanis, A. (1982). What do professional persons think about computers? *Behavioral and Information Technology, 1*, 55–68.

■ ■ ■

4832

Test Name: GOALS AND STRATEGIES FOR STUDYING SCIENCE QUESTIONNAIRE

Purpose: To measure students' study strategy beliefs and perceptions of teacher goals.

Number of Items: Items in each scale ranged from 3 to 4.

Format: Includes two parts: strategy value beliefs scale with four subscales: memorization, monitoring, elaboration, and organization; and perceived teacher goals scale with three subscales: mastery, independent thinking, and performance.

Reliability: Alpha coefficients ranged from .64 to .81.

Author: Nolen, S. B., and Haladyma, T. M.

Article: A construct validation of measures of students' study strategy beliefs and perceptions of teacher goals.

Journal: *Educational and Psychological Measurement*, Spring 1990, *50*(1), 191–202.

Related Research: Nolen, S. B. (1988). Reasons for studying:

Motivational orientations and study strategies. *Cognition and Instruction, 5*, 269–287.

■ ■ ■

4833

Test Name: GROUP THERAPY SURVEY

Purpose: To assess expectations about and attitudes toward group therapy.

Number of Items: 25

Format: Items are rated on a 4-point scale from *strongly agree* to *strongly disagree*. Includes three factors: positive attitudes, misconceptions, and self-disclosure fears.

Reliability: Test–retest (2 weeks) reliability was .80. Internal consistency was .59.

Author: Broday, S. F., et al.

Article: Factor analysis and reliability of the group therapy survey.

Journal: *Educational and Psychological Measurement*, Summer 1989, *49*(2), 457–459.

Related Research: Slocum, Y. S. (1987). A survey of expectations about group therapy among clinical and nonclinical populations. *International Journal of Group Psychotherapy, 37*, 39–54.

■ ■ ■

4834

Test Name: HELPFULNESS OF ASSERTIVE INTERVIEW BEHAVIORS

Purpose: To assess the perception of how helpful a series of specific job interview behaviors are relative to making a good impression on an interviewer.

Number of Items: 16

Format: Responses are made on a 5–point scale ranging from 1 (*not at all helpful*) to 5 (*very helpful*). A sample item is presented.

Reliability: Internal consistency reliability was .75.

Validity: Correlations with variables ranged from .06 to .71.

Author: Phillips, S. D., and Bruch, M. A.

Article: Shyness and dysfunction in career development.

Journal: *Journal of Counseling Psychology*, April 1988, *35*(2), 159–165.

Related Research: Cianni-Surridge, M., & Horan, J. J. (1983). On the wisdom of assertive job-seeking behavior. *Journal of Counseling Pyschology*, *30*, 209–214.

■ ■ ■

4835

Test Name: HELPING EFFICACY SCALE

Purpose: To measure to what extent people believe that helping behavior is beneficial to society.

Number of Items: 10

Format: Five-point Likert format. Sample items presented.

Reliability: Alpha was .69.

Author: Amato, P. R.

Article: Personality and social network involvement as predictors of helping behavior in everyday life.

Journal: *Social Psychology Quarterly*, March 1990, *53*(1), 31–43.

Related Research: Bandura, A. (1982). Self-efficacy mechanism in human agency. *American Psychology*, *37*, 127–147.

■ ■ ■

4836

Test Name: HEALTH BELIEF MODEL QUESTIONNAIRE

Purpose: To measure health beliefs.

Number of Items: 28

Format: Five-point Likert format.

Reliability: Alphas ranged from .58 to .80.

Author: Brooks, C. H.

Article: A hierarchical analysis of the effects of an activity-centered health curriculum on general health beliefs and self-reported behavior.

Journal: *Journal of Educational Research*, January/February 1987, *81*(3), 149–154 .

Related Research: Cummings, K. M., et al. (1978). Construct validation of the health belief model. *Health Education Monographs*, *6*, 394–405.

■ ■ ■

4837

Test Name: HEALTH BELIEF SCALE

Purpose: To measure health beliefs, locus of control, and value expectancies of adults with advanced cancer.

Reliability: Cronbach's alphas ranged from .56 to .84 across subscales.

Validity: Correlations between subscales ranged from –.12 to .55. The multiple correlation of the best subscales with receiving unorthodox treatment was .31.

Author: Newell, S. M., et al.

Article: Utility of the Modified Health Belief Model in predicting compliance with treatment by adult patients with advanced cancer.

Journal: *Psychological Reports*, October 1986, *59*(2)II, 783–791.

Related Research: Becker, M. H., et al. (1977). Selected psychosocial models and correlates of individual health related behaviors. *Medical Care*, *15*(Suppl.), 27–46.

■ ■ ■

4838

Test Name: HOMOSEXUAL EMPLOYMENT BELIEF SCALE

Purpose: To measure beliefs about the consequences of employing homosexuals.

Number of Items: 13

Format: Likert format. All items presented.

Reliability: Cronbach's alpha was .95. Test–retest (2 weeks) reliability was .90.

Validity: A single factor accounted for 64% of the common variance. Correlations with other variables ranged from .55 to .69.

Author: O'Brien, F. P., and Vest, M. J.

Article: A proposed scale to measure beliefs about the consequences of employing homosexuals.

Journal: *Psychological Reports*, October 1988, *63*(2), 547–551.

■ ■ ■

4839

Test Name: IDEA INVENTORY

Purpose: To measure irrational beliefs.

Number of Items: 33

Format: Four-point agreement scale.

Validity: A total of 73 of 110 correlations with the MMPI were statistically significant, and all negative indicating pathology was related to greater irrationality.

Author: Jacobsen, R. H., et al.

Article: Factor analytic study of irrational beliefs.

Journal: *Psychological Reports*, December 1988, *63*(3), 803–809.

Related Research: Kassinove, H., et al. (1977). Developmental trends in rational thinking: Implications for rational-emotive school mental health programs. *Journal of Community Psychology*, *5*, 266–274.

■ ■ ■

4840

Test Name: IMPRESSIONS OF COUNSELOR CHARACTERISTICS SCALE

Purpose: To measure impressions of counselor characteristics.

Number of Items: 12

Format: Responses are made on an 8-point rating scale.

Reliability: Coefficient alpha was .95.

Validity: Correlation with the subjects' perceptions of the counselor's expected helpfulness was .67.

Author: Green, C. F., et al.

Article: Effects of counselor and subject race and counselor physical attractiveness on impressions and expectations of a female counselor.

Journal: *Journal of Counseling Psychology*, July 1986, *33*(3), 349–352.

Related Research: Cash, T. F., et al. (1975). When counselors are heard but not seen: Initial impact of physical attractiveness. *Journal of Counseling Psychology, 22*, 273–279.

■ ■ ■

4841

Test Name: INCEST EXPERIENCES QUESTIONNAIRE

Purpose: To measure perceived incestuousness and its cognitive consequences.

Number of Items: 15

Format: Five-point Likert format.

Reliability: Test–retest ranged from .67 to .95.

Validity: Consequences of incest correlated significantly with depression, self-esteem, and social role functioning (standardized regression coefficients ranged from −.23 to −.42).

Author: Draucker, C. B.

Article: Cognitive adaptation of female incest survivors.

Journal: *Journal of Consulting and Clinical Psychology*, December 1989, *57*(5), 668–670.

■ ■ ■

4842

Test Name: INDEX OF ADJUSTMENT AND VALUES

Purpose: To measure self-characterization, self-acceptance, and ideal self.

Number of Items: 49

Format: Five-point characterization scales.

Reliability: Internal consistency was .88. Test–retest reliability was .87.

Author: Jennings, P. S., et al.

Article: Personality correlates of reflectivity.

Journal: *Psychological Reports*, August 1986, *59*(1), 87–94.

Related Research: Bills, R. G. (1954). Acceptance of self as measured by interviews and the Index of Adjustment and Values. *Journal of Consulting Psychology, 18*, 22.

■ ■ ■

4843

Test Name: INTELLECTUAL ACHIEVEMENT RESPONSIBILITY QUESTIONNAIRE

Purpose: To measure locus of control involving learning-related activities primarily in the school setting.

Number of Items: 32

Format: Half of the items are concerned with successes in the academic achievement domain and half with failures. Each item involves two response alternatives.

Reliability: Internal consistency was .62.

Validity: Correlations with other variables ranged from −.19 to .26.

Author: Caracosta, R., and Michael, W. B.

Article: The construct and concurrent validity of a measure of academic self-concept and one of locus of control for a sample of university students.

Journal: *Educational and Psychological Measurement*, Autumn 1986, *46*(3), 735–744.

Related Research: Crandall, V. C., et al. (1965). Children's beliefs in their control of reinforcements in intellectual academic achievement behaviors. *Child Development, 36*, 91–109.

■ ■ ■

4844

Test Name: INTELLECTUAL ACHIEVEMENT RESPONSIBILITY QUESTIONNAIRE—REVISED

Purpose: To assess locus of control.

Number of Items: 16

Format: Success experiences are described by seven items and failure experiences are described by nine items. In responding to each item children choose one of two alternatives representing either internal or external control.

Reliability: Kuder-Richardson formula reliability coefficient was .63.

Author: Mevarech, Z. R.

Article: Computer-assisted instructional methods: A factorial study within mathematics disadvantaged classrooms.

Journal: *Journal of Experimental Education*, Fall 1985, *54*(1), 22–27.

Related Research: Crandall, V. C., et al. (1965). Children's beliefs in their own control of reinforcements in intellectual academic achievement situations. *Child Development, 36*, 91–111.

■ ■ ■

4845

Test Name: INTELLECTUAL ACHIEVEMENT RESPONSIBILITY QUESTIONNAIRE

Purpose: To measure locus of control.

Number of Items: 34

Format: Forced-choice items. Includes four subscales: failure due to effort, success due to effort, failure due to ability, and success due to ability.

Reliability: Coefficient alpha was .75. Test–retest (12 weeks) reliability was .60.

Validity: Correlations with other variables ranged from −.38 to .60.

Author: Reynolds, W. M., and Miller, K. L.

Article: Assessment of adolescents' learned helplessness in achievement situations.

Journal: *Journal of Personality Assessment*, Summer 1989, *53*(2), 211–228.

Related Research: Crandall, V. C., et al. (1965). Children's beliefs in their own control of reinforcements in intellectual-academic situations. *Child Development*, *36*, 91–109.

■ ■ ■

4846

Test Name: INTERNAL CONTROL INDEX

Purpose: To measure locus of control.

Number of Items: 28

Format: Responses are made on a 5-point response scale.

Reliability: Coefficient alpha was .85.

Validity: Correlations with other variables ranged from −.52 to .56.

Author: Meyers, L. S., and Wong, D. T.

Article: Validation of a new test of locus of control: The Internal Control Index.

Journal: *Educational and Psychological Measurement*, Autumn 1988, *48*(3), 753–761.

Related Research: Duttweiler, P. C. (1984). The Internal Control Index: A newly developed measure of locus of control. *Educational Psychological Measurement*, *44*, 209–221.

■ ■ ■

4847

Test Name: I-E LOCUS OF CONTROL SCALE

Purpose: To measure locus of control.

Number of Items: 29

Format: Includes 23 forced-choice items plus 6 filler items.

Reliability: Internal reliability ranged from .65 to .79.

Author: Martin, N. K., & Dixon, P. N.

Article: The effects of freshman orientation and locus of control on adjustment to college.

Journal: *Journal of College Student Development*, July, 1989, *30*(4), 362–367.

Related Research: Rotter, J. B. (1966). Generalized expectancies for internal vs. external control of reinforcement. *Psychological Monographs*, *80*, 1–28.

■ ■ ■

4848

Test Name: INTERNAL–EXTERNAL CORRESPONDENCE SCALE (REVISED)

Purpose: To assess whether an individual's behavior corresponds to internal feelings and external consequences.

Number of Items: 21

Format: Four-point scaled ratings of preferences for one of two paired statements. All items presented.

Reliability: Alpha was .77. Test–retest reliability (1 month) was .81.

Validity: Correlations with other variables ranged from −.38 to .50.

Author: Ickes, W., and Teng, G.

Article: Refinement and validation of Brickman's measure of internal–external correspondence.

Journal: *Journal of Research in Personality*, September 1987, *21*(3), 287–305.

Related Research: Brickman, P. (1978). Is it real? In J. H. Harvey, W. Ickes, & R. F. Kidd (Eds.), *New*

directions in attribution research (Vol. 2, pp. 5–34). Hillsdale, NJ: Erlbaum.

■ ■ ■

4849

Test Name: INTERNAL–EXTERNAL SCALE

Purpose: To measure client's locus of control.

Number of Items: 20

Format: Single-stimulus format.

Reliability: Coefficient alpha was .86.

Author: Foon, A. E.

Article: Effects of locus of control on counseling expectations of clients.

Journal: *Journal of Counseling Psychology*, October 1986, *33*(4), 462–464.

Related Research: Rotter, J. B. (1966). Generalized expectancies for internal versus external control of reinforcement. *Psychological Monographs*, *80*(1, Whole No. 609).

■ ■ ■

4850

Test Name: INTERNAL, POWERFUL OTHERS, AND CHANCE SCALES

Purpose: To measure beliefs of control over daily events.

Number of Items: 24

Format: Includes three scales of internal, powerful others, and chance control over daily events. Responses are made on a 6-point disagree–agree format.

Reliability: Alpha coefficients ranged from .66 to .75 (*N* = 77).

Validity: Correlations with the Nuclear Locus of Control scale ranged from −.24 to .39.

Author: Rounds, J. B., and Erdahl, P.

Article: Nuclear Locus of Control scales: Information on development, reliability, and validity.

Journal: *Educational and Psychological Measurement*, Summer 1988, *48*(2), 387–395.

Related Research: Levenson, H. (1973). Multidimensional locus of control in psychiatric patients. *Journal of Consulting and Clinical Psychology*, *41*, 397–404.

■ ■ ■

4851

Test Name: INTERNS' EXPECTANCY AND ATTITUDE SCALES

Purpose: To measure expectations, perceptions, and reactions of student interns to internship experiences.

Number of Items: 46

Format: Seven-point Likert format. Sample items presented.

Reliability: Alphas ranged from .37 to .95.

Author: Feldman, D. C.

Article: Summer interns: Factors contributing to positive developmental experiences.

Journal: *Journal of Vocational Behavior*, December 1990, *37*(3), 267–284.

Related Research: Feldman, D. C. (1976). A contingency theory of socialization. *Administrative Science Quarterly*, *21*, 433–452.

■ ■ ■

4852

Test Name: INTERPERSONAL FUTURE LIKELIHOOD INVENTORY

Purpose: To measure future time perspective.

Number of Items: 15

Format: Each item is a lifestyle characteristic or event to which subjects respond on a 5-point scale from *extremely unlikely* to *extremely likely*.

Reliability: Alpha reliabilities ranged from .55 to .73.

Author: McClam, T., and Blinn, L. M.

Article: Interpersonal lives in the future: Projections of undergraduate women.

Journal: *Perceptual and Motor Skills*, February 1988, *66*(1), 71–78.

Related Research: Plante, J. (1977). *A study of future time perspective and its relationship to self-esteem and social responsibility of high school students*. Unpublished doctoral dissertation, University of Massachusetts, Amherst.

■ ■ ■

4853

Test Name: INTERVIEWER PERCEPTION SCALE

Purpose: To measure a job applicant's perceptions of an interviewer.

Number of Items: 20

Format: 5-point scales. Sample item presented.

Reliability: Alphas ranged from .71 to .84 across subscales.

Author: Liden, R. C., and Parsons, C. K.

Article: A field study of job applicant interview perceptions, alternative opportunities, and demographic characteristics.

Journal: *Personnel Psychology*, Spring 1986, *39*(1), 109–122.

Related Research: Schmitt, N., & Cagle, B. W. (1976). Applicant decisions in the employment interview. *Journal of Applied Psychology*, *61*, 184–192.

■ ■ ■

4854

Test Name: INTOLERANCE OF AMBIGUITY SCALE

Purpose: To measure the tendency to perceive ambiguous situations as sources of threat.

Number of Items: 16

Format: Subjects respond to each item on a 6-point Likert format. Examples are presented.

Reliability: Test–retest reliability was .85.

Validity: Correlations with other intolerance of ambiguity scales were reported to range from .36 to .54.

Author: Anderson, K. L.

Article: Androgyny, flexibility, and individualism.

Journal: *Journal of Personality Assessment*, Summer 1986, *50*(2), 265–278.

Related Research: Budner, S. (1962). Intolerance of ambiguity as a personality variable. *Journal of Personality*, *32*, 29–56.

■ ■ ■

4855

Test Name: I, P, & C SCALE

Purpose: To measure locus of control.

Number of Items: 24

Format: Employs a 6-point Likert scale.

Reliability: Kuder-Richardson formula reliability coefficients ranged from .64 to .78. Split-half reliabilities ranged from .60 to .79.

Validity: Correlations with Rotter's E scale ranged from −.41 to .56.

Author: Ellermann, N. C., and Johnston, J.

Article: Perceived life roles and locus of control differences of women pursuing nontraditional and traditional academic majors.

Journal: *Journal of College Student Development*, March 1988, *28*(2), 142–146.

Related Research: Levinson, H. (1973). Multidimensional locus of control in psychiatric patients. *Journal of Consulting and Clinical Psychology*, *41*, 397–404.

4856

Test Name: IRRATIONAL BELIEF MEASURE

Purpose: To assess irrational beliefs.

Number of Items: 20

Format: Five-point Likert format. Sample items presented.

Reliability: Cronbach's alpha was .80. Test–retest (2 weeks) reliability was .89.

Validity: Correlations with other variables ranged from .55 to –.27.

Author: Malouff, J. M., and Schutte, N. S.

Article: Development of validation of a measure of irrational belief.

Journal: *Journal of Consulting and Clinical Psychology*, December 1986, *54*(6), 860–862.

■ ■ ■

4857

Test Name: IRRATIONAL BELIEFS TEST

Purpose: To assess extent of irrational beliefs.

Number of Items: 100

Format: Five-point agreement scale.

Reliability: Test–retest (2 weeks) reliability was .88.

Validity: Correlated –.72 with Rational Behavior Inventory.

Author: Gitlin, D. E., and Tucker, C. M.

Article: Ability to discriminate rational responses to items in the Irrational Beliefs Test as a predictor of rationality and trait anxiety.

Journal: *Psychological Reports*, April 1988, *62*(2), 483–487.

Related Research: Jones, R. G. (1969). A factored measure of Ellis' irrational belief system, with personality and maladjustment correlates. *Dissertation Abstracts International, 29,* 4379B. (University Microfilms No. 69–6443)

4858

Test Name: IRRATIONAL HETEROSOCIAL BELIEFS SCALE

Purpose: To measure rational and irrational beliefs in heterosocial situations.

Number of Items: 34

Format: Includes rational and irrational subscales.

Reliability: Cronbach alphas were .74 and .70.

Author: Myszka, M. T., et al.

Article: Comparison of cognitive assessment methods with heterosocially anxious college women.

Journal: *Journal of Counseling Psychology*, October 1986, *33*(4), 401–407.

Related Research: Ellis, A. (1962). *Reason and emotion in psychotherapy.* New York: Lyle Street Press.

■ ■ ■

4859

Test Name: JOB DIAGNOSTIC SURVEY

Purpose: To provide a perceptual measure of job characteristics.

Number of Items: 15

Format: Includes five core job characteristics: task identity, task significance, skill variety, autonomy, and feedback. Employed 7-point Likert-type items.

Reliability: Internal consistency reliabilities ranged from .71 to .59.

Author: Idaszak, J. R., and Drasgow, F.

Article: A revision of the Job Diagnostic Survey: Elimination of a measurement artifact.

Journal: *Journal of Applied Psychology*, February 1987, *72*(1), 69–74.

Related Research: Hackman, J. R., & Oldham, G. R. (1975).

Development of the Job Diagnostic Survey. *Journal of Applied Psychology, 60,* 159–170.

■ ■ ■

4860

Test Name: JOB PERFORMANCE SCALE

Purpose: To measure a sales person's self-evaluation of his or her job.

Number of Items: 23

Reliability: Alphas ranged from .89 to .90.

Validity: Correlations with other job-role related constructs ranged from –.36 (role ambiguity) to .04 (role overload).

Author: Lagare, R. P.

Article: Role-stress differences between salesmen and saleswomen: Effect on job satisfaction and performance.

Journal: *Psychological Reports*, June 1988, *62*(3), 815–825.

Related Research: Behrman, D. N., & Perreault, Jr., W. O. (1982) Measuring the performance of industrial salespersons. *Journal of Business Research, 10,* 335–370.

■ ■ ■

4861

Test Name: KHATENA-MORSE MULTITALENT PERCEPTION INVENTORY

Purpose: To identify leadership, music, art, and creative talent of people aged 10 years and over.

Number of Items: 50

Format: Affirmative responses are counted to obtain a total score. There are Forms A and B. Sample items are presented.

Reliability: Coefficient alpha ranged from .71 to .92 (Form A) and from .84 to .91 (Form B). Split-half corrected coefficients ranged from .77 to .95 (Form A) and from .63 to .98 (Form B). Alternate form reliability ranged from .76 to .93. Test–retest (2 weeks) reliability was .78 (Form A) and .74 (Form B).

Validity: Correlations with other variables ranged from .02 to .81 (Form A) and from .03 to .76 (Form B).

Author: Khatena, J., and Morse, D. T.

Article: Preliminary study of the Khatena-Morse Multitalent Perception Inventory.

Journal: *Perceptual and Motor Skills*, June 1987, *64*(3, Part 2), 1187–1190.

■ ■ ■

4862

Test Name: LAU-WARE HEALTH LOCUS OF CONTROL SCALE—SHORT FORM

Purpose: To measure health locus of control.

Number of Items: 20

Format: Includes the following subscales: Self-control, Provider control, Chance, and General Health Threat. Responses are made on a 6-point scale ranging from 1 (*strongly disagree*) to 6 (*strongly agree*). Abbreviated items are presented.

Reliability: Alpha coefficients ranged from .32 to .50.

Validity: Correlations with other variables ranged from −.20 to .38.

Author: Marshall, G. N., et al.

Article: A comparison of two multidimensional health locus of control instruments.

Journal: *Journal of Personality Assessment*, Spring 1990, *54*(1/2), 181–190.

Related Research: Lau, R. R. (1982). Origins of health locus of control beliefs. *Journal of Personality and Social Psychology*, *42*, 322–334.

■ ■ ■

4863

Test Name: LIFE OPTIMISM TEST

Purpose: To measure dispositional optimism.

Number of Items: 8

Reliability: Test–retest (9 weeks) reliability was .75.

Author: Staats, S.

Article: Hope: A comparison of two self-report measures for adults.

Journal: *Journal of Personality Assessment*, Summer 1989, *53*(2), 366–375.

Related Research: Scheier, M., & Carver, C. (1985). Optimism, coping, and health: Assessment and implications of generalized outcome expectancies. *Health Psychology*, *4*, 219–247.

■ ■ ■

4864

Test Name: LOCUS OF CONTROL

Purpose: To measure internal–external locus of control.

Number of Items: 60

Format: Responses are made on a Likert-type format.

Reliability: Split-half reliabilities ranged from .84 to .96. Test–retest reliabilities ranged from .71 to .86.

Author: Lutz, F. W., and Maddirala, J.

Article: Stress, burnout in Texas teachers and reform mandated accountability.

Journal: *Educational Research Quarterly*, 1990, *14*(2), 10–21.

Related Research: Rotter, J. B. (1966). Generalized expectancies for internal versus external control of reinforcement. *Psychological Monographs*, *80* (1 Whole No. 609).

■ ■ ■

4865

Test Name: LOCUS OF CONTROL FOR THREE ACHIEVEMENT DOMAINS

Purpose: To measure perceived acceptance of responsibility for both success and failure in three domains.

Number of Items: 47

Format: Includes activity domains of intellectual, physical, and social and six independent subscales.

Reliability: Kuder-Richardson Formula 20 internal consistency estimates of reliability ranged from .52 to .54.

Validity: Correlations with other variables ranged from −.07 to −.57.

Author: Ormize, M. M., et al.

Article: Relationship of Locus of Control Inventory for Three Achievement Domains (LOCITAD) to two other locus of control measures: A construct validity study.

Journal: *Educational and Psychological Measurement*, Autumn 1987, *47*(3), 737–742.

Related Research: Bradley, R., et al. (1977). A new scale to assess locus of control in three achievement domains. *Psychological Reports*, *41*, 656–661.

■ ■ ■

4866

Test Name: LOCUS OF CONTROL SCALE

Purpose: To measure three locus of control dimensions.

Number of Items: 24

Format: Includes subscales of: chance, powerful others, and internality.

Reliability: Internal consistency reliability estimates ranged from .64 to .78.

Validity: Correlations with other variables ranged from −.36 to .55.

Author: Goodman, S. H., and Waters, L. K.

Article: Convergent validity of five locus of control scales.

Journal: *Educational and Psychological Measurement*, Autumn 1987, 47(3), 743–747.

Related Research: Walkey, F. H. (1979). Internal control, powerful others, and chance: A confirmation of Levenson's factor structure. *Journal of Personality Assessment, 43,* 532–535.

■ ■ ■

4867

Test Name: LOCUS OF CONTROL SCALE

Purpose: To measure three dimensions of locus of control.

Number of Items: 18

Format: Includes three dimensions of fatalism, social systems control, and self-control.

Reliability: Coefficient alpha reliability estimates ranged from .62 to .72.

Validity: Correlations with other variables ranged from –.29 to .55.

Author: Goodman, S. H., and Waters, L. K.

Article: Convergent validity of five locus of control scales.

Journal: *Educational and Psychological Measurement*, Autumn 1987, 47(3), 743–747.

Related Research: Dragutinovich, S., et al. (1983). Factor analysis and norms for an 18-item version of Reid and Ware's internal-external scale. *Canadian Journal of Behavioral Science, 15,* 259–265.

■ ■ ■

4868

Test Name: LOCUS OF CONTROL SCALE

Purpose: To measure locus of control.

Number of Items: 29

Reliability: Coefficient alpha was .88.

Validity: Correlations with other variables ranged from –.18 to .05.

Author: Hollenbeck, J. R., et al.

Article: An empirical examination of the antecedents of commitment to difficult goals.

Journal: *Journal of Applied Psychology*, February 1989, 74(1), 18–23.

Related Research: Spector, P. E. (1982). Behavior in organizations as a function of employee's locus of control. *Psychological Bulletin, 91,* 482–497.

■ ■ ■

4869

Test Name: LOCUS OF CONTROL SCALE

Purpose: To indicate locus of control.

Format: Responses are made on a 4-point scale ranging from 1 (*strongly agree*) to 4 (*strongly disagree*).

Reliability: Internal consistency was .71.

Validity: Correlations with other variables ranged from –.01 to .33.

Author: Noe, R. A., and Steffy, B. D.

Article: The influence of individual characteristics and assessment center evaluation or career exploration behavior and job involvement.

Journal: *The Journal of Vocational Behavior*, April 1987, 30(2), 187–202.

Related Research: Andrisani, P. J., & Nestel, G. (1976). Internal–external control as a contributor to and outcome of work experience. *Journal of Applied Psychology, 61,* 156–165.

■ ■ ■

4870

Test Name: LOCUS OF CONTROL SCALE

Purpose: To measure locus of control.

Number of Items: 45

Format: Forced-choice pairs.

Validity: Factor structure is similar for college age and older adults.

Author: Prichard, K. K., et al.

Article: Reliability of a multidimensional locus of control construct for older adults anticipating transitions in careers.

Journal: *Psychological Reports*, December 1986, 59(2)II, 1007–1012.

Related Research: Ried, D. W., & Ware, E. E. (1974). Multidimensionality of internal–external control: Implications for past and future research. *Canadian Journal of Behavioral Science, 5,* 265–271.

■ ■ ■

4871

Test Name: LOCUS OF CONTROL SCALE—MODIFIED

Purpose: To assess individual differences in perceptions of control about environmental events.

Number of Items: 15

Format: A Likert response format was used.

Reliability: Test–retest reliability coefficients ranged from .18 to .75.

Validity: Correlations with other variables ranged from –.18 to .14.

Author: Blustein, D. L.

Article: Social cognitive orientations and career development: A theoretical and empirical analysis.

JournaL: *Journal of Vocational Behavior*, August 1987, 31(1), 63–80.

Related Research: Collins, B. E. (1974). Four components of the Rotter Internal-External Scale: Belief in a difficult world, a just world, a predictable world, and a politically responsive world. *Journal of Personality and Social Psychology, 29,* 381–391.

4872

Test Name: LOGIC OF CONFIDENCE SCALE

Purpose: To measure belief in teacher professionalism.

Number of Items: 27

Format: Includes three factors: myth of professionalism, avoidance, and overlooking. A 6-point Likert scale was used. All items are presented.

Reliability: Cronbach's alpha coefficients ranged from .75 to .95.

Validity: Correlations with other variables ranged from −.47 to .56.

Author: O'Keafor, K. R., et al.

Article: Toward an operational definition of the logic of confidence.

Journal: *Journal of Experimental Education*, Fall 1987, *56*(1), 47–54.

■ ■ ■

4873

Test Name: LONG-TERM PERSONAL DIRECTION SCALE

Purpose: To operationally define future time perspective.

Number of Items: 20

Format: Responses are made on a 7-point Likert scale.

Reliability: Alpha coefficients ranged from .69 to .87.

Author: Savickas, M. L.

Article: The career decision-making course: Description and field test.

Journal: *The Career Development Quarterly*, March 1990, *38*(3), 275–284.

Related Research: Wessman, A. E. (1973). Personality and the subjective experience of time. *Journal of Personality Assessment*, *37*, 103–114.

■ ■ ■

4874

Test Name: MANAGER'S ROLE QUESTIONNAIRE

Purpose: To measure how different types of managers are perceived to need given qualities.

Number of Items: 10

Format: Rating scales (essential to role to not expected). All items presented.

Reliability: Alpha was .84.

Validity: Confirmatory factor analysis marginally confirmed the Mintzkerg hypothesis.

Author: Sen, J., and Das, J. P.

Article: Roles of managers as perceived by business students.

Journal: *Psychological Reports*, April 1990, *66*(2), 391–400.

Related Research: McCall, M. W., & Segrist, C. A. (1980). *In pursuit of the manager's job: Building on Mintzberg*. Greensboro, NC: Center for Creative Leadership.

■ ■ ■

4875

Test Name: MATHEMATICS ATTRIBUTION SCALE

Purpose: To measure students' attributions of success and failure in algebra.

Format: Five-point Likert format.

Reliability: Reliabilities ranged from .30 to .80 across eight subscales.

Validity: No differences in scores between males and females.

Author: Choroszy, M., et al.

Article: Attributions for success and failure in algebra among men and women attending American Samoa community college.

Journal: *Psychological Reports*, February 1987, *60*(1), 47–51.

Related Research: Fennema, E., et al. (1979). Mathematics Attribution Scale: An instrument to measure student's attributions of the causes of their successes and failures in mathematics. *Journal Abstract Service of the American Psychological Association: Catalog of Selected Documents in Psychology*, *9*(2), No. 26.

■ ■ ■

4876

Test Name: MATHEMATICS SELF-EFFICACY SCALE

Purpose: To measure one's mathematics self-efficacy.

Number of Items: 52

Format: Includes three subscales: mathematics tasks, mathematics courses, and mathematics problems. Confidence ratings for all scales were recorded on a 10-point continuum ranging from 0 (*no confidence*) to 10 (*complete confidence*).

Reliability: Alpha coefficients ranged from .90 to .96.

Author: Lapan, R. T., et al.

Article: Self-efficacy as a mediator of investigative and realistic general occupational themes on the Strong-Campbell Interest Inventory.

Journal: *Journal of Counseling Psychology*, April 1989, *36*(2), 176–182.

Related Research: Betz, N. E., & Hackett, G. (1983). The relationship of mathematics self-efficacy expectations to the selection of science-based majors. *Journal of Vocational Behavior*, *23*, 329–345.

■ ■ ■

4877

Test Name: MATHEMATICS SELF-EFFICACY SCALE (JAPANESE VERSION)

Purpose: To assess math self-efficacy.

Number of Items: 52

Format: Varied formats covering basic math, algebra, geometry, and math-related courses.

Reliability: Test–retest (4 weeks) reliability ranged from .68 to .75. Alpha was .91.

Author: Matsui, T., et al.

Article: Mechanisms underlying math self-efficacy learning of college students.

Journal: *Journal of Vocational Behavior,* October 1990, *37*(2), 225–238.

Related Research: Betz, N. E., & Hackett, G. (1983). The relationship of mathematics self-efficacy expectations to the selection of science-based college majors. *Journal of Vocational Behavior, 23,* 329–345.

■ ■ ■

4878

Test Name: MEANS-ENDS BELIEFS SCALE

Purpose: To assess children's beliefs about the effectiveness of causes, or their means-ends beliefs.

Number of Items: 40

Format: Children rate the effectiveness of five different potential means for producing outcomes in the school domain. Examples are presented.

Reliability: Spearman-Brown split-half reliabilities ranged from .70 to .90.

Author: Skinner, E. A.

Article: Age differences in the dimensions of perceived control during middle childhood: Implications for developmental conceptualizations and research.

Journal: *Child Development,* December 1990, *61*(6), 1882–1890.

Related Research: Skinner, E. A., et al. (1988). Beliefs about control, means-ends, and agency: A new conceptualization and its measurement during childhood. *Journal of Personality and Social Psychology, 54,* 117–133.

■ ■ ■

4879

Test Name: MEDICAL STUDENT SELF-CONFIDENCE SCALE

Purpose: To measure self-confidence of medical students.

Number of Items: 5

Format: Each item is based on the stem "How confident are you that you can ___?" Responses are made on 7-point scale from 1 (*not at all confident*) to 7 (*very confident*).

Validity: Correlations with measures of masculinity and femininity were .32 and .12 respectively (*N* = 99).

Author: Zeldow, P. B., et al.

Article: Masculinity, femininity, and psychosocial adjustment in medical students: A 2-year follow-up.

Journal: *Journal of Personality Assessment,* Spring 1987, *51*(1), 3–14.

Related Research: Zeldow, P. B., et al. (1985). Masculinity, femininity, Type A behavior, and psychosocial adjustment in medical students. *Journal of Personality and Social Psychology, 48,* 481–492.

■ ■ ■

4880

Test Name: MENTAL IMAGERY QUESTIONNAIRE

Purpose: To measure vividness of image, absorption of image, and effort required to form a mental image.

Number of Items: 20

Format: Includes two parts: visual scenes and personal actions, each of which has three scales: clarity and vividness of image, absorption of image, and effort required to form a mental image. Each item is scored on a 5-point scale.

Validity: Correlations with the Vividness of Movement Imagery Questionnaire ranged from −.65 to .60.

Author: Campos, A., and Perez, M. J.

Article: Vividness of Movement Imagery Questionnaire: Relations with other measures of mental imagery.

Journal: *Perceptual and Motor Skills,* October 1988, *67*(2), 607–610.

Related Research: Farthing, G. W., et al. (1983). Relationship between two different types of imagery vividness questionnaire items and three hypnotic susceptibility scale factors. *International Journal of Clinical and Experimental Hypnosis, 31,* 8–13.

■ ■ ■

4881

Test Name: MISFORTUNE ATTRIBUTION SCALE

Purpose: To assess the extent to which people attribute the success or failure of others to controllable or uncontrollable factors.

Number of Items: 10

Format: 5-point Likert format. Sample items presented.

Reliability: Alpha was .61.

Author: Amato, P. R.

Article: Personality and social network involvement as predictors of helping behavior in everyday life.

Journal: *Social Psychology Quarterly,* March 1990, *53*(1), 31–43.

Related Research: Weiner, B. (1980). A cognitive (attribution)-emotion-action model of motivated behavior. An analysis of judgments of help-giving. *Journal of Personality and Social Psychology, 39,* 186–200.

■ ■ ■

4882

Test Name: MOTIVATED STRATEGIES FOR LEARNING QUESTIONNAIRE

Purpose: To measure students' motivational beliefs and self-regulated learning.

Number of Items: 56

Format: Seven-point Likert format. All items presented.

Reliability: Alphas ranged from .74 to .89 across subscales.

Validity: Correlations with student performance measures ranged from −.24 to .36.

Author: Pintrich, P. R., and DeGroot, E. V.

Article: Motivational and self-regulated learning components of classroom academic performance.

Journal: *Journal of Educational Psychology*, March 1990, *82*(1), 33–40.

■ ■ ■

4883

Test Name: MOTIVATION TO SHOP SCALES

Purpose: To measure shopping locus of control, enjoyment and competence to shop, shopping self-determination, exploratory shopping, and shopping satisfaction.

Number of Items: 15

Format: Nine-point Likert format. All items presented.

Reliability: Alphas ranged from .53 to .75 across subscales.

Validity: Relationships between subscales were adequate for high lifestyle activity shoppers, but marginal for low lifestyle activity shoppers (LISREL).

Author: Lesser, J. A., et al.

Article: Antecedents and consequences of the intrinsic motivation to shop.

Journal: *Psychological Reports*, June 1989, *64*(3, Part II), 1183–1191.

■ ■ ■

4884

Test Name: MULTIDIMENSIONAL HEALTH LOCUS OF CONTROL SCALE

Purpose: To measure health locus of control.

Number of Items: 18

Format: Includes three subscales: Internal Control, Powerful Others, and Chance. Abbreviated items are presented.

Reliability: Alpha coefficients ranged from .63 to .75.

Validity: Correlations with other variables ranged from −.20 to .38.

Author: Marshall, G. N., et al.

Article: A comparison of two multidimensional health locus of control instruments.

Journal: *Journal of Personality Assessment*, Spring 1990, *54*(1/2), 181–190.

Related Research: Walston, K. A., et al. (1978). Development of the Multidimensional Health Locus of Control (MHCL) Scales. *Health Education Monographs*, *6*, 161–170.

■ ■ ■

4885

Test Name: NATURE–NURTURE ATTRIBUTION SCALE

Purpose: To gauge beliefs about the relative importance of heredity and environment as determinants of ability.

Number of Items: 10

Format: Five-point scale ranging from 1 (*heredity only*) to 5 (*environment only*). All items presented.

Reliability: Alpha was .80.

Author: Zeider, M., and Beit-Hallahmi, B.

Article: Israeli students' perspectives concerning determinants of intelligence.

Journal: *The Journal of Social Psychology*, August 1988, *128*(4), 517–523.

Related Research: Zeider, M. (1987). Test of the cultural bias hypothesis: Some Israeli findings. *The*

Journal of Applied Psychology, *72*, 38–48.

■ ■ ■

4886

Test Name: NEGATIVE SELF-EVALUATION SCALE

Purpose: To assess children's negative self-evaluations.

Number of Items: 34

Format: True–false items consisting of four domains: general self-worth, intellectual competence, social acceptance, and physical competence.

Reliability: Cronbach's alpha was .86.

Author: Groot, M., and Prins, P.

Article: Children's social behavior: Reliability and concurrent validity of two self-report measures.

Journal: *Journal of Psychopathology and Behavioral Assessment*, September 1989, *11*(3), 195–207.

Related Research: Meijers, J. J., & Fournier, E. P. (1982). Negatieve zelfevaluatic bÿ kinderen van 9–12 jaar. De constructie van een meetinstrument (The development of the Negative Self-Evaluation Scale). *Nederlands Tijdschrift voor de Psychologie*, *37*, 279–292.

■ ■ ■

4887

Test Name: NOWICKI-STRICKLAND LOCUS OF CONTROL SCALE

Purpose: To measure locus of control for children.

Number of Items: 40

Format: Items describing reinforcement situations across interpersonal and motivational areas of affiliation, achievement, and dependency are answered either *yes* or *no*.

Reliability: Reliability coefficients reportedly ranged from .68 to .81.

Validity: Correlations with other variables ranged from −.09 to −.57.

Author: Omizo, M. M., et al.

Article: Relationship of Locus of Control Inventory for Three Achievement Domains (LOCITAD) to two other locus of control measures: A construct validity study.

Journal: *Educational and Psychological Measurement*, Autumn 1987, *47*(3), 737–742.

Related Research: Nowicki, S., & Strickland, B. (1973). A locus of control scale for children. *Journal of Consulting and Clinical Psychology*, *40*, 148–154.

■ ■ ■

4888

Test Name: NOWICKI-STRICKLAND INTERNAL EXTERNAL CONTROL SCALE FOR EARLY ELEMENTARY CHILDREN

Purpose: To measure locus of control in children at the first and second grade.

Number of Items: 13

Format: Responses are *yes* or *no*. All items are presented.

Reliability: Test–retest (6 weeks) reliability was .77 (*N* = 40). Kuder-Richardson Formula 20 internal consistency was .74.

Validity: Correlation with Preschool and Primary Nowicki-Strickland Internal–External Control Scale was .91 (*N* = 30). Correlation with Iowa Basic Skills Achievement Test was −.34.

Author: Nowicki, S., Jr., and Duke, M. P.

Article: A brief self report form of the Cartoon Scale of Preschool and Primary Nowicki-Strickland Internal-External Control Scale.

Journal: *Educational and Psychological Measurement*, Spring 1989, *49*(1), 205–208.

4889

Test Name: NUCLEAR LIKELIHOOD QUESTIONNAIRE

Purpose: To provide an estimate of the likelihood of nuclear war.

Number of Items: 8

Format: Items are time frames ranging from *the next week* to *ever*.

Reliability: Alpha coefficients ranged from .84 to .91 (*N* = 84).

Validity: Correlations with the Nuclear Locus of Control Scales ranged from −.12 to .10 (*N* = 84).

Author: Rounds, J. B., and Erdahl, P.

Article: Nuclear Locus of Control Scales: Information on development, reliability, and validity.

Journal: *Educational and Psychological Measurement*, Summer 1988, *48*(2), 387–395.

Related Research: Erdahl, P., & Rounds, J. B. (1986, August). *Locus of control and likelihood of nuclear war: Two studies.* Paper presented at the 94th Annual Convention of the American Psychological Association, Washington, DC (ERIC Document Reproduction Service No. ED 277924).

■ ■ ■

4890

Test Name: NUCLEAR LOCUS OF CONTROL SCALES

Purpose: To assess beliefs about whether nuclear war and nuclear policy decisions are, or can be, influenced by ourself, powerful others, or chance.

Number of Items: 15

Format: Responses to each item are made on a 6-point scale ranging from *strongly disagree* to *strongly agree*. All items are presented.

Reliability: Coefficient alphas ranged from .62 to .91.

Validity: Correlations with other variables ranged from −.24 to .39.

Author: Rounds, J. B., and Erdahl, P.

Article: Nuclear Locus of Control Scales: Information on development, reliability, and validity.

Journal: *Educational and Psychological Measurement*, Summer 1988, *48*(2), 387–395.

Related Research: Levenson, H. (1981). Differentiating among internality, powerful others, and chance. In H. M. Lefcourt (Ed.), *Research with the Locus of Control Construct* (Vol. 1, pp. 15–63). New York: Academic Press.

■ ■ ■

4891

Test Name: NUTRITIONAL LOCUS OF CONTROL

Purpose: To measure locus of control in the domain of family eating habits.

Number of Items: 27

Format: Four-point true–false format. All items presented.

Reliability: Alphas ranged from .47 to .91 across subscales.

Validity: Correlations with general locus of control ranged from .18 to .46.

Author: Mitchell, S. E., et al.

Article: Dietary quality and family environment.

Journal: *Psychological Reports*, December 1987, *61*(3), 791–801.

■ ■ ■

4892

Test Name: OUTCOME-EXPECTATIONS QUESTIONNAIRE

Purpose: To measure children's beliefs about the reinforcing and punishing consequences of aggression.

Number of Items: 48

Format: For each item the children imagine themselves performing a behavior toward a specified classmate and then they indicate, by checking one of four response alternatives, their level of confidence in the occurrence of a particular consequence. Examples are presented.

Reliability: Coefficient alphas ranged from .51 to .67.

Author: Perry, D. G., et al.

Article: Cognitive social learning mediators of aggression.

Journal: *Child Development*, June 1986, *57*(3), 700–711.

Related Research: Wheeler, V. A., & Ladd, G. W. (1982). Assessment of children's self-efficacy for social interactions with peers. *Developmental Psychology, 18,* 795–805.

∎ ∎ ∎

4893

Test Name: OUTCOME EXPECTANCIES QUESTIONNAIRE

Purpose: To measure subjects' outcome expectancies.

Number of Items: 10

Format: Responses are made on a 5-point scale ranging from 1 (*severe punishment*) to 5 (*major reward*). Two examples are presented.

Reliability: Coefficient alpha was .75.

Validity: Correlations with other variables ranged from −.29 to .24.

Author: Trevino, L. K., and Youngblood, S. A.

Article: Bad apples in bad barrels: A causal analysis of ethical decision-making behavior.

Journal: *Journal of Applied Psychology,* August 1990, *75*(4), 378–385.

∎ ∎ ∎

4894

Test Name: PERCEIVED CLOTHING DEPRIVATION QUESTIONNAIRE

Purpose: To measure perceived clothing deprivation.

Number of Items: 27

Format: Includes seven dimensions or constructs: suitability, overall appearance of clothing, fashionability, quality of clothing, appropriate clothing for various activities and seasons, ability to buy, and general perceived clothing deprivation. Responses are made on a 5-point Likert scale ranging from *never* to *always.*

Validity: Correlations with eight clothing values ranged from −.14 to .26. Split-half corrected coefficient was .91.

Author: Francis, S. K., and Liu, Q.

Article: Effects of clothing values on perceived clothing deprivation among adolescents.

Journal: *Perceptual and Motor Skills,* December 1990, *71*(3) part 2, 1191–1199.

Related Research: Liu, Q. (1987). *Effects of clothing values on clothing deprivation among high school students.* Unpublished Master's thesis, Oregon State University.

∎ ∎ ∎

4895

Test Name: PERCEIVED COMPETENCE SCALE

Purpose: To measure perceived competence in children.

Number of Items: 28 pairs of statements

Format: Children select which of two statements best describe them and then how true it is of them.

Reliability: Alphas ranged from .79 to .82 across subscales.

Validity: Correlations with other variables ranged from −.11 to .74.

Author: Marsh, H. W., and Gouvernet, P. J.

Article: Multidimensional self-concepts and perceptions of control: Construct validation of responses by children.

Journal: *Journal of Educational Psychology,* March 1989, *81*(1), 57–69.

Related Research: Harter, S. (1982). The perceived competence scale for children. *Child Development, 53,* 87–97.

∎ ∎ ∎

4896

Test Name: PERCEIVED CONFLICT INVENTORY

Purpose: To measure how much conflict subjects perceive in common choice situations.

Number of Items: 10

Time Required: Less than 15 minutes.

Format: Multiple-choice, yes–no, and frequency scales. Sample item presented.

Reliability: Cronbach's alpha ranged from .86 to .92.

Author: Shiloh, S., and Melamed, S.

Article: Anxiety, conflict and perception of everyday decisions.

Journal: *Psychological Reports,* June 1988, *62*(3), 799–805.

∎ ∎ ∎

4897

Test Name: PERCEIVED CONTROL AT SCHOOL SCALE

Purpose: To assess students' perceived control at school.

Number of Items: 16

Format: Responses are made on a 6-point Likert scale from 1 (*never*) to 6 (*always*). All items are presented.

Reliability: Alpha coefficients ranged from .22 to .82. Test–retest (2 weeks) ranged from .55 to .80 (*N* = 22).

Validity: Correlations with other variables ranged from .28 to .58.

Author: Adelman, H. S., et al.

Article: An instrument to assess students' perceived control at school.

Journal: *Educational and Psychological Measurement*, Winter 1986, *46*(4), 1005–1017.

Related Research: Taylor, L., et al. (1985). Minors' attitude and competence toward participation in psychoeducational decisions. *Professional Psychology: Research and Practice, 16*, 226–235.

■ ■ ■

4898

Test Name: PERCEIVED OPPORTUNITIES FOR EXERCISE QUESTIONNAIRE

Purpose: To measure perceived opportunities for exercise.

Number of Items: 32

Format: Includes several scales: physical fitness congruency, health benefits congruency, affiliation congruency, coping with stress congruency, mastery congruency, recognition congruency, and competition congruency.

Reliability: Cronbach's alpha ranged from .79 to .94.

Author: Duda, J. L., and Tappc, M. K.

Article: Predictors of personal investment in physical activity among middle-aged and older adults.

Journal: *Perceptual and Motor Skills*, April 1988, *66*(2), 543–549.

Related Research: Maehr, M. L., & Braskamp, L. A. (1986). *The motivation factor: A theory of personal investment*. Lexington, MA: Lexington Press.

■ ■ ■

4899

Test Name: PERCEIVED PHYSICAL FITNESS SCALE

Purpose: To measure perceived physical fitness.

Number of Items: 12

Format: Responses are made on a Likert scale format ranging from *strongly agree* to *strongly disagree*.

Reliability: Test–retest (1 week) reliability was .95.

Validity: Correlations with trait anxiety was −.39. Correlations with actual cardiovascular physical fitness was .38.

Author: Abadie, B. R.

Article: Relating trait anxiety to perceived physical fitness.

Journal: *Perceptual and Motor Skills*, October 1988, *67*(2), 539–543.

■ ■ ■

4900

Test Name: PERCEIVED SELF-EFFICACY SCALE

Purpose: To measure perceived self-efficacy.

Number of Items: 15

Format: Job attendance situations are described and trainees indicate whether they would be able to come to work in each situation and rated their confidence for *yes* answers on a 0–100 scale.

Reliability: Coefficient alphas ranged from .88 to .91. Test–retest reliabilities were .92 and .94.

Author: Frayne, C. A., and Latham, G. P.

Article: Application of social learning theory to employee self-management of attendance.

Journal: *Journal of Applied Psychology*, August 1987, *72*(3), 387–392.

Related Research: Condiotte, M. M., & Lichtenstein, E. C. (1981). Self-efficacy and relapse in smoking cessation programs. *Journal of Consulting and Clinical Psychology, 49*, 648–658.

■ ■ ■

4901

Test Name: PERCEIVED SOVIET THREAT

Purpose: To measure perceptions of Soviet military threat.

Number of Items: 10

Format: Responses are made on a 6-point scale ranging from *strongly disagree* to *strongly agree*.

Reliability: Coefficient alpha was .87 (*N* = 151).

Validity: Correlations with the Nuclear Locus of Control Scales ranged from −.20 to .24 (*N* = 151).

Author: Rounds, J. B., and Erdahl, P.

Article: Nuclear Locus of Control Scales: Information on development, reliability, and validity.

Journal: *Educational and Psychological Measurement*, Summer 1988, *48*(2), 387–395.

■ ■ ■

4902

Test Name: PERCEPTION OF COUNSELOR BEHAVIORS QUESTIONNAIRE

Purpose: To assess participant's perception of counselor behaviors.

Number of Items: 14

Format: Utilizes a 5-point Likert scale ranging from 1 (*never*) to 5 (*always*). Includes two dimensions: perceived empathic involvement and perceived directive counseling style.

Reliability: Alpha coefficients were .64 and .74.

Validity: Correlations with other variables ranged from −.58 to .55.

Author: Akutsu, P. D., et al.

Article: Predictors of utilization intent of counseling among Chinese and white students: A test of the proximal–distal model.

Journal: *Journal of Counseling Psychology*, October 1990, *37*(4), 445–452.

■ ■ ■

4903

Test Name: PERCEPTIONS OF PARENTAL BELIEFS CONCERNING TEACHERS

Purpose: To ascertain teachers' perceptions of the beliefs parents hold about them.

Number of Items: 18

Format: A sample item is presented.

Reliability: Cronbach's alpha was .94.

Validity: Correlations with other variables ranged from .29 to .56.

Author: Feldman, D., et al.

Article: Teachers' beliefs about administrators and parents of handicapped and nonhandicapped students.

Journal: *Journal of Experimental Education*, Fall 1989, *58*(1), 43–54.

Related Research: Feldman, D., & Gerstein, L. H. (1988). A factor analytic study of three teacher belief scales. *Measurement and Evaluation in Counseling and Development, 21,* 72–80.

■ ■ ■

4904

Test Name: PERFORMANCE SELF-ESTEEM SCALE

Purpose: To assess self-esteem in job performance.

Number of Items: 47

Format: Subjects rate positive and negative descriptors on 7-point scales.

Reliability: Alpha was .90.

Validity: Correlations with other variables ranged from −.13 to .49.

Author: Hackett, G., et al.

Article: The relationship of role model influences to the career salience and educational and career plans of college women.

Journal: *Journal of Vocational Behavior,* October 1989, *35*(2), 164–180.

Related Research: Stake, J. E. (1979). Women's self-estimates of competence and the resolution of the

home/career conflict. *Journal of Vocational Behavior, 14,* 33–42.

■ ■ ■

4905

Test Name: PERFORMANCE SELF-ESTEEM SCALE

Purpose: To measure the performance dimension of self-esteem.

Number of Items: 27

Format: Utilized a true–false format.

Reliability: Internal consistency was .91. Corrected split-half reliability was .82.

Author: Pickering, G. S., and Galvin-Schaefers, K.

Article: An empirical study of reentry women.

Journal: *Journal of Counseling Psychology*, July 1988, *35*(3), 298–303.

Related Research: Stake, J. E. (1979). The ability/performance dimension of self-esteem. *Psychology of Women Quarterly, 3,* 365–377.

■ ■ ■

4906

Test Name: PERFORMANCE SELF-ESTEEM SCALE

Purpose: To measure self-confidence.

Number of Items: 40.

Format: Seven-point true–false format.

Reliability: Alpha was .90.

Author: Stake, J. E.

Article: Exploring attributions in natural settings: Gender and self-esteem effects.

Journal: *Journal of Research in Personality,* December 1990, *24*(4), 468–486.

Related Research: Stake, J. E. (1979). The ability/performance dimension of self-esteem: Implications for women's achievement

behavior. *Psychology of Women Quarterly, 3,* 365–377.

■ ■ ■

4907

Test Name: PERSONAL AND ACADEMIC SELF-CONCEPT INVENTORY

Purpose: To measure global, social, physical, and academic components of self-concept in addition to social anxiety.

Format: Includes seven subscales: self-regard, social acceptance, math ability, verbal ability, physical appearance, physical ability, and social anxiety. Sample items are presented. A seven point Likert-type format is used which ranges from *very often* to *practically never*.

Reliability: Alpha coefficients ranged from .69 to .91. Test–retest correlations ranged from .81 to .98.

Validity: Correlations with other variables ranged from −.80 to .74 (*N* = 37).

Author: Fleming, J. S., and Whalen, D. J.

Article: The Personal and Academic Self-Concept Inventory: Factor structure and gender differences in high school and college samples.

Journal: *Educational and Psychological Measurement,* Winter 1990, *50*(4), 957–967.

Related Research: Fleming, J. S., & Courtney, B. E. (1984). The dimensionality of self-esteem: II. Hierarchical facet model for revised measurement scales. *Journal of Personality and Social Psychology, 46,* 404–421.

■ ■ ■

4908

Test Name: PERSONAL ATTRIBUTES QUESTIONNAIRE—SHORT FORM

Purpose: To assess the degree to which respondents believe that they possess a wide range of social and emotional attributes.

Number of Items: 24

Format: Each item is rated on a 5-point scale from 1 (*give up easily*) to 5 (*never give up*).

Reliability: Reliability ranged from .75 to .85.

Author: Andrews, M., et al.

Article: Student characteristics as predictors of perceived academic advising needs.

Journal: *Journal of College Student Personnel*, January 1987, *28*(1), 60–65.

Related Research: Wilson, R. F., & Cook, E. P. (1984). Concurrent validity of four androgyny instruments. *Sex Roles, 11*, 813–837.

■ ■ ■

4909

Test Name: PERSONAL REACTION SCALE

Purpose: To measure locus of control.

Number of Items: 41

Format: Responses made on 1–99 scale of certainty of belief.

Validity: Correlations with locus of control scales ranged from −.45 to .62.

Author: Waters, L. K., et al.

Article: Congruent validity of the Personal Reaction Scale.

Journal: *Psychological Reports*, August 1987, *61*(1), 314.

Related Research: Gelejs, I., et al. (1984). Personal Reaction Scale for college and noncollege adults: Its development and factorial validity. *Educational and Psychological Measurement, 44*, 383–393.

■ ■ ■

4910

Test Name: PERSONAL TEACHING EFFICACY SCALE

Purpose: To measure how much teachers believe they can influence student achievement.

Number of Items: 5

Format: Five-point Likert format. All items presented.

Reliability: Alpha was .65.

Author: Midgley, C., et al.

Article: Change in teacher efficacy and student self- and task-related beliefs in mathematics during the transition to junior high school.

Journal: *Journal of Educational Psychology*, June 1989, *81*(2), 247–258.

Related Research: Midgley, C., et al. (1988). The transition to junior high school: Beliefs of pre- and post-transition teachers. *Journal of Youth and Adolescence, 17*, 543–562.

■ ■ ■

4911

Test Name: PHENOMENOLOGY OF CONSCIOUSNESS INVENTORY

Purpose: To assess phenomenological experiences.

Number of Items: 53

Format: Includes 12 major and 14 minor dimensions. There are two forms.

Reliability: Coefficient alphas ranged from .70 to .90.

Author: Pekala, R. J., et al.

Article: Measurement of phenomenological experiences: Phenomenology of consciousness inventory.

Journal: *Perceptual and Motor Skills*, October, 1986, *63*(2, Part 2), 983–989

Related Research: Pekala, R. J., et al. (1985). Individual differences in phenomenological experience: States of consciousness as a function of absorption. *Journal of Personality and Social Psychology, 48*, 125–132.

4912

Test Name: PHYSICAL APPEARANCE EVALUATION SCALE

Purpose: To measure satisfaction with physical appearance.

Number of Items: 19

Format: Five-point agreement scales.

Reliability: Alpha was .89. Test–retest (3 weeks) reliability was .85.

Author: Bruch, M. A., et al.

Article: Differences between fearful and self-conscious shy subtypes in background and current adjustment.

Journal: *Journal of Research in Personality*, June 1986, *20*(2), 172–186.

Related Research: Winstead, B. A., & Cash, T. F. (1984). *Reliability and validity of the Body-Self Relations Questionnaire: A new measure on body image*. Paper presented at the Southeastern Psychological Association Convention, New Orleans.

■ ■ ■

4913

Test Name: PHYSICAL ATTRACTIVENESS RATING SCALES

Purpose: To measure attractiveness in four dimensions: grooming, traits, dynamic attractiveness, and static (posed) attractiveness.

Number of Items: 16

Time Required: 15–30 seconds.

Format: Raters view videotaped subjects and rate them on 5- and 7-point Likert scales.

Reliability: Alphas ranged from .32 to .92.

Author: Brown, T. A., et al.

Article: Perceptions of physical attractiveness among college students: Selected determinants and methodological matters.

Journal: *The Journal of Social Psychology*, June 1986, *126*(3), 305–316.

Related Research: Noles, S. W., et al. (1985). Body image, physical attractiveness, and depression. *Journal of Consulting and Clinical Psychology*, *53*, 88–94.

■ ■ ■

4914

Test Name: PHYSICAL FITNESS EXPECTANCY OF REINFORCEMENT SCALE

Purpose: To measure expectancies that specific health-related physical fitness behaviors will lead to specific health-related reinforcement.

Number of Items: 15

Format: Employs a 6-point Likert-type format ranging from 1 (*strongly disagree*) to 6 (*strongly agree*). Examples are presented.

Reliability: Coefficient alpha was .88.

Validity: Correlations with other variables ranged from −.01 to .10.

Author: Bezjak, J. E., and Lee, J. W.

Article: Relationship of self-efficacy and locus of control constructs in predicting college students' physical fitness behaviors.

Journal: *Perceptual and Motor Skills*, October 1990, *71*(2), 499–508.

■ ■ ■

4915

Test Name: PHYSICAL FITNESS LOCUS OF CONTROL

Purpose: To measure physical fitness locus of control.

Number of Items: 27

Format: Includes three subscales: internal physical fitness locus of control, powerful other physical fitness locus of control, and chance physical fitness locus of control. A 6-point Likert format was used.

Reliability: Alpha coefficients ranged from .82 to .86.

Validity: Correlations with other variables ranged from −.14 to .14.

Author: Bezjak, J. E., and Lee, J. W.

Article: Relationship of self-efficacy and locus of control constructs in predicting college students' physical fitness behaviors.

Journal: *Perceptual and Motor Skills*, October 1990, *71*(2), 499–508.

■ ■ ■

4916

Test Name: PHYSICAL FITNESS SELF-EFFICACY SCALE

Purpose: To measure a person's perceived competence and confidence in performing tasks involving components of health-related physical fitness.

Number of Items: 15

Format: Employs a 6-point Likert scale ranging from 1 (*strongly disagree*) to 6 (*strongly agree*). Examples are presented.

Reliability: Coefficients alpha was .84.

Validity: Correlations with other variables ranged from .15 to .45.

Author: Bezjak, J. E., and Lee, J. W.

Article: Relationship of self-efficacy and locus of control constructs in predicting college students' physical fitness behaviors.

Journal: *Perceptual and Motor Skills*, October 1990, *71*(2), 499–508.

■ ■ ■

4917

Test Name: PICTORIAL SCALE OF PERCEIVED COMPETENCE AND SOCIAL ACCEPTANCE FOR YOUNG CHILDREN.

Purpose: To assess children's perceptions of their cognitive and physical competence, and peer and maternal acceptance as well as

teachers' assessment of each child's cognitive and physical competence and peer acceptance.

Reliability: Internal consistencies ranged from .66 to .85.

Validity: Correlations with parental acceptance ranged from −.05 to .37. Correlations with the relationship dimension of the Family Environment Scale ranged from −.40 to .49.

Author: Bullock, J. R., and Pennington, D.

Article: The relationship between parental perceptions of the family environment and children's perceived competence.

Journal: *Child Study Journal*, 1988, *18*(1), 17–31.

Related Research: Harter, S., & Pike, R. (1984). The Pictorial Scale of Perceived Competence and Social Acceptance for Young Children. *Child Development*, *55*, 1969–1982.

■ ■ ■

4918

Test Name: POLITICAL CAUSAL ATTRIBUTION SCALE (QUEBEC)

Purpose: To measure four forms of political attribution: directiveness, consensus, consistency over time, and consistency over modality.

Number of Items: 24

Format: Six-point Likert format. Sample items presented.

Reliability: Split-half reliability was .85.

Author: Chebat, J., and Filiatrault, P.

Article: Preference for forms of political attributions.

Journal: *The Journal of Social Psychology*, October 1986, *126*(5), 633–638.

Related Research: Kelly, H. H. (1973). The process of causal attributions. *American Psychologist*, *28*, 107–128.

4919

Test Name: POLITICAL EFFICACY SCALE

Purpose: To measure internal and external political efficacy.

Number of Items: 14

Format: Employs a 7-point scale.

Reliability: Alpha coefficients were .72 (internal) and .82 (external).

Validity: Correlations with other variables ranged from −.52 to .34 (external) and from −.27 to .51 (internal).

Author: Zimmerman, M. A.

Article: The relationship between poitical efficacy and citizen participation: Construct validation studies.

Journal: *Journal of Personality Assessment*, Fall 1989, *53*(3), 544–566.

Related Research: Craig, S. C., & Maggiotto, M. A. (1982). Measuring political efficacy. *Political Methodology*, 8, 85–109.

■ ■ ■

4920

Test Name: POPULARITY SCALE

Purpose: To measure self-esteem.

Number of Items: 20

Format: Ten true-keyed and 10 false-keyed items that reflect the person's perception of the degree to which the self is accepted, included, approved of, liked, and looked up to by significant others.

Reliability: Coefficient alphas were .78, .81, and .69 (*N*s were 189, 521, and 178, respectively).

Validity: Correlations with: Confidence Scale was .42 (*N* = 178); Rosenberg's Self-Esteem Scale was .39 (*N* = 178).

Author: Lorr, M., and Wunderlich, R. A.

Article: Two objective measures of self-esteem.

Journal: *Journal of Personality Assessment*, Spring 1986, *50*(1), 18–23.

■ ■ ■

4921

Test Name: POTENTIAL TEACHER'S ATTITUDE QUESTIONNAIRE

Purpose: To assess general self-efficacy beliefs and self-efficacy beliefs specific to the teaching and learning process.

Number of Items: 13

Format: Items are rated on a 6-point scale. An example is presented.

Reliability: Internal consistency was .53 (unequal-length Spearman-Brown formula). Test–retest reliability was .77.

Author: Gorrell, J., and Capron, E. W.

Article: Cognitive modeling effects on preservice teachers with low and moderate success expectations.

Journal: *Journal of Experimental Education*, Spring 1989, *57*(3), 231–244.

Related Research: Bandura, A. (1982). Self-efficacy mechanism in human agency. *American Psychologist*, 37, 122–147.

■ ■ ■

4922

Test Name: PREDICTING FUTURE EVENTS SCALE

Purpose: To measure the cognitive dimensions people use to predict their futures.

Number of Items: 21

Format: Five-point Likert format. All items presented.

Reliability: Test–retest reliability ranged from .59 to .90 across subscales.

Validity: Correlations with other variables ranged from .11 to .24.

Author: Tobacyk, J., et al.

Article: Prediction of Future Events Scale: Assessment of beliefs about predicting the future.

Journal: *The Journal of Social Psychology*, December 1989, *129*(6), 819–823.

■ ■ ■

4923

Test Name: PREMENSTRUAL EXPERIENCE ASSESSMENT

Purpose: To assess history and perceptions of types and intensity of premenstrual symptoms.

Number of Items: 88

Format: Four-point severity rating scale.

Reliability: Alphas ranged from .74 to .92 across factors.

Validity: Discriminated between groups created by self-report of discomfort. Congruence of factors was .99 after partialing out oral contraceptive influence.

Author: Futterman, L. A., et al.

Article: Assessing premenstrual syndrome using the Premenstrual Experience Assessment.

Journal: *Psychological Reports*, August 1988, *63*(1), 19–34.

■ ■ ■

4924

Test Name: PRESCHOOL AND PRIMARY NOWICKI-STRICKLAND INTERNAL–EXTERNAL CONTROL SCALE

Purpose: To measure locus of control in children.

Number of Items: 26

Format: Responses are *yes* or *no* to items in a cartoon format.

Validity: Correlation with the Nowicki-Strickland Internal–External Control Scale for Early Elementary Children was .91 (*N* = 30).

Author: Nowicki, Jr., S., and Duke, M. P.

Article: A brief self report form of the Cartoon Scale of Preschool and Primary Nowicki-Strickland Internal-External Control Scale.

Journal: *Educational and Psychological Measurement*, Spring 1989, *49*(1), 205–208.

Related Research: Nowicki, S., & Duke, M. P. (1974). A preschool and primary internal–external control scale. *Developmental Psychology, 10*, 874–880.

■ ■ ■

4925

Test Name: PRESCHOOL BEHAVIOR QUESTIONNAIRE

Purpose: To measure teacher perceptions of child adjustment.

Number of Items: 30

Format: Three-point rating scale format.

Reliability: Interrater reliabilities ranged from .67 to .81. Test–retest reliability ranged from .60 to .99.

Author: Webster-Stratton, C.

Article: Mothers' and fathers' perceptions of child deviance: Roles of parent and child behaviors and parent adjustment.

Journal: *Journal of Consulting and Clinical Psychology*, December 1988, *56*(6), 909–915.

Related Research: Behar, L. (1977). The preschool behavior questionnaire. *Journal of Abnormal Child Psychology, 5*, 265–275.

■ ■ ■

4926

Test Name: PROFESSIONAL EXPECTATIONS SCALE

Purpose: To assess expectations or attitudes about professional life.

Number of Items: 47

Format: 11-point rating scale. Sample item presented.

Reliability: Cronbach's alpha was .90.

Validity: Correlation with burnout was −.36 ($p < .01$).

Author: Kahill, S.

Article: Relationship of burnout among professional psychologists to professional expectations and social support.

Journal: *Psychological Reports*, December 1986, *59*(3), 1043–1053.

■ ■ ■

4927

Test Name: PSYCHOTHERAPY EXPECTANCY INVENTORY— REVISED

Purpose: To measure how the client expects each participant to behave.

Number of Items: 30

Format: Includes four client role expectations: approval, advice, audience, and relationship. Responses are made on a 7-point Likert scale ranging from 1 (*not at all*) to 7 (*very strongly*).

Reliability: Internal consistency ranged from .75 to .87. Test–retest (1 week) reliability ranged from .54 to .68.

Author: Tracey, T. J., and Dundon, M.

Article: Role anticipations and preferences over the course of counseling.

Journal: *Journal of Counseling Psychology*, January 1988, *35*(1), 3–14.

Related Research: Rickers-Ovsiankina, M. A., et al. (1971). Patients' role expectancies in psychotherapy: A theoretical and measurement approach. *Psychotherapy: Theory, Research, and Practice, 8*, 124–126.

■ ■ ■

4928

Test Name: PUPIL CONTROL IDEOLOGY

Purpose: To measure control orientations of faculties.

Number of Items: 20

Format: Likert-type items with higher scores indicating more custodial orientation.

Reliability: Spearman-Brown corrected coefficients ranged from .91 to .95. Alpha reliability was .77.

Author: Kottkamp, R. B., and Mulhern, J. A.

Article: Teacher expectancy motivation, open to closed climate and pupil control ideology in high schools.

Journal: *Journal of Research and Development in Education*, Winter 1987, *20*(2), 9–18.

Related Research: Willower, D. J., et al. (1967). *The school and pupil control ideology* (Pennsylvania State University Studies Monograph No. 24). University Park: Pennsylvania State University.

■ ■ ■

4929

Test Name: RACIAL SELF-ESTEEM SCALE

Purpose: To measure the belief that blacks possess positive characteristics and not negative characteristics.

Number of Items: 15

Format: Four-point "true" scale. Sample items presented.

Reliability: Alpha was .80.

Validity: Correlations with other variables ranged from −.08 to .18.

Author: Hughes, M., and Demo, D. H.

Article: Self-perceptions of Black Americans: Self-esteem and self-efficacy.

Journal: *American Journal of Sociology*, July 1989, *95*(1), 132–159.

■ ■ ■

4930

Test Name: RA LIFE CONFLICT SCALE

Purpose: To assess role conflict.

Number of Items: 6

Format: Responses are made on a 5-point Likert type scale ranging from 1 (*not at all*) to 5 (*very frequently*).

Reliability: Coefficient alpha was .74.

Validity: Correlations with other variables ranged from −.42 to .39.

Author: Delugar, R. J., and Winters, J. J., Jr.

Article: The impact of role ambiguity and conflict on resident assistants.

Journal: *Journal of College Student Development*, May 1990, *31*(3), 230–236.

■ ■ ■

4931

Test Name: RAPE AVERSIVENESS SCALE

Purpose: To measure perceptions of the consequences of rape.

Number of Items: 7

Format: Items rated on 11-point awareness scales.

Reliability: Alpha was .82.

Validity: Correlations with other variables ranged from −.50 to .19.

Author: Hamilton, M., and Yee, J.

Article: Rape knowledge and propensity to rape.

Journal: *Journal of Research in Personality*, March 1990, *24*(1), 111–122.

■ ■ ■

4932

Test Name: RAPE MYTH ACCEPTANCE SCALE

Purpose: To indicate level of agreement with rape myths.

Number of Items: 11

Format: Subjects indicate level of agreement with each rape myth. Subjects are also asked how likely

they are to believe reports of rape and what percentage of rapes they believe are invented.

Reliability: Cronbach's alpha was .88.

Author: Muehlenhard, C. L., and Linton, M. A.

Article: Date rape and sexual aggression in dating situations: Incidence and risk factors.

Journal: *Journal of Counseling Psychology*, April 1987, *34*(2), 186–196.

Related Research: Burt, M. R. (1980). Cultural myths and supports for rape. *Journal of Personality and Social Psychology*, *38*, 217–230.

■ ■ ■

4933

Test Name: RATING STUDENT SELF-REGULATING LEARNING OUTCOMES

Purpose: To measure teachers' perceptions of student self-regulation behavior.

Number of items: 12

Format: Five-point frequency scales, *never* to *always*.

Reliability: Kuder-Richardson Formula 20 was .95.

Validity: Correlations with the cannonical root ranged from −.23 to .48 across items.

Author: Zimmerman, B. J., and Martinez-Pons, M.

Article: Construct validation of a strategy model of student self-regulated learning.

Journal: *Journal of Educational Psychology*, September 1988, *80*(3), 284–290.

■ ■ ■

4934

Test Name: RATIONAL BELIEFS INVENTORY

Purpose: To assess beliefs that are inherently irrational and conducive to maladjustment.

Number of Items: 37

Format: Responses to each item are made on a 5-point Likert scale indicating degree of agreement–disagreement.

Validity: Correlations with other variables ranged from −.25 to .64.

Author: Rich, A. R., and Bonner, R. L.

Article: Support for a pluralistic approach to the treatment of depression.

Journal: *Journal of College Student Development*, September 1989, *30*(5), 426–431.

Related Research: Shorkey, C., & Whiteman, J. (1977). Development of the Rational Beliefs Inventory: Initial validity and reliability. *Educational and Psychological Measurement*, *37*, 327–334.

■ ■ ■

4935

Test Name: REALISTIC EXPECTATIONS QUESTIONNAIRE

Purpose: To assess realism of expectations.

Number of Items: 9

Format: Includes an assessment of: number of trade-related courses, number of years of trade-related work experience, and extent to which the apprentice was well-informed about various program aspects prior to entry.

Reliability: Coefficient alpha was .76.

Validity: Correlations with other variables ranged from −.26 to .40.

Author: Latack, J. C., et al.

Article: Carpenter apprentices: Comparison of career transitions for men and women.

Journal: *Journal of Applied Psychology*, August 1987, *72*(3), 393–400.

■ ■ ■

4936

Test Name: REALISTIC JOB EXPECTATIONS SCALE

Purpose: To assess job expectations.

Number of Items: 4

Format: Five-point Likert scale. Sample items presented.

Reliability: Internal consistency was .71.

Author: Blau, G.

Article: Exploring the mediating mechanisms affecting the relationship of recruitment source to employee performance.

Journal: *Journal of Vocational Behavior*, December 1990, *37*(3), 303–320.

Related Research: Breaugh, J., & Mann, P. (1984). Recruiting source effects: A test of two alternative explanations. *Journal of Occupational Psychology, 57*, 261–267.

■ ■ ■

4937

Test Name: RELIGIOUS LOCUS OF CONTROL SCALE

Purpose: To measure locus of control in religious populations.

Number of Items: 16

Format: Forced-choice. All items presented.

Validity: Validity coefficients ranged from .15 to .81.

Author: Gabbard, C. E., et al.

Article: Assessing locus of control with religious populations.

Journal: *Journal of Research in Personality*, September 1986, *20*(3), 292–308.

Related Research: Benson, P., & Spilkar, B. (1973). God image as a function of self-esteem and locus of control. *Journal for the Scientific Study of Religion, 12*, 297–310.

■ ■ ■

4938

Test Name: REPRESENTATIONAL SYSTEMS INVENTORY

Purpose: To measure a subject's degree of absorption in imagery activities selected from hypnotherapy treatment programs.

Number of Items: 30

Format: Likert format.

Reliability: Test–retest (4 weeks) reliability was .92.

Author: Cochrane, G., and Friesen, J.

Article: Hypnotherapy in weight loss treatment.

Journal: *Journal of Consulting and Clinical Psychology*, August 1986, *54*(4), 489–492.

Related Research: Available from University Microfilms, 300 North Zeeb Road, Ann Arbor, MI 48106, or from G. Cochrane, 2095 West 45th Avenue, Vancouver, BC, Canada V6M 2H8.

■ ■ ■

4939

Test Name: REWARD INEQUITY SCALE

Purpose: To assess the extent to which rewards were perceived to be fair or unfair.

Number of Items: 5

Format: Responses are made on a 5-point Likert scale ranging from 1 (*very fairly*) to 5 (*very unfairly*). An example is presented.

Reliability: Coefficient alpha was .91.

Validity: Correlations with other variables ranged from −.54 to .53.

Author: Frone, M. R., and McFarlin, D. B.

Article: Chronic occupational stressors, self-focused attention, and well being: Testing a cybernetic model of stress.

Journal: *Journal of Applied Psychology*, December 1989, *74*(6), 876–883.

Related Research: Price, J. L., & Mueller, C. W. (1986). *Handbook of organizational measurement.* Marshfield, Ma: Pitman.

■ ■ ■

4940

Test Name: ROLE AMBIGUITY SCALE

Purpose: To measure role ambiguity.

Number of Items: 4

Format: Five-point Likert format. All items presented.

Reliability: Alpha was .69.

Validity: Correlation with supervisor satisfaction was −.43.

Author: Beehr, T. A., et al.

Article: Social support and occupational stress: Talking to supervisors

Journal: *Journal of Vocational Behavior*, February 1990, *36*(1), 61–81.

Related Research: Beehr, T. A. (1976). Perceived situational moderators of the relationship between subjective role ambiguity and role strain. *Journal of Applied Psychology, 72*, 683–690.

■ ■ ■

4941

Test Name: ROLE AMBIGUITY SCALE

Purpose: To measure the extent to which an individual is unclear about the role expectations of others, as well as the degree of uncertainty associated with one's role performance.

Number of Items: 6

Format: Responses are made on a 5-point scale ranging from 1 (*strongly disagree*) to 5 (*strongly agree*).

Validity: Correlations with other variables ranged from −.36 to .46.

Author: Netemayer, R. G., et al.

Article: Analysis of role conflict and roles ambiguity in a structural equations framework.

Journal: *Journal of Applied Psychology,* February 1990, *75*(2), 148–157.

Related Research: Rizzo, J. R., et al (1970). Role conflict and ambiguity in complex organizations. *Administrative Science Quarterly, 15,* 150–163.
Schuler, R. S., et al. (1977). Role conflict and ambiguity: A scale analysis. *Organizational Behavior and Human Performance, 20,* 111–128.

■ ■ ■

4942

Test Name: ROLE CONFLICT SCALE

Purpose: To measure the degree to which expectations of a role are incompatible or incongruent with the reality of the role.

Number of Items: 8

Format: Responses are made on a 5-point scale from 1 (*strongly disagree*) to 5 (*strongly agree*).

Validity: Correlations with other variables ranged from –.55 to .48.

Author: Netemayer, R. G., et al.

Article: Analysis of role conflict and role ambiguity in a structural equations framework.

Journal: *Journal of Applied Psychology,* February 1990, *75*(2), 148–157.

Related Research: Rizzo, R. S., et al. (1970). Role conflict and ambiguity in complex organizations. *Administrative Science Quarterly, 15,* 150–163.
Schuler, R. S., et al. (1977). Role conflict and ambiguity: A scale analysis. *Organizational Behavior and Human Performance, 20,* 111–128.

■ ■ ■

4943

Test Name: ROLE CONFLICT SCALE

Purpose: To measure role conflict.

Number of Items: 4

Format: Responses are made on a 7-point scale from 1 (*very little extent*) to 7 (*a great extent*).

Reliability: Coefficient alpha was .61.

Validity: Correlations with other variables ranged from –.52 to .52.

Author: Tetrick, L. E., and LaRocco, J. M.

Article: Understanding, prediction, and control as moderators of the relationships between perceived stress, satisfaction, and psychological well-being.

Journal: *Journal of Applied Psychology,* November 1987, *72*(4), 538–543.

Related Research: House, R. J., & Rizzo, J. R. (1972). Role conflict and ambiguity as critical variables in a model of organizational behavior. *Organizational Behavior and Human Performance, 7,* 467–505.

■ ■ ■

4944

Test Name: ROLE CONFLICT AND ENHANCEMENT SCALE

Purpose: To measure perceptions of combining work and family roles (career–family, career–marriage, career–parenting).

Number of Items: 18

Format: Open-ended interview format.

Reliability: Alphas ranged from .71 to .74.

Author: Thedje, L. B., et al.

Article: Women with multiple roles: Role-compatibility perceptions, satisfaction, and mental health.

Journal: *Journal of Marriage and the Family,* February 1990, *52*(1), 63–72.

Related Research: Thedje, L. B., et al. (1985). Role conflict study: Conflict and enhancement subscales. Unpublished instrument. University of Michigan.

4945

Test Name: ROLE PLAYING SCALE

Purpose: To measure role playing and role taking.

Number of Items: 12

Format: 4-point scale.

Reliability: Alpha was .75.

Author: Hensley, W. E., and Waggenspack, B. M.

Article: A brief scale of role playing.

Journal: *Journal of Research in Personality,* March 1986, *20*(1), 62–65.

Related Research: Fletcher, K. E., & Averill, J. R. (1984). A scale for the measurement of role-playing ability. *Journal of Research in Personality, 18,* 131–149.

■ ■ ■

4946

Test Name: ROLE STRAIN SCALE

Purpose: To measure the spillover of pressures of one role on another.

Number of Items: 32

Format: Likert format implied. Sample items presented.

Reliability: Alphas ranged from .90 to .92.

Author: Greenberger, E., and O'Neil, R.

Article: Parents' concerns about their child's development: Implications for fathers' and mothers' well-being and attitudes toward work.

Journal: *Journal of Marriage and the Family,* August 1990, *52*(3), 621–635.

Related Research: Greenberger, E., & Goldberg, W. (1989). Work, parenting and the socialization of children. *Development Psychology, 25,* 22–35.

■ ■ ■

4947

Test Name: ROTTER I-E SCALE

Purpose: To measure internal versus external locus of control orientation.

Number of Items: 29

Reliability: Test–retest (1 week to 2 months) reliability coefficients ranged from .49 to .83. Internal consistency estimates of reliability ranged from .65 to .79.

Validity: Correlations with other variables ranged from –.07 to –.37.

Author: Omizo, M. M., et al.

Article: Relationship of Locus of Control Inventory for Three Achievement Domains (LOCITAD) to two other locus of control measures: A construct validity study.

Journal: *Educational and Psychological Measurement*, Autumn 1987, *47*(3), 737–742.

Related Research: Rotter, J. B. (1966). Generalized expectancies for internal versus external control of reinforcement. *Psychological Monographs*, *80*(Whole No. 609).

■ ■ ■

4948

Test Name: ROSENBERG SELF-ESTEEM SCALE

Purpose: To measure attitudes of approval or disapproval toward the self.

Number of Items: 10

Format: Responses are made on a 6-point Likert scale ranging from 1 (*strongly disagree*) to 6 (*strongly agree*).

Reliability: Test–retest (2 weeks) reliability was .85. Coefficient of reproducability was .92.

Validity: Correlations with other variables ranged from .56 to .83.

Author: Cranston, P., and Leonard, M. M.

Article: The relationship between undergraduates' experiences of campus micro-inequities and their self-esteem and aspirations.

Journal: *Journal of College Student Development*, September 1990, *31*(5), 395–401.

Related Research: Silber, W., & Tippet, J. S. (1965). Self-esteem: Clinical assessment and measurement validation. *Psychological Reports*, *16*, 1017–1071.

■ ■ ■

4949

Test Name: ROSENBERG SELF-ESTEEM SCALE

Purpose: To measure self-esteem.

Number of Items: 7

Format: Includes feelings of self-worth, self-respect, pride, and personal satisfaction. True–false format.

Validity: Correlations with measures of masculinity and femininity were .38 and .08, respectively.

Author: Zeldow, P. B., et al.

Article: Masculinity, femininity, and psychosocial adjustment in medical students: A 2-year follow-up.

Journal: *Journal of Personality Assessment*, Spring 1987, *51*(1), 3–14.

Related Research: Rosenberg, M. (1965). *Society and the adolescent self image*. Princeton, NJ: Princeton University Press.

■ ■ ■

4950

Test Name: SCALE TO ASSESS WORLD VIEWS

Purpose: To assess an individual's perception of his or her relationship to nature, institutions and people.

Number of Items: 45

Format: Five-point Likert format.

Reliability: Item-total reliability was .98. Split-half reliabilities were .95 and .96.

Validity: Kruskal's MDSCAL method yielded a five-dimension solution: human nature, relationships, nature, time, and activity.

Author: Ibrahim, F. A., and Kahn, H.

Article: Assessment of world views.

Journal: *Psychological Reports*, February 1987, *60*(1), 163–176.

■ ■ ■

4951

Test Name: SCHOOL SENTIMENT INVENTORY

Purpose: To measure children's school-related perceptions.

Number of Items: 32

Format: Responses to each item are either *yes* or *no*. Sample items are presented.

Reliability: Kuder-Richardson Formula 20 reliability coefficients exceeded .82.

Author: Ladd, G. W.

Article: Having friends, keeping friends, making friends, and being liked by peers in the classroom: Predictors of children's early school adjustment.

Journal: *Child Development*, August 1990, *61*(4), 1081–1100.

Related Research: Ladd, G. W., & Price, J. M. (1987). Predicting children's social and school adjustment following the transition from preschool to kindergarten. *Child Development*, 58, 1168–1189.

■ ■ ■

4952

Test Name: SCHOOL VISION INVENTORY

Purpose: To measure the concept of moral imagination or vision.

Number of Items: 14

Format: True or false format. Sample items are presented.

Reliability: Alpha was .85.

Author: Licatar, J. W., et al.

Article: Principal vision, teacher sense of autonomy and environmental robustness.

Journal: *The Journal of Educational Research*, November–December 1990, *84*(2), 93–99.

Related Research: Greenfield, W. D. (1989). *A Guide to Interpreting the Vision Instrument*. College of Education, Louisiana State University, Baton Rouge, LA.

■ ■ ■

4953

Test Name: SELF-ACTUALIZATION SCALE

Purpose: To measure self actualization in youth.

Number of Items: 62

Time Required: 15–20 minutes.

Format: Four-point Likert format.

Author: Karnes, F. A., and D'Ilio, V. R.

Article: Self-actualization of gifted youth as measured on the reflections of self by youth.

Journal: *Psychological Reports*, October 1990, *67*(1), 465–466.

Related Research: Schatz, E. M., & Buckmaster, L. R. (1984). Development of an instrument to measure self-actualizing growth in preadolescents. *Journal of Creative Behavior*, *18*, 263–272.

■ ■ ■

4954

Test Name: SELF-APPRAISAL INVENTORY—SCHOOL RELATIONS

Purpose: To measure the self-concepts of children in the area of school relations.

Number of Items: 20

Format: A self-report instrument.

Reliability: Internal consistency reliability was .81. Test–retest reliability (2 months) was .78.

Author: Fenn, L. M., and Iwanicki, E. F.

Article: An investigation of the relationship between student affective characteristics and student achievement within more and less effective school settings.

Journal: *Journal of Research and Development in Education*, Summer 1986, *19*(4), 10–18.

Related Research: Delisle, J. R. (1981). *The revolving door model of identification and programming for the academically gifted*. Unpublished doctoral dissertation, University of Connecticut, Storrs, CT.

■ ■ ■

4955

Test Name: SELF-CATHEXIS SCALE

Purpose: To measure one's feelings about self.

Number of Items: 35

Format: A 5-point Likert scale is used to rate each item.

Reliability: Reported reliability is .88. Split-half reliability was .90.

Author: Dworkin, S. H., and Kerr, B. A.

Article: Comparison of interventions for women experiencing body image problems.

Journal: *Journal of Consulting Psychology*, April 1987, *34*(2), 136–140.

Related Research: Secord, P. F., & Jourard, S. M. (1953). The appraisal of body cathexis and the self. *Journal of Consulting Psychology*, *17*, 343–347.

■ ■ ■

4956

Test Name: SELF-CONCEPT INVENTORY—REVISED

Purpose: To measure nine aspects of a child's self.

Number of Items: 20

Format: Includes such aspects as: physical ability, attractive appearance, convergent mental ability, divergent mental ability, social relations, happy qualities, social virtues, school subjects, and work habits.

Reliability: Coefficient alpha was .88.

Validity: Correlations with the other variables ranged from –.10 to .40.

Author: Feshbach, N. D., and Feshbach, S.

Article: Affective processes and academic achievement.

Journal: *Child Development*, October 1987, *58*(5), 1335–1347.

Related Research: Sears, D. S. (1964). Self-concept in the service of educational goals. *California Journal of Institutional Improvement*.

■ ■ ■

4957

Test Name: SELF-CONCEPT SCALE

Purpose: To measure general self-concept.

Number of Items: 4

Format: Likert-format

Reliability: Alphas ranged from .82 to .97.

Author: Pottebaum, S. M., et al.

Article: Is there a causal relation between self-concept and academic achievement?

Journal: *Journal of Educational Research*, January/February 1986, *79*(3), 140–144.

Related Research: Riccobono, J., et al. (1981). *National Longitudinal Study: Data file users manual* (Vol. 2). Research Triangle Park, N.C.: Research Triangle Institute.

■ ■ ■

4958

Test Name: SELF-CONSCIOUSNESS SCALE

Purpose: To measure self-consciousness.

Number of Items: 25

Format: Includes three components: private self-consciousness, public self-consciousness, and social anxiety. Responses are made on a scale ranging from 0 (*extremely uncharacteristic*) to 4 (*extremely characteristic*).

Validity: Correlations with other variables ranged from −.27 to .74.

Author: Edelmann, R. J.

Article: Chronic blushing, self-consciousness, and social anxiety.

Journal: *Journal of Psychopathology and Behavioral Assessment*, June 1990, *12*(2), 119–127.

Related Research: Fenigstein, A., et al. (1975). Public and private self-consciousness: Assessment and theory. *Journal of Consulting and Clinical Psychology*, *43*, 522–527.

■ ■ ■

4959

Test Name: SELF-CONSCIOUSNESS SCALE

Purpose: To measure self-consciousness in several dimensions: public self-consciousness, anxiety, reflectiveness, and internal state awareness.

Number of Items: 13

Format: Response categories not specified but all items are presented.

Reliability: LISREL goodness of fit statistics ranged from .79 to .90 across several models.

Author: Gould, S. J.

Article: The Self-Consciousness Scale: A confirmatory Analysis.

Journal: *Psychological Reports*, October 1986, *59*(2)II, 809–810.

Related Research: Fenigstein, A., et al. (1975). Public and private self-consciousness: Assessment and theory. *Journal of Consulting and Clinical Psychology*, *43*, 522–527.

4960

Test Name: SELF-CONSCIOUSNESS SCALE

Purpose: To tap dispositional differences in the degree to which individuals' primary focus of attention is the self rather than the environment.

Number of Items: 17

Format: Sample items are presented.

Reliability: Internal consistency estimate of reliability was .78.

Validity: Correlations with other variables ranged from −.17 to .40.

Author: Hollenbeck, J. R., and Williams, C. R.

Article: Goal importance, self-focus, and the goal-setting process.

Journal: *Journal of Applied Psychology*, May 1987, *72*(2), 204–211.

Related Research: Carver, C. S., & Glass, D. G. (1976). The self-consciousness scale: A discriminant validity study. *Journal of Personality Assessment*, *40*, 169–172.

■ ■ ■

4961

Test Name: SELF-CONSCIOUSNESS SCALE

Purpose: To measure self-consciousness.

Number of Items: 23

Format: Includes three subscales: private self-consciousness, public self-consciousness, and social anxiety.

Validity: Correlations with other variables ranged from −.30 to .18.

Author: Thomas, C. D., and Freeman, R. J.

Article: The Body Esteem Scale: Construct validity of the female subscales.

Journal: *Journal of Personality Assessment*, Spring 1990, *54*(1/2), 204–212.

Related Research: Fenigstein, A., et al. (1975). Public and private self-consciousness: Assessment and theory. *Journal of Consulting and Clinical Psychology*, *43*, 522–527.

■ ■ ■

4962

Test Name: SELF-CONSCIOUSNESS SCALE—REVISED

Purpose: To assess three dimensions of self-attention.

Number of Items: 19

Format: Includes three dimensions of self-intention: public self-consciousness, private self-consciousness, and social anxiety. Responses are made on a 5-point Likert scale ranging from *extremely uncharacteristic* to *extremely characteristic*. Examples are presented.

Reliability: Alpha coefficients ranged from .74 to .79.

Author: Abe, J. S., and Zane, N. W. S.

Article: Psychological maladjustment among Asian and white American college students: Controlling for confounds.

Journal: *Journal of Counseling Psychology*, October 1990, *37*(4), 437–444.

Related Research: Fenigstein, A., et al. (1975). Public and private self-consciousness: Assessment and theory. *Journal of Consulting and Clinical Psychology*, *43*, 522–527.

■ ■ ■

4963

Test Name: SELF-CONTROL QUESTIONNAIRE

Purpose: To measure locus of control.

Number of Items: 51

Format: Rated on 4- (external) and 3- (internal) point scales.

Reliability: Test–retest was .96 (total) .83 (internal), and .96 (external).

Author: Werch, C. E., and Gorman, D. R.

Article: Factor analysis and internal and external self-control practices for alcohol consumption.

Journal: *Psychological Reports,* December 1986, *59*(3), 1207–1213.

Related Research: Werch, C. E., & Gorman, D. R. (1986). Relationship between external and internal self-control and the alcohol consumption patterns and problems of college students. *Journal of Studies on Alcohol, 46,* 30–37.

■ ■ ■

4964

Test Name: SELF DESCRIPTION QUESTIONNAIRE III

Purpose: To measure multidimensional academic and nonacademic self-conepts for late adolescents.

Number of Items: 136

Format: Includes 13 self-conepts: general, English, mathematics, general school, physical ability, physical appearance, social (same sex), social (opposite sex), parent relations, emotional stability, problem solving/creative thinking, religion/spitiruality, and honesty/reliability. Responses are made on an 8-point Likert scale ranging from 1 (*definitely false*) to 8 (*definitely true*).

Reliability: Internal consistency reliability ranged from .79 to .95 for general and academic self-concepts. Test–retest reliability ranged from .66 to .94 for general and academic self-concepts.

Author: Byrne, B. M.

Article: The Self Description Questionnaire III: Testing for equivalent factorial validity across ability.

Journal: *Educational and Psychological Measurement,* Summer 1988, *48*(2), 397–406.

Related Research: Marsh, H. W., & O'Neill, R. (1984). Self Description Questionnaire: The construct validity of multidimensional self-concept ratings by late adolescents. *Journal of Educational Measurement, 21,* 153–174.

■ ■ ■

4965

Test Name: SELF-DESCRIPTION QUESTIONNAIRE III

Purpose: To measure self-concept for late adolescents.

Number of Items: 42

Format: Eight-point Likert format from (*definitely true*) to (*definitely false*).

Reliability: Median alpha was .90.

Author: Bryne, B., and Shavelson, R. J.

Article: On the structure of adolescent self-concept.

Journal: *Journal of Educational Psychology,* December 1986, *78*(6), 474–481.

Related Research: Marsh, H. W., & O'Neill, R. (1984). Self-Description Questionnaire III: The construct validity of multidimensional self-concept ratings by late adolescents. *Journal of Educational Measurement, 21,* 153–174.
Marsh, H. W. (1986). Self-serving effect bias in academic attributions: Its relation to academic achievement and self concept. *Journal of Educational Psychology, 78,* 190–200.

■ ■ ■

4966

Test Name: SELF-EFFICACY/ INTEREST RATINGS SCALE

Purpose: To assess self-efficacy and task interest.

Number of Items: 3

Format: Items measure self-efficacy strength, level of task self-efficacy, and task interest. All items are presented.

Reliability: Test–retest (1 week) reliabilities ranged from .55 to .70.

Author: Hackett, G., and Campbell, N. K.

Article: Task self-efficacy and task interest as a function of performance on a gender-neutral task.

Journal: *Journal of Vocational Behavior,* April 1987, *30*(2), 203–215.

Related Research: Hackett, G., & O'Halloran, S. (1985). Test–retest reliabilities of career self-efficacy measures. Unpublished manuscripts.

■ ■ ■

4967

Test Name: SELF-EFFICACY INVENTORY

Purpose: To measure the degree to which a student feels efficacious about specific behaviors related to creative production.

Number of Items: 20

Format: The instrument employs a 5-point summed rating.

Reliability: Alpha coefficient was .92.

Author: Burns, D. E.

Article: The effects of group training activities on students' initiation of creative investigations.

Journal: *Gifted Child Quarterly,* Winter 1990, *34*(1), 31–36.

Related Research: Starko, A. (1986). *The effects of creative investigations on extracurricular creativity.* Unpublished doctoral dissertation, University of Connecticut.

■ ■ ■

4968

Test Name: SELF-EFFICACY INVENTORY

Purpose: To examine trainees' expectations for the supervisory process.

Number of Items: 21

Format: Respondents indicate their confidence in their ability to perform each activity effectively on a 9-point scale ranging from 0 (*not confident*) to 9 (*completely confident*).

Reliability: Cronbach's alpha was .93.

Validity: Correlations with other variables ranged from −.14 to .30.

Author: Efstation, J. F., et al.

Article: Measuring the working alliance in counselor supervision.

Journal: *Journal of Counseling Psychology*, July 1990, *37*(3), 322–329.

Related Research: Friedlander, M. L., & Snyder, J. (1983). Trainees' expectations for the supervisory process: Testing a developmental model. *Counselor Education and Supervision*, 22, 342–348.

■ ■ ■

4969

Test Name: SELF-EFFICACY QUESTIONNAIRE

Purpose: To measure children's perceptions of their abilities to perform aggression and related behaviors.

Number of Items: 46

Format: Each item describes a social situation and the children indicate their ability to perform a specified behavior in that situation. Examples are presented.

Reliability: Alpha coefficients of internal consistency ranged form .67 to .86.

Author: Perry, D. G., et al.

Article: Cognitive social learning mediators of aggression.

Journal: *Child Development*, June 1986, *57*(3), 700–711.

Related Research: Wheeler, V. A., & Ladd, G. W. (1982). Assessment of children's self-efficacy for social interactions with peers. *Developmental Psychology*, 18, 795–805.

4970

Test Name: SELF-EFFICACY SCALE

Purpose: To assess the general expectation that one is able to successfully execute behaviors that are required to produce desired outcomes.

Number of Items: 22

Format: Items are rated on a 5-point scale ranging from *not at all like me* to *very much like me*. Sample items are presented.

Reliability: Cronbach's alpha was .91. Test–retest (2 weeks) reliability was .86.

Author: Smith, R. E., and Nye, S. L.

Article: Comparison of induced affect and covert rehearsal in the acquisition of stress management coping skills.

Journal: *Journal of Counseling Psychology*, January 1989, *36*(1), 17–23.

Related Research: Coppel, D. B. (1980). *The relationship of perceived social support and self-efficacy to major and minor stressors.* Unpublished doctoral dissertation, University of Washington, Seattle.

■ ■ ■

4971

Test Name: SELF-EFFICACY SCALE—REVISED

Purpose: To measure self-efficacy in an academic setting.

Number of Items: 27

Format: Includes seven task areas: class concentration, memorization, exam concentration, understanding, explaining concepts, discriminating concepts, and note-taking. Examples are presented.

Reliability: Interitem correlation coefficients ranged from .46 to .83.

Validity: Criterion validity coefficients ranged from .10 to .26.

Criterion validity coefficients corrected for alteration ranged from .11 to .31.

Author: Wood, R. E., and Locke, E. A.

Article: The relation of self-efficacy and grade goals to academic performance.

Journal: *Educational and Psychological Measurement*, Winter 1987, *47*(4), 1013–1024.

Related Research: Locke, E. A., et al. (1984). Effect of self-efficacy, goals, and task strategies on task performance. *Journal of Applied Psychology*, 69, 241–251.

■ ■ ■

4972

Test Name: SELF-EFFICACY SCALE

Purpose: To measure self-efficacy.

Number of Items: 10

Format: Employs a 7-point scale.

Validity: Correlations with the Political Efficacy Scale were .14 (external) and .16 (internal).

Author: Zimmerman, M. A.

Article: The relationship between political efficacy and citizen participation: Construct validation studies.

Journal: *Journal of Personality Assessment*, Fall 1989, *53*(3), 554–566.

Related Research: Tipton, R., & Worthington, E. (1984). The measurement of generalized self-efficacy: A study of construct validity. *Journal of Personality Assessment*, 48, 545–548.

■ ■ ■

4973

Test Name: SELF-ESTEEM INVENTORY

Purpose: To measure global self-esteem.

Number of Items: 10

Format: Responses are made on a 4-point scale ranging from *strongly agree* to *strongly disagree*.

Reliability: Test–retest (2 weeks) reliability was .85.

Validity: Correlations with other variables ranged from –.49 to . –.60.

Author: Serling, D. A., and Betz, N. E.

Article: Development and evaluation of a measure of fear of commitment.

Journal: *Journal of Counseling Psychology*, January 1990, *37*(1), 91–97.

Related Research: Silber, E., & Tippett, J. (1965). Self-esteem: Clinical assessment and measurement validation. *Psychological Reports, 16,* 1017–1071.

■ ■ ■

4974

Test Name: SELF-ESTEEM QUESTIONNAIRE

Purpose: To measure a general manifestation of self-esteem and general self-confidence in the work setting.

Number of Items: 11

Format: Employs a 5-point response scale. Sample items are presented.

Reliability: Coefficient alpha was .68.

Author: James, L. A., and James, L. R.

Article: Integrating work environment perceptions: Explorations into the measurement of meaning.

Journal: *Journal of Applied Psychology,* October 1989, *74* (5), 739–751.

Related Research: James, L. R., & Jones, A. P. (1980). Perceived job characteristics and job satisfaction: An examination of reciprocal causation. *Personnel Psychology, 33,* 97–135.

4975

Test Name: SELF-ESTEEM RATING SCALE FOR CHILDREN

Purpose: To provide a teacher's rating scale of children's self-esteem.

Number of Items: 12

Format: Responses to each item are *always, frequently, occasionally, seldom,* or *never.* All items are presented.

Reliability: Alpha coefficients ranged from .70 to .91 (*N*s ranged from 11 to 27).

Validity: Correlations with other variables ranged from .05 to .89.

Author: Chiu, L.

Article: Development of the Self-Esteem Rating Scale for Children (Revised).

Journal: *Measurement and Evaluation in Counseling and Development*, April 1987, *20*(1), 36–41.

■ ■ ■

4976

Test Name: SELF-ESTEEM SCALE

Purpose: To measure self-esteem.

Number of Items: 25

Format: Sample items presented.

Reliability: Alphas ranged from .74 to .90 across subscales.

Author: de Turk, M. A., and Miller, G. R.

Article: The effects of husbands' and wives' social cognition on their marital adjustment, conjugal power, and self-esteem.

Journal: *Journal of Marriage and the Family,* November 1986, *48*(4), 715–724.

Related Research: Berger, C. R. (1966). *A factor analytic study of self-esteem.* Unpublished master's thesis, Michigan State University.

■ ■ ■

4977

Test Name: SELF-ESTEEM SCALE

Purpose: To measure self-esteem.

Number of Items: 14

Format: Semantic differential format.

Reliability: Test–retest reliability was .87.

Author: Gecas, V., and Seff, M. A.

Article: Social class and self-esteem: Psychological centrality, compensation, and the relative effects of work and home.

Journal: *Social Psychology Quarterly,* June 1990, *53*(2), 165–173.

Related Research: Gecas, V., & Seff, M. A. (1989). Social class, occupational conditions, and self-esteem. *Sociological Perspectives, 32,* 353–365.

■ ■ ■

4978

Test Name: SELF-ESTEEM SCALE

Purpose: To measure self-esteem.

Number of Items: 6

Format: Four-point true–false format. Sample items are presented.

Reliability: Alpha was .66.

Author: Hughes, M., and Demo, D. H.

Article: Self-perceptions of Black Americans: Self-esteem and personal efficacy.

Journal: *American Journal of Sociology,* July 1989, *95*(1), 132–159.

Related Research: Bachman, J. G., & Johnston, L. D. (1978). *The monitoring the future project: Design and procedures.* Ann Arbor: University of Michigan, Institute for Social Research.

■ ■ ■

4979

Test Name: SELF-IMAGE DISPARITY QUESTIONNAIRE

Purpose: To identify self-image disparity.

Number of Items: 20

Format: Items are bipolar semantic differentials. Subjects first indicate how they see themselves, then how they would like to be. All items are presented.

Validity: Correlations with other variables were .48 and .61.

Author: Furnham, A., and Osborne, A.

Article: Repression-sensitization, self-image disparity, and mental health.

Journal: *Educational and Psychological Measurement*, Spring 1986, *46*(1), 125–133.

Related Research: Furnham, A., & Kirris, P. (1983). Self-image disparity, ethnic identity and sex-role stereotypes in British and Cypriot adolescents. *Journal of Adolescence*, *6*, 275–292.

■ ■ ■

4980

Test Name: SELF-IMAGE QUESTIONNAIRE

Purpose: To measure the maturity of a student's self-image.

Number of Items: 30

Format: Items are bipolar traits rated on an 8-point scale.

Reliability: Test–retest reliabilities ranged from .64 (13 days) to .58 (56 days).

Validity: Correlations with other variables ranged from −.60 to .42.

Author: Jones, L. K.

Article: Adapting to the first semester of college: A test of Heath's model of maturing.

Journal: *Journal of College Student Personnel*, May 1987, *28*(3), 205–211.

Related Research: Heath, D. H. (1965). *Explorations of maturity*. New York: Appleton-Century-Crafts.

■ ■ ■

4981

Test Name: SELF-IMAGE QUESTIONNAIRE FOR YOUNG ADOLESCENTS

Purpose: To measure three aspects of adolescent's self-image.

Number of Items: 29

Format: Includes three parts: body image scale, peer relationships scale, and superior adjustment scale.

Reliability: Alpha coefficients ranged from .74 to .83.

Validity: Correlations with other variables ranged from −.10 to .41.

Author: Brooks-Gunn, J., and Warren, M. P.

Article: The psychological significance of secondary sexual characteristics in nine-to-eleven-year-old girls.

Journal: *Child Development*, August 1988, *59*(4), 1061–1069.

Related Research: Petersen, A. C., et al. (1984). A self-image questionnaire for young adolescents (SIQYA): Reliability and validity studies. *Journal of Youth and Adolescence*, *13*, 93–111.

■ ■ ■

4982

Test Name: SELF-MONITORING SCALE

Purpose: To tap self-observation and self-control guided by situational cues to social appropriateness.

Number of Items: 25

Format: Includes three factors: Other-directedness, Acting, and Extraversion. Examples are presented. True–false format.

Reliability: Kuder-Richardson formula reliability ranged from .63 to .70. Test–retest (1 month) reliability was .83.

Author: Abe, J. S., and Zane, N. W. S.

Article: Psychological maladjustment among Asian and white American college students: Controlling for comfounds.

Journal: *Journal of Counseling Psychology*, October 1990, *37*(4), 437–444.

Related Research: Snyder, M. (1974). Self-monitoring of expressive behavior. *Journal of Personality and Social Psychology*, *30*, 526–537.

■ ■ ■

4983

Test Name: SELF-MONITORING SCALE

Purpose: To assess self-monitoring.

Number of Items: 18

Reliability: Coefficient alpha was .70.

Validity: Correlations with other variables ranged from −.27 to .17.

Author: Brown, M. T., et al.

Article: Self-monitoring processes and Holland vocational preferences among college students.

Journal: *Journal of Counseling Psychology*, April 1989, *36*(2), 183–188.

Related Research: Snyder, M., & Gangestad, S. (1986). On the nature of self-monitoring: Matters of assessment, matters of validity. *Journal of Personality and Social Psychology*, *51*, 125–139.

■ ■ ■

4984

Test Name: SELF-REPORTED SELF-APPRAISAL SCALE

Purpose: To provide a self-report of one's ability to accurately appraise oneself.

Number of Items: 5

Format: Response to Item 1 is on a Likert scale from *definitely no* to *definitely yes*. Responses to Items 2 through 5 are made on a Likert scale from *very ineffective* to *very effective*. All items are presented.

Reliability: Split-half reliabilities were .84 and .86. Test–retest reliability was .42.

Validity: Correlations with other variables ranged from −.13 to .66.

Author: Westbrook, B. W., et al.

Article: The relationship between cognitive career maturity and self-reported career maturity of high school students.

Journal: *Measurement and Evaluation in Counseling and Development*, July 1987, *20*(2), 51–61.

■ ■ ■

4985

Test Name: SENSE OF COHERENCE SCALE

Purpose: To measure the extent to which a person views the world as ordered and predictable.

Number of Items: 29

Reliability: Alphas ranged from .83 to .88.

Validity: Correlations with A-trait, A-state T, and A-state T2 ranged from −.62 to .06.

Author: Antonovsky, H., and Sagy, S.

Article: The development of sense of coherence and its impact on responses to stress situations.

Journal: *The Journal of Social Psychology*, April 1986, *126*(2), 213–225.

Related Research: Antonovsky, A. (1983). The sense of coherence: Development of a research instrument. *The William S. Schwartz Newsletter and Research Reports* (Tel-Aviv University), 11–22.

■ ■ ■

4986

Test Name: SENSE OF COMPETENCE SCALE

Purpose: To measure sense of competence.

Number of Items: 23

Format: Six-point Likert format.

Reliability: Alpha was .96.

Author: Bhagat, R. S., and Allie, S. M.

Article: Organizational stress, personal life stress, and symptoms of

life strains: An examination of the moderating role of sense competence.

Journal: *Journal of Vocational Behavior*, December 1989, *35*(3), 231–253.

Related Research: Wagner, F. R., & Morse, J. J. (1975). A measure of individual sense of competence. *Psychological Review, 5,* 451–459.

■ ■ ■

4987

Test Name: SENSE OF COMPETENCE QUESTIONNAIRE

Purpose: To gauge an individual's sense of competence.

Number of Items: 19

Format: Responses are made on a 7-point agree–disagree response scale. Includes four subscales: competence thema, task knowledge, influence, and confidence.

Reliability: Alhpa coefficients ranged from .76 to .82.

Validity: Correlations with other variables ranged from .18 to .45.

Author: Steel, R. P., et al.

Article: Psychometric properties of a measure of sense of competence.

Journal: *Educational and Psychological Measurement*, Summer 1989, *49*(2), 433–446.

Related Research: Wagner, F. R., & Morse, J. J. (1975). A measure of individual sense of competence. *Psychological Reports, 36,* 451–459.

■ ■ ■

4988

Test Name: SENSE OF COMPETENCE SCALE

Purpose: To assess perceived interpersonal and intellectual skills.

Number of Items: 23

Format: Responses are made on a 4-point Likert scale ranging from 1

(*strongly agree*) to 4 (*strongly disagree*). All items are presented.

Reliability: Cronbach's alphas were .76 and .79.

Author: Janosik, S., et al.

Article: The relationship of residence halls' student-environment fit and sense of competence.

Journal: *Journal of College Student Development*, July 1988, *29*(4), 320–236.

Related Research: Janosik, S. M. (1987). *Relationship of residence hall environments and student sense of competence and academic achievement.* Unpublished doctoral dissertation, Virginia Polytechnic Institute and State University.

■ ■ ■

4989

Test Name: SENSE OF COMPETENCE AND TIME-DIMENSION SCALE

Purpose: To measure sense of personal competence in roles.

Number of Items: 90

Format: Semantic differential sample items are described.

Reliability: Alphas ranged from .78 to .87.

Author: Dreman, S., et al.

Article: Competence or dissonance? Divorcing mothers' perceptions of sense of competence and time perspective.

Journal: *Journal of Marriage and the Family*, May 1989, *51*(2), 405–415.

Related Research: Dreman, S., & Orr, E. (1985). *Changes perceived by mothers occurring in the social, familial, and personal constellation after filing for divorce in the rabbinical court in Israel.* Unpublished manuscript, Ben Gurion University of the Negev, Beer Sheva, Israel.

4990

Test Name: SHORT INDEX OF SELF-ACTUALIZATION

Purpose: To measure self-actualization as defined by Fromm, Rogers, Maslow and Goldstein.

Number of Items: 15

Format: Likert format (implied). All items presented.

Validity: Confirmatory factor analysis (LISREL algorithm) identified five hypothesized dimensions, but an oblique rotation solution may fit the data better than an orthogonal solution.

Author: Tucker, R. K., and Weber, D. R.

Article: Factorial validity of Jones and Crandall's Short Index of Self-Actualization.

Journal: *Psychological Reports*, August 1988, *63*(1), 39–45.

Related Research: Jones, A., & Crandall, R. (1986). Validation of a short index of self-actualization. *Personality and Psychology Bulletin*, *12*, 63–73.

■ ■ ■

4991

Test Name: SOCIAL IDENTITY SURVEY

Purpose: To elicit and record student's idiosyncratic social identities.

Number of Items: 25

Time Required: 30 minutes.

Format: Subjects list 10 identities of their choice and rate each on 25 bipolar scales.

Reliability: Alphas ranged from .67 to .85.

Author: Garza, R. T., and Herringer, L. G.

Article: Social Identity: A multidimensional approach.

Journal: *The Journal of Social Psychology*, June 1987, *127*(3), 299–308.

■ ■ ■

4992

Test Name: SOCIAL REACTION INVENTORY

Purpose: To measure locus of control.

Number of Items: 29

Format: Forced-choice items.

Reliability: Split-half estimate of .65; Kuder-Richardson Formula 20 coefficients ranged from .69 to .76; test–retest (1 month) reliabilities ranged from .60 to .83.

Validity: Correlations with other variables ranged from −.07 to −.24.

Author: Martel, J., et al.

Article: Validity of an intuitive personality scale: Personal responsibility as a predictor of academic achievement.

Journal: *Educational and Psychological Measurement*, Winter 1987, *47*(4), 1153–1163.

Related Research: Rotter, J. B. (1966). Generalized expectancies for internal versus external locus of control of reinforcement. *Psychological Monographs*, *80*, 1–26.

■ ■ ■

4993

Test Name: SORENSON RELATIONSHIP QUESTIONNAIRE

Purpose: To assess perceptions of the therapist's empathy and expertness.

Number of Items: 24

Format: Likert-type format.

Reliability: Internal consistency was .85.

Author: Carter, R. L., and Motta, R. W.

Article: Effects of intimacy of therapist's self-disclosure and

formality on perceptions of credibility in an initial interview.

Journal: *Perceptual and Motor Skills*, February 1988, *66*(1), 167–173.

Related Research: Sorenson, A. G. (1967). *Toward an instructional model for counseling*. Occasional Report No. 6, Center for the Study of Instructional Program, University of California, Los Angeles.

■ ■ ■

4994

Test Name: SPATIAL DIMENSIONALITY TEST

Purpose: To measure the spatial constructs of visualization, spatial orientation, and spatial relations.

Number of Items: 60

Format: Includes six subtexts: Hidden Figures, Card Rotations, Paper Folding, Surface Development, Horizontal/Vertical Rotations, and Cube Perspectives.

Reliability: Internal consistency reliability ranged from .51 to .96.

Validity: Correlations with other variables ranged from −.14 to .46.

Author: Olson, D. M., and Eliot, J.

Article: Relationships between experiences, processing style, and sex-related differences in performance on spatial tests.

Journal: *Perceptual and Motor Skills*, April 1986, *62*(2), 447–460.

■ ■ ■

4995

Test Name: STRESSOR AND COPING RESPONSE INVENTORIES FOR CHILDREN

Purpose: To elicit a child's perception of experienced stress.

Number of Items: 87 (subsets of this total are subscales for various grade levels and types of stress). All items presented.

Format: Four-point Likert format.

Reliability: Alpha ranged from .50 to .86 across subscales. Item-total correlations ranged from .03 to .63.

Validity: Several nonquantitative assessments of content, concurrent, and construct validity are reported that suggest the scales are valid.

Author: Elwood, S. W.

Article: Stressor and Coping Response Inventories for Children.

Journal: *Psychological Reports*, June 1987, *60*(3)I, 931–947.

■ ■ ■

4996

Test Name: SUBJECTIVE EXPECTANCIES INVENTORY

Purpose: To measure the utility or one's expectancy that desirable outcomes will occur when initiating heterosocial interactions.

Number of Items: 4

Format: Each item is in the form of a situation to which the respondent provides two affective responses that reflect how he would feel if the woman accepted his overture and if she rejected it. An example is presented.

Reliability: Test–retest (4 weeks) reliability was .85.

Author: Zane, N. W. S.

Article: Change mechanisms in placebo procedures: Effects of suggestion, social demand, and contingent success on improvement in treatment.

Journal: *Journal of Counseling Psychology*, April 1989, *36*(2), 234–243.

Related Research: Gormally, J., et al. (1981). The relationship between maladaptive cognitions and social anxiety. *Journal of Consulting and Clinical Psychology*, *49*, 300–301.

■ ■ ■

4997

Test Name: SUPERNATURALISM QUESTIONNAIRE

Purpose: To assess belief in the paranormal.

Number of Items: 32

Format: Six-point Likert format. Sample item presented.

Reliability: Cronbach's alpha was .87. Split-half reliability was .76. Test–retest was .76.

Validity: Predicted validity was .98.

Author: Randall, T. M.

Article: Belief in the paranormal declines: 1977–1987.

Journal: *Psychological Reports*, June 1990, *66*(3, Part II), 1347–1351.

Related Research: Randall, T. M., & Desrosiers, M. (1980). Measurement of supernatural belief: Sex differences and locus of control. *Journal of Personality Assessment*, *44*, 493–498.

■ ■ ■

4998

Test Name: SURVEY OF ACHIEVEMENT RESPONSIBILITY

Purpose: To measure attributions for success.

Number of Items: 40

Format: Students choose between four reasons (effort, luck, task or ability) for success or failure for each of 40 tasks

Reliability: Alphas ranged from .39 to .75. Test–retest ranged from .44 to .75.

Author: Ryckman, D. B., and Peckham, P.

Article: Gender differences in attributions form success and failure in situations across subject areas.

Journal: *Journal of Educational Research*, November/December 1987, *81*(2), 120–125.

Related Research: Ryckman, D. B., et al. (1985). *The Survey of Achievement Responsibility (SOAR): Some reliability and validity data on a new acacemically oriented attribution scale.* Paper presented at the AERA convention in Chicago.

4999

Test Name: SURVEY OF STUDENT COUNSELING NEEDS

Purpose: To identify the perceived counseling needs of community college students.

Number of Items: 25

Format: Includes 24 forced-choice items and one open-ended item.

Reliability: Cronbach's alpha reliability was .95 (forced-choice items). Test–retest (6 weeks) reliability coefficients ranged from .82 to .98.

Author: Warchal, P., and Southern, S.

Article: Perceived importance of counseling needs among adult students.

Journal: *Journal of College Student Personnel*, January 1986, *27*(1), 43–48.

Related Research: Corrado, T. J., & Mangano, J. A. (1980, August). Toward a taxonomy of adult 2-year college student needs. *Research in Education*.

■ ■ ■

5000

Test Name: SYDNEY ATTRIBUTION SCALE

Purpose: To measure attributions for academic achievement.

Number of Items: 72

Format: Five-point falseness to truth scales.

Reliability: Median alpha was .75.

Author: Watkins, D., and Gutierrez, M.

Article: Causal relationships among self-concept, attributions, and achievement in Filipino students.

Journal: *The Journal of Social Psychology*, October 1990, *130*(5), 625–631.

Related Research: Marsh, H. W. (1984). Relations among dimensions of self-attribution, dimensions of self-concept, and academic achievement. *Journal of Educational Psychology, 76,* 1291–1308.

■ ■ ■

5001

Test Name: TEACHER EFFICACY SCALE

Purpose: To measure whether teachers feel certain that their instructional skills are effective.

Number of Items: 11

Format: Five-point Likert format. Sample item presented.

Reliability: Alpha was .76.

Validity: Correlations with other variables ranged from −.21 to .56.

Author: Brissie, J. S., et al.

Article: Individual, situational contributions to burnout.

Journal: *Journal of Educational Research,* November/December 1988, *82*(2), 106–112.

■ ■ ■

5002

Test Name: TEACHER EFFICACY SCALE

Purpose: To measure general and personal teaching efficacy.

Number of Items: 30

Format: Likert format.

Reliability: Alpha coefficients ranged from .75 to .78.

Author: Evans, E. O., and Tribble, M.

Article: Perceived teaching problems, self-efficacy, and commitment to teaching among preservice teachers.

Journal: *Journal of Educational Research,* November–December 1986, *80*(2), 81–85.

Related Research: Gibson, S., & Dembo, M. H. (1984). Teacher efficacy: A construct validation.

Journal of Educational Psychology, 76, 569–582.

■ ■ ■

5003

Test Name: TEACHER EFFICACY SCALE

Purpose: To measure beliefs teachers have about their skills and their abilities to achieve desirable learning outcomes in students.

Number of Items: 24

Format: Six-point agreement scales.

Reliability: Cronbach's alphas ranged from .62 to .82.

Validity: Factor analysis extracted two dimensions (personal efficacy and outcome expectancy).

Author: Saklofske, D. H., et al.

Article: Teachers' efficacy and teaching behaviors.

Journal: *Psychological Reports,* October 1988, *63*(2), 407–414.

Related Research: Gibson, S., & Dembo, M. H. (1984). Teacher efficacy: A construct validation. *Journal of Educational Psychology, 76,* 569–582.

■ ■ ■

5004

Test Name: TEACHER EFFICACY SCALE

Purpose: To measure personal and teaching efficacy among classroom teachers.

Number of Items: 22

Format: Likert format.

Reliability: Alphas ranged from .74 to .82.

Validity: Correlations with other variables ranged from −.42 to .61.

Author: Woolfolk, A. E., and Hoy, W. K.

Article: Prospective teachers' sense of efficacy and beliefs about control.

Journal: *Journal of Educational Psychology,* March 1990, *82*(3), 81–91.

Related Research: Gibson, S., & Dembo, M. (1984). Teacher efficacy: A construct validation. *Journal of Educational Psychology, 76,* 569–582.

■ ■ ■

5005

Test Name: TEACHER LOCUS OF CONTROL SCALE

Purpose: To measure teachers' tendencies to attribute student success and failure in the classroom to an internal or external locus of control.

Number of Items: 28

Format: Teachers react to classroom events by selecting either an internal or external locus of control attribute.

Reliability: Kuder-Richardson Formula 20 reliabilities were .81 and .71.

Validity: Correlations with other variables ranged from −.26 to .24.

Author: Parkay, F. W., et al.

Article: A study of the relationships among teacher efficacy, locus of control, and stress.

Journal: *Journal of Research and Development in Education,* Summer 1988, *21*(4), 13–22.

Related Research: Rose, J. S., & Medway, F. J. (1981). Measurement of teachers' beliefs in their control over student outcome. *Journal of Educational Research, 74,* 185–190.

■ ■ ■

5006

Test Name: TEACHER PUPIL SURVEY

Purpose: To measure how closely a child corresponds to the idealized perceptions of a teacher.

Number of Items: 31

Format: Eight-point Likert format.

Reliability: Interrater agreement was .75.

Author: Bender, W. N.

Article: Teachability and behavior of learning disabled children.

Journal: *Psychological Reports*, October 1986, *59*(2)I, 471–476.

Related Research: Kornblau, B. W. (1982). Teacher pupil survey: A technique for assessing teachers' perceptions of pupil attributes. *Psychology in the Schools, 19,* 170–174.

■ ■ ■

5007

Test Name: TEACHERS' BELIEFS ABOUT ADMINISTRATORS

Purpose: To appraise respondents' beliefs concerning administrators.

Number of Items: 12

Format: A sample item is presented.

Reliability: Cronbach's alpha was .92.

Validity: Correlations with other variables ranged from .29 to .56.

Author: Feldman, D., et al.

Article: Teachers' beliefs about administrators and parents of handicapped and nonhandicapped students.

Journal: *Journal of Experimental Education*, Fall 1989, *58*(1), 43–54.

Related Research: Feldman, D., & Gerstein, L. H. (1988). A factor analytic study of three teacher belief scales. *Measurement and Evaluation in Counseling and Development, 21,* 72–80.

■ ■ ■

5008

Test Name: TEACHER TOLERANCE SCALE

Purpose: To measure teachers' perceptions of students' tolerance for teachers.

Number of Items: 35

Format: Five-point Likert format.

Reliability: Cronbach's alpha ranged from .91 to .92 across two subscales.

Author: Cunningham, B., and Sugarwara, A.

Article: Preservice teacher's perceptions of childrens' problem behaviors.

Journal: *Journal of Educational Research*, September/October 1988, *82*(1), 34–39.

Related Research: Algozzine, B. (1987). The emotionally disturbed child: Disturbed or disturbing? *Journal of Abnormal Child Psychology, 5,* 205–211.

■ ■ ■

5009

Test Name: TEACHER WORK AUTONOMY SCALE

Purpose: To measure beliefs about teacher work autonomy.

Number of Items: 10

Format: Responses are made on 7-point bipolar scales. Examples are presented.

Reliability: Reliability coefficients ranged from .80 to .90.

Author: Okeafor, K. R., and Teddlie, C.

Article: Organizational factors related to administrators' confidence in teachers.

Journal: *Journal of Research and Development in Education*, Fall 1989, *23*(1), 28–36.

Related Research: Okeafor, K., et al. (1987). Toward an operational definition of the logic of confidence. *Journal of Experimental Education, 56,* 47–54.

■ ■ ■

5010

Test Name: TEXAS SOCIAL BEHAVIOR INVENTORY

Purpose: To assess student's self-esteem and competence in social situations.

Number of Items: 16

Format: Statements are rated on a 5-point scale from 1 (*not at all characteristic*) to 5 (*very much characteristic*).

Reliability: Coefficient alpha was .91.

Author: Ponzetti, J. J., Jr., and Cate, R. M.

Article: The relationship of personal attributes and friendship variables in predicting loneliness.

Journal: *Journal of College Student Development*, July 1988, *29*(4), 292–298.

Related Research: Spence, J., & Helmreich, R. (1978). *Masculinity and femininity*. Austin: University of Texas Press.

■ ■ ■

5011

Test Name: THE SELF-PERCEPTION OF ATTAINMENT SCALE

Purpose: To measure students' self-concepts of academic attainment.

Number of Items: 28

Format: Items are depictions of children ranked from best to poorest. Respondents are asked to rate themselves.

Reliability: Test–retest reliability (2 weeks) was .83.

Validity: Correlations between teachers' ratings and self-ratings ranged from .67 to .76. Correlation with the CAT was .36.

Author: Midkiff, R. M., et al.

Article: Role of self-concept of academic attainment in achievement-related behaviors.

Journal: *Psychological Reports*, February 1986, *58*(1), 151–158.

Related Research: Nicholls, J. G. (1979). Development of perception of own attainment and causal attribution for success and failure in reading. *Journal of Educational Psychology, 71,* 94–99.

5012

Test Name: TRAIT ASCRIPTION SCALE

Purpose: To provide a measure of location of identity.

Number of Items: 20

Format: Items are bipolar trait terms and a "depends on the situation" option for each of the items.

Reliability: Split-half reliability was .82.

Validity: Correlations with other variables ranged from –.08 to .12.

Author: Blustein, D. L.

Article: Social cognitive orientations and career development: A theoretical and empirical analysis.

Journal: *Journal of Vocational Behavior*, August 1987, *31*(1), 63–80.

Related Research: Nisbett, R. E., et al. (1973). Behavior as seen by the actor and as seen by the observer. *Journal of Personality and Social Psychology*, 27, 154–165.

■ ■ ■

5013

Test Name: UNEMPLOYMENT ATTRIBUTION SCALE

Purpose: To assess a subject's attributions for being unemployed.

Number of Items: 16

Format: Seven-point rating scales. All items presented.

Reliability: Internal reliabilities ranged from .65 to .73 across subscales.

Author: Feather, N. T., and O'Brien, G. E.

Article: A longitudinal study of the effects of employment and unemployment on school leaving.

Journal: *Journal of Occupational Psychology*, June 1986, *59*(2), 121–144.

Related Research: Feather, N. T. (1983). Caused attributions and

beliefs about work and unemployment among adolescents in state independent secondary schools. *Australian Journal of Psychology*, 35, 211–232.

■ ■ ■

5014

Test Name: UNIVERSAL FORCES SCALE

Purpose: To measure supernatural locus of control without reference to God as conceptualized by any particular religion.

Number of Items: 8

Format: Likert format. All items presented.

Reliability: Cronbach's alpha was .56.

Validity: Correlations with other locus of control measures ranged from –.10 to .60.

Author: Richards, D. G.

Article: A "Universal Forces" dimension of locusal control in a population of spiritual seekers.

Journal: *Psychological Reports*, December 1990, *67*(3, Part I), 847–850.

■ ■ ■

5015

Test Name: UNIVERSITY HOMOPHOBIA SCALE

Purpose: To measure the degree to which people perceive the environment to be homophobic.

Number of Items: 25

Format: Responses are graded on a scale from 1 to 100.

Reliability: Coefficient alpha was .90.

Author: Reynolds, A. J.

Article: Social environmental conceptions of male homosexual behavior: A university climate analysis.

Journal: *Journal of College Student Development*, January 1989, *30*(1), 62–69.

Related Research: Hudson, W. W., & Ricketts, W. A. (1980). A strategy for the measurement of homophobia. *Journal of Homosexuality*, 5, 357–372.

■ ■ ■

5016

Test Name: UNSUBSTANTIATED BELIEFS SCALE

Purpose: To measure belief in superstitions and other unsubstantiated "knowledge."

Number of Items: 30

Format: True–false responses. All items presented.

Validity: Sex differences are not significant, but differences by sex across time (1925–1983) are significant.

Author: Tupper, V., and Williams, R. J.

Article: Unsubstantiated beliefs and beginning psychology students: 1925, 1952, 1983.

Journal: *Psychological Reports*, April 1986, *58*(2), 383–388.

Related Research: Nixon, H. K. (1925). Popular answers to some psychological questions. *American Journal of Psychology*, 36, 418–423.

■ ■ ■

5017

Test Name: VACATION DISCREPANCY SCALE

Purpose: To measure pre–post discrepancy in vacation satisfaction.

Number of Items: 67

Format: Five-point responses. Sample items presented.

Reliability: Alphas ranged from .78 to .90.

Author: Lounsberry, J. W., and Franz, C. P. G.

Article: Vacation discrepancy: A leisure motivation approach.

Journal: *Psychological Reports*, April 1990, *66*(2), 699–700.

Related Research: Utecht, K. M., & Aldag, R. J. (1989). Vacation discrepancy: Correlates of individual differences and outcomes. *Psychological Reports*, *65*, 867–882.

■ ■ ■

5018

Test Name: VACATION DISCREPANCY INDICES

Purpose: To assess the gap between ideal and actual vacations.

Number of Items: 40

Format: 20 statement pairs (ideal vs. actual).

Reliability: Alphas ranged from .49 to .75 across five subscales.

Validity: Correlations with other variables ranged from −.33 to .33.

Author: Lounsberry, J. W., and Franz, C. P. G.

Article: Vacation discrepancy: A leisure motivation approach.

Journal: *Psychological Reports*, April 1990, *66*(2), 699–700.

■ ■ ■

5019

Test Name: VIVIDNESS OF MOVEMENT IMAGERY QUESTIONNAIRE

Purpose: To assess movement imagery.

Number of Items: 24

Format: Includes six groups of items: basic body movements, basic movement with more precision, movement with control but some unplanned risk, movement controlling an object, movement which causes imbalance and recovery, and movement demanding control in aerial situations. Subjects' vividness of imagery on a 5-point rating scale ranging from 5 (*no image at all, you only know that you are thinking of the skill*) to 1 (*perfectly clear and as vivid as normal vision*).

Validity: Correlations with other variables ranged from −.65 to .60.

Author: Campos, A., and Perez, M. J.

Article: Vividness of Movement Imagery Questionnaire: Relations with other measures of mental imagery.

Journal: *Perceptual and Motor Skills*, October 1988, *67*(2), 607–610.

Related Research: Isaac, A., et al. (1986). An instrument for assessing imagery of movement: The Vividness of Movement Imagery Questionnaire. *Journal of Mental Imagery*, *10*, 23–30.

■ ■ ■

5020

Test Name: WOMEN AS PROFESSORS SCALE

Purpose: To assess stereotypes toward women as professors.

Number of Items: 21

Format: Responses are made on a 7-point scale ranging from 1 (*strongly disagree*) to 7 (*strongly agree*).

Reliability: Alpha coefficients were .92 and .94.

Validity: Correlation with sex of the rater was −.35. Correlations with performance ratings ranged from −.35 to .39 (men) (*N*s ranged from 16 to 103) and from −.27 to .65 (women) (*N*s ranged from 18 to 147).

Author: Dobbins, G. H., et al.

Article: The effects of purpose of appraisal and individual differences in stereotypes of women on sex differences in performance ratings: A laboratory and field study.

Journal: *Journal of Applied Psychology*, August 1988, *73*(3), 551–558.

■ ■ ■

5021

Test Name: WORK LOCUS OF CONTROL SCALE

Purpose: To measure locus of control at work.

Number of Items: 16

Format: Likert format. Sample itmes presented.

Reliability: Aphas was .80.

Validity: Correlations with other variables ranged from .11 to .17.

Author: Storms, P. L., and Spector, P. E.

Article: Relationships of organizational frustration with reported behavioral reactions: The moderating effect of locus of control.

Journal: *Journal of Occupational Psychology*, September 1987, *60*(3), 227–234.

Related Research: Spector, P. E. (1984). *Development of the work locus of control scale.* Unpublished manuscript. Tampa: University of South Florida.
Spector, P. E. (1988). Development of the work locus of control scale. *Journal of Occupational Psychology*, *61*, 335–340.

CHAPTER 17
Personality

5022

Test Name: ADAPTED SHAME AND GUILT SCALE

Purpose: To measure shame and guilt proneness.

Number of Items: 24

Format: Includes two factors: shame and guilt.

Reliability: Cronbach's alpha was .83 for shame and .89 for guilt. Test–retest (2 weeks) reliability was .93 for shame and .95 for guilt ($N = 27$).

Validity: Correlations with other variables ranged from –.48 to .46 for shame ($N = 63$) and from –.30 to .43 for guilt ($N = 63$).

Author: Harder, D. H., and Zalma, A.

Article: Two promising shame and guilt scales: A construct validity comparison.

Journal: *Journal of Personality Assessment*, Winter 1990, *55*(3 & 4), 729–745.

Related Research: Hoblitzelle, W. (1982). *Developing a measure of shame and guilt and the role of shame in depression.* Unpublished predissertation, Yale University, New Haven, CT.

■ ■ ■

5023

Test Name: ADJECTIVE RATINGS FORM

Purpose: To measure personality characteristics attributed to children by children.

Number of Items: 17

Format: Likert format. All items presented.

Reliability: Alpha was .94.

Validity: Correlation with positive general impressions scale was .47.

Author: Wheeler, P. T., et al.

Article: Effect of a child's physical attractiveness on verbal scoring of the Wechsler Intelligence Scale for Children (Revised) and personality attributions.

Journal: *Journal of General Psychology*, April 1987, *114*(2), 109–116.

Related Research: Anderson, N. H. (1968). Likableness ratings of 555 personality trait words. *Journal of Personality and Social Psychology*, 9, 272–279.

■ ■ ■

5024

Test Name: AFFECT INTENSITY MEASURE

Purpose: To measure intensity of positive and negative emotions.

Number of Items: 40

Format: Agree–disagree format. Sample items presented.

Validity: Correlations with self-consciousness ranged from –.05 to .33 in male and female samples.

Author: Flett, G. L., et al.

Article: Affect intensity and self-consciousness in college students.

Journal: *Psychological Reports*, February 1986, *58*(1), 148–150.

Related Research: Larsen, R. J., & Diener, E. (1985). A multitrait-

multimethod examination of affect structure: hedonic level and emotional intensity. *Personality and Individual Differences*, 6, 631–636.

■ ■ ■

5025

Test Name: ASCRIPTION OF RESPONSIBILITY QUESTIONNAIRE

Purpose: To measure willingness to ascribe specific responsibility.

Number of Items: 40

Format: Includes four factors: traditional focused responsibility, diffuse responsibility, exercised responsibility, and individual focused responsibility. Items are presented.

Reliability: Coefficient alpha ranged from .56 to .76 ($Ns = 251$ to 403).

Validity: Correlations with other variables ranged from –.31 to .59 ($Ns = 58$ to 251).

Author: Hakstian, A. R., et al.

Article: The Ascription of Responsibility Questionnaire: Development and empirical extensions.

Journal: *Journal of Personality Assessment*, Summer 1986, *50*(2), 229–246.

■ ■ ■

5026

Test Name: BIOGRAPHICAL QUESTIONNAIRE

Purpose: To measure adolescent general life experiences.

Number of Items: 118

Format: Includes questions about: Parental and sibling relationships, socioeconomic status, religious activities, athletic interests, scientific interests and activities, and a range of other feelings, activities, and interests.

Reliability: Factors produced reliability coefficients above .75.

Author: Shaffer, G. S.

Article: Patterns of work and nonwork satisfaction.

Journal: *Journal of Applied Psychology*, February 1987, 72(1), 115–124.

Related Research: Owens, W. A., & Schoenfeldt, L. F. (1979). Toward a classification of persons. *Journal of Applied Psychology, 64*, 569–597.

■ ■ ■

5027

Test Name: BRAND EMOTIONS SCALE FOR WRITERS

Purpose: To measure emotions involved in writing.

Number of Items: 20

Format: Varied formats measure emotion traits and emotion states.

Reliability: Split-half reliability ranged from .70 into .87 across subscales.

Author: Brand, A. G., and Powell, J. L.

Article: Emotions and the writing process: A description of apprentice writers.

Journal: *Journal of Educational Research*, May/June 1986, 79(5), 280–285.

Related Research: Brand, A. G. (1984, Fall). *Emotions and the writing process: Developing a research methodology*. Temple University working papers in composition. Philadelphia, PA: Temple University.

5028

Test Name: CHILDREN'S PERSONAL ATTRIBUTES QUESTIONNAIRE—SHORT FORM

Purpose: To measure masculine, feminine, and gender-neutral personality characteristics.

Number of Items: 21

Format: Children respond to each item on a 5-point scale ranging from *never* to *always*. Examples are presented.

Validity: Correlations with parents' ratings were .25 and .32.

Author: Mitchell, J. E., et al.

Article: Masculinity and femininity in twin children: Genetic and environmental factors.

Journal: *Child Development*, December 1989, 60(6), 1475–1485.

Related Research: Hall, J. A., & Halberstadt, A. G. (1980). Masculinity and femininity in children: Development of the Children's Personal Attributes Questionnaire. *Developmental Psychology, 16*, 270–280.

■ ■ ■

5029

Test Name: COGNITIVE ERROR QUESTIONNAIRE

Purpose: To measure catastrophizing, overgeneralization, personalization, and selective abstraction.

Number of Items: 24

Format: Five-point rating scales. Sample item presented.

Reliability: Parallel form correlations have ranged from .87 to .88.

Author: Scogin, F., et al.

Article: Validity of the Cognitive Error Questionnaire with depressed and nondepressed older adults.

Journal: *Psychological Reports*, August 1986, 59(1), 267–272.

Related Research: Lefebvre, M. F. (1981). Cognitive distortion and cognitive errors in depressed psychiatric and low back pain patients. *Journal of Consulting and Clinical Psychology, 49*, 517–525.

■ ■ ■

5030

Test Name: CYNICAL DISTRUST SCALE

Purpose: To measure cynical distrust as a type of hostility.

Number of Items: 9

Format: Five-point Likert format. All items presented.

Validity: Correlations with other variables ranged from −.32 to .77.

Author: Greenglass, E. R., and Julkunen, J.

Article: Cook-Medley hostility, anger and the Type A behavior pattern in Finland.

Journal: *Psychological Reports*, December 1990, 67(3) II, 1059–1066.

Related Research: Cook, W. W., & Medley, D. M. (1954). Proposed hostility and pharisaic-virtue scales for the MMPI. *Journal of Applied Psychology, 38*, 414–418.

■ ■ ■

5031

Test Name: DEFENSIVENESS SCALE FOR CHILDREN

Purpose: To measure children's defensiveness.

Number of Items: 40

Format: The questions ask children whether they experience common anxieties, vulnerabilities, and dependency. Examples are presented.

Reliability: Internal consistency coefficient was .82.

Validity: Correlations with other variables ranged from −.36 to .32.

Author: Wapner, J. G., and Connor, K.

Article: The role of defensiveness in cognitive impulsivity.

Journal: *Child Development*, December 1986, *57*(6), 1370–1374.

Related Research: Ruebush, B. K., & Waite, R. R. (1961). Oral dependency in anxious and defensive children. *Merrill-Plamer Quarterly*, 7, 181–190.

■ ■ ■

5032

Test Name: DIFFERENTIAL EMOTIONS SCALE

Purpose: To identify intensity of feelings.

Number of Items: 64

Format: Includes three scores: positive emotions, negative emotions, and denied emotions. Intensity of feelings are recorded on a 5-point scale.

Validity: Correlations with the Levels of Emotional Awareness Scale ranged from −.27 to .08.

Author: Lane, R. D., et al.

Article: The Levels of Emotional Awareness Scale: A cognitive-developmental measure of emotion.

Journal: *Journal of Personality Assessment*, Fall 1990, *55*(1 and 2), 124–134.

Related Research: Izard, C. E. (1972). *Patterns of emotions*. New York: Academic.

■ ■ ■

5033

Test Name: DIFFERENTIAL EMOTIONS SCALE

Purpose: To measure interest, enjoyment, surprise, distress, anger, disgust, fear, guilt, contempt and shame.

Number of Items: 60

Format: Five-point Likert format.

Reliability: Alphas ranged from .72 to .93.

Author: Mosher, D. L., and Anderson, R. D.

Article: Macho personality, sexual aggression, and reactions to guided imagery of rape.

Journal: *Journal of Research in Personality*, March 1986, *20*(1), 77–94.

Related Research: Mosher, D. L., & White, B. B. (1981). On differentiating shame from shyness. *Motivation and Emotion*, 5, 61–74.

■ ■ ■

5034

Test Name: DIMENSIONS OF TEMPERAMENT SURVEY

Purpose: To measure activity level, approach-withdrawal, flexibility-rigidity, mood, distractibility, and persistence.

Number of Items: 34

Format: Four-point true–false format.

Reliability: Alphas ranged from .74 to .89. Test–retest (10 weeks) ranged from .59 to .75.

Author: Windle, M.

Article: Predicting temperament-mental health relationships: A covariance structure latent variable analysis.

Journal: *Journal of Research in Personality*, March 1989, *23*(1), 118–144.

Related Research: Windle, M., & Lerner, R. M. (1986). Reassessing the dimensions of temperamental individuality across the life span: The revised dimensions of temperament survey (DOTS-R). *Journal of Adolescent Research*, *1*, 213–230.

■ ■ ■

5035

Test Name: DIMENSIONS OF TEMPERAMENT SURVEY— REVISED

Purpose: To assess dimensions of temperament.

Number of Items: 54

Format: Responses are on a 4-point scale ranging from 1 (*usually false*) to 4 (*usually true*). Included 10 factors: activity level—general; activity level—sleep; approach—withdrawal; flexibility—rigidity; quality of mood; rhythmicity—sleep; rhythmicity—eating; rhythmicity—daily habits; distractibility; and persistence.

Reliability: Alpha coefficients ranged from .62 to .75 (*N* = 300). Test–retest (6 weeks) correlations ranged from .59 to .75 (*N* = 179).

Author: Windle, M.

Article: Temperament and personality: An interinventory study of the DOTS-R, EASI-II, and EPI.

Journal: *Journal of Personality Assessment*, Fall 1989, *53*(3), 487–501.

Related Research: Windle, M., & Lerner, R. M. (1986). Reassessing the dimensions of temperamental individuality across the life span: The revised dimensions of temperament survey (DOTS-R). *Journal of Adolescent Research*, *1*, 213–230.

■ ■ ■

5036

Test Name: DOT ESTIMATION TASK

Purpose: To measure compulsiveness versus decisiveness.

Number of Items: 50

Time Required: 6 minutes.

Format: Subjects determine on each trial which of two fields presented on a CRT screen contains one more dot than the other.

Reliability: Test–retest reliabilities were .46 and .64 (*N* = 90).

Author: Lambirth, T. T., et al.

Article: Use of behavior-based personality instrument in aviation selection.

Journal: *Educational and Psychological Measurement*, Winter 1986, *46*(4), 973–978.

Related Research: Mullins, C. (1962). *Two measures of decisiveness.* Technical Memorandum PR-TM-62–5, Personnel Research Laboratory, Lackland Air Force Base, San Antonio, Texas.

■ ■ ■

5037

Test Name: DREAM EXTRAVERSION SCALE

Purpose: To measure content of dreams by using revised items from the Eysenck Extraversion Scale.

Number of Items: 12

Format: Yes–no.

Reliability: Interjudge agreement was .72 on one dream.

Validity: Correlation between dream extraversion and Eysenck scores was −.29 for subjects scoring low on neuroticism.

Author: Samson, H., and DeKoninck, J.

Article: Continuity or compensation between waking and dreaming: An exploration using the Eysenck Personality Inventory.

Journal: *Psychological Reports*, June 1986, *58*(3), 871–874.

■ ■ ■

5038

Test Name: EASI-III

Purpose: To measure four temperaments.

Number of Items: 51

Format: Includes the temperaments of: emotionality, activity, sociability, and impulsiveness each with one or more sub-factors. Responses to each item are either *true* or *false*.

Validity: Correlations with other variables ranged from −.66 to .48.

Author: Sipps, G. J., and DiCaudo, J.

Article: Convergent and discriminant validity of the Myers-Briggs Type Indicator as a measure of sociability and impulsivity.

Journal: *Educational and Psychological Measurement*, Summer 1988, *48*(2), 445–451.

Related Research: Buss, A. H., & Plomin, R. (1975). *A temperament theory of personality development.* New York: Wiley.

■ ■ ■

5039

Test Name: EAS TEMPERAMENT SURVEY

Purpose: To assess maternal perceptions of the child's temperament.

Number of Items: 20

Format: Responses are made on a 5-point scale ranging from *not characteristic* to *very characteristic.*

Reliability: Test–retest reliabilities ranged from .58 to .80.

Author: Cohn, D. A.

Article: Child–mother attachment of six-year-olds and social competence at school.

Journal: *Child Development*, February 1990, *61*(1), 152–162.

Related Research: Buss, A. D., & Plomin, R. (1984). *Temperament: Early developing personality traits.* Hillsdale, New Jersey: Erlbaum.

■ ■ ■

5040

Test Name: EGO IDENTITY SCALE

Purpose: To measure identity.

Number of Items: 72

Format: Includes six subscales. Each statement is answered either by *agree* or by *disagree.*

Reliability: Reliability estimated by the Spearman-Brown prophecy formula was .85.

Validity: Correlations with other variables ranged from −.10 to .29.

Author: Larkin, L.

Article: Identity and fear of success.

Journal: *Journal of Applied Psychology*, January 1987, *34*(1), 38–45.

Related Research: Rasmussen, J. E. (1964). Relationship of ego identity to psychological effectiveness. *Psychological Reports, 15*, 815–825.

■ ■ ■

5041

Test Name: EGO IDENTITY SCALE

Purpose: To measure ego identity.

Number of Items: 12

Format: Items are paired. Examples are presented.

Reliability: Odd-even, split-half reliability was .68.

Validity: Correlations with other variables ranged from −.22 to −.39.

Author: Sperling, M. B.

Article: Ego identity and desperate love.

Journal: *Journal of Personality Assessment*, Winter 1987, *51*(4), 600–605.

Related Research: Tan, A. L., et al. (1977). A short measure of Eriksonian ego identity. *Journal of Personality Assessment, 41*, 279–284.

■ ■ ■

5042

Test Name: EMOTION ASSESSMENT SCALE

Purpose: To measure emotional reactivity.

Number of Items: 24

Format: Includes eight emotion categories: anger, anxiety, disgust, fear, guilt, happiness, sadness, and surprise. For each item subjects place a mark on a 10–cm visual analogue scale ranging from least possible to most possible. All items are presented.

Reliability: Internal reliability coefficients ranged from .70 to .91. Split-half reliability was .94.

Validity: Correlations with other variables ranged from −.42 to .69.

Author: Carlson, C. R., et al.

Article: The assessment of emotional reactivity: A scale development and validation study.

Journal: *Journal of Psychopathology and Behavioral Assessment*, December 1989, *11*(4), 313–325.

Related Research: Izard, C. (1977). *Human Emotions*. New York: Plenum.

■ ■ ■

5043

Test Name: ERWIN IDENTITY SCALE

Purpose: To measure Chickering's vector identity.

Number of Items: 58

Format: Response to each item is made on a 5-point scale from 1 (*very true of me*) to 5 (*not at all true of me*). Includes three subscales: confidence, sexual identity, and conceptions about body and appearance.

Reliability: Cronbach's alpha ranged from .75 to .85.

Validity: Correlations with other variables ranged from −.14 to .39.

Author: Hood, A. B., et al.

Article: Changes in ego identity during the college years.

Journal: *Journal of College Student Personnel*, March 1986, *27*(2), 107–113.

Related Research: Erwin, T. D. (1979). The validation of the Erwin Identity Scale (Doctoral dissertation, The University of Iowa, 1978). *Dissertation Abstracts International*, *39*, 4818A.

■ ■ ■

5044

Test Name: EXPERIENCE QUESTIONNAIRE

Purpose: To measure self-reported experiential data.

Number of Items: 47

Format: Likert-scale responses are made to each item. All items are presented in abbreviated form.

Reliability: Over-all reliability is reported to be "something above .70."

Author: Privett, G., and Bundrick, C. M.

Article: Measurement of experience: Construct and content validity of the Experience Questionnaire.

Journal: *Perceptual and Motor Skills*, August 1987, *65*(1), 315–332.

Related Research: Privette, G. (1984). *Experience Questionnaire*. Pensacola, FL: The University of West Florida.

■ ■ ■

5045

Test Name: EXPRESSED EMOTION QUESTIONNAIRE

Purpose: To measure expressed emotion.

Number of Items: 99

Format: Four-point frequency rating scales. Sample items presented.

Reliability: Mean-item total correlation was .52. Alphas ranged from .90 to .96 across subscales.

Validity: Correlations with other variables ranged from .43 to .66.

Author: Docherty, N. M., et al.

Article: Development and preliminary validation of a questionnaire assessment of expressed emotion.

Journal: *Psychological Reports*, August 1990, *67*(1), 279–287.

■ ■ ■

5046

Test Name: EXTENDED OBJECTIVE MEASURE OF EGO IDENTITY STATUS

Purpose: To assess the relative degree of prevalence of each of the four ego-identity statuses.

Number of Items: 64

Format: Includes four subscales, each to measure one ego identity status: diffusion, foreclosure, moratorium, and identity achievement. A 6-point Likert response format was used.

Reliability: Alpha coefficients ranged from .66 to .90. Test–retest (2 weeks) correlation coefficients ranged from .82 to .90.

Validity: Correlations with other variables ranged from −.39 to .41.

Author: Blustein, D. L., and Phillips, S. D.

Article: Relation between ego identity statuses and decision-making styles.

Journal: *Journal of Counseling Psychology*, April 1990, *37*(2), 160–168.

Related Research: Bennion, L. D., and Adams, G. R. (1986). A revision of the Extended Version of the Objective Measure of Ego Identity Status: An identity instrument for use with late adolescents. *Journal of Adolescent Research*, *1*, 183–198.

■ ■ ■

5047

Test Name: EXTENDED PERSONAL ATTRIBUTES QUESTIONNAIRE

Purpose: To assess subject gender traits.

Number of Items: 40

Format: Includes six scales employing a 5-point Likert format.

Reliability: Reliability coefficients for two scales ranged from .72 to .76.

Author: Sipps, G. J., and Janeczek, R. G.

Article: Expectancies for counselors in relation to subject gender traits.

Journal: *Journal of Counseling Psychology*, April 1986, *33*(2), 214–216.

Related Research: Spence, J. T., & Helmreich, R. (1979). *Personal Attributes Questionnaire*. Unpublished manuscript. University of Texas at Austin, Department of Psychology.

■ ■ ■

5048

Test Name: FORCED-CHOICE GUILT INVENTORY

Purpose: To measure the generalized expectancy for self-mediated punishment in the face of transgressions.

Number of Items: 17

Format: Forced-choice format.

Reliability: Alpha was .76.

Author: Corcoran, K. J., and Rotler, J. B.

Article: Morality-conscience guilt scale as a predictor of ethical behavior in a cheating situation among college females.

Journal: *Journal of General Psychology*, April 1987, *114*(2), 117–123.

Related Research: Mosher, D. L. (1968). Measurement of guilt in females by self-report inventories. *Journal of Consulting and Clinical Psychology*, *32*, 690–695.

■ ■ ■

5049

Test Name: GENERAL TRUST SCALE

Purpose: To measure general trust.

Number of Items: 8

Format: Five-point Likert format. All items presented.

Reliability: Alpha was .77.

Author: Yamagishi, T.

Article: The provision of a sanctioning system in the United States and Japan.

Journal: *Social Psychology Quarterly*, September 1988, *51*(3), 173–189.

Related Research: Yamagishi, T., & Sato, K. (1986). Motivational basis of

the public goods problem. *Journal of Personality and Social Psychology*, *50*, 67–73.

■ ■ ■

5050

Test Name: HARDINESS SCALE

Purpose: To assess personality hardiness.

Number of Items: 20

Reliability: Coefficient alpha was .71. Test–retest reliability was .73.

Validity: Correlations with other variables ranged from –.39 to .45.

Author: Barling, J., et al.

Article: Psychological functioning following an acute disaster.

Journal: *Journal of Applied Psychology*, November, 1987, *72*(4), 683–690

Related Research: Barling, J. (1986). Interrole conflict and marital functioning amongst employed fathers. *Journal of Occupational Behavior*, *7*, 1–8.

■ ■ ■

5051

Test Name: INDEX OF EMPATHY

Purpose: To measure the vicarious emotional response to the perceived emotional experience of others.

Number of Items: 22

Format: Responses are yes–no. An example is presented.

Reliability: Test–retest reliability was .83 (seventh graders).

Validity: Convergent validity was .76 with the Fleshbach and Roe measure of empathy. Correlations with other variables ranged from –.33 to .44.

Author: Chalmers, J. B., and Townsend, M. A. R.

Article: The effects of training in social perspective taking on socially maladjusted girls.

Journal: *Child Development*, February 1990, *61*(1), 178–190.

Related Research: Bryant, B. K. (1982). An index of empathy for children and adolescents. *Child Development*, *53*, 413–425.

■ ■ ■

5052

Test Name: INFANT BEHAVIOR QUESTIONNAIRE

Purpose: To assess temperament.

Number of Items: 87

Format: Includes six dimensions: activity level; positive emotionality; fear; anger/ frustration; soothability; and undisturbed persistence.

Reliability: Internal reliability coefficients ranged from .72 to .82 (*N* = 463).

Author: Broberg, A., et al.

Article: Inhibition: Its stability and correlates in sixteen- to forty-month-old children.

Journal: *Child Development*, August 1990, *61*(4), 1153–1163.

Related Research: Rothbart, M. K. (1981). Measurement of temperament in infancy. *Child Development*, *52*, 569–578.

■ ■ ■

5053

Test Name: INFANT TEMPERAMENT QUESTIONNAIRE

Purpose: To assess perception of infant temperament.

Format: Responses are made on a 6-point scale.

Reliability: Test–retest (2 weeks) reliability was .84.

Validity: Correlated with mothers' general evaluations of their infants' difficulty was .52.

Author: Donovan, W. L., et al.

Article: Maternal self-efficacy: Illusory control and its effect on susceptibility to learned helplessness.

Journal: *Child Development*, October 1990, *61*(5), 1638–1647.

Related Research: Carey, W. B., & McDevitt, S. C. (1978). Revision of the infant temperament questionnaire. *Journal of Pediatrics, 61*, 735–739.

■ ■ ■

5054

Test Name: LEVELS OF EMOTIONAL AWARENESS SCALE

Purpose: To measure emotional structure.

Number of Items: 20

Format: Each item is a scene. They are constructed to elicit four types of emotion (anger, fear, happiness, and sadness) at five levels of increasing complexity. An example is presented.

Reliability: Interrater reliability was .84. Cronbach's alpha was .81 ($N = 35$).

Validity: Correlations with other variables ranged from −.27 to .40.

Author: Lane, R. D., et al.

Article: The Levels of Emotional Awareness Scale: A cognitive-developmental measure of emotion.

Journal: *Journal of Personality Assessment*, Fall 1990, *55*(1 and 2), 124–134.

■ ■ ■

5055

Test Name: MEASURES OF TEMPERAMENT

Purpose: To assess temperament.

Number of Items: 98

Format: Includes three dimensions: a semantic differential measure of trait pleasure-displeasure, a questionnaire measure of trait arousability, and a questionnaire measure of trait dominance-submissiveness. Examples are given.

Validity: Correlations with measures of eating-related characteristics ranged from −.18 to .28.

Author: Mehrabian, A., and Riccioni, M.

Article: Measures of eating-related characteristics for the general population. Relationships with temperament.

Journal: *Journal of Personality Assessment*, Winter 1986, *50*(4), 610–629.

Related Research: Mehrabian, A. (1978). Measures of individual differences in temperament. *Educational and Psychological Measurement, 38*, 1105–1117. Mehrabian, A. (1977). Individual differences in stimulus screening and arousability. *Journal of Personality, 45*, 237–250.

■ ■ ■

5056

Test Name: MULTIDIMENSIONAL PERSONALITY QUESTIONNAIRE

Purpose: To measure eleven personality traits: well-being, social potency, achievement, social closeness, stress reaction, alienation, aggression, control, harm avoidance, traditionalism, and absorption.

Number of Items: 300

Format: True–false format.

Reliability: Internal consistency ranged from .80 to .92.

Author: Almagor, M., and Ehrlich, S.

Article: Personality correlates and cyclicity in positive and negative affect.

Journal: *Psychological Reports*, June 1990, *66*(3, Part II), 1159–1169.

Related Research: Tellegen, A. (1982). *Multidimensional Personality Questionnaire.* (Unpublished manual, University of Minnesota)

■ ■ ■

5057

Test Name: MULTIDIMENSIONAL PERSONALITY QUESTIONNAIRE

Purpose: To measure personality.

Number of Items: 247

Format: Includes 11 primary scales. Responses to each statement are either *true* or *false*. Sample items are presented.

Reliability: Internal consistency ranged from .77 to .89.

Author: George, J. M.

Article: Personality, affect, and behavior in groups.

Journal: *Journal of Applied Psychology*, April 1990, *75*(2), 107–116.

Related Research: Tellegen, A. (1985). Structure of mood and personality and their relevance to assessing anxiety, with an emphasis on self-report. In A. H. Tuma and J. D. Maser (Eds.), Anxiety and the anxiety disorders (pp. 681–706). Hillsdale, N.J.: Erlbaum.

■ ■ ■

5058

Test Name: OBJECTIVISM SCALE

Purpose: To measure individual differences in objectivism.

Number of Items: 11

Format: Responses to each item are made on a 5-point scale from *not at all* to *extremely characteristic of me.*

Reliability: Alpha was .83 ($N = 60$).

Validity: Correlations with other variables ranged from −.41 to .47.

Author: Leary, M. R., et al.

Article: Objectivism in information utilization: Theory and measurement.

Journal: *Journal of Personality Assessment*, Spring 1986, *50*(1), 32–43.

■ ■ ■

5059

Test Name: PERSISTENCE SCALE FOR CHILDREN

Purpose: To measure persistence in children.

Number of Items: 40

Format: Response to each item is either *yes* or *no.* All items are presented.

Reliability: Cronbach's alpha was .66. Test–retest reliability (6 months) was .77.

Author: Lufi, D., and Cohen, A.

Article: A scale for measuring persistence in children.

Journal: *Journal of Personality Assessment*, Summer 1987, *51*(2), 178–185.

Related Research: Lufi, D. (1979). Development of scale for determining persistency in academic field (Doctoral dissertation, Washington State University). *Dissertation Abstracts International*, *40*, 2019–A.

■ ■ ■

5060

Test Name: PERSONAL ATTRIBUTES QUESTIONNAIRE

Purpose: To measure personal attributes including sex-role status, hand preference, and age.

Number of Items: 33

Format: Bipolar scales were used for the sex-role status items.

Validity: Correlations with book-carrying styles ranged from –.81 to .49.

Author: Alley, T. R., and Kolker, J. I.

Article: Psychological gender, hand preferences, and sex differences in book-carrying styles.

Journal: *Perceptual and Motor Skills*, June 1988, *66*(3), 815–822.

Related Research: Spence, J. T., & Helmreich, R. L. (1978). *Masculinity and femininity: Their psychological dimensions, correlates, and antecedents*. Austin, TX: University of Texas.

■ ■ ■

5061

Test Name: PERSONAL FEELINGS QUESTIONNAIRE—2

Purpose: To measure shame and guilt proneness.

Number of Items: 16

Format: Includes two subscales: shame and guilt. Responses are made on a 4-point scale ranging from *you never experience the feeling* to *you experience the feeling continuously or almost continuously.* All items are presented.

Reliability: Alpha coefficients were .78 (shame) and .72 (guilt). Test–retest (2 weeks) reliability coefficients were .91 (shame) and .85 (guilt).

Validity: Correlations with other variables ranged form –.25 to .46.

Author: Harder, D. H., and Zalma, A.

Article: Two promising shame and guilt scales: A construct validity comparison.

Journal: *Journal of Personality Assessment*, Winter 1990, *55*(3 & 4), 729–745.

Related Research: Harder, D. W., & Lewis, S. J. (1987). The assessment of shame and guilt. In J. N. Butcher & C. D. Spielberger (Eds.), *Advances in personality assessment* (Vol. 6, pp. 89–114). Hillsdale, NJ: Erlbaum.

■ ■ ■

5062

Test Name: PERSONALITY DISORDER EXAMINATION

Purpose: To assess the 12 DSM-III-R personality disorders.

Number of Items: 249

Format: Items are rated as either clinically significant, present but of uncertain clinical significance, or absent.

Reliability: Interrater reliability provided kappa coefficients which ranged from .70 to .96.

Author: Schmidt, N. B., and Telch, M. J.

Article: Prevalence of personality disorders among bulimics,

nonbulimic binge eaters, and normal controls.

Journal: *Journal of Psychopathology and Behavioral Assessment*, June 1990, *12*(2), 169–185.

Related Research: Loranger, A. W., et al. (1986). *Personality Disorder Examination.* Unpublished manuscript (May 1985 version).

■ ■ ■

5063

Test Name: PERSONALITY PRIORITIES INVENTORY FOR ADOLESCENTS

Purpose: To assess the personality priorities of adolescents.

Number of Items: 50

Format: Includes four factors: pleasing, significance, detaching, and avoiding.

Reliability: Coefficient alphas ranged from .68 to .85. Test–retest reliability ranged from .75 to .86.

Author: DeLaet, T. J., and Wise, S. L.

Article: The development and validation of the Personality Priorities Inventory for Adolescents.

Journal: *Educational and Psychological Measurement*, Summer 1986, *46*(2), 455–459.

Related Research: Langenfeld, S. D., & Main, F. O. (1983). Personality priorities: A factor analytic study. *Individual Personality*, *39*, 40–51.

■ ■ ■

5064

Test Name: PERSONALITY TRAIT RATING SCALE

Purpose: To assess general traits such as happiness and anxiety.

Number of Items: 10

Format: Nine-point rating scales.

Reliability: Test–retest ranged from .87 to .88.

Author: Goldstein-Hendley, S., and Green, S.

Article: Effects of teachers' marital status and child's family's marital status on teacher's rating of a child.

Journal: *Psychological Reports*, June 1986, *58*(3), 959–964.

Related Research: Santrock, J. W., & Tracy, R. L. (1978). Effects of children's family structure status on the development of stereotypes by teachers. *Journal of Educational Psychology*, *70*, 754–757.

■ ■ ■

5065

Test Name: PERSONAL RESPONSIBILITY SCALE

Purpose: To measure personal responsibility in a wide range of concrete situations.

Number of Items: 30

Format: Subjects indicate on a 5-point scale how frequently they engage in each activity. All items are presented.

Reliability: Split-half corrected reliability was .83. Test–retest (1 week) reliability was .79.

Validity: Correlations with other variables ranged from –.24 to .38.

Author: Martel, J., et al.

Article: Validity of an intuitive personality scale: Personal responsibility as a predictor of academic achievement

Journal: *Educational and Psychological Measurement*, Winter 1987, *47*(4), 1153–1163.

■ ■ ■

5066

Test Name: PERSON PERCEPTION QUESTIONNAIRE

Purpose: To assess six personal dimensions: adjustment, competence, likability, roll-over load, masculinity, and femininity.

Number of Items: 42

Format: Semantic differential format.

Reliability: Alphas ranged from .81 to .88.

Author: Jackson, L. A., and Sullivan, L. A.

Article: Perceptions of multiple role participants.

Journal: *Social Psychology Quarterly*, September 1990, *53*(3), 274–282.

Related Research: Jackson, L. A., & Cash, T. F. (1984). Components of gender-stereotypes and their implications for stereotyped and nonstereotyped inferences. *Personality and Social Psychology Bulletin*, *11*, 326–344.

■ ■ ■

5067

Test Name: PROCESS OF CHANGE QUESTIONNAIRE

Purpose: To measure processes of change including: consciousness raising, dramatic relief, self-liberation, social liberation, counter conditioning, stimulus control, self-reevaluation, environmental reevaluation, reinforcement management, and helping relationship.

Number of Items: 40

Format: Five-point Likert, frequency of occurrence scales. All items presented.

Reliability: Alphas ranged from .69 to .92.

Validity: Convergent validity ranged from .34 to .72.

Author: Prochaska, J. O., et al.

Article: Measuring processes of change: Applications to the cessation of smoking.

Journal: *Journal of Consulting and Clinical Psychology*, August 1988, *56*(4), 520–528.

■ ■ ■

5068

Test Name: PURPOSE-IN-LIFE TEST (FOR THE ELDERLY)

Purpose: To assess meaningful life experiences (making sense out of component parts of one's existence).

Number of Items: 7

Format: Checklist/rating scale format.

Validity: No relationships were found between age or sex and current purpose. Most meaningful events occur in the first half of life.

AUTHOR: Baum, S. K.

ARITICLE: Meaningful life experiences for elderly persons.

JOURNAL: *Psychological Reports*, October 1988, *63*(2), 427–433.

Related Research: Chang, R., & Dodder, R. (1984). The modified Purpose in Life Scale: A cross-national validity study. *International Journal of Aging and Human Development*, *18*, 207–217. Yarnell, T. (1971). Purpose in Life Test: Further correlates. *Journal of Individual Psychology*, *27*, 36–39.

■ ■ ■

5069

Test Name: REVISED INFANT TEMPERAMENT QUESTIONNAIRE

Purpose: To assess mothers' perceptions of their infants' temperamental difficulty.

Number of Items: 95

Format: Mothers rate each item on a 6-point scale from 1 (*almost never*) to 6 (*almost always*) to indicate the behavior frequency of her child.

Reliability: Test–retest (2 weeks) reliability ranged from .72 to .93.

Author: Cutrona, C. E., and Troutman, B. R.

Article: Social support, infant temperament, and parenting self-efficacy: A mediational model of postpartum depression.

Journal: *Child Development*, December 1986, *57*(6), 1507–1518.

Related Research: Carey, W. B., & McDevitt, S. C. (1978). Revision of the Infant Temperament Questionnaire. *Pediatrics*, *61*, 735–739.

. . .

5070

Test Name: SELF-CONSCIOUSNESS SCALE

Purpose: To measure self-consciousness.

Number of Items: 27

Format: Includes three subscales: private self-consciousness, public self-consciousness, and social anxiety.

Reliability: Test–retest reliabilities ranged from .73 to .84.

Validity: Correlations with the Dating Anxiety Survey ranged from .04 to .36.

Author: Calvert, J. D., et al.

Article: Psychometric evaluation of the Dating Anxiety Survey: A self-report questionnaire for the assessment of dating anxiety in males and females.

Journal: *Journal of Psychopathology and Behavioral Assessment*, September 1987, *9*(3), 341–350.

Related Research: Fenigstein, A., et al. (1975). Public and private self-consciousness: Assessment and theory. *Journal of Consulting and Clinical Psychology*, *43*, 522–527.

. . .

5071

Test Name: SELF-DECEPTION AND IMPRESSION MANAGEMENT SCALES

Purpose: To measure self-deception and need for approval.

Number of Items: 10

Format: True–false format.

Reliability: Alpha for self-deception was .62. Alpha for impression management was .29.

Author: Mellor, S., et al.

Article: Comparative trait analysis of long-term recovering alcoholics.

Journal: *Psychological Reports*, April 1986, *58*(2), 411–418.

Related Research: Paulhus, D. L. (1984). Two-component models of socially desirable responding. *Journal of Personality and Social Psychology*, *46*, 598–609.

. . .

5072

Test Name: SELF-DEFEATING PERSONALITY SCALE

Purpose: To measure self-defeating personality disorder.

Number of Items: 48

Format: True–false format.

Reliability: Cronbach's alpha was .68. Test–retest (3 weeks) reliability ranged from .71 to .75.

Validity: Correlations with items from the Adjective Checklist ranged from −.47 to .50.

Author: Schill, T.

Article: A measure of self-defeating personality.

Journal: *Psychological Reports*, June 1990, *66*(3, Part II), 1343–1346.

. . .

5073

Test Name: SHALLING SIFNEOS PERSONALITY SCALE

Purpose: To measure alexithymia.

Number of Items: 20

Format: Includes three factors: difficulty in expression of feelings, unimportance of feelings, and daydreaming/introspection. Responses are made on a scale ranging from 1 (*does not apply at all*) to 4 (*applies completely*).

Reliability: Coefficient alpha was .51.

Validity: Correlations with other variables ranged from −.25 to .26.

Author: Norton, N. C.

Article: Three scales of alexithymia: Do they measure the same thing?

Journal: *Journal of Personality Assessment*, Fall 1989, *53*(3), 621–637.

Related Research: Apfel, R. J., & Sifneos, P. E. (1979). Alexithymia: Concept and measurement. *Psychotherapy and Psychosomatics*, *32*, 180–190.

. . .

5074

Test Name: SITUATIONAL GUILT SCALE

Purpose: To provide a self-report measure of guilt.

Number of Items: 22

Format: Includes three factors: interpersonal harm guilt, norm violation guilt, and self-control failure guilt.

Reliability: Cronbach alpha's ranged from .74 to .92 ($N = 122$). Test–retest (2 to 3 weeks) Pearson correlations ranged from .84 to .90 ($N = 45$).

Validity: Correlations with self-report measures ranged from −.03 to .57 (N 122).

Author: Klass, E. T.

Article: Situational approach to assessment of guilt: Development and validation of a self-report measure.

Journal: *Journal of Psychopathology and Behavioral Assessment*, March 1987, *9*(1), 35–48.

. . .

5075

Test Name: STATE SPORT-CONFIDENCE INVENTORY

Purpose: To measure state self-confidence when competing in a sport.

Number of Items: 13

Format: Responses to each item are made on a 9-point Likert scale ranging from *low* to *high*.

Validity: Correlation with: predicted finishing time was −.35; actual finishing time was −.36.

Author: Gayton, W. F., and Nickless, C. J.

Article: An investigation of the validity of the trait and state sport-confidence inventories in predicting marathon performance.

Journal: *Perceptual and Motor Skills*, October 1987, *65*(2), 481–482.

Related Research: Vealey, R. S. (1986). Conceptualization of sport-confidence and competitive orientation: Preliminary investigation and instrument development. *Journal of Sport Psychology*, 8, 221–246.

■ ■ ■

5076

Test Name: SUBJECTIVISM SCALE

Purpose: To measure subjectivism.

Number of Items: 11

Format: Sample items are presented.

Reliability: Interitem reliability was .72.

Validity: Correlation with objectivism was −.32.

Author: Leary, M. R., et al.

Article: Objectivism in information utilization: Theory and measurement.

Journal: *Journal of Personality Assessment*, Spring 1986, *50*(1), 32–43.

5077

Test Name: TOUGHNESS AND CONSISTENCY SCALE

Purpose: To measure toughness and consistency as elements of personality important for the study of political attitudes.

Number of Items: 14

Format: Adjective pairs format. All items presented.

Reliability: Alphas were .74 (toughness) and .71 (consistency).

Validity: Correlations with other variables ranged from −.28 to .71.

Author: Goertzel, T. G.

Article: Authoritarianism of personality and political attitudes.

Journal: *The Journal of Social Psychology*, February 1987, *127*(1), 7–18.

■ ■ ■

5078

Test Name: TRUST AND SUSPICION SCALE

Purpose: To measure trust and suspicion by self-report.

Number of Items: 8

Format: Likert.

Reliability: Alpha was .70.

Validity: Two factor solution confirmed by LISREL. Trust and suspicion were negatively correlated (−.17).

Author: Lagace, R., and Gassenheimer, J. B.

Article: A measure of global trust and suspicion: Replication.

Journal: *Psychological Reports*, October 1989, *65*(2), 473–474.

Related Research: MacDonald, A. P., et al. (1972). Self disclosure and two kinds of trust. *Psychological Reports*, *30*, 143–148.

■ ■ ■

5079

Test Name: YN-2 SCALE

Purpose: To measure the tendency to respond affirmatively.

Number of Items: 20

Format: Responses are made on a 7-point Likert-type response format where 1 indicates complete disagreement.

Reliability: Coefficient alpha was .76.

Validity: Correlations with the Kirton Adaptation-Innovation Inventory ranged from −.19 to .41.

Author: Goldsmith, R. E., et al.

Article: Yeasaying and the Kirton Adaptation-Innovation Inventory.

Journal: *Educational and Psychological Measurement*, Summer 1986, *46*(2), 433–436.

Related Research: Wells, W. D. (1961). The influence of yeasaying response style. *Journal of Advertising Research*, *1*(4), 1–12.

5080

Test Name: ADOLESCENT SELF-PERCEPTION INVENTORY

Purpose: To measure sex-role endorsement.

Number of Items: 60

Format: Responses to each item are made on a 4-point scale ranging from *not at all true of me* to *very true of me*.

Validity: Correlation with another measure of sex-role endorsement was .88.

Author: Mitchell, J. E., et al.

Article: Masculinity and femininity in twin children: Genetic and environmental factors.

Journal: *Child Development*, December 1989, *60*(6), 1475–1485.

Related Research: Thomas, S. J., (1983). *Providing a concrete context for sex role endorsement in adolescents: Some measurement considerations*. Paper presented at the annual meeting of the American Educational Research Association, Montreal, Quebec, Canada.

■ ■ ■

5081

Test Name: COMMITMENT TO PHYSICAL ACTIVITY SCALE

Purpose: To measure a subject's commitment to physical activity.

Number of Items: 12

Format: Employs a 5-point Likert scale with scores ranging from 60 (*extremely committed*) to 12 (*not at all committed*).

Reliability: Reliability coefficients were .91 (2 weeks) and .92 (4 weeks).

Author: Lock, R. S.

Article: College women's decision-making skills relating to voluntary participation in physical activity during leisure time.

Journal: *Perceptual and Motor Skills*, August 1990, *71*(1), 141–146.

Related Research: Neilson, A. B., & Corbin, C. B. (1986). *Physical activity commitment*. Paper presented at North American Society for Psychology of Sport and Physical Activity, Scottsdale, Arizona.

■ ■ ■

5082

Test Name: GENDER ROLE CONFLICT SCALE-I

Purpose: To measure aspects of male gender role conflict.

Number of Items: 37

Format: Responses to each item are made on a 6-point scale from 1 (*strongly disagree*) to 6 (*strongly agree*). Includes four factors: success, power, and competition; restrictive emotionality; restrictive affectionate behavior between men; and conflicts between work and family relationships.

Reliability: Test–retest (4 weeks) reliability ranged from .72 to .86. Alpha coefficients ranged from .75 to .89.

Author: Good, G. E., et al.

Article: Male role and gender role conflict: Relations to help-seeking in men.

Journal: *Journal of Counseling Psychology*, July 1989, *36*(3), 295–300.

Related Research: O'Neil, J. M., et al. (1986). Gender-role conflict scale: College men's fear of femininity. *Sex Roles, 14*, 335–350.

■ ■ ■

5083

Test Name: GENDER ROLE SCALE

Purpose: To measure attitudes toward gender roles.

Number of Items: 7

Format: Five-point Likert format.

Reliability: Alphas ranged from .63 and .79.

Author: Funk, R. B., and Willits, F. K.

Article: College attendance and attitude change: A panel study, 1970–1981.

Journal: *Sociology of Education*, July 1987, *60*(4), 224–231.

Related Research: Thornton, A., & Freedman, D. (1979). Changes in the sex role attitudes of women, 1962–1977: Evidence from a panel study. *American Sociological Review, 44*, 831–842.

■ ■ ■

5084

Test Name: GENDER ROLE PREFERENCES SCALE

Purpose: To measure modernity of gender role preferences.

Number of Items: 24

Format: Seven-point scale from 0 (*not true at all*) to 6 (*definitely true*).

Reliability: Alphas ranged from .88 to .90.

Author: Godwin, D. D., and Scanzoni, J.

Article: Couple consensus during marital joint decision-making: A context, process outcome model.

Journal: *Journal of Marriage and the Family*, November 1989, *51*(4), 943–956.

Related Research: Scanzoni, J., & Szinovacz, M. (1980). *Family decision-making: A developmental sex role model*. Beverly Hills, CA: Sage.

■ ■ ■

5085

Test Name: HEALTH OPINION SURVEY

Purpose: To measure preferences for treatment approaches. High scores indicate favorable attitudes toward self-directed care.

Number of Items: 16

Format: Agree–disagree format (2 categories).

Reliability: Reliability ranged in the .70s.

Validity: Correlations with various self-directed care variables ranged from −.58 to .20.

Author: Dinning, W. D., and Crampton, J.

Article: The Krantz Health Opinion Survey: Correlations with preventive health behaviors and intentions.

Journal: *Psychological Reports*, February 1989, *64*(1), 59–64.

Related Research: Krantz, D. S., et al. (1980). Assessment of preferences for self-treatment and information in health care. *Journal of Personality and Social Psychology*, *39*, 977–990.

■ ■ ■

5086

Test Name: INDEX OF SEX ROLE ORIENTATION

Purpose: To measure sex-role orientation.

Number of Items: 16

Format: Responses are made on a 5-point Likert scale ranging from *strongly agree* to *strongly disagree*.

Reliability: Reliability was .92.

Author: Horn, H., et al.

Article: A comparative study of Israeli female students in nontraditional (engineering) and traditional (humanities) fields of study.

Journal: *Research in Higher Education*, April 1990, *31*(2), 177–192.

Related Research: Dreyer, N. A., et al. (1981). ISRO: A scale to measure sex-role orientation. *Sex Roles*, *7*(2), 173–183.

■ ■ ■

5087

Test Name: INSTRUCTIONAL PREFERENCES INVENTORY

Purpose: To measure preference for course structure and for course difficulty.

Number of Items: 33

Format: A forced choice format was employed. Includes two subscales: preference for course structure and preference for course difficulty.

Reliability: Coefficient alphas ranged from .78 to .83 (preference for course structure) and from .58 to .74 (preference for course difficulty).

Author: Hocevar, D., et al.

Article: The measurement of preference for course structure and preference for course difficulty. The Instructional Preferences Inventory (IPI).

Journal: *Educational and Psychological Measurement*, Winter 1987, *47*(4), 997–1003.

Related Research: Strom, B., et al. (1982). The Course Structure Inventory: Discriminant and construct

validity. *Educational and Psychological Measurement*, *42*, 1125–1133.

■ ■ ■

5088

Test Name: LEAST PREFERRED CO-WORKER—REVISED

Purpose: To measure a leader's relationships or task orientation.

Number of Items: 22

Format: Items are semantic differentials describing the person with whom the leader can work least well. The items are presented.

Reliability: Test–retest (6 weeks) correlation coefficients ranged from .24 to .50.

Author: Ashworth, S. D., and Hazer, J. T.

Article: Scale content, respondent classification, referent stereotyping, and stability in four LPC measures.

Journal: *Educational and Psychological Measurement*, Spring 1986, *46*(1), 107–123.

Related Research: Rice, R. W., & Seaman, F. J. (1981). Internal analyses of the least preferred coworker (LPC) scale. *Educational and Psychological Measurement*, *41*, 109–120.

■ ■ ■

5089

Test Name: LEAST PREFERRED CO-WORKER SCALE

Purpose: To measure leadership style.

Number of Items: 18

Format: Eight-point semantic differentials are employed.

Validity: Correlations with other variables ranged from −.38 to .51.

Author: Kennedy, J. K., Jr., et al.

Article: Construct space of the Least Preferred Co-Worker (LPC) Scale.

Journal: *Educational and Psychological Measurement*, Autumn 1987, 47(3), 807–814.

Related Research: Fiedler, F. E., et al. (1976). *Improving leadership effectiveness: The leader-match concept.* New York: Wiley.

■ ■ ■

5090

Test Name: LIKING SCALE

Purpose: To measure how well a man likes a woman

Number of Items: 3

Format: On 9-point Likert scales men rate how well they liked, would like to date, and would like to work with the woman.

Reliability: Correlation was .69. Cronbach's alpha was .96.

Validity: Correlations with other variables ranged from –.02 to .40.

Author: Jones, G. N., et al.

Article: Criterion-related validity of self-report measures of female heterosocial functioning.

Journal: *Journal of Psychopathology and Behavioral Assessment*, March 1988, 10(1), 1–7.

Related Research: Shrout, P. E., & Fleiss, J. L. (1979). Intraclass correlations: Uses in assessing rater reliability. *Psychological Bulletin, 86,* 420–428.

■ ■ ■

5091

Test Name: MANAGEMENT-OF-DIFFERENCE EXERCISE

Purpose: To measure preferences for five conflict modes in addition to a number of personality measures.

Number of Items: 30

Format: An ipsative questionnaire consisting of sets of paired items, each describing one of five conflict modes.

Validity: Correlations with other variables ranged from –.18 to .49.

Author: Kabanoff, B.

Article: Predictive validity of the MODE conflict instrument.

Journal: *Journal of Applied Psychology*, February 1987, 72(1), 160–163.

Related Research: Kilmann, R. H., & Thomas, K. W. (1977). Developing a forced-choice measure of conflict handling behavior: The "Mode" instrument. *Educational and Psychological Measurement, 37,* 309–325.

■ ■ ■

5092

Test Name: MODIFIED PERSONAL INVOLVEMENT INVENTORY

Purpose: To assess an individual's enduring involvement with a stimulus object.

Number of Items: 16

Format: Each item consists of a pair of words in a semantic differential format. All items are presented.

Reliability: Test–retest (1 month) reliability coefficients ranged from .20 to .74.

Author: Munson, J. M., and McQuarrie, E. F.

Article: The factorial and predictive validities of a revised measure of Zaichkowsky's Personal Involvement Inventory.

Journal: *Educational and Psychological Measurement*, Autumn 1987, 47(3), 773–782.

Related Research: Zaichkowsky, J. L. (1985). Measuring the involvement construct. *Journal of Consumer Research, 12* (December), 341–352.

■ ■ ■

5093

Test Name: NEOPHILIA SCALE

Purpose: To measure a liking for, or an openness to, the new.

Number of Items: 38

Format: Responses are made on a 5-point scale. All items are presented.

Reliability: Alpha was. 85.

Validity: Correlations with other variables ranged from –.01 to .71.

Author: Walker, I., and Gibbins, K.

Article: Expecting the unexpected: An explanation of category width.

Journal: *Journal of Perceptual and Motor Skills,* June 1989, 68(3) Part 1, 715–724.

■ ■ ■

5094

Test Name: OPINIONS ABOUT PSYCHOLOGY SCALE

Purpose: To measure objective/subjective preferences in the study of psychology.

Number of Items: 15

Format: Forced-choice. All items presented (high scores coded objective).

Validity: Factor analysis revealed one primary polarized factor (objectivity—subjectivity). Correlation with an understanding science scale was .30; with numbered psychology courses taken was .21.

Author: McCall, N. J., and Carlin, D.

Article: Psychology of the scientist: LX. Relation of training about science to preference for objective psychology.

Journal: *Psychological Reports*, April 1989, 64(2), 383–390.

Related Research: Coan, R. W. (1979). *Psychologists: Personal and theoretical pathways.* New York: Irvington Press.

■ ■ ■

5095

Test Name: PERCEPTUAL PREFERENCES AND SENSITIVENESS AMONG ENVIRONMENTAL SENSORY STIMULI CHECK LIST—REVISED

Purpose: To ascertain subjects' preferences among environmental stimuli in vision, audition, tactile sense, and olfaction, and to estimate their subjective sensitiveness to weak or intense and prolonged sensory stimuli in their environment.

Number of Items: 60

Format: The instrument is a check list. All items are presented.

Reliability: Test–retest product-moment correlations ranged from .30 to .72.

Author: Satow, A.

Article: An ecological approach to mechanisms determining individual differences in perception.

Journal: *Perceptual and Motor Skills*, June 1986, *62*(3), 983–998.

Related Research: Satow, A. (1983). Nonparallel relationship between tolerance and sensitiveness for visual and auditory environmental stimuli. *Journal of Light & Visual Environment*, 7, 18–24.

• • •

5096

Test Name: PERSONAL ATTRIBUTES QUESTIONNAIRE

Purpose: To assess instructional and expressive dimensions of gender-role orientation.

Number of Items: 24

Format: Five-point responses to each descriptive adjective.

Reliability: Alphas ranged from .79 to .94.

Validity: Correlations with other variables ranged from −.20 to .46.

Author: Hackett, G., et al.

Article: The relationship of role model influences to the career salience and educational and career plans of college women.

Journal: *Journal of Vocational Behavior*, October 1988, *35*(2), 164–180.

Related Research: Spence, J. T., et al. (1975). Ratings of self and peers on sex role attributes and their relation to self-esteem and conceptions of masculinity and femininity. *Journal of Personality and Social Psychology, 32,* 29–39.

• • •

5097

Test Name: PERSONAL ATTRIBUTES QUESTIONNAIRE

Purpose: To measure sex role stereotypes and masculinity–femininity.

Number of Items: 55

Format: Responses are made using 5-point Likert scales.

Reliability: Internal consistency was .73 (men) and .91 (women).

Author: Lash, S. J., and Polyson, J A.

Article: Reassessment of gender perception in projected animal content.

Journal: *Perceptual and Motor Skills*, October 1988, *67*(2), 547–553.

Related Research: Spence, J. T., et al. (1974). The Personal Attributes Questionnaire: A measure of sex role stereotypes and masculinity–femininity. *JSAS Catalog of Selected Documents in Psychology, 4*(43, Ms. No. 617).

• • •

5098

Test Name: PERSONAL ATTRIBUTES QUESTIONNAIRE

Purpose: To assess sex-role orientation.

Number of Items: 16

Format: Includes masculinity and femininity subscale scores. A sample item is presented.

Reliability: Internal consistency ranged from .73 to .76.

Validity: Correlations with other variables ranged from .40 to .75.

Author: Vrendenburg, K., et al.

Article: Depression in college students: personality and experiential factors.

Journal: *Journal of Counseling Psychology*, October 1988, *35*(4), 419–425.

Related Research: Spence, J. T., et al. (1974). The Personal Attributes Questionnaire: A measure of sex role stereotypes and masculinity–femininity. *JSAS: Catalog of Selected Documents in Psychology*, 4, 43(Ms. No. 617).

• • •

5099

Test Name: PERSONALITY ATTRIBUTES QUESTIONNAIRE— FEMININITY SCALE

Purpose: To measure femininity.

Number of Items: 8

Format: Consists of 8 trait descriptions in a bipolar format.

Reliability: The 2-year stability coefficient was .73.

Validity: Correlations with other variables ($N = 99$) ranged from −.29 to .46.

Author: Zeldow, P. B., et al.

Article: Masculinity, femininity, and psychosocial adjustment in medical students: A 2-year follow-up.

Journal: *Journal of Personality Assessment*, Spring 1987, *51*(1), 3–14.

Related Research: Spence, J. T., & Helmreich, R. L. (1978). *Masculinity and femininity: Their psychological dimensions, correlates, and antecedents.* Austin: University of Texas Press.

• • •

5100

Test Name: PERSONALITY ATTRIBUTES QUESTIONNAIRE— MASCULINITY SCALE

Purpose: To measure masculinity.

Number of Items: 8

Format: Consists of eight trait descriptions in a bipolar format.

Reliability: The 2-year stability coefficient was .65.

Validity: Correlations with other variables ($N = 99$) ranged from −.19 to .38.

Author: Zeldow, P. B., et al.

Article: Masculinity, femininity, and psychosocial adjustment in medical students: A 2-year follow-up.

Journal: *Journal of Personality Assessment*, Spring 1987, *51*(1), 3–14.

Related Research: Spence, J. T., & Helmreich, R. L. (1978). *Masculinity and femininity: Their psychological dimensions, correlates, and antecedents*. Austin: University of Texas Press.

■ ■ ■

5101

Test Name: PERSONAL INVOLVEMENT INVENTORY

Purpose: To assess an individual's enduring involvement with a stimulus object.

Number of Items: 20

Format: Each item consists of a pair of words in a semantic differential format. Sixteen of the items are presented.

Reliability: Test–retest (1 month) reliability ranged from .60 to .93. Cronbach's alpha reliability estimates ranged from .95 to .97.

Author: Munson, J. M., and McQuarrie, E. F.

Article: The factorial and predictive validities of a revised measure of Zaichkowsky's Personal Involvement Inventory.

Journal: *Educational and Psychological Measurement*, Autumn 1987, *47*(3), 773–782.

Related Research: Zaichkowsky, J. L. (1985). Measuring the involvement

construct. *Journal of Consumer Research*, *12* (December), 341–352.

■ ■ ■

5102

Test Name: PHYSICAL ACTIVITY STEREOTYPING INDEX

Purpose: To measure the extent to which parents, teachers, and children label physical activites according to gender.

Number of Items: 24

Format: Five response choices are used: *a lot more for boys, a little more for boys, equally for boys and girls, a little more for girls, a lot more for girls*.

Reliability: Test–retest reliability ranged from .77 to .95.

Validity: Correlation between groups of judges ranged from .98 for male activities to .82 for female activities.

Author: Ignacio, A. A.

Article: Development and verification of a gender-role stereotyping index for physical activities.

Journal: *Journal of Perceptual and Motor Skills*, June 1989, *68*(3) Part 2, 1067–1075.

■ ■ ■

5103

Test Name: POSITIVE SEX ROLE INVENTORY

Purpose: To measure professionally related positive sex-role characteristics.

Number of Items: 60

Format: Students rate each item on a 1 to 5-point scale from 1 (*fairly desirable*) to 5 (*extremely desirable*), indicating the desirability of each item as an attribute for counseling psychologists. Includes three subscales: masculine, feminine, and neutral.

Reliability: Coefficient alphas ranged from .76 to .84.

Author: Speth, C. A., and Plake, B. S.

Article: Assessment of positive sex-role characteristics.

Journal: *Educational and Psychological Measurement*, Summer 1986, *46*(2), 443–447

Related Research: Williams, J. E., & Best, D. L. (1977). Sex stereotypes and trait favorability on the Adjective Check List. *Educational and Psychological Measurement*, *37*, 101–110.

■ ■ ■

5104

Test Name: PREFERRED CIVIL-LIBERTIES CLIMATE SCALE

Purpose: To measure an individual's preference for civil-liberties tolerance at his or her place of work.

Number of Items: 19

Format: Likert.

Reliability: Alpha was .86.

Validity: Correlation with perceived climate was .17 (not significant).

Author: Sheinfeld, D., and Zalkind, S. S.

Article: Does civil-liberties climate in organizations correlate with job satisfaction and work alienation?

Journal: *Psychological Reports*, April 1987, *60*(2), 467–477.

Related Research: Zalkind, S. S., et al. (1975). Civil liberties attitudes and personality measures: Some exploratory research. *Journal of Social Issues*, *31*, 77–83.

■ ■ ■

5105

Test Name: PRODUCT PREFERENCE SCALE

Purpose: To measure consumer preference for various products.

Number of Items: 11

Format: Item responses are made on a 9-point Likert scale from *disagree* to *agree*. Sample items are presented.

Reliability: Kuder-Richardson Formula 20 reliability coefficient was .99.

Author: Mehrabian, A., and deWetter, R.

Article: Experimental test of an emotion-based approach to fitting brand names to products.

Journal: *Journal of Applied Psychology*, February 1987, *72*(1), 125–130.

Related Research: Mehrabian, A., & Wixen, W. J. (1986). Preferences for individual video games as a function of their emotional effects on players. *Journal of Applied Social Psychology*, *16*, 3–15.

■ ■ ■

5106

Test Name: REVISED— INDIVIDUAL QUESTIONNAIRE

Purpose: To assess preference for visual and verbal processing style.

Number of Items: 54

Format: Includes two scales: visual and verbal.

Reliability: Alpha coefficients were .80 (verbal) and .82 (imagery).

Author: Olson, D. M., et al.

Article: Relationships between activities and sex-related differences in performance on spatial tests.

Journal: *Perceptual and Motor Skills*, August 1988, *67*(1), 223–232.

Related Research: Paivio, A., & Harshman, R. (1983). Factor analysis of a questionnaire on imagery and verbal habits and skills. *Canadian Journal of Psychology*, *37*, 461–483.

■ ■ ■

5107

Test Name: ROLE CONFLICT SCALE

Purpose: To measure role conflict.

Number of Items: 8

Format: Responses are made on a 7-point scale ranging from *very rarely* to *continually*. An example is presented.

Reliability: Coefficient alpha was .82.

Validity: Correlations with other variables ranged from –.37 to .51.

Author: Greenhaus, J. H., et al.

Article: Work experiences, job performance, and feelings of personal and family well-being.

Journal: *Journal of Vocational Behavior*, October 1987, *31*(2), 200–215.

Related Research: Rizzo, J. R., et al. (1970). Role conflict and ambiguity in complex organizations. *Administrative Science Quarterly*, *15*, 150–163.

■ ■ ■

5108

Test Name: SELF-EFFICACY/ INTEREST RATING SCALE

Purpose: To measure self-interest and interest in tasks.

Number of Items: 3

Format: Items rated on 10- and 13-point scales.

Reliability: Test–retest (1 week) reliability ranged from .60 to .76.

Author: Campbell, N. K., and Hackett, G.

Article: The effects of mathematics task performance on math self-efficacy and task interest.

Journal: *Journal of Vocational Behavior*, April 1986, *28*(2), 149–162.

Related Research: Hackett, G., & O'Halloran, S. (1986). *Test–retest reliability of career self-efficacy measures*. Unpublished manuscript.

■ ■ ■

5109

Test Name: SEX-ROLE ANTECEDENTS SCALES

Purpose: To classify personal and perceived parental sex-role orientations as masculine, feminine, androgynous or undifferentiated.

Number of Items: 28

Time Required:

Format: Includes equivalent masculine and feminine scales. Items are all unipolar.

Reliability: Kuder-Richardson formula reliability coefficients ranged from .70 to .79.

Validity: Correlations with the Personal Attributes Questionnaire ranged from .82 to .93.

Author: Mast, D. L., and Herron, W. G.

Article: The sex-role antecedents scales.

Journal: *Perceptual and Motor Skills*, August, 1986, *63*(1), 27–56

■ ■ ■

5110

Test Name: SEX ROLE BEHAVIOR SCALE

Purpose: To sample the interest/ behavior domain of sex roles comprehensively.

Number of Items: 240

Format: Includes male- and female-valued and sex-specific interests and behaviors in four areas: Leisure activity preferences; vocational interests, social interaction; and marital, or primary relationship behavior. Responses are made on a 5-point scale.

Reliability: Alpha coefficients ranged from .65 to .98.

Author: Orlofsky, J. L. and O'Heron, C. A.

Article: Development of a short-form sex role behavior scale.

Journal: *Journal of Personality Assessment*, Summer, 1987, *51*(2), 267–277.

Related Research: Orlofsky, J. L., et al. (1982). Development of the revised sex role behavior scale. *Journal of Personality Assessment, 46,* 632–638.

■ ■ ■

5111

Test Name: SEX ROLE BEHAVIOR SCALE—SHORT FORM

Purpose: To sample the interest/behavior domain of sex roles comprehensively.

Number of Items: 96

Format: Includes male- and female-valued and sex-specific interests and behaviors in four areas: leisure activity preferences, vocational interests, social interaction, and marital or primary relationship behaviors. Responses are made on a 5-point scale.

Reliability: Alpha coefficients ranged from .61 to .92.

Validity: Correlations with other variables ranged from −.37 to .40.

Author: Orlofsky, J. L., and O'Heron, C. A.

Article: Development of a short-form sex role behavior scale.

Journal: *Journal of Personality Assessment,* Summer, 1987, *51*(2), 267–277

Related Research: Orlofsky, J. L., et al. (1982). Development of the revised sex role behavior scale. *Journal of Personality Assessment, 46,* 632–638.

■ ■ ■

5112

Test Name: SEX-ROLE CONFLICT SCALE

Purpose: To measure sex-role conflict.

Number of Items: 17

Format: Likert format.

Reliability: Alpha was .94. Split-half reliability ranged from .73 to .82.

Test–retest (2 weeks) reliability was .96.

Author: Soled, S., and Blair, E. D.

Article: Relationship of age and sex-role conflict for professional women in human services.

Journal: *Psychological Reports,* October 1990, *67*(2), 523–527.

Related Research: Chusmir, L. H., & Koberg, C. S. (1986). Development and validation of the Sex-Role Conflict Scale. *Journal of Applied Behavioral Science, 22,* 397–409.

■ ■ ■

5113

Test Name: SEX ROLE IDEOLOGY SCALE

Purpose: To measure normative beliefs about gender-role behavior.

Number of Items: 30

Format: Seven-point Likert format.

Reliability: Split-half reliability was .91. Test–retest (3 weeks) reliability was .87.

Author: Fitzgerald, L. F., and Hesson-McInnis, M.

Article: The dimensions of sexual harassment: A structural analysis.

Journal: *Journal of Vocational Behavior,* December 1989, *35*(3), 309–326.

Related Research: Kalin, R., & Tilby, P. J. (1978). Development and validation of a sex-role ideology scale. *Psychological Reports, 43,* 731–738.

■ ■ ■

5114

Test Name: SEX-ROLE ORIENTATION SCALE

Purpose: To asses the traditional-egalitarian sex role continuum.

Number of Items: 5

Format: Likert format.

Reliability: Cronbach's alpha was .69.

Author: Bowen, G. L., and Neenan, P. A.

Article: Sex-role orientations among married men in the military: The generational factor.

Journal: *Psychological Reports,* April 1988, *62*(2), 523–526.

Related Research: Bowen, G. L., & Orthner, D. K. (1983). Sex-role congruency and marital quality. *Journal of Marriage and the Family, 45,* 223–230.

■ ■ ■

5115

Test Name: TOY PREFERENCE TEST

Purpose: To measure sex-role identification.

Number of Items: 22

Format: Each item is a photo of a pair of masculine and feminine toys. For each item the children point to the toy they would prefer to play with.

Validity: Correlations with gender-based affiliation preference was zero order (*df* = 126) .40 and controlling for age (*df* = 125) .30.

Author: Serbin, L. A., and Sprafkin, C.

Article: The salience of gender and the process of sex typing in three- to seven-year-old children.

Journal: *Child Development,* October 1986, *57*(5), 1188–1199.

Related Research: DeLucia, L. A. (1963). The toy preference test: A measure of sex-role identification. *Child Development, 34,* 107–117.

■ ■ ■

5116

Test Name: VISUALIZER–VERBALIZER QUESTIONNAIRE

Purpose: To assess preference for visual or verbal modes of processing.

Number of Items: 15

Format: True–false items.

Reliability: Test–retest (2 weeks) reliability coefficient was .91.

Author: Holt, P. A., and Stone, G. L.

Article: Needs, coping strategies, and coping outcomes associated with long-distance relationships.

Journal: *Journal of College Student Development*, March 1988, *29*(2), 136–141.

Related Research: Richardson. (1977). Verbalizer-Visualizer: A cognitive style dimension. *Journal of Mental Imagery, 1*, 109–126.

CHAPTER 19
Problem Solving and Reasoning

5117

Test Name: APHASIA SCREENING TEST—PARTIAL

Purpose: To measure dysphasic errors.

Number of Items: 10

Format: Includes naming errors, articulation errors, and sentence interpretation errors.

Reliability: Interrater reliability coefficient was .82.

Author: Horn, J. L., et al.

Article: Phonetically inaccurate spelling among learning-disabled, head-injured, and nondisabled young adults.

Journal: *Brain and Language*, January 1988, *33*(1), 55–64.

Related Research: Russell, E. W., et al. (1970). *Assessment of brain damage.* New York: Wiley.

■ ■ ■

5118

Test Name: ASSESSMENT OF CAREER DECISION-MAKING SCALE

Purpose: To measure the extent to which the individual uses a rational, intuitive, and dependent decision-making style.

Number of Items: 30

Format: Includes three scales: rational, intuitive, and dependent decision-making styles.

Reliability: Test–retest (2 weeks) reliabilities were .85 and .76 ($N = 76$).

Author: York, D. C., and Tinsley, H. E. A.

Article: The relationship between cognitive styles and Holland's personality types.

Journal: *Journal of College Student Personnel*, November 1986, *27*(6), 535–541.

Related Research: Harren, V. A., & Biscardi, D. L. (1980). Sex roles and cognitive styles as predictors of Holland typologies. *Journal of Vocational Behavior, 17*, 231–241.

■ ■ ■

5119

Test Name: AUTOMATIC THOUGHTS INVENTORY

Purpose: To assess positive thinking/positive automatic cognition.

Number of Items: 30

Format: Five-point Likert format. All items presented.

Reliability: Alpha was .94. Split-half reliability was .95.

Validity: Correlated .29 with the Automatic Thoughts Questionnaire (negative thoughts). Correlations with other variables ranged from –.33 to .60.

Author: Ingram, R. E., and Wiscinski, K. S.

Article: Assessment of positive automatic cognition.

Journal: *Journal of Consulting and Clinical Psychology*, December 1988, *56*(6), 898–892.

Related Research: Hollon, S. D., & Kendall, P. C. (1980). Cognitive self-statements in depression: Development of an automatic thoughts questionnaire. *Cognitive Therapy and Research, 4*, 383–395.

■ ■ ■

5120

Test Name: CHILDREN'S PROBLEM-SOLVING SKILLS MEASURE

Purpose: To assess children's problem-solving skills.

Number of Items: 10

Format: In response to each vignette the child has 4 minutes to write all the things he/she might say or do if found in the situation. A sample item is presented.

Reliability: Alpha coefficients ranged from .72 to .89.

Validity: Correlations with other variables ranged from –.31 to .35.

Author: Dubow, E. F., and Tisak, J.

Article: The relation between stressful life events and adjustment in elementary school children: The role of social support and social problem-solving skills.

Journal: *Child Development*, December 1989, *60*(6), 1412–1423.

Related Research: Deluty, R. H. (1981). Alternative-thinking ability of aggressive, assertive, and submissive children. *Cognitive Therapy and Research, 5*, 309–312.

■ ■ ■

5121

Test Name: COGNITIVE FAILURES QUESTIONNAIRE

Purpose: To measure self-reported frequency of lapses in cognitive control.

Number of Items: 25

Format: At least two factors are identified: a general cognitive failures factor and a factor concerned with failures in processing people's names. All items are presented.

Validity: Correlations with other variables ranged from −.13 to .37.

Author: Matthews, G., et al.

Article: Multiple factors of cognitive failure and their relationships with stress vulnerability.

Journal: *Journal of Psychopathology and Behavioral Assessment*, March 1990, *12*(1), 49–65.

Related Research: Broadbent, D. E., et al. (1982). The cognitive failures questionnaire (CFQ) and its correlates. *British Journal of Clinical Psychology*, *21*, 1–16.

■ ■ ■

5122

Test Name: COGNITIVE INTERFERENCE QUESTIONNAIRE

Purpose: To measure intrusive and off-task thoughts.

Number of Items: 21

Format: Five-point frequency rating scales.

Reliability: Alpha was .76.

Author: Mikulincer, M., et al.

Article: Learned helplessness, reactance and cue utilization.

Journal: *Journal of Research in Personality*, June 1989, *23*(2), 235–247.

Related Research: Sarason, I. G., et al. (1986). Cognitive interference: Situational determinants and traitlike characteristics. *Journal of Personality and Social Psychology*, *51*, 215–226.

5123

Test Name: COGNITIVE STATUS EXAMINATION

Purpose: To asses cognitive status quickly in a patient-care setting.

Number of Items: 37

Time Required: 15–30 minutes.

Format: Varied format. All items briefly summarized.

Reliability: Interrater concurrence was 92%.

Validity: Significantly ($p < .001$) differentiated five criterion patient groups: psychiatric, medical, acute brain damage, chronic-stable brain damage, chronic-progressive brain damage.

Author: Barrett, Jr., E. T., and Gleser, G. C.

Article: Development and validation of the Cognitive Status Examination.

Journal: *Journal of Consulting and Clinical Psychology*, December 1987, *55*(6), 877–882.

Related Research: Barrett, Jr., E. T. (1985). *Cognitive status examination administration and scoring manual*. Unpublished manuscript.

■ ■ ■

5124

Test Name: COMMON BELIEF INVENTORY FOR STUDENTS

Purpose: To measure rational thinking in children.

Number of Items: 44

Format: A self-report scale employing a 5-point Likert format. Examples are presented.

Reliability: Internal consistency estimates and 6 week stability were in the mid-.80s.

Validity: Correlation with the Revised Children's Manifest Anxiety Scale was .56.

Author: Hooper, S. R., et al.

Article: Concurrent validity of the Common Belief Inventory for Students.

Journal: *Perceptual and Motor Skills*, February 1987, *64*(1), 331–334.

Related Research: Hooper, S. R., & Layne, C. C. (1983). The Common Belief Inventory for Students: A measure of rationality in children. *Journal of Personality Assessment*, *47*, 85–90.

■ ■ ■

5125

Test Name: COMMON BELIEFS SURVEY III

Purpose: To measure irrational thinking: blame-proneness, self-downing, perfectionism, locus of control.

Number of Items: 54

Format: Five-point Likert format.

Reliability: Internal consistency ranged from .79 to .95 across subscales.

Author: Tosi, D. J., et al.

Article: Factor analysis of the Common Beliefs Survey III: A replication study.

Journal: *Journal of Consulting and Clinical Psychology*, June 1986, *54*(3), 404–405.

Related Research: Bassai, J. L. (1978). *The Common Beliefs Survey III*. Unpublished manuscript.

■ ■ ■

5126

Test Name: DEFINING ISSUES TEST

Purpose: To measure type of moral reasoning when respondents react to moral dilemmas.

Number of Items: 6 (long version); 3 (short version).

Format: Consists of long and short versions. For each dilemma respondents react to 12 issues.

Reliability: Test–retest correlations for the short form ranged from .58 to .77.

Author: Locke, D. C., and Zimmerman, N. A.

Article: Effects of peer-counseling training on psychological maturity of Black students.

Journal: *Journal of College Student Personnel*, November 1987, *28*(6), 525–532.

Related Research: Tucker, D. O., Jr., & Locke, D. C. (1986). The manipulation of race in moral dilemmas: Implications for moral education and human relations. *Educational and Psychological Research*, *13*, 99–109.

■ ■ ■

5127

Test Name: EXPERIMENTAL TEST OF TESTWISENESS

Purpose: To assess testwiseness.

Number of Items: 70

Format: Multiple-choice. Includes seven subscales: alliterative association, grossly unrelated alternatives, inclusionary language, more precise correct alternatives, longer correct alternatives, grammatical cues, and give-aways answered in other items.

Reliability: Kuder-Richardson Formula 20 reliability coefficient was .72. Stability coefficient was .64.

Author: Miller, P. M., et al.

Article: Factor structure of the Gibb experimental test of testwiseness.

Journal: *Educational and Psychological Measurement*, Spring 1990, *50*(1), 203–208.

Related Research: Miller, P. M., et al. (1988). Stability of the Gibb (1964) Experimental Test of Testwiseness. *Educational and Psychological Measurement*, *48*, 1123–1127.

5128

Test Name: GLOBAL JOB SKILL ASSESSMENT

Purpose: To measure ability to evaluate information and define problems.

Number of Items: 8

Format: Graphic rating scale format.

Reliability: Internal consistency ranged from .63 to .85. Interrater reliability ranged from .36 to .65.

Validity: Campbell and Fiske's four criteria of validity presented and suggest the scale is valid.

Author: Schippmann, J. S., and Prien, E. P.

Article: Psychometric Evaluation of an Integrated Assessment Procedure.

Journal: *Psychological Reports*, August 1986, *59*(1), 111–222.

■ ■ ■

5129

Test Name: HERMANN BRAIN DOMINANCE PROFILE

Purpose: To provide a self-report measure of hemisphere specialization.

Number of Items: 120

Reliability: Test–retest (30 months) reliability coefficients ranged from .43 to .84 ($N = 19$).

Validity: Correlations with GRE scores ranged from −.40 to .51.

Author: Payne, D. A.

Article: Brain dominance cognitive style and Graduate Record Examination Aptitude Test.

Journal: *Educational and Psychological Measurement*, Spring 1988, *48*(1), 175–179.

Related Research: Herrmann, N. (1982). The creative brain: Part Two. *Training and Developmental Journal*, *36*, 75–88.

5130

Test Name: INDIVIDUAL DIFFERENCES QUESTIONNAIRE

Purpose: To measure imagined and verbal thinking habits and skills.

Number of Items: 86

Format: Responses are either *true* or *false*.

Validity: Correlations with the Vividness of Movement Imagery Questionnaire ranged from −.15 to −.49.

Author: Campos, A., and Perez, M. J.

Article: Vividness of Movement Imagery Questionnaire: Relations with other measures of mental imagery.

Journal: *Perceptual and Motor Skills*, October 1988, *67*(2), 607–610.

Related Research: Paivio, A. (1971). *Imagery and verbal processes*. New York: Holt, Rinehart and Winston.

■ ■ ■

5131

Test Name: INVENTORY OF LEARNING PROCESSES

Purpose: To measure learning processes including: deep processing, elaborative processing, fact retention, and methodical study.

Number of Items: 122

Format: True–false.

Reliability: Test–retest reliability ranged from .79 to .88.

Validity: Correlations between an examination and deep and elaborative processing were .42 and .51, respectively.

Author: Gadzella, B. M., et al.

Article: Study skills, learning process, and academic achievement.

Journal: *Psychological Reports*, August 1987, *61*(1), 167–172.

Related Research: Shmeck, R. R., et al. (1977). Development of a self-report inventory for assessing individual differences in learning processes. *Applied Psychological Measurement*, *1*, 413–431.

■ ■ ■

5132

Test Name: INVENTORY OF LEARNING PROCESSES

Purpose: To assess individual differences in learning processes.

Number of Items: 63

Format: Includes four subscales: deep processing, elaborate processing, fact retention, and methodical study.

Reliability: Interim consistency (Kuder-Richardson Formula 20) ranged from .58 to .82 ($N = 434$). Test–retest reliabilities (2 weeks) ranged from .79 to .88 ($N = 95$).

Author: Miller, C. D., et al.

Article: Learning approaches and motives: male and female differences and implications for learning assistance programs.

Journal: *Journal of College Student Development*, March 1990, *31*(2), 147–154.

Related Research: Schmeck, R. R., & Ribich, F. D. (1978). Construct validation of the inventory of learning processes. *Applied Psychological Measurement*, *2*, 551–562.

■ ■ ■

5133

Test Name: INVENTORY OF LEARNING PROCESSES—SHORT FORM

Purpose: To assess individual differences in learning processes.

Number of Items: 37

Format: Includes four dimensions: synthesis-analysis, fact retention, elaborative processes, and study methods.

Reliability: Test–retest reliability coefficients ranged from .67 to .91. Internal consistency coefficients ranged from .36 to .67.

Validity: Correlations with other variables ranged from −.49 to .72.

Author: Bartling, C. A.

Article: Reliability and validity of a shortened form of the Inventory of Learning Processes.

Journal: *Educational and Psychological Measurement*, Spring 1987, *47*(1), 253–260.

Related Research: Schmeck, R. R., et al. (1977). Development of a self-report inventory for assessing individual differences in learning processes. *Applied Psychological Measurement*, *1*, 413–431.

■ ■ ■

5134

Test Name: KIRTON ADAPTATION–INNOVATION INVENTORY

Purpose: To identify stylistic differences in individual approaches to problem solving.

Number of Items: 32

Format: Contains three component dimensions of adaptation–innovation: efficiency, conformity, and originality.

Reliability: Coefficient alphas ranged from .75 to .85.

Validity: Correlations with the YN-2 Scale ranged from −.19 to .41.

Author: Goldsmith, R. E., et al.

Article: Yeasaying and the Kirton Adaptation-Innovation Inventory.

Journal: *Educational and Psychological Measurement*, Summer 1986, *46*(2), 433–436.

Related Research: Kirton, M. J. (1976). Adaptors and innovators: A description and measure. *Journal of Applied Psychology*, *61*, 622–629.

■ ■ ■

5135

Test Name: LEARNING AND STUDY STRATEGY INVENTORY

Purpose: To measure how students learn and study.

Number of Items: 90

Format: Five-point rating scales.

Reliability: Test–retest reliability ranged from .64 to .70.

Validity: Concurrent validity ranged from .40 to .60.

Author: Haynes, N. M., et al.

Article: Gender and achievement status differences on learning factors among black high school students.

Journal: *Journal of Educational Research*, March/April 1987, *81*(4), 233–237.

Related Research: Weinstein, C. E., et al. (1985). *Assessing Learning Strategies: The Design and Development of the LASSI*. Austin, Texas: University of Texas.

■ ■ ■

5136

Test Name: LEARNING STYLE INVENTORY

Purpose: To measure learning styles such as alone, with peers, with a teacher and others.

Number of Items: 23

Format: Five-point Likert format.

Reliability: Reliability was .83.

Author: Dunn, R., et al.

Article: Grouping students for instruction: Effects of learning style on achievement and attitudes.

Journal: *The Journal of Social Psychology*, August 1990, *130*(4), 485–494.

Related Research: Dunn, R. (1987). Research on instructional environments: Implications for student achievement and attitudes. *Professional School Psychology*, *2*, 43–52.

■ ■ ■

5137

Test Name: LEARNING STYLE QUESTIONNAIRE

Purpose: To assess individual learning styles within an experiential learning model.

Number of Items: 40

Format: Employs bipolar scales responded to a 5-point response mode.

Reliability: Alpha reliabilities ranged from .78 to .88 for individual scales and .90 and .93 for the two bipolar scales.

Author: Marshall, J. C., and Merritt, S. L.

Article: Reliability and construct validity of the Learning Style Questionnaire.

Journal: *Educational and Psychological Measurement*, Spring 1986, *46*(1), 257–262.

Related Research: Merritt, S. L., & Marshall, J. C. (1984). Reliability and construct validity of ipsative and normative forms of the Learning Style Inventory. *Educational and Psychological Measurement*, *44*, 463–472.

■ ■ ■

5138

Test Name: LEVELS OF LEARNING SCALES

Purpose: To measure Bloom's taxonomy of educational objectives for the cognitive domain (knowledge, comprehension, applications, analysis, synthesis, evaluation).

Number of Items: 333

Format: Subjects must learn rare English words and answer questions about stories that contain them.

Reliability: Alphas ranged from .59 to .93 across subscales.

Validity: Factor analysis did not yield six scales as suggested by Bloom's theory. Knowledge accounted for 45% of the common variance.

Author: Kottke, J. L., and Schuster, D. H.

Article: Development tests for measuring Bloom's learning outcomes.

Journal: *Psychological Reports*, February 1990, *66*(1), 27–32.

Related Research: Bloom, B. S. (1956). *Taxonomy of educational objectives. Handbook I: Cognitive domain*. New York: McKay.

■ ■ ■

5139

Test Name: MEANS–ENDS PROBLEM-SOLVING TEST

Purpose: To measure problem solving among adolescents.

Number of Items: 5

Format: Adolescents provide a solution to each problem (item) which is then rated by judges.

Reliability: Interrater reliability was .94. Test–retest reliability ranged from .43 to .59. Internal consistency ranged from .80 to .84.

Validity: Correlation with IQ was .30.

Author: Rotheram-Borus, M. J., et al.

Article: Cognitive style and pleasant activities among adolescent suicide attempters.

Journal: *Journal of Consulting and Clinical Psychology*, October 1990, *58*(5), 554–561.

Related Research: Platt, J., & Spivack, G. (1975). Mean–ends problem solving: The MEPS procedure manual. Philadelphia: Hahnemann University, Department of Mental Health Sciences.

■ ■ ■

5140

Test Name: MORAL JUDGMENT INTERVIEW

Purpose: To measure an individual's moral reasoning capability.

Format: Includes three hypothetical moral dilemmas read to the subjects who are asked how they would resolve each dilemma.

Reliability: Interrater reliability was .91.

Validity: Correlations with other variables ranged from .37 to .47.

Author: Bakken, L., and Ellsworth, R.

Article: Moral development in adulthood: Its relationship to age, sex, and education.

Journal: *Educational Research Quarterly*, 1990, *14*(2), 2–9.

Related Research: Colby, A., et al. (1979). *Standard form scoring manual, part three, form A*. Center for Moral Education, Harvard University, Cambridge, MA.

■ ■ ■

5141

Test Name: MULTIDIMENSIONAL RATING SCALE

Purpose: To evaluate display formats.

Number of Items: 155

Format: Includes six cognitive dimensions: content density, content integration, format, cognitive fidelity, cognitive processing, and general acceptance.

Reliability: Cronbach's alpha ranged from .83 to .98 ($N = 54$). Test–retest reliability ranged from .44 to .63.

Author: Gertman, D. I., and Blackman, H. S.

Article: Application of multidimensional rating techniques to CRT-generated display formats.

Journal: *Perceptual and Motor Skills*, December 1987, *65*,(3), 731–739.

Related Research: Siegel, A. I., et al. A forced-choice instrument for evaluating visual information displays. Technical Report Office of Naval Research Contact N00014–66–C0183, Project No. NR-196–076/6–29/67.

■ ■ ■

5142

Test Name: NEED FOR COGNITION SCALE

Purpose: To measure differences among individuals in their tendency to engage in and enjoy thinking.

Number of Items: 34

Format: Employs a Likert-type response scale.

Reliability: Split-half reliability was .76. Coefficient alpha was .91.

Author: Waters, L. K., and Zakrajsek, T.

Article: Correlates of need for cognition total and subscale scores.

Journal: *Educational and Psychological Measurement*, Spring 1990, *50*(1), 213–217.

Related Research: Cacioppo, J. T., & Petty, R. E. (1982). The need for cognition. *Journal of Personality and Social Psychology, 42*, 116–131.

■ ■ ■

5143

Test Name: PERSONAL PHILOSOPHY INVENTORY

Purpose: To measure temporal lobe signs in normal populations.

Number of Items: 140

Format: 20–30 minutes.

Reliability: Yes–no format. Sample items presented.

Validity: Subscale test–retest reliabilities ranged from .60 to .95.

Author: Persinger, M. A., and Makarec, K.

Article: Temporal lobe epileptic signs and correlative behaviors displayed by normal populations.

Journal: *Journal of General Psychology*, April 1987, *114*(2), 179–195.

■ ■ ■

5144

Test Name: PREFERENCE FOR IDEATION IN PROBLEM SOLVING SCALE

Purpose: To measure the active divergence in problem solving attitude.

Number of Items: 6

Format: Utilizes a 5-point Likert agreement scale.

Reliability: Cronbach's alphas ranged from .72 to .98.

Author: Basadur, M., et al.

Article: Training effects on attitudes toward divergent thinking among manufacturing engineers.

Journal: *Journal of Applied Psychology*, November 1986, *71*(4), 612–617.

Related Research: Basadur, M. S., & Finkbeiner, C. T. (1985). Measuring preference for ideation in creative problem solving training. *Journal of Applied Behavioral Science, 21*(1), 37–49.

■ ■ ■

5145

Test Name: PROBLEM-SOLVING INVENTORY

Purpose: To assess self-appraised, interpersonal problem-solving behaviors, and attitudes.

Number of Items: 32

Format: Response to each item was made on a 6-point Likert scale indicating degree of agreement–disagreement.

Reliability: Internal consistency was .90. Test–retest (2 weeks) reliability was .89.

Validity: Correlation with students' ratings of level of problem-solving skills was .46. Correlations with other variables ranged from −.49 to .58.

Author: Rich, A. R., and Bonner, R. L.

Article: Support for a pluralistic approach to the treatment of depression.

Journal: *Journal of College Student Development*, September 1989, *30*(5), 426–431.

Related Research: Heppner, P. P., and Petersen, C. H. (1982). The development and implications of a personnel problem-solving inventory. *Journal of Counseling Psychology, 29*, 66–75.

■ ■ ■

5146

Test Name: PROBLEM-SOLVING STRATEGY SURVEY

Purpose: To identify elementary school pupils' problem-solving strategies that they report using in solving mathematical word problems.

Number of Items: 22

Format: Responses to each item are made on a 4-point scale from 1 (*strategy used none of the time*) to 4 (*strategy used all of the time*).

Reliability: Cronbach's alpha was .74.

Author: Waxman, H. C.

Article: Investigating sex-related differences in mathematical problem-solving strategies of elementary school students.

Journal: *Perceptual and Motor Skills*, December 1987, *65*(3), 925–926

Related Research: Waxman, H. C. (1986). *The Problem-Solving Strategy Survey, technical manual* (Tech. Rep. No. 107). Houston, TX: University of Houston, Educational Research Center.

■ ■ ■

5147

Test Name: PROPOSITIONAL LOGIC TEST

Purpose: To measure the ability to interpret truth-functional operators by identifying instances that are consistent or inconsistent with a stated rule.

Number of Items: 16

Format: Includes four subtests of: conjunction, disjunction, biconditional, and implication. Examples are presented.

Reliability: Kuder-Richardson Formula 20 reliabilities were .82 ($N = 226$), .90 ($N = 30$), and .94 ($N = 34$).

Validity: Correlations with the Test of Logical Reasoning was .63 and with grade in science was .57.

Author: Piburn, M. D.

Article: Reliability and validity of the Propositional Logic Test.

Journal: *Educational and Psychological Measurement*, Autumn 1989, *49*(3), 667–672.

■ ■ ■

5148

Test Name: PROVERBS TEST

Purpose: To measure thinking via proverb interpretation.

Number of Items: 12

Format: Proverbs of differing abstractness presented to subjects.

Reliability: Test–retest was .96.

Author: Cunningham, D. A., et al.

Article: Relationship between proverb familiarity and proverb interpretation: Implications for clinical practice.

Journal: *Psychological Reports*, June 1987, *60*(3)I, 895–898.

Related Research: Gorham, D. R. (1956). A proverbs test for clinical and experimental use. *Psychological Reports*, *20*, 1–12.

■ ■ ■

5149

Test Name: REFLECTIVE JUDGMENT SCALE

Purpose: To measure the development of reasoning from equaling one's own views with the truth to more complex reasoning based on relativistic assumptions.

Number of Items: 7 (see format)

Format: Subjects are interviewed about an issue such as handgun control and abortion rights with seven probes. All probes presented.

Reliability: Interrater reliability ranged from .94 to .96.

Author: Liberto, J. C.

Article: Levels of reflective judgement among non college trained adults.

Journal: *Psychological Reports*, June 1990, *66*(3, Part II), 1091–1100.

Related Research: Kitchener, K. S., & King, P. M. (1985). *Reflective judgment scoring rules*. (Unpublished manuscript, University of Minnesota)

■ ■ ■

5150

Test Name: REFLECTIVE JUDGMENT INTERVIEW

Purpose: To asses reflective judgment.

Number of Items: 4

Format: Consists of four dilemmas on science, current events, religion, and history. Respondents give their views and justification concerning the contradictions in each dilemma.

Reliability: Internal consistency ranged from .63 to .96. Interrater reliability ranged from .53 to .96.

Author: Magolda, M. B. B.

Article: Measuring gender differences in intellectual development: A comparison of assessment methods.

Journal: *Journal of College Student Development*, November 1988, *29*(6), 528–537.

Related Research: Kitchener, K. S., & King, P. M. (1981). Reflective judgment: Concepts of justification and their relationship to age and education. *Journal of Applied Development Psychology*, *2*, 89–116.

■ ■ ■

5151

Test Name: SOCIAL STUDIES STRATEGIES SURVEY

Purpose: To assess students' perceptions of the cognitive strategies that they use in social studies and students' perception of classroom instruction.

Number of Items: 12

Format: Likert format. All items presented.

Reliability: Internal consistency ranged from .60 to .80.

Author: Knight, S. L., et al.

Article: Students' perceptions of relationships between social studies instruction and cognitive strategies.

Journal: *Journal of Educational Research*, May/June 1989, *82*(5), 270–276.

Related Research: Waxman, H., & Knight, S. (1985). *Social Studies Strategies Survey*. Houston, TX: University of Houston.

■ ■ ■

5152

Test Name: STRATEGIES SCALE

Purpose: To measure how likely teachers would be to use helping and restrictive strategies to manage a child's behavior.

Number of Items: 12

Format: Five-point Likert format.

Reliability: Cronbach's alpha ranged from .63 to .66.

Author: Cunningham, B., and Sugarwara, A.

Article: Preservice teacher's perceptions of childrens' problem behaviors.

Journal: *Journal of Educational Research*, September/October 1988, *82*(1), 34–39.

Related Research: Brophy, J., & Rohrkemper, M. (1981). The influence of problem ownership on teacher's perceptions of ad strategies for coping with problem students. *Journal of Educational Psychology*, *73*, 295–311.

5153

Test Name: STUDY PROCESS QUESTIONNAIRE

Purpose: To assess learning-approach and motive.

Number of Items: 42

Format: Includes three learning-approach scales: reproduction approach (largely memorization), meaning approach (personal value and meaning of the information), and the organizing approach (being organized); and three motive scales: intrinsic (study to pass courses); achievement (earn a degree), and instrumental (get a job).

Reliability: Alpha coefficients ranged from .53 to .73.

Validity: Correlations between scales and grade point average ranged from −.39 to .40.

Author: Miller, C. D., et al.

Article: Learning approaches and motives: male and female differences and implications for learning assistance programs.

Journal: *Journal of College Student Development*, March 1990, *31*(2), 147–154.

Related Research: Biggs, J. B. (1976). Dimensions of study behavior: Another look at ATI. *British Journal of Educational Psychology*, *46*, 68–80.

■ ■ ■

5154

Test Name: SURVEY OF PERSONAL BELIEFS

Purpose: To measure irrational thinking.

Number of Items: 50

Format: Includes five factors: awfulizing, self-directed shoulds, other-directed shoulds, low-frustration tolerance, and self-worth. Items are scored on a 6-point Likert scale format.

Reliability: Alpha correlations ranged from .57 to .89 (*N* = 280).

Test–retest (21 days) reliability ranged from .65 to .87 (*N* = 97).

Validity: Correlations with other variables ranged from −.27 to −.52.

Author: Demaria, T. P., et al.

Article: Psychometric properties of the Survey of Personal Beliefs: A rational-emotive measure of irrational thinking.

Journal: *Journal of Personality Assessment*, Summer 1989, *53*(2), 329–341.

Related Research: Kassinove, H. (1986). Self-reported affect and core irrational thinking: A preliminary analysis. *Journal of Rational-Emotive Therapy*, *42*(2), 119–130.

■ ■ ■

5155

Test Name: TEMPORAL LOBE SCALE

Purpose: To assess temporal lobe signs and complex partial epilepsy signs.

Number of Items: 30

Format: True–false. All items presented.

Reliability: Test–retest (10 days) reliability was .90, and test–retest (100 days) reliability was .70.

Author: Makarec, K., and Persinger, M. A.

Article: Electroencephalographic validation of a temporal lobe signs inventory in a normal population.

Journal: *Journal of Research in Personality*, September 1990, *24*(3), 323–337.

Related Research: Persinger, M. A., & Makarec, K. (1987). Temporal lobe epileptic signs and correlative behaviors in normal populations. *The Journal of General Psychology*, *114*, 179–195.

■ ■ ■

5156

Test Name: TENDENCY FOR PREMATURE CRITICAL

EVALUATIONS OF IDEAS IN PROBLEM SOLVING SCALE

Purpose: To measure the premature convergence in problem solving attitude.

Number of Items: 8

Format: Utilizes a 5-point Likert agreement scale.

Reliability: Cronbach's alpha ranged from .80 to .97.

Author: Basadur, M., et al.

Article: Training effects on attitudes toward divergent thinking among manufacturing engineers.

Journal: *Journal of Applied Psychology*, November 1986, *71*(4), 612–617.

Related Research: Basadur, M. S., & Finkbeiner, C. T. (1985). Measuring preference for ideation in creative problem solving training. *Journal of Applied Behavioral Science*, *21*(1), 37–49.

■ ■ ■

5157

Test Name: TEST OF CRITICAL THINKING

Purpose: To measure the ability of fourth and fifth graders to make inferences, evaluate source reliability, use deductive reasoning and to generalize.

Number of Items: 54

Time Required: 45 minutes.

Format: Multiple-choice.

Reliability: Test–retest reliabilities (2 months) was .85.

Author: Hudgins, B. B., and Edelman, S.

Article: Teacher critical thinking skills to fourth and fifth graders through teacher-led small group discussions.

Journal: *The Journal of Educational Research*, July/August, 1986, *79*(6), 333–342.

Related Research: Edelman, S., & Hudgins, B. B. (1984). *Test of critical thinking.* Unpublished test, Washington University.

■ ■ ■

5158

Test Name: TEST OF LOGICAL REASONING

Purpose: To measure logical thinking.

Number of Items: 10

Format: Measures five modes of formal reasoning: controlling variables, proportional reasoning, combinatorial reasoning, probabilistic reasoning, and correlational reasoning.

Reliability: Coefficient alpha was .85 ($N = 682$).

Validity: Correlation with the Propositional Logic Test was .63.

Author: Piburn, M. D.

Article: Reliability and validity of the Propositional Logic Test.

Journal: *Educational and Psychological Measurement,* Autumn 1989, *49*(3), 667–672.

Related Research: Tobin, K., & Capie, W. (1981). The development and validation of a group test of logical thinking. *Educational and*

Psychological Measurement, 41, 413–423.

■ ■ ■

5159

Test Name: VERBALIZER–VISUALIZER QUESTIONNAIRE

Purpose: To assess verbal (sequential information processing) and visual (parallel reasoning) thinking.

Number of Items: 15

Format: True–false.

Reliability: Internal consistency ranged from .54 to .70 across subscales.

Validity: Correlations with other cognitive style and aptitude measures ranged from −.43 to .70.

Author: Green, K. E., and Shroeder, D. H.

Article: Psychometric quality of the Verbalizer-Visualizer Questionnaire as a measure of cognitive style.

Journal: *Psychological Reports,* June 1990, *66*(3)1, 939–945.

Related Research: Richardson, A. (1977). Verbalizer–visualizer: A cognitive style dimension. *Journal of Mental Imagery, 1,* 109–126.

5160

Test Name: YOUR STYLE OF LEARNING AND THINKING

Purpose: To measure right, left, and integrated hemispheric preferences.

Number of Items: 40

Format: In each item, the subject selects one of three responses. A sample item is presented.

Reliability: Alternate-form reliability ranged from .63 to .85. Test–retest (10 weeks) coefficients ranged from .50 to .69.

Validity: Correlations with other variables ranged from −.63 to .40.

Author: Payne, D. A., and Evans, K. A.

Article: Interrelationships among three measures of preference for cognitive style based on hemisphere specialization theory.

Journal: *Perceptual and Motor Skills,* August, 1986, *63*(1), 19–25

Related Research: Torrance, E. P., & Reynolds, C. R. (1980). Norms-technical manual for Your Style of Learning and Thinking (Form C). Athens, GA: Department of Educational Psychology, University of Georgia.

CHAPTER 20
Status

5161

Test Name: PERCEIVED ECONOMIC STATUS

Purpose: To measure economic status.

Number of Items: 11

Format: Five-point Likert format.

Reliability: Alpha was .85.

Author: Singh, A. K., and Pandey, J.

Article: Social support as a moderator of the relationship between poverty and coping behaviors.

Journal: *The Journal of Social Psychology,* August 1990, *130*(4), 533–541.

Related Research: Pandey, J., & Singh, A. K. (1985). Social psychological responses to perceived and objective indicators of poverty in India. In R. I. Langunes & Y. H. Poortinga (Eds.), *From a different perspective: Studies of behavior across cultures* (pp. 148–156). Lisse, Holland: Swets and Zeitlinger.

5162

Test Name: STATUS CONCERN SCALE

Purpose: To measure attitudes toward social status and upward mobility including the value placed upon traditional symbols of status and attainment of upward mobility in conventional ways.

Number of Items: 10

Format: Sample items are presented.

Reliability: Split-half reliability coefficient was .78.

Validity: Correlation with the F scale was .71.

Author: Anderson, K. L.

Article: Androgyny, flexibility, and individualism.

Journal: *Journal of Personality Assessment,* Summer 1986, *50*(2),265–278.

Related Research: Kaufman, W. C. (1957). Status, authoritarianism and anti-Semitism. *American Journal of Sociology, 62,* 379–382.

5163

Test Name: STATUS DEFERENCE SCALE

Purpose: To measure status obeisance.

Number of Items: 29

Format: Responses are made on a 6-point scale ranging from disagree strongly to agree strongly. Examples are presented.

Reliability: Reliability coefficients ranged from .90 to .99.

Author: Okeafor, K. R., and Teddlie, C.

Article: Organizational factors related to administrators' confidence in teachers.

Journal: *Journal of Research and Development in Education,* Fall 1989, *23*(1), 28–36.

Related Research: Helsel, A. R. (1971). Status obeisance and pupil control ideology. *Journal of Educational Administration, 9,* 38–47.

CHAPTER 21
Trait Measurement

5164

Test Name: A-B RATING SCALE

Purpose: To measure Type A behavior.

Number of Items: 24. All items are presented.

Format: Sample item: "I eat slowly—I eat fast."

Reliability: Alpha ranged from .43 to .86 across three subscales. Total scale alpha was .68.

Validity: Kaiser criterion yielded seven factors, but the screen test indicated a three factor solution was desirable.

Author: Leak, G., and Flotte, K.

Article: Factor structure and factorial replication of a new measure of the Type A behavior pattern.

Journal: *Psychological Reports*, February 1987, *60*(1), 35–38.

· · ·

5165

Test Name: A-B RATING SCALE

Purpose: To assess Type A behavior in highly literate older children.

Number of Items: 17

Format: Children respond to 7-point bipolar items. An example is presented.

Reliability: Spearman-Brown test–retest reliability estimates ranged from .52 to .59.

Author: Nay, R. E., and Wagner, M. K.

Article: The assessment of Type A behavior in children and adolescents: An overview.

Journal: *Journal of Psychopathology and Behavioral Assessment*, March 1987, *9*(1), 1–12.

Related Research: Wolf, T. M., et al. (1982). Validation of a measure of Type A behavior pattern in children: Bogalusa heart study. *Child Development*, *53*, 126–135.

· · ·

5166

Test Name: ACADEMIC INTERACTION INVENTORY

Purpose: To assess college student assertiveness.

Number of Items: 30

Format: Items are descriptions of problematic situations typical of college life. Each item is rated on a 5-point scale. An example is presented.

Reliability: Test–retest reliability estimates ranged from .82 to .86.

Validity: Correlations with other variables ranged from .51 to .55.

Author: Vredenburg, K., et al.

Article: Depression in college students: Personality and experiential factors.

Journal: *Journal of Counseling Psychology*, October 1988, *35*(4), 419–425.

Related Research: Blankstein, K. R., et al. (1981, November). *A new measure of assertion in college students: Development and validation of the Academic Interaction Inventory (AII)*. Paper presented at the 15th annual meeting of the Association for Advancement of Behavior Therapy, Toronto.

5167

Test Name: ADOLESCENT EGOCENTRISM SCALE

Purpose: To measure adolescent egocentrism.

Number of Items: 15

Format: Subscale of the Adolescent Egocentrism-Sociocentrism Scale. Each item is rated for degree of personal importance on a 5-point Likert scale ranging from 1 (*no importance*) to 5 (*very important*). Includes three subscales: personal fable, self-focus, and imaginary audience. Sample items are presented.

Reliability: Cronbach's alphas ranged from .63 to .85.

Validity: Correlations with other variables ranged from −.06 to .22.

Author: Cohn, L. D.

Article: A comparison of two measures of egocentrism.

Journal: *Journal of Personality Assessment*, Summer 1988, *52*(2), 212–222.

Related Research: Enright, R. D., et al. (1980). Adolescent egocentrism-sociocentrism and self-consciousness. *Journal of Youth and Adolescence*, *9*(2), 101–116.

· · ·

5168

Test Name: ANGER CONTROL INVENTORY

Purpose: To assess the situational components and multiple response factors that determine anger control.

Number of Items: 134

Format: Includes 10 anger stimulus scales and 6 anger response scales.

Reliability: Alpha coefficients ranged from .54 to .89 ($N = 236$). Test–retest (1 month) correlations ranged from .72 to .83 ($N = 49$).

Validity: Correlations with criterion (clinical sample of 118) ranged from .13 to .47. Correlations with criterion (normal sample of 190) ranged from .12 to .56.

Author: Hoshmand, L. T., and Austin, G. W.

Article: Validation studies of a multifactor cognitive-behavioral anger control inventory.

Journal: *Journal of Personality Assessment*, Fall 1987, *51*(3), 417–432.

Related Research: Hoshmand, L. T., et al. (1981, August). *The diagnosis and assessment of anger control problems.* Paper presented at the meeting of the American Psychological Association, Los Angeles.

■ ■ ■

5169

Test Name: ANGER EXPRESSION IN AND OUT SCALES

Purpose: To measure the self-reported tendencies to generally suppress or exhibit anger when provoked.

Number of Items: 16

Format: Includes two 8-item scales. Items are rated on a 4-point Likert scale ranging from 1 (*almost never*) to 4 (*almost always*).

Reliability: Alpha reliabilities ranged from .73 to .84.

Validity: Correlations with other variables ranged from −.24 to .59.

Author: Deffenbacher, J. L., et al.

Article: Cognition-relaxation and social skills interventions in the treatment of general anger.

Journal: *Journal of Counseling Psychology*, April 1987, *34*(2), 171–176.

Related Research: Lopez, F. G., & Thurman, C. W. (1986). A cognitive-behavioral investigation of anger among college students. *Cognitive Therapy and Research, 10,* 245–256.

■ ■ ■

5170

Test Name: ANGER INVENTORY

Purpose: To measure anger.

Number of Items: 90

Format: Responses are made on a 5-point Likert scale.

Reliability: Cronbach alpha was .96.

Validity: Correlation with the reaction inventory was .82.

Author: Hains, A. A., and Szyjakowski, M.

Article: A cognitive stress-reduction intervention program for adolescents.

Journal: *Journal of Counseling Psychology*, January 1990, *37*(1), 79–84.

Related Research: Novaco, R. W. (1975). *Anger control: The development and evaluation of an experimental treatment.* Lexington, MA: D. C. Heath.

■ ■ ■

5171

Test Name: ASSERTION INVENTORY

Purpose: To measure assertiveness.

Number of Items: 18

Format: *Never* to *almost always* response categories. Sample item described.

Reliability: Alphas ranged from .70 to .82.

Author: Botvin, G. J., et al.

Article: Preventing adolescent drug abuse through a multimodal

cognitive-behavioral approach: Results of a 3–year study.

Journal: *Journal of Consulting and Clinical Psychology*, August 1990, *58*(4), 437–446.

Related Research: Gambrill, E. D., & Richey, C. A. (1975). An assertion inventory for use in assessment research. *Behavior Therapy, 6,* 550–561.

■ ■ ■

5172

Test Name: ASSERTION INVENTORY

Purpose: To assess the probability of engaging in assertive behavior and the degree of discomfort in being assertive.

Number of Items: 40

Format: A self-report scale providing response probability and discomfort scores.

Reliability: Test–retest reliabilities were .87 and .81.

Author: Stoppard, J. M., and Henri, G. S.

Article: Conceptual level matching and effects of assertion training.

Journal: *Journal of Counseling Psychology*, January 1987, *34*(1), 55–61.

Related Research: Gambrill, E. D., & Richey, C. A. (1975). An assertion inventory for use in assessment and research. *Behavior Therapy, 6,* 550–561.

■ ■ ■

5173

Test Name: ASSERTIVENESS–RESPONSIVENESS MEASURE

Purpose: To measure assertiveness and responsiveness.

Number of Items: 20

Format: Five-point Likert format.

Reliability: Split-half was .88 for assertiveness and .93 for responsiveness.

Author: Richmond, V. P., and McCroskey, J. C.

Article: Reliability and separation of factors on the Assertiveness–Responsiveness Measure.

Journal: *Psychological Reports*, October 1990, *67*(2), 449–450.

Related Research: Thompson, C. A., et al. (1990). Japanese and Americans compared on assertiveness/responsiveness. *Psychological Reports*, *66*, 829–830.

■ ■ ■

5174

Test Name: BARTNER SCALE—REVISED

Purpose: To measure Pattern A behavior.

Number of Items: 14

Format: Responses are made on a 11-point scale, centered at 0 and ascending to 5 in both directions.

Reliability: Coefficient alpha was .68

Validity: Correlations with other variables ranged from .14 to .65.

Author: Edwards, J. R., et al.

Article: Examining the relationship among self-report measure of the Type A behavior pattern: The effects of dimensionality, measurement error, and differences in underlying constructs.

Journal: *Journal of Applied Psychology*, August 1990, *75*(4), 440–454.

Related Research: Bortner, R. W. (1969). A short rating scale as a potential measure of pattern A behavior. *Journal of Chronic Diseases*, *22*, 87–91.

■ ■ ■

5175

Test Name: BRESKIN RIGIDITY TEST

Purpose: To assess cognitive mobility and fixity.

Number of Items: 15

Format: Each item is a pair of abstract visual symbols for which the subjects indicate the one they like better. Of the pair, one represents a good Gestalt (1) and the other does not (0). The more rigid subjects select the good Gestalt, which has the most closure.

Reliability: Kuder-Richardson formula coefficient was .98. Split-half coefficient was .78.

Author: Cunningham, D. M., et al.

Article: Performance of field-independent and -dependent college students, and their "fixed" and "mobile" subtypes, on two formats of a cognitive task.

Journal: *Perceptual and Motor Skills*, February 1988, *66*(1), 311–317.

Related Research: Breskin, S. (1968). Measurement of rigidity: A non-verbal test. *Perceptual and Motor Skills*, *27*, 1203–1206.

■ ■ ■

5176

Test Name: CALIFORNIA F SCALE

Purpose: To assess a style of cognitive rigidity.

Number of Items: 29

Format: Responses are made on a 7-point Likert scale.

Validity: Correlations with other variables ranged from −.46 to .19.

Author: Rich, A. R., and Bonner, R. L.

Article: Interpersonal moderators of depression among college students.

Journal: *Journal of College Student Personnel*, July 1987, *28*(4), 337–342.

Related Research: Adorno, T. W., et al. (1950). *The Authoritarian Personality*. New York: Harper.

5177

Test Name: CALIFORNIA F SCALE

Purpose: To measure authoritarian personality.

Number of Items: 20

Format: Likert response scale is used.

Reliability: Reliability coefficients ranged from .79 to .88.

Author: Wyatt, R. C., and Meyers, L. S.

Article: Psychometric properties of four 5-point Likert response scales.

Journal: *Educational and Psychological Measurement*, Spring 1987, *47*(1), 27–35.

Related Research: Adorno, T. W., et al. (1950). *The authoritarian personality*. New York: Harper.

■ ■ ■

5178

Test Name: CAUSAL DIMENSION SCALE—MODIFIED

Purpose: To provide a trait measure of attributions of success and failure.

Number of Items: 18

Format: Half the items relate to attributions of success and the other half relate to attributions of failure. Each statement was rated on a 5-point Likert scale.

Reliability: Coefficient alpha was .88.

Author: Rothblum, E. D., et al.

Article: Affective, cognitive, and behavioral differences between high and low procrastinators.

Journal: *Journal of Counseling Psychology*, October 1986, *33*(4), 387–394.

Related Research: Russell, D. (1982). The Causal Dimension Scale: A measure of how individuals perceive causes. *Journal of Personality and Social Psychology*, *42*, 1137–1145.

5179

Test Name: CHILDREN'S HOSTILITY INVENTORY

Purpose: To measure different facets of child hostility and aggression.

Number of Items: 38

Format: Subscales include: assaultiveness, indirect hostility, irritability, negativism, resentment, suspicion, and verbal hostility. Items are true–false.

Validity: Correlation with the Interview for Antisocial Behavior was .68.

Author: Kazdin, A. E., and Esveldt-Dawson, K.

Article: The interview for antisocial behavior: Psychometric characteristics and concurrent validity with child psychiatric inpatients.

Journal: *Journal of Psychopathology and Behavioral Assessment*, December 1986, *8*(4), 289–303.

Related Research: Buss, A. H., & Durkee, A. (1957). An inventory for assessing different kinds of hostility. *Journal of Consulting Psychology, 21,* 343–349.

■ ■ ■

5180

Test Name: COGNITIVE-SOMATIC ANXIETY QUESTIONNAIRE

Purpose: To measure cognitive and somatic anxiety.

Number of Items: 14

Format: Each item is rated on a 5-point scale from 1 (*not at all*) to 5 (*very much so*). All items are presented.

Validity: Correlations with other self-report measures ranged from −.40 to .50.

Author: DeGood, D. E., and Tait, R. C.

Article: The Cognitive-Somatic Anxiety Questionnaire: Psychometric and validity data.

Journal: *Journal of Psychopathology and Behavioral Assessment*, March 1987, *9*(1), 75–87.

Related Research: Schwartz, G. E., et al. (1978). Patterning of cognitive and somatic processes in the self-regulation of anxiety: Effects of mediation versus exercise. *Psychomatic Medicine, 40,* 321–328.

■ ■ ■

5181

Test Name: COLLEGE SELF-EXPRESSION SCALE (SPANISH VERSION)

Purpose: To measure assertion.

Number of Items: 50

Reliability: Test–retest (one month) was .87. Cronbach's alpha was .89.

Validity: When factor analyzed, the Spanish data revealed the same general factor structure as American data.

Author: Caballo, V. E., and Buela, G.

Article: Factor analyzing the College Self-Expression Scale with a Spanish population.

Journal: *Psychological Reports*, October 1988, *63*(2), 503–507.

Related Research: Galassi, J. P., et al. (1974). The College Self-Expression Scale: A measure of assertiveness. *Behavior Therapy, 5,* 165–171.

■ ■ ■

5182

Test Name: COLLEGE WOMEN'S ASSERTIVENESS SAMPLE

Purpose: To assess assertive behavior through a role-play measure.

Number of Items: 52

Format: Each item represents a typical social conflict presented by tape recorder to which the respondent responds verbally as if the event were actually happening.

Reliability: Internal consistency ranged from .29 to .80. Test–retest

reliabilities were .85 (1 week), .84 (4 weeks), and .57 (10 weeks).

Validity: Correlations with other variables ranged from .21 to .61.

Author: Lohr, J. M., et al.

Article: Internal consistency and reliability of alternate short forms of the College Women's Assertion Sample: Clinical and research implications.

Journal: *Journal of Psychopathology and Behavioral Assessment*, June 1990, *12*(2), 129–142.

Related Research: MacDonald, M. L. (1978). Measuring assertion: A model and method. *Behavior Therapy, 9,* 889–899.

■ ■ ■

5183

Test Name: COMPETITIVE–COOPERATIVE ATTITUDE SCALE

Purpose: To measure strength of competitiveness.

Number of Items: 28

Format: Responses are made on a 5-point scale ranging from 1 (*strongly disagree*) to 5 (*strongly agree*). Examples are presented.

Validity: Correlations with other variables were −.34 to −.08.

Author: Ryckman, R. M., et al.

Article: Construction of a hypercompetitive attitude scale.

Journal: *Journal of Personality Assessment*, Winter 1990, *55*(3 and 4), 630–639.

Related Research: Martin, H. J., & Larsen, S. (1976). Measurement of competitive-cooperative attitudes. *Psychological Reports, 39,* 303–306.

■ ■ ■

5184

Test Name: DOGMATISM SCALE

Purpose: To assess intolerance and rigidity of an individual's belief system.

Number of Items: 40

Format: Responses are made on a 5-point scale ranging from 1 (*strongly disagree*) to 5 (*strongly agree*).

Validity: Correlation with the Hypercompetitive Attitude Scale was .46 (N = 45). Examples are presented.

Author: Ryckman, R. M., et al.

Article: Construction of a hypercompetitive attitude scale.

Journal: *Journal of Personality Assessment*, Winter 1990, *55*(3 and 4), 630–639.

Related Research: Rokeach, M. (1960). *The open and closed mind: Investigations into the nature of belief systems and personality systems.* New York: Basic Books.

■ ■ ■

5185

Test Name: FRAMINGHAM SCALE

Purpose: To measure Type A behavior.

Number of Items: 10

Reliability: Coefficient alpha was .69.

Validity: Correlations with other variables ranged from .17 to .61.

Author: Edwards, J. R., et al.

Article: Examining the relationship among self-report measure of the Type A behavior pattern: The effects of dimensionality, measurement error, and differences in underlying constructs.

Journal: *Journal of Applied Psychology*, August 1990, *75*(4), 440–454.

Related Research: Haynes, S. G., et al. (1978). The relationship of psychosocial factors to coronary heart disease in the Framingham study: I. Methods and risk factors. *American Journal of Epidemiology, 107*, 362–383.

5186

Test Name: GENDER-FREE MACH IV

Purpose: To measure Machiavellianism using the Christie and Geis items with sexist terminology removed.

Format: The word *men* was changed to *people* and *father* changed to *parent* in questions 8, 14, and 20.

Reliability: Alpha was .68. Mean-item total was .38. Test–retest (6 weeks) was .76.

Validity: Sex differences were attenuated on the revised gender free version compared to the original. Lower correlations with social desirability, especially for men, were obtained compared to the original.

Author: Zook, A. II, and Sipps, G. J.

Article: Reliability data and sex differences with a Gender-Free Mach IV.

Journal: *The Journal of Social Psychology*, February 1986, *126*(1), 131–132.

Related Research: Hanson, D. I., & Vleeming, R. G. (1982). Machiavellianism: A bibliography. *JSAS Catalog of Selected Documents in Psychology, 12* (Ms. No. 2448).

■ ■ ■

5187

Test Name: HAMILTON ANXIETY SCALE

Purpose: To provide a clinician-rating scale for anxiety.

Number of Items: 14

Format: Items focus on affective, cognitive, and behavioral dimensions as well as on somatic symptoms. Responses to each item are made on a scale of 0 (*absence of symptoms*) to 4 (*very severe symptoms*).

Validity: Correlation with the State-Trait Anxiety Inventory was .75.

Author: Deluty, B. M., et al.

Article: Concordance between clinicians' and patients' ratings of anxiety and depression as mediated by private self-consciousness.

Journal: *Journal of Personality Assessment*, Spring 1986, *50*(1), 93–106

Related Research: Hamilton, M. (1959). The assessment of anxiety states by rating. *British Journal of Medical Psychology, 32*, 50–55.

■ ■ ■

5188

Test Name: HOSTILITY INVENTORY

Purpose: To measure anger and hostility.

Number of Items: 75

Format: True–false.

Validity: Correlations with trait measures of anger ranged from .66 to .71.

Author: Maiuro, R. D., et al.

Article: Anger, hostility and depression in domestically violent versus generally assaultive men and nonviolent control subjects.

Journal: *Journal of Consulting and Clinical Psychology*, February 1988, *56*(1), 17–23.

Related Research: Buss, A. H., & Durkee, A. (1975). An inventory for assessing different kinds of hostility. *Journal of Consulting Psychology, 21*, 343–349.

■ ■ ■

5189

Test Name: IMAGINARY AUDIENCE SCALE

Purpose: To measure egocentrism.

Number of Items: 12

Format: Each item is a brief vignette depicting a potentially embarrassing situation for which the subject chooses one of three responses indicating degree of self-consciousness ranging from 1 (*low*) to 3 (*high*). Includes two subscales: abiding self and transient self.

Reliability: Coefficient alphas ranged from .59 to .65.

Validity: Correlations with other variables ranged from −.28 to .32.

Author: Cohn, L. D., et al.

Article: A comparison of two measures of egocentrism.

Journal: *Journal of Personality Assessment*, Summer 1988, *52*(1), 212–222.

Related Research: Elkind, D., & Bowen, R. (1979). Imaginary audience behavior in children and adolescents. *Developmental Psychology*, *15*(1), 38–44.

■ ■ ■

5190

Test Name: MACH IV

Purpose: To assess Machiavellianism.

Number of Items: 20

Reliability: Split-half reliabilities averaged .79. Cronbach's alpha was .73.

Validity: Correlations with other variables ranged from .10 to .52.

Author: Mullins, L. S., and Kopelman, R. E.

Article: Toward an assessment of the construct validity of four measures of narcissism.

Journal: *Journal of Personality Assessment*, Winter 1988, *52*(4), 610–625.

Related Research: Christie, R., & Geis, F. L. (Eds.). (1970). *Studies in Machiavellianism*. New York: Academic.

■ ■ ■

5191

Test Name: MANIFEST ANXIETY SCALE

Purpose: To measure trait anxiety.

Number of Items: 50

Format: Contains descriptions of manifest anxiety taken from the Minnesota Multiphasic Personality Inventory. The student indicates whether each is either *true* or *false*.

Reliability: Test–retest (3-weeks, 5-months, and greater than 5 months) reliabilities were .88, .82, and .81, respectively.

Author: Chapin, T. J.

Article: The relationship of trait anxiety and academic performance to achievement anxiety: Students at risk.

Journal: *Journal of College Student Development*, May 1989, *30*(3), 229–236.

Related Research: Taylor, J. A. (1953). A personality scale of manifest anxiety. *Journal of Abnormal and Social Psychology*, *30*, 367–374.

■ ■ ■

5192

Test Name: MARGOLIS-THOMAS MEASURE OF NARCISSISM—REVISED

Purpose: To measure narcissism.

Number of Items: 24

Format: Items are paired statements: one narcissistic, the other nonnarcissistic.

Reliability: Kuder-Richardson Formula 20 was .69.

Validity: Correlations with other variables ranged from −.34 to .52.

Author: Mullins, L. S., and Kopelman, R. E.

Article: Toward an assessment of the construct validity of four measures of narcissism.

Journal: *Journal of Personality Assessment*, Winter 1988, *52*(4), 610–625.

Related Research: Margolis, H. D., & Thomas, V. (1980). *The*

measurement of narcissism in adolescents with and without behavioral and emotional disabilities. Unpublished master's thesis. United States International University, San Diego, CA.

■ ■ ■

5193

Test Name: MATTHEWS YOUTH TEST FOR HEALTH

Purpose: To assess Type A behavior of preadolescents.

Number of Items: 17

Format: Teachers indicate on a 5-point scale from 1 (*extremely uncharacteristic*) to 5 (*extremely characteristic*) how characteristic each item is of the student.

Reliability: Test–retest (3 months) reliability ranged from .79 to .82. Cronbach's alphas were .89 and .88. Interrater reliability was .61.

Validity: Correlations with other variables ranged from −.12 to .42.

Author: Smith, J. C., and Gerace, T. A.

Article: Validity of the Miami Structured Interview—1 for assessing Type A behavior, competitiveness, and aggression in children.

Journal: *Journal of Psychopathology and Behavioral Assessment*, December 1987, *9*(4), 369–382.

Related Research: Matthews, K. A., & Angulo, J. (1980). Measurement of the Type A behavior pattern in children: Assessment of children's competitiveness, impatience-anger, and aggression. *Child Development*, *51*, 466–475.

■ ■ ■

5194

Test Name: NARCISSISM INVENTORY

Purpose: To measure narcissistic pathology.

Number of Items: 41

Format: Yes–no format. All items presented.

Reliability: Alphas ranged from .76 to .84.

Validity: Congruence coefficients ranged from .95 to .96.

Author: O'Brien, M. L.

Article: Further evidence on the validity of the O'Brien multiphasic narcissism inventory.

Journal: *Psychological Reports*, June 1988, *62*(3), 879–882.

■ ■ ■

5195

Test Name: NARCISSISTIC PERSONALITY DISORDER SCALE

Purpose: To measure narcissism.

Number of Items: 9

Format: Items are answered *true* or *false*.

Reliability: Kuder-Richardson Formula 20 was .42.

Validity: Correlations with other variables ranged from –.29 to .30.

Author: Mullins, L. S., and Kopelman, R. E.

Article: Toward an assessment of the construct validity of four measures of narcissism.

Journal: *Journal of Personality Assessment*, Winter 1988, *52*(4), 610–625.

Related Research: Watson, P. J., et al. (1984). Narcissism and empathy: Validity evidence for the Narcissistic Personality Inventory. *Journal of Personality Assessment, 48*, 301–305.

■ ■ ■

5196

Test Name: NARCISSISTIC PERSONALITY INVENTORY

Purpose: To measure narcissism.

Number of Items: 54

Format: Forced-choice.

Reliability: Alternate forms (8 week interval) was .72.

Author: Carroll, L.

Article: A comparative study of narcissism, gender, and sex-role orientation among bodybuilders, athletes, and psychology students.

Journal: *Psychological Reports*, June 1989, *64*(3, Part I), 999–1006.

Related Research: Raskin, R., & Hall, C. S. (1979). A Narcissistic Personality Inventory. *Psychological Reports, 45*, 590.

■ ■ ■

5197

Test Name: NARCISSISTIC PERSONALITY INVENTORY

Purpose: To measure narcissism.

Number of Items: 27

Format: Forms A and B.

Reliability: Internal consistency of both forms was .87.

Validity: Correlations with other variables ranged from –.13 to .42.

Author: Mullins, L. S., and Kopelman, R. E.

Article: Toward an assessment of the construct validity of four measures of narcissism.

Journal: *Journal of Personality Assessment*, Winter 1988, *52*(4), 610–625.

Related Research: Raskin, R. N., & Hall, C. S. (1981). The Narcissistic Personality Inventory: Alternate form reliability and further evidence of construct validity. *Journal of Personality Assessment, 45*, 159–162.

■ ■ ■

5198

Test Name: NARCISSISTIC PERSONALITY SCALE

Purpose: To measure narcissism.

Number of Items: 75

Format: Yes–no format. All items presented.

Reliability: Alphas ranged from .71 to .76. Test–retest reliability ranged from .71 to .74.

Validity: Correlated from –.23 to .65 with neuroticism and extraversion.

Author: O'Brien, M. L.

Article: Examining the dimensionality of pathological narcissism: Factor analysis and construct validity of the O'Brien Multiphasic Inventory.

Journal: *Psychological Reports*, October 1987, *61*(2), 499–510.

Related Research: Raskin, R. N., & Hall, C. S. (1981). The Narcissistic Personality Inventory: Alternate form reliability and further evidence of construct validity. *Journal of Personality Assessment, 45*, 159–162.

■ ■ ■

5199

Test Name: NARCISSISTIC PERSONALITY INVENTORY— REVISED

Purpose: To measure narcissism.

Number of Items: 40

Format: Includes seven factors: authority, exhibitionism, superiority, vanity, explorativeness, entitlement, and self-sufficiency.

Validity: Correlations with other variables ranged from –.48 to .57.

Author: Raskin, R., and Novacek, J.

Article: An MMPI description of the narcissistic personality.

Journal: *Journal of Personality Assessment*, Spring 1989, *53*(1), 66–80.

Related Research: Raskin, R., & Hall, C. S. (1979). A narcissistic personality inventory. *Psychological Reports, 45*, 590.

■ ■ ■

5200

Test Name: PERFECTIONISM SCALE

Purpose: To measure neurotic perfectionism.

Number of Items: 10

Reliability: Test–retest (2 weeks) reliability was .74. Internal consistency was .73.

Validity: One factor accounted for 57 percent of common variance and 30 percent of total variance.

Author: Broday, S. F., and Sedlacek, W. E.

Article: Factor analysis and reliability of the Burns Perfectionism Scale.

Journal: *Psychological Reports*, June 1988, *62*(3), 806.

Related Research: Burns, D. D. (1983). The spouse who is a perfectionist. *Medical Aspects of Human Sexuality*, *17*, 219–230.

■ ■ ■

5201

Test Name: PERSONALITY STYLE SCALE

Purpose: To measure assertiveness and responsiveness.

Number of Items: 40

Format: Five-point Likert format.

Reliability: Alpha was .91.

Author: Morgan, M. Y., and Scanzoni, J.

Article: Religious orientations and women's expected continuity in the labor force.

Journal: *Journal of Marriage and the Family*, May 1987, *49*(2), 367–379.

Related Research: Elias, J. (1979, March). *Identification of a personality style*. Paper presented at the Missouri Department of Education Workshop for Home Economics Teachers, Lake Ozark, MO.

■ ■ ■

5202

Test Name: RAPE EMPATHY SCALE—REVISED

Purpose: To assess empathy toward both rapists and rape victims.

Number of Items: 20

Format: Responses are made on a 7-point Likert scale from 1 (*strongly agree*) to 7 (*strongly disagree*).

Validity: Correlation with the Attitudes toward Rape Questionnaire was .64.

Author: Border, L. A., et al.

Article: Effects of a university rape prevention program on attitudes and empathy toward rape.

Journal: *Journal of College Student Development*, March 1988, *29*(2), 132–136.

Related Research: Deitz, S. R., et al. (1982). Measurement of empathy toward rape victims and rapists. *Journal of Personality and Social Psychology*, *43*, 372–384.

■ ■ ■

5203

Test Name: RATHUS ASSERTIVENESS SCHEDULE

Purpose: To measure global assertiveness.

Number of Items: 30

Reliability: Test–retest reliability was .78. Split-half reliability was .77.

Validity: Correlations with other variables ranged from −.32 to .36.

Author: Elliott, T. R., and Gramling, S. E.

Article: Personal assertiveness and the effects of social support among college students.

Journal: *Journal of Counseling Psychology*, October 1990, *37*(4), 427–436.

Related Research: Rathus, S. (1973). A 30-item schedule for assessing assertive behavior. *Behavior Therapy*, *4*, 398–406.

■ ■ ■

5204

Test Name: RELATIONSHIP INVENTORY EMPATHY SCALE— OS FORM

Purpose: To assess an individual's perceptions of another's empathic responsivity.

Number of Items: 16

Format: Responses are made on a 6-point anchored scale, ranging from −3 to +3.

Reliability: Split-half reliability coefficient was .86.

Author: Harman, J. I.

Article: Relations among components of the empathic process.

Journal: *Journal of Counseling Psychology*, October, 1986, *33*(4), 371–376.

Related Research: Barrett-Lennard, G. T. (1981). The empathy cycle: Refinement of a nuclear concept. *Journal of Counseling Psychology*, *28*, 91–100.

■ ■ ■

5205

Test Name: REVISED CHEEK AND BUSS SHYNESS SCALE

Purpose: To measure shyness.

Number of Items: 13

Format: Responses are made on a 5-point scale ranging from 1 (*very uncharacteristic, strongly disagree*) to 5 (*very characteristic, strongly agree*).

Reliability: Internal consistency coefficient was .90. Test–retest (45 days) reliability was .88.

Validity: Correlations with ratings of shyness were .63 and .79.

Author: Phillips, S. D., and Bruch, M. A.

Article: Shyness and dysfunction in career development.

Journal: *Journal of Counseling Psychology*, April 1988, *35*(2), 159–165.

Related Research: Cheek, J. M., & Buss, A. H. (1981). Shyness and sociability. *Journal of Personality and Social Psychology*, *41*, 330–339.

5206

Test Name: RIGIDITY QUESTIONNAIRE

Purpose: To measure rigidity based on a need for certainty.

Number of Items: 12

Format: Employs a 5-point response scale. Examples are presented.

Reliability: Coefficient alpha was .74.

Author: James, L. A., and James, L. R.

Article: Integrating work environment perceptions: Explorations into the measurement of meaning.

Journal: *Journal of Applied Psychology*, October 1989, *74*(5), 739–751.

Related Research: James, L. R., et al. (1979). Correlates of psychological influence: An illustration of the psychological climate approach to work environment perceptions. *Personnel Psychology, 32*, 563–588.

■ ■ ■

5207

Test Name: SELF-CONTROL SCHEDULE

Purpose: To provide a trait measure of self-control.

Number of Items: 35

Format: Items are rated on a 4-point Likert scale ranging from 2 to −2.

Reliability: Alpha coefficients ranged from .78 to .86. Test–retest reliability was .86.

Author: Rothblum, E. D., et al.

Article: Affective, cognitive, and behavioral differences between high and low procrastinators.

Journal: *Journal of Counseling Psychology*, October 1986, *33*(4), 387–394.

Related Research: Rosenbaum, M. (1980). A schedule for assessing self-control behaviors: Preliminary

findings. *Behavior Therapy, 11*, 109–121.

■ ■ ■

5208

Test Name: SELF-FOCUS SENTENCE COMPLETION TEST

Purpose: To assess level of narcissism.

Number of Items: 30

Format: Sentence completion utilizing one of six categories: self-focus, self-focus negative, external world focus, external world focus affective, ambivalence, and neutral.

Reliability: Interrater reliabilities ranged from .90 to .97 for self-focus and .77 to .90 for self-focus negative.

Author: Gacono, C. B.

Article: An empirical study of object relations and defensive operation in antisocial personality disorder.

Journal: *Journal of Personality Assessment*, Summer 1990, *54*(3 and 4), 589–600.

Related Research: Exner, J. (1973). The self-focus sentence completion: A study of egocentricity. *Journal of Personality Assessment, 37*, 437–455.

■ ■ ■

5209

Test Name: SELF-RIGHTEOUSNESS SCALE

Purpose: To measure self-righteousness.

Number of Items: 4

Format: Five-point Likert format. All items presented.

Reliability: Alpha was .73.

Author: Falbo, T., and Sheppard, J. A.

Article: Self-righteousness: Cognitive, power, and religious characterisitics.

Journal: *Journal of Research in Personality*, June 1986, *20*(2), 145–157.

Related Research: Falbo, T., & Belk, S. S. (1985). A short scale to measure

self-righteousness. *Journal of Personality Assessment, 49*, 172–177.

■ ■ ■

5210

Test Name: SHYNESS RESPONSE SCALE

Purpose: To measure responses to shyness.

Number of Items: 24

Format: Five-point frequency scales.

Reliability: Alphas ranged from .66 to .81.

Author: Bruch, M. A., et al.

Article: Differences between fearful and self-concious shy subtypes in background and current adjustment.

Journal: *Journal of Research in Personality*, June 1986, *20*(2), 172–186.

Related Research: Zimbardo, P. G. (1977). *Shyness*. Reading, MA: Addison Wesley.

■ ■ ■

5211

Test Name: SHYNESS SCALE

Purpose: To measure shyness.

Number of Items: 11

Format: Likert format.

Reliability: Spearman-Brown odd-even was .78.

Author: Maroldo, G. K.

Article: Shyness, boredom and grade point average among college students.

Journal: *Psychological Reports*, August 1986, *59*(1)I, 395–398.

Related Research: Cheek, J. N., & Buss, A. H. (1981). Shyness and sociability. *Journal of Personality and Social Psychology, 5*, 592–600.

■ ■ ■

5212

Test Name: SPORT COMPETITION ANXIETY TEST

Purpose: To measure competitive trait anxiety.

Number of Items: 15

Format: Responses to each item are made on a 3-point scale (*hardly ever, sometimes, often*).

Validity: Correlation with state anxiety was .52.

Author: Cooley, E. J.

Article: Situational and trait determinants of competitive state anxiety.

Journal: *Perceptual and Motor Skills*, June 1987, *64*(3, Part 1), 767–773.

Related Research: Martens, R. (1977). *Sport competition anxiety test.* Champaign, IL: Human Kinetics.

■ ■ ■

5213

Test Name: STATE-TRAIT ANGER SCALE—TRAIT

Purpose: To assess general anger.

Number of Items: 10

Format: Likert scale with each item rated from 1 (*almost never*) to 4 (*almost always*) indicating how the person generally feels.

Reliability: Internal consistency ranged from .81 to .91.

Validity: Correlations with other variables ranged from −.01 to .31.

Author: Deffenbacher, J. L., et al.

Article: Cognitive-relaxation and social skills interventions in the treatment of general anger.

Journal: *Journal of Counseling Psychology*, April 1987, *34*(2), 171–176.

Related Research: Spielberger, C. D., et al. (1983). Assessment of anger: The State-Trait Anger Scale. In J. N. Butcher & C. D. Spielberger (Eds.), *Advances in personality assessment* (Vol. 2, pp. 112–134). Hillsdale, NJ: Erlbaum.

5214

Test Name: TELLEGEN ABSORPTION SCALE

Purpose: To measure openness to absorbing and self-altering experiences.

Number of Items: 34

Format: Subjects rate on a scale ranging from 1 (*strongly disliked*) to 5 (*strongly liked*) 20 slides of 15th century representational painting and 10 slides of 20th century abstract painting.

Validity: Correlations with other variables ranged from −.02 to .48.

Author: Combs, A. L., et al.

Article: Absorption and appreciation of visual art.

Journal: *Perceptual and Motor Skills*, October 1988, *67*(2), 453–454.

Related Research: Tellegen, A., & Atkinson, G. (1974). Openness to absorbing and self-altering experiences ("absorption"), a trait related to hypnotic susceptibility. *Journal of Abnormal Psychology, 83,* 268–277.

■ ■ ■

5215

Test Name: THE ANXIETY SCALE

Purpose: To provide a clinician-rating scale for anxiety.

Number of Items: 9 categories.

Format: Each category is rated on a 5-point scale from 1 (*absent or minimal manifestation*) to 5 (*maximal manifestation*).

Reliability: Interrater reliability ranged from .56 to .93.

Validity: Correlations with the patients' Taylor Manifest Anxiety scores was .63.

Author: Deluty, B. M., et al.

Article: Concordance between clinicians' and patients' ratings of anxiety and depression as mediated by private self-consciousness.

Journal: *Journal of Personality Assessment*, Spring 1986, *50*(1), 93–106.

Related Research: Buss, A. H., et al. (1955). The measurement of anxiety in clinical situations. *Journal of Consulting Psychology, 19,* 125–129.

■ ■ ■

5216

Test Name: TOLERANCE OF AMBIGUITY SCALE

Purpose: To measure tolerance of ambiguity.

Number of Items: 20

Format: Six-point Likert format. Sample items presented.

Reliability: Split-half reliability was .86. Test–retest reliability was .63 (6 months).

Author: Tegano, D. W.

Article: Relationships of tolerance of ambiguity and playfulness to creativity.

Journal: *Psychological Reports*, June 1990, *66*(3)1, 1047–1056.

Related Research: Rydell, S. T. (1966). Tolerance of ambiguity and semantic differential ratings. *Psychological Reports, 19,* 1303–1312.

■ ■ ■

5217

Test Name: TRAIT SPORT-CONFIDENCE INVENTORY

Purpose: To measure trait self-confidence when competing in a sport.

Number of Items: 13

Format: Responses to each item are made on a 9-point Likert scale ranging from *low* to *high*. Respondents answer in terms of how they usually feel.

Validity: Correlation with: predicted finishing time, −.42; actual finishing time, −.43.

Author: Gayton, W. F., and Nickless, C. J.

Article: An investigation of the validity of the trait and state sport-confidence inventories in predicting marathon performance.

Journal: *Perceptual and Motor Skills*, October 1987, *65*(2), 481–482.

Related Research: Vealey, R. S. (1986). Conceptualization of sport-confidence and competitive orientation: Preliminary investigation and instrument development. *Journal of Sport Psychology*, *8*, 221–246.

■ ■ ■

5218

Test Name: TYPE A BEHAVIOR QUESTIONNAIRE (FINNISH)

Purpose: To measure type A behavior.

Number of Items: 17

Format: Five-point Likert format.

Reliability: General reliabilities ranged from .72 to .81.

Validity: Correlations with Hunter-Wolf A-B Rating Scale was .62.

Author: Räikkönen, K., and Keltikangas-Järvinen, L.

Article: Prevalence and sociodemographic variance of Type A behavior in Finnish preadolescents, adolescents, and young adults.

Journal: *Journal of General Psychology*, July 1989, *116*(3), 271–283.

Related Research: Mathews, K. A., & Angulo, J. (1980). Measurement of type A behavior pattern in children: Assessment of children's

competitiveness, impatience-anger, and aggression. *Child Development*, *51*, 466–475.

■ ■ ■

5219

Test Name: TYPE A COGNITIVE QUESTIONNAIRE

Purpose: To provide a self-report measure to reflect specific Type A cognitions.

Number of Items: 41

Format: Responses to each item are made on a 9-point Likert scale indicating the degree to which each item is descriptive of the person's thinking. Examples are presented.

Reliability: Coefficient alphas were .94 and .95. Test–retest (1 week) reliability was .84.

Validity: Correlations with other variables ranged from .18 to .60.

Author: Watkins, P. L., et al.

Article: Empirical support for a Type A belief system.

Journal: *Journal of Psychopathology and Behavioral Assessment*, June 1987, *9*(2), 119–134.

■ ■ ■

5220

Test Name: TYPE A INVENTORY

Purpose: To measure type A behavior.

Number of Items: 9

Format: Employs a 7-point scale ranging from *very true of me* to *not at all true of me*.

Validity: Correlations with other variables ranged from –.30 to .79.

Author: Kirschner, C., et al.

Article: Personality and performance: An examination of Type A and B constructs.

Journal: *Journal of Perceptual and Motor Skills*, June 1989, *68*(3) Part 2, 1104–1106.

Related Research: Caplan, R. D. Organized stress and individual strain: a social-psychological study of risk factors in coronary heart disease among administrators, engineers, and scientists. (Doctoral dissertation, University of Michigan, 1971) *Dissertation Abstracts International*, 1971, 690. (University Microfilm No. 72-14822)

■ ■ ■

5221

Test Name: YOUNG CHILDREN'S EMPATHY MEASURE

Purpose: To measure preschool childrens' empathy.

Number of Items: 4 vignettes, each with 2 questions.

Format: Child is asked questions about vignettes describing fear, sadness, anger, and happiness.

Reliability: Total alpha was .69. Interrater reliability ranged from .93 to .99.

Validity: Correlated .41 with age, and .13 with the Peabody Picture Vocabulary.

Author: Poresky, R. H.

Article: The Young Children's Empathy Measure: Reliability and effects of Companion animal bonding.

Journal: *Psychological Reports*, June 1990, *66*(3)1, 931–936.

CHAPTER 22
Values

5222

Test Name: CAREER IMPORTANCE SCALE

Purpose: To measure the importance of work in a person's life.

Number of Items: 3

Format: Seven-point Likert format.

Reliability: Alpha was .72.

Author: Posner, B. Z., and Powell, G. N.

Article: A longitudinal investigation of work preferences among college graduates.

Journal: *Psychological Reports*, June 1990, *66*(3, Part II), 1125–1134.

Related Research: Posner, B. Z., & Schmidt, W. H. (1984). Values and the American manager: An update. *California Management Review*, 26, 202–216.

• • •

5223

Test Name: CAREER VALUES SCALE

Purpose: To measure managerial and technical career values.

Number of Items: 14

Format: Seven-point Likert format.

Reliability: Alphas were .72 (mangerial values) and .79 (technical values).

Author: Rynes, S. L., et al.

Article: Aspirations to manage: A comparison of engineering students and working engineers.

Journal: *Journal of Vocational Behavior*, April 1988, *32*(2), 239–253

Related Research: Shein, E. H. (1978). *Career dynamics*. Reading, MA: Addison Wesley.

• • •

5224

Test Name: CLOTHING VALUES INVENTORY

Purpose: To measure clothing values.

Number of Items: 33

Format: Responses are made on a 5-point Likert scale ranging from *never* to *always*.

Reliability: Split-half corrected coefficient was .78.

Validity: Correlations with the Perceived Clothing Deprivation Questionnaire ranged from −.14 to .26.

Author: Francis, S. K., & Liu, Q.

Article: Effects of clothing values on perceived clothing deprivation among adolescents.

Journal: *Perceptual and Motor Skills*, December 1990, *71*(3, Part 2), 1191–1199.

Related Research: Creekmore, A. M. (1966). *Methods of Measuring Clothing Variables*. East Lansing: Michigan State University Press.

• • •

5225

Test Name: COLLECTIVISM/POWER DISTANCE MEASURE

Purpose: To measure collectivism and power distance.

Number of Items: 7

Format: Four items measured collectivism and three items measured power distance. Responses were made on a 5-point Likert scale ranging from 1 (*strongly disagree*) to 5 (*strongly agree*). All items are presented.

Reliability: Cronbach's alphas were .69 (collectivism) and .75 (power distance).

Author: Erez, M., and Earley, P. C.

Article: Comparative analysis of goal-setting strategies across cultures.

Journal: *Journal of Applied Psychology*, November 1987, *72*(4), 658–665.

Related Research: Hofstede, G. (1984). *Culture's consequences: International differences in work related values* (abridged). Beverly Hills, CA: Sage.

• • •

5226

Test Name: FAITH SCALE

Purpose: To measure faith in people, self, supreme being, and technology.

Number of Items: 35

Format: Five-point Likert format. Sample items presented.

Validity: Correlations of two subscales with other variables ranged from −.20 to .28.

Author: Van De Water, D. A., and McAdams, D. P.

Article: Generativity and Erikson's "Belief in the Species."

Journal: *Journal of Research in Personality*, December 1989, *23*(4), 435–449.

Related Research: Tipton, R. M., et al. (1980). Faith and locus of control. *Psychological Reports*, *46*, 1151–1154.

■ ■ ■

5227

Test Name: FIVE DIMENSIONAL RELIGIOSITY SCALE

Purpose: To measure religiosity.

Number of Items: 24

Format: Includes five subscales: ideological, ritualistic, intellectual, experiential, and consequential.

Reliability: Coefficients of reproducibility ranged from .90 to .94 for the five subscales.

Author: Young, M.

Article: Religiosity and satisfaction with virginity among college men and women.

Journal: *Journal of College Student Personnel*, July 1986, *27*(4), 339–344.

Related Research: Faulkner, J. E., & DeJong, G. F. (1966). Religiosity in 5–D: An empirical analysis. *Social Forces*, *45*, 246–254.

■ ■ ■

5228

Test Name: INTERCULTURAL VALUES INVENTORY

Purpose: To identify value orientations and their alternative solutions.

Number of Items: 150

Format: Includes five orientation scales, each containing three subscales of 10 items each. Responses are yes–no. The five orientations are: human nature mode, person/nature mode, time sense mode, activity mode, and social relations mode.

Reliability: Coefficients ranged from .54 to .79.

Author: Carter, R. T.

Article: Cultural value differences between African-Americans and White Americans.

Journal: *Journal of College Student Development*, January 1990, *31*(1), 71–79.

Related Research: Carter, R. T. (1984). *The relationship between Black American college students value-orientations and their racial identity attitudes.* Unpublished manuscript, University of Maryland, College Park, Maryland.

■ ■ ■

5229

Test Name: ISLAMIC WORK ETHIC AND INDIVIDUALISM SCALES

Purpose: To measure the belief that work is obligatory and a virtue and that self-reliance is a source of success.

Number of Items: 53

Format: Five-point Likert format. All items presented.

Reliability: Alphas were .89 (work ethic) and .79 (individualism).

Author: Ali, A.

Article: Scaling on Islamic work ethic.

Journal: *The Journal of Social Psychology*, October 1989, *128*(5), 575–583.

Related Research: Ali, A. (1986/87). The Arab executive: A study of values and work orientations. *American-Arab Affairs*, *19*, 94–100.

■ ■ ■

5230

Test Name: LAM SCALE

Purpose: To measure literal, antiliteral and antireligious theological orientations.

Number of Items: 17

Format: Forced-choice.

Reliability: Alphas ranged from .71 to .92.

Author: Clark, C. A., et al.

Article: The transmission of religious beliefs and practices from parents to firstborn early adolescent sons.

Journal: *Journal of Marriage and the Family*, May 1988, *50*(2), 463–472.

Related Research: Hunt, R. A. (1972). The LAM scales. *Journal for the Scientific Study of Religion*, *11*, 42–52.

■ ■ ■

5231

Test Name: LIFE ESTEEM SURVEY

Purpose: To measure the importance of 22 life goals.

Number of Items: 22

Format: Nine-point (weighted) scales. All items and weights are presented.

Reliability: Alphas ranged from .61 to .78. Test–retest reliability ranged from .79 to .81.

Author: Wheeler, R. J., et al.

Article: Life goals and general well-being.

Journal: *Psychological Reports*, February 1990, *66*(1), 307–312.

Related Research: Wheeler, R. J. (1977). Measuring sense of purpose. Unpublished Master's thesis: St. Louis University.

■ ■ ■

5232

Test Name: MORAL ORIENTATION SCALE USING CHILDHOOD DILEMMAS

Purpose: To measure adult preference for "justice-" or "care-" oriented moral thinking.

Number of Items: 12

Format: Respondents read each dilemma and rank the four accompanying considerations in order of preference. An example is presented.

Reliability: Test–retest (2–3 weeks) reliability was .71 (*N* = 25).

Author: Yacker, N., and Weinberg, S. L.

Article: Care and justice moral orientation: A scale for its assessment.

Journal: *Journal of Personality Assessment*, Fall 1990, *55*(1 and 2), 18–27.

Related Research: Orenstein, S. H. (1988). *Parental preference in moral dilemma resolution with girls and boys*. Unpublished dissertation proposal, New York University, New York.

■ ■ ■

5233

Test Name: OCCUPATIONAL VALUES SCALE

Purpose: To measure how important each value would be in an ideal job.

Number of Items: 10

Format: Each item is rated on a 3-point scale from 1 (*low*) to 3 (*high*). All items are presented.

Validity: Correlations with vocational identity ranged from −.60 to .69.

Author: Leong, F. T. L., and Morris, J.

Article: Assessing the construct validity of Holland, Daiger, and Power's measure of vocational identity.

Journal: *Measurement and Evaluation in Counseling and Development*, October 1989, *22*(3), 117–125.

Related Research: Rosenberg, M. (1957). *Occupations and values*. Glencoe, IL: The Free Press.

■ ■ ■

5234

Test Name: OHIO WORK VALUES INVENTORY

Purpose: To measure the work values of elementary school children.

Number of Items: 77

Format: Includes 11 scales: altruism, object orientation, job security, control, self-realization, independence, money, task satisfaction, solitude, ideas-data, and prestige. Responses are made on a 5-point scale ranging from 1 (*not much*) to 5 (*very much*).

Reliability: Internal consistency reliability ranged from .61 to .95.

Author: Leong, F. T. L., and Tata, S. P.

Article: Sex and acculturation differences in occupational values among Chinese-American children.

Journal: *Journal of Counseling Psychology*, April 1990, *37*(2), 208–212.

Related Research: Hales, L. W., & Fenner, B. J. (1975). Measuring the work values of children: The Ohio Work Values Inventory. *Measurement and Evaluation in Guidance*, 8, 20–25.

■ ■ ■

5235

Test Name: OUTCOME VALUES QUESTIONNAIRE

Purpose: To measure children's values of aggression outcomes.

Number of Items: 40

Format: Includes six scales: tangible rewards, control of the victim, suffering by the victim, retaliation from the victim, peer rejection, and negative self-evaluation. Sample items are presented.

Reliability: Coefficient alphas ranged from .58 to .85.

Author: Boldizar, J. P., et al.

Article: Outcome values and aggression.

Journal: *Child Development*, June 1989, *60*(3), 571–579.

Related Research: Harter, S. (1982). The Perceived Competence Scale for children. *Child Development, 53,* 87–97.

■ ■ ■

5236

Test Name: PARARELIGIOUS BELIEF INVENTORY

Purpose: To measure parareligious beliefs.

Number of Items: 30

Format: Three-point belief scale (*unqualified belief* to *disbelief*).

Reliability: Alpha was .89.

Author: Zeidner, M., and Beit-Hallahmi, B.

Article: Sex, ethnic, and social class differences in parareligious beliefs among Israeli adolescents.

Journal: *The Journal of Social Psychology,* June 1988, *128*(3), 333–343.

Related Research: Plug, C. (1975). The psychology of superstition: A review. *Psychologia Africana, 16,* 93–115.

■ ■ ■

5237

Test Name: PERSONAL RELIGIOSITY INVENTORY

Purpose: To measure religiosity in nine dimensions.

Number of Items: 45

Format: Likert format.

Reliability: Highest alpha was .94.

Author: Handal, P. J., et al.

Article: Preliminary investigation of the relationship between religion and psychological distress in Black women.

Journal: *Psychological Reports,* December 1989, *65*(3, Part I), 971–975.

Related Research: Lipsmeyer, M. B. (1984). The measurement of religiosity and its relationship to mental health impairment.

Dissertation Abstracts International, 45, 1918–1919.

■ ■ ■

5238

Test Name: PHYSICAL FITNESS-VALUE SCALE

Purpose: To measure general value held toward health-related physical fitness.

Number of Items: 9

Format: Employs a 6-point Likert-type scale ranging from 1 (*strongly disagree*) to 6 (*strongly agree*). An example is presented.

Reliability: Coefficient alpha was .85.

Validity: Correlations with other variables ranged from .18 to .36.

Author: Bezjak, J. E., and Lee, J. W.

Article: Relationship of self-efficacy and locus of control constructs in predicting college students' physical fitness behaviors.

Journal: *Perceptual and Motor Skills,* October 1990, 71(2), 499–508.

Related Research: Rokeach, M. (1973). *The nature of human values.* New York: Free Press.

■ ■ ■

5239

Test Name: PRO-PROTESTANT WORK ETHIC

Purpose: To measure the Protestant work ethic.

Number of Items: 4

Format: Responses are made on a 6-point scale ranging from 1 (*strongly disagree*) to 6 (*strongly agree*). An example is presented.

Reliability: Alpha coefficients were .65 and .67 (*N* = 90). Test–retest reliability (7 month) was .60 (*N* = 90).

Author: Blau, G. J.

Article: Using a person–environment fit model to predict job involvement and organizational commitment.

Journal: *Journal of Vocational Behavior,* June 1987, 30(3), 240–257.

Related Research: Blood, M. (1969). Work values and job satisfaction. Work values and job satisfaction. *Journal of Applied Psychology, 53,* 456–459.

■ ■ ■

5240

Test Name: PROTESTANT ETHIC SCALE

Purpose: To measure the perceived virtues of industriousness, asceticism, and individualism.

Number of Items: 19

Format: 6-point agreement scales.

Reliability: Internal reliabilities ranged from .74 to .75.

Author: Feather, N. T., and O'Brien, G. E.

Article: A longitudinal study of the effects of employment and unemployment on school leaving.

Journal: *Journal of Occupational Psychology,* June 1986, 59(2), 121–144.

Related Research: Mirels, H. L., & Garrett, J. B. (1971). The protestant ethic as a personality variable. *Journal of Consulting and Clinical Psychology, 36,* 40–44.

■ ■ ■

5241

Test Name: RELIGIOSITY SCALE

Purpose: To measure religiosity.

Number of Items: 23

Format: Likert format.

Reliability: Test–retest ranged from .84 (10 weeks) to .43 (2 years).

Author: Gladding, S. T., and Clayton, G. A.

Article: The Gladding, Lewis and Adkins Scale of Religiosity: Differences among a sample of Protestants, Catholics, Jews and nonaffiliates.

Journal: *Psychological Reports,* October 1986, 59(2)II, 995–998.

Related Research: Gladding, S. T., et al. (1981). Religious beliefs and positive mental health: The GLA scale and counseling. *Counseling and Values, 25,* 206–215.

■ ■ ■

5242

Test Name: RELIGIOUS IDENTIFICATION SCALE

Purpose: To assess religious identification.

Number of Items: 2

Format: Assess how religious the youth is and how much the youth participate in religious activities.

Reliability: Coefficient alpha was .85.

Validity: Correlations with other variables ranged from −.44 to .33.

Author: Oetting, E. R., and Beauvais, F.

Article: Peer cluster theory, socialization characteristics, and adolescent drug use: A path analysis.

Journal: *Journal of Counseling Psychology,* April 1987, 34(2), 205–213.

■ ■ ■

5243

Test Name: RELIGIOUS ORIENTATION SCALE—ALLPORT-ROSS VERSION

Purpose: To assess religious orientation.

Number of Items: 20

Format: Employed 5-point Likert scale ranging from *strongly agree* to *strongly disagree.* Includes three factors.

Reliability: Alpha coefficients ranged from .62 to .90.

Author: Leong, F. T. L., and Zachar, P.

Article: An evaluation of Allport's Religious Orientation Scale across one Australian and two United States samples.

Journal: *Educational and Psychological Measurement,* Summer 1990, *50*(2), 359–368.

Related Research: Allport, G. W., & Ross, M. J. (1967). Personal religious orientation and prejudice. *Journal of Personality and Social Psychology, 5,* 432–433.

• • •

5244

Test Name: STRENGTH OF RELIGIOUS BELIEFS SCALES

Purpose: To assess strength of participants' religious beliefs.

Number of Items: 30

Format: Responses are made on a 7-point Likert scale. Includes three subscales: approach to human authorities, approach to scripture or doctrine, and identification with a religious group.

Reliability: Cronbach's alphas ranged from .76 to .92.

Author: Keating, A. M., and Fretz, B. R.

Article: Christians' anticipations about counselors in responses to counselor descriptions.

Journal: *Journal of Counseling Psychology,* July 1990, *37*(3), 293–296.

Related Research: Worthington, E. L. (1986). Religious counseling: A review of published empirical research. *Journal of Counseling and Development, 64,* 421–431.

• • •

5245

Test Name: STUDENT PERCEPTIONS OF THE VALUE OF MATHEMATICS SCALES

Purpose: To measure students' perceptions of the intrinsic value of math as well as its importance and usefulness.

Number of Items: 15

Format: Most of the items are responded to on a 7-point Likert-type scale. All items are presented.

Reliability: Cronbach's alphas were .76 and .80.

Author: Midgley, C., et al.

Article: Student/teacher relations and attitudes toward mathematics before and after the transition to junior high school.

Journal: *Child Development,* August 1989, *60*(4), 981–992.

Related Research: Parsons, J. E. (1980). *Self-perceptions, task perceptions, and academic choice: Origins and change* (Final Technical Report to the National Institute of Education). Ann Arbor: University of Michigan. (ERIC Document Reproduction Service No. ED186 477)

• • •

5246

Test Name: VALENCE SCALES FOR MATHEMATICS AND ENGLISH

Purpose: To measure the subjective value of mathematics and English.

Number of Items: 6

Format: Seven-point importance rating scales. All items presented.

Reliability: Alphas were .69 (mathematics) and .79 (English).

Validity: Correlations with other variables ranged from −.40 to .22.

Author: Feather, N. T.

Article: Values, valences and course enrollment: Testing the role of personal values within and expectancy-valence framework.

Journal: *Journal of Educational Psychology,* September 1988, *80*(3), 381–391.

• • •

5247

Test Name: VALUES INVENTORY

Purpose: To measure individualistic values.

Number of Items: 8

Format: Seven-point scale. All items presented.

Reliability: Alphas ranged from .62 to .81.

Author: Simons, R. L., et al.

Article: Husband and wife differences in determinants of parenting: A social learning and exchange model of parental behavior.

Journal: *Journal of Marriage and the Family,* May 1990, *52*(2), 375–392.

Related Research: Braithwaite, J., & Law, H. (1983). Structure of human values: Testing the adequacy of the Rokeach Value Survey. *Journal of Personality and Social Psychology, 49,* 250–263.

• • •

5248

Test Name: VALUES QUESTIONNAIRE

Purpose: To assess the values associated with the impact of undergraduate education.

Number of Items: 36

Format: Five-point Likert scale. All items presented.

Reliability: Alphas ranged from .41 to .79.

Validity: Correlations between subscales ranged from −.02 to .45.

Author: Biddle, B. J., et al.

Article: Modality of thought, campus experiences, and the development of values.

Journal: *Journal of Educational Psychology,* December 1990, *82*(4), 671–682.

• • •

5249

Test Name: VALUES SCALE

Purpose: To assess values that affect work motivation.

Number of Items: 100

Format: The importance of each item is indicated on a scale ranging from 1 (*little or no importance*) to 4 (*very important*).

Reliability: Internal consistency coefficients ranged from .68 to .91. Test–retest reliability ranged from .63 to .82.

Author: Macnab, D., and Fitzsimmons, G. W.

Article: A multitrait-multimethod study of work-related needs, values, and preferences.

Journal: *The Journal of Vocational Behavior*, February 1987, *30*(1), 1–15.

Related Research: Work importance study (1980). Report of the fourth working conference of the Work Importance Study. Dubrovnik, Yugoslavia: WIS.

■ ■ ■

5250

Test Name: WORK BELIEFS SCALE

Purpose: To assess work beliefs.

Number of Items: 18

Format: Includes two work belief systems: the work ethic and the Marxist-related beliefs.

Validity: Correlations with other variables ranged from −.63 to .49.

Author: Fullagar, C., and Barling J.

Article: A longitudinal test of a model of the antecedents and consequences of union loyalty.

Journal: *Journal of Applied Psychology*, April 1989, *74*(2), 213–227.

Related Research: Buchholz, R. (1978). An empirical study of contemporary beliefs about work in American society. *Journal of Applied Psychology*, *63*, 219–227.

5251

Test Name: WORK ETHIC ENDORSEMENT SCALE

Purpose: To measure one's belief in the importance of hard work and frugality.

Number of Items: 19

Format: Responses are made on a 7-point scale ranging from 1 (*strongly disagree*) to 7 (*strongly agree*). Sample items are presented.

Reliability: Coefficient alpha was .79.

Validity: Correlations with other variables ranged from −.19 to .38.

Author: Morrow, P. C., and McElroy, J. C.

Article: Work commitment and job satisfaction over the career stages.

Journal: *Journal of Vocational Behavior*, June 1987, *30*(3), 330–346.

Related Research: Morrow, P. C., & McElroy, J. C. (1986). On assessing measures of work commitment. *Journal of Occupational Behavior*, 7, 139–145.

■ ■ ■

5252

Test Name: WORK ETHIC SCALE

Purpose: To measure the belief in hard work and frugality.

Number of Items: 19

Format: Seven-point Likert format. Sample items presented.

Reliability: Alpha was .76.

Author: Morrow, P. C., and Goetz, J. F., Jr.

Article: Professionalism as a form of work commitment.

Journal: *Journal of Vocational Behavior*, Febrauary 1988, *32*(1), 92–111.

Related Research: Mirels, H. L., & Garrett, J. B. (1971). The protestant work ethic as a personality variable. *Journal of Consulting and Clinical Psychology*, *36*, 40–44.

5253

Test Name: WORK VALUES SCALE

Purpose: To measure sex differences in work values.

Number of Items: 25

Format: Five-point Likert format.

Validity: A set of 18 of the 25 items discriminated between male and female respondents (84% correctly classified).

Author: Beutell, N. J., and Brenner, O. C.

Article: Sex differences in work values.

Journal: *Journal of Vocational Behavior*, February 1986, *28*(1), 29–41.

Related Research: Manhardt, P. J. (1972). Job orientation among male and female college graduates in business. *Personnel Psychology*, *25*, 361–368.

■ ■ ■

5254

Test Name: WORK VALUES SCALES

Purpose: To measure desired skill-utilization, desired variety, and desired influence in an ideal job.

Number of Items: 13

Format: Five-point rating scales.

Reliability: Alphas ranged from .65 to .74.

Author: Feather, N. T., and O'Brien, G. E.

Article: A longitudinal study of the effects of employment and unemployment on school leaving.

Journal: *Journal of Occupational Psychology*, June 1986, *59*(2), 121–144.

Related Research: O'Brien, G. E., & Dowling, P. (1980). The effects of congruency between perceived and desired job attributes upon job satisfaction. *Journal of Occupational Psychology, 53*, 121–130.

■ ■ ■

5255

Test Name: WORLDMINDEDNESS SCALE

Purpose: To measure an orientation favoring a world-view of humanity.

Number of Items: 32

Format: Seven-point rating scales.

Reliability: Split-half reliability was .93. Test–retest reliability was .93. Other reliability readings ranged from .33 to .80.

Author: Schell, B., et al.

Article: An investigation of worldmindedness, satisfaction, and commitment for hirers of foreign students exchanges.

Journal: *Psychological Reports,* October 1986, *59*(2)II, 911–920.

Related Research: Sampson, D. L., & Smith, H. P. (1957). A scale to measure world-minded attitudes. *Journal of Social Psychology, 69*, 33–37.

Vocational Evaluation

5256

Test Name: BARRETT-LENNARD RELATIONSHIP INVENTORY

Purpose: To measure Roger's necessary and sufficient conditions.

Number of Items: 85

Format: Seven-point rating scales.

Reliability: Test–retest reliability ranged from .79 to .89.

Author: Scott, T., et al.

Article: Further evidence for unidimensionality of measures of counseling performance.

Journal: *Psychological Reports*, June 1986, *58*(3), 983–990.

Related Research: Barrett-Lennard, G. T. (1962). Dimensions of therapist response as causal factors in therapeutic changes. *Psychological Monographs, 76*(12, Whole No. 562).

. . .

5257

Test Name: BARRETT-LENNARD RELATIONSHIP INVENTORY—REVISED

Purpose: To measure subjects' rating of their relationship with their counselor.

Number of Items: 36

Format: Includes five parts: empathetic understanding, unconditional regard, level of regard, congruence, and resistance.

Reliability: Cronbach's alpha reliability coefficients ranged from .54 to .85.

Author: Dowd, E. T., et al.

Article: Compliance-based and defiance based intervention strategies and psychological reactance in the treatment of free and unfree behavior.

Journal: *Journal of Counseling Psychology*, October 1988, *35*(4), 370–376.

Related Research: Strong, S. R., et al. (1979). Motivational and equipping functions of interpretation in counseling. *Journal of Counseling Psychology, 26*, 98–107.

. . .

5258

Test Name: BEHAVIORAL OBSERVATION SCALE—ADAPTED

Purpose: To rate instructor performance.

Number of Items: 10

Format: Employs a 7-point Likert-type format.

Reliability: Internal consistency was .80.

Author: Steiner, D. D., and Rain, J. S.

Article: Immediate and delayed primacy and recency effects in performance evaluation.

Journal: *Journal of Applied Psychology*, February 1989, *74*(1), 136–142.

Related Research: Murphy, K. R., et al. (1982). Do behavioral observation scales measure observation? *Journal of Applied Psychology, 67*, 562–567.

5259

Test Name: BEHAVIORAL RATING SCALE

Purpose: To measure police effectiveness in domestic disputes.

Number of Items: 24

Format: Yes–no format. All items presented.

Reliability: Spearman-Brown coefficients ranged from .71 to .92.

Validity: No statistically significant differences were found between trained and untrained officers in a simulated domestic dispute.

Author: Bandy, C., et al.

Article: Police performance in resolving family disputes: What makes the difference.

Journal: *Psychological Reports*, June 1986, *58*(3), 743–576.

Related Research: Axelberd, M., & Valle, T. (1978). Development of the behavioral scale for measuring police effectiveness in domestic disputes. *Crisis Interventions, 9*, 69–80.

. . .

5260

Test Name: BEHAVIOR RATING SCALE

Purpose: To evaluate the performance of graduate students delivering videotaped lectures.

Number of Items: 12

Format: Each speaker is evaluated on the occurrence of each of 12 teacher behaviors (eye contact, reading from notes, etc.). Evaluations are made on a 7-point scale ranging from 1 (*never*) to 7 (all of the time).

Validity: Convergent validity was .57. Discriminant validity was .21.

Author: Murphy, K. R., and Balzer, W. K.

Article: Systematic distortions in memory-based behavior ratings and performance evaluations: Consequences for rating accuracy.

Journal: *Journal of Applied Psychology*, February 1986, *71*(1), 39–44.

Related Research: Murphy, K., et al. (1982). Relationship between observational accuracy and accuracy in evaluating performance. *Journal of Applied Psychology*, *67*, 320–325.

■ ■ ■

5261

Test Name: CLIENT SATISFACTION FORM

Purpose: To assess client satisfaction with the counselor and the interview.

Number of Items: 25

Format: Includes positively and negatively worded items with higher scores reflecting greater client satisfaction.

Reliability: .92.

Author: Schneider, L. J., and Hayslip, Jr., B.

Article: Female counselor-client dyads: Effects of counselor age, client marital status, and intimacy level of presenting problem on perceptions of counselors.

Journal: *Journal of Counseling Psychology*, July 1986, *33*(3), 242–248.

Related Research: Ashby, J. D., et al. (1957). Effects on clients of a reflective and a leading type of psychotherapy. *Psychological Monographs*, *71*(24, Whole No. 453). Robiner, W. N., & Storandt, M. (1983). Client perceptions of the therapeutic relationship as a function

of client and counselor age. *Journal of Counseling Psychology*, *30*, 96–99.

■ ■ ■

5262

Test Name: COGNITIVE THERAPY SCALE

Purpose: To evaluate therapist competence in cognitive therapy for depression.

Number of Items: 11

Format: Seven-point Likert format.

Reliability: Interrater reliability was .59 (one inter), .77 (two raters), and .84 (three raters). Item-total correlations ranged from .59 to .94.

Validity: A discriminant function increased the base rate of classification by 35%.

Author: Vallis, T. M., et al.

Article: The Cognitive Therapy Scale: Psychometric properties.

Journal: *Journal of Consulting and Clinical Psychology*, June 1986, *54*(3), 381–385.

Related Research: Young, J., & Beck, A. (1980). *Cognitive Therapy Scale: Rating manual*. Unpublished manuscript, Center for Cognitive Therapy, Philadelphia, PA.

■ ■ ■

5263

Test Name: COLLABORATIVE STUDY PSYCHOTHERAPY RATING SCALE

Purpose: To test whether therapists adhered to their prescribed treatments in the National Institute of Mental Health Treatment of Depression Collaborative Research Program.

Number of Items: 96

Format: Includes six subscales: interpersonal, clinical management, facilitative conditions, and explicit directiveness. Responses are made on a 7-point Likert scale.

Reliability: Alpha coefficients ranged from .63 to .94.

Validity: Correlations with a rater-bias scale ranged from −.11 to .67.

Author: Hill, C. E., et al.

Article: A method for investigating sources of rater bias.

Journal: *Journal of Counseling Psychology*, July 1988, *35*(3), 346–350.

Related Research: Hollon, S. D., et al. (1984, May). *Systems for rating therapies for depression*. Paper presented at the annual meeting of the American Psychiatric Association, Los Angeles.

■ ■ ■

5264

Test Name: CONFIDENCE IN MANAGEMENT SCALE

Purpose: To rate one's immediate supervisor.

Number of Items: 7

Reliability: Coefficient alpha was .83.

Validity: Correlations with other variables ranged from −.29 to .40.

Author: Puffer, S. M.

Article: Prosocial behavior, noncompliant behavior, and work performance among commission sales people.

Journal: *Journal of Applied Psychology*, November 1987, *72*(4), 615–621.

Related Research: Cook, J., & Wall, T. D. (1980). New work attitude measures of trust, organizational commitment and personal need fulfillment. *Journal of Occupational Psychology*, *53*, 39–52.

■ ■ ■

5265

Test Name: COUNSELOR EVALUATION INVENTORY

Purpose: To rate counselor effectiveness.

Number of Items: 21

Format: Includes three dimensions: counseling climate, client satisfaction, and counselor comfort. Responses are made on a 5-point Likert scale.

Reliability: Test–retest (2 weeks) reliabilities ranged from .63 to .78.

Author: Hayes, T. J., and Tinsley, H. E. A.

Article: Identification of the latent dimensions of instruments that measure perceptions of and expectations about counseling.

Journal: *Journal of Counseling Psychology*, October 1989, *36*(4), 492–500.

Related Research: Linden, J. D., et al. (1965). Development and evaluation of an inventory for rating counseling. *Personnel and Guidance Journal, 44*, 267–276.

■ ■ ■

5266

Test Name: COUNSELING EVALUATION INVENTORY

Purpose: To measure counseling climate, counselors' comfort and clients' satisfaction.

Number of Items: 19

Format: Five-point Likert format.

Reliability: Test–retest reliability was .72.

Author: Scott, T., et al.

Article: Further evidence for unidimensionality of measures of counseling performance.

Journal: *Psychological Reports*, June 1986, *58*(3), 983–990.

Related Research: Linden, J. D., et al. (1965). Development and evaluation of an inventory for rating counseling. *Personnel and Guidance Journal, 44*, 267–276. Bachelor, A. (1987). The Counseling Evaluation Inventory and the Counselor Rating Form: Their relationship to improvement and to

each other. *Psychology Reports, 61*, 567–575.

■ ■ ■

5267

Test Name: COUNSELOR EFFECTIVENESS RATING SCALE

Purpose: To measure the participant's perception of counselor credibility.

Number of Items: 10

Format: Responses are made on a 5-point Likert scale ranging from 1 (*strong disagreement*) to 5 (*strong agreement*).

Reliability: Coefficient alpha was .86.

Validity: Correlations with other variables ranged from –.14 to .71.

Author: Akutsu, P. D., et al.

Article: Predictors of utilization intent of counseling among Chinese and White students. A test of the proximal-distal model.

Journal: *Journal of Counseling Psychology*, October 1990, *37*(4), 445–452.

Related Research: Atkinson, D. R., & Wampold, B. E. (1982). A comparison of the Counselor Rating Form and the Counselor Effectiveness Rating Scale. *Counselor Education Supervision, 22*, 25–36.

■ ■ ■

5268

Test Name: COUNSELOR EFFECTIVENESS RATING SCALE

Purpose: To identify client perceptions of counselor credibility and utility.

Number of Items: 7

Format: Ratings are made on a 7-point bipolar scale ranging from 1 (*bad*) to 7 (*good*).

Reliability: Internal consistency reliabilities ranged from .75 to .90.

Author: Haley, T. J., and Dowd, E. T.

Article: Responses of deaf adolescents to differences in

counselor method of communication and disability status.

Journal: *Journal of Counseling Psychology*, July 1988, *35*(3), 258–262.

Related Research: Atkinson, D. R., & Carskaddon, G. (1975). A prestigious introduction, psychological jargon, and perceived counselor credibility. *Journal of Counseling Psychology, 22*, 180–186.

■ ■ ■

5269

Test Name: COUNSELOR EFFECTIVENESS RATING SCALE

Purpose: To measure counselor effectiveness.

Format: Each item is rated on a 7-point rating scale ranging from 7 (*good*) to 1 (*bad*).

Reliability: Reliability coefficients ranged from .75 to .88.

Validity: Correlations with the Counselor Rating Form ranged form .78 to .79.

Author: Hayes, T. J., and Tinsley, H. E. A.

Article: Identification of the latent dimensions of instruments that measure perceptions of and expectations about counseling.

Journal: *Journal of Counseling Psychology*, October 1989, *36*(4), 492–500.

Related Research: Atkinson, D. R., & Wampold, B. E. (1982). A comparison of the Counselor Rating Form and Counselor Effectiveness Rating Scale. *Counselor Education and Supervision, 22*, 25–36.

■ ■ ■

5270

Test Name: COUNSELOR EFFECTIVENESS SCALE

Purpose: To measure client attitudes towards the counselor.

Number of Items: 25

Format: Semantic differential adjectives are rated on a 7-point scale. There are two forms.

Reliability: Parallel-forms reliability was .97.

Author: Hayes, T. J., and Tinsley, H. E. A.

Article: Identification of the latent dimensions of instruments that measure perceptions of and expectations about counseling.

Journal: *Journal of Counseling Psychology*, October 1989, *36*(4), 492–500.

Related Research: Ivey, A. E. (1971). *Microcounseling: Innovations in interviewing, counseling, psychotherapy, and psychoeducation* (2nd ed.). Springfield, IL: Charles C Thomas.

■ ■ ■

5271

Test Name: COUNSELOR EFFECTIVENESS SCALE

Purpose: To measure effective and noneffective counseling.

Number of Items: 50

Format: Seven-point semantic differential.

Reliability: Parallel Form was .98.

Author: Scott, T., et al.

Article: Further evidence for unidimensionality of measures of counseling performance.

Journal: *Psychological Reports*, June 1986, *58*(3), 983–990.

Related Research: Ivey, A. C., et al. (1968). Microcounseling and attending behavior: An approach to practicum counselor training. *Journal of Counseling Psychology, 15*, 1–12.

■ ■ ■

5272

Test Name: COUNSELOR EVALUATION RATING SCALE

Purpose: To rate student performance in counseling and supervision.

Number of Items: 13

Format: Seven-point Likert format.

Reliability: Internal was .95. Test–retest (4 weeks) reliability was .94.

Author: Scott, T. B., et al.

Article: Further evidence for unidimensionality of measures of counseling performance.

Journal: *Psychological Reports*, June 1986, *58*(3), 983–990.

Related Research: Myrick, D. R., & Kelly, R. D. (1971). A scale for evaluating practicum students in counseling and supervision. *Counselor Education and Supervision, 10*, 330–336.

■ ■ ■

5273

Test Name: COUNSELOR RATING FORM

Purpose: To measure respondents' perceptions of counselor expertness, attractiveness, and trustworthiness.

Number of Items: 36

Format: Includes three scales consisting of bipolar adjectives rated on a 7-point scale.

Reliability: Split-half reliability coefficients ranged from .85 to .91.

Validity: Correlations with the Goal Attainment Scale ranged from .37 to .56.

Author: Hayes, T. J., and Tinsley, H. E. A.

Article: Identification of the latent dimensions of instruments that measure perceptions of and expectations about counseling.

Journal: *Journal of Counseling Psychology*, October 1989, *36*(4), 492–500.

Related Research: Barak, A., & LaCrosse, M. B. (1975). Multidimensional perception of

counselor behavior. *Journal of Counseling Psychology, 22*, 471–476.

■ ■ ■

5274

Test Name: COUNSELOR RATING FORM—SHORT

Purpose: To measure subjects' ratings of counselor attractiveness, trustworthiness, and expertness.

Number of Items: 12

Format: A list of adjectives are rated on a 7-point scale from 1 (*not very descriptive*) to 7 (*very descriptive*).

Reliability: Internal consistency reliabilities ranged from .82 to .91.

Author: Enns, C. Z., and Hackett, G.

Article: Comparison of feminist and nonfeminist women's reactions to variants of nonsexist and feminist counseling.

Journal: *Journal of Counseling Psychology*, January 1990, *37*(1), 33–40.

Related Research: Corrigan, J. D., & Schmidt, L. D. (1983). Development and validation of revisions in the Counselor Rating Form. *Journal of Counseling Psychology, 30*, 64–75.

■ ■ ■

5275

Test Name: COUPLE THERAPY ALLIANCE SCALE

Purpose: To measure client's perceptions of the therapeutic alliance.

Number of Items: 29

Format: Includes interpersonal subscales: self-therapist alliance, other-therapist alliance, and group therapist alliance. Responses are made on a 7-point Likert scale ranging from 1 (*completely agree*) to 7 (*completely disagree*). Examples are presented.

Reliability: Test–retest reliability for the self subscale was .83. Internal consistency reliability for the self-therapist subscale was .85.

Author: Heatherington, L., and Friedlander, M. L.

Article: Complimentarity and symmetry in family therapy communication.

Journal: *Journal of Counseling Psychology*, July 1990, *37*(3), 261–268.

Related Research: Pinsof, W. M., & Catherall, D. R. (1986). The integrative psychotherapy alliance: Family, couple, and individual therapy scales. *Journal of Marital and Family Therapy*, *12*, 137–151.

■ ■ ■

5276

Test Name: CROSS-CULTURAL COMPETENCY SCALE

Purpose: To measure participants' perceptions of the counselor's cross-cultural competence.

Number of Items: 12

Format: The items were about the counselor's interview behavior. Extent of agreement with each item was made on a 5-point scale. Examples are presented.

Reliability: Alpha coefficients were .88 and .92.

Author: Pomales, J., et al.

Article: Effects of Black students' racial identity on perceptions of White counselors varying in cultural sensitivity.

Journal: *Journal of Counseling Psychology*, January 1986, *33*(1), 57–61.

Related Research: Sue, D. W., et al. (1982). Position papers: Cross-cultural counseling competencies. *The Counseling Psychologist*, *10*(2), 45–52.

■ ■ ■

5277

Test Name: EMPLOYEE RATING SCALE

Purpose: To assess the superior's view of the subordinate's performance level.

Number of Items: 7

Reliability: Cronbach's alpha was .88.

Validity: Correlations with other variables ranged from .30 to .47.

Author: Scandura, T. A., et al.

Article: When managers decide not to decide autocratically: An investigation of leader–member exchange and decision influence.

Journal: *Journal of Applied Psychology*, November 1986, *71*(4), 579–584.

Related Research: Graen, G., et al. (1972). Dysfunctional leadership styles. *Organizational Behavior and Human Performance*, 7, 216–236.

■ ■ ■

5278

Test Name: FAMILY THERAPY ALLIANCE SCALE

Purpose: To measure client's perceptions of the therapeutic alliance.

Number of Items: 29

Format: Includes three interpersonal subscales: Self–therapist alliance, other–therapist alliance, and group–therapist alliance. Responses are made on a 7-point Likert scale ranging from 1 (*completely agree*) to 7 (*completely disagree*). Examples are presented.

Reliability: Test–retest reliability for the self subscale was .83. Internal consistency reliability for the self-therapist subscale was .85.

Author: Heatherington, L., and Friedlander, M. L.

Article: Complimentarity and symmetry in family therapy communication.

Journal: *Journal of Counseling Psychology*, July 1990, *37*(3), 261–268.

Related Research: Pinsof, W. M., & Catherall, D. R. (1986). The

integrative psychotherapy alliance: Family, couple, and individual therapy scales. *Journal of Marital and Family Therapy*, *12*, 137–151.

■ ■ ■

5279

Test Name: 15 PERSONAL PROBLEMS INVENTORY

Purpose: To measure the degree of confidence placed in a counselor's effectiveness.

Number of Items: 15

Format: Includes four factors: performance anxiety problems, interpersonal problems, intrapersonal problems, and substance abuse problems.

Reliability: Alpha coefficients ranged from .64 to .81.

Author: Johnson, M. E., and Holland, A. L.

Article: Measuring clients' expectations: The 15 Personal Problems Inventory.

Journal: *Measurement and Evaluation in Counseling and Development*, October 1986, *19*(3), 151–156.

Related Research: Cash, T., et al. (1975). When counselors are heard but not seen: Initial impact of physical attractiveness. *Journal of Counseling Psychology*, 4, 273–279.

■ ■ ■

5280

Test Name: IDEA FORM H

Purpose: To evaluate high school teacher effectiveness.

Number of Items: 50

Format: Five-point response scales are used. All items except 9 that were not germane to the study were presented.

Reliability: Median interrater reliabilities for student and teacher ratings ranged from .17 to .30.

Author: Aubrecht, J. D., et al.

Article: High school student ratings of teaching effectiveness compared with teacher self-ratings.

Journal: *Educational and Psychological Measurement*, Summer 1986, *46*(2), 415–423.

Related Research: Center for Faculty Evaluation and Development. (1981). *Student Reaction to Course and Teacher: IDEA Form H.* Manhattan, KS: Author.

■ ■ ■

5281

Test Name: IDEAL TEACHER CHECKLIST

Purpose: To enable students to identify criteria of the ideal teacher using characteristics measuring personal–social and cognitive–intellectual attributes.

Number of Items: 39

Format: Students indicate by a single check the characteristics they feel should be encouraged, a double check for the five characteristics they consider the most important, and crossing out the characteristics they think should be discouraged.

Reliability: Test–retest (6 weeks) reliability was .92 (*N* = 100). Interscorer reliability among trained scorers was 1.00.

Author: Dehlari, N. S.

Article: Iranian students' perception of ideal teacher.

Journal: *Perceptual and Motor Skills*, February 1987, *64*(1), 143–146.

Related Research: Dehlari, N. S. (1977). Ideal Teacher Checklist. Isfahan University of Isfahan Studies of Creative Behavior.

■ ■ ■

5282

Test Name: IDEAL THERAPEUTIC RELATIONSHIP SCALE

Purpose: To measure the ideal therapeutic relationship.

Number of Items: 14

Format: Five-point rating scales.

Reliability: Interrater ranged from .41 to .91.

Author: Scott, T., et al.

Article: Further evidence for unidimensionality of measures of counseling performance.

Journal: *Psychological Reports*, June 1986, *58*(3), 983–990.

Related Research: Ivey, A. C., et al. (1968). Microcounseling and attending behavior: An approach to practicum training. *Journal of Counseling Psychology*, *15*, 1–12.

■ ■ ■

5283

Test Name: INTERVIEWER'S PREINTERVIEW QUESTIONNAIRE

Purpose: To provide interviewer's preinterview impressions of the job applicant.

Number of Items: 16

Format: One item employs a 9-point scale ranging from 1 (*very good fit*) to 9 (*very poor fit*), one item uses a 5-point scale ranging from 1 (*definitely recommend for hire*) to 5 (*definitely not recommend for hire*), and 14 items use a 5-point scale ranging from 1 (*high*) to 5 (*low*).

Reliability: Coefficient alpha was .91.

Validity: Correlations with other variables ranged from –.19 to .63.

Author: Phillips, A. P., and Dipboye, R. L.

Article: Correlational tests of predictions from a process model of the interview.

Journal: *Journal of Applied Psychology*, February 1989, *74*(1), 41–52.

■ ■ ■

5284

Test Name: INTERVIEWER'S POSTINTERVIEW QUESTIONNAIRE

Purpose: To provide interviewer's postinterview impressions of the job applicant.

Number of Items: 16

Format: One item employs a 9-point scale ranging from 1 (*very good fit*) to 9 (*very poor fit*), one item uses a 5-point scale ranging from 1 (*definitely recommend for hire*) to 5 (*definitely not recommend for hire*), and 14 items use a 5-point scale ranging from 1 (*high*) to 5 (*low*).

Reliability: Coefficient alpha was .92.

Validity: Correlations with other variables ranged from –.15 to .81.

Author: Philips, A. P., and Dipboye, R. L.

Article: Correlational tests of predictions from a process model of the interview.

Journal: *Journal of Applied Psychology*, February 1989, *74*(1), 41–52.

■ ■ ■

5285

Test Name: JOB ASSOCIATE-BISOCIATE REVIEW INDEX

Purpose: To measure innovativeness among research and development professionals.

Number of Items: 19

Format: Seven-point enjoyment rating scales. Sample item presented.

Reliability: Alpha ranged from .80 to .87.

Validity: Two predicted factors emerged corresponding to the associate and bisociate dimensions.

Author: Jabri, M. M.

Article: A new scale for the measurement of individual innovativeness amongst research and development scientists.

Journal: *Psychological Reports*, June 1988, *62*(3), 951–952.

5286

Test Name: JOB PERFORMANCE RATING FORM

Purpose: To enable supervisors to assess employees.

Number of Items: 13

Format: Ratings are made on a 7-point scale ranging from *unsatisfactory* to *satisfactory*.

Reliability: Coefficient alpha was .93.

Validity: Correlations with other variables ranged from −.20 to .11.

Author: Greenhaus, J. H., et al.

Article: Work experiences, job performance, and feelings of personal and family well-being.

Journal: *Journal of Vocational Behavior*, October 1987, *31*(2), 200–215.

■ ■ ■

5287

Test Name: JOB PERFORMANCE RATING SCALE

Purpose: To enable supervisors to evaluate work competence.

Number of Items: 8

Format: The eight scales comprising this instrument included: oral communication skills, written communication skills, learning ability, dependability, practical judgment and reasoning, observational skills, initiative to work independently, and interpersonal relations.

Reliability: Reliabilities ranged from .21 to .49.

Validity: Correlations with the Police Procedures Test ranged from .10 to .32.

Author: Friedland, D. L., and Michael, W. B.

Article: The reliability of a promotional job knowledge examination scored by number of items right and by four confidence weighting procedures and its corresponding concurrent validity

estimates relative to performance criterion ratings.

Journal: *Educational and Psychological Measurement*, Spring 1987, *47*(1), 179–188.

■ ■ ■

5288

Test Name: JOB SKILLS RATING SCALE

Purpose: To measure and rate manager skills such as ability to work with mechanical devices, to supervise, and to follow through.

Number of Items: 8

Format: Five-point rating scales.

Reliability: Internal consistency ranged from .63 to .85. Interrater reliability ranged from .37 to .63.

Validity: Campbell and Fiske's four criteria of validity are presented and suggest the scale is valid.

Author: Schippmann, J. S., and Prien, E. P.

Article: Psychometric evaluation of an integrated assessment procedure.

Journal: *Psychological Reports*, August 1986, *59*(1), 111–122.

■ ■ ■

5289

Test Name: MENTORING FUNCTIONS SCALES

Purpose: To assess the extent to which protégés believe mentors provide career and psychosocial functions.

Number of Items: 21

Format: Five-point Likert format. All items presented.

Reliability: Alphas ranged from .89 to .92 across subscales.

Validity: Correlations with other variables ranged from −.06 to .26.

Author: Noe, R. A.

Article: An investigation of the determinants of successful assigned mentoring relationships.

Journal: *Personnel Psychology*, Summer 1988, *41*(2), 457–479.

■ ■ ■

5290

Test Name: ORGANIZATIONAL CITIZENSHIP BEHAVIOR SCALE

Purpose: To obtain supervisory assessments of each subordinate's characteristic pattern of organizational citizenship behavior.

Number of Items: 16

Format: Responses are made on a 5-point scale ranging from 1 (*never*) to 5 (*almost always*). All items are presented.

Reliability: Alpha coefficients were .81 and .91.

Validity: Correlations with other variables ranged from −.17 to .21.

Author: Organ, D. W., and Konovsky, M.

Article: Cognitive versus affective determinants of organizational citizenship behavior.

Journal: *Journal of Applied Psychology*, February 1989, *74*(1), 157–164.

Related Research: Smith, C. A., et al. (1983). Organizational citizenship behavior: It's nature and antecedents. *Journal of Applied Psychology*, *68*, 653–663.

5291

Test Name: PERCEPTIONS OF COUNSELOR'S EXPECTED HELPFULNESS

Purpose: To evaluate subjects' perceptions of the counselor's expected helpfulness with a variety of specific problems.

Number of Items: 15

Format: Responses are made on a 6-point rating scale.

Reliability: Coefficient alpha was .94.

Validity: Correlation with Impressions of Counselor Characteristics Scale was .67.

Author: Green, C. F., et al.

Article: Effects of counselor and subject race and counselor physical attractiveness on impressions and expectations of a female counselor.

Journal: *Journal of Counseling Psychology*, July 1986, *33*(3), 349–352.

Related Research: Lewis, K. N., & Walsh, W. B. (1978). Physical attractiveness: Its impact on the perception of a female counselor. *Journal of Counseling Psychology*, *25*, 210–216.

■ ■ ■

5292

Test Name: PERFORMANCE EFFECTIVENESS SCALE

Purpose: To measure effectiveness of teacher performance.

Number of Items: 19

Format: Five-point Likert format. Sample items are presented.

Reliability: Alpha was .94.

Author: Bhagat, R. S., and Allie, S. M.

Article: Organizational stress, personal life stress, and symptoms of life strains: An examination of the moderating role of sense competence.

Journal: *Journal of Vocational Behavior*, December 1989, *35*(3), 231–253.

Related Research: Smith, P. C., et al. (1969). The measurement of satisfaction in work and retirement. Chicago: Rand McNally.

■ ■ ■

5293

Test Name: PERFORMANCE EVALUATION SCALE

Purpose: To evaluate the performance of graduate students delivering vidoetaped lectures.

Number of Items: 8

Format: Evaluation is made on performance dimensions including: thoroughness of preparation, grasp of material, etc. Raters used a 5-point Likert scale ranging from 1 (*very bad*) to 5 (*very good*).

Validity: Convergent validity was .70. Discriminant validity was .47.

Author: Murphy, K. R., and Balzer, W. K.

Article: Systematic distortions in memory-based behavior ratings and performance evaluations: Consequences for rating accuracy.

Journal: *Journal of Applied Psychology*, August 1986, *71*(3), 39–44.

Related Research: Murphy, K., et al. (1982). Relationship between observational accuracy and accuracy in evaluating performance. *Journal of Applied Psychology*, *67*, 320–325.

■ ■ ■

5294

Test Name: PRIMARY GRADE PUPIL REPORT

Purpose: To enable 4-year-olds to respond to items describing teachers.

Number of Items: 11

Format: Pupils responded to each item by marking one of three faces (smiley, neutral, and frowning) representing yes, sometimes, and no responses. All items are presented.

Reliability: Alpha reliabilities were .70 to .62.

Author: Driscoll, A., et al.

Article: Teacher evaluation in early childhood education: What information can young children provide?

Journal: *Child Study Journal*, 1990, *20*(2), 67–79.

Related Research: Driscoll, A., et al. (1985). Student reports for primary teacher evaluation. *Education Research Quarterly*, *9*(3), 43–50.

5295

Test Name: QUALITY OF INSTRUCTION QUESTIONNAIRE

Purpose: To assess quality of instruction.

Number of Items: 36

Format: Includes three subscales: cues, participation, and reinforcement. Responses to each item are made on a 5-point scale ranging from *never* to *always*.

Reliability: Alpha coefficients ranged from .71 to .91. Test–retest (2 weeks) correlations ranged from .81 to .90.

Author: Tenenbaum, G.

Article: The relationship between the quality of instruction and intellectual achievement responsibility following positive and negative outcomes.

Journal: *Journal of Experimental Education*, Spring 1988, *56*(3), 154–159.

Related Research: Nordin, A. B. (1979). *The effects of different qualities of instruction on selective, effective, and time variables.* Unpublished doctoral dissertation, University of Chicago.

■ ■ ■

5296

Test Name: RESIDENT ASSISTANT EVALUATION FORM–R

Purpose: To assess the resident assistant's performance by the RA's residents.

Number of Items: 16

Format: Responses to 15 items are on a scale ranging from 4 (*strongly agree*) to 1 (*strongly disagree*) or *Don't know*. One item was responded to on a scale ranging from 4 (*excellent*) to 1 (*poor*).

Reliability: Coefficient alpha was .94.

Validity: Correlations with other variables ranged from −.01 to −.18.

Author: Deluga, R. J., and Winters, Jr., J. J.

Article: The impact of role ambiguity and conflict on resident assistants.

Journal: *Journal of College Student Development*, May 1990, *31*(3), 230–236.

■ ■ ■

5297

Test Name: RESIDENT ASSISTANT EVALUATION FORM—RD

Purpose: To assess the resident assistant's performance by the resident assistant's supervising resident director.

Number of Items: 49

Format: Responses are made on a scale ranging from 4 (*outstanding*) to 1 (*needs improvement*). Two other options include: *don't know* and *not applicable*. Includes eight subscales: personal characteristics, managerial skills, student conduct programming, administrative duties, and relationships with supervisors, peer staff, and students.

Reliability: Alpha coefficients ranged from .44 to .87.

Validity: Correlations with other variables ranged from −.42 to .31.

Author: Deluga, R. J., and Winters, Jr., J. J.

Article: The impact of role ambiguity and conflict on resident assistants.

Journal: *Journal of College Student Development*, May 1990, *31*(3), 230–236.

■ ■ ■

5298

Test Name: SALESPERSON'S JOB PERFORMANCE QUESTIONNAIRE

Purpose: To obtain manager's indication of the performance of their sales personnel.

Number of Items: 15

Format: Employs 5-point Likert scales. Includes three factors: sales, territory management, and job knowledge.

Reliability: Alpha coefficients ranged from .76 to .86.

Author: Stout, S. K., et al.

Article: Career transitions of superiors and subordinates.

Journal: *The Journal of Vocational Behavior*, April 1987, *30*(2), 124–137.

Related Research: Cron, W. L., & Slocum, J. W. Jr. (1986). The influence of career stages on salespeople's job attitudes, work perceptions, and performance. *Journal of Marketing Research, 23*, 119–129.

■ ■ ■

5299

Test Name: SELF-ASSESSMENT OF RELATIVE STRENGTHS IN TEACHING

Purpose: To enable teachers to identify their competence in teaching techniques.

Number of Items: 25

Format: Subjects respond to each item on a 5-point Likert scale from 1 (*practically incompetent*) to 5 (*very competent*).

Reliability: Coefficient alpha was .92. Test–retest (3 weeks) reliability was .77 (N = 50).

Author: Gretes, J. A., and Wolfe, D. M.

Article: Self-expressed competence and the preservice teacher: An instrument validation study.

Journal: *Educational and Psychological Measurement*, Summer 1987, *47*(2), 499–504.

Related Research: Hoover, K. H., et al. (1965). A comparison of expressed teaching strength before and after student teaching. *Journal of Teacher Education, 16*, 324–328.

■ ■ ■

5300

Test Name: SESSION EVALUATION QUESTIONNAIRE

Purpose: To assess session impact.

Number of Items: 10

Format: Includes two dimensions: depth–value and smoothness–ease. Each dimension includes five bipolar adjective scales presented in a 7-point semantic differential format. All items are presented.

Reliability: Alpha coefficients ranged from .87 to .93.

Author: Tryon, G. S.

Article: Session depth and smoothness in relation to the concept of engagement in counseling.

Journal: *Journal of Counseling Psychology*, July 1990, *37*(3), 248–253.

Related Research: Stiles, W. B., & Snow, J. S. (1984). Counseling session impact as viewed by novice counselors and their clients. *Journal of Counseling Psychology, 31*, 3–12.

■ ■ ■

5301

Test Name: SESSION EVALUATION QUESTIONNAIRE—FORM 2

Purpose: To enable clients and counselors to evaluate treatment sessions.

Number of Items: 22

Format: The respondents show how they feel about the session by marking 7-point bipolar adjective scales. All items are presented.

Reliability: Alpha coefficients for counselor and client indexes ranged from .84 to .93. Internal consistency of external rater SEQ indexes ranged from .80 to .93.

Author: Stiles, W. B., et al.

Article: Do sessions of different treatments have different impacts?

Journal: *Journal of Counseling Psychology*, October 1988, *35*(4), 391–396.

Related Research: Stiles, W. B. (1980). Measurement of the impact of psychotherapy sessions. *Journal of Consulting and Clinical Psychology, 48*, 176–185.

■ ■ ■

5302

Test Name: STUDENT TEACHING RATING FORM

Purpose: To measure teaching attitudes, subject matter knowledge, mastery of instruction, discipline, and emotional maturity.

Number of Items: 32

Format: Five-point Likert format.

Reliability: Alphas ranged from .76 to .81.

Validity: Multiple correlations between subscales ranged from .87 to .95 in a five-step stepwise regression.

Author: Philips, L., et al.

Article: The effects of halo and leniency on cooperating teacher reports using Likert rating scales.

Journal: *Journal of Educational Research,* January/February 1986, *79*(3), 151–154.

5303

Test Name: THERAPIST AND CLIENT RATING SCALES

Purpose: To measure therapist skills.

Number of Items: 67

Format: Three-point and nine-point effectiveness rating scales.

Reliability: Alphas ranged from .66 to .87 across subscales.

Validity: Partial correlations with Dyadic Adjustment Scale ranged from −.13 to .63.

Author: Holtzworth-Munroe, A., et al.

Article: Relationship between behavioral marital therapy outcome and process variables.

Journal: *Journal of Consulting and Clinical Psychology,* December 1989, *57*(5), 658–662.

■ ■ ■

5304

Test Name: VIRGILIO TEACHER BEHAVIOR INVENTORY

Purpose: To assess effectiveness in the classroom.

Number of Items: 35

Format: Includes five factors. Responses were made on a six-point Likert-type rating scale ranging from 5 (*excellent*) to 1 (*poor*).

Reliability: Alpha coefficients ranged from .88 to .96. Interrater reliability ranged from .80 to .84 (total score).

Validity: Correlation with the Stallings' Classroom Snapshot ranged from .50 to .64.

Author: Teddlie, C., et al.

Article: Development and validation of the Virgilio Teacher Behavior Instrument.

Journal: *Educational and Psychological Measurement,* Summer 1990, *50*(2), 421–430.

Related Research: Virgilio, I., & Teddlie, C. (1989). *Technical manual for the Virgilio Teacher Behavior Inventory.* Unpublished manuscript, University of New Orleans.

CHAPTER 24
Vocational Interest

5305

Test Name: AFFECTIVE COMMITMENT SCALE

Purpose: To measure commitment.

Number of Items: 8

Format: Responses are made on 7-point disagree–agree scales.

Reliability: Alpha coefficients ranged from .74 to .88.

Validity: Correlations with other variables ranged from −.14 to .86.

Author: Meyer, J. P., et al.

Article: Organizational commitment and job performance: It's the nature of the commitment that counts.

Journal: *Journal of Applied Psychology*, February 1989, *74*(1), 152–156.

Related Research: McGee, G. W., & Ford, R. C. (1987). Two (or more?) dimensions of organizational commitment: Reexamination of the affective and continuance commitment scales. *Journal of Applied Psychology*, *72*, 638–641.

■ ■ ■

5306

Test Name: ASSESSMENT OF CAREER DECISION MAKING— STYLES SCALE

Purpose: To assess the manner in which people make decisions.

Number of Items: 30

Format: Includes three subscales. Items are true–false.

Reliability: Test–retest reliability ranged from .76 to .85.

Author: Read, N. O., et al.

Article: The effects of marital status and motherhood on the career concerns of reentry women.

Journal: *The Career Development Quarterly*, September 1988, *37*(1), 46–55.

Related Research: Harren, V. A., et al. (1979). Influence of gender, sex-role attitudes, and cognitive complexity on gender-dominant career choices. *Journal of Counseling Psychology*, *26*, 227–234.

■ ■ ■

5307

Test Name: CAREER COMMITMENT SCALE

Purpose: To measure attitudes toward profession or vocation.

Number of Items: 7

Format: Five-point Likert format.

Reliability: Alpha was .83.

Author: Blau, G. J.

Article: Further exploring the meaning and measurement of career commitment.

Journal: *Journal of Vocational Behavior*, June 1988, *32*(3), 284–297.

Related Research: Blau, G. J. (1985). The measurement and prediction of career commitment. *Journal of Occupational Psychology*, *58*, 277–288.
McGinnis, S., & Morrow, P. C. (1990). Job attitudes among full- and part-time employees. *Journal of Vocational Behavior*, *36*, 82–96.
Arnold, J. (1990). Predictors of career commitment: A test of three

theoretical models. *Journal of Vocational Behavior*, *37*, 285–302.
Blau, G. (1989). Testing the generalizability of a career commitment measure and its impact on employee turnover. *Journal of Vocational Behavior*, *35*, 88–103.

■ ■ ■

5308

Test Name: CAREER COMMITMENT SCALE

Purpose: To measure identification with a career.

Number of Items: 5

Format: Seven-point Likert format. Sample items presented.

Reliability: Alpha was .79.

Author: Steffy, B. D., and Jones, J. W.

Article: The impact of family and career planning variables on the organizational, career, and community commitment of professional women.

Journal: *Journal of Vocational Behavior*, April 1988, *32*(2), 196–212.

Related Research: Gould, S. (1979). Characteristics of career planners in upwardly mobile occupations. *Academy of Management Journal*, *22*, 539–550.

■ ■ ■

5309

Test Name: CAREER CONCERN INVENTORY—ADULT FORM

Purpose: To assess awareness of and concern for the tasks of career development.

Number of Items: 60

Format: Five-point concern scales.

Reliability: Alphas ranged from .91 to .95.

Author: Ornstein, S., and Isabella, L.

Article: Age versus stage models of career attitudes of women: A partial replication and extension.

Journal: *Journal of Vocational Behavior*, February 1990, *36*(1), 1–19.

Related Research: Super, D. E., et al. (1981). *Career development inventory*: Adult form I. New York: Teachers' College, Columbia University.

■ ■ ■

5310

Test Name: CAREER DECISION-MAKING QUESTIONNAIRE

Purpose: To measure possible changes in planfulness following interventions.

Number of Items: 60

Format: Measures three styles of decision-making: Planning, intuitive, and dependent.

Reliability: Internal consistency ranged form .33 to .46.

Author: Lucas, M. S., and Epperson, D. L.

Article: Types of vocational undecidedness: A replication and refinement.

Journal: *Journal of Counseling Psychology*, October 1990, *37*(4), 382–388.

Related Research: Lunneborg, P. M. (1978). Sex and career decision-making styles. *Journal of Counseling Psychology*, 25, 299–305.

■ ■ ■

5311

Test Name: CAREER DECISION-MAKING SELF-EFFICACY SCALE

Purpose: To measure the confidence an individual expresses in being able to complete the tasks necessary to make career decisions.

Number of Items: 50

Format: Responses are made on a scale ranging from 0 (*no confidence*) to 9 (*complete confidence*).

Reliability: Coefficient alpha was .97.

Author: Fukuyama, M. A., et al.

Article: Effects of discover on career self-efficacy and decision making of undergraduates.

Journal: *The Career Development Quarterly*, September 1988, *37*(1), 56–62.

Related Research: Taylor, K. M., & Betz, N. E. (1983). Applications of self-efficacy theory to the understanding and treatment of career indecision. *Journal of Vocational Behavior*, 22, 63–81.

■ ■ ■

5312

Test Name: CAREER EXPLORATION SURVEY

Purpose: To measure the extent to which subjects have engaged in various environmental and self-exploratory activities in the last 3 months.

Number of Items: 11

Format: Five-point Likert format.

Reliability: Alphas ranged from .82 to .89.

Author: Blustein, D. L.

Article: The role of goal instability and career self-efficacy in the career exploration process.

Journal: *Journal of Vocational Behavior*, October 1989, *35*(2), 194–203.

Related Research: Stumpf, S. A., et al. (1983). Development of the career exploration survey (CES). *Journal of Vocational Behavior*, 22, 191–226.

Steffy, B. D. (1989). Antecedents and consequences of job search behaviors. *Journal of Vocational Behavior, 35*, 254–269.

■ ■ ■

5313

Test Name: CAREER EXPLORATION SURVEY— ADAPTED

Purpose: To provide a comprehensive assessment of career exploration.

Number of Items: 22

Format: Includes five subscales: Environmental exploration, Self-exploration, External search instrumentality, Internal search instrumentality, and Method instrumentality. Responses are made on 5-point Likert scales.

Reliability: Internal consistency reliabilities ranged from .67 to .89.

Validity: Correlations with other variables ranged from −.32 to .30.

Author: Blustein, D. L.

Article: The role of career exploration in the career decision making of college students.

Journal: *Journal of College Student Development*, March 1989, *30*(2), 111–117.

Related Research: Stumpf, S. A., et al. (1983). Development of the Career Exploration Survey (CES). *Journal of Vocational Behavior*, 22, 191–226.

■ ■ ■

5314

Test Name: CAREER EXPLORATORY SURVEY

Purpose: To measure several aspects of exploratory behavior.

Number of Items: 23

Format: Five-point response scales were used. Examples are presented.

Reliability: Internal consistency reliability estimates ranged from .70 to .89.

Validity: Correlations with other variables ranged from −.31 to .53.

Author: Noe, R. A., and Steffy, B. D.

Article: The influence of individual characteristics and assessment center evaluation on career exploration behavior and job involvement.

Journal: *The Journal of Vocational Behavior,* April 1987, *30*(2), 187–202.

Related Research: Stumpf, S. A., et al. (1983). Development of the Career Exploration Survey (CES). *Journal of Vocational Behavior,* 22, 191–226.

■ ■ ■

5315

Test Name: CAREER FACTORS INVENTORY

Purpose: To facilitate differential diagnosis of career indecision by measuring both personal–emotional and informational content areas.

Number of Items: 21

Format: Includes four factors: career choice anxiety, generalized indecisiveness, need for career information, and need for self-knowledge.

Reliability: Test–retest (23 weeks) reliability coefficients ranged from .79 to .84. Internal consistency coefficients ranged from .73 to .86.

Author: Chartrand, J. M., and Robbins, S. B.

Article: Using multidimensional career decision instruments to assess career decidedness and implementation.

Journal: *The Career Development Quarterly,* December 1990, *39*(2), 166–177.

Related Research: Chartrand, J. M., et al. (1990). Development and validation of the Career Factors Inventory. *Journal of Counseling Psychology,* 37, 491–501.

5316

Test Name: CAREER INDECISION SCALE

Purpose: To assess sources of career indecision.

Number of Items: 32

Format: Varied formats. All items presented.

Reliability: Alphas ranged from .51 to .81 across subscales. Test–retest reliability ranged from .77 to .96.

Validity: Correlations with other variables ranged from −.30 to .40.

Author: Callanan, G. A., and Greenhaus, J. H.

Article: The career indecision of managers and professionals: Development of a scale and test of a model.

Journal: *Journal of Vocational Behavior,* August 1990, *37*(1), 79–103.

■ ■ ■

5317

Test Name: CAREER PLANNING QUESTIONNAIRE

Purpose: To measure six theoretically different aspects of career maturity.

Number of Items: 120

Format: Includes six scales: career decisions, career activities, career salience, self knowledge, career concerns, and career values. Examples are presented.

Reliability: Kuder-Richardson Formula 20 reliability coefficients ranged from .35 to .85 (*N*s ranged from 51 to 178).

Validity: Coefficients of equivalence for four scales ranged from .70 to .79.

Author: Westbrook, B. W., et al.

Article: Reliability and construct validity of new measures of career maturity for 11th-grade students.

Journal: *Measurement and Evaluation in Counseling and Development,* April 1987, *20*(1), 18–26.

Related Research: Westbrook, B. W. (1983). *Career Planning Questionnaire revised research edition.* Unpublished test, North Carolina State University, Department of Psychology, Raleigh.

■ ■ ■

5318

Test Name: CAREER PLANNING SCALE

Purpose: To measure clarity of career objectives and plans.

Number of Items: 6

Format: Four-point Likert format. Sample items presented.

Reliability: Internal consistency was .89.

Author: Noe, R. A.

Article: An investigation of the determinants of successful assigned mentoring relationships.

Journal: *Personnel Psychology,* Summer 1988, *41*(2), 457–479.

Related Research: Gould, S. (1979). Characteristics of career planners in upwardly mobile occupations. *Academy of Management Journal,* 22, 539–550.

■ ■ ■

5319

Test Name: CAREER PREFERENCES SCALES

Purpose: To measure education and training aspirations, career-entry expectations, and career-task self-efficacy.

Number of Items: 11

Format: Seven-point Likert format. All items presented.

Reliability: Internal consistency ranged from .82 to .94.

Validity: Congruence of factors among subsamples was .99.

Author: Brodzinski, J. D., et al.

Article: Differentiating among three measures of career preference.

Journal: *Psychological Reports,* December 1989, *65*(3, Part II), 1275–1281.

■ ■ ■

5320

Test Name: COMMITMENT TO THE UNION SCALE

Purpose: To provide a union commitment scale.

Number of Items: 28

Format: Responses are made on a 3-point scale from 3 (*agree*) to 1 (*disagree*). Includes five factors: union loyalty, responsibility to the union, organization/work loyalty, belief in the union, and union instrumentality. Items are presented.

Reliability: Cronbach's alphas ranged from .70 to .86.

Author: Fullagar, C.

Article: A factor analytic study on the validity of a union commitment scale.

Journal: *Journal of Applied Psychology,* February 1986, *71*(1), 129–136.

Related Research: Ladd, R. T., et al. (1982). Union commitment: Replication and extension. *Journal of Applied Psychology, 67,* 640–644.

■ ■ ■

5321

Test Name: COMMITMENT TO THE UNION SCALE

Purpose: To assess union commitment.

Number of Items: 29

Format: Includes four factors: union loyalty, responsibilty for the union, willingness to work for the union, and belief in unionism. All items presented.

Reliability: Test–retest reliability ranged from .66 to .89.

Author: Tetrick, L. E., et al.

Article: Evidence for the stability of the four dimensions of the Commitment to the Union Scale.

Journal: *Journal of Applied Psychology,* October 1989, *74*(5), 819–822.

Related Research: Gordon, M. E., et al. (1980). Commitment to the union: Development of a measure and an examination of its correlates. *Journal of Applied Psychology, 65,* 479–499.

■ ■ ■

5322

Test Name: CONTINUANCE COMMITMENT SCALE

Purpose: To measure the behavioral view of organizational commitment.

Number of Items: 8

Format: All items are presented.

Reliability: Cronbach's alphas were .73 and .74.

Validity: Correlation with the affective commitment scale was .08.

Author: McGee, G. W., and Ford, R. C.

Article: Two (or more?) dimensions of organizational commitment: Reexamination of the affective and continuous commitment scales.

Journal: *Journal of Applied Psychology,* November 1987, *72*(4), 638–642.

Related Research: Meyer, J. P., & Allen, N. J. (1984). Testing the "side-bet theory" of organizational commitment: Some methodological considerations. *Journal of Applied Psychology, 69,* 372–378.

■ ■ ■

5323

Test Name: COPING SCALE

Purpose: To measure coping with career decision making.

Number of Items: 54

Format: Responses are made on a 5-point scale ranging from 1 (*hardly ever do this*) to 5 (*almost always do this*).

Reliability: Alphas ranged from .52 to .85.

Author: O'Hare, M. M., and Tamburri, E.

Article: Coping as a moderator of the relation between anxiety and career decision-making.

Journal: *Journal of Counseling Psychology,* July 1986, *33*(3), 255–264.

Related Research: Von Sell, M., et al. (1980). Empirical indices of coping with job stress: Problems and directions for research. Paper presented at the meeting of the Midwest Academy of Management, Cincinnati, OH.

■ ■ ■

5324

Test Name: JOB CHOICE SCALE

Purpose: To measure growth need strength.

Number of Items: 11

Format: Respondents choose between two different job situations on a 5-point scale ranging from 1 (*strongly prefer job A*) to 5 (*strongly prefer job B*).

Reliability: Alpha coefficients were .66 and .69 (*N* = 90). Test–retest (7–month) reliability was .65 (*N* = 90).

Author: Blau, G. J.

Article: Using a person–environment fit model to predict job involvement and organizational commitment.

Journal: *Journal of Vocational Behavior,* June 1987, *30*(3), 240–257.

Related Research: Hackman, J. R., & Oldham, G. (1974). The job diagnostic survey: An instrument for the diagnosis of jobs and evaluation of job redesign projects (Tech. rep.). Yale University.

5325

Test Name: JOB-INVOLVEMENT/ CENTRAL-LIFE-INTEREST MEASURE

Purpose: To assess the degree to which a person's work role dominates other life roles.

Number of Items: 6

Format: Employs a 5-point Likert scale. A sample item is presented.

Reliability: Alpha coefficients were .91 and .93.

Validity: Correlations with other variables ranged from .47 to −.30.

Author: Lounsbury, J. W., and Hoopes, L. L.

Article: A vacation from work: Changes in work and nonwork outcomes.

Journal: *Journal of Applied Psychology*, August 1986, *71*(3), 392–401.

Related Research: Saleh, S. D., & Hosek, J. (1976). Job involvement: Concepts and measurements. *Academy of Management Journal, 1,* 213–224.

■ ■ ■

5326

Test Name: JOB INVOLVEMENT MEASURE

Purpose: To measure job involvement.

Number of Items: 10

Format: Responses are made on a 5-point scale ranging from 1 (*strongly disagree*) to 5 (*strongly agree*). An example is presented.

Reliability: Alpha coefficients ranged from .74 to .84 (*N* = 90). Test–retest reliabilities ranged from .48 to .58 (*N* = 90).

Author: Blau, G. J.

Article: Using a person–environment fit model to predict job involvement and organizational commitment.

Journal: *Journal of Vocational Behavior*, June 1987, *30*(3), 240–257.

Related Research: Kanungo, R. (1982). Measurement of job and work involvement. *Journal of Applied Psychology*, *67*, 341–349.

■ ■ ■

5327

Test Name: JOB INVOLVEMENT QUESTIONNAIRE—SHORT FORM

Purpose: To determine job involvement.

Number of Items: 6

Format: Respondents rate their level of involvement in work and on the job on a 4-point scale ranging from *strongly agree* to *strongly disagree*.

Reliability: Split-half reliability was .73.

Validity: Correlations with other variables ranged from .29 to .38.

Author: Chusmir, L. H., and Koberg, C. S.

Article: Creativity differences among managers.

Journal: *Journal of Vocational Behavior*, October 1986, *29*(2), 240–253.

Related Research: Lodahl, T. M., & Kejner M. (1965). The definition and measurement of job involvement. *Journal of Applied Psychology, 49,* 24–33.

■ ■ ■

5328

Test Name: JOB INVOLVEMENT SCALE

Purpose: To measure job involvement.

Number of Items: 10

Format: Employed a 5-point Likert scale from *strongly agree* to *strongly disagree.*

Reliability: Internal consistency was .82.

Validity: Correlations with other variables ranged from −.35 to .46.

Author: Hollenbeck, J. R., and Williams, C. R.

Article: Turnover functionality versus turnover frequency: A note on work attitudes and organizational effectiveness.

Journal: *Journal of Applied Psychology*, November 1986, *71*(4), 606–611.

Related Research: Kanungo, R. N. (1982). Measurement of job and work involvement. *Journal of Applied Psychology, 67,* 341–349.

■ ■ ■

5329

Test Name: JOB INVOLVEMENT SCALE

Purpose: To measure job involvement.

Number of Items: 20

Format: Responses are made on a 5-point scale ranging from 1 (*strongly agree*) to 5 (*strongly disagreee*).

Reliability: Internal consistency reliabiltiy was .67.

Validity: Correlations with other variables ranged from −.08 to .36.

Author: Noe, R. A., and Steffy, B. D.

Article: The influence of individual characteristics and assessment center evaluation or career exploration behavior and job involvement.

Journal: *The Journal of Vocational Behavior*, April 1987, *30*(2), 187–202.

Related Research: Lodahl, T. M., & Kejner, M. (1965). The definition and measurement of job involvement. *Journal of Applied Psychology, 49,* 24–33.

■ ■ ■

5330

Test Name: JOB INVOLVEMENT SCALE—SHORT FORM

Purpose: To assess job involvement.

Number of Items: 6

Format: Responses are made on a 5-point Likert scale ranging from 1 (*strongly agree*) to 5 (*strongly disagree*).

Reliability: Coefficient alpha was .73.

Validity: Correlations with other variables ranged from −.40 to .45.

Author: Baba, V. V.

Article: Methodological issues in modeling absence: A comparison of least squares and Tobit analyses.

Journal: *Journal of Applied Psychology*, August 1990, *75*(4), 428–432.

Related Research: Lodahl, T. M., & Kejner, M. (1965). The definition and measurement of job involvement. *Journal of Applied Psychology*, *49*, 24–33.

■ ■ ■

5331

Test Name: JOB INVOLVEMENT/ VALUED SELF MEASURE

Purpose: To assess the degree to which persons consider their performance important to self-worth.

Number of Items: 5

Format: Employs a 5-point Likert scale. A sample item is presented.

Reliability: Alpha coefficients were .72 and .73.

Validity: Correlations with other variables ranged from .47 to −.31.

Author: Lounsbury, J. W., and Hoopes, L. L.

Article: A vacation from work: Changes in work and nonwork outcomes.

Journal: *Journal of Applied Psychology*, August 1986, *71*(3), 392–401.

Related Research: Saleh, S. D., & Hosek, J. 91976). Job involvement:

Concepts and measurements. *Academy of Management Journal, 1,* 213–224.

■ ■ ■

5332

Test Name: JOB SEARCH SCALES

Purpose: To measure methods and flexibility in searching for a job.

Number of Items: 13

Format: Seven-point scales. All items described.

Reliability: Alphas ranged from .55 to .82.

Validity: Correlations with other variables ranged from −.28 to .15.

Author: Shamir, B.

Article: Self-esteem and the psychological impact of unemployment.

Journal: *Social Psychology Quarterly*, March 1986, *49*(1), 61–72.

■ ■ ■

5333

Test Name: MATURITY OF CAREER CHOICE SCALE

Purpose: To assess the maturity of an individual's choice.

Number of Items: 6

Format: Responses to Items 1 through 3 are on a scale from 1 (*none*) to 5 (*more than a whole lot*) and responses to Items 4 through 6 are on a Likert scale from *strongly disagree* to *strongly agree*. All items are presented.

Reliability: Test–retest (1 year) reliability coefficient was .57. Split-half reliability was .89.

Validity: Correlations with other variables ranged from −.07 to .66.

Author: Westbrook, B. W., et al.

Article: The relationship between cognitive career maturity and self-reported career maturity of high school students.

Journal: *Measurement and Evaluation in Counseling and Development*, July 1987, *20*(2), 51–61.

■ ■ ■

5334

Test Name: NORMATIVE COMMITMENT SCALES

Purpose: To measure attitude and behavioral intentions that reflect commitment to organizations.

Number of Items: 9

Format: Likert. Sample items presented.

Reliability: Alphas ranged from .76 to .85 across two subscales.

Author: Vardi, Y., et al.

Article: The value content of organizational mission as a factor in the commitment of members.

Journal: *Psychological Reports*, August 1989, *65*(1), 27–34.

Related Research: Popper, M. (1984). Dimensions and expressions of organizational commitment. Unpublished doctoral dissertation. Tel-Aviv University, Israel.

■ ■ ■

5335

Test Name: ORGANIZATIONAL ATTRACTION SCALE

Purpose: To measure interest in working for an organization.

Number of Items: 6

Format: Likert format.

Reliability: Alphas ranged from .91 to .92.

Validity: Correlated significantly with three measures of organizational image.

Author: Schein, V. E., and Diamante, T.

Article: Organizational attraction and the person–environment fit.

Journal: *Psychological Reports*, February 1988, *62*(1), 167–173.

5336

Test Name: ORGANIZATIONAL COMMITMENT QUESTIONNAIRE—SHORT FORM

Purpose: To assess respondents' attachment to the company.

Number of Items: 9

Format: Employed a 3-point rating scale: disagree, not sure, agree.

Reliability: Coefficient alpha was .87. Test–retest reliability was .84.

Validity: Correlations with other variables ranged from −.20 to .52.

Author: Barling, T. et. al.

Article: Psychological functioning following an acute disaster.

Journal: *Journal of Applied Psychology*, November, 1987, *72*(4), 683–690.

Related Research: Mowday, R. T., et al. (1982). Employee–organization linkages: The psychology of commitment, absenteeism and turnover. New York: Academic Press.

■ ■ ■

5337

Test Name: ORGANIZATIONAL COMMITMENT SCALE

Purpose: To measure organizational commitment.

Number of Items: 15

Format: Employs a 5-point Likert scale ranging from *strongly disagree* to *strongly agree*.

Reliability: Alpha was .84.

Validity: Correlations with other variables ranged from −.68 to .46.

Author: Hollenbeck, J. R., and Williams, C. R.

Article: Turnover functionality versus turnover frequency: A note on work attitudes and organizational effectiveness.

Journal: *Journal of Applied Psychology*, November 1986, *71*(4), 606–611.

Related Research: Mowday, R. T., et al. (1982). *Employee-organization linkages: The psychology of commitment, absenteeism, and turnover.* New York: Academic Press.

■ ■ ■

5338

Test Name: ORGANIZATIONAL COMMITMENT QUESTIONNAIRE

Purpose: To provide general indicator of employee satisfaction with the company as a whole.

Number of Items: 9

Format: Responses one made on a 7-point scale ranging from 1 (*strongly disagree*) to 7 (*strongly agree*). An example is presented.

Reliability: .89.

Validity: Correlations with other variables ranged from −.18 to .13.

Author: Klein, K. J., and Hall, R. J.

Article: Correlates of employee satisfaction with stock ownership: Who likes an ESOP most?

Journal: *Journal of Applied Psychology*, November 1988, *73*(4), 630–638.

Related Research: Mowday, R. T., et al. (1979). The measurement of organizational commitment. *Journal of Vocational Behavior*, *14*, 224–247.

■ ■ ■

5339

Test Name: ORGANIZATIONAL COMMITMENT SCALE

Purpose: To assess the degree to which persons are committed to the values, goals, philosophy, and practices of the organization for which they work.

Number of Items: 4

Reliability: Alpha coefficients were .72 and .76.

Validity: Correlations with other variables ranged from .55 to −.38.

Author: Lounsbury, J. W., and Hoopes, L. L.

Article: A vacation from work: Changes in work and nonwork outcomes.

Journal: *Journal of Applied Psychology*, August 1986, *71*(3), 392–401.

Related Research: Porter, L. W., et al. (1974). Organizational commitment, job satisfaction, and turnover among psychiatric technicians. *Journal of Applied Psychology*, *59*, 603–609.

■ ■ ■

5340

Test Name: ORGANIZATIONAL COMMITMENT SCALE

Purpose: To assess organizational commitment.

Number of Items: 9

Format: Responses were made on a 5-point Likert scale ranging from 1 (*strongly disagree*) to 5 (*strongly agree*).

Reliability: Coefficient alpha was .88.

Validity: Correlations with other variables ranged from −.24 to .70.

Author: Mathieu, J. E., and Kohler, S. S.

Article: A cross-level examination of group absence influences on individual absence.

Journal: *Journal of Applied Psychology*, April 1990, *75*(2), 217–220.

Related Research: Mowday, R. T., et al. (1979). The measurement of organizational commitment. *Journal of Vocational Behavior*, *14*, 224–247.

■ ■ ■

5341

Test Name: ORGANIZATIONAL COMMITMENT SCALE

Purpose: To measure an individual's identification with and involvement in a particular vorganization.

Number of Items: 15

Format: Responses are made on a 7-point Likert scale ranging from 1 (*strongly disagree*) to 7 (*strongly agree*). Sample items are presented.

Reliability: Coefficient alpha was .91.

Validity: Correlations with other variables from −.13 to .58.

Author: Morrow, P. C., and McElroy, J. C.

Article: Work commitment and job satisfaction over three career stages.

Journal: *Journal of Vocational Behavior*, June 1987, *30*(3), 330–346.

Related Research: Mowday, R. T., et al. (1979). The measurement of organizational commitment. *Journal of Vocational Behavior*, *14*, 224–247.

■ ■ ■

5342

Test Name: ORGANIZATIONAL COMMITMENT SCALE

Purpose: To measure the degree to which people are committed to their organization.

Number of Items: 8

Format: Includes three aspects of commitment: belief in the organization's goals and values, willingness to exert effort to achieve organizational goals, and desire to maintain membership in the organization. Responses are made on a 6-point scale ranging from 1 (*strongly disagree*) to 6 (*strongly agree*).

Reliability: Reliability was .82.

Validity: Correlations with other variables ranged from −.21 to .62.

Author: Pazy, A., and Zin, R.

Article: A contingency approach to consistency: A challenge to prevalent views.

Journal: *The Journal of Vocational Behavior*, February 1987, *30*(1), 84–101.

Related Research: Mowday, R. T., et al. (1979). The measurement of

organizational commitment. *Journal of Vocational Behavior*, *14*, 227–247.

■ ■ ■

5343

Test Name: ORGANIZATIONAL COMMITMENT SCALE

Purpose: To measure commitment to a job in a particular organization.

Number of Items: 4

Format: Three-point scales that rate desire to leave current job.

Reliability: Alphas ranged from .74 to .84.

Author: Yammarino, F. Y., and Dubinsky, A. J.

Article: Employee responses: Gender- or job-related differences?

Journal: *Journal of Vocational Behavior*, June 1988, *32*(3), 366–383.

Related Research: Hrebiniak, L. G., & Alluto, J. A. (1972). Personal and role-related factors in the development of organizational commitment. *Administrative Science Quarterly*, *17*, 555–573.

■ ■ ■

5344

Test Name: PROFESSIONAL COMMITMENT SCALE

Purpose: To measure desire for professional autonomy, professional identification, professional ethics, and maintenance of collegiality.

Number of Items: 20

Format: Seven-point Likert format.

Reliability: Alpha was .63.

Author: Koberg, C. S., and Chusmir, L. H.

Article: Relationships between sex-role conflict and work related variables: Gender and hierarchical differences.

Journal: *The Journal of Social Psychology*, December 1989, *129*(6), 779–791.

Related Research: Bartol, K. M. (1979). Professionalism as a predictor of organizational commitment, role stress, and turnover: A multidimensional approach. *Academy of Management Journal*, *22*, 815–821.

■ ■ ■

5345

Test Name: PROFESSIONAL COMMITMENT SCALE

Purpose: To measure attitudes toward and identification with one's professional choice.

Number of Items: 5

Format: Items pertain to loyalty and pride in one's profession, acceptance of its values, and sense of professional fulfillment.

Reliability: Cronbach's alpha was .72.

Validity: Correlations with other variables ranged from −.18 to .62.

Author: Pazy, A., and Zin, R.

Article: A contingency approach to consistency: A challenge to prevalent views.

Journal: *The Journal of Vocational Behavior*, February 1987, *30*(1), 84–101.

Related Research: Lachman, R., & Aranya, N. (1986). Job related attitudes and turnover intentions among professionals in different work settings. *Organization Studies*, *7*, 279–293.

■ ■ ■

5346

Test Name: PROFESSIONALISM SCALE

Purpose: To measure commitment to careers involving using career as a major referent, belief in public service, belief in self-regulation by colleagues, belief in a sense of calling, and a desire for autonomy.

Number of Items: 45

Format: Five-point self-rating scales.

Reliability: Alphas ranged from .69 to .76.

Author: Morrow, P. C., and Goetz, J. F., Jr.

Article: Professionalism as a form of work commitment.

Journal: *Journal of Vocational Behavior*, February 1988, *32*(1), 92–111.

Related Research: Hall, R. H. (1968). Professionalism and bureaucratization. *American Sociological Review, 33*, 92–104.

■ ■ ■

5347

Test Name: READINESS FOR VOCATIONAL PLANNING, REVISED EDITION

Purpose: To measure career maturity.

Number of Items: 18

Format: An open-ended, written test.

Reliability: Interrater reliability ranged from .83 to .90. Kuder-Richardson Formula 20 reliability coefficients ranged from .70 to .86.

Author: Westbrook, B. W., et al.

Article: Reliability and construct validity of new measures of career maturity for 11th-grade students.

Journal: *Measurement and Evaluation in Counseling and Development*, April 1987, *20*(1), 18–26.

Related Research: Gribbons, W. D., & Lohnes, P. R. (1968). *Emerging careers*. New York: Teachers College Press, Columbia University.

■ ■ ■

5348

Test Name: SALIENCE AND CLARITY OF CAREER STRATEGY SCALE

Purpose: To assess the clarity of participants' career objectives and strategies.

Number of Items: 6

Format: Responses are made on a 5-point scale ranging from 1 (*strongly agree*) to 5 (*strongly disagree*). An example is presented.

Reliability: Internal consistency reliability was .82.

Validity: Correlations with other variables ranged from .01 to .51.

Author: Noe, R. A., and Steffy, B. D.

Article: The influence of individual characteristics and assessment center evaluation or career exploration behavior and job involvement.

Journal: *The Journal of Vocational Behavior*, April 1987, *30*(2), 187–202.

Related Research: Gould, S. (1979). Characteristics of career planning in upwardly mobile occupations. *Academy of Management Journal, 22*, 539–550.

■ ■ ■

5349

Test Name: SATISFACTION OPINIONNIARE

Purpose: To assess high school students' satisfaction with career exploration experiences.

Number of Items: 9

Format: Likert-type format. Each item is rated on a 5-point scale ranging from 1 (*strongly disagree*) to 5 (*strongly agree*).

Reliability: Alpha coefficients ranged from .79 to .81.

Author: Jones, L. K.

Article: The career key: An investigation of the reliability and validity of its scales and its helpfulness to college students.

Journal: *Measurement and Evaluation in Counseling and Development*, July 1990, *23*(2), 67–76.

Related Research: Cooper, J. F. (1976). Comparative impact of the SCII and the vocational card sort on career salience and career exploration of women. *Journal of Counseling psychology, 23*, 340–352.

■ ■ ■

5350

Test Name: SCALE OF VOCATIONAL INDECISION

Purpose: To provide an overall index of undecidedness.

Number of Items: 18

Format: Each item is rated on a 4-point scale from *not at all like me* to *exactly like me*. Indecision is reflected by a high score. An example is provided.

Reliability: Internal consistency reliability was .85.

Author: Clarke, K. M., & Greenberg, L. S.

Article: Differential effects of the Gestalt two-chair intervention and problem solving in resolving decisional conflict.

Journal: *Journal of Counseling Psychology*, January 1986, *33*(1), 11–15.

Related Research: Osipow, S. G., et al. (1976). A scale of educational–vocational undecidedness: A typological approach. *Journal of Vocational Behavior, 9*, 233–243.

■ ■ ■

5351

Test Name: SELF-UNCERTAINTY SCALE

Purpose: To assess the degree to which participants report uncertainty about their career decision.

Number of Items: 4

Format: A subscale of the Vocational Decision Scale. Responses are made on a Likert scale ranging from 1 (*completely disagree*) to 6 (*completely agree*).

Reliability: Test–retest (3 months) reliability was .77.

Validity: Correlations with variables ranged from −.23 to .10.

Author: Phillips, S. D., and Bruch, M. A.

Article: Shyness and dysfunction in career development.

Journal: *Journal of Counseling Psychology*, April 1988, *35*(2), 159–165.

Related Research: Jones, L. K., & Chenery, M. F. (1980). Multiple subtypes among vocationally undecided college students: A model and assessment instrument. *Journal of Consulting Psychology*, *27*, 469–477.

■ ■ ■

5352

Test Name: TEACHER COMMITMENT AND JOB SCALES

Purpose: To measure teachers' commitment to teaching and teachers' perception of job conditions.

Number of Items: 47

Format: Likert format. All items presented.

Reliability: Alphas ranged from .61 to .82. Item-total correlations ranged from .25 to .67.

Validity: Correlations between commitment and job perceptions ranged from −.06 to .63.

Author: Rosenholtz, S. J., and Simpson, C.

Article: Workplace conditions and the rise and fall of teachers' commitment.

Journal: *Sociology of Education*, October 1990, *64*(4), 241–257.

■ ■ ■

5353

Test Name: UNION COMMITMENT SCALE

Purpose: To assess union commitment.

Number of Items: 20

Format: Includes two subscales: union attitudes and opinions; and prounion behavioral intentions.

Responses are made on a 5-point scale ranging from 1 (*strongly disagree*) to 5 (*strongly agree*). Sample items are presented.

Reliability: Alpha coefficients ranged from .81 to .89.

Validity: Correlations with other variables ranged from −.21 to .50.

Author: Mellor, S.

Article: The relationship betweeen membership decline and union commitment: A field study of local unions in crisis.

Journal: *Journal of Applied Psychology*, June 1990, *75*(3), 258–267.

Related Research: Friedman, L., & Harvey, R. J. (1986). Factors of union commitment: The case for lower dimensionality. *Journal of Applied Psychology*, *71*, 371–376.

■ ■ ■

5354

Test Name: UNION PARTICIPATION SCALE

Purpose: To measure participation in labor unions.

Number of Items: 9

Format: Yes–no and frequency formats. All items described.

Reliability: Alphas ranged from .73 to .90 across subscales.

Validity: Correlations with other variables ranged from −.21 to .63.

Author: McShane, S. L.

Article: The multidimensionality of union participation.

Journal: *Journal of Occupational Psychology*, September 1986, *59*(3), 177–187.

5355

Test Name: VOCATIONAL ACTIVITY PREFERENCE PROFILE SCALE

Purpose: To identify vocational activity preferences.

Number of Items: 210

Format: Includes 21 scales of 10 items each. Responses are made by indicating either: *would like to perform the activity, no opinion about the activity*, or *would not like to perform the activity*.

Reliability: Reliability estimates ranged from .79 to .97.

Author: Cunningham, J. W., et al.

Article: Interest factors derived from job analytically based activity preference scales.

Journal: *Journal of Vocational Behavior*, June 1987, *30*(3), 270–279.

Related Research: Cunningham, J. W., et al (1975). The development of activity preference scales based on systematically derived work dimensions: An ergometric approach to interest measurement. *JSAS Catalog of Selected Documents in Psychology*, *5*, 355(Ms. No. 1154).

■ ■ ■

5356

Test Name: VOCATIONAL DECISION SCALE

Purpose: To measure three dimensions of vocational decision status.

Number of Items: 38

Format: Includes three dimensions: degree of decidedness, level of comfort about the state of decidedness, and reasons for being undecided. Responses are made on a 5-point Likert scale.

Reliability: Test–retest reliabilities ranged from .36 to .85. Coefficient alpha was .90.

Validity: Correlations with other variables ranged from −.63 to .80.

Author: Fuqua, D. R., et al.

Article: The relationship of career indecision and anxiety: A multivariate examination.

Journal: *The Journal of Vocational Behavior*, April 1987, *30*(2), 175–186.

Related Research: Jones, L. L., & Chenery, M. F. (1980). Multiple subtypes among vocationally undecided college students: A model and assessment instrument. *Journal of Counseling Psychology, 27,* 469–477.

■ ■ ■

5357

Test Name: VOCATIONAL DECISION SCALE

Purpose: To measure career indecision.

Number of Items: 38

Format: Items are rated on a 6-point scale from 1 (*completely disagree*) to 6 (*completely agree*).

Reliability: Test–retest reliabilities ranged from .36 to .65. Cronbach's alpha was .90.

Author: Hartman, B. W., et al.

Article: Multivariate generalizability analysis of three measures of career indecision.

Journal: *Educational and Psychological Measurement*, Spring 1988, *48*(1), 61–68.

Related Research: Jones, L. K. (1977). *The Vocational Decision Scale.* Unpublished Scale, 1977. (Available from Lawrence K. Jones, Department of Counselor Education, North Carolina State University, Raleigh, North Carolina 27695.)

■ ■ ■

5358

Test Name: VOCATIONAL DECISION-MAKING DIFFICULTY SCALE

Purpose: To assess the reasons given by individuals for vocational indecision.

Number of Items: 13

Format: Responses are either true or false. Includes four factors: lack of information about the world of work, lack of clarity about where the

subject fits into the world of work, choice anxiety, and questions about one's abilities.

Reliability: Kuder-Richardson Formula 20 values ranged from .63 to .86. Test–retest (6 weeks) reliability ranged from .38 to .66.

Author: Gianakos, I., and Subich, L. M.

Article: The relationship of gender and sex-role orientation to vocational undecidedness.

Journal: *Journal of Vocational Behavior*, August 1986, *29*(1), 42–50.

Related Research: Holland, J. L., & Holland, J. E. (1977). Vocational indecision: More evidence and speculation. *Journal of Counseling Psychology, 24,* 404–414.

■ ■ ■

5359

Test Name: VOCATIONAL INFORMATION-SEEKING BEHAVIOR INVENTORY

Purpose: To assess the tendency to engage in career-information-seeking behaviors.

Number of Items: 15

Format: Responses are made on a 5-point scale from 1 (*never*) to 5 (*frequently*). A sample item is presented.

Reliability: Internal reliability coefficient was .82.

Validity: Correlations with variables ranged from −.23 to .15.

Author: Phillips, S. D., and Bruch, M. A.

Article: Shyness and dysfunction in career development.

Journal: *Journal of Counseling Psychology*, April 1988, *35*(2), 159–165.

Related Research: Krumboltz, J. D., & Thoresen, C. E. (1964). The effect of behavioral counseling in group and individual settings on information-seeking behavior. *Journal of*

Counseling Psychology, 11, 324–333.

■ ■ ■

5360

Test Name: WORK CHALLENGE SCALE

Purpose: To assess perceived interest in one's work.

Number of Items: 6

Format: Four-point true–false scales.

Reliability: Alpha was .79.

Author: Dornstein, M., and Matalon, Y.

Article: A comprehensive analysis of the predictors of organizational commitment: A study of voluntary army personnel in Israel.

Journal: *Journal of Vocational Behavior*, April 1989, *34*(2), 192–203.

Related Research: Quinn, R. P., & Staines, G. L. (1979). In J. D. Cook et al. (Eds.), *The experience of work* (chapter 3, p. 67). London: Academic Press.

■ ■ ■

5361

Test Name: WORK HOMEMAKING SALIENCE SCALES

Purpose: To measure salience of careers and homemaking.

Number of Items: 29

Format: Five-point Likert format.

Reliability: Alpha was .84.

Author: Klein, H.

Article: Job satisfaction in professional dual-career couples: Psychological and socioeconomic variables.

Journal: *Journal of Vocational Behavior*, June 1988, *32*(3), 225–268.

Related Research: Super, D., & Culha, M. (1976). *Work Salience Inventory.* Available from the first author. Teachers' College, New York, New York 19927.

5362

Test Name: WORK PREFERENCES QUESTIONNAIRE

Purpose: To measure work preferences.

Number of Items: 10

Format: Responses are made on a 5-point Likert scale. Examples are presented.

Reliability: Coefficient alpha was .82.

Validity: Correlations with other variables ranged from .06 to .26.

Author: Stumpf, S. A., and Lockhart, M. C.

Article: Career exploration: Work-role salience, work preferences, beliefs, and behavior.

Journal: *Journal of Vocational Behavior,* June 1987, *30*(3), 258–269.

Related Research: Mitchell, T. R., & Knudson, B. W. (1973). Institutionality theory predictions of students' attitudes toward business and their choice of business as a career. *Academy of Management Journal, 16,* 41–51.

■ ■ ■

5363

Test Name: WORK-ROLE SALIENCE

Purpose: To measure work-role salience.

Number of Items: 8

Format: Responses are made on a 5-point Likert format.

Reliability: Coefficient alpha was .61.

Validity: Correlations with other variables ranged from .01 to .47.

Author: Stumpf, S. A., and Lockhart, M. C.

Article: Career exploration: Work-role salience, work preferences, beliefs, and behavior.

Journal: *Journal of Vocational Behavior,* June 1987, *30*(3), 258–269.

Related Research: Greenhaus, J. H., & Sklarew, N. D. (1981). Some sources and consequences of career exploration. *Journal of Vocational Behavior, 18,* 1–12.

Author Index

• • •

All numbers refer to test numbers for the current volume. Volumes 1 and 2 did not include an author index.

Bartling, C. A., 5133
Bartol, K. M., 3580, 5344
Baruch, G., 4027
Basadur, M., 5144, 5156
Bass, B. M., 4417
Bassai, J. L., 5125
Battista, J., 3869
Baugh, B. T., 4725
Baum, S. K., 5068
Beach, S. R. H., 3764, 4083, 4814
Beauvais, F., 3729, 4423, 4560, 4562, 5242
Bech, A. J., 4815
Beck, A., 3846, 3942, 5262
Beck, A. T., 3764, 3768, 3770, 3924, 4289
Becker, M. H., 4837
Beckham, E. E., 3788
Beckwith, J., 4386
Beder, B. A., 3698
Beehr, T. A., 3807, 4170, 4478, 4940
Behar, L., 4427, 4925
Behrman, D. N., 4860
Beit-Hallahmi, B., 4885, 5236
Belk, S. S., 5209
Bell, M., 3772
Bell, R. C., 4216
Bell, Y., 4754
Bemo, D. H., 4978
Benbow, C. P., 4755
Bender, W. N., 5006
Benedict, J. O., 4440
Benjamin, L. S., 4098
Benn, M., 4327
Bennett, J. B., 4712
Bennion, L. D., 5046
BenPorath, Y. S., 3886
Benson, J., 4280
Bentler, P., 3842, 4937
Berg, B., 3981, 4529, 4791
Berg, K. M., 4462
Berger, E., 4823
Berger, E. M., 4065
Berger, R. E., 4425
Bergin, A. E., 4441
Berkman, L. F., 3891
Berkowitz, L., 3919
Berrenberg, J. L., 4767
Bersheid, E., 4778
Bertock, M. R., 3810, 4210
Besemer, S. P., 4495
Best, D. L., 5103
Bettenhausen, K., 4008
Betz, E. L., 3704
Betz, N. E., 3716, 3818, 4876, 4877, 4973, 5311

Beutell, N. J., 5253
Bezjak, J. E., 4914, 4915, 4916, 5238
Bezruckzko, N., 3681
Bhagat, R. S., 4666, 4986, 5292
Bianchi, L., 4746
Biddle, B. J., 5248
Biggs, J. B., 5153
Bihm, E. M., 4718
Bills, R. G., 4842
Bitter, R. G., 4612
Blackman, H. S., 5141
Blair, E. D., 5112
Blank, J. R., 3678
Blankstein, K. R., 3743, 5166
Blatt, S. J., 4499
Blau, G., 4412, 4936
Blau, G. J., 4215, 4788, 5307, 5324, 5239, 5326
Blegen, M. ., 4577
Bleumenfeld, W. S., 4262
Blinn, L. M., 4852
Block, J., 4524
Blood, M., 5239
Bloom, B. S., 5138
Bluedorn, A. C., 4184
Bluen, S. D., 4173
Bluestein, D. L., 4391
Blumenfield, P. C., 3722
Blustein, D. L., 4871, 5012, 5046, 5312, 5313
Boerma, F. J., 3736
Bogardus, E. S., 4011
Bokemeier, J., 4341
Boldizar, J. P., 5235
Bond, M. J., 4475
Bonner, R. L., 3867, 4934, 5145, 5176
Bonneson, M. G., 4374
Bonnington, S. B., 4824
Booth, A., 4612
Borden, L. A., 4246
Border, L. A., 5202
Bordin, E. S., 4492
Borduin, C. M., 4630
Borgen, F. H., 4164
Borrello, G. M., 4033
Bortner, R. W., 5174
Bosscher, R. J., 3768
Botvin G. J., 5171
Botvin, G. J., 4470
Bouman, T. K., 3809
Bouton, R. A., 4293, 4297
Bowd, A. D., 4337
Bowen, G. L., 5114
Bowen, R., 5189

Bowlby, R. A., 4250
Boyd, J. R., 4439
Boylan, C. P., 4337
Boyne, J., 4356
Bracken, D., 4161
Bradburn, N. M., 3755, 3756
Bradley, R., 4865
Braiker, H. B., 3998
Braithwaite, J., 5247
Braly, K. W., 4291
Branch, C. W., 3976
Brand, A. G., 5027
Brandt, P. A., 4050
Brant, K. W., 4385
Braskamp, L. A., 4898
Braunstein, D. N., 4715, 4716, 4717
Bray, J., 4571
Breakwell, G. M., 4721
Breaugh, J., 4936
Breiter, H. J., 3813
Brenner, O. C., 5253
Breskin, S., 5175
Breslau, N., 3781
Breslin, F. A., 3874
Breslow, L., 3891
Bretherton, I., 4001
Brickman, P., 4848
Brief, A. P., 3762, 3779, 3862, 4133, 4143
Briere, J., 4521
Brissie, J. S., 4046, 4142, 4203, 4429, 4465, 4672, 5001
Broad, J., 4363
Broadbent, D. E., 5121
Broberg, A., 5052
Broday, S. F., 4833, 5200
Brodbar-Nemzer, J. Y., 4583
Brodsky, S. L., 3874
Brodzinski, J. D., 5319
Brookings, J. B., 3806
Brooks, C. H., 4836
Brooks, G. C., Jr., 3702
Brooks, L. A., 4650
Brooks-Gunn, J., 4979
Brophy, J., 5152
Brown, M. T., 4983
Brown, R., 4009, 4782
Brown, S. A., 4813
Brown, S. D., 4057, 4089
Brown, T. A., 4913
Brownlee-Duffeck, M., 4381
Bruch, M. A., 3987, 4398, 4834, 4912, 5205, 5210, 5351, 5359
Bryant, B. K., 5051
Bryant, F., 4437
Bryman, A., 4025

Connor, K., 5031
Connors, C. K., 4346
Conte, H. R., 3776
Cook, D. A., 4765
Cook, E. P., 4908
Cook, J., 5264
Cook, W. W., 5030
Cooley, E. J., 5212
Cooper, J. F., 5349
Cooper, S. E., 4519
Coppel, D. B., 4970
Corbin, C. B., 5081
Corcoran, K. J., 5048
Corrado, T. J., 4999
Corrigan, J. D., 5274
Corroll, J. L., 4388
Coryel, W., 3859
Cosier, R. A., 4480
Courtney, B. E., 4907
Coyne, J. C., 4042
Craig, D., 4274
Craig, J. M., 4006
Craig, S. C., 4919
Craig, S. S., 4819
Craighead, W. E., 4789
Craik, K. H., 4714
Cramer, P., 3875
Crampton, J., 5085
Crandall, R., 3923, 4301, 4990
Crandall, V. C., 3856, 4760, 4843,
    4844, 4845
Cranston, P., 4948
Craske, M. G., 3758, 3882
Crawford, J. D., 3887
Creekmore, A. M., 5224
Crimmins, D. B., 4718
Crisp, A. H., 3849
Crnic, K. A., 4603, 4617
Crockenberg, S., 4589
Crocker, L., 3712, 3744
Croft, D. B., 4663
Cron, W. L., 5298
Crook, J. C., 4141
Cross, D., 4216
Crown, S., 3849
Crowne, D. P., 4036
Cuellar, I., 3967
Culha, M., 5361
Cullen, F., 4377
Cummings, J. S., 4626
Cummings, K. M., 4836
Cunningham, B., 5008, 5152
Cunningham, D. A., 5148
Cunningham, D. M., 5175
Cunningham, J. W., 5355
Curran, J. P., 4072

Curry, J. F., 4789
Curry, S., 4734
Curtis, J., 3994
Cutrona, C. E., 4084, 4085, 4606,
    5069
Cuyjet, M. J., 4647

• • •

D'Angelli, A. R., 4242
D'llio, V. R., 3670, 4953
Dahlhauser, M. M., 4805
Daley, J. A., 3750
Dalton, D. R., 4480
Daly, J. A., 3707
Dambrot, F. H., 4224, 4225, 4254,
    4284
Dansereau, F., 4189
Darling-Fisher, C. S., 4514
Das, J. P., 4351, 4874
Dastmalchian, A., 4652
Daugherty, C. G., 4254
Davis, A. S., 4181
Davis, L. L. 4773
Davis, M. H., 4106
Davis, P. S., 4653
Dawson, C., 4486
de Turk, M. A., 4533, 4976
Deal, J. E., 4524, 4605
Dean, D. G., 3969
Debats, D. L., 3869
Deci, E. L., 4391
Deffenbacher, J. L., 3759, 5169,
    5213
DeGood, D. E., 5180
DeGroot, E. V., 4881
Dehlari, N. S., 5281
Deitz, S. R., 4436, 5202
DeJong, G. F., 5227
Dekking, Y. M., 4075
DeKoninck, J., 5037
DeLaet, T. J., 5063
Delisle, J. R., 4954
DeLuccie, M. F., 4507
DeLucia, L. A., 5115
Deluga, R. J., 4135, 4198, 4930,
    5296, 5297
Deluty, B. M., 3838, 5187, 5215
Deluty, R. H., 4354, 4363, 5120
Demba, M. H., 5002, 5003
Demo, D. H., 3977, 4526, 4539,
    4929
Derber, M., 4652
Derogatis, L. R., 3777, 3810, 3848,
    3944, 4376, 4449
deRuiter, C., 3817, 4073
Desrosiers, M., 4997

Dess, G. G., 4653
Devereux, E., 4537
Diamante, T., 5335
DiCaudo, J., 5038
Diener, E., 3924, 4705, 5024
Dillard, B. G., 4308
Dillon, K. M., 3737
DiMatteo, M. R., 4107, 4106, 4108
Dinning, W. D., 5085
Dipboye, R. L., 5283, 5284
Dishman, R. K., 4737
Dittrich, J. E., 4664
DiVesta, F. J., 4269
Dixon, P. N., 3709, 4847
Dobbins, G. H., 5020
Dobson, K. S., 3813
Docherty, N. M., 5045
Doctor, R. M., 3960
Dodder, R., 5068
Dodrill, C. B., 4112
Doherty, M. L., 4404, 4481, 4688
Dohrenwend, B. S., 3864, 3908
Dolan, S., 4218
Dollinger, S. J., 3875
Domino, G., 4503
Donatelli, M. J., 3936
Donovan, W. L., 4570, 5053
Dooley, D., 3908
Dorn, F. J., 4820
Dornic, S., 3892
Dornstein, M., 4677
Dougherty, T. W., 4180
Doverspike, D., 3667
Dowd, E. T., 4473, 5257, 5268
Dowling, P., 5254
Downs, A. C., 4245
Dragutinovich, S., 4867
Drake, M. F., 4450
Drasgow, F., 4859
Draucker, C. B., 4841
Dreman, S., 4989
Dreyer, N. A., 5086
Driedger, L., 4009
Driscoll, A., 5294
Dubinsky, A. J., 4189, 5343
Dubow, E. F., 4464, 4620, 5120
Dubrin, A. J., 4425
Duda, J. L., 4730, 4731, 4898
Duffy, G. G., 3669
Duke, M. P., 3963, 4752, 4888, 4924
Dukes, R. L., 3774, 3792, 3795
Duncan, O. D., 4136
Duncan, P., 4361
Dundon, M., 4375, 4648, 4766, 4927
Dunham, R. B., 4138
Dunn, E. J. 3926

Fretz, B. R., 3824, 4084, 5244
Frice, J. M., 4792
Friedland, D. L., 3683, 5287
Friedlander, M. L., 4611, 4811, 4968, 5275, 5278
Friedman, L., 5353
Friedman, G. H., 3828, 3873, 3929
Friedrich, W. N., 3979, 4616
Friend, R., 3822, 4076, 4082
Friesen, J., 4938
Froebhle, T. C., 3951
Frone, M. R., 4188, 4219, 4479, 4643, 4659, 4939
Fuchs, D., 3688, 3921
Fukeyama, M. A., 5311
Fullagar, C., 4110, 4174, 5250, 5320
Funk, R., 5083
Fuqua, D. A., 4482
Fuqua, D. R., 3935, 4639, 4640, 5356
Furman, W., 4004, 4619
Furnham, A., 3920, 4979
Futterman, L. A., 4923

■ ■ ■

Gabbard, C. E., 4937
Gacono, C. B., 3913, 5208
Gadzella, B. M., 5131
Gaen, G. B., 4404
Gail, L., 4748
Galambos, N. L., 4260
Galassi, J. P., 3861, 5181
Galvin-Schaefers, K., 4472, 4905
Gambrill, E. D., 5171, 5172
Gandour, M., 4614
Gangestad, S., 4983
Ganong, L., 4426
Ganong, L. H., 4003, 4296, 4540
Ganster, D. C., 4194
Garcia, P. A., 4488
Garden, A. M., 4127
Gardner, D. C., 4812
Gardner, D. G., 4202
Garfinkel, P. E., 4290
Garner, D. M., 4290
Garrard, M., 4244
Garrett, J. B., 5240, 5252
Garssen B., 3817, 4073
Garza, R. T., 4991
Gassenheimer, J. B., 5078
Gaston, L., 4621
Gay, E. G., 4163
Gayton, W. F., 5075, 5217
Gecas, V., 4977
Gehring, T. M., 4564

Geiger, M. A., 4240
Geisler, J. S., 4488
Gelejs, I., 4909
Gelso, C. J., 4471
Gelso, C. J., 3804
Gentley, R. R., 4185
Gentry, C. S., 4080
George, A. A., 4205
George, J. M., 3862, 4008, 4143, 4212, 5057
Gerace, T. A., 5193
Gerhart, B., 4154
Gerstein, L. H., 4629, 4903, 5007
Gerstein, L. H., 4272
Gerth, A., 4732
Gertman, D. I., 5141
Getter, H., 4573, 4574
Geyer, P. D., 4159, 4179
Ghiu, L., 4975
Gianakos, I., 5358
Gibaud-Wallson, J. A., 4606
Gibb, G., 3893
Gibbins, K., 3839, 4817, 5093
Gibson, S., 5002, 5003
Gil, K. M., 3802
Gilmore, J., 4261
Gim, R. H., 4100
Gitlin, D. E., 4857
Gladding, S. T., 5241
Glass, C. R., 4081
Glass, D. G., 4960
Gleghorn, A. A., 4273, 4779
Glenwick, D. S., 3756
Gleser, G. C., 5123
Glezer, H., 4556
Glidden, C. E., 4248
Glow, R. A., 4346
Gobdel, B. C., 4481
Godwin, D. D., 4534, 5084
Goertzel, T. G., 5077
Goetz, J. F., Jr., 5252, 5346
Goheen, M. D., 3946
Gold, S., 4227
Goldberg, D. P., 3826, 3830
Goldberg, W., 4946
Golden, B. R., 4369, 4385
Goldin, L., 4303
Goldsmith, R. E., 4024, 4139, 4713, 5134, 5079
Goldstein, A. P., 4086
Goldstein-Hendley, S., 5064
Gonzalez, G. M., 4457
Good, G. E., 4245, 4247, 5082
Good, K. C., 4741
Good, L. R., 4741
Goodman, S. H., 4866, 4867

Gopher, D., 3667
Gordon, D. A., 3728
Gordon, M. E., 4110, 4250, 5321
Gordon, R. A., 4661
Gore, E. J., 4492
Gormally, J., 4996
Gorman, D. R., 4963
Gorrell, J., 4921
Gottlieb, B. H., 3981
Gottman, J. M., 3992, 3997
Gough, H. G., 4060
Gould, J. W., 3765
Gould, S., 5308, 5348
Gould, S. J., 4959
Gould, S. U., 4120
Gouvernet, P. J., 4790, 4895
Gove, W. R., 3911
Govender, R., 4808
Graen, G., 4405, 5277
Graen, G. B., 4133
Graham, J. A., 4705
Gralnick, W. S., 3741, 4345
Gramling, S. E., 3710, 3859, 5203
Granberg, B., 4229
Granberg, D., 4229
Granger, C., 3676, 4502
Greeley, A. T., 4251, 4342
Green, C. F., 4840, 5291
Green, G. K., 4781
Green, K. E., 5159
Green, S. 5064
Greenberg, J., 4250
Greenberg, L. S., 4491, 5350
Greenberg, M. T., 4020, 4603, 4617
Greenberger, E., 4523, 4632, 4946
Greene, R., 4490
Greenfield, W. D., 4952
Greenglass, E. R., 4719, 5030
Greenhaus, J. H., 3915, 4579, 4631, 4690, 5107, 5286, 5316, 5363
Gregorich, S. E., 4277
Gregson, T., 4146
Gresham, F. M., 4087
Gressard, C., 3795
Gressard, C. P., 4280
Gretes, J. A., 5299
Gribbons, W. D., 5347
Griffeth, R. W., 4171
Griffin-Pierson, S., 4700
Griffore, R. J., 4746
Groot, M., 4075, 4364, 4365, 4886
Gross, W. C., 4805
Gross, P. R., 3827
Grossarth-Maticek, R., 3900
Guilfoyle, G. R., 4642
Gullo, D. F., 3676, 4052, 4502

Hudburg, R. A., 3796, 3797
Hudgins, B. B., 5157
Hudson, W., 3855, 4323
Hudson, W. W., 5015
Hueftle, S., 4321
Hughes, K. R., 4699
Hughes, M., 3977, 4929, 4978
Hughes, M. D., 3911
Hughey, J. B., 4279
Hui, C. H., 4012
Humphrey, L. L., 4466
Humphrys, P., 4183
Hunsley, J., 3706, 3718
Hunt, D. E., 4493
Hunt, D. M., 4035
Hunt, J., 3705
Hunt, R. A., 5230
Hurley, J. R., 4650
Hurt, H. T., 4713
Huston, T. L., 3998
Hyman, R. B., 4027
Hynes, M. J., 3987

■ ■ ■

Ibrahim, F. A., 4950
Ickes, W., 4848
Idaszak, J. R., 4859
Ignacio, A. A., 5102
Ihinger-Tallman, M., 4003
Ilardi, B. C., 3697, 4736, 4738
Ilgen, D. R., 4017
Ingilis, A., 4719
Ingram, R. E., 5119
Insel, P. M., 4276
Isaac, A., 5019
Isabella, L., 4166, 5309
Isom, S., 3742
Ivey, A. C., 5282
Ivey, A. E., 5270
Iwanicki, E. F., 4954
Izard, C. E., 5032

■ ■ ■

Jabri, M. M., 5285
Jackson, L. A., 4054, 4235, 5066
Jackson, S. E., 4653
Jacobsen, R. H., 4839
Jacobson, L. I., 4066
Jaloweic, A., 3860
James, L. A., 4693, 4974, 5206
James, L. R., 4662, 4667, 4693,
 4974, 5206
James, R. K., 4196
Janeczek, R. G., 5047

Janosik, S., 4988
Jansen, A., 4319
Jarjoura, D., 3769
Jason, L. A., 4459
Jay, S. M., 4600
Jeffers, D. L., 4054, 4235
Jencks, C., 4136
Jenkins, J. O., 3868
Jenkins, S. J., 4330
Jenner, J. R., 4059, 4197
Jennings, P. S., 4842
Jensen, G. F., 4735
Jermier, J. M., 4678
Jewman, J., 4690
John, J. P., 3691
Johnson, B. K., 4267
Johnson, D. H., 3804
Johnson, D. W., 4238
Johnson, E. S., 3671, 3673, 3674,
 3680
Johnson, J., 4226, 4855
Johnson, M. A., 3985
Johnson, M. E., 5279
Johnson, P., 3752
Jones, A., 4990
Jones, A. P., 4662, 4667, 4974
Jones, G. N., 4102
Jones, J. W., 3983, 4584, 5308
Jones, L. K., 3700, 4501, 4510,
 4980, 5090, 5349, 5351
Jones, L. L., 5356
Jones, R. G., 4857
Jones, T. S., 4483
Jorgensen, R. S., 3831
Jourard, S. M., 4489, 4771, 4955
Joyce, W. F., 4688
Juel, C., 4512
Jung, J., 3800

■ ■ ■

Kabanoff, B., 5091
Kaefe, F. J., 3802
Kagan, D. M., 3812, 4206, 4368,
 4492
Kahill, S., 3950, 4622
Kahl, J. A., 4547, 4825
Kahn, H., 4950
Kahn, S. E., 4309
Kalin, R., 5113
Kalliopuska, M., 3996
Kandel, D. B., 4219
Kanner, A., 3710, 3797
Kanungo, R., 5326
Kaplan, A., 4091
Kaplan, H. S., 4740
Karasek, R., 4643

Karasek, R. A., 4689
Kardash, C. A., 3675
Karnes, F. A., 4953
Karr, S. K., 4567
Kashani, J. H., 3845
Kaslow, N. J., 4793
Kass, S. J., 3775
Kassinove, H., 4839, 5154
Katoff, L., 4505
Katstra, J., 4343
Katz, D., 4291
Katz, I., 4590, 4794
Katz, M. M., 3752
Katz, S., 4288
Katz, V. J., 4276
Katz, Y. J., 4324, 4329
Kaufman, W. C., 5162
Kazdin, A. E., 3845, 3847, 4357,
 4399, 5179
Keane, T. M., 3881, 3707
Keaveny, T. J., 4292
Keenan, A., 4129
Keeton, W. P., 4778
Kejner, M., 5327, 5329, 5330
Kejner, M. M., 4300
Kekating, A. M., 5244
Keller, C., 3860
Kelley, H. H., 3998
Kelly, H. H., 4918
Kelly, R. D., 5272
Kelson, T. R., 4775
Keltikangas-JÑrvinen, L., 3922, 5218
Kendall, P. C., 5119
Kennedy, J. K., Jr., 5089
Kenny, M. E., 3992, 3997, 4594
Kerr, B. A., 4771, 4955
Kerr, S., 4460, 4678
Kettenis, P. T., 4075
Kettke, J. L., 4115
Khalsa, H. K., 3800
Khatena, J., 4861
Kickstein, E., 4750
Kiger, G., 4325, 4451
Kilmann, R. H., 5091
Kilpatrick, D. G., 3884
Kilpatrick, D. L., 4361
King, B., 4343
King, D. W., 4322
King, S., 4642
Kings, L. A., 4322
Kinicki, A. J., 4125, 4171
Kinnaird, K. L., 4244
Kipnis, D., 4201, 4428
Kirelä, S., 3962
Kirmeyer, S. L., 4180
Kirris, P., 4979

Lichtenstein, E., 4048
Liden, R. C., 4853
Liebert, R. M, 3742
Lief, H. I., 3687
Lim, C. U., 4664
Linden, J. D., 4639, 4641, 5265
Linehan, M. M., 3917
Link, B. G., 4377
Linn, B. S., 3928
Linn, M. 3885
Linn, M. W., 3928
Linton, M. A., 3964, 4255, 4753, 4932
Lips, H. M., 4278
Lipsmeyer, M. B., 5237
Liu, A., 4894
Liu, Q., 5224
Livneh, C. L., 4121
Livneh, H., 3876, 4121, 4243
Lo Presto, C. T., 4354
Lobel, S. A., 4291
Lock, R. S., 5081
Locke, D. C., 4517, 5126
Locke, E. A., 4971
Locke, H. J., 4579, 4618
Lockhart, M. C., 5362, 5363
Lodahl, T. M., 4300, 5327, 5329, 5330
Loeb, P. A., 4367
Loerch, K. J., 4555
Loevinger, J., 4516, 4517, 4520
Lofland, L. A., 4097
Lohr, J. M., 5182
Long, B. C., 4207, 4209
Long, E. C. J. 4043, 4067
Lopez, F. G, 3701, 3735, 3909, 4231, 4553, 4563, 4613, 5169
Loranger, A. W., 5062
Lorr, M., 4800, 4920
Lounsbury, J. W., 3872, 4157, 5017, 5018, 5325, 5331, 5339
Loyd, B. H., 3795, 4280, 4282
Loyd, D. E., 4282
Lucas, M. S., 5310
Lufi, D., 5059
Luftig, R. L., 4031, 4053
Luiton, S. J., 3751
Lummis, G., 3698
Lunneborg, C. E., 4389
Lunenburg, F. C., 4314, 4434, 4435
Lunneborg, P. N., 5310
Lunneborg, P. W., 4389
Luria, R. E., 3954
Lutz, F. W., 4864
Lyerly, S. B., 3752
Lynch, J. H., 4000, 4001, 4020, 4070, 4550

Lynn, R., 4694
Lyon, M. A., 3736
Lyons, J. S., 4047, 4610
Lyons, T. F., 4134
Lysons, A., 4667

■ ■ ■

Macan, T. H., 4474
MacDonald, A. P., 4069, 5078
MacDonald, A. P., Jr., 4241
MacDonald, M. L., 5182
MacDonald, N. T., 3736
Mackenzie,K. R., 4650
MacKinnon, C., 3677
MacKinnon, C. E., 4696
Macnab, D., 5249
MacPhillamy, D. J., 3902
Mactin, J. L., 4104
Maddirala, J., 4864
Madsen, D. B., 4739
Maehr, M. L., 4898
Maggiotto, M. A., 4919
Magolda, M. B. B., 4506, 5150
Mahalik, J. R., 4442
Mainiero, L. A., 4145
Maiuro, R. D., 5188
Major, B., 4479
Makarec, K., 5143, 5155
Makaremi, A., 3849
Makosky, V. P., 3737
Malamuth, N. M., 4328, 4521
Malby, J. N., 4504
Mallinckrodt, B., 3702, 3771, 3824, 4084, 4701
Malouff, J. M., 4856
Mancini, J. A, 3901, 4079
Mangano, J. A., 4999
Mangrum, C. T., 4227
Mann, B. J., 4630
Mann, P., 4936
Mannheim, B., 4220
Manning, M. R., 4190
Marchant, G. J., 4332
Marcoulides, G. A., 3705
Marcus-Mendoza, S. T., 4698
Margalit, M., 4086
Margolis, H. D., 5192
Margoribanks, K., 4266
Markee, N. L., 4773
Marks, I. M., 3823
Marlowe, D., 4036
Maroldo, G. K., 5211
Marlowe, H. A., Jr., 4088
Marrow-Tlucak, 4505
Marsh, H. W., 4747, 4790, 4791, 4895, 4964, 4965, 5000

Marshall, J. C., 5137
Marshall, G. N., 4862, 4884
Marso, R. N., 4205, 4211, 4269
Martel, J., 4992, 5065
Martelli, T., 4182
Martens, R., 3790, 5212
Martin, H. J., 5183
Martin, N. K., 3709, 4847
Martin, R. A., 3798, 3933
Martinetti, R. F., 4796
Martinez-Pons, M., 4933
Marullo, D., 4566
Marx, J. A., 4471
Marx, M. S., 4349
Mason, S. E., 4725
Mast, D. L., 5109
Masten, A. S., 4061
Matalon, Y., 4677
Mathes, E. W., 4016
Mathieu, J. E., 3830, 4148, 5340
Matsui, T., 3720, 4877
Matthews, A. M., 3823
Matthews, G., 5121
Matthews, K. A., 4414, 5193, 5218
Mazmanian, D. 3944
McAdams, D. P., 5226
McCall, M. W., 4874
McCall, N. J., 5094
McCarron, M. M., 4259
McCarthy, M. E., 3723, 3773, 4674
McClam, T., 4852
McCollum, E. E. 4575
McCombs, A., 3685
McConocha, D. M., 4370
McCrady, B., 4383
McCroskery, J. H., 4452
McCroskey, J. C., 5173
McCubbin, H. I., 3799, 4535
McCutcheon, L. E., 3698
McDaniel, P. S., 3737
McDevitt, S. C., 5053, 5069
McDonald, R. D., 4418
McElroy, J. C., 5251, 5341
McEwen, M. K., 4252
McFall, R. M., 4101
McFarlin, D. B., 4188, 4219, 4479, 4643, 4659, 4939
McGee, G. W., 5305, 5322
McGinnis, S., 5307
McGinnis, S. K., 3990, 4140
McHale, S. M., 4255, 4593
McIntosh, E. G., 4402
McIntyre, L. L., 3711
McIvor, G. P., 3887
McKeel, A. J., 3901
McKell, A. J., 4079

O'Brien, P., 4658
O'Bryant, S. L., 3755
O'Callaghan, K. W., 4228
O'Connor, E. J., 4130, 4149, 2472, 2623
O'Dell, S. L., 3679
O'Halloran, S., 4966
O'Hara, M. W., 3769
O'Hare, M. M., 5323
O'Heron, C. A., 4270, 5110, 5111
O'Keafor, K. R., 4872
O'Leary, K. D., 4531, 4591, 4625
O'Malley, S. S., 4687
O'Neil, J. M., 5082
O'Neill, R., 4523, 4946, 4965
O'Quin, K., 4495
O'Reilly, C. A., III, 4008
Oberleder, M., 4308
Ochiltree, G., 3672
Oetting, E. R., 3729, 4423, 4560, 4562, 5242
Offermann, L. R., 4311
Okada, M., 3935
Okeafor, K. R., 4029, 5009, 5163
Oldham, G., 5324
Oldham, G. R., 4147, 4178, 4191, 4763, 4859
Ollilia, L. O., 4223
Olson, D. H., 4550, 4801, 4994, 5106
Olver, R., 4611, 4811
Omizo, M. M., 4887, 4947
Ondercin, P., 4369
Orenstein, S. H., 5232
Organ, D. W., 3904, 4144, 5290
Orlofsky, J. L., 4270, 5110, 5111
Ormize, M. M., 4865
Ornstein, S., 4166, 5309
Orr, E., 4989
Osborne, A., 3920, 4979
Osipow, S. H., 4181
Ostini, R., 4433
Ostrander, D. L., 3937
Otis, S. W., 4327
Ottens, A. J., 3958, 4420
Owen, S. V., 4748
Owens, W. A., 5026

■ ■ ■

Pace, L. W., 4309
Page, M. H., 4558
Page, M. M., 4038
Page, S., 4733
Pahkala, K., 3962
Paivio, A., 3675, 5106
Paludi, M. 3676

Pandey, J., 5161
Parham, T. A., 4316, 4320
Parish, T. S., 4669
Park, K., 4601
Parkay, F. W., 5005
Parker, G., 3752, 4595
Parker, K. D., 3819
Parkes, K. R., 3811, 3943, 4117, 4689
Parrish, T. S., 4032
Parsons, C. K., 4853
Parsons, J. E., 5245
Parsons, J. J., 4211
Parsons, N. K., 4318
Partlo, C., 3727, 4668
Pascaarela, E., 3708
Pascarella, E. T., 3734, 4633
Pascual-Leone, J., 4226
Pasley, K., 4003
Patton, J. J., 4500
Patton, M., 3835
Patton, M. J., 4442, 4742
Paulhus, D., 4096
Paulhus, D. L., 3972, 4764, 5071
Paykel, E. S., 4568
Payne, D. A., 5129, 5160
Payne, P. A., 3828, 3873, 3929
Payne, R., 3952, 4109, 4218
Pazy, A., 4158, 5342, 5345
Pearlin, L., 3894
Pearlin, L. I., 3814, 3824, 4623
Pearson, H. M., 4309
Pearson, J. E., 4484
Pease, D., 4504, 4615
Peckering, G. S., 4905
Peckham, P., 4998
Pedersen, D. M., 4055
Pekala, R. J., 4911
Pelsma, D. M., 4186
Peng, S. S., 4755
Penley, L., 4120
Pennington, D., 4592, 4917
Pennington, D. C., 3704
Pepe, V., 3937
Perez, M. J., 4880, 5019, 5130
Perkel, A., 4808
Perkins, D., 4305
Perlman, D. S., 4582
Perman, S., 4455
Perosa, L. M., 4552, 4627
Perosa, S. L., 4552, 4627
Perri, M., III, 4727
Perri, M. G., 3905
Perry, D. G., 4892, 4969
Perry, M. A., 3979
Perry, S. W., 3954

Persinger, M. A., 5143, 5155
Peters, L. H., 4130, 4253, 4340
Petersen, A. C., 4981
Petersen, C. H., 5145
Peterson, C., 4570, 4761
Peterson, D. L., 4328
Peterson, P., 4762
Pettegrew, L. S., 4209, 4210
Pettigrew, T. F., 4817
Petty, R. E., 4725, 4726, 4727, 5142
Pfost, K. S., 4328
Philips, A. P., 5284
Philips, L., 5302
Phillips, A. P., 5283
Phillips, S. D., 4398, 4834, 5046, 5205, 5351, 5359
Piburn, M. D., 5147, 5158
Picano, J. J., 3854
Pickering, G. S., 4472
Piedmont, R. L., 4714
Pigge, F. L., 4205, 4211, 4269
Pike, R., 4052, 4917
Pinchot, P., 3848
Pines, A., 3950
Pinof, W. M., 5275, 5278
Pinto, J. N., 4285
Pinto, P., 4412
Pintrich, P., 3722
Pintrich, P. R., 4881
Pitner, N. J., 4413, 4460
Plake, B. S., 5103
Plante, J., 4852
Platt, J., 5139
Plomin, R., 5038, 5039
Plug, C., 5236
Pokay, P., 3722
Pollio, H. R., 4393
Polyson, J. A., 5097
Pomales, J., 3967, 5276
Ponce, F. Q., 3966
Pond, S. B., III, 4179, 4159, 4829
Ponterotto, J. G., 4320
Ponzetti, J. J., Jr. 5010
Popovich, P. M., 4237
Popper, M., 5334
Poresky, R. H., 3984, 4545, 4546, 4596, 4798, 5221
Porter, A. W., 4663
Porter, B., 4591
Porter, L. W., 5339
Porterfield, A. L., 3789, 3798, 3933
Posner, B. Z., 4119, 4128, 4373, 4407, 5222
Pottebaum, S. M., 4957
Potvin, L, 3899
Powell, F. C., 4411

Russ, S. W., 4468
Russel, J. H., 3748
Russell, D., 4107, 4108, 4787, 5178
Russell, D. W., 4084
Russell, E. W., 5117
Russell, I., 4696
Russell, J. E. A., 4340, 4670
Ryan, R., 4736
Ryan, R. M., 3741, 4000, 4001,
    4020, 4070, 4345, 4391, 4550
Ryckman, D. B., 4998
Ryckman, R. M., 4019, 4339, 4711,
    5183, 5184
Rydell, S. T., 5216
Rynes, S. L., 4120, 5223

■ ■ ■

Sabourin, S., 3945, 3972, 4636
Sagy, S., 4985
Saidla, D. D., 4064
Saklofske, D. H., 5002
Saleh, S. D., 5325, 5331
Sallbrown, F. H., 4232
Sampson, D. L., 5255
Samson, H., 5037
Sandler, I. N., 3789
Santrock, J., 4426
Santrock, J. W., 5064
Saracho, O. N., 4313, 4758
Sarason, I. G., 3863, 3865, 3712,
    3743, 3868, 5122
Sato, K. 5049
Satow, A., 5095
Savickas, M. L., 4873
Scandura, T. A., 4379, 4404, 5277
Scardino, T. J., 4256
Scarpello, V., 4163, 4164, 4177
Schacht, A. J., 3974
Schaefer, E. S., 4438, 4526, 4599,
    4604
Schaer, B., 3742, 4185
Schag, C. C., 3778
Schatz, E. M., 4953
Scheier, M., 3844, 4863
Schein, V. E., 5335
Schell, B., 5255
Schere, R. F., 3957
Schill, T., 3850, 5072
Schilling, D. J., 4356
Schippman, J. S., 5128, 5288
Schlottmann, R. S., 4040
Schmeck, R. R., 3723, 4400, 5132,
    5134
Schmida, M., 4329
Schmidt, L. D., 5274
Schmidt, L. J., 4314, 4434, 4435

Schmidt, N., 3996
Schmidt, N. B., 5062
Schmidt, W. H., 5222
Schmitt, A., 3712
Schmitt, A. P., 3744
Schmitt, N., 4853
Schnake, M. E., 4690
Schneider, B. H., 4061, 4077
Schneider, L. J., 5261
Schoenfeldt, L. F., 5026
Scholl, R. W., 4144
Schooler, C., 3894
Schotte, D. E., 3846
Schram, J. L., 4111
Schriber, J. B., 4683
Schrier, P. E., 4311
Schriesheim, C., 4410
Schuler, R. S., 4942
Schulman, R. G., 4783
Schumaker, J. F., 3805
Schuman, W., 4344
Schumm, W. R., 4576
Schunk, D. H., 4800
Schuster, D. H., 5138
Schutte, N. S., 4856
Schutz, R. W., 4207, 4209
Schwab, D. P., 4177
Schwab, J. J., 3771
Schwab, R. E., 4176
Schwartz, G. E., 3787, 5180
Schwartz, J. C., 4599
Schwartzwald, J., 3852
Schwarz, J. C., 4572, 4573, 4574
Schwitzer, A. M., 3695, 4742, 4500
Scogin, F., 5929
Scott, R. L., 4616
Scott, T., 5256, 5266, 5271
Scott, T. B., 5272
Seaman, F. J., 5088
Searight, H. R., 3791, 3926, 4367
Sears, D. S., 4956
Seashore, S. E., 4141, 4188
Secord, P. F., 4771, 4955
Sedlacek, W. E.,3702, 3724, 3725,
    5200
Sedlacek, W. I., 4228
Seeman, M., 4054
Seff, M. A., 4977
Segrist, C. A., 4874
Seidman, S. A., 4204
Seligman, M. E. P., 4761, 4789
Sen, J., 4874
Serban, G., 3776
Serbin, L. A., 5115
Serling, D. A., 3818, 4973
Sermat, W., 3996

Sexton, C. S., 4582
Shaffer, G. S., 5026
Shama, A., 4477
Shamir, B., 3761, 5332
Shanas, E., 3851
Shapiro, S. B., 3547, 4336
Sharafinski, C. E., 4681, 4682
Sharking, B. S., 4720
Shatford, L. A., 4462
Shavelson, R. J., 4747, 4965
Shein, E. H., 5223
Sheinfeld, D., 4795, 5104
Shell, D. F., 3726, 3916
Shepard, L., 4159, 4221
Sheppard, J. A., 5209
Sherman, J. A., 3716
Sherman, L. W., 4053
Sherrill, C., 4275
Sherry, D., 4421
Sherry, P., 4457
Shields, S., 4777
Shields, S. A., 4770
Shiloh, S., 4896
Shim, S., 4450
Shinkle, R., 3748
Shmeck, R. R., 5131
Shooler, S., 4623
Shorkey, C., 4934
Shoskes, J. E., 3756
Shotland, R. L., 4006
Shouksmith, G., 4167
Shroeder, D. H., 5159
Shrout, P. E., 5090
Shuptrine, F. K., 4062, 4068
Shurka, E., 4288
Siegel, A. I., 5141
Siegal, S. M., 4611, 4811
Sigalman, C. K., 4447
Signorella, M. L., 4453
Silber, E., 4973
Silber, W., 4948
Silva, P. A., 4443
Silverberg, S., 4000
Silverberg, S. B., 4544
Simkins, L., 3843
Simmons, C. H., 4286
Simmons, D. D., 4501
Simons, R. L., 4569, 5247
Simos, R. L., 3814
Simpson, C., 5352
Sinclair, R. J., 3799, 4531, 4574,
    4708
Singh, A. K., 5161
Singleton, L. C., 3965
Sinha, J. B. P., 4380
Sinisi, C., 4271

...

Subject Index

All numbers refer to test numbers. Numbers 1 through 339 refer to entries in Volume 1, numbers 340 through 1034 refer to entries in Volume 2, numbers 1035 through 1595 refer to entries in Volume 3, numbers 1596 through 2369 refer to entries in Volume 4, numbers 2370 through 3665 refer to entries in Volume 5, and numbers 3666 through 5363 refer to entries in Volume 6.

separation, 3910; states, 1638; stress, 3894; stress response, 3852; task-associated, 3762; work-related, 4143; in writing process, 3750, 5027

Affection(ate): nurturant, 652; social, 417

Affectivity, 600: assessment, 1964

Affiliation, 1720: need, 44, 745, 986, 2007; need, Mexican-American, 738; peer, 228; toward others, 1706

Affiliative tendency, 44

African: children, 1740; society, malaise in, 65, 301

African Americans: attitudes toward, 4325, 4327; commitment to separatism, 3977; ethnocentrism, 3976; racial identity, 4316;, 4317, 4320; self-concept, 4929; self-consciousness, 4754

Aggress(ion)(iveness), 216, 397, 403, 417, 651, 920, 927, 940, 1510, 1870, 2247, 3452, 3455, 3463, 3470, 4357: anxiety, 2437; –assertiveness, 1842; attitude toward, 2706; authoritarian, 2253; behavioral, 1843, 2295, 2800, 2801, 2858; child(ren), 1840, 2277, 2878, 3453, 3464, 3498, 4364, 5179; children's outcome expectations, 4892; children's values, 5235; –conducive activities, 2190; delay, 1212; interpersonal, 1221; job, 1033; lack of, 2251; marriage, 4625; peer relations, 946, 4078; potential, 1476; self, 242; self-efficacy beliefs, 4969; sexual, 131. *See also* Rape

Aging, 407, 415: successful, 33

Agoraphobia, 3758, 3882, 3883: behavior, 2812, 3883; cognitions, 2438

Agree(ableness)(ment), 1720: –disagreement, 483; disagreement response set, 281

Aide(s), 577: child-interactions, 577

AIDS: attitudes, 4233, 4236; attitudes toward fear of, 4293; employer beliefs, 4756; fear response, 3959; traumatic stress response, 4104

Ailments, common, 407

Air cadets, 478

Alcohol(ic)(s), 405, 526, 1122, 1674, 3159, 3160, 4383; 4386, 4459:

abuse, 2802, 2849; addict, 1639; adolescents, 4470; college students, 4457; drug use, 563; expectancies, 4813; treatment behaviors, 4350

Alexithymia, 5073

Alienat(ed)(ing)(ion), 45, 64, 65, 430, 437, 453, 533, 809, 1090, 1093, 1699, 1701, 1709, 1725, 3969: adolescent, 2549; attitudes, 83; college student, 3747, 4111; conditions, 430; consumer, 1700; cultural, 1093; general, 442, 1091; interpersonal, 1110; manifest, 443, 1103; social, 1098; student(s), 64, 455, 582; university, 465, 1730; work, 2671

Aloneness, 413

Aloofness, 688

Alternate uses, 608

Alternatives, correct, 385

Altitude, high, 571

Altruis(m)(tic), 624, 2317: in children, 926; motivation, 3134

Alumni, follow up, 158

Alzheimer's Disease, 3666

Ambigu(ity)(ous), 2122: intolerance of, 1796; role, 2357, 2525, 3288, 3292, 4940, 4941; situation, threat perceived, 2077; tolerance (for) (of), 481, 612, 646, 955, 965, 1505, 2245, 4854, 5216

Ambition, teacher, 1363, 1364

Ambivalence, 2486

American: Catholic priest, 1668; political behavior, 368; values, 1524

American Indian values, 3545

Anagram fluency, 1903

Analog(ies)(y), 887: figure, 2059; verbal, 1065

Analysis, 600: auditory, 1374; early childhood education, 678; schedule, 601; visual, 1041, 1441

Analytic: abilities, 661; empathy, 1370

Anaphora comprehension, 5, 2370

Anatomy test, 658

Anger, 832, 950, 1501, 2246, 2252, 2283, 3106, 3454, 3455, 3494, 5188, 5213: college student, 3759; control, 5168; expression, 5169; measurement, 5170

Anhedonia, 910: physical, 2507

Animal studies, attitude toward, 4337

Anomia, 424, 1685, 2563, 2612

Anomie, 1078, 1091, 1638, 1640, 1684: psychological, 413

Anthropology achievement: elementary grades, 1044; concepts, 1269

Anthropomorphism, 4051

Anti: –authoritarianism, 481; –democratic attitudes, 77; –intraception, 2253; –sexism, 1123;-social behavior, 578; –war, demonstrators, 552; –worldminded, 1795

Anticipations, personal, 2107

Anxiety, 283, 286, 387, 405, 417, 487, 841, 860, 925, 928, 945, 947, 948, 966, 1496, 1500, 1641, 1642, 1681, 2248, 2270, 2440, 2473, 2523, 3785, 3825, 3927, 3929, 3954, 5187, 5215: academic, 400; achievement, 908, 1625, 2433, 2439; adolescent worries, 3960; aggression, 2437; agoraphobia, 3758, 3882; assessment, 3760; behavioral, 2456; in children, 3921, 4075, 4468; cognitive-somatic, 3787, 5180; competition, 3790, 5212; computer, 3705, 3774, 3792-3797; concept, 1381; coping styles, 3920; criticism, 3822; dating, 3993; death, 410, 1649, 1650, 1651, 2447, 2459, 2541, 3805, 3806; debilitating, 1625, 1626, 1633, 2240; depression, 773, 1686; elementary children, 933; existential, 1657; facilitating, 1625, 2240; financial, 3824; first graders, 948; generalized, 3827, 3876; graduate school, test, 2427; health, 3841; heterosocial, 3987; job-induced, 1666; major choice, 1648; manifest, 1478, 2524, 3488; maternal separation, 4588; mathematics, 394, 1630, 2417, 2418, 3714-3720; multidimensional measure, 3935; neurotic, 749; piano, 2508; preschool, 2509; prolonged, 3761; in psychiatric patients, 3764; reactions, 402; self-rating, 911; separation, 3932; sexual functioning, 3842; situational, 26 sixth graders, 947; social, 2604, 2605, 4072-4076, 4082; state, 1682; –stress, 1643; student, 3737; symptoms 1632, 2441; task-

2945; development, responsibility, 762; disadvantaged, 7, 531, 621; disadvantaged, Mexican-American, 380, 384, 390; disadvantaged, Negro, 376; disadvantaged, preschool, causality, 886; disadvantaged, preschool consequential thinking, 885; disadvantaged, problem-solving, 894; disadvantaged, self-esteem, 830; disobedience, 953; disruptive, 397; disturbed, 38; divorce beliefs, 4529; drug use, 2819; echoic response, 7; egocentricism, 1443, 1485, 1503; ego strength, 3206; eight-year-old, 1771; elementary school, 101, 1043, 1136; elementary school anxiety, 933; emotional disturbance, 1082; empathy, 5221; entering school, 3; ethnic attitudes, 1184; exploratory behavior, 260; evaluation of teacher, 5294; everyday skills, 3672; expectations of aggressive behavior outcomes, 4892; fear, 2490, 3875; feelings, family, 41, 4530; feelings-judgments, 243; fifth grade, verbal absurdities, 895; fine-motor task development, 4504; first graders, anxiety, 948; first graders, vowel selection, 1045; five to ten years, 382; fourth and fifth grade, school attitudes, 155; fourth-sixth grade, cognitive style, 939; frustration, 2528; future time perspective, 772; handwriting, 2373; gifted, 1124, 3250; guilt, 964; handicapped peers, 4275; health resources, 2414; helplessness, 3782, 3856; home environment, 4545, 4546, 4567, 4596; home stimulation, 1952; hopelessness, 2482, 3847; hospitalization behavior, 1230, 1488; hyperactive, 397, 2827, 2878; impulsive-reflective, 291; innovative behavior, 1926; instrumental competence, 3677; intellectual ability, 888; intelligent vs. unintelligent behavior, 4397; intent judgment, 626; interaction aide, 577; intermediate level, science interest, 864; intermediate level, rating subjects, 871; interpersonal attraction, 55; interracial attitude, 1183;

introversion-extroversion, 956; intrusive parenting, 4611; investigatory activity, 724; judgment, 4116; knowledge of sexual abuse, 3682; language arts for, 277; learning, 17, 521, 2677; learning behavior, 4400; learning disabled, 2853; learning, teachers' perception, 2038; literacy, 3257; locus of control, 754, 797, 799, 2041, 2092, 2101, 2146, 2148, 3182, 3183, 4887, 4888, 4924; loneliness, 2554, 2583, 3241, 3242, 4031; management confidence, 2051; manifest anxiety, 1478, 1493, 2524; maternal employment, 4523; mathematics anxiety, 3717; maturity, 621, 4510, 4511, 4516; mentally retarded, 1759; minority, 502; moral judgment, 977, 2311; moral values, 978; mother's perception of temperament, 5039; motivation to achieve, 718, 737; multitalent, 4861; negative self-evaluation, 4886; normative beliefs, 535; one-year-old, 649; painful medical therapy, 4600; parent child communication, 640, 646, 654, 3005, 3034; parent ratings of feelings, 4528; parental acceptance, 4592, 4593; parents' daily reports, 4602; parents' satisfaction with, 4598; parents, emotionally disturbed, 148; part-whole perception, 19; peer relations, 1104, 2601; perceptions, 659, 3260; perception, auditory-visual, 1414; perception, control, 3252; perception, environment, 178; perception, mother behavior, 761; peer nominations, 4061; peer relations, 4053; perceived competence in, 4895; perceived self-efficacy, 4917; perceived social acceptance, 4052; perceived social support, 4620; perception, 4366; perception of academic failure, 4697; perception of control, 4790; perception of parental behavior, 4536; perception of parental conflict, 4591; perception of social skills, 4792; perception of teacher behavior, 4469; performance attribution, 3268; personality, 842,

927, 1450; personality assumptions, 5023; personality characteristics, 5028; phonics, 2398; pictorial attitude, 1770; play behavior, 2861, 2862; play socialization, 61; playfulness, 4362; preference, 1464; prejudice, 1176; preliterate, 1812; preschool, 383, 397, 425, 459, 477, 616–618, 635, 1397; preschool-aged, 2195; preschool anxiety, 2509; preschool cognitive functioning, 59; preschool disadvantaged, 403; preschool disadvantaged, problem solving, 892, 894; preschool frustration, 1229; preschool prejudice, 1174; preschool problem behavior, 4427; primary grades, 718; problem behavior traits, 1844, 2799, 2808, 2816, 2831; problem solving, 893, 1468, 3436, 5120; prosocial behavior, 963; provocative, 397; psychiatric pathology, 2514; rational thinking in, 5124; readiness, 1118; reading readiness, 4227; rearing, 553, 1304, 2855, 2971, 3042; rearing attitudes, 496, 1148, 3032; rearing problems, 38; reasoning, 3418, 3441; reinforcement, 1853; response styles, 843; retarded, flexibility, 923; reward preference, 261; role taking, 1236; school age, 629; school motivation, 731; school perceptions, 4951; school-related self-concept, 4954; security, 3037; self-assessment of social skills, 3980; self-concept, 230, 807, 3186, 3213, 3221, 3232, 3254, 3279, 3297, 4791, 4956; self-concept, poverty, 798; self-concept, primary, 763; self-control, 3185, 4466; self-enhancement–self-derogation, 843; self-esteem 458, 2039, 3197, 3206, 4975; self-regulation, 4345; self-social construct, 434; self-perception, 3187; self-reported social support, 3981; sex role, 881, 3188; silent, 397; sixth grade, anxiety, 947; social acceptance, 2593, 3965; social anxiety, 4075; social attitudes, 4276; social behavior, 842, 964; social class, 3189; social competence, 2567, 2606; social desirability, 251,

1708, 2557; social intelligence, 2564; social reinforcement, 725; social responsibility, 58; social situation, 2613; spatial conservation, 1061; stimulus, 1852; stress, 2536, 3184; study conflict, 1466; –teacher, interpersonal perceptions, 2076; teaching rating, 1063; teacher values of disadvantaged, 990; temperament, see, temperament, child and infant; text anxiety, 32, 1076, 1635; twenty-four and thirty-six months, 641; tolerance of individual differences, 3963; Type A, 3450, 3489, 4414, 5193; unhappy, 397; verbal absurdities, 895; work values, 2317, 5234; working parents, 4538; young, 349, 370, 381

Child care, 4527: attitude toward work and, 4265; infant behavior, 4422

Childhood, 625: early, 623; early education, 658, 678; middle, 412

Choice, 3390: vocational, 1574, 1587, 1594

Christianity, 4259

Chronicity, 421

Church: attitudes, 80, 3062; faith-religion, 1668

Cigarettes, 1122

Clark-Trow subtypes, 714

Class(room): activities, 1380; activities, new, 564; adjustment, 2406; atmosphere, 1027; attendance, 3698; behavior, 390, 565, 566, 574, 578, 581, 681, 718, 1108, 1209, 1211, 1237, 1854, 1855, 1878, 1885, 2820–2823, 2828, 2865, 2880, 2882, 3056; climate, 583, 3100; environments, 680, 686, 1324, 1539, 3057, 3058, 3078, 3093, 3094; experience, child's, 532; integrated, 2189; interaction, 1261, 1894, 1897; management strategy, 880; methods, junior high school, 700; misconduct, 578; peer performance, 575; planes and procedures, 679; process, 681; quality, 3116; questions, 600; status, 659, 1474; structure, 1969

Classification: job, 3073, 3095; skills, 627, 2946; socioeconomic, 1471

Classifying, 2215

Clerical, 2178: text, 73

Client: assessment, 1080; attitude, counseling, 999; beliefs, 3190; centered counseling, 249; change, 691; expectancy, 3191, 2308, 3210; expectations about counseling, 4819-4822, 4833, 4927, 5291; growth, 646; perception, 227, 309; perception, problem solving, 764; reaction, 589; reaction to interview, 998; satisfaction, 182, 999, 2335, 3059, 4635-4637, 4684, 5261, 5265, 5266; self-rating, 310; therapist, 2903; verbal behavior system, 587

Climate: bank, 3054; classroom, 3100; counseling, 999; job, 1967; learning, 1323; organization, 1308, 3050, 3097–3099, 3102; school, 3108

Close-mindedness, 413

Closed-mindedness, 2292

Closure, speed, 1612, 1617

Clothing: deprivation, perception of, 4894, 5224; orientation, 875; values, 5224

Coding, 2215

Coffee, 1122

Cognit(ion)(ive), 3, 1255: ability, 2678, 2961; affect, 404; agoraphobic, 2438; anxiety assessment, 3787; assessment, children, 2405; automatic thoughts, 5119; Beck's cognitive triad, 3788; behavioral changes, 572; behavior, infant, 1287; behavior, student, 568; belief systems, 4492; career decision-making, 5118; child critical thinking strategies, 5157; child problem-solving skills, 5120; coherence in daily living, 3931; complexity, 47, 1279, 1465, 1913, 2229, 3408, 3421; complexity, children, 2203; complexity, interpersonal, 433; complexity, simplicity, 433; complexity, vocational, 707; components, 1209; conceptual level, 4492, 4493; control, 913, 924, 1506, 2289; couple functioning, 4533; dealing with strangers, 4097; decision-making needs, 4702; in depression, 3784; development,

623, 627, 635, 4515, 5149; differentiation, 2230; difficulty, 1670; distortion avoidance, 3811; distortion in rheumatoid arthritis, 3786; educational objectives, 5138; egocentricism, 1491; emotional autonomy, 4000, 4001; error, 3192, 5028; evaluation of display formats, 285; flexibility, 923; functioning, 260, 1121, 2213; functioning, adolescents, 605; functioning, preschool, 59; future expectation, 3845-3847, 4922; hemisphere specialization, 5129, 5160; home environment, 642; hope, 3844; impairment, 2681; individual differences, 5142; information processing style, 5106, 5116, 5128, 5159; intellectual development, 4506; intelligent vs. unintelligent behavior, 4397; intention to quit job, 4141, 4212, 4215; intrusive thoughts, 5122; irrational thinking, 5125, 5154; job outcomes appraisal, 4144; knowledge of, 3669; lapses in control, 5121; learning, 175, 5131-5133, 5135-5137, 5153; level, children, 2224; logic of confidence, 4029; logical thinking, 5158; moral reasoning, 5126, 5140, 5232; need, 3367, 4725-4727; objectivism, 5058; obsessive-compulsive, 3893; optimism, 4863; pessimism, 3834; predisposition to depression, 3813; preference, 2179, 3391, 3410; problem solving styles, 5134; process, 265, 3193, 3423; processing, children, 1905; propositional logic, 5147; proverb interpretation, 5148; quick assessment in patient-care setting, 5123; rational thinking in children, 5124; reflective judgment, 5149, 5150; regulation 3669; rigidity, 5175, 5176, 5184, 5206; social studies strategies, 5151; structure, 218; style, 1479, 1498, 3369; style, field dependence, 815; style, flexibility, 939; style, fourth-sixth graders, 939; subjectivism, 5076; suicidal ideation, 3917, 3925, 3942; teacher decision-making, 5152; tempo, 603, 942; temporal lobe

Content, 596, 689
Contentment, 3828
Continuity, residence, 466
Contraception, 3987
Control(s), 655, 2317: of anger, 5168;
    child perception of, 4790;
    cognitive, 913, 924, 1506;
    environment, 1997; homicide, 970;
    imagery, 2052; internal, 238;
    internal-external, 467, 810;
    interpersonal, 2075, 4113;
    maternal, 1954; motor impulse,
    386; multidimensional assessment,
    4096; organization, 1962; parental,
    145; perception, 239; personal,
    1415; problems, behavior, 403;
    procrastination attribution, 4802;
    pupil, 810, 1523, 3105; social, 52,
    163, 4054; social, in school, 100;
    student control ideologies, 4314,
    4434, 4928. *See also* Locus of
    control
Controlling-punitive, 652
Controvers(ial)(y): attitude, 2733;
    lectures, campus, 586
Conventionalism, 2253, 2734
Cooperation, 338, 397, 1775, 1802,
    3412: attitude toward, 1371;
    student, 24
Coordination, 575: general dynamic,
    348; general static, 348
Coping: adequacy, 215; with anxiety,
    3920; behavior, 2830; cancer
    patients, 3778; with career
    decision-making, 5323; child,
    3697; classroom, 1211;
    conceptual process approach,
    3957; difficult situations, 3799;
    environment, 1095; family, 2984,
    4535; humor, 3798; jealousy,
    4402; in marriage, 4581;
    mechanisms, 3355; with pain,
    3802; perception of others'
    helpfulness, 4115; strategies,
    1085, 2974, 3801, 3811, 3860,
    3956-3958; style, 3803;
    unemployment, 3952, 4125
Correctional center, 1202
Cosmopolitanism orientation, 2306
Counselee behavior, 427
Counseling, 699: appropriateness,
    409, 1336; attitude toward, 2698,
    2708, 2788; attitudes of Blacks,
    999; center, 409, 703, 1313; client
    attitude, 999; client beliefs, 3190;
    client expectations, 3191,

3208-3210; client reaction, 311;
    climate, 999, 2335; disadvantaged
    youth, 27; effects of, 689;
    elementary children, 25, 28;
    elementary school, 70, 671;
    evaluation, 1000, 3063;
    expectations, 2058, 3198; follow
    up, 1010; goals, 1358; individual,
    43; influence, 258; information,
    2374; interview, student rating,
    699; inventory 689; marriage, 146,
    240, 1349; micro, 10, 85; need for,
    1689; outcome, 34, 500; practicum
    evaluation, 1003; preference,
    3409; pre-marital, 147; rating of,
    311; rehabilitation, 692, 1057;
    relationship(s), 1003, 1268, 2335;
    relationship, perceptions of, 2037;
    residence vs. nonresidence, 546;
    satisfaction, 3564; self-evaluation,
    328; sensitivity-repression, 921;
    skills, 1543, 2343, 3578; student-
    student, 1000; underachievers,
    1069; vocational, 670
Counselor(s), 427, 484, 702, 2909:
    activity, 584; appraisal position,
    665; attitudes, 89, 309, 560, 1173;
    attractiveness, 2336, 2341, 2342;
    behavior, 1543, 3325, 3565;
    certification, teaching
    requirement, 702; client,
    2899-2901; client perception,
    1372; comfort, 999, 2335;
    competence, 3571; construction-
    impulsivity, 961; contracts, 665;
    education, 255; education,
    graduate, 1004; effectiveness, 307,
    312, 316, 325, 1001, 1002, 1057,
    1559, 2335, 3566, 3567, 3569;
    empathy, 309, 3505, 3506; ethical
    discrimination, 969; evaluation,
    999, 1021; evaluation, residence
    hall, 1006, 1019; experience,
    1004; expertness, 2336, 2341,
    2342; facilitative conditions, 2344;
    function, 232; high school, 612,
    660; impulsivity-constriction, 961;
    interpersonal relations, 1003;
    interest and effort, 1003; interview
    behavior, 584; nonverbal behavior,
    2351; orientation, 2340;
    paraprofessional residence hall,
    2354; perception of counseling,
    3200; perception of residence,
    1020; performance, 2339, 3599;
    personal characteristics, 1004;

philosophy, 968; preference, 1544,
    3392; professional
    responsibilities, 314, 1003;
    qualification, 687; rating, 317,
    3572, 3573, 3595; rehabilitation
    effectiveness, 1561;
    reinforcement, 1545; restrictive-
    nonrestrictive, 2163; role, 332,
    820, 3195, 3199; role concepts,
    313; selection, 1004; self-concept,
    822, 1426; self-rating, 769;
    service, 820; stress, 2620; student,
    1021; tasks 837; theory
    preference, 54; trainee, 596, 1250,
    1317; trainee's effectiveness,
    2337; training, 3568, 3570;
    training, community college, 664;
    trustworthiness, 2336, 2341,
    2342; undergraduate residence,
    2355; verbal behaviors, 2351;
    verbal response, 588; viewed by
    students, 993
Counting, 345
Couples, married, 648
Courage, social and existential, 1832
Course(s), 527, 667: academic and
    vocational, 75; attitude, 2735;
    evaluation, 168, 666-668, 698,
    1546, 1547, 3064; expectation,
    3158; nursing, 3639, 3641; rating,
    college, 1024; satisfaction, 175;
    structure, 667
Courtship, 2597
Coworker esteem, 1458
Creative(ly): activity, 1921, 2940;
    attitudes, 130; behavior, 531;
    behavior, child's, 1926; behavior,
    disadvantaged, 1922; behavior,
    underlying elements, 2168; gifted
    adolescents, 1935; gifted adults,
    615, 1935; gifted children, 615;
    ideas, physics, 1930;
    inquisitiveness, 578; motivation,
    607; person, 1929; personality,
    620; potential, engineers, 1933;
    potential, scientists, 1933;
    predisposition, 1928; productions,
    130, 613; remote associates, 2941;
    students, 2942; thinking, 1924;
    thinking, strategies, 615
Creativity, 126-133, 281, 296,
    606-620, 688, 861, 1280-1283,
    1885, 1920-1935, 4494, 4495:
    differences, 132; disadvantaged,
    1283; elementary children, 1927,
    1932; encouragement, 487;

4572, 4574, 4626; interpersonal communication, 4525; interpersonal relations, 4018; intrusive parenting, 4611; job role conflict, 4944; kinship restraints, 4577; learning environment, 2985; life changes, 3863; marriage decision-making, 4573; maltreatment, 2989; maternal developmental history, 4589; maternal separation anxiety, 4588; mother's parenting satisfaction, 4617; mother's perception of husband's support, 4624; nurturance, 4590, 4597; orientation, 2302; parent-adolescent relationship, 4532; parent-child interaction, 4524, 4587, 4595, 4601, 4603; parent competence, 4608; parental, 593; parental acceptance, 4592, 4593; parental emotional stress, 3894; parental response to child medical care, 4600; parental self-efficacy, 4606; parenting beliefs, 4569; parenting style, 4609, 4615; parents' satisfaction with child, 4598; perceived support from, 4610, 4620, 4621; proverbs, 4558; psychological separation, 4613; relations, 141, 142, 645, 1296, 2982, 2983; relationships, 1951; relations, peer counseling, 1973; richness, 466; role, 302; role behavior, 4559; role expectations, 4578; satisfaction, 4548, 4575; sibling relations, 4619; sibling support expectancies, 4565; social support, 2988, 4622; strengths assessment, 4562; structure, 4563, 4564, 4627, 4628; substance abuse intervention, 4560; ties, 302; traditional values, 4556; well-being, 2987; work conflicts, 4555, 4631, 4632; workers', 4538
Fantasy, 40, 1243, 2886: projections, 579; sexual, 2876
Fat, fear of, 2477
Fatalism, 985, 4825
Father(s): acceptance, 645; attitudes, 645; dominance, 647, 673; esteem, 788; identification with, 434, 830; relationship with, 653
Fatigue, 841, 1670
Fear, 253, 3823, 3884: AIDS, 3959, 4293; bodily sensations, 3817;

children, 2490, 3875; commitment, 3818; crime, 3819; death, 3820; dying, 406, 1081, 1650, 1651, 2453, 2467–2469, 2497; failure, 19, 204, 392, 1342, 3821; fat, 2477; litigation, 3874; negative evaluation, 3822; psychotherapy, 2451; rating of, 414; success, 1658–1660, 1667, 2410–2412, 2470, 2471, 2478, 2500, 2545, 3897; survey, 1966
Feedback, 2908: amount of, 487; analysis, 1259; interpersonal, 1899; job, 3083; teacher, 333, 1885
Feelings, 593: dysphoric, 416; expressing, 1753; expression of, 500, 773; inadequacy, 773; inferiority, 515; openness, 293; perception, 102; personal, 804; positive-negative, 555; sensitivity to, 500; toward school, 1825; toward Whites, 2157
Fees, attitudes, 2787
Felt figure replacement, 440
Female(s): career choice, 710; need achievement, 728; professional competence, 975, 3243; professors, 1754; social roles, 1755
Femin(ine)(inity)(ism)(ist), 1789, 1790: –antifeminist, 1791; attitudes, 1834, 4239; ideology, 3557; liberal attitudes, 1767; –masculinity, 795, 927; orientation, 1768; rating scale, 284; women's self-concept, 4294
Field dependence/independence, 770, 776, 815, 3231, 4758: practice, 1317
Figure: analogies, 2059; copying, 1734; drawing, 888; human, 32
Film test, 765
Financial status, 5161: employment compensation, satisfaction with, 4177, 4178; pay disclosure effects, 4190; satisfaction, 215, 3923; stress, 3814, 3824; stress for families, 4543
Firearm registration, attitude toward, 1125
Fireman: job perception, 1012; leadership, 1549
First grade(rs), 371, 374: achievement, 469, 474; anxiety, 948; auditory perception, 750;

home environment, 1946; racial attitude, 1813; readiness, 1118; readiness for, 1735; reading achievement, 602
Five-year-olds, 1744
Flexibility, 15, 481, 893: conceptual, 923; cognitive, 923, 939; constricted, 924; educational, 131; interpersonal, 217; perceptual, 923; rigidity, 1486; speed, 15; spontaneous, 923
Fluency: anagram, 1903; ideational, 1911
Focus(ing), 596, 1859
Follow-up, student counseling, 1010
Food preference, 3396, 3417
Foreclosure, 628
Foreign: language aptitude, 1733; language attitude, 2744; policy, 510
Foreigners, attitude toward, 2798
Foreman, perception of job, 1012; production, 1013; responsibilities, 1011
Formal reasoning abilities, 2227
Formalistic, 2186
Form discrimination, 2143
Fourth, fifth, and sixth grade, 1647
Fraternit(ies)(y): activities, 486; social, 300, 486
Free: speech commitment, 973; time, 570
Freedom, expression, campus, 586; from cynicism, 481; students, 586
Freshmen: camp experience, 774; year, college, 628
Friend(liness)(s)(ship), 447, 1097, 2565, 4004, 4047, 4093: identification with, 434, 830; Black-White, 452
Frustration(s), 796, 1216, 2472, 4129, 4130, 4364, 4403: delay, 1212; job, 2623; reactions to, 1675, 2528; response, 1229
Functional literacy: high school, 1611; reading skills, 1602
Functioning, facilitative, 1716
Future: goal success expectancy, 220; orientation, 207, 301, 976; time perspective, 50, 56

∎∎∎

Games, 1218
Gay men and lesbians: attitudes toward, 4233, 4241, 4242, 4297; employer attitudes, 4838; jealousy, 4016; perception of homophobic

environments, 5015; social distance, 4080

Gender, 1219: behavior, 1285; identity, 630, 3403; role attitude, 2746; role, middle childhood, 243

General ability, perceptions, 2147

General anxiety, 1638

General health, 3826, 3830, 3831, 3833; beliefs, 4836, 4837

General information, 1738

Generations, relations, 76

Genuineness, 328, 1438: facilitative, 2344

Geograph(ic)(y), 347, 3070: Japan, 351

Geometry, 4, 474: aptitude, 74

Geriatric: depression, 2475, 2520; hopelessness, 2476; outpatients, 2566

Gestalt completion, 1617

Gifted: adults, creative, 615; children, 1124, 1387; children, creative, 615, 1283, 2940, 2942; children, self-concept, 3250; children, teacher attitude, 558; teacher, 1049

Girls: adolescent, 2866; delinquent, 463; delinquent, parents of, 656; social competence, 2595

Goal(s): attainment of, 714; college, 719; deficiency, 1994; educational, 511, 3068; instability, 4132, 4500, 4709; job, 709; marital, 3021; Neotic, 821; orientation, 400; personal, 829; pre-counseling, 1358; success, future expectancy, 2020; therapy, 1365; vocational, 511

God, 1748

Grad(es)(ing), 487: attitude toward, 166, 2757; contract attitude, 513; contract system, 513; high school, 700; practices, 1748; predictor, 75; systems, 487

Graduate(s): business programs, 661; education, 685; programs, 676; school, case of entry, 487; students, 528; student education, 131; students' environmental perception, 2062; student intellectual attitude, 86

Grammatical: clues, 385; structure, 380

Grandiosity, 4442, 4519, 4742

Grandparents, foster, 33

Grapheme-phoneme, 366

Graphic expression, 715

Gratification, postponement, 207

Grievance, 2656

Grooming, hygiene, 1603

Group(s): activity, 681; arousal, 1998; atmosphere, 2568, 3074; attachment, 4009; attitudes about controversy, 4238; attractiveness, 1712; behavior, affective, 596; behavior, self perception, 778; cohesion, 1710, 1711, 2569, 4008; conformity, 445, 3985; counseling disadvantaged, 53; decision-making, 2912; direction by supervisor, 1005; importance, 4010; in-group/out-group communication, 4481; individualism-collectivism, 4012; interaction, 1722; judgment, 1392; minority, 480; need strength, 1999; participation, 53; practicum, 1259; process, 523, 880; religious, 183; solidarity, 4007, 4012; work, 598

Group therapy, 4650, 4651: expectations, 4833

Guidance: administrator, 677; assessment, 687; classes, elementary, 31; counseling attitudes, 85, 189; director's roles, 318; function, 325; needs, elementary, 31; practices, 185; process, 687; school evaluation, 687; state director, 318, 697

Guilt, 289, 841, 1638, 1670, 2247, 2252, 2279, 2284, 5048, 5061, 5074: dispositional, 2276; –innocence, 381; proneness, 5022

■ ■ ■

Habits, 593: work, 1033, 1047

Hair loss, 3836

Handicapped, 1756, 2702: attitude toward, 2784; children, 1384, 1386, 1388, 1390, 1411, 1433, 1435–1437, 3688, 4351, 4566, 4616; children, mainstreaming, 1783, 2694; children, peer attitudes, 4275; educationally, 583; preschoolers, 1597

Handwriting: children, 2373; cursive, 2375; kindergarten, 1051; legibility, 2376

Happiness, 1661, 3756: marital, 3022

Harmony: familial, 466; within group, 1711

Hazard perception, 2065

Head start, 637

Health: behavior, 2864; engenderingness, 1487; habits, 1220; locus of control, 2066, 3217–3219, 3251, 3339; mental, 42; opinion, 2067; organizational, 1330; physical, 215, 2860; resources, 2414; self-perception, 779; status, 2835

Health professionals, 4134. *See also* Nurses

Hebrew, visual discrimination, 2377

Help-seeking behaviors, 4247, 4303

Helpfulness: of others, perceived, 4115; self-concept, 4114

Helpgivers, campus, 993

Helping dispositions, 2267, 3578

Helplessness: child, 3856; child, teacher report, 3941; institutional, 1670; learned, 1670; psychiatric patients, 3895

Heterosocial: assessment, 2570; behavior, 2885

Hierach(ical)(y), 695: influence, 1892; occupational, 269

High school, 436, 471: achievement motivation, 729; alienation, 1090; counselors, 612, 660; curriculum, 473; functional literacy, 1611; occupational aspiration, 897, 901; personality, 851; seniors, 517; sex education, 668; social studies, 601; stress, 2481; students, 401, 472, 645, 650, 653; students, self-esteem, 827; vocational plans, 1590

Higher education, opportunities, 167

Higher learning, 347

Higher order need strength, 2000

Hindrance, 688

History: Black, 157; case, 856; school, 625; social, 466

Hobbies, 593

Home, 497, 516: behavior, 1957; economics, behavioral change, 572; economic interest, 3631; environment, 1294, 1298, 1947; environment, cognitive, 642; environment, first graders, 1946; index, 344; interview, 647; learning environment, 647, 2993, 2994, 2997, 2998; observation, 1948; self-esteem, 2064; stimulation, 642; stimulations, child's, 1952, 2969; teachers, 572

detention, 4808; diabetes, 4809; dieting beliefs, 4810; family eating habits, 4891; fetal health, 4826; health, 2066, 3217–3219, 3251, 3339, 3340, 4837, 4887, 4888, 4924, 4862; individual perceptual differences, 4871; intellectual, social physical, 2086; internal-external, 576, 2049, 2081, 3164; interpersonal relationships, 2087; learning, 4843-4845; mental health, 2096; mother's perception, 4751; peer counseling, 1973; personal reaction scale, 4909; physical fitness, 4915; preschool, primary, 2113; rehabilitation clients, 29; religious, 4937; supernatural, 5014; teacher, 3332 3334; in workplace, 5021
Logic(al), 474, 884: ability, children, 3441; additions, 19; connectives, 123; operations, 2946
Loneliness, 1703–1705, 1729, 2552–2554, 2561, 2615, 3982, 3996, 4031, 4106-4108: adolescent, 4030; children, 2583
Long-term memory, 1601
Love, 3989, 3995, 4032, 4033, 4105, 4264: addiction, 2584; punishment, symbolic, 654; reward, symbolic, 654; romantic, 2599, 2600; sickness, 3012
Loving, styles, 1871
Lower class, 349: children, test anxiety, 1076
Loyalty: to coworkers, 3990; supervisor, 1005; teacher, 1883; union, 4110
Lunar effects, 3172
Lying, 4425

■ ■ ■

Machiavelliansim, 1492, 1517, 1721, 3486, 3487, 3514, 5186, 5190
Magic, 3539
Majors, college, 222, 662
Maladjustment, 2492
Malaise, African society, 65
Male(s): influence on female career choice, 710; need achievement, 728; self-esteem, 826; sex-role attitude, 2760; young adult, 636
Management, 388: strategy, classroom, 880; style, 1333
Manager(ial)(s), 4412, 4413, 4461: AIDS beliefs, 4756; attitudes, 523,

1536; autocratic personality, 787; behavior, 3560; changes in practice, 1129; description, 1447; employee evaluation, 5264; employee perception of support, 4680-4682; employee relations, 4655; needs, 1348; perceived qualities for, 4874; positions, 3104; rating, 1560, 3580, 3585, 3586; sex-role stereotypes, 1482; supervisor-employee race relations, 4765; traits, 2265; values, 5223; vocational evaluation, 5288
Manifest: alienation, 443, 1102; anxiety, 29, 1478, 1493, 1647, 2524, 3488; needs, 211, 2005; rejection, 496
Marginality, 249
Marijuana, 353, 1214, 1223: attitude toward, 1133
Marital: activities, 3013; alternatives, 3016; communication, 2972, 3017; conflict, 2973; dependency, 3029, 3046; instability, 3023; interaction, 3024, 3025; quality, 3026; relationships, 1766, 3018, 3021; satisfaction, 2976, 3007, 3020, 3022, 3027, 3028, 3035
Marri(age)(ed), 503, 593, 1056, 1161: adjustment, 648, 1299, 2962, 2978, 2980, 3011, 3014, 3015, 3019, 4541, 4542, 4579; aggressive behavior in, 4625; attitude toward, 4244; attitudes toward married women's employment, 4309; complaints, 2966; conflict scale, 4580; cooperativeness in conflict, 4534; coping strategies, 4581; counseling, 146; couple cognitions, 4533; couples, 648; dating, 503; difficulties, psychiatric patients, 773; family decision-making, 4573; husband-wife social support, 4623; influence strategies, 4582; interaction, 240; interactional problem-solving, 4013; jealousy, 3006; motivation for, 4719; perspective-taking, 4043, 4067; premarital sexual permissiveness, 4312; provocative behavior, 4586; quality, 4583; reward, 3041; satisfaction, 648, 1305, 3765, 3923, 4576, 4584, 4585, 4618;

social support from husbands, 4568; students, 1349; termination, 2963, 2968, 2977
Masculine: attitudes, 2759; transcendence, 1757
Masculinity-femininity, 795, 927, 2265; concepts, 114
Masochistic-self effacing personality, 787
Mass media, 302
Mastery, 301
Masturbation, attitude toward, 4302
Materials and facilities: junior high school, 700; learning, 1325
Maternal: acceptance, perceived, 759; attitude, perceived, 759; controls, 1954; encouragement measure, 651; interview, 927; involvement, 578; perceived nurturance, 646; responsiveness, 2273; vocalization, 649; warmth, 652
Mathematics, 4, 19, 21, 508, 525, 1758, 2371: achievement in, 1740, 2383; anxiety, 394, 1630, 2417, 2418, 3714-3720; attitude toward, 153, 524, 2715, 2740, 2761, 2762, 2795, 4303; attribution, 3246, 4760-4762, 4875; early behaviors, 345; lecture, quality, 3086; locus of control, 3244; problem-solving strategies, 3722, 5146; remedial, 508; self-concept, 1409, 3247, 3248, 3722; self-efficacy, 3249, 4876, 4877; statistics, attitude toward, 4249, 4268, 4326; stereotype, 3245; student perceptions, 3722; students' valuation of, 5245, 5246
Maturity, 2265: adult vocational, 1936; behavior, 621, 1206, 1937; children, 621; emotional, 621; personal, 636; reading, 1053; social, 636; students', 2349; vocational, 308, 2618
Meaning: assimilation of, 380; concept, 106–125, 1269–1279; implied, 1278; unusual, 1914
Meaningful(ness): in life, 821; words, 360
Meaninglessness, 413, 424, 1700
Mechanics, word association, 119
Mechanization, attitude toward, 1162
Media therapy, 98, 307

university residence, 704; practices effectiveness, 1972; preference, 259; pride, 3649; research, 1331; structure, 1332; subject matter, 679; supervision, 1023

Organized demeanor, 1885

Organizers, advance, 8

Orientation, 2213: achievement, 248, 713; career, 1576, 3617, 3618; college, 879; environmental, 302; future, 207, 301; goal, 400; interpersonal, 54, 67, 216; lifestyle, 2186; other, 989; peer group, 534; person, 1994; professional, 539; research, 1816; school, 547; work, 2676

Originality, 617, 861, 1281

Outcomes: instrumental, 3416; measurement, 3804, 4375

Outpatients, geriatric, 2566

Overexcitability, 3495

Overprotection, 496

Overt aggression, 1638

■ ■ ■

Pain: apperception, 2095; behavior, 2854, 2867; coping, 3955; daily living activities and, 3751; pediatric, 2857; sickle cell disease, 3802

Paintings, assessment, 1457

Panic, 2438

Parachute jumpers, 406

Paragraph completion, 120, 891, 1498, 1499

Paranoid: behavior, 646; ideation, 1681

Paranormal belief, 3211

Paraplegics, 418

Parent(al)(ing)(s), 451, 498, 1304, 3036: adolescent interaction, 640, 3001, 3030; approval, 499; as teacher, 1808; attitude, 144, 504, 532, 533, 640, 1148, 1193, 3010; authority, 640; behavior, 643, 655, 1295, 3033; behavior, loving-rejecting, 149; –child communication, 103, 640; –child interaction, 646, 1955, 2979, 3005; child rearing, 2855, 2971; child relations, 148, 654, 3034; control, 145; delinquent girls, 656; disturbed children, 38; dominance, 229, 1301; encouragement, 713; expectation, 1302; family, 593;

frustration, 1216; identification, 143; interest, 650; motivation, 1945; normal adolescent girls, 656; perceptions, 1956; punishment intensity, 1949; questionnaire, 463; rating, 643, 1303; relations, adolescent, 760; satisfaction, 3008; support, 640, 3038; transition to, 3048; warmth, 3031

Participation, 1687: group, 53; psychological, 1419

Passive speech, 397

Past, remembered, 812

Paternal reactions to birth, 1958

Pathological behavior, 1226, 1310

Patient(s): adjustment, 418; behavior, 1870; depressive, 420; psychogeriatric, 2213; schizophrenic, 306; symptoms, 1663; terminally ill, 1656; therapist, 995; therapy, 191

Pattern(s): activity, 400; communication, 597; copying, 801; meanings, 608

Pay, 2367, 2651, 2652, 3258

Peer(s), 497, 516, 523: acceptance, 1105; affiliation, 228; aggressiveness in children, 946; attitude toward, 541; classroom performance, 575; counseling effectiveness, 1973; evaluation, 1168, 3374; group, 163; group orientation, 534; influence on behavior, 556; network, 2591; perceptions, 256; rating, 802, 2556, 3449; relations, 70, 397, 472, 675, 2601, 4078; relations in adolescents, 760, 3968, 3979; relations in children, 4053, 4792; roles, 2590, 3259; self-esteem, 2064; teacher, 4046; tutoring, 1240

Penmanship and neatness: children, 2373; perception of, 2147

People: concepts, 502; liking, 2582; test, 535

Perceived: decision-making, 3262; depth of interaction, 1722; environment, behavioral press, 2050; external barriers, 2208; identity, 3261; isolation, 453; lunar effects, 3172; maternal nurturance, 646; power, 3214 problems, Black/White somatotype, 3263; students, 1980; stress, 2501;

supervision influence, 2359; work influence, 2653

Perception(s), 1, 227–256, 748–838, 1367–1443, 2030–2157, 2280: academic climate, 1335, 3322; adequacy by college teachers, 785; aesthetic, 254; alcohol consumption, 3159, 3160; of Alzheimer's disease, 3666; of appraisal interview and supervisor, workers, 2036, 3162; of assertive job interview techniques, 4834; attractiveness, 3275; auditory, first graders, 750; auditory, Spanish language-oriented children, 1613; auditory and visual stimuli, 765; authentic ability, 2147; body, 3175–3177, 4769–4781, 4827; boss, 3326; campus by student, 187; causes, 3181, 3327; children, 659, 1414; classroom, 1227; client, 227, 2336, 4803, 5265–5279; of clients by therapists, 4766; clothing deprivation, 4894; college environment, 177; college students, 706; college students of instructor effectiveness, 2358; competence, 3243; complexity of, 768; about computers, 3705, 4800, 4830; control, 239, 3168, 3252; of counseling relationship, 2037; counseling session, 3200; counselor-client, 1372; counselor role, 332, 3199; counselor by students, 993; curriculum, 694; environment by children, 178; environment by employee, 164; environmental, 179; features, 1391; first graders, 1423; general ability, 2147; graduate students' perception, 2062; hazard, 2065; of helping behavior, 4114, 4115, 4835; of homophobic environments, 5015; illness, 3220; individual world views, 4950; instructor's, 2349; interpersonal, 428, 433; job, 4140, 4144, 4164, 4172, 4853, 4859; of job complexity, 2083; job, by firemen, 1012; job, by foreman, 1012; of leadership behavior, 2084; learning behavior, 838; life stresses, 2047; of love, 4032, 4033; of manager qualities, 4874; marriage, 240; maternal

frustration, 1229; children, handicapped, 1597; children, prejudice, 1174; children, reflexivity, 1490; children, self-perception, 835; to primary, 390; primary locus of control, 2113; problem solving, disadvantaged children, 892, 894; program, 642; racial attitude, 1814; screener, 1714; social-emotional behavior, 1237

Presentation, self, 2558

Presenter competence, 3591

Press(ure), 487, 1666: achievement, 496, 647, 673; activeness, 647, 673; English, 647, 673; ethlanguage, 647, 673; independence, 647, 673; intellectuality, 647, 673; job, 1687

Prestige, 269, 2317: among sociology journals, 906; college major, 896; occupational, 269, 273–275, 897, 900, 3447, 3651; perception of vocational, 204

Priesthood, 1668

Priests, American Catholic, 1668

Primary: children, reinforcement preferences, 739; grade, 367; grade children, 718; grades, primary and elementary, 1743; grades, reading attitude, 1775; grades, reading comprehension, 14; preschool locus of control, 2113; roles, 73; self-concept, 2114, 2115; teacher directiveness, 936

Principal(s), 484, 495: elementary school, 1680; evaluation, 1558; perception, 1407; role, 538; teacher, 595; teacher communication, 688

Principalization, 850

Principle(s): business, 661; identification, 884

Print, awareness, 2390

Privacy, 4055: attitude, 2751, 2752; invasion, 1320, 2079

Probability, 2224

Probation administrators, 523

Probing, 689

Problem(s): assessment, 1674; behavior, 28, 389, 495, 2807; behavior control, 403; behavior traits, children and adolescents, 1844; centeredness, 583; child-rearing, 38; client, 1080; conduct,

2251; –defining skills, 5128; educational, 131; educational-vocational, 38; elementary school, 1108; emotional, child, 1082; industrial, 150, 151; instructional television, 488; job, 1968; sexual marital, 38; social interpersonal, 38; solving, 264–267, 456, 884–895, 1465–1469, 2200–2234, 3316, 3429, 3435, 3437–3440, 5145; solving ability, 2226; solving, adequacy, 764; solving, adolescent, 5139; solving, behavior, 3280; solving, children, 893, 1468, 3433, 3436, 5120; solving, client perceptions, 764; solving, disadvantaged children, 892, 894; solving, interactional, 4013; solving, interpersonal, 2576; solving, preference, 5144; solving, preschool, 892; solving, skills, 2225; solving, strategies, 1467, 3432, 5146; solving, stylistic differences, 5134; solving, teacher, 1232, 2804; solving, therapist perception, 764; student, 1336, 2859; supervisor, 996; wives, 1306

Procedure(s), 600, 694, 695: sampling, 161

Processing: activity, 577; cognitive, 3193; reactive, 421

Procrastination, 3281, 4431, 4432, 4802: attitudes, 2769; behavior, 2868, 2869

Production, 676, 688: consumption, 302; foreman, 1013

Productivity, creative, 130

Profession, employee commitment, 1996

Professional(ism), 326, 327, 1816: activities, 657; attitudes, 82, 1815; commitment, 1815; identification, 1815; orientation, 539; responsibilities, counselors', 1003; role orientation, 539; self-attitudes, 82

Professors: female, 1754; preference for, 866

Proficiency, job, 320

Program: innovation, 160; planning, 694

Programmed instruction, 153

Prohibitions, 649

Project: complexity, 3103; Head Start, 637

Projection(s), 41, 850: fantasy, 579; role, 2512

Projectivity, 2253

Promotion, desire for, 2359

Pronunciation, 371

Propensity, social, 2611

Property, 593

Proportion, 1614

Protest: behavior, 1817; situational attitude, 1817

Protestant ministers, 519

Provocative child, 397

Proverbs, 1818

Pro-worldminded, 1795

Proxemic distance, 68

Psychiatric aide employees, 3592

Psychiatric: behavior, 1205; complaints, 773; evaluation, children, 2514; marital difficulties, 773; outpatients, 1681; patients, 489, 1654, 3895, 3907, 3944, 4377; progress, 2452; symptoms, 2515, 2539; treatment, 773, 3120; vocational problems, 773

Psychiatric rating, 405, 1079

Psychodynamic mental health, 880

Psychological: adjustment, 28–43, 421; androgyny, 2176; anomie, 413; dependence, 2199; distance, 50, 56; distress, 35, 2493; health, attitude, 1137; help, attitude, 2743; influence, 3324; moods, 1669; needs, 1339; reports and service, attitude toward, 154; separation, 3040; state, 841; stress, 2517; testing, 1127; well-being, 2493

Psychologist: attitudes, 154; burnout, 3950; perceived, 3265; stress, 2662

Psychology: attitude toward, 1127; occupations in, 142, 903

Psychopath(ic)(y), 855–857: criminal, 2518

Psychopathology, dimensions of, 412, 2448, 3346

Psychosexual maturity, 1668

Psychosocial: development, 632, 1941, 2945, 2947, 2955; environment, 1960

Psychosomatic: complaints, 2480, 2516; symptoms, 3858

Psychotherapists and patients, 306

Psychotherapy, 1137: check list, 2519; evaluation, 1080; fear of, 2451; process, 2352, 2616

Psychotic symptoms, 773, 853
Psychoticism, 1681
Public exposure to sexual stimuli, 1761
Public policy issues, 1797
Public school(s), 687: teaching, 539
Puerto Ricans, 3967
Pun, 613
Punishment: capital, 1750; direct object, 654; parental intensity, 1949; symbolic love, 654
Punitive-controlling, 652
Punitiveness, attitudes, 2770
Pupil: affect, 1217; attitude, 455, 540; behavior, 574, 578; control, 810; control ideology, 1819, 2117, 2771, 3105, 3282, 3283; development, 637; evaluation, 3374; ideal, 1929; information acquisition, 1; interaction, 1027; interest by teacher, 1027; observation by teacher, 1027; opinion, 541, 1820; ratings, 2870; ratings by teachers, 297, 298; responses, 1267; self-esteem, 3276; teacher, 600

■ ■ ■

Q sort, 822, 831, 1678
Qualit(ies)(y), 681: class, 3116; college departments, 3067; education, 663; leadership, 338; of life, 3914, 3915; of life, workplace, 4187; mathematics, lecture, 3086
Quantitative, achievement, 1043, 1063; aptitude, 1732
Questions, classroom, 1266

■ ■ ■

Races, tolerance of, 1792
Racial: academic predictor, 2684; attitudes, 46, 78, 79, 87, 88, 482, 520, 542, 1147, 1176, 1804, 1812, 1813, 4325, 4327; attitude, first grade, 1813; attitude, preliterate children, 1814; attitude, preschool, 1814; cultural values, 5228; discriminatory behavior, 4451; evaluation, 3448; factors, 386; identity attitudes, 2772, 2773, 4315–4317, 4320; intermarriage attitudes, 90; mistrust, 3991; preference, 865, 1459; relations, 76, 99; self-concept, 4929; stereotype, 520, 1154, 4291, 4327;

subjective identification, 4818; supervisor-employee relations, 4765
Radicalism, 280, 529: –conservatism, 1821
Rape, 3684; attitudes, 4246, 4436; empathy, 5202; perceptions, 4931, 4932
Rapport: with students, 33; teacher, 1891
Rating: applicant, 3588; college course, 1024; counseling interviews, 699, 3594; counselor, 35, 72, 3573, 3595; curriculum, 706; managers, 3580; peer, 2556; police, 3577, 3579, 3587; sales person, 3596, 3598; scales, descriptive, 215; students, 24; teacher, 1028, 2395; work trainee, 338
Rational, 2205, 2206: behavior, 1679, 1874, 2774, 2871
Rationality, 1679, 2931
Reaction, counseling, 311
Reactive, inhibition, 399
Readers, retarded, 340
Readiness, for first grades: reading, 352, 356, 357, 1118; school, 469; vocational planning, 470; words, 337
Reading, 2, 12, 15, 21, 340, 516, 543, 1048, 3916: achievement, 350, 1035–1037, 1043, 1063, 1598; achievement, first-grade, 602; adult and college, 20; adult attitudes, 4232; and spelling ability, perception of, 2147; attitude, 543, 544, 1175, 1787, 1822, 1823, 2741, 2763, 2775, 4313; attitude, elementary school, 1822; Black and White students, 2; comprehension, 14, 20, 1055, 1062, 1609, 2388, 2688, 3669; comprehension, child, 4513; comprehension, college students, 1615; confidence, 3726; consultant, 1334; difficulty, source of, 340; failures, 475; formal, 352; functional skills, 1602; informal, 350; input, 372; instruction, fourth grade, 544; instruction, individualizing, 545; kindergarten, 352; levels, 375; maturity, 1053; miscue, 2391; oral, 2388, 2391; performance, 1744; performance predictors, 4223; phonemic

analysis, 3690, 4512; pre-, 352; preference, 1455, 1460; rate, 1039; readiness, 352, 356, 357, 1121, 4227; retention, 1616; skills, 366, 1038; span, 2392; storage, 373; student perception of ability, 3736; teacher survey, 545; teaching in content classrooms, 1763; teaching of, 559
Real estate, success, 2686
Realism: color, 830; size, 434, 830, 2296
Reality: perceptions, 3173; testing, 3772
Rearing adolescents, 490
Reasoning, 889, 1738: ability, 2204; ability, formal, 2231, 3419, 3428, 3442; abilities, concrete, 2227; abstract, 2201, 2202, 3424; abstract, junior high, 884; analogical, 3418; deductive-inductive, 3426; logical, 3427, 3441; moral, 2212, 2218, 2219, 2222, 3531, 3558; proportional, 3420; scientific, 2232
Rebellious independence, 481
Recall, 4, 8, 346, 359, 360, 361, 382: perception, adults, 533
Receptivity to change, 301
Reciprocal inhibitions, 399
Recognition, 2, 363, 366, 374, 663: interrogative patterns, 380, 384; word, 342
Reconstruction, 13
Recruit(ers)(ment): job, 518; student athletes, 3413
Referential communication, 2923
Referral, 2191: process, 2119
Reflection, 689: impulsivity, 285, 290, 291, 1490, 1494, 2170, 2272
Reflective observation, 2216
Reflectivity, 2262
Reflexes, interpersonal, 448
Refusal behavior, 1857, 2803
Regard: level, 1538; unconditional positive, 431
Regression, adaptive, 606
Rehabilitation, 337: clients, 29; counseling, 692, 1057; counselor effectiveness, 1561; gain, 693; industrial, 515; services, 182; vocational, 691
Reinforcement: by others, 44; children, 1853; contingencies, 1434; counselors, 1545; delay of, 58, 239; expectation, 69; positive,

2116, 2144; relations, 2060; visualization, 2097

Speakers, 1765, 2913

Speech, 388: active, 397; aphasic, 1887; forms, private, 1491; imitation, 349; passive, 397

Speed, 1361: of closure, 1612, 1617; motor, 1610; perceptual, 1604, 1608, 1618

Spelling, 108: and reading ability, perception of, 2147; sound, 1062

Spouse: abuse, 3000, 4521; relationship, 3045; self-concept, 3298

Stability of self-concept, 2145

Staff, 523, 3112, 3113

State anxiety, 1682, 2440

State guidance office function, 697

Statistics: attitude toward, 2701, 2786; basic, 2372

Status, 268–277, 896–906, 1470–1475, 2235–2239: academic, college freshmen, 904; classroom, 659; concern, 1475; developmental, 481; distance, Mexican-American migrants, 902; ego identity, 628; family, 2987; identity achievement, 271; jobs, 273, 275, 276, 2645; occupational, 276, 1470; socioeconomic, 270, 482, 898, 899, 1471–1474, 3444; socioeconomic, college freshmen, 905

Stereotype(s), 2253, 3169: banking, 156; body build, 561; girls, activity, 2032; Italian, 3228; mathematics, 3245; occupational, 270, 3642; political, 1186; racial, 520, 1154, 1198; sex role, 1482, 2196, 3318, 3319; vocational role, 3660

Stimulation, 666: auditory, 1233; home, 642; seeking, 741

Stimulus: child, 185; expressions, 38; seeking, 2847; varying input need, 1992

Strain: occupational, 1686, 2627, 2638; role, 1667

Stratification, social, 268

Street language, 378

Stress: 423, 841, 1672, 1673, 1677, 1687, 2434, 2466, 2488, 2489, 2501, 2532, 2535, 2537, 2543, 3812, 3945, 3954: administrative, 2617; adolescent, 2435, 3753, 3754; arousal and, 3936; athlete,

3868; children, 2536; college student, 3691, 3710, 3789; combat related, 2454; coping behavior, 2830, 3958; counselor, 2620; disease risk and, 3900; economic, 3814, 4543; elderly, 2531; environmental, 3071; evaluative, 1627, 1694; health professional, 4134; high school, 2481; humor and, 3798; job related, 2621, 2638, 2639, 2641, 2642, 2649, 2650, 2654, 2658, 4161, 4181, 4195, 4199, 4222; life events, 2531, 2533, 3866, 3867, 3885; medical school, 2419, 2425; nursing, 2639, 2648, 4169; organizational, 4197; parental, 3894, 4566; perception, 3898; physical response, 4452; police work, 4182; psychological, 2517; psychological symptoms, 3771, 3948; and race, 3868; role, 2525–2527, 4198; school, 4666; school psychologist, 2662; subjective, 1086, 2484; suppression, 3943; symptoms, 3939, 3940, 3946; teacher, 2655, 2665, 2666, 3117, 3810, 4186, 4203, 4204, 4207–4210; undergraduates, 833, 2415, 2423; vulnerability, 3938; work load, 4180, 4188

Striving, achievements, 716

Structure(d): bureaucratic, 1309; cognitive, 218; conceptual, 604; job, 3084; need for, 2208; need for in adolescents, 760, 1070, 1378, 1991; organizational, 1332; situation, 656

Student(s), 581, 662, 680: ability, junior college, 766; academic aspiration, 2027; academic attitude, 1126; activism, 1483, 2879; activities, university, 705, 1293; adolescent, 1430; affective behavior, 568; alienated, 455, 582; aspiration, disadvantaged, 740; athlete, 3413; attainment satisfaction, 714; attitudes and beliefs, 556, 859, 1160, 1163, 1188–1190, 1193, 1194; autonomy, 333; behavior, 578, 603, 737, 2824; –centered characteristics, 581; –centered classroom, 1969; –centeredness, junior high, middle school

teachers, 1867; cognitive behavior, 568; cognitive processing, 3423; counselor, 1021; counselor contacts, 665; disadvantaged, 679; drug attitudes, 1145; effects on White fifth-grade, 88; engineering, 829; evaluation of teachers, 690, 698, 1009, 1014, 1022, 1027, 1029, 1032, 1562–1565, 1567–1572; evaluation of instructors, 2348; efforts, 2349; faculty perceptions about academic advising, 1959; faculty relations, 675, 694; feelings toward Whites, 2157; foreign, 1094; freedom, 586; graduate, 528, 2426; high risk, 1189; high school occupational aspiration, 897, 901; influence, university residence, 704; interracial attitudes, 535; junior high school, 700; learning environment, 3114; male high school occupational aspiration, 901; notes, 379; opinion, 95; outcomes, 687; perception, 175, 3322; perception of advisers, 993; perceptions of teacher, 1027; performance aspects, 568; performance attribution, 3323; personal, 859; philosophical orientation, 3552; preference, 263; problem behavior, 2589; relations with, 679; roles, 2590; satisfaction, 159, 1071; satisfaction, university, 705; self-concept, 1429, 3304; self-esteem, 2134, 3310, 3313; social work majors, 674; sociometric analysis, 1695; stress, 2415, 2423, 2424; suicide, 1087, 1088; superior, 680; survey of school situations, 700; teacher, 701; teacher, concerns of, 701; teacher, elementary school, 495, 701; teacher evaluation, 3590, 3602; teacher relationships, 2416, 2911; teachers, social studies, 600; test anxiety, 387; –student counseling, 1000; tutors, 322; university, 442, 586; White & Black, 2

Study: habits, 23, 1105, 2883; individualized, 6; practices, 169; strategy, 1072, 1073

Style: behavioral, 564; categorization, 1464; cognitive, 1479; ideational expressive, 594; instructional, 288;